HUMAN RIGHTS POLICY IN ONTARIO

Ontario Human Rights Commission

Ontario
Human Rights Commission
Commission ontarienne des
droits de la personne

THOMSON
CARSWELL

[illegible] position on disability, accommodation, [illegible] guidance on compliance with the Ontario *Human* [illegible] policies and guidelines are developed through public con- [illegible] extensive study of applicable Canadian and international human rights law. Members of the public can expect that the Commission will apply its policies and guidelines in the enforcement and interpretation of the *Code*. These Guidelines are not legal advice and should be read in conjunction with applicable decisions and the specific language of the *Code*.

Library and Archives Canada Cataloguing in Publication

Human rights policy in Ontario / Ontario Human Rights Commission. — 4th ed.

4th ed.
Issued also in French under the title: Politiques des droits de la personne en Ontario

Includes index.
ISBN 978-0-7798-14336-7

1. Civil Rights — Ontario. 2. Ontario. Ontario Human Rights Code.
I. Ontario Human Rights Commission

KEO819.H85 2007 342.71308'5 C2007-905147-2
KF4483.C5H85 2007

Published by the Ontario Human Rights Commission
Province of Ontario, Toronto, Canada

ISBN 978-0-7798-14336-7
Disponible en français

THOMSON
CARSWELL

One Corporate Plaza
2075 Kennedy Road
Toronto, Ontario
M1T 3V4

Customer Relations
Toronto 1-416-609-3800
Elsewhere in Canada/U.S. 1-800-387-5164
Fax 1-416-298-5082
World Wide Web: http://www.carswell.com
E-mail: carswell.orders@thomson.com

PREFACE TO THE FOURTH EDITION

On this 45th anniversary of the Ontario *Human Rights Code*, I am pleased to present the fourth edition of *Human Rights Policy in Ontario*, a publication first introduced in 1998. I am also pleased that Thomson Carswell, a respected publisher of employment and human rights related material, is our partner in putting together this latest compendium of the Ontario Human Rights Commission's policies and guidelines.

Since the *Code* was introduced, society's understanding of human rights has evolved, and protections under it have expanded to reflect these changes. Where the *Code* once covered six grounds — race, creed, colour, nationality, ancestry and place of origin, today there are 15 protected grounds including the right to be free from discrimination on the basis of gender, marital and family status, disability, and sexual orientation.

Despite 45 years of work, discrimination still persists, calling for continued efforts to address new and varied human rights issues. In this regard, the Commission's research and policy function is essential because it educates as well as advances awareness and understanding of existing and emerging human rights issues.

Over the years, the Commission has accordingly developed a considerable collection of policy statements on a wide range of human rights issues, many of which have received national and even international attention.

The purpose of Commission policies and guidelines is to set out how the *Code* will be interpreted and applied in dealing with human rights complaints. For this reason, the general public, human rights lawyers, community advocates and the courts, including the Supreme Court of Canada, often refer to them for clarification of rights and responsibilities.

Key features of this particular edition include new policies and guidelines on racism and racial discrimination, family status and accessible education, as well as updated versions of policies on discrimination against older people because of age, pregnancy and breastfeeding, and sexual orientation.

In keeping with the Commission's new vision for "an Ontario in which everyone is valued, treated with dignity and respect, and where human rights are nurtured by us all," this compendium will serve as an indispensable tool for ensuring that these "written rights" become "lived rights."

Barbara Hall, B.A., LL.B., Ph.D. (hon.)
Chief Commissioner
November 2007

Summary Table of Contents

DETAILED TABLE OF CONTENTS

HUMAN RIGHTS CODE

PART I — FREEDOM FROM DISCRIMINATION

PART II — INTERPRETATION AND APPLICATION

PART III — THE ONTARIO HUMAN RIGHTS COMMISSION

290/98 — BUSINESS PRACTICES PERMISSIBLE TO LANDLORDS IN SELECTING PROSPECTIVE TENANTS FOR RESIDENTIAL ACCOMMODATION

642 — SEARCH AND ENTRY WARRANTS

PART I — POLICIES AND GUIDELINES

Guidelines on Accessible Education

Approved by the Commission: September 29, 2004

1. — Introduction

In October 2003, the Ontario Human Rights Commission (the "Commission") released its consultation report entitled *The Opportunity to Succeed: Achieving Barrier-free Education for Students with Disabilities ("The Opportunity to Succeed")*. The Report was the product of the Commission's research and consultation with a wide array of interested parties during the fall of 2002 on human rights issues affecting students with disabilities.

Feedback received throughout the consultation indicated that, while there is a highly regulated and complex educational framework in place to address the needs of students, and while in many cases education providers are doing much to meet the diverse needs of the student population, a significant number of students with disabilities continue to face obstacles in their attempts to access educational services in Ontario. *The Opportunity to Succeed* identified key barriers at the primary, secondary and postsecondary levels of education. These barriers include: inadequate funding, physical inaccessibility, cumbersome and time-consuming accommodation processes, negative attitudes and stereotypes, and a lack of understanding of Commission policy and the rights and responsibilities of all parties under the Ontario *Human Rights Code* (the "*Code*").

The Report outlined actions required by schools and school boards, postsecondary institutions, government and other responsible parties to promote compliance with human rights law and policy. It defined the responsibilities of students and/or their parent(s) and guardian(s) as participants in the accommodation process. In addition, it set out the Commission's own commitments to take steps to ensure that students with disabilities have equal access to educational services. In this regard, the Commission has committed to monitoring progress with the recommended actions required by the Report and will follow up with education providers to assess levels of compliance. The Commission also committed to developing *Guidelines on Ac-*

cessible Education (the "*Guidelines*") to help parties better understand their obligations in the education of students with disabilities.

While the *Guidelines* are a companion piece to *The Opportunity to Succeed*, each document serves a distinct purpose. Whereas *The Opportunity to Succeed* reported the feedback received by the Commission during its education consultation and recommended specific actions for the parties involved in order to address systemic issues in educational services, the *Guidelines* take key principles from the Commission's *Policy and Guidelines on Disability and the Duty to Accommodate* ("*Disability Policy*")[1] and apply them to the educational context. They are intended to provide guidance to support education providers[2] and students with disabilities in the fulfilment of their duties and rights under the *Code*.

The *Guidelines* provide clarification with respect to the following areas:

- The principles of accommodation
- Creating a welcoming environment for all students
- The accommodation process
- The right to confidentiality and the disclosure of information
- Appropriate accommodation
- Accommodation planning
- The undue hardship standard
- Roles and responsibilities of those involved in the accommodation process

It should be noted that the *Guidelines* are not intended to provide prescriptive solutions for accommodating specific disabilities, as accommodation must always be based on an individualized assessment. Where appropriate, however, examples are provided which apply the principles outlined to situations involving students with specific types of disabilities.

For a full understanding of how the Commission approaches disability issues, the *Guidelines* should be read in conjunction with the Commission's *Disability Policy* and the consultation report, *The Opportunity to Succeed*.

By clearly setting out the Commission's interpretation of the responsibilities of all parties to the accommodation process, and by providing direction

---

[1] Ontario Human Rights Commission, *Policy and Guidelines on Disability and the Duty to Accommodate*, (March 2001), available online at Commission's website: www.ohrc.on.ca.

[2] "Education providers" includes, but is not limited to, school boards, school staff, educators, post-secondary institutions, and where appropriate, government.

to these parties on how to best achieve compliance, it is hoped that the *Guidelines* will help to prevent discrimination, reduce disputes throughout the process, and where disputes continue to occur, provide strategies to help avoid their escalation.

2. — Scope of Application

2.1 — Education is a "Service" under the *Code*

Section 1 of the *Code* guarantees the right to equal treatment in services, without discrimination on the ground of disability. Education, in its broadest sense, is a "service" within the meaning of the *Code*.[3] The scope of "educational services" will include the mastery of knowledge, academic standards, evaluation and accreditation. It may also encompass the development of a student's personality, talents and mental and physical abilities to their fullest potential, and may include co-instructional activities such as school-related sports, arts and cultural activities and school functions and field trips. At the lower grade levels, the service of education will typically be defined more broadly and may include the student's overall social, physical and academic development in the educational setting. At the higher levels of education, formal educational services will be defined more narrowly and will focus increasingly on academic standards and accreditation.

2.2 — Duty to Accommodate Disability

Once a disability-related need has been identified, or where a *prima facie* case of discrimination has been established, education providers have a duty to accommodate the needs of students with disabilities in order to allow them to access educational services equally, unless to do so would cause undue hardship.[4]

2.3 — Applies to Public and Private Educational Institutions

The right to equal treatment and the duty to accommodate exist for publicly funded and privately funded early childhood pre-schools, elementary and secondary schools, colleges and universities. This includes special schools which exist in the province such as hospital schools, care and treatment pro-

---

[3] *Peel Board of Education v. Ontario (Human Rights Commission)* (1990), 12 C.H.R.R. D/91 (Ont. S.C.)

[4] See section 17 of the Ontario *Human Rights Code* (the "*Code*"), R.S.O. 1990, c. H-19. It should be noted that, in some situations, equality may require different treatment that does not offend an individual's dignity.

grams, schools in correctional facilities, and provincial schools.[5] It would also include separate schools, French language schools, and trade, business and professional accreditation courses.

2.4 — Defining Disability

The definition of "disability" in the *Code* is broad.[6] It includes past, present and perceived conditions. When considering whether a student has been discriminated against because of disability, the focus may be on how the student was treated rather than on proving that he or she has physical limitations or an ailment.

> *What the Courts Say*: The Supreme Court has established that a disability may be the result of a physical limitation, an ailment, a perceived limitation or a combination of all these factors. The focus is on the *effects* of the preference, exclusion, or other type of differential treatment experienced by the person and not on proof of physical limitations or the presence of an ailment. The Court has stated: "By placing the emphasis on human dignity, respect, and the right to equality rather than a simple biomedical condition, this approach recognizes that the attitudes of society and its members often contribute to the idea or perception of a 'handicap.' In fact, a person may have no limitations in everyday activities other than those created by prejudice and stereotypes."[7]

Protection for persons with disabilities under the *Code* explicitly includes physical disability, developmental disabilities and learning disabilities. Discrimination may be based as much on perceptions, myths and stereotypes, as on the existence of actual functional limitations.[8]

---

[5]Provincial schools are residential schools geared to students with specific exceptionalities, for example, students who are blind, deaf, deafened or hard of hearing.

[6]See section 10 of the *Code*, *supra*, note 4.

[7]*Quebec (Commission des droits de la personne et des droits de la jeunesse) v. Montréal (City)*; *Quebec (Commission des droits de la personne et des droits de la jeunesse) v. Boisbriand (City)*, ["*Mercier*"], 1 S.C.R. 665 at para. 77.

[8]*Ibid.*, at para. 39.

2.5 — Forms of Discrimination

Discrimination can take many forms. It can occur when an education provider adopts a rule that, on its face, discriminates against persons with disabilities.

> *Example*: As a condition of enrolment, a college requires deaf students to sign a waiver stating that the college is not responsible for providing or funding accommodations.

Discrimination can also take place through another person or other means.

> *Example*: A private school instructs an admissions scout not to recruit students with disabilities who have costly accommodation requirements. In this case, the person or persons giving the instructions are discriminating indirectly.

Education rules, policies, procedures, requirements, eligibility criteria or qualifications may appear neutral but may nonetheless amount to constructive, or "adverse effect" discrimination.

> *Example*: A university policy of awarding scholarships only to students in fulltime attendance would likely have an adverse effect on students whose disabilities only permit them to attend school on a part-time basis.

3. — Principles of Accommodation

Accommodation is a means of preventing and removing barriers that impede students with disabilities from participating fully in the educational environment in a way that is responsive to their own unique circumstances. The principle of accommodation involves three factors: dignity, individualization and inclusion.[9]

---

[9] In *Eaton v. Brant County Board of Education*, [1997] 1 S.C.R. 241, the Supreme Court of Canada recognized that while specialized or segregated education may be appropriate where it is in a child's best interest, integration should be recognized as a norm of general application.

3.1 — Respect for Dignity

Students with disabilities have the right to receive educational services in a manner that is respectful of their dignity. Human dignity encompasses individual self respect and self worth. It is concerned with physical and psychological integrity and empowerment. It is harmed when individuals are marginalized, stigmatized, ignored or devalued.

Education providers must fashion accommodation solutions in a manner that respects the dignity of students with disabilities.[10] Accommodations should be considered along a continuum from those that most respect a student's right to privacy, autonomy and dignity, to those that least respect them. Accommodations that do not take into account a student's right to respectful and dignified treatment will not be appropriate.[11] Respect for dignity also includes taking into account how an accommodation is provided and the student's (and/or their parent(s)' or guardian(s)') own participation in the process.

Educators have a duty to maintain a positive school environment for all persons they serve.[12] Throughout the Commission's consultation, participants emphasized that the attitudes of educators towards disability issues play a major role in influencing how other students treat and relate to students with disabilities. Teachers should make efforts to sensitize students about disability issues and to model respectful attitudes and behaviour to-

---

[10]The Supreme Court of Canada has confirmed that dignity is a factor to be considered in determining disability accommodation in the education context. In commenting on its decision in *Eaton v. Brant County Board of Education*, the Court stated

> . . . Emily's claim might have succeeded if . . .the Court had been persuaded that the Board's response to the challenge posed by Emily's placement [the accommodation] *had itself violated Emily's dignity as a human being equally deserving of consideration*, or placed discriminatory obstacles in the way of her self-fulfillment. [Emphasis added.]

Granovsky v. Canada (Minister of Employment and Immigration), [2000] 1 S.C.R. 703 at para. 74 making reference to *Eaton* decision, *ibid.*

[11]The Supreme Court's decisions in *Law v. Canada (Minister of Employment and Immigration)*, [1999] 1 S.C.R. 497, and *Granovsky*, *ibid*, have confirmed that the concept of human dignity is central to discrimination analysis. These cases indicate that if an accommodation marginalizes, stigmatizes or demeans the person with a disability's sense of worth or dignity as a human being, it will not be appropriate.

[12]*Ross v. New Brunswick School District No. 15*, [1996] 1 S.C.R. 825, 25 C.H.R.R. D/175.

wards students with disabilities. Education providers need to address any behaviour that may be injurious to the dignity of students with disabilities.

3.2 — Individualized Accommodation

There is no set formula for accommodation. Each student's needs are unique and must be considered afresh when an accommodation request is made. At all times, the emphasis must be on the individual student and not on the category of disability. Blanket approaches to accommodation that rely solely on categories, labels and generalizations are not acceptable.

Although many accommodations will benefit large numbers of students with similar needs, it must be kept in mind that an accommodation solution that meets one student's requirements may not meet the needs of another. Two students with the same disability may have very different needs; for example, while some students with visual impairments read Braille, many do not. Different effects of a disability and different learning styles may call for different approaches.[13]

> *In Practice*: An appropriate accomodation for a student who is Deaf and whose primary language of communication is American Sign Language or Langue des signes québecoise might be a Provincial School for the Deaf or a sign language instructional program in a local community school. At the same time, an appropriate accommodation for another student, who is also profoundly deaf, and who primarily uses auditory-verbal communication, might be inclusion in a regular classroom.

Individualized assessment includes being aware of the ways in which students with disabilities are affected by also being members of other historically disadvantaged groups. These students may sometimes be subjected to discriminatory treatment that is based on more than one protected *Code*

---

[13]In the *Eaton* decision, the Supreme Court of Canada recognized the unique nature of disability and emphasized the need for individualized accommodation because the ground of disability "means vastly different things depending upon the individual and the context", *Eaton*, *supra*, note 9 at para. 69.

ground (*e.g.* race, sex, sexual orientation or ethnic origin). These grounds may intersect thus producing a unique experience of discrimination.[14]

> *In Practice*: An eight-year-old boy with attention deficit hyperactivity disorder, whose family has recently immigrated to Ontario from Sri Lanka, registers at his neighbourhood public school. In order to ensure that the boy's parents are fully informed about the workings of the special education system and the resources available to students with disabilities, the school principal provides the family with written information about these services in Tamil, the family's first language.
>
> *In Practice*: A university organization providing support services to lesbian, gay, bisexual and transgendered students ensures that its literature is available in alternative formats so that it is accessible to students with visual disabilities.

Education providers must also ensure that testing and evaluation materials and procedures used to grade and place students with disabilities are not selected or implemented in a manner that is racially or culturally biased, or otherwise infringes the rights protected by the *Code*.

3.3 — Inclusion and Full Participation

As the Commission noted in its *Disability Policy*, "in some circumstances, the best way to ensure the dignity of persons with disabilities may be to provide separate or specialized services."[15] However, education providers must first make efforts to build or adapt educational services to accommodate students with disabilities in a way that promotes their inclusion and full participation. Preventing and removing barriers means all students should be able to access their environment and face the same duties and requirements with dignity and without impediment.

> *Did You Know*: Internationally, inclusion is recognized as an essential part of ensuring that students with disabilities have equal opportunities

---

[14]The Commission has explored this "contextualized" or "intersectional" approach to discrimination analysis at length in its Discussion Paper entitled *An Intersectional Approach to Discrimination: Addressing Multiple Grounds in Human Rights Claims* (2001), available online at the Commission's website: www.ohrc.on.ca.

[15]*Disability Policy, supra*, note 1 at Part 3.1.3.

in school. In this regard, the United Nations Educational, Scientific, and Cultural Organization (UNESCO) noted:

> Inclusion is to be seen as part of the wider struggle to overcome exclusive discourse and practices, and against the ideology that each individual is completely separate and independent. Inclusion is about the improving of schooling. Rather than being a marginal theme concerned how a relatively small group of pupils might be attached to mainstream schools, it lays the foundations for an approach that could lead to the transformation of the system itself.[16]

Other Jurisdictions: In the United States, the *Individuals with Disabilities Education Act* also recognizes the importance of including students with disabilities in the regular curriculum. The *Act* states:

> To the maximum extent appropriate, children with disabilities. . .are educated with children who are not disabled, and special classes, separate schooling, or other removal of children with disabilities from the regular educational environment occurs only when the nature or severity of the disability of a child is such that education in regular classes with the use of supplementary aids and services cannot be achieved satisfactorily.[17]

Education providers must take steps to include students with disabilities in classroom and extra-curricular activities, wherever possible. Education policies, programs, services and activities must be designed inclusively with the needs of all students in mind, so as not to exclude or single out any student. Education policies must take into account the diverse needs of the student population, and must plan for alternative measures to address the needs of students with disabilities.

In Practice: Workplace tensions have culminated to the point where a labour strike by school staff appears imminent. Thinking ahead, the school board in question works together with school principals to draft a contingency plan for students that would permit them to continue attending school should there be a work stoppage. The plan includes specific provisions addressing the needs of students with disabilities, and includes a back-up plan in the event that educational assistants, special needs assistants and other special education staff are part of a walkout.

---

[16]UNESCO, *Salamanca Five Years On: A Review of UNESCO Activities in the Light of The Salamanca Statement and Framework for Action on Special Needs Education* (1999) at p. 9

[17]*Individuals with Disabilities Education Act*, 20 U.S.C., ss. 612(a)(5)(A).

The following are steps education providers can take to provide students with disabilities with the greatest opportunity to participate fully in educational services:

STEP 1: — Promoting Inclusive Design

In order to ensure that students with disabilities have equal access to education, academic facilities, programs, policies, and services must be structured and designed for inclusiveness. This means education providers have an obligation to be aware of both the differences between students and differences that characterize groups of individuals when making design choices so as not to create barriers. This approach is referred to as "inclusive design" or "universal design."[18]

Course curriculum, delivery methods and evaluation methodologies should be designed inclusively from the outset. This may mean creative use of technology, such as putting materials online, or selecting software that is compatible with screen readers. When courses are online, web-based or CD based, accessibility issues should be addressed up-front, in the development stage.

> *Did You Know*: UNESCO's 1994 World Conference on Special Needs Education, which resulted in the *Salamanca Statement and Framework for Action on Special Needs Education*, emphasized that educational systems and programs should be designed and implemented to take into account the wide diversity of children's needs and characteristics. Article 28 of the *Salamanca Statement* provides: "Curricula should be adapted to children's needs, not vice-versa. Schools should therefore provide curricular opportunities to suit children with different abilities and interests."[19]

---

[18]The Center for Universal Design at North Carolina State University defines universal design as "the design of products and environments to be usable by all people, to the greatest extent possible, without the need for adaptation or specialized design. The intent of universal design is to simplify life for everyone by making products, communications, and the built environment more usable by as many people as possible at little or no extra cost. Universal design benefits people of all ages and abilities." Please see http://www.tiresias.org/guidelines/inclusive.htm. Information accessed July 30, 2004.

[19]Document available at www.unesco.org/education/pdf/SALAMA_E.PDF. Information accessed May 12, 2004.

When constructing new buildings, undertaking renovations, purchasing new computer systems, launching new Web sites, designing courses, setting up programs, services, policies and procedures, education-providers should keep in mind the principles of universal design. New barriers should never be created in the construction of new facilities or in the renovation of old ones. Rather, design plans should incorporate current accessibility standards such as the Canadian Standards Association's Barrier Free Design[20] and Principles of Universal Design.[21]

> *In Practice*: A college takes steps to ensure that course handouts and other curriculum materials are available in electronic text format at the time print materials are provided to all students so that students who require alternative formats (*e.g.*, students with visual impairments or learning disabilities) do not experience delay. The college also makes efforts to provide course materials to all students by e-mail or the internet to promote even greater inclusiveness.

Inclusive design emphasizes equal participation and recognizes that *all* students have varying abilities and needs. This method of design may involve an entirely different approach and it is based on positive steps needed to ensure equal access for those who have experienced historical disadvantage and exclusion from society's benefits.[22] This positive approach is more effective because it is accessible and inclusive from the start. Barrier preven-

---

[20]Document available at www.csa-intl.org/onlinestore/GetCatalogItemDetails.asp?mat=2004958&pa. Information accessed May 12, 2004.

[21]See www.design.ncsu.edu:8120/cud/univ_design/princ_overview.htm.

[22]In *Eaton*, the Supreme Court of Canada stated:

> Exclusion from the mainstream of society results from the construction of a society based solely on "mainstream" attributes to which the disabled will never be able to gain access. . . [I]t is the failure to make reasonable accommodation, to fine-tune society so that its structures and assumptions do not result in the relegation and banishment of disabled persons from participation, which results in discrimination against them. [*Eaton*, note 9 at para. 67 of Quicklaw version]

And in another decision, the Court also affirmed that standards should be designed to reflect all members of society, insofar as this is reasonably possible. See *British Columbia (Public Service Employee Relations Commission) v. BCGSEU*, [1999] 3 S.C.R. 3 ["*Meiorin*"] at para. 68.

tion is much more preferable to barrier removal, and it is consistent with the notion of disability as a social model.

STEP 2: — Removing Barriers

Students with disabilities currently face many obstacles in the education system, including physical, attitudinal and systemic barriers. Students with mobility disabilities, for example, may face barriers in the form of inaccessible school buildings and student housing. Negative attitudes towards and stereotypes about students with disabilities continue to act as obstacles in themselves, with some students not feeling welcome or included in class activities, or social situations at school.

The removal of barriers is necessary in order to give meaning to the right to equality and freedom from discrimination guaranteed to persons with disabilities under Part 1 of the *Code*.

Where barriers already exist, the duty to accommodate requires education providers to make changes up to the point on undue hardship to provide equal access for students with disabilities.

> *In Practice*: A university arranges sensitivity training for all faculty and academic staff on issues facing students with learning disabilities. The training focuses on creating greater awareness of different learning needs and addressing misperceptions and misinformation which in themselves can create barriers to equal access to educational services.

STEP 3: — Accommodating Remaining Needs

Even where the principles of universal design have been fully implemented and schools have adopted a comprehensive approach to removing barriers, some barriers may continue to exist for students with disabilities.

Where barriers continue to exist because it is impossible to remove those barriers at a given point in time, then, as part of the duty to accommodate, next-best alternatives or temporary solutions must be explored and implemented, if to do so would not result in undue hardship.

Differential treatment may sometimes be required in order to provide students with an equal opportunity to achieve full benefit from the education service. When accommodating the needs of students through differential treatment, educators must still keep in mind and maximize the principles of respect for dignity, individualization, and inclusion and full participation.

How to Achieve Accessibility

- Develop an accessibility policy and student complaint procedure.
- Review and identify accessibility barriers across educational facilities.
- Develop a standardized accessibility plan for future locations based not only on the Ontario *Building Code*, but also on the Ontario *Human Rights Code* and current standards and best practices in barrier-free design.
- For existing facilities, develop a plan, and begin removing barriers.
- Monitor progress toward achieving accessibility.

4. — Creating a Welcoming Environment

4.1 — Preventing Bullying and Harassment

Part of an educational institution's duty to maintain a safe learning environment for students includes addressing bullying and harassing behaviour. Students who are being harassed are entitled to the *Code's* protection where the 15 harassment creates a poisoned educational environment. This protection would apply to sanction: (i) education providers who themselves harass students based on *Code* grounds, and (ii) education providers who know or ought to know that a student is being harassed based on *Code* grounds, and who do not take effective individualized and systemic steps to remedy that harassment.

4.1.1 — Responsibilities of Education Providers

Education providers have a responsibility to take immediate steps to intervene in situations where bullying and harassment may be taking place. The harassment of students because of disability will amount to discrimination where it poisons the educational setting and impairs access to educational services. Every person has the right to be free from humiliating or annoying behaviour that is based on one or more grounds in the *Code*. If left unchecked, harassment can impede a student's ability to access educational services equally and to participate fully in the educational experience.

> *Example*: In a classroom, a student with Tourette's Syndrome is repeatedly subjected to taunting and teasing by a group of other students for no apparent reason. The same group of students exclude him from recess activities stating that he is "different"and "weird." It may be inferred from the particular circumstances that the treatment is due to the

student's disability even though none of the other students ever made a direct reference to his disability. The student's ability to access the educational program is, as a result of this harassment, impaired.

The courts have established that schools have a duty to maintain a positive, nondiscriminatory learning environment.[23] In this regard, education providers should take steps to educate students about human rights and implement strategies to prevent discrimination and harassment. An education provider has a responsibility to take immediate remedial action once made aware of harassing conduct. If an allegation of harassment has been substantiated, appropriate action must be taken. This may include disciplinary action.

A student who is a target of harassment may be in a vulnerable situation. Therefore, there is no requirement that he or she formally object to the behaviour before a violation of the *Code* can be considered to have taken place, where the conduct is or should have been known to be unwelcome. It may be unrealistic to require a student who is the target of harassment to object as a condition of seeking the right to be free from such treatment.

An education provider who knew of, or should have had knowledge of, the harassment and could have taken steps to prevent or stop it, may be liable in a human rights complaint.

4.1.2 — Prevention Through Education

Anti-harassment training for educators and school staff is an important first step in creating a climate of mutual respect in an educational environment. Educators will then be in a position to appropriately address issues of bullying and harassment that arise in the classroom.

---

[23] See *Ross, supra*, note 12; *Quebec (Comm. Des droits de la personne) c. Deux-Montagnes, Comm. Scolaire* (1993), 19 C.H.R.R. D/1 (T.D.P.Q.) ("*Kafe*"); *Jubran v. North Vancouver School District No. 44,* (2002), 42 C.H.R.R. D/273, 2002 BCHRT 10 (In *Jubran*, the Tribunal held that the School Board (i) had a duty to provide an educational environment that did not expose students to discriminatory harassment, (ii) knew that students were harassing another student, and (iii) was liable for failing to take adequate measures to stop that harassment. The B.C. Supreme Court quashed the Tribunal's decision on the ground that the harassment was not linked to a protected ground under the legislation, and stated that it did not have to decide any other issues in disposing of the case. The B.C. Court of Appeal is scheduled to hear a further appeal in October of 2004: see *North Vancouver School District No. 44 v. Jubran*, [2003] B.C.J. No. 10.)

Education providers can help to prevent incidents of bullying and harassment before they occur by:

- Exhibiting a clear attitude of non-tolerance towards bullying and harassment.
- Communicating clearly to the student body the consequences of bullying and harassment.
- Educating students about disability issues and encouraging awareness of differing needs and acceptance of diversity.
- Engaging in role-playing and educational exercises to help students develop increased compassion and a greater awareness of the impact that bullying behaviour may be having on others.
- Respecting the confidentiality of students who do report bullying. This will encourage other students who are being harassed to report it in its early stages.

4.1.3 — Anti-harassment Policies

Educational institutions can go a long way toward promoting a harassment-free environment for students with disabilities, and other individuals protected by the *Code*, by having a clear, comprehensive anti-harassment policy in place. In cases of alleged harassment, the policy will alert all parties to their rights, roles and responsibilities. Such a policy should clearly set out ways in which the harassment will be dealt with promptly and efficiently. Please see the Appendix for suggested contents of an anti-harassment policy.

In Practice: All students and school staff should be aware of the existence of an anti-harassment policy and the procedures in place for resolving complaints. This can be done by:

- distributing policies to everyone as soon as they are introduced
- making new students aware of them by including the policies in any orientation material
- training educators and school staff on the contents of the policies, and
- providing ongoing education on human rights issues.

4.2 — Accounting for Non-evident Disabilities

Part of creating a welcoming environment involves being sensitive to the many ways in which a student's disability might manifest and the unique needs which may arise as a result. Some types of disabilities are not apparent to the average onlooker. This can be because of the nature of the specific disability in question: it may be episodic, its effects may not be visible, or it may not manifest consistently in all environments. Examples of non-evident disabilities include mental disabilities, learning disabilities, chronic fatigue syndrome, environmental sensitivities and epilepsy.

Students with non-evident disabilities often face unique challenges in the education system. For some, requesting an accommodation may be especially difficult if a teacher or professor doubts the authenticity of the request because they cannot "see" it. Sensitivity and informed understanding on the part of educators, school staff, and fellow students alike can combat stereotypes, stigma and prejudice, all of which can have a discriminatory effect on students with non-evident disabilities.

Mental disability is a form of non-evident disability that raises unique issues in the educational context. Much misinformation continues to exist about mental illness and too often persons with mental disabilities are labelled and judged according to inaccurate preconceptions and assumptions. Rules, preconditions, policies or practices that treat persons with mental disabilities differently from other persons with disabilities may be discriminatory on their face.[24]

Academic environments must be sensitive to the needs of all students, including students with mental disabilities. It is important to keep in mind that some mental illnesses may render the student incapable of identifying his or her needs. An education provider has a responsibility to take an active role in addressing situations that may be linked to mental disability. Where an education provider has reason to believe that a student may require assistance or accommodation due to a mental disability, further inquiries should be made, and support offered. Even if an education provider has not been formally advised of a mental disability, affording differential treatment to a student based on the perception of a disability may still engage the protection of the *Code*.

> *In Practice*: A third-year university student begins to exhibit erratic behaviour. Although she has been a successful student to date, she begins

[24]For example, see *Gibbs v. Battlefords and Dist. Cooperative Ltd.*, [1996] 3 S.C.R. 566, 27 C.H.R.R. D/87.

missing classes and fails to submit her coursework on time. In the middle of a lecture, she suddenly starts shouting inexplicably. The professor arranges to meet with the student after class to inquire into her situation. As a result of this discussion, the professor contacts the university's Office for Students with Disabilities. A meeting is arranged and the student is offered assistance. The university helps arrange counselling and support services for the student who, ultimately, is diagnosed with schizophrenia. The Office for Students with Disabilities then works with the student and her professors to arrange academic accommodations.

Education providers should educate themselves, school staff and students about nonevident disabilities, including mental illness, so as to provide a welcoming and safe environment for all students with disabilities. Schools should ensure that all students are provided with learning opportunities that foster an awareness and appreciation of diversity issues in the educational environment, and combat negative attitudes and stereotypes.

4.3 — Discipline, Safe Schools and Students with Disabilities

The stated purposes of safe schools legislation, regulations and related school board policies — to promote respect, non-violent conflict resolution and the safety of people in schools — are reasonable and *bona fide* and of paramount importance.[25] At the same time, in some cases, discipline policies may have an adverse effect on students with disabilities.[26] Education providers have a duty to assess each student with a disability individually before imposing disciplinary sanctions. Disciplinary sanctions include detentions, exclusions, suspensions, expulsions, and other forms of punish-

[25]In 2000, the Ontario Legislature passed the *Safe Schools Act*. The Act gives force to the provincial Code of Conduct and provides principals, teachers, and school boards with more authority to suspend and expel students and involve the police. The *Safe Schools Act* specifies infractions which require mandatory suspensions, expulsions and police involvement. It also permits school board policies to add infractions for which suspensions or expulsions are either mandatory or discretionary.

[26]The potential discriminatory effect of safe school legislation and policies on individuals protected by the *Code* was a prominent concern raised during the Commission's disability and education consultation, and is discussed at length in *The Opportunity to Succeed*. This issue was also raised extensively in the Commission's inquiry into racial profiling, and is discussed in the Commission's report entitled *Paying the Price: The Human Cost of Racial Profiling*. Both documents are available online at the Commission's website: www.ohrc.on.ca.

ment. Educators should attempt to determine whether the behaviour in question is a manifestation of the student's disability by considering:

- formal assessments and evaluations of the student
- relevant information supplied by the student or the student's parents
- observations of the student
- the student's accommodation plan[27]
- whether the accommodations provided for in the student's accommodation plan were appropriate, and whether these accommodations were being provided consistent with the student's accommodation plan
- whether the student's disability impaired his or her ability to understand the impact and consequences of the behaviour subject to disciplinary action
- whether the student's disability impaired his or her ability to control the behaviour subject to disciplinary action, and
- whether the student has undetected disability-related needs that require accommodation.

Under the *Code*, education providers have a legal obligation to accommodate students with disabilities up to the point of undue hardship. All students with disabilities, even those whose behaviour is disruptive, are entitled to receive accommodation.

> *Did You Know*: Other jurisdictions have implemented safeguards to protect students with disabilities from being disciplined for behaviour that is disability-related. For example, in the United States, the *Individuals with Disabilities Education Act* requires that, where certain disciplinary action is taken or contemplated against a student with a disability, a review must be conducted of the relationship between the child's disability and the behaviour subject to the disciplinary action.[28]

Educators must consider a range of strategies to address disruptive behaviour. Such strategies will include reassessing and, where necessary, modifying the student's accommodation plan, providing additional supports, implementing alternative learning techniques, and other forms of positive behavioural intervention.

---

[27]For a more detailed discussion on accommodations plans, please refer to the section of the Guidelines entitled "Accommodation Planning"

[28]See *Individuals with Disabilities Education Act*, *supra*, note 17, ss. 615(k)(4)(A)(ii).

If a student's behaviour is not a manifestation of his or her disability, that is, where there is no causal relationship between the student's disability and the behaviour in question, then that student would be subject to the normal consequences of his or her misconduct. Where discipline is warranted, however, it is to be implemented with discretion and with regard to the student's unique circumstances.[29]

There may be rare situations in which a student's behaviour, even where it is a manifestation of his or her disability, poses a health and safety risk to him or herself, other students, teachers and/or school staff. While an education provider in this type of situation continues to have a duty to accommodate the student up to the point of undue hardship, it is recognized that there may be legitimate health and safety concerns that need to be addressed. In some situations involving health and safety risks, placement in a mainstream classroom may not be the most appropriate accommodation. This issue is discussed in the "Undue Hardship Standard" section of the Guidelines under "Health and Safety Requirements".

5. — Accommodation Process

5.1 — Basic Principles

The principles of respect for dignity, individualization, and inclusion and full participation apply both to the substance of an accommodation and to the accommodation process. The manner in which an accommodation is provided and the methods by which it is implemented are subject to human rights standards.

At the heart of the accommodation process is the responsibility, shared by all parties, to engage in meaningful dialogue about accommodation, and to seek out expert assistance as needed. Everyone involved should co-operatively engage in the process, share information, and avail themselves of potential accommodation solutions.[30]

5.2 — Sharing Information

Information about accommodation procedures should be readily available to students and, where applicable, their parents. It is important to create an educational environment that encourages and supports accommodation re-

[29]The Ontario Court of Appeal has commented that discipline measures pursuant to the regulations under the *Education Act* must take into account a student's individual circumstances. See *Bonnah (Litigation Guardian of) v. Ottawa-Carlton District School Board* (2003), 64 O.R. (3d) 454 (Ont. C.A.) at para. 37.

[30]See *Disability Policy*, *supra*, note 1 at Part 3.4.

quests, and educators and school staff should be encouraged to show a positive attitude toward accommodation. Educational institutions can demonstrate their support for and commitment to providing accommodation by making public announcements during meetings or through the institution's communication channels. All students should be informed that students with disabilities are entitled to accommodation, the process for requesting an accommodation, their right to participate in such a process, and any other information that may be helpful in making the accommodation process more understandable and accessible. In addition, the accommodation process should be part of the regular life and discourse of the educational institution. At the same time, it should respect confidentiality and the process itself should not result in an undue burden on individual students and/or their parent(s)/guardian(s).

5.3 — Timeliness

Accommodations must be provided in a timely manner. Delays in the provision of accommodation have the potential to directly impede a student's ability to access and participate in the educational curriculum. As such, unreasonable delays may be found to violate the procedural duty to accommodate, and thus constitute a breach of the *Code*.

> Examples of delays that students with disabilities may experience include:
>
> - waiting long periods of time for textbooks and other academic materials in alternative formats
> - delays in the receipt of professional assessments
> - delays in the provision of support staff (*e.g.*, educational assistants, special needs assistants, sign language interpreters, *etc.*)
> - waiting lists for other types of special education services (*e.g.*, identification hearings, classroom placements, preparation of accommodation plans, implementation of accommodation plans, processing of claims for funding, *etc.*), and
> - delays in receiving needed adjustments to accommodations.

When making accommodation requests, students have a responsibility to give education providers ample time to ensure that accommodations will be available when needed.

Where the most appropriate accommodation cannot be provided right away, education providers have a duty to provide for interim accommodation as the next-best and timely solution while planning for a more appropriate and permanent solution. In the meantime, this will enable students to be as productive and involved as possible.

> *In Practice:* A personal reader may be an interim accommodation for a person who has low vision, while she is waiting for an electronic transcription of course materials to be provided.

5.4 — Dispute Resolution

Education providers should provide an effective and transparent mechanism to resolve disputes that arise in the accommodation process. At the primary and secondary levels, students and their parents should have timely access to a mechanism that will hear and resolve issues related to the identification of a student's disability-related needs, placement, programs and services, and any other process issues that may arise. The mechanism should be comprised of or have access to qualified individuals representing a range of interests. At the post-secondary level, students should also have an avenue to address and resolve accommodation disputes in a timely fashion.

The purpose of a dispute resolution mechanism should be to identify problems and determine ways to solve them which would permit the student access to educational services with a minimum of delay. Educational institutions should facilitate this process and provide reasonable assistance to students and, where applicable, their parents/guardians. Dispute resolution procedures that are not timely or effective could amount to a failure of the duty to accommodate.

Where there is a dispute regarding a proposed accommodation, and an education provider alleges undue hardship, the education provider must demonstrate it. It is not the responsibility of a student seeking accommodation to prove that a proposed accommodation would *not* cause undue hardship.[31]

5.5 — Training

Staff training is one of the critical supports that an educational institution can provide in the accommodation process. Disability awareness training should be a mandatory part of professional training for all teachers, faculty and school staff, and should be available on an ongoing basis throughout the school year. The student being accommodated, those responsible for

---

[31] The elements of undue hardship will be discussed in greater detail in the section of the Guidelines entitled "Undue Hardship Standard."

providing accommodation, and other staff should learn about disability issues, accommodation and the implemented choices.

> *In Practice*: At the primary and secondary levels, effective training will enable teachers to deal effectively with disability issues in the classroom. Training will also help teachers educate students about issues of diversity and difference.
>
> *In Practice*: At the post-secondary level, computer systems staff may need to learn about the interaction of a new access device with the organization's computer system.

Training should be repeated if changes in the educational institution or in the student's accommodation plan make it necessary to modify the accommodation.

6. — Confidentiality and Disclosure of Information

When requesting accommodation from an education provider, students (and/or their parent(s)/guardian(s)) have a responsibility to provide sufficient information about their disability-related needs in order to facilitate the accommodation. Educational services at the lower levels of education are broad and may include cultivating aspects of the student's development beyond those which are strictly academic. Since the accommodations that younger students may require will often relate to their overall wellbeing, it may be appropriate for education providers at the primary and sometimes at the secondary levels to require more extensive and detailed information about a student's disability-related needs. At the higher levels of schooling, where educational services are defined more narrowly and the focus is more on academic standards and accreditation, accommodations will generally be related to the student's academic needs and the degree and type of information required by education providers will not likely be as broad.

In an ideal world, all students, including students with disabilities, would be comfortable discussing all aspects of their personal identities in an open manner without fear of discrimination and/or harassment. However, in reality, some students may be reluctant to disclose their disabilities at school, particularly at the secondary and post-secondary levels, for fear of being stigmatized, denied opportunities, or of arousing unwanted curiosity and unnecessary concern from others. Some will have had bad experiences in the past that may have included being on the receiving end of intolerant attitudes and other forms of discriminatory treatment.

6.1 — Protecting Disability-Related Information

It is important that an education provider take steps to ensure that students feel safe disclosing a disability. In order to avoid labelling or stereotyping, it is essential that education-providers take precautions to safeguard the disability-related information of students. This is especially important for individuals with disabilities that continue to carry a strong social stigma, such as mental illness and HIV/AIDS. Maintaining confidentiality for students with disabilities is an important procedural component of the duty to accommodate. The degree of confidentiality afforded to students will likely vary according to the level of education being offered. For example, confidentiality may be less of an issue for students at the primary school level where the educational service being offered is broad and student autonomy is less of an issue. For students at the secondary and post-secondary levels, privacy and confidentiality will likely be of greater importance, particularly as students, in many cases, are developing greater independence and will often be more in control of managing their own accommodation needs.

Personal information that either directly or indirectly identifies that a student has a disability should remain exclusively with designated personnel in a secure filing system away from the student's academic record in order to protect the student's privacy. This is meant to protect the institution from allegations of discrimination, as well as the student from potential discriminatory practices.

> *In Practice:* In the day-to-day activities of the educational institution, education providers must take care to avoid disclosing a student's disability. For example, faculty should not speak about a student's disability in front of their class or other students, disclose a student's personal disability information without permission to other faculty/staff, leave written information regarding a student's disability in a public place or in plain view, or use names when discussing general disability issues.

Any data collected on students with disabilities (such as numbers of students served, types of disabilities, or accommodations received) should be collected in aggregate, and must not include any information that would reveal a student's identity. Particularly at the secondary and post-secondary levels, educational institutions must ensure that data on disability do not appear on academic documents including test results, transcripts, student records, or graduation documentation. Distinguishing the score results of a student who received accommodation has the potential of revealing the existence of a disability and exposing that student to discrimination.

> *In Practice*: Transcripts, entrance test result forms, or licensing exam result forms should not indicate that a student received accommodation, or that academic requirements were met under "special" or "non-standard conditions."

For some students, disclosing a disability may not be necessary because the disability may not impact upon their study. This will especially be the case where educational institutions have designed their technology structures, curricula, programs and services inclusively, and adaptation or modification to meet the needs of students with disabilities is therefore unnecessary.

6.2 — Information to be Provided

While a student seeking accommodation must provide information about his or her disability-related needs, and in some cases may have to provide medical confirmation that a disability exists, it is not generally necessary, particularly at the secondary and post-secondary levels, for the student to explicitly inform the education provider of the specific type of disability, or to provide specific medical information (*e.g.*, a diagnosis) about a disability. A diagnosis of a student's medical condition will not usually be relevant to or necessary for planning accommodation and, wherever possible, an education provider should attempt to ascertain the disability-related needs of a student without requiring a formal diagnosis.

There will be some cases, however, where there may be overlap between a description of the student's needs and an actual diagnosis. In these circumstances, it may be necessary for an education provider to require a diagnosis in order to appropriately accommodate a student.

> *Example*: In the course of providing information to her school principal to facilitate the provision of accommodation, a Grade 11 student provides an assessment of her learning needs from an outside expert. The assessment outlines the learning supports required by the student, and in doing so, identifies the student as having a learning disability.

The staff in offices for students with disabilities at colleges and universities have expertise in dealing with accommodation issues in the academic environment and, as such, can play a vital role in assisting with the accommodation process.

Students may choose to provide these offices with more detailed information about their disabilities, including, for example, a diagnostic assessment, where to do so would facilitate the provision of accommodation. Offices for students with disabilities must ensure that the disability-related information of students is kept strictly confidential.

There may also be some instances where a student will be asked to produce a medical diagnosis of his or her disability for the purposes of establishing eligibility for student funding programs.

> *Example*: A government-sponsored fund developed specifically to assist college and university students who are deaf, deafened or hard of hearing requires that students provide a medical diagnosis in order to be considered eligible.

In situations where a diagnosis is necessary, the educational institution is responsible for implementing procedures to ensure that student confidentiality is maximized, the information requested is limited to that which is specifically needed for the program, and the information is disseminated only to those responsible for administering the program.

In some instances, there may be a reasonable and *bona fide* basis for an education provider to question the legitimacy of a student's request for accommodation or the adequacy of the information provided. In such cases, the education provider may request confirmation or additional information from a qualified health care professional. No one can be forced to submit to an independent medical examination, but failure to respond to reasonable requests may delay the provision of accommodation until such information is provided.

7. — Appropriate Accommodation

7.1 — Basic Principles

It is the Commission's position that the duty to accommodate requires that the most appropriate accommodation be determined and then undertaken, short of undue hardship. The most appropriate accommodation is one that most respects the dignity of the student with a disability, meets individual needs, best promotes inclusion and full participation, and maximizes confidentiality.

An accommodation will be considered appropriate if it will result in equal opportunity to attain the same level of performance, or to enjoy the same level of benefits and privileges enjoyed by others, or if it is proposed or adopted for the purpose of achieving equal opportunity, and meets the student's disability-related needs.

The aim of accommodation is the inclusion and full participation of students with disabilities in educational life. Education providers must make efforts to build or adapt educational services to accommodate students with disabilities in a way that promotes their full participation. Barriers must be prevented or removed so that students with disabilities are provided with equal opportunities to access and benefit from their environment and face the same duties and requirements as everyone else, with dignity and without impediment.

7.2 — Forms of Accommodation

Depending on a student's individual needs and the nature of the educational service being provided, accommodations that students with disabilities may require may include:

- modifications to improve the physical accessibility of educational buildings, facilities, resources and student housing
- support services, such as assessment or advice on learning strategies
- a modified curriculum
- modification to evaluation methodologies, such as extended time when taking tests and completing assignments, or alternative evaluation formats
- academic materials in alternative formats (*e.g.*, Braille, large print, digitized text, voice activated software, assisted hearing devices)
- sign language interpretation services
- provision of and training on adaptive technology
- in-class assistance from specialized professionals
- in-class supports (*e.g.*, tutors, interpreters, notetakers, personal readers), and
- transportation to and from school.

7.3 — Placement

At the primary and secondary levels, before considering placing a student in a selfcontained or specialized classroom, education providers must first consider inclusion in the regular classroom.[32] In most cases, appropriate

[32]The Ministry of Education has articulated its policy position on this issue stating its commitment to the principle that "the integration of exceptional students should

accommodation will be accommodation in the regular classroom with supports.[33] However, every student with a disability is unique. In order to provide appropriate accommodation to all students with disabilities, education providers must, with the assistance of parental input, assess each student's particular strengths and needs, and consider these against a full range of placements, programs and services. Ultimately, appropriate accommodation will be decided on an individual basis.

In determining the most appropriate accommodation, education providers should consider factors such as:

- the student's preferred learning style
- the student's academic performance (grades and other signs of advancement or regression)
- the length of time the accommodation will take to arrange
- whether supports provided are compatible with accommodation supports used at home
- the geographical proximity of a placement to the student's home (ideally, the student should be able to attend his or her neighbourhood school)
- the extent to which a placement affords the student with opportunities to socialize and interact with other students
- the degree to which a placement addresses health and safety issues.

In the *Eaton* decision, the Supreme Court of Canada established that equality may sometimes require different treatment that does not offend an individual's dignity.[34] Emily Eaton, a student with a disability, was initially placed in an integrated classroom. However, after three years, her teachers and assistants concluded that this placement was not in her best interests

---

be the normal practice in Ontario, when such a placement meets the pupil's needs and is in accordance with parental wishes." Please see MEDU Memorandum dated June 9, 1994 to directors of education, superintendents of special education, and principals as quoted in Ministry of Education, *Special Education: A Guide for Educators*, 2001 at D10.

[33]In situations where an education provider makes a determination that home instruction is the most appropriate accommodation for a student with a disability, even if it is only an interim placement while other more permanent accommodation solutions are being explored, the education provider continues to have a duty to accommodate the student up to the point of undue hardship and to bear the costs of the accommodation.

[34]*Eaton*, *supra*, note 9.

and she was moved to a specialized classroom. Her parents disputed the change and appealed the decision up to the Supreme Court of Canada. The Court stated that the failure to place Emily Eaton in an integrated setting did not create a burden or disadvantage for her, because such a placement was not in her best interests. According to the Court,

> While integration should be recognized as the norm of general application because of the benefits it generally provides, a presumption in favour of integrated schooling would work to the disadvantage of pupils who require special education in order to achieve equality . . . Integration can be either a benefit or a burden depending on whether the individual can profit from the advantages that integration provides.

At the same time, the Supreme Court has also said that the search for accommodation is a multi-party inquiry.[35] In education, this means that students with disabilities, their parents or guardians, as well as educators, administrators and any necessary experts together must consider the best interests of the student in determining the most appropriate placement accommodation. In some circumstances, the best way to meet the individual needs of students with disabilities with dignity may be to provide separate or specialized services. This may include education in a self-contained classroom within a neighbourhood school, or it may involve enrolment in a specialized school, including a provincial school or a demonstration school. However, it is the Commission's view that, before considering placing a student in a self-contained, or specialized classroom, education providers must first consider inclusion in the regular classroom.

Where placement outside the regular classroom is determined to be the most appropriate accommodation, the education provider should still make reasonable efforts to include the student in school programs and activities with students without disabilities, wherever possible. For example, the student should be afforded the opportunity to participate in music and art classes, lunch, recess, gym, school trips, *etc*.

7.4 — Accommodation Process as a Continuum

Accommodation is a process and a matter of degree, rather than an all-or-nothing proposition, and can be seen as a continuum. At one end of this continuum would be the most appropriate accommodation that meets a student's needs. Alternative accommodation (that which would be less than "ideal") might be next on the continuum and might also be implemented as an interim solution until the most appropriate accommodation is imple-

---

[35]*Central Okanagan School District No. 23 v. Renaud*, [1992] 2 S.C.R. 970, at para. 43.

mented or restored. This also means that in the course of exploring other appropriate alternatives, the most appropriate accommodation known at that given point in time should still be implemented or maintained.

It is the Commission's view that short of undue hardship, the highest point in the continuum of accommodation must be achieved. However, if there is a choice between two accommodations which are equally responsive to the student's needs in a dignified manner, then those responsible for accommodation may select the one that is less expensive or that is less disruptive to the organization.

> *In Practice*: While in Grade 3, a student with dyslexia received the one-onone services of a full-time Special Needs Assistant as an accommodation. Based on an assessment of the nature and extent of the student's needs along with a review of her academic and social progress, this level of intensive support was no longer necessary once the student was in Grade 4 and the school board decided that the services of a part-time Special Needs Assistant would be an appropriate accommodation.

The *Code* does not guarantee the right to any one particular form of accommodation. Before opting for the less expensive or disruptive option, however, an accommodation provider must first demonstrate, considering the student's specific needs, that two accommodations are in fact equally responsive and equally dignified.

7.5 — Modifying Educational Requirements

Section 17 of the *Code* states that a right is not infringed if the person with a disability is incapable of performing or fulfilling the essential duties or requirements attending the exercise of the right. Once appropriate accommodation is received, students must still be able to perform the essential requirements of the service. While courts and tribunals have provided little guidance on the nature of essential duties and requirements, terms that have been used include indispensable, vital, and very important.

Depending on the level of education in question, essential requirements may be defined quite differently. At the primary and secondary levels, for instance, there is a statutory right to education for all. Each child is entitled to the opportunity to develop his or her unique abilities and talents. Therefore, the essential requirements of the educational service at these levels would be defined broadly, and would likely include the student's overall physical and social development, in addition to the student's academic performance.

At the post-secondary level of education, the educational right would be defined more narrowly, and the essential requirements of the educational service at this level would likely be more focused on academic performance. An appropriate accommodation at the post-secondary level would enable a student to successfully meet the essential requirements of the programme, with no alteration in standards or outcomes, although the manner in which the student demonstrates mastery, knowledge and skills may be altered. In this way, education providers are able to provide all students with equal opportunities to enjoy the same level of benefits and privileges and meet the requirements for acquiring an education without the risk of compromising academic integrity.[36]

> *In Practice*: A college policy requires students to fulfil a minimum number of in-class hours in order to receive credit for a course. However, in response to the needs of students whose disabilities make it difficult or impossible to attend school full-time, the policy states that the attendance requirements may be modified where appropriate.

A requirement should not lightly be considered to be essential, but should be carefully scrutinized. This includes course requirements and standards. For example, at the post-secondary level, it may likely be an essential requirement that a student master core aspects of a course curriculum. It is much less likely that it will be an essential requirement to demonstrate that mastery in a particular format, unless mastery of that format (*e.g.*, oral communication) is also a vital requirement of the program.

> *In Practice*: A university professor in a nursing program requires all students to demonstrate proficiency in her course by passing an in-class essay test worth 100% of the student's final grade. The primary aim of the course is to teach students clinical evaluation methodology. Unless the education provider can show that the 100% essay mode of evaluation is an essential requirement of the course, it may be found to discriminate against students with learning disabilities and other types of disabilities that make it difficult to process large amounts of written material under strict time constraints.

The onus is on the education provider to show that a student is incapable of

[36]For a more detailed discussion on academic integrity, please see *The Opportunity to Succeed* at pages 61-62.

performing the essential requirements of the educational service, even with accommodation. Conclusions about inability to perform essential requirements must not be reached without actually testing the ability of the student. It is not enough for an education provider to assume that a student cannot perform an essential requirement. Rather, there must be an objective determination of that fact.

Non-essential requirements are those requirements that would not detract from the main purpose of the educational service if they were waived. Accommodation for nonessential requirements may include finding another way for the student to meet the requirement, having it done differently, or dropping it altogether.

8. — Accommodation Planning

As part of the duty to accommodate, education providers are responsible for taking steps to plan for the accommodation of students with disabilities. Effective planning will take place both on an organizational level and on an individual level in relation to each student with accommodation needs. Individual planning should also address the transition needs of a student as he or she moves from one level or type of education to another. Accommodation planning may also require education providers to collect and analyze aggregate data on students with disabilities in order to ensure that education policies and practices do not have an adverse effect on these students.

Accommodation is an ongoing process and accessibility plans and accommodation plans should be reviewed on a regular basis. As with any other plan, documenting progress in writing helps with monitoring, accountability and future planning. Where academic requirements or facilities change over time, education providers are required to review, modify or upgrade accommodations. Plans should be revised as the individual's needs, or the educational institution, changes.

> *Example*: A change in the computer network could interrupt a student's efficient use of a technical aid connected to the system. New equipment in the school or educational institution may require additional accommodation or modifications to existing accommodations.

8.1 — Institutional Accessibility Plans

Education providers must take steps to ensure that accessibility plans comply with the requirements of human rights law and policy. To be effective, an accessibility plan should set out an educational institution's specific commitments to providing equal access to educational services for all students. In this regard, accessibility plans should

- set goals, identify steps being taken and report on achievements made by the educational institution with respect to adhering to the principles of inclusion by design, barrier removal, most appropriate or next-best or interim accommodation of remaining needs, individualization, confidentiality, and shared responsibilities in the accommodation process
- report on policies, procedures and mechanisms for implementation, monitoring, education and training, input, dispute resolution and accountability, and
- include timelines, performance measures and accountability structures, and respect the dignity and the right to inclusion and participation of students with disabilities, in the process of planning for and implementing accessibility.

In Practice: Education providers might wish to prepare and make available to the public a formal report outlining their commitment to providing accessible education for all students. The report might include the educational institution's accessibility plan, and the findings of data collection and analysis. Where the data reveals discrepancies, the report could also set out steps that will be taken to address inequities and bring the education provider's practices into compliance with the *Code* and Commission policy.

8.2 — Individual Accommodation Plans

Education providers should also develop an accommodation plan for each student with a disability who requires accommodation, in consultation with that student and/or his or her parent or guardian. At the primary and secondary levels, accommodation plans will likely be more prescriptive and structured and include learning objectives; whereas, at the post-secondary level, students might prefer to have more control over their accommodation planning, and plans would likely focus on specific accommodation services or modifications to evaluation methods, and would not be as tied to learning outcomes. Depending on the student's individual needs and preferences, an effective accommodation plan may include:

- a statement of the student's individual limitations and needs as they relate to accessing the service of education, including any necessary assessments and information from experts or specialists
- arrangements for necessary assessments by a health or other professional

- identification of the most appropriate accommodation
- a statement of the specific services and supports required by the student (*e.g.*, assistive technology devices)
- the ordering of any necessary products or services
- the student's present levels of educational performance and a statement of current educational status (may not be required at the post-secondary level)
- a statement of annual goals (including specific performance indicators and short-term objectives)
- incorporation of input from student and/or parent(s)/guardian(s)
- clear timelines for the various stages of the accommodation process
- specific steps to be taken to meet annual goals
- criteria, procedure and schedule to determine whether the accommodation is facilitating the student's educational goals
- a mechanism for review and re-assessment, where necessary, to determine whether the student's accommodation needs are being met, and/or
- an accountability mechanism (for example, if plan not implemented, or if not implemented effectively or in a timely fashion.

8.3 — Transitioning

At the primary and secondary levels, accommodation plans should also include a statement with respect to the student's transition needs. It might include, for example, a plan to have the student take specific courses designed to prepare him or her for postsecondary study, or it might outline a strategy to have the student participate in a vocational educational program or other type of "co-op" placement. The focus should be on how the student's educational program can be planned to facilitate a successful transition to his or her goals after secondary school. Each student is unique, and goals may include post-secondary schooling, vocational training, integrated employment, continuing and adult education, independent living, or community participation. School staff should inform students that, where the student so desires, staff will communicate with the student's prospective educational institution or employers with regard to accommodation practices or effective learning strategies to help facilitate the student's transition.

Transition planning will also be appropriate in situations where students are transferring from one type of educational setting to another.

Example: An 11-year-old girl with a history of behavioural difficulties has made significant progress in a section 20 program.[37] She has learned effective anger management techniques and is ready to be re-integrated into the regular school system with supports. Working together, her former and prospective teachers, her parents and medical professionals develop a plan in order to facilitate this transition.

8.4 — Data Collection

Effective planning requires education providers to ensure that education policies and practices do not have an adverse impact on students with disabilities, or other individuals protected by the *Code*. In order to make sure that education environments are free from social phenomena widely recognized as discriminatory such as profiling, institutionalized barriers, socio-economic disadvantage or unequal opportunity on the basis of protected *Code* grounds, education providers should collect statistical information for the purposes of monitoring, preventing and ameliorating systemic and adverse discrimination.

Did you know: In 2004, the Toronto District School Board (TDSB), in conjunction with provincial organizations, established the *Safe and Compassionate Schools Task Force* to review the Board's Safe Schools Policy and its implementation. In its submission to the Task Force, the Commission recommended that the TDSB collect and analyze data on suspensions and expulsions under the *Safe Schools Act* and that this data be used to prevent and correct any discriminatory effect.[38]

Statistics and data collection may also be warranted in situations where an

---

[37]Section 20 programs provide educational programming to students who, for a variety of reasons, require their educational needs to be met outside of the regular school system in specialized settings.

[38]See Recommendation #3 of the *Submission of the Ontario Human Rights Commission to the Toronto District School Board Safe and Compassionate Schools Task Force* (April 2004) available online at the Commission's website: www.ohrc.on.ca. In addition, in *The Opportunity to Succeed*, the Commission recommended that school boards collect and analyze data on suspensions and expulsions under the *Safe Schools Act* to ensure that the *Act* is not having an adverse effect on individuals protected by the *Code*. The Commission also recommended that the Ministry of Education collect and analyze data on placements of students with disabilities for the purpose of addressing iniquities and promoting compliance with the *Code* and Commission policy. See *The Opportunity to Succeed*, *supra*, note 26 at pp. 25 and 40 respectively.

education provider has an objective basis to believe that systemic infringement of rights may be occurring, or where there are persistent allegations or perceptions of systemic discrimination, or where it is an organization's intent to prevent or ameliorate disadvantage already known to be faced by persons with disabilities. Where problems are identified, data analysis can provide useful direction for remedies to address systemic discrimination as well as evaluate the success of such measures. This is in keeping with the remedial purpose of the *Code* and with recent human rights jurisprudence that finds organizations have an obligation to take into account a person's already disadvantaged position within Canadian society.[39]

> *Other Jurisdictions*: In the United States, the *Individuals with Disabilities Education Act* requires states to collect and provide data on students with disabilities on an annual basis. Internationally, the United Nations has also recommended that "States Parties should encourage the collection, analysis and codification of statistics and information on disabilities and on the effective enjoyment of human rights by persons with disabilities."[40]

Data collection and the use of data should only ever be undertaken for legitimate purposes not contrary to the *Code* such as ameliorating disadvantage, removing systemic barriers and promoting substantive equality for individuals and groups protected by the *Code*. Collecting information about characteristics based on enumerated grounds under the *Code* may lead to an inference that the information might be used to treat an individual or group in a discriminatory manner. To address such concerns, measures should be

---

[39] The notion that substantive differential treatment can result because of a distinction, exclusion or preference, or because of a failure to take into account a person's already disadvantaged position within Canadian society was first articulated in *Law*, *supra*, note 11. The approach has been affirmed in several subsequent cases, most notably two cases dealing with discrimination on the basis of disability: *Mercier*, *supra*, note 7, and *Granovsky*, *supra*, note 10.

[40] *Individuals with Disabilities in Education Act*, *supra*, note 17, s. 618(c); Draft Comprehensive and Integral International Convention on the Protection and Promotion of the Rights and Dignity of Persons with Disabilities, at Article 6, United Nations Ad Hoc Committee, January 2004.

taken in order to ensure that the collection and use of data is done in a legitimate and appropriate manner.[41]

In Practice: At the primary and secondary levels, data collected could include numbers of students in mainstream classrooms versus self-contained classrooms, number of students in each placement according to type of disability, number of students who also belong to other historically disadvantaged groups, *etc*. At the post-secondary level, data collected could include numbers of students who leave their programs before graduating, and lengths of time taken to provide accommodations.

Where an analysis of this data reveals significant discrepancies with respect to trends in identification, placement, disciplinary action, graduation and/or drop-out rates, education providers should review and revise their policies, practices and procedures accordingly to ensure that they are in compliance with the *Code*.

9. — Undue Hardship Standard

Under the *Code*, every student with a disability is entitled to accommodation up to the point of undue hardship. The *Code* sets out only three elements that may be considered in assessing whether an accommodation would cause undue hardship:

- cost
- outside sources of funding, if any, and
- health and safety requirements, if any.

It is the Commission's position that this means that only factors that can be brought within these three elements will be considered.[42]

Example: A union opposes the hiring of a specialized educational pro-

---

[41]For more information, please see the Ontario Human Rights Commission's *Guidelines for Collecting Data on Enumerated Grounds Under the Code*, available online at the Commission's website: www.ohrc.on.ca.

[42]The broad and purposive interpretation of the *Code* and human rights generally means that rights must be construed liberally and defences to those rights should be construed narrowly. There are a number of cases that confirm this approach to the interpretation of human rights statutes. Most recently, in *Mercier, supra* note 7, the Supreme Court summarized these cases and outlined the relevant principles of

fessional to assist in the accommodation of a student with a learning disability because the professional is not part of the bargaining unit. Unless the union can show that the hiring will cause undue hardship on the basis of one of the three elements set out above, disruption to the collective agreement will not, in and of itself, be enough to establish undue hardship.

In order to claim the undue hardship defence, the education provider has the onus of proof. The student requesting accommodation does not have to prove that the accommodation can be accomplished without undue hardship. The nature of the evidence required to prove undue hardship must be objective, real, direct and, in the case of cost, quantifiable. The education provider must provide facts, figures and scientific data or opinion to support a claim that the proposed accommodation in fact causes undue hardship. A mere statement, without supporting evidence, that the cost or risk is "too high" based on impressionistic views or stereotypes will not be sufficient.

Objective evidence includes, but is not limited to:

- financial statements and budgets
- scientific data, information and data resulting from empirical studies
- expert opinion
- detailed information about the activity and the requested accommodation, and
- information about the conditions surrounding the activity and their effects on the person or group with a disability.

9.1 — Elements of the Undue Hardship Defence

9.1.1 — Costs

What the Courts Say: The Supreme Court of Canada has said that, "One must be wary of putting too low a value on accommodating the disabled. It is all too easy to cite increased cost as a reason for refusing to accord the disabled equal treatment."[43]

---

human rights interpretation. Moreover, the *Code* has primacy over other legislation (see sub-section 47(2) of the *Code*). relevant principles of human rights interpretation. Moreover, the *Code* has primacy over other legislation (see sub-section 47(2) of the *Code*).

[43] *British Columbia (Superintendent of Motor Vehicles) v. British Columbia (Council of Human Rights)*, [1999] 3 S.C.R. 868 ["*Grismer*"] at para. 41.

The costs standard is a high one. Where possible, an education provider must take steps to recover the costs of accommodation. This can be done, for example, by obtaining grants, subsidies and other outside sources of funding[44] which help to offset accommodation expenses. Tax deductions and other government benefits flowing from the accommodation must also be considered. In addition, inclusive design and other creative design solutions can often avoid expensive capital outlay.

In determining whether a financial cost would alter the essential nature or substantially affect the viability of the educational institution, consideration will be given to:

- The size of the institution — what might prove to be a cost amounting to undue hardship for a small educational institution will not likely be one for a larger educational institution.
- Can the costs be recovered in the normal course of operation?
- Can other divisions, departments, *etc.* of the educational institution help to absorb part of the costs?
- Can the costs be phased in — so much per year?
- Can the education provider set aside a certain percentage of money per year to be placed in a reserve fund to be used for accommodation issues?[45]

---

[44]Outside sources of funding may include:

- *Funds that may be available to the student only, provided through government programs and that are linked to the student's disability.* Students might be expected to take advantage of these programs when making accommodation requests of an education provider. However, such resources should most appropriately meet the accommodation needs of the student, including respect for dignity.
- *Funds that would assist education providers defray the costs of accommodation.* Other outside accommodation resources might be available to a student with a disability when more than one organization has an overlapping or interconnected sphere of responsibility for the duty to accommodate.
- *Funding programs to improve accessibility for persons with disabilities — a corporate or organizational responsibility.*

[45]It should be noted that both phasing in and the establishment of a reserve fund are to be considered only *after* the accommodation provider has demonstrated that the most appropriate accommodation could not be accomplished immediately.

- Will the educational programs and services for all students be substantially and permanently altered? For example, will a school board be forced to cancel its music programs to fund an accommodation?

The government is required to ensure that school boards have access to sufficient funding to ensure equal access to education. School boards, in turn, have a responsibility to provide adequate funding to schools to enable the provision of accommodations. Where an education provider receives funding from government for the purposes of promoting accessibility and meeting the needs of students with disabilities, the education provider should track accommodation data and alert the government to any funding deficiencies that exist.

Education providers cannot use limited resources or budgetary restrictions as a defence to the duty to accommodate without first meeting the formal test for undue hardship based on costs. Further, education providers are not to decide which accommodations are most appropriate for a student based on financial considerations or budgetary constraints. Whether an accommodation is "appropriate" is a determination completely distinct and separate from whether the accommodation would result in "undue hardship." If the accommodation meets the student's needs and does so in a way that most respects dignity, then a determination can be made as to whether or not this "most appropriate" accommodation would result in undue hardship.

Where the most appropriate accommodation would result in undue hardship, education providers should consider "next-best" alternatives or interim measures while the most appropriate accommodation is being phased in or implemented at a later date.

If an accommodation exceeds an education provider's pre-determined special education budget, the education provider must look to its global budget, unless to do so would cause undue hardship.[46]

> *Example*: A publicly-funded school informs the parents of a student with a learning disability that they cannot provide their son with the services of a special needs assistant. The school principal states that he only has a certain amount of resources to fund accommodations to students with disabilities, and that he has already spent the money on the "most needy" students. The school board in this instance would be re-

---

[46]This is consistent with the Commission's approach in the employment context, where an employer or other entity cannot refuse to accommodate an employee with a disability because the accommodation would exhaust the funds that the employer had earmarked for employees with disabilities.

> quired to review its overall budget before supporting a conclusion that the accommodation could not be provided without causing undue hardship based on costs.

Costs of accommodation must be distributed as widely as possible within the institution responsible for accommodation so that no single school, or academic department is disproportionately burdened with the costs of accommodation. The appropriate basis for evaluating the costs is based on the budget of the institution as a whole, not the school or academic department in which the student with the disability has requested an accommodation.

> *Example*: A college student requires the services of a sign language interpreter in his classes. The college has received several accommodation requests in the given academic year and has depleted its disability accommodation budget. Before denying the student's request, however, the college reviews its overall budget and finds a surplus in the budget of the business department which is then used to fund the student's request.

Larger organizations, in particular governments, may be in a better position to set an example or provide leadership in accommodating persons with disabilities. Accommodation costs will likely be more easily absorbed by larger organizations.

9.1.2 — Health and Safety Requirements

Maintaining a safe learning environment for students, school staff and educators alike is an important objective. Health and safety issues will arise in various educational contexts and have the potential to affect individual students with disabilities, other students, educators and school staff. Depending on the nature and degree of risk involved, it may be open to education providers to argue that accommodating a student with a disability would amount to an undue hardship.

Where a health and safety requirement creates a barrier for a student with a disability, the education provider should assess whether the requirement can be modified or waived. However, modifying or waiving health and safety requirements may create risks that have to be weighed against the student's right to equality.

> *In Practice*: A teacher has reservations about allowing a student who uses a wheelchair to accompany the class on a field trip to a local zoo because of her belief that it will be too dangerous. The school principal

decides to make further inquiries, including contacting the zoo's management, and determines that most of the facility is accessible, and that patrons who use wheelchairs and other motorized devices regularly visit the premises without incident. It is important to substantiate the actual degree of risk in question, rather than acting on inaccurate or stereotypical perceptions that may have little to do with a student's actual limitations.

An education provider may believe that accommodation that would result in the modification or waiver of a health or safety requirement could place the student at risk. The education provider is obliged to explain the potential risk to the student or his or her parent, where appropriate. The student, or his or her parent, will usually be in the best position to assess the risk. This applies only if the potential risk is to the student's health or safety alone. Where the risk that remains after considering alternatives and after accommodation is so significant as to outweigh the benefits of enhancing equality, it will be considered to be undue hardship.

Where a student is placed in an educational setting outside the regular classroom due to health and safety risks, the student is entitled to periodic reassessment to determine, in cases where the student's status changes, whether re-inclusion in the regular educational program is appropriate.

In Practice: A student with bi-polar disorder is unable to attend college due to uncontrollable and violent outbursts associated with his disability. After a period of medical treatment and with the aid of medication, he is able to manage his disability effectively. At this point, the college arranges to meet with and reassess the student's accommodation needs. The duty to accommodate is dynamic and ongoing and must be responsive to changes in the nature of a student's disability.

Where modification or waiver of a health or safety requirement is believed to result in a risk to the health or safety of others, the degree of risk must be evaluated. The education provider must consider other types of risks assumed within the institution. A potential risk created by accommodation should be assessed in light of those other more common sources of risk in the educational institution. The seriousness of the risk is to be judged based on taking suitable precautions to reduce it.

An education provider can determine whether modifying or waiving a health or safety requirement creates a significant risk by considering the following:

- Is the student (or his or her parents) willing to assume the risk in circumstances where the risk is solely to his or her own health or safety?[47]
- Would changing or waiving the requirement be reasonably likely to result in a serious risk to the health or safety of other students, educators or school staff?[48]
- What other types of risks are assumed within the institution or sector, and what types of risks are tolerated within society as a whole?

In evaluating the seriousness or significance of risk, the following factors may be considered:

- The nature of the risk: What could happen that would be harmful?
- The severity of the risk: How serious would the harm be if it occurred?
- The probability of the risk: How likely is it that the potential harm will actually occur? Is it a real risk, or merely hypothetical or speculative? Could it occur frequently?
- The scope of the risk: Who will be affected by the event if it occurs?

If the potential harm is minor and not very likely to occur, the risk should not be considered serious. If there is a risk to public safety, consideration will be given to the increased numbers of people potentially affected and the likelihood that the harmful event may occur.

Where a student with a disability engages in behaviour that impacts upon the well-being of others, it may be open to education providers to argue that to accommodate that student would cause undue hardship on the basis of health and safety concerns, specifically, that the accommodation would pose a risk to public safety. However, the seriousness of the risk will be evaluated only *after* accommodation has been provided and only after appropriate precautions have been taken to reduce the risk. It will be up to the education provider to provide objective and direct evidence of the risk. Suspicions or impressionistic beliefs about the degree of risk posed by a student, without supporting evidence, will not be sufficient.

A claim of undue hardship must stem from a genuine interest in maintaining a safe learning environment for all students, rather than as a punitive action. Even where a student poses a risk to him or herself or the safety of

---

[47] Risk is evaluated after all accommodations have been made to reduce it.

[48] *Ibid.*

others, an education provider still has a duty to canvass other accommodation options, including separate services, where possible and appropriate.

Ultimately, an education provider must balance the rights of the student with a disability with the rights of others. There may be situations where a student poses a health and safety risk to him or herself or to others that would amount to an undue hardship, or an otherwise appropriate accommodation is impossible to implement in the particular circumstances. However, it is important that education providers not rush to such a conclusion. Further training for staff, or further supports for the student may resolve the issue. The accommodation process must be fully explored, to the point of undue hardship.

10. — Roles and Responsibilities

Often, a number of parties might be involved in the accommodation process, rendering it quite complex. Everyone should co-operatively engage in the process, share information and avail themselves of potential accommodation solutions. It is in everyone's best interests that congenial and respectful relationships be maintained throughout the accommodation process.

The *student with a disability* (or his or her parent/guardian) has a responsibility to:

- advise the education provider of the need for accommodation related to a disability
- make his or her needs known to the best of his or her ability, in order that the education provider may make the requested accommodation
- answer questions or provide information regarding relevant restrictions or limitations, including information from health care professionals, where appropriate, and as needed
- participate in discussions regarding possible accommodation solutions
- co-operate with any experts whose assistance is required
- fulfill agreed upon responsibilities, as set out in the accommodation plan
- work with the education provider on an ongoing basis to manage the accommodation process, and
- advise the education provider of difficulties they may be experiencing in accessing educational life, including problems with arranged accommodations.

As a party to the accommodation process, the *education provider* has a responsibility to:

- take steps to include students with disabilities in in-class and extra-curricular activities
- advise students, or their parent(s)/guardian(s), of available accommodations and support services, and the process by which these resources may be accessed
- accept a student's request for accommodation in good faith (even when the request does not use any specific formal language), unless there are legitimate reasons for acting otherwise
- take an active role in ensuring that alternative approaches and possible accommodation solutions are investigated, and canvass various forms of possible accommodation and alternative solutions, as part of the duty to accommodate
- obtain expert opinion or advice where needed, and bear the costs of any required disability-related information or assessment
- maximize a student's right to privacy and confidentiality, including only sharing information regarding the student's disability with those directly involved in the accommodation process
- limit requests for information to those reasonably related to the nature of the need or limitation, and only for the purpose of facilitating access to educational services
- deal with accommodation requests in a timely manner
- ensure that the school environment is welcoming and that all students treat one another with respect
- take immediate remedial action in situations where bullying and harassment is or may be taking place, and
- educate all faculty, staff and students about disability-related issues.

In the provision of educational services, the *education provider* has a responsibility to:

- review the accessibility of the educational institution as a whole, including all educational services
- design and develop new or revised facilities, services, policies, processes, courses, programs or curricula inclusively, with the needs of persons with disabilities in mind, and
- ensure that the costs of accommodation are spread as widely as possible.

Unions, professional associations, and third party educational service providers are required to:

- take an active role as partners in the accommodation process
- facilitate accommodation efforts, and
- support accommodation measures irrespective of collective agreements, unless to do so would create undue hardship.

The duty to accommodate a disability exists for needs that are known. Education providers are not, as a rule, expected to accommodate disabilities of which they are unaware. However, some students may be unable to identify or communicate their needs because of the nature of their disability. In such circumstances, education providers should attempt to assist a student who is perceived to have a disability, by offering assistance and accommodation. Once disability-related needs are known, the legal onus shifts to those with the duty to accommodate.

Appendix A — Anti-Harassment Policy

The following are suggested contents for an anti-harassment policy that is broad enough to cover all forms of harassment in the educational setting.

- A statement setting out the education provider's commitment to a fair and equitable learning environment free of discrimination and harassment and that discrimination/harassment will not be tolerated by the educational institution.
- A statement of rights and obligations, including:
  - student rights
  - education provider, educator, and school staff obligations, and
  - a statement indicating that no reprisals are permitted or will be taken against a student making a complaint.
- A list of the prohibited grounds of discrimination listed in the *Code*.
- The *Code* definitions of "harassment" and of "sexual harassment/solicitation."
- An explanation of the concept of a "poisoned environment" as a violation of the *Code*.[49]
- Description/examples of unacceptable behaviour, such as:
  - examples of harassment based on a ground listed in the *Code*
  - refusal to evaluate fairly based on a ground listed in the *Code*, and
  - examples of what would constitute sexual harassment, *etc*.
- How internal complaints will be handled, including:
  - to whom the complaint should be made
  - confidentiality, and
  - length of time for complaint to be investigated, *etc*.
- Disciplinary measures that will be applied if a claim of harassment or discrimination is proven.
- Remedies that will be available if the claim of harassment or discrimination is proven, such as:
  - an oral or written apology from the harasser/person who discriminated and educational institution

---

[49]See Part 3.1.6 of the Commission's Policy on *Sexual Harassment and Inappropriate Gender-Related Comments and Conduct* available online at the Commission's website: www.ohrc.on.ca.

  - recovery of lost class time, fair evaluation, or academic credit that was denied, and/or
  - compensation for injury to dignity.
- A statement reinforcing the right of students to go to the Commission at any time during the internal process, as well as an explanation of the 6-month time requirement in the *Code*.

Guidelines on Collecting Data on Enumerated Grounds under the *Code*

Approved by the Commission: September 24, 2003

1. — Introduction

It is the position of the Ontario Human Rights Commission (the "Commission") that the Ontario *Human Rights Code* (the *"Code"*) permits the collection and analysis of data based on enumerated grounds, such as race, disability or sex as long as it is for legitimate purposes not contrary to the *Code.*[1] *Code*-legitimate purposes include monitoring and evaluating discrimination, identifying and removing systemic barriers, ameliorating disadvantage and promoting substantive equality.

Statistics collected in an appropriate manner on a periodic or on-going basis can provide an effective means of monitoring for and preventing social phenomena widely recognized as discriminatory, such as profiling, institutionalized barriers, socio-economic disadvantage or unequal opportunity on the basis of race, disability, sex or other enumerated grounds. Where problems are identified, data analysis can provide useful direction for remedies to ameliorate systemic discrimination as well as evaluate the success of such measures.

In several of its recent public inquiry reports and submissions, the Commission has recommended that data collection, based on the grounds of race and disability, be undertaken in key public services, including policing and the education system, in order to monitor, prevent and ameliorate reported systemic and adverse discrimination.[2]

---

[1]See the Commission's publication, *Guidelines on Special Programs* (1997). Also see the American *Individuals with Disabilities in Education Act* 20 U.S.C. at 1418(c), and the *Draft Comprehensive and Integral International Convention on the Protection and Promotion of the Rights and Dignity of Persons with Disabilities*, at Article 6, United Nations Ad Hoc Committee, January 2004.

[2]See the following Commission documents available at *www.ohrc.on.ca*: *Paying the Price: The Human Cost of Racial Profiling*; *The Opportunity to Succeed: Achieving Barrier-free Education for Students with Disabilities*; *Submission of the Ontario Human Rights Commission to the Toronto District School Board Safe and Compassionate Schools Task Force* (April 2004); and, *Comment of the Ontario Human Rights Commission on the Draft Comprehensive and Integral International Convention on the Protection and Promotion of the Rights and Dignity of Persons*

The Commission recognizes that collecting information about characteristics based on enumerated grounds under the *Code* may lead to an inference that the information might be used to treat an individual or group in a discriminatory manner. To address such concerns, the following measures should be taken in order to ensure that the collection and use of data is done in a legitimate and appropriate manner:

2. — *Code*-legitimate Purpose

- A data collection program should clearly set out a *Code*-legitimate purpose: to monitor and evaluate potential discrimination, identify and remove systemic barriers, ameliorate or prevent disadvantage and/or promote substantive equality for individuals identified by enumerated grounds.

3. — Reasonable Belief

- Organizations establishing data collection programs should set out the sources of their reasonable belief for the necessity of such a program. These might include, for example:
  - Census data and/or other social science research demonstrating that individuals identified by race, disability, sex or other enumerated grounds of discrimination face socio-economic disadvantage, increased discipline or drop-out rates in education, or disproportional rates of interaction with law enforcement or the criminal justice system
  - Persistent allegations or perceptions of systemic discrimination
- A data collection program can be contextualized within an organization's obligation to take into account a person's already disadvantaged position within Canadian society.

4. — Inform the Public

- Regardless of the method of data collection, the individuals on whom data is being collected, or the broader public in general, must be informed why such information is being collected and how the collection

---

with Disabilities (April 2004) available at www.un.org/esa/socdev/enable/rights/ahc3ohrc.htm.

and use of such data will assist to relieve disadvantage or discrimination and achieve equal opportunity.

5. — Consult Affected Communities

- Where public interest allegations are involved, service providers should consult with affected communities regarding the need for data collection and appropriate methodology.

6. — Use Least Intrusive Means

- The form that data collection takes should be the least intrusive alternative that most respects dignity and privacy of individuals.
- One standard method to identify types of individuals within or served by an organization is the use of self-identification surveys. When using this method it should be made clear to individuals that their participation is voluntary.
- Another method might have an employee or an external expert record data through observation.
- Anonymity of individuals must be assured.

7. — Distinguishing Collection, Use and Disclosure

- The methodology should distinguish between the appropriate collection, use and disclosure of information.
- There should be a rational and objective connection between the nature of the information being collected and its intended use.
- Data should be aggregated so that any identifying information such as name, driver's license number or student number is removed from the data.
- Data should be separate from and unconnected to any other records that contain personal identifying information, unless it is being used to determine a person's eligibility for a specific special program.
- Data collection procedures, storage, access and disclosure must be carefully controlled.
- Confidentiality and dignity should always be respected.

8. — Information and Privacy

- In addition to the *Human Rights Code*, data collection must also comply with freedom of information and privacy protection legislation.

Guidelines on Special Programs

Approved by the Commission: November 19, 1997

1. — Introduction

The Ontario *Human Rights Code* (the *"Code"*) states that it is public policy in Ontario to recognize the inherent dignity and worth of every person and to provide for equal rights and opportunities without discrimination. The provisions of the *Code* are aimed at creating a climate of understanding and mutual respect for the dignity and worth of each person, so that each person feels a part of the community and feels able to contribute to the community.

Special programs are a way to help people who experience discrimination, economic hardship and disadvantage by putting into place measures that respond to particular needs and that help to reduce discrimination. These special measures or "programs" are protected by section 14 of the *Code*.

To assist employers, landlords and others who adopt such measures, the Commission has developed these *Guidelines on Special Programs*. The *Guidelines* are intended to encourage the voluntary adoption and use of special programs as well as to clarify how section 14 of the *Code* works. Finally, the Commission's role in dealing with special programs will be addressed.

2. — What Does the *Code* Say?

Section 14 allows special programs to be implemented that might otherwise be considered to be discriminatory under the *Code*. Section 14 of the *Code* defines a special program as a program that is:

- designed to relieve hardship or economic disadvantage or
- designed to assist disadvantaged persons or groups to achieve equal opportunity or
- likely to contribute to the elimination of the infringement of rights protected under the *Code*.

A program must satisfy one of the above criteria before it can be a special program as defined by the *Code*. There are many types of programs that might fall within section 14.

> *Example*: A housing co-op reserves a certain number of spaces for women who are leaving a relationship in which they have been battered.

Example: A job program for persons under 25 is put into place to combat youth unemployment.

Example: A community legal clinic provides services only to persons with disabilities to help them fight some of the systemic barriers that have prevented them from fully participating in society.

It is important to make sure that people are aware that a special program exists and that there are restrictions or limits as to who is eligible to apply for a job, or who is entitled under a special program to obtain certain services. For example, a job ad in the context of a job program for youth under 25 should clearly explain to potential applicants or to the public that the employment is part of a special program designed to assist youth under 25 years of age.

3. — What is the Relationship between Section 14 and the *Charter*?

The *Charter of Rights and Freedoms* has an equality section that protects Canadians from discrimination by all levels of government. There is a specific section in the *Charter* that protects or "safeguards" special programs from being attacked. In the United States, people were using the Constitution successfully to challenge special programs on the basis that they were "reverse discrimination." Section 15(2) of the *Charter* was intended to prevent such challenges from successfully eroding or undermining special programs in Canada.

The *Code* applies not only to municipal and provincial governments in Ontario, but it also applies to acts of discrimination between individuals, for example, on the job, or in services or housing. Because of the similarities between the *Charter* and the *Code*, cases decided under the *Charter* can help us understand how section 14 is to be properly interpreted.

4. — Why are Special Programs Protected?

4.1 — Substantive Equality

Historically, "equality" has been interpreted to mean that everyone should receive the same or similar treatment. Over time, however, we have come to recognize that providing the same or similar treatment to all persons or groups does not always address their needs or even lead to equal treatment. Similar treatment ignores diversity and special needs. A basic principle of substantive equality is that it allows us to meet the needs of disadvantaged persons or groups using historical, legal and social contexts.[1]

4.2 — Systemic Discrimination

Direct and constructive[2]discrimination can create formidable and ongoing barriers to the participation of some people in society. Sometimes, these barriers are "systemic". Systemic discrimination was defined by the Supreme Court of Canada in *Canadian National Railway Co. v. Canada (Canadian Human Rights Commission) and Action travail des femmes* (1987), 8 C.H.R.R. D/4210 at 4227:

> . . . systemic discrimination in an employment context is discrimination that results from the simple operation of established procedures of recruitment, hiring and promotion, none of which is necessarily designed to promote discrimination. The discrimination is then reinforced by the very exclusion of*the disadvantaged group because the exclusion fosters the belief, both within and outside the group, that the exclusion is the result of "natural" forces; for example, that women "just can't do the job."

Where systemic discrimination exists, efforts to treat everyone the "same" may not result in equality. In fact, identical treatment may simply perpetuate inequality:

> *Example*: There are few racial minority staff members working with company "X," even though company "X" does not tolerate overt discrimination in its hiring. For years, however, company "X" has hired only by word-of-mouth, which results in most of its applicants coming from family members and friends of the largely white staff. Moreover, some employees display a negative attitude towards the few racial minority colleagues working there. Word has gotten out to potential applicants from other racial groups who see the work environment as hostile to them.

5. — How Do You Put a Special Program in Place?

Landlords, service providers and other organizations may initiate their own special programs. No special or advance approval is required by the Com-

---

[1]*Andrews v. Law Society of British Columbia*, [1989] 1 S.C.R. 143.

[2]Direct discrimination usually refers to intentional discrimination that results in unequal treatment. Constructive discrimination refers to rules or practices that are neutral on their face but that have an adverse impact resulting in discriminatory treatment or results.

mission or provided for by the *Code*. This ensures that special programs can be implemented with a minimum of delay and expense.

If there is doubt as to whether a special program satisfies the requirements of section 14, the Commission may make an order that the special program does not satisfy legal requirements or that modifications are necessary. The procedures to follow in the event that a person wishes to challenge an existing program are set out in the Commission's operational guidelines. Part 7 of the *Guidelines* also provides further information.

These *Guidelines* will help you ensure that the special programs you choose to implement are consistent with the underlying purpose of the *Code*. Here are a few things to keep in mind.

6. — What Should Special Programs Look Like?

6.1 — Eligibility Criteria

The program should clearly identify who the program is intended to assist. For example:

- through grounds of the *Code*: race, ancestry, place of origin, colour, ethnic origin, citizenship, creed, sex, sexual orientation, age (employment for 18+), marital status, family status, disability, record of offenses (in employment), receipt of public assistance (in accommodation)
- disadvantaged persons/groups: persons who are experiencing hardship or economic disadvantage

Care should be taken to ensure that the program does not unreasonably restrict who will benefit, especially when the restrictions might be considered to be "discriminatory" under the *Code*. There should be a rational connection between any restrictions in eligibility and the purpose of the special program itself.

For example, the Ontario Government offered financial assistance to blind persons who purchased reading devices through its Assistive Devices Program. This assistance, however, was only available to young individuals. The Court of Appeal said the program discriminated on the basis of age by excluding elderly applicants and stated that there was no rational or logical connection between the age requirements and the purpose of the program. The program was struck down by the Court.

This does not mean, however, that special programs have to include all disadvantaged groups to avoid the risk of being viewed as discriminatory. A special program that is designed to relieve the disadvantage experienced by a particular group, and which, in fact, targets that particular group is not required to expand its eligibility criteria beyond the targeted group.[3]

6.2 — Rationale for Program

The special program should:

- identify the persons or groups
- state clearly the reasons why the identified persons or groups are considered to be experiencing hardship, disadvantage, or discrimination
- explain how the proposed measures will relieve this hardship, economic disadvantage or discrimination, or how they will assist in achieving equal opportunity
- indicate that the special program is for a specific time period and is of a temporary nature.

Evidence of hardship or disadvantage should be objective and where possible, quantifiable. It should not be subjective or based on personal impressions. Always ask, is there a real problem and does this program address it?

As a rule, questions relating to grounds in the *Code* as criteria for offering employment or promotion or, in the context of services, housing, contracts or membership in vocational associations, are discriminatory and are prohibited. However, data collection for monitoring and evaluation purposes is permitted by the *Code* in the context of a special program.

Data may also be collected if the information is used to demonstrate under-representation of particular groups or other forms of hardship or disadvantage. Data collection of this type can, for example, determine the racial profile of a workforce in order to put into place a program:

> *Example*: An employer is planning to expand the company and hire new staff. The employer conducts a work survey to see whether the workforce is representative of the community that it serves. Employees

---

[3]See generally *Lovelace v. Ontario* (1997), 33 O.R. (3d) (Ont. C.A). *Lovelace* dealt with a challenge to an affirmative action program under the Canadian *Charter of Rights and Freedoms*. The case was brought by Aboriginal groups who were excluded from a program that was designed for a particular First Nations community and who challenged the program as being under-inclusive. The Court of Appeal disagreed. It held that as long as the program accords with the historical records pertaining to the group's situation and it recognizes the distinct circumstances of the group, and is consistent with the goals of section 15 of the *Charter*, it should be upheld.

are asked to self-identify and to submit the information anonymously to human resources.

Statistics collected on an on-going basis also provide a means of assessing the results of special-program initiatives and can serve as a tool for assessing the need for further measures.

The *Code* does not specify how or even if the collection of data should take place. There are some standard methods to identify groups within, or served by, an organization:

- self-identification surveys
- use of an employee to a conduct a survey
- use of an external consultant or expert to collect the data.

Each method has its own advantages and disadvantages in terms of associated costs to the organization, rate of return, accuracy of results and protection of the privacy of the individual. As a rule, self-identification surveys are a straightforward way to collect such information, but organizations should select the method that best suits the program goals and organizational culture.

Privacy and dignity should always be a concern in the collection of data. Those organizations which are subject to freedom of information and privacy legislation should ensure that the identification method they choose complies with section 41 of the *Freedom of Information and Protection of Privacy Act*, R.S.O. 1990, c. F-31. Further information may be obtained directly from the Information and Privacy Commissioner.

Organizations that are not subject to privacy legislation should nonetheless attempt to collect data in a manner that respects dignity and privacy. For example, organizations can develop internal policies on privacy, or codes of ethics.

Participants must be told how the information will be used. This assurance will help them feel more comfortable when asked to provide the information. Data collected in the context of a special program must be used for special program purposes only. For this reason, storage and access should be carefully controlled.

6.3 — Follow a Plan

6.3.1 — Consultation

Appropriate steps should be taken to identify and consult with those who may be affected by the proposed special program. Depending on the nature of the program, this could include labour unions or employee associations, tenant associations, service-users or community organizations. The program provider should prepare a plan that includes the following information:

6.3.2 — Developing a Plan

- an outline of how the special program will be implemented, including terms and conditions of the program
- how long the program will run
- special measures to be implemented and
- goals, timetables and anticipated results.

Goals, timetables and anticipated results should be expressed in objective and, where possible, quantifiable terms to show how the program is designed to address existing hardship, economic disadvantage, or discrimination. Special programs are for a specific time period and therefore of a temporary nature.

6.3.3 — Monitoring and Evaluation Mechanisms

The program should include a mechanism to monitor and evaluate the progress towards the desired results. It is important to:

- evaluate the effectiveness of the program
- facilitate accountability within the organization and
- communicate program results to the organization and/or its client groups.

> *Example*: Tracking target-group members through the system and collecting data to monitor and evaluate the changing composition of client groups is an example of an appropriate monitoring mechanism.

7. — What is the Commission's Authority to Inquire into Special Programs?

7.1 — Powers of the Commission

The Commission can initiate a complaint against an organization that is infringing the *Code*. In appropriate cases, the Commission can require a remedy in the form of a special program.

> *Example*: In 1991, at the request of employers who were using the services of two Toronto-area employment agencies, the Commission initiated a complaint against the employment agencies that were screening applicants on the basis of race. A settlement was reached which in-

cluded a requirement that the companies set up an employment equity program.

The *Code* also permits the Commission to investigate complaints against special programs or to initiate its own inquiry into a special program. The Commission may also inquire into that program to determine whether it qualifies as a special program pursuant to section 14(2) of the *Code*.

7.2 — Crown Special Programs

Because of section 14(5) of the *Code*, the Commission cannot itself inquire into or make orders against special programs that are implemented by the Crown.

However, once the government provides a benefit, it cannot exclude disadvantaged groups on a discriminatory basis. If a special program is challenged because it denies eligibility to the program in a discriminatory way, the Commission may decide to refer the matter to the Board of Inquiry, which, in turn, would review the special program.

7.3 — Specials Programs Cannot Discriminate on Other Grounds

Even where a program appears to qualify as a special program under section 14(1), the program provider cannot arbitrarily discriminate based on other prohibited grounds under the *Code*.

Where special programs must allocate scarce resources (for example, training courses, assistive devices, etc.), the resources should be allocated in a manner that reduces or eliminates disadvantage and that is rationally connected to the purpose of the program. (See further, *Ontario (Human Rights Commission) v. Ontario (Ministry of Health)*.[4]

8. — Relevant *Human Rights Code* Provisions

The Ontario *Human Rights Code* (Part II of this book) includes provisions relevant to this policy in the following sections: 14(1)(2)(3)(4)(5), 23(1) and 41(1).

---

[4](1994), 21 C.H.R.R. D/259.

Policy and Guidelines on Disability and the Duty to Accommodate

Revised Version Approved by the Commission: November 23, 2000

1. — Introduction

Under the Ontario *Human Rights Code*[1] (the "*Code*"), everyone has the right to be free from discrimination because of handicap or perceived handicap in the social areas of employment, services, goods, facilities, housing, contracts and membership in trade and vocational associations. This right means that persons with disabilities[2] have the right to equal treatment, which includes the right to accessible workplaces, public transit, health services, restaurants, shops and housing.

Almost one-third of complaints filed with the Ontario Human Rights Commission are on the ground of disability. Most are in the area of employment, with services constituting the second largest area. For this reason, this Policy focuses on the workplace, with specific guidance to support employers, unions and employees in the fulfilment of their duties and rights under the *Code*.[3]

In 1989, the Ontario Human Rights Commission published its *Guidelines on Assessing Accommodation Requirements for Persons with Disabilities*. These Guidelines were introduced after extensive consultations with stakeholders, and created for the first time a standard for the interpretation of "undue hardship." The Guidelines have been cited before Boards of Inquiry and the Courts, and have become an important interpretative tool. Since that time, there have been several important legal decisions, notably from the Supreme Court of Canada, with respect to the ground of disability and the duty to accommodate. These decisions have assisted the Commission in its

---

[1] R.S.O. 1990, c. H.19.

[2] The terms "disability" and "person with a disability" are used throughout this document instead of "handicap" or "handicapped person." Although the term "handicap" is used in the *Code*, many people with disabilities prefer the term "disability."

[3] During consultations held in 1999 by the Ontario Human Rights Commission, stakeholders highlighted the particular issues facing educational institutions and those persons seeking access to them. Many of the principles set out in this Policy apply to service sectors as well, but the Commission will be undertaking new Guidelines for the educational sector in order to address these concerns.

evolving understanding of equality for persons with disabilities. Significantly, the Supreme Court has noted the need to adapt society so that its structures and attitudes include persons with disabilities. This requires a shift in our approach to the entire area, one that affirms the centrality of human dignity in achieving equality.

In 1999, the Commission invited stakeholders to provide input on the revisions to the Guidelines. Over 150 stakeholders were approached. They represented a broad spectrum of interests, including consumers and organizations from the disability community, employer associations, educational institutions, law firms, labour, provincial and municipal government agencies, business and trade associations and service providers.

Several themes emerged from these consultations, and have informed these revisions:

- There is a need to reaffirm the standard of undue hardship that was created in 1989.
- While undue hardship is a high standard, it is necessary to ensure equality. It is, in this sense, "reasonable" and accommodation to the point of undue hardship is "reasonable accommodation."
- Individual accommodation has grown in significance as a central principle of human rights law.
- More guidance is needed on the definition of disability, as well as more practical direction on the steps required in the accommodation process.
- The principle of design by inclusion and barrier removal has to be underscored.
- More information on the needs of persons with mental disabilities is a priority.
- Unions and employee associations have a critical role to play in the accommodation process.
- There is a need to clarify the impact of accommodation on performance standards and on access to jobs other than the "pre-disability" job.
- The principle of dignity with risk (i.e., the ability of persons with disabilities to assume risk to themselves) has to be balanced with health and safety considerations.

As a result, there are several new features in these Guidelines. The reader will find references to case law and international human rights obligations, as well as a resource section.

The right to be accommodated and the corresponding duty of the employer and union are now well established in statute and case law. Accommodation is a fundamental and integral part of the right to equal treatment. The duty to accommodate means that the terms and conditions of the workplace, or the functions of a job, may have to be changed. The *Code* recognizes that an employer may have operating rules, policies and procedures that may be necessary for business reasons, or that there may be certain legal requirements, such as health and safety legislation. There may also be collective agreements that set out the terms and conditions governing the workplace.

Accommodation with dignity is part of a broader principle, namely, that our society should be structured and designed for inclusiveness. This principle, which is sometimes referred to as integration, emphasizes barrier-free design and equal participation of persons with varying levels of ability. Integration is also much more cost effective than building parallel service systems, although it is inevitable that there will be times when parallel services are the only option. Inclusive design and integration are also preferable to "modification of rules" or "barrier removal," terms that, although popular, assume that the *status quo* (usually designed by able-bodied persons), simply needs an adjustment to render it acceptable. In fact, inclusive design may involve an entirely different approach. It is based on positive steps needed to ensure equal participation for those who have experienced historical disadvantage and exclusion from society's benefits.[4] The right to equality can be breached by a failure to address needs related to disadvantage.

---

[4]In *Granovsky v. Canada (Minister of Employment and Immigration)* (18 May 2000), 2000 SCC 28, online: Supreme Court of Canada www.lexum.umontreal.ca/csc-scc/en/index.html [hereinafter "*Granovsky*"], the Supreme Court recognized that the primary focus in the disability analysis is on the inappropriate legislative or administrative response (or lack thereof) of the State (at para. 39). The Court states (at para. 33):

> Section 15(1) ensures that governments may not, intentionally or *through a failure of appropriate accommodation*, stigmatize the underlying physical or mental impairment, or attribute functional limitations to the individual that the underlying physical or mental impairment does not entail, or fail to recognize the added burdens which persons with disabilities may encounter in achieving self-fulfillment in a world relentlessly oriented to the able-bodied. [emphasis added.]

Although in *Granovsky* the focus was State action, similar principles apply to persons responsible for accommodation under human rights law.

As the Supreme Court of Canada has observed:

> The principle that discrimination can accrue from a failure to take positive steps to ensure that disadvantaged groups benefit equally from services offered to the general public is widely accepted in the human rights field.[5]

This positive approach is more effective because it is accessible and inclusive from the start. Employers and others who set standards or requirements "owe an obligation to be aware of both the differences between individuals, and differences that characterize groups of individuals. They must build conceptions of equality into workplace [or other] standards."[6] A proactive approach to disability accommodation is therefore necessary.

Those responsible for accommodation[7] should be aware of the standards for accommodation. The following guiding principles should be kept in mind:

- The needs of persons with disabilities must be accommodated in the manner that most respects their dignity, to the point of undue hardship.
- There is no set formula for accommodation — each person has unique needs and it is important to consult with the person involved.
- Taking responsibility and showing willingness to explore solutions is a key part of treating people respectfully and with dignity.
- Voluntary compliance may avoid complaints under the *Code*, as well as save the time and expense needed to defend against them.

2. — What is Disability?

2.1 — The Definition in the *Human Rights Code*

Section 10(1) of the *Code* defines "handicap" as follows:

> "because of handicap" means for the reason that the person has or has had, or is believed to have or have had,
>
> > (a) any degree of physical disability, infirmity, malformation or disfigurement that is caused by bodily injury, birth defect or illness, and without limiting the generality of the foregoing, including diabetes

[5] *Eldridge v. British Columbia (Attorney General)*, [1997] 3 S.C.R. 624 at para. 78, online: www.lexum.umontreal.ca/csc-scc/en/index.html [hereinafter *"Eldridge"*].

[6] *British Columbia (Public Service Employee Relations Commission) v. BCGSEU*, [1999] 3 S.C.R. 3 at para. 68 [hereinafter "*Meiorin*"].

[7] The term "person (or organization or company) responsible for accommodation" includes individuals, partnerships, corporations, companies, unions, joint ventures and organizations. More than one "person" may be responsible for accommodation, and where this term is used, it refers to all parties who are obliged to take part in the accommodation.

mellitus, epilepsy, any degree of paralysis, amputation, lack of physical co-ordination, blindness or visual impediment, deafness or hearing impediment, muteness or speech impediment, or physical reliance on a guide dog or on a wheelchair or other remedial appliance or device,

(b) a condition of mental retardation or impairment,

(c) a learning disability, or a dysfunction in one or more of the processes involved in understanding or using symbols or spoken language,

(d) a mental disorder, or

(e) an injury or disability for which benefits were [illegible] ceived under the insurance plan estab[illegible] *y and Insurance Act, 1997.*

"Disability" should be interpreted i[illegible] present and past conditions, as well as a sub[illegible] based on perception of disability. Althoug[illegible] various types of conditions, it is clear that th[illegible] ot exhaustive. Protection for persons with [illegible] n explicitly includes mental illness,[8] devel[illegible] g disabilities. Even minor illnesses or infirm[illegible] sabilities," if a person can show that she was treated unfairly because of the perception of a disability.[9] Conversely, a person with an ailment who cannot show she was treated unequally because of a perceived or actual disability will be unable to meet even the *prima facie* test for discrimination. It will always be critical to assess the context of the differential treatment in order to determine whether discrimination has taken place, and whether the ground of disability is engaged.

---

[8]Mental illness has been described as "significant clinical patterns of behaviour or emotions associated with some level of distress, suffering (pain, death), or impairment in one or more areas of functioning (school, work, social and family interactions). At the root of this impairment are symptoms of biological, psychological or behavioural dysfunction, or a combination of these." See Canadian Psychiatric Association, *Mental Illness and Work*, (brochure), online: Canadian Psychiatric Association homepage http://cpa.medical.org/MIAW/MIAW.asp at pg. 1

[9]The *Code*'s definition of "handicap" includes perceived handicap.

2.2 — A Broader Approach to Understanding Disability: A Social Perspective

The Supreme Court of Canada has recently shed new light on the approach to be taken in understanding disability. In *Mercier*,[10] a case arising in Quebec, the Supreme Court made it clear that disability must be interpreted to include its subjective component, since discrimination may be based as much on perceptions, myths and stereotypes, as on the existence of actual functional limitations.

In *Mercier*, the complainants were denied employment or dismissed when it was discovered that they had medical conditions. However, their conditions did not result in any functional limitations. The employers argued that since the conditions did not give rise to any functional limitations, they could not be "disabilities" under Quebec's human rights law. The Supreme Court of Canada disagreed.

The Court chose not to create an exhaustive definition of disability. Instead, it opted for an equality-based framework that takes into account evolving biomedical, social and technological developments. This includes a socio-political dimension that emphasizes human dignity, respect and the right to equality. Thus, a disability may be the result of a physical limitation, an ailment, a perceived limitation or a combination of all these factors. The focus is on the effects of the distinction, preference or exclusion experienced by the person and not on proof of physical limitations or the presence of an ailment.

Another Supreme Court of Canada decision[11] has since confirmed that "social handicapping," *i.e.*, society's response to a real or perceived disability, should be the focus of the discrimination analysis.

This approach is consistent with the *Code*, which includes past, present and perceived conditions. It affords a broad and liberal interpretation and promotes the objectives of the *Code*.

2.3 — Non-evident Disabilities

The nature or degree of certain disabilities might render them "non-evident" to others. Chronic fatigue syndrome and back pain, for example, are not apparent conditions. Other disabilities might remain hidden because they

---

[10] *Quebec (Commission des droits de la personne et des droits de la jeunesse) v. Montréal (City)*; *Quebec (Commission des droits de la personne et des droits de la jeunesse) v. Boisbriand (City)* (3 May 2000), 2000 SCC 27, online: Supreme Court of Canada www.lexum.umontreal.ca/csc-scc/en/index.html [hereinafter "*Mercier*"].

[11] *Granovsky*, *supra* note 4.

are episodic. Epilepsy is one example. Similarly, environmental sensitivities can flare up from one day to the next, resulting in significant impairment to a person's health and capacity to function, while at other times, this disability may be entirely non-evident. Other examples might include:

- persons whose disabilities do not actually result in any functional limitations but who experience discrimination because others believe their disability makes them less able
- persons who have recovered from conditions but are treated unfairly because of their past condition
- persons whose disabilities are episodic or temporary in nature.

Other disabilities may become apparent based on the nature of the interaction, such as when there is a need for oral communication with an individual who is deaf, or there is a need for written communication with an individual who has a learning disability. A disability might become apparent over time through extended interaction. It might only become known when a disability accommodation is requested or, simply, the disability might remain "non-evident" because the individual chooses not to divulge it for personal reasons.

Regardless of whether a disability is evident or non-evident, a great deal of discrimination faced by persons with disabilities is underpinned by social constructs of "normality" which in turn tend to reinforce obstacles to integration rather than encourage ways to ensure full participation. Because these disabilities are not "seen," many of them are not well understood in society. This can lead to stereotypes, stigma and prejudice.

2.4 — Mental Disability

Although mental disability is a form of non-evident disability, it raises particular issues that merit independent consideration. Over the years, many employers have expressed the need for specific guidance on the issue of mental disability. Section 10 of the *Code* expressly includes mental disabilities. Persons with mental disabilities face a high degree of stigmatization and significant barriers to employment opportunities.[12] Stigmatization can foster a climate that exacerbates stress, and may trigger or worsen the person's condition. It may also mean that someone who has a problem and needs help may not seek it, for fear of being labelled.

The Supreme Court of Canada has recognized the distinct disadvantage and negative stereotyping faced by persons with mental disabilities, and has held that discrimination against individuals with mental disabilities is un-

---

[12] *Mental Illness and Work, supra* note 8.

lawful. In *Gibbs v. Battlefords*[13] the Court struck down an insurance plan for employees with disabilities that limited benefits for mental disabilities to a lower level as compared to physical disabilities. It is therefore the Commission's position that such distinctions are *prima facie* discriminatory.

3. — *Prima Facie* Discrimination Because of Disability

Once a disability within the meaning of section 10 of the *Code* is established, the individual has the burden of showing a *prima facie* case of discrimination.

Discrimination under the *Code* can be direct (refusal to grant a job or provide access to services or housing, for example, because of a disability), indirect, constructive (adverse effect) or based on society's failure to accommodate actual differences.

In some cases, it will be clear that discrimination has occurred. In others, a preliminary assessment tool may be helpful. The Supreme Court of Canada has suggested three broad inquiries to determine if discrimination has taken place:[14]

(1) Differential Treatment

Was there substantively differential treatment, either because of a distinction, exclusion or preference, or because of a failure to take into account the complainant's already disadvantaged position within Canadian society?

(2) An Enumerated Ground

Was the differential treatment based on an enumerated ground?

(3) Discrimination in a Substantive Sense

Finally, does the differential treatment discriminate by imposing a burden upon, or withholding a benefit from, an individual? The discrimination might be based on stereotypes of a presumed group or personal characteristics, or might perpetuate or promote the view that an indivi-

---

[13] *Gibbs v. Battlefords and Dist. Co-operative Ltd.* (1996), 27 C.H.R.R. D/87 (S.C.C.).

[14] This was first articulated in *Law v. Canada (Minister of Employment and Immigration)*, [1999] 1 S.C.R. 497, online: Supreme Court of Canada www.lexum.umontreal.ca/csc-scc/en/index.html (date accessed: 4 August 2000) [hereinafter "*Law*"]. The approach has been affirmed in several subsequent cases, most notably two cases dealing with discrimination on the basis of disability: *Mercier*, *supra* note 10 and *Granovsky*, *supra* note 4.

dual is less capable or worthy of recognition or value as a human being or as a member of Canadian society who is equally deserving of concern, respect and consideration. Does the differential treatment amount to discrimination because it makes distinctions that are offensive to human dignity?

Given the clear historical disadvantage experienced by persons with disabilities, it is likely that most differential treatment because of disability will result in a finding of *prima facie* discrimination.[15] This would include not only unfair treatment because of disability, but also neutral factors or requirements that have an adverse impact on persons with disabilities. It would also include inappropriate responses, or a lack of response to the complainant's condition or stated need for accommodation.

3.1 — Discrimination and Insurance

Discrimination may also take place where a term or condition of employment requires enrolment in a group insurance contract and an applicant does not qualify for the insurance plan because of disability. The term or condition of employment itself would be viewed as a violation of the *Code*.[16]

If an employee is excluded because of a disability from a benefit, pension or superannuation plan or fund or a contract of group insurance, an employer must compensate the employee an amount equivalent to the contribution that the employer would have otherwise made on behalf of an employee who does not have a disability.[17]

Compensation to employees takes on different forms, such as contributions to benefit premiums or accrual of vacation credits. Where employers, as a matter of course, pay a certain form of compensation to other employees who are absent from work, employees absent due to disability are also entitled to such compensation.[18]

---

[15]The facts of *Granovsky*, *supra* note 4 illustrate an exception to this general proposition. Where a scheme targets a particular group, for example, those who are less fortunate than the complainant, it is unlikely to be considered discriminatory to exclude more advantaged groups.

[16]Subsection 25(1) of the *Code*.

[17]Subsection 25(4) of the *Code*.

[18]Conversely, in *O.N.A. v. Orillia Soldiers Memorial Hospital* (1999), 169 D.L.R. (4th) 489; leave to appeal to S.C.C. refused [1999] S.C.C.A. No. 118, online: QL (SCCA) [hereinafter "*Orillia*"], nurses on unpaid leave of absence due to disability did not accumulate service after periods set out in the collective agreement, and the employer was not required to contribute premiums to employee benefit plans after

4. — The Duty to Accommodate

4.1 — General Principles

4.1.1 — Respect for Dignity

The duty to accommodate persons with disabilities means accommodation must be provided in a manner that most respects the dignity of the person, if to do so does not create undue hardship.[19] Dignity includes consideration of how accommodation is provided and the individual's own participation in the process.

Human dignity encompasses individual self-respect and self-worth. It is concerned with physical and psychological integrity and empowerment. It is harmed when individuals are marginalized, stigmatized, ignored or devalued.[20] Privacy, confidentiality, comfort, autonomy, individuality and self-esteem are important factors as well as to whether an accommodation maximizes integration and promotes full participation in society.

Different ways of accommodating the needs of persons with disabilities should be considered along a continuum from those ways which are most respectful of privacy, autonomy, integration and other human values, to those which are least respectful of those values.

Perhaps the most common example of an accommodation that demonstrates little respect for the dignity of a person with a disability is a wheelchair entrance over a loading dock or through a service area or garbage room. Persons with disabilities should have the same opportunity as others to enter

---

the employees had received long-term disability payments for a specified time. The Ontario Court of Appeal held that there was no contravention of the *Code* because these nurses were not treated differently from those in the appropriate comparator group, namely employees who were not working for other reasons.

[19]The Supreme Court's recent decisions in *Law, supra* note 14 and *Granovsky, supra* note 4 have confirmed that the concept of human dignity is central to discrimination analysis. These cases indicate that if an accommodation marginalizes, stigmatizes or demeans the person with a disability's sense of worth or dignity as a human being, it will not be appropriate. In commenting on the *Eaton* case, the Court said in *Granovsky, supra* note 4 at para. 74:

> . . .Emily's claim might have succeeded if . . .the Court had been persuaded that the Board's response to the challenge posed by Emily's placement [the accommodation] *had itself violated Emily's dignity as a human being equally deserving of consideration*, or placed discriminatory obstacles in the way of her self-fulfillment. [Emphasis added.]

[20]*Law, supra* note 14 at para. 53.

a building in a manner that is as convenient and pleasant for them as it is for others.

4.1.2 — Individualized Accommodation

The essence of accommodating people with disabilities is individualization. As a result of the new three-step test proposed by the Supreme Court of Canada and re-affirmed by the Ontario Court of Appeal in *Entrop*,[21] each person with a disability must be considered, assessed and accommodated individually.

> *Example*: A corporate policy provides for obligatory termination in the event that an employee in a safety-sensitive position tests positive after a breathalyzer test. This blanket policy does not provide for individualized assessment or the appropriateness of the outcome in the circumstances and, accordingly, does not accommodate employees on an individual basis.

There is no set formula for accommodating people with disabilities. Each person's needs are unique and must be considered afresh when an accommodation request is made. A solution may meet one person's requirements but not another's, although it is also the case that many accommodations will benefit large numbers of persons with disabilities.

4.1.3 — Integration and Full Participation

International human rights standards point to the importance of full participation and enjoyment of life for persons with disabilities.

The United Nations' *Declaration of the Rights of Disabled Persons*[22] provides in sections 3 and 8 that:

> 3. Disabled persons have the inherent right to respect for their human dignity. Disabled persons, whatever the origin, nature and seriousness of their handicaps and disabilities, have the same fundamental rights as their fellow citizens of the same age, which implies first and foremost the right to enjoy a decent life, as normal and full as possible.
>
> [. . .]

---

[21] *Entrop v. Imperial Oil Limited* (21 July 2000), Docket C29762, at paras. 77-81 (Ont. C.A.), online: Court of Appeal for Ontario www.ontariocourts.on.ca [hereinafter "*Entrop*"].

[22] United Nations, *Declaration of the Rights of Disabled Persons*, proclaimed by General Assembly resolution 3447 (XXX) of 9 December 1975.

8. Disabled persons are entitled to have their special needs taken into consideration at all stages of economic and social planning.

With these principles in mind, achieving integration and full participation for persons with disabilities requires barrier-free and inclusive designs and removal of existing barriers. Preventing and removing barriers means persons with disabilities should be able to access their environment and face the same duties and requirements as everyone else with dignity and without impediment. Where barriers continue to exist because it is impossible to remove those barriers at a given point in time, then accommodation should be provided to the extent possible, short of undue hardship.

It is well established in human rights law that equality may sometimes require different treatment that does not offend the individual's dignity. In some circumstances, the best way to ensure the dignity of persons with disabilities may be to provide separate or specialized services. However, employment, housing, services and facilities must be built or adapted to accommodate individuals with disabilities in a way that promotes their integration and full participation. Segregated treatment in services, employment, or housing for individuals with disabilities is less dignified and is unacceptable, unless it can be shown that integrated treatment would pose undue hardship or that segregation is the only way to achieve equality.[23]

4.1.3(a) — Design by Inclusion

Integration requires up-front barrier-free design and inclusion-by-design in order to fully integrate persons with disabilities into all aspects of society as much as possible.

This approach combats "social handicapping" and recognizes that social attitudes and actions often contribute to "handicaps": a person may have few or even no limitations other than those created by non-inclusive thinking. The Supreme Court has noted the need to "fine-tune" society so that structures and assumptions do not exclude persons with disabilities from participation in society[24] and it has more recently affirmed that standards should

[23] *Eaton v. Brant County Board of Education*, [1997] 1 S.C.R. 241 [hereinafter "*Eaton*"].

The Supreme Court stated that "integration should be recognized as the norm of general application because of the benefits it generally provides" (at para. 69); however, the Court found that in Emily Eaton's circumstances, segregated accommodation was in her best interests. The Court was of the view that this was one of those unusual cases where segregation was a more appropriate accommodation.

[24] *Eaton*, *ibid.* at para. 67.

be designed to reflect all members of society, insofar as this is reasonably possible.[25]

When constructing new buildings, undertaking renovations, purchasing new computer systems, launching new websites, setting up new policies and procedures, offering new services, or implementing new public transit routes, design choices should be made that do not create barriers for persons with disabilities.

Inclusive design is the approach that is most respectful of the dignity of persons with disabilities.

4.1.3(b) — Removing Barriers

Persons with disabilities are currently excluded by many kinds of barriers, including physical, attitudinal and systemic ones. Significant changes are required as part of the duty to accommodate in order to provide equal access to employment (including collective agreements), transportation systems, buildings (except private residences), rental accommodation, services, restaurants, shopping centres, stores and other places and activities. These changes are necessary in order to give meaning to the right to equality and freedom from discrimination guaranteed to persons with disabilities under Part I of the *Code*.

A systemic barrier is not just a single rule or policy but a combination of policies and/or guidelines that result in the exclusion of people identified by a *Code* ground such as disability. Organizations should understand and be aware of the possibility that systemic barriers may exist within their organization and actively seek to identify and remove them.

Barrier removal maximizes integration with one's environment so ideally everyone is able to participate fully and with dignity. Identifying and removing systemic barriers also makes good business sense. It may reduce and prevent the filing of human rights complaints and can make facilities and procedures more comfortable for other groups such as seniors and for all people in general.

4.1.3(c) — Accommodating Remaining Needs

Even up-front barrier-free or inclusive design and systematic removal of existing barriers may not result in full participation for persons with disabilities. At this point, differential treatment might be required in order to provide equal opportunity to full participation.

---

[25] *Meiorin*, *supra* note 6 at para. 68.

Again, accommodating remaining needs through differential treatment must be done in a manner that maximizes integration and dignity.

4.2 — Legal Principles

Once a *prima facie* case of discrimination is found to exist, the legal burden shifts to the person responsible for accommodation to show that the discrimination is justifiable. The following sections will deal with the basic legal test that persons responsible for accommodation must meet, and with the shared responsibilities of all parties to the accommodation process.

Section 11 of the *Code*, combined with section 9, operates to prohibit discrimination that results from requirements, qualifications, or factors that may appear neutral but which have an adverse effect on persons with disabilities. This is often called "adverse effect," or "constructive" discrimination. Section 11 allows the person responsible for accommodation to demonstrate that the requirement, qualification or factor is reasonable and bona fide by showing that the needs of the group to which the complainant belongs cannot be accommodated without undue hardship.

Section 17 also creates an obligation to accommodate, specifically under the ground of disability. Section 17 states that a right is not infringed if the person with a disability is incapable of performing or fulfilling the essential duties or requirements attending the exercise of the right. However, this defence is not available unless it can be shown that the needs of the person cannot be accommodated without undue hardship.

Section 17 addresses two important differences between disability and other *Code* grounds.[26] Firstly, it recognizes that discrimination against persons with disabilities is not always grounded in negative stereotypes but rather can be based on society's failure to accommodate actual differences. Secondly, it emphasizes the need for individualized accommodation, because the ground of disability "means vastly different things depending upon the individual and the context."[27]

The Ontario Court of Appeal has confirmed recently that both sections 11 and 17 apply to persons with disabilities.[28] However, as a result of two

---

[26] *Eaton*, *supra* note 23 at paras. 66-7. The unique nature of disability has been recognized by the Supreme Court of Canada.

[27] *Ibid.*, at para. 69.

[28] *Supra*, note 21.

landmark decisions of the Supreme Court of Canada,[29] the distinction between direct discrimination and adverse effect discrimination has become of much less practical significance. The Ontario Court of Appeal has confirmed that this "unified approach" should be applied to Ontario human rights law as well.[30] The practical result is that in most cases of discrimination on the ground of disability, individualized accommodation will be necessary.

The Supreme Court of Canada sets out a framework for examining whether the duty to accommodate has been met.[31] If *prima facie* discrimination is found to exist, the person responsible for accommodation must establish on a balance of probabilities that the standard, factor, requirement or rule

1. was adopted for a purpose or goal that is rationally connected to the function being performed,
2. was adopted in good faith, in the belief that it is necessary for the fulfilment of the purpose or goal, and
3. is reasonably necessary to accomplish its purpose or goal, in the sense that it is impossible to accommodate the claimant without undue hardship.

As a result of this test, the rule or standard itself must be inclusive and must accommodate individual differences up to the point of undue hardship rather than maintaining discriminatory standards supplemented by accommodation for those who cannot meet them. This ensures that each person is assessed according to his or her own personal abilities instead of being judged against presumed group characteristics.[32]

The ultimate issue is whether the person responsible for accommodation has shown that accommodation has been provided up to the point of undue hardship. In this analysis, the procedure to assess accommodation is as important as the substantive content of the accommodation.[33]

---

[29]*Meiorin, supra* note 6, and *British Columbia (Superintendent of Motor Vehicles) v. British Columbia (Council of Human Rights)*, [1999] 3 S.C.R. 868, [hereinafter "*Grismer*"].

[30]*Entrop v. Imperial Oil Limited* (21 July 2000), Docket C29762 at paras. 77-81 (Ont. C.A.), online: Court of Appeal for Ontario www.ontariocourts.on.ca [hereinafter "*Entrop*"].

[31]*Meiorin, supra* note 6.

[32]*Grismer, supra* note 29 at para. 20.

[33]*Ibid.*, at para. 66.

The following non-exhaustive factors should be considered in the course of the analysis:[34]

- whether the person responsible for accommodation investigated alternative approaches that do not have a discriminatory effect
- reasons why viable alternatives were not implemented
- ability to have differing standards that reflect group or individual differences and capabilities
- whether persons responsible for accommodation can meet their legitimate objectives in a less discriminatory manner
- whether the standard is properly designed to ensure the desired qualification is met without placing undue burden on those to whom it applies
- whether other parties who are obliged to assist in the search for accommodation have fulfilled their roles.

4.3 — Most Appropriate Accommodation

The duty to accommodate requires that the most appropriate accommodation be determined and then be undertaken, short of undue hardship. The most appropriate accommodation is one that most respects the dignity of the individual with a disability, meets individual needs, best promotes integration and full participation, and ensures confidentiality.

Accommodation is a process and is a matter of degree, rather than an all-or-nothing proposition, and can be seen as a continuum. At one end of this continuum would be full accommodation that most respects the person's dignity. Next is phased-in accommodation over time, followed by the most appropriate accommodation only being implemented once sufficient reserve funds have been set aside. Alternative accommodation (that which would be less than "ideal") might be next on the continuum when the most appropriate accommodation is not feasible. Alternative accommodation might also be accomplished at a later date if immediate implementation would result in undue hardship. Or, alternative accommodation might be implemented as an interim solution while the most appropriate accommodation is being phased in or implemented at a later date.

Whether an accommodation is "appropriate" is a determination completely distinct and separate from whether the accommodation would result in "undue hardship" (the test that has to be met under sections 11 and 17(2) of the *Code*).

---

[34]*Meiorin*, *supra* note 6 at para. 65.

Accommodation will be considered appropriate if it will result in equal opportunity to attain the same level of performance, or to enjoy the same level of benefits and privileges experienced by others or if it is proposed or adopted for the purpose of achieving equal opportunity, and meets the individual's disability-related needs. If the accommodation meets the individual's needs and does so in a way that most respects dignity, then a determination can be made as to whether or not this "most appropriate" accommodation would result in undue hardship.

An Ontario Board of Inquiry has ruled that short of undue hardship, the highest point in the continuum of accommodation must be achieved.[35] However, if there is a choice between two accommodations which are equally responsive to the person's needs in a dignified manner, then those responsible are entitled to select the one that is less expensive or that is less disruptive to the organization.

4.3.1 — Essential Duties and the Current Job

The *Code* guarantees equal treatment to all persons capable of performing the essential duties or requirements of the job or service. No one can be judged incapable of performing those duties until efforts have been made to accommodate the individual up to the point of undue hardship. The first step is to separate the essential from the nonessential duties of the job. Where possible, non-essential tasks can be reassigned to another person. The person with the disability should then be assessed in terms of his or her ability to perform the essential duties and, on that basis, accommodation should be considered.

There is little guidance as to how to distinguish between essential duties and others. In one Ontario Board of Inquiry decision, the word "essential" was defined as follows:

> "Essential" means that which is "needed to make a thing what it is; very important; necessary" — Synonyms are "indispensable, requisite, vital." Thus, peripheral or incidental, non-core or non-essential aspects of a job are not pertinent to a determination under [s. 17(1)].[36]

Conclusions about inability to perform essential duties should not be reached without actually testing the ability of the person. It is not enough for the employer or person to assume that the person cannot perform an

---

[35] *Quesnel v. London Educational Health Centre* (1995), 28 C.H.R.R. D/474 at para. 16 (Ont. Bd. of Inq.) [hereinafter "*Quesnel*"].

[36] *Cameron v. Nel-gor Nursing Home* (1984), 5 C.H.R.R. D/2170 at D/2192 (Ont. Bd. of Inq.) [dictionary citations omitted].

essential requirement. Rather, there must be an objective determination of that fact.[37]

The duty to accommodate may require employers to consider modifying performance standards or productivity targets. The term "performance standard" refers broadly to qualitative or quantitative standards that may be imposed on some or all aspects of work, whether they are set by the employer or through collective bargaining. A productivity target is a performance standard that relates specifically to the output of work expected by the employer. Performance standards generally can be distinguished from qualification standards, which are the skills or attributes that one must have to be eligible for a particular job:

> Production standards identify the level at which an employee must perform job functions in order to perform successfully. Qualification standards, on the other hand, identify the skills and abilities necessary to perform the functions at the required level.[38]

The central issue in determining whether or how performance standards should be modified is whether the standards in question are essential duties or requirements within the meaning of section 17 of the *Code*. If the person is unable to perform the standard, but the standard is not considered an essential part of the job, it can be changed or the function removed from the employee altogether and reassigned.

If the standard is essential, the employer is nevertheless required to accommodate the employee under section 17(2) of the *Code*. Keeping in mind the overall objective of the inclusion of employees with disabilities in the workplace, sections 17 (1) and (2) of the *Code* together include an obligation on an employer to accommodate a person. This accommodation may include an adjustment of that performance standard so long as doing so does not result in undue hardship. If it does amount to undue hardship, the employer has a defence.

This does not preclude the employer from enforcing performance standards that are unrelated to the disability. The employer is entitled to a productive employee and to develop standards and targets that maximize organizational objectives.

---

[37] *Ibid.* See also *Crabtree v. 671632 Ontario Ltd. (c.o.b. Econoprint (Stoney Creek))*, [1996] O.H.R.B.I.D. No. 37 (Ont. Bd. of Inq.), online: QL (HRBD).

[38] Robert L. Burgdorf, *Disability Discrimination in Employment Law* (Washington D.C.: Bureau of National Affairs, 1995) at 241.

4.3.2 — Alternative Work

Although accommodation in the pre-disability job is always preferable, it may not always be possible. The issue of whether an employee is entitled to have access to a job other than the pre disability job is a matter of some debate. Nothing in the *Code* or in section 17 specifically restricts the requirement to accommodate a worker with disability to the pre-disability position. Conversely, nothing in section 17 expressly authorizes it either. Nevertheless, in light of the broad and purposive interpretation that should be afforded to human rights legislation, it is the Commission's view that accommodation in a job other than the pre-disability job may be appropriate in some circumstances. Section 17 may therefore include access to alternative work. Some of the following considerations may assist employers in determining whether such accommodation is available under section 17(2).

The following questions should be considered:

- Is alternative work possible and available, at present or in the near future?
- If it is not available, can a new position be created without causing undue hardship?
- Does it require additional training and does the training impose undue hardship?
- Do the tasks performed match the job description, or is there flexibility in the workplace with regard to an employee's responsibilities?
- Does the alternative work policy contravene a collective agreement?
- What are the terms of the collective agreement or individual contract of employment?
- What are the past practices of the workplace? How interchangeable are workers? Do employees frequently change positions either permanently or temporarily for reasons other than disability accommodation?[39]

Depending on how the previous questions are answered, accommodation may therefore include job restructuring, reassignment to open positions, re-

[39]See M. K. Joachim, "The Duty To Accommodate Disabled Workers and the Provision of Alternative Work: An Unexplained Assumption" (2000) 7 *Charter and Human Rights Litigation* 407 for an excellent review of labour and human rights case law. Although Joachim locates the right to alternative employment in section 17(1), it can also be viewed as being located in the section 17(2) and the duty to accommodate. Whichever is the correct reasoning, employees should have some access to alternative employment.

training for alternative positions or job bundling if that would not constitute undue hardship for the employer. This will depend on the circumstances of the employment and the labour environment at a given workplace. In the final analysis, the employee must be able to perform a useful and productive job for the employer.[40]

Three of these options are discussed in the following sections.

4.3.2(a) — Temporary Alternative Work

The term "alternative work" means different work or work that does not necessarily involve similar skills, responsibilities and compensation. Temporary alternative work may be an appropriate accommodation either in a return to work context, or in a situation where a disability renders an employee temporarily unable to accomplish the pre-disability job.

Temporary alternative work can be an appropriate accommodation to assist an individual where the nature of the disability and its limitations are temporary or episodic.

4.3.2(b) — Permanent Alternative Work

An employer-initiated alternative work arrangement must consider the circumstances of the individual's return to work. When an employee asks to be reinstated in a previous position, the employer may make the appropriate inquiries to assess whether the employee is fully able to carry out the essential functions of the job. Whenever possible, the returning employee should be given an opportunity to prove his or her ability to perform the pre-disability job.[41]

Where the employee can no longer perform his or her current job and if alternative work is appropriate based on the analysis described above, the Commission is of the view that the employer should consider permanent alternative work. This is consistent with a line of labour arbitration cases that have found that the duty to accommodate may include significant

---

[40] *Hamilton Civic Hospitals and CUPE, Local 794* (1994), 44 L.A.C. (4th) 31 [Ont. Arb. Award.]

[41] In *Chamberlin v. 599273 Ontario Ltd cob Stirling Honda* (1989), 11 C.H.R.R. D/110 (Ont. Bd. of Inq.), the Board of Inquiry found that the employer should have given the complainant the opportunity to prove he could still perform his old job.

workplace reorganization[42] as well as with the obligation to provide suitable work in order to satisfy the duty to re-employ injured workers.[43]

Reassignment to a vacant position should be considered an appropriate accommodation only when accommodation in the current position would cause undue hardship. The vacant position must be vacant within a reasonable amount of time, but the employer is not required to "promote" the employee. Reassignment is not available to job applicants. If reassignment creates a conflict because of a collective agreement, accommodation needs should prevail over the collective agreement. When reassignment takes place, the person must be qualified for the reassigned position. The vacant position must be equivalent to the current one, although a less equivalent position would be acceptable if no equivalent one exists.

4.3.3 — Return to Work

Accommodating a person who has been absent from work may involve any of the above forms of accommodation but also raises unique issues. People who return to work after an absence related to a ground in the *Code* are protected by the *Code*.[44] They generally have the right to return to their jobs, and this is frequently referred to as the "pre-disability job." Both employers and unions must co-operate in accommodating employees who are returning to work. Accommodation is a fundamental and integral part of the right to equal treatment in the return to work context.

---

[42]An employer may have to move an employee to a job more consistent with the employee's health status; *Re Calgary District Hospital Group and U.N.A. Loc. 121-R* (1994), 41 L.A.C. (4th) 319 (Alta. Lab. Rel. Bd.). The employer may have to look for work comparable to the original job rather than giving the employee an inferior position; *Re York County Hospital and Ontario Nurses' Association* (1992), 26 L.A.C. (4th) 384 (Ont. Lab. Rel. Bd.). The employer may even need to create a new job by joining together all the light duties and then reassigning the heavy duties to other employees; *Re Greater Niagara Hospital and Ontario Nurses Association* (1995), 50 L.A.C. (4th) 34 (Ont. Lab. Rel. Bd.). In one decision, the employer's duty to accommodate included not only the duties and requirements associated with the current job but also the duties and requirements associated with a bundle of tasks within the ability of an employee with a disability; *Re Mount Sinai Hospital and the O.N.A.* (1996), 54 L.A.C. (4th) 261 (Ont. Lab. Rel. Bd.).

[43]*Workplace Safety and Insurance Act*, S.O. 1997, c. 16, Sch. A, ss. 40 and 41 [hereinafter "*WSIA*"].

[44]There are also rights and obligations pertaining to return to work set out in the WSIA that may exist concurrently with human rights protections.

The right to return to work for persons with disabilities only exists if the worker can fulfil the essential duties of the job after accommodation short of undue hardship.[45] If a person cannot fulfil the essential duties of the job, despite the employer's effort to accommodate short of undue hardship, there is no right to return to work. As noted in the preceding section, there may also be a right to alternative work.

Under the *Code*, there is no fixed rule as to how long an employee with a disability may be absent before the duty to accommodate has been met. This will depend on the ability of the employee to perform the essential duties of the job considering the unique circumstances of every absence and the nature of the employee's condition, as well as circumstances in the workplace. Also important is the predictability of absence, both in regards to when it will end and if it may recur and the frequency of the absence. The employee's prognosis and length of absence are also important considerations. It is more likely that the duty to accommodate will continue with a better prognosis, regardless of the length of absence.

The duty to accommodate does not necessarily guarantee a limitless right to return to work. On the other hand, a return to work program that relies on arbitrarily selected cutoffs or that requires an inflexible date of return may be challenged as a violation of the *Code*. Ultimately the test of undue hardship is the relevant standard for assessing return to work programs.

4.4 — Duties and Responsibilities in the Accommodation Process

The accommodation process is a shared responsibility. Everyone involved should cooperatively engage in the process, share information, and avail themselves of potential accommodation solutions.

The *person with a disability* is required to:

- advise the accommodation provider of the disability (although the accommodation provider does not generally have the right to know what the disability is)
- make her or his needs known to the best of his or her ability, preferably in writing, in order that the person responsible for accommodation may make the requested accommodation
- answer questions or provide information regarding relevant restrictions or limitations, including information from health care professionals, where appropriate, and as needed

[45] See Section 17 of the *Code*.

- participate in discussions regarding possible accommodation solutions
- co-operate with any experts whose assistance is required to manage the accommodation process or when information is required that is unavailable to the person with a disability
- meet agreed-upon performance and job standards once accommodation is provided[46]
- work with the accommodation provider on an ongoing basis to manage the accommodation process
- discuss his or her disability only with persons who need to know. This may include the supervisor, a union representative or human rights staff.

The *employer* is required to:

- accept the employee's request for accommodation in good faith, unless there are legitimate reasons for acting otherwise
- obtain expert opinion or advice where needed
- take an active role in ensuring that alternative approaches and possible accommodation solutions are investigated,[47] and canvass various forms of possible accommodation and alternative solutions, as part of the duty to accommodate[48]
- keep a record of the accommodation request and action taken
- maintain confidentiality
- limit requests for information to those reasonably related to the nature of the limitation or restriction so as to be able to respond to the accommodation request
- grant accommodation requests in a timely manner, to the point of undue hardship, even when the request for accommodation does not use any specific formal language

---

[46]In some cases, accommodation may require the modification of job standards. See the section entitled *Essential Duties and the Current Job.*

[47]*Meiorin, supra* note 6 at paras. 65-66.

[48]*Human Rights Digest*, vol. 1 no. 2 (February/March 2000) citing *Conte v. Rogers Cablesystems Ltd.* (1999), C.H.R.R. Doc. 99-227 (Can. Human Rights Tribunal), *Mazuelos v. Clark* (2000), C.H.R.R. Doc. 00-011 (B.C. Human Rights Tribunal) and *Gordy v. Oak Bay Marine Management Ltd.* (2000), C.H.R.R. Doc. 00-040 (B.C. Human Rights Tribunal).

- bear the cost of any required medical information or documentation. For example, doctors' notes and letters setting out accommodation needs, should be paid for by the employer.

Unions and professional associations are required to:

- take an active role as partners in the accommodation process[49]
- share joint responsibility with the employer to facilitate accommodation[50]
- support accommodation measures irrespective of collective agreements, unless to do so would create undue hardship.

The duty to accommodate a disability exists for needs that are known. Organizations and persons responsible for accommodation are not, as a rule, expected to accommodate disabilities of which they are unaware. However, some individuals may be unable to disclose or communicate their needs because of the nature of their disability. In such circumstances, employers should attempt to assist a person who is clearly unwell or perceived to have a disability, by offering assistance and accommodation. On the other hand, employers are not expected to diagnose illness or "second-guess" the health status of an employee.

> *Example*: An employer is unaware of an employee's drug addiction but perceives that a disability might exist. The employer sees that the employee is having difficulty performing, and is showing signs of distress. If the employer imposes serious sanctions or terminates the employee for poor performance, without any progressive performance management and attempts to accommodate, these actions may be found to have violated the *Code*.[51]

Before terminating or sanctioning an employee for "unacceptable behaviour," an employer might first consider whether the actions of the employee are caused by a disability, especially where the employer is aware or perceives that the employee has a disability. Employers should always in-

---

[49]The Supreme Court of Canada's decision in *Central Okanagan School District No. 23 v. Renaud*, [1992] 2 S.C.R. 970, [hereinafter "*Renaud*"] sets out the obligations of unions.

[50]*Ibid.* at 988.

[51]For further information about drug and alcohol related disabilities, see Ontario Human Rights Commission, *Policy on Drug and Alcohol Testing* (1996, revised September 27, 2000), Online: Ontario Human Rights Commission website www.ohrc.on.ca.

form all employees that a disability-related assessment or accommodation can be provided as an option to address performance issues. Progressive performance management and discipline as well as employee assistance supports ensure that all employees have a range of opportunities to address performance issues on an individualized basis before sanctions or termination are considered. For example, severe change in an employee's behaviour could signal to an employer that the situation warrants further examination.

Mental illness should be addressed and accommodated in the workplace like any other disability. In some cases, an employer may be required to pay special attention to situations that could be linked to mental disability. Even if an employer has not been formally advised of a mental disability, the perception of such a disability will engage the protection of the *Code*. Prudent employers should try to offer assistance and support to employees before imposing severe sanctions. It should be borne in mind that some mental illnesses may render the employee incapable of identifying his or her needs.

> *Example*: John has bipolar disorder, which he has chosen not to disclose to his employer because he is concerned about how he would be treated at work if it were known that he had a mental disability. He experiences a crisis at work, followed by a failure to appear at work for several days. The employer is concerned about John's absence and recognizes that termination for failure to report to work may be premature. The employer offers John an opportunity to explain the situation after treatment has been received and the situation has stabilized. Upon learning that a medical issue exists, the employer offers assistance and accommodation.

Once disability-related needs are known, the legal onus shifts to those with the duty to accommodate. For example, counselling or referral through Employee Assistance Programs (EAPs) could be the solution for an underlying disability that might be aggravated by workplace or personal stress.

There may be instances where there is a reasonable and *bona fide* basis to question the legitimacy of a person's request for accommodation or the adequacy of the information provided. In such cases, the accommodation provider may request confirmation or additional information from a qualified health care professional in order to obtain the needed information. No one can be forced to submit to an independent medical examination, but failure to respond to reasonable requests may delay the provision of accommodation until such information is provided.

4.4.1 — Confidentiality

Persons with disabilities are not necessarily required to disclose private or confidential matters, and should disclose information to the accommodation provider only as it pertains to the need for accommodation and any restrictions or limitations.

> *Example*: An employee with AIDS has provided documentation to demonstrate her need for a flexible schedule and rest periods to manage periods of fatigue, and time to attend appointments with health care professionals. However, it is not necessary for the employee to disclose that she has AIDS. The employer is entitled to know that the employee has a disability and that she needs certain accommodations in order to remain productive at work.

Maintaining confidentiality for individuals with mental illness may be especially important because of the strong social stigmas and stereotyping that still persist about such disabilities.

Documentation supporting the need for particular accommodation (flexible hours, a different supervisor, a particular technical aid, for example) should be provided only to those who need to be aware of the information. It may be preferable in some circumstances for information to be provided to the company's health department or human resources staff rather than directly to the supervisor, so as to further protect confidentiality. Medical documentation should be kept separate from the person's corporate file.

5. — Undue Hardship

The *Code* prescribes three considerations in assessing whether an accommodation would cause undue hardship. These are:

- cost
- outside sources of funding, if any
- health and safety requirements.

Accommodating someone with a disability is seldom as expensive or difficult as is sometimes imagined. Over two-thirds of job accommodations cost under $500; many cost nothing at all.[52]

---

[52] A. Cantor, "The Costs and Benefits of Accommodating Employees with Disabilities" (Toronto: 1996), online: Cantor + Associates Workplace Accommodation Consultants www.interlog.com/~acantor/.

The *Code* sets out only three considerations. This means that no other considerations, other than those that can be brought into those three standards, can be properly considered under Ontario law. There have been cases originating from other jurisdictions or from Ontario prior to the amendment of the *Code* that have included such other factors as employee morale, or conflict with a collective agreement. However, the Ontario legislature has seen fit to enact a higher standard by specifically limiting undue hardship to three particular components. The broad and purposive interpretation of the *Code* and human rights generally means that rights must be construed liberally and defences to those rights should be construed narrowly.[53] Moreover, the *Code* has primacy over legislation,[54] and also prevails over agreements such as collective agreements.[55]

Several factors are therefore excluded from considerations that are frequently raised by respondents. These are business inconvenience, employee morale, customer preference, and collective agreements or contracts.[56]

5.1 — Excluded Factors

5.1.1 — Business Inconvenience

"Business inconvenience" is not a defence to the duty to accommodate. If there are demonstrable costs attributable to decreased productivity, efficiency or effectiveness, they can be taken into account in assessing undue hardship under the cost standard, providing they are quantifiable and demonstrably related to the proposed accommodation.

---

[53]There are a number of cases that confirm this approach to the interpretation of human rights statutes. Most recently, in *Mercier*, *supra* note 10 the Supreme Court summarized these cases and outlined the relevant principles of human rights interpretation.

[54]Section 44 of the *Code*.

[55]*Renaud*, *supra* note 49

[56]This is not an exclusive list. During the consultations, the issue of whether academic freedom may be a component of undue hardship was raised. Academic freedom is unrelated to the duty to accommodate and should not be a defence to accommodating persons with disabilities. For example, a student may require a more accessible classroom, or need more time in an examination because of a disability-related need. These are legitimate requests that do not diminish academic freedom. If an accommodation need places such a financial burden on the institution that it would amount to undue hardship by reason of cost or because it would substantially change the nature of the enterprise, or its viability, it would then meet the undue hardship standard. This issue will be dealt with at greater length in the Commission's planned guidelines on accommodation in the educational sector.

5.1.2 — Employee Morale

In some cases, accommodating an employee may generate negative reactions from coworkers who are either unaware of the reason for the accommodation or who believe that the employee is receiving an undue benefit. The reaction may range from resentment to hostility. However, the person responsible for providing accommodation should ensure that staff are supportive and are helping to foster an environment that is positive for all employees. It is not acceptable to allow discriminatory attitudes to fester into workplace hostilities that poison the environment for disabled workers.

Moreover, individuals with disabilities have a right to accommodation with dignity. It is an affront to an individual's dignity if issues of morale and misconception stemming from perceived unfairness are not prevented or dealt with. In such cases, those responsible will not have met their duty to provide accommodation with dignity.

5.1.3 — Third-party Preference

Human rights case law notes that third-party preferences do not constitute a justification for discriminatory acts, and the same rule applies to customer preferences.[57]

5.1.4 — Collective Agreements or Contracts

Collective agreements or other contractual arrangements cannot act as a bar to providing accommodation. The Courts have determined that collective agreements and contracts must give way to the requirements of human rights law. To allow otherwise would be to permit the parties to contract out of their *Code* rights under the auspices of a private agreement. Accordingly, subject to the undue hardship standard, the terms of a collective agreement or other contractual arrangement cannot justify discrimination that is prohibited by the *Code*.

A union may cause or contribute to discrimination by participating in formulating a work rule, *e.g.*, a provision in the collective agreement, that has a discriminatory effect.[58] Unions and employers are jointly responsible for

[57]The issue of customer, third party and employee preference is discussed in J. Keene, *Human Rights in Ontario*, 2nd ed. (Toronto: Carswell, 1992) at 204-5.

[58]*Renaud*, *supra* note 49.

negotiating collective agreements that comply with human rights laws. They should build conceptions of equality into collective agreements.[59]

> *Example*: When a union and employer are negotiating a collective agreement, the principle of seniority is maintained as a general principle. However, the union and employer can together address how employees with disabilities will be accommodated.

However, if an employer and a union cannot reach an agreement on how to resolve an accommodation issue, the employer must make the accommodation in spite of the collective agreement. If the union opposes the accommodation, or does not co-operate in the accommodation process, then the union may be named as a respondent in a complaint filed with the Commission.

Unions will have to meet the same requirements of demonstrating undue hardship having regard to costs, and health and safety. For example, if the disruption to a collective agreement can be shown to create direct financial costs, this can be taken into account under the cost standard. Issues surrounding terms of a collective agreement relating to health or safety are dealt with under the section dealing with Health and Safety.

In non-unionized environments, employers can make flexible employment arrangements to meet their duty to accommodate. The same sort of flexible employment arrangements should be considered in unionized environments, although they may fall outside the collective agreement where the duty to accommodate arises.

5.2 — Onus of Proof and Objective Evidence

In order to claim the undue hardship defence, the person who is responsible for making the accommodation has the onus of proof.[60] It is not up to the person with a disability to prove that the accommodation can be accomplished without undue hardship.

The nature of the evidence required to prove undue hardship must be objective, real, direct, and, in the case of cost, quantifiable. The person responsible for accommodation must provide facts, figures, and scientific data or opinion to support a claim that the proposed accommodation in fact causes

---

[59] *Meirion*, *supra* note 6 at para. 68. Those setting standards and rules must be aware of the differences between individuals and groups of individuals. Standards and rules should not just be based on the "mainstream" *e.g.*, employees who do not have disabilities.

[60] *Grismer*, *supra* note 29 at para. 42.

undue hardship. A mere statement, without supporting evidence, that the cost or risk is "too high" based on impressionistic views or stereotypes will not be sufficient.[61]

> *Example*: A deaf patient requires a sign language interpreter in a hospital. The hospital administrator refuses to provide the accommodation, stating "if everyone wanted signers, it would bankrupt us." The hospital administrator does not provide financial information to justify this claim, nor does he provide demographic evidence to show the likely number of patients who may require signers. As a result, the hospital's defence will be unlikely to succeed.

Objective evidence includes, but is not limited to:

- financial statements and budgets
- scientific data, information and data resulting from empirical studies
- expert opinion
- detailed information about the activity and the requested accommodation
- information about the conditions surrounding the activity and their effects on the person or group with a disability.

5.3 — Elements of the Undue Hardship Defence

5.3.1 — Cost

The Supreme Court of Canada has said that, *"one must be wary of putting too low a value on accommodating the disabled. It is all too easy to cite increased cost as a reason for refusing to accord the disabled equal treatment."*[62] The cost standard is therefore a high one.

Costs will amount to undue hardship if they are:

- quantifiable
- shown to be related to the accommodation
- so substantial that they would alter the essential nature of the enterprise, or so significant that they would substantially affect its viability.

---

[61] *Meiorin*, *supra* note 6 at paras. 78-79 and *Grismer*, *supra* note 29 at para. 41. Cases since *Meiorin* and *Grismer* have also applied this stringent requirement for objective evidence; see, for example, *Miele v. Famous Players Inc.* (2000), 37 C.H.R.R. D/1 (B.C.H.R.T.).

[62] *Grismer*, *supra* note 32 at para. 41

This test will apply whether the accommodation will benefit one individual or a group.

The costs that remain after all costs, benefits, deductions and other factors have been considered will determine undue hardship.

All projected costs that can be quantified and shown to be related to the proposed accommodation will be taken into account. However, mere speculation, for example, about monetary losses that may follow the accommodation of the person with a disability will not generally be persuasive.

The financial costs of the accommodation may include:

- capital costs, such as the installation of a ramp, the purchase of screen magnification or software
- operating costs such as sign language interpreters, personal attendants or additional staff time
- costs incurred as a result of restructuring that are necessitated by the accommodation
- any other quantifiable costs incurred directly as a result of the accommodation.

Concerns may arise about the potential increase in liability insurance premiums by the perceived health and safety risks of having persons with disabilities on particular job sites. Increased insurance premiums or sickness benefits would be included as operating costs where they are quantified, such as actual higher rates (not hypothetical), and are shown not to be contrary to the principles in the *Code* with respect to insurance coverage.[63] Where the increased liability is quantifiable and provable, and where efforts to obtain other forms of coverage have been unsuccessful, insurance costs can be included.

For the purposes of determining whether a financial cost[64] would alter the essential nature or substantially affect the viability of the organization, consideration will be given to:

- the ability of the person responsible for accommodation to recover the costs of accommodation in the normal course of business (see section 5.4.1)
- the availability of any grants, subsidies or loans from the federal, provincial or municipal government or from non-government sources which could offset the costs of accommodation

---

[63]Section 25(1) of the *Code*.

[64]For further discussion on minimizing costs, please refer to section 5.4 "Minimizing Undue Hardship."

- the ability of the person responsible for accommodation to distribute the costs of accommodation throughout the whole operation (see section 5.4.2)
- the ability of the person responsible for accommodation to amortize or depreciate capital costs associated with the accommodation according to generally accepted accounting principles
- the ability of the person responsible for accommodation to deduct from the costs of accommodation any savings that may be available as a result of the accommodation, including:
  - tax deductions and other government benefits (see section 5.4.4)
  - an improvement in productivity, efficiency or effectiveness (see section 5.4.5)
  - any increase in the resale value of property, where it is reasonably foreseeable that the property might be sold
  - any increase in clientele, potential labour pool, or tenants
  - the availability of the Workplace Safety and Insurance Board's *Second Injury and Enhancement Fund*[65] (see section 5.4.6).

Larger organizations, including businesses and governments, may be in a better position to set an example or provide leadership in accommodating persons with disabilities. Accommodation costs will likely be more easily absorbed by larger organizations. Large employers, for example, are more likely to have the opportunities and the means to provide employment opportunities for greater numbers of persons with disabilities in a manner that accommodates their needs.

The phrase "benefits of enhancing equality" is intended to include consideration of benefits from the accommodation which may accrue to a person's co-workers, family, friends, fellow students, or the general public by the accommodation being made.

5.3.1(a) — Heritage Buildings

The accessibility of heritage buildings raises controversial issues. A general exemption from accessibility requirements for heritage properties is not included in the Policy because it would result in broad exclusions as more and more buildings gain protection because of their heritage status. In a situation involving a heritage property, it is recognized that the cost of making

[65] *Second Injury and Enhancement Fund (S.I.E.F), Policy Document (08-01-05) in the Pre-Bill 99 Operational Policy Manual of the Workplace Safety and Insurance Board (W.S.I.B).*

the proposed accommodation may be increased by the necessity to preserve defining historic design features. However, aesthetic features, in and of themselves, that are not historic design features, are not to be included in the assessment.

The test of altering the essential nature or substantially affecting the viability of the enterprise allows the preservation of the defining features of a heritage property to be taken into account as a justifiable factor in assessing undue hardship.

5.3.2 — Outside Sources of Funding

The availability of outside sources of funding may alleviate accommodation costs.[66] Organizations can make use of outside resources in order to meet their duty to accommodate and must first do so before claiming undue hardship.

There are three potential sources of funding to consider:

1. *Funds that may be available to the individual only, provided through government programs and that are linked to the individual's disability*

   Resources, such as services or programs, might be available to accommodate the needs of persons with disabilities that could also aid them at work, in their apartment or while accessing a service.

   Persons with disabilities might be expected to first avail themselves of outside resources available to them when making accommodation requests to an employer or service provider. However, such resources should most appropriately meet the accommodation needs of the individual, including respect for dignity.

2. *Funds that would assist employers and service providers defray the cost of accommodation*

   Other outside accommodation resources might be available to an individual with a disability when more than one organization has an overlapping or interconnected sphere of responsibility for the duty to accommodate.

> *Example*: A lawyer who is deaf, and who works for a large law

[66]The Access Fund is an example of an outside source of funding. It helps community organizations develop barrier-free facilities, so persons with disabilities can be active volunteers and participate in potential employment opportunities. The Access Fund is part of Ontario's Equal Opportunity and Disability Partnerships and designed in partnership with the Ontario Trillium Foundation, which delivers the program.

firm, receives real-time captioning or sign language interpreter accommodation funded and provided by a court. While the lawyer is acting in court, the court takes responsibility for the duty to accommodate, relieving the lawyer's employer of its responsibility during this time period only.

3. *Funding programs to improve accessibility for persons with disabilities — a corporate or organizational responsibility*

Governments have a positive duty to ensure that services generally available to the public are also available to persons with disabilities. Governments should not be allowed to evade their human rights responsibilities by delegating implementation of their policies and programs to private entities.[67] An organization that assumes responsibility for a government program must attend to the accommodation needs of its users.

5.3.3 — Health and Safety

Health and safety requirements may be contained in a law or regulation, or result from rules, practices or procedures that have been established independently or in conjunction with other businesses or services engaged in similar kinds of activity.

Organizations have a responsibility to undertake health and safety precautions that would ensure that the health and safety risks in their facilities or services are no greater for persons with disabilities than for others. Where a health and safety requirement creates a barrier for a person with a disability, the accommodation provider should assess whether the requirement can be waived or modified. If waiving the health and safety requirement is likely to result in a violation of the *Occupational Health and Safety Act (OHSA)*, the employer should generate alternative measures based on the equivalency clauses of the *OHSA*.[68] The employer is required to show an objective assessment of the risk as well as demonstrate how the alternative measure provides equal opportunity to the person with a disability. The employer might be able to claim undue hardship after these measures were undertaken and a significant risk still remains.

---

[67] *Eldridge*, *supra* note 5.

[68] R.S.O. 1990, c. 0-1. The *OHSA* regulations have equivalency clauses that allow for the use of alternative measures to those specified in its regulations, provided the alternative measures afford equal or better protection to workers.

5.3.3(a) — Bona Fide *and Reasonable Requirements*

Health and safety risks will amount to undue hardship if the degree of risk that remains after the accommodation has been made outweighs the benefits of enhancing equality for persons with disabilities. The person responsible for accommodation will have to satisfy the three-step test set out in section 4.2.

Health and safety standards that are genuinely adopted for the protection of workers, clients or the public will usually meet the second step of the test. On the other hand, a standard that is established to circumvent human rights legislation will not meet this test.

The third step requires the organization to demonstrate that the standard is reasonably necessary and that accommodation cannot be accomplished without incurring undue hardship.

Health or safety risks that result in undue hardship could be reduced to acceptable levels over time, for example, by adding safety features, or changing job descriptions to accommodate an employee with a disability. Development of a new technology to allow an employee with a disability to operate certain machinery more safely, for example, may take some time. In principle, therefore, a person responsible for accommodation could be required to phase in an accommodation that would lessen the health or safety risk over time, provided that the delay is reasonable and justified in relation to the development time attributed to the accommodation.

5.3.3(b) — Assumption of Risk

A person with a disability may wish to assume a risk. The risk created by modifying or waiving a health and safety requirement is to be weighed against the right to equality of the person with a disability. Where the risk is so significant as to outweigh the benefits of equality, it will be considered to create undue hardship.

In determining whether an obligation to modify or waive a health or safety requirement, whether established by law or not, creates a significant risk to any person, consideration will be given to:

- the significance, probability and seriousness of the risk
- the other types of risks that the person responsible for accommodation is assuming within the organization
- the types of risks tolerated within society as a whole, reflected in legislated standards such as licensing standards, or in similar types of organizations.

The "risk" that remains after all precautions including accommodations (short of undue hardship based on cost) have first been made to reduce the risk will determine undue hardship.

Where a modification or waiver of a health and safety requirement could place an individual with a disability at risk, the person responsible for accommodation is obliged to explain the potential risk to the individual. Where possible, persons with disabilities should be allowed to assume risk with dignity, subject to the undue hardship standard. At the same time, the organization has an obligation under health and safety legislation not to place individuals in a situation of direct threat of harm. High probability of substantial harm to anyone will constitute an undue hardship.

Seriousness of the Risk

The fact that a person has a disability, in and of itself, is not sufficient to establish that there is a risk. Evidence will be required to prove the nature, severity, probability and scope of the risk.

In determining the seriousness or significance of a risk, the following factors should be considered:

- the nature of the risk
  - what could happen that would be harmful?
- the severity of the risk
  - how serious would the harm be if it occurred?
- the probability of the risk
  - how likely is it that the potential harm will actually occur?
  - is it a real risk, or merely hypothetical or speculative?
  - could it occur frequently?
- the scope of the risk
  - who will be affected by the event if it occurs?

These four factors should be considered together to determine the seriousness of the risk. If the potential harm is minor and not very likely to occur, the risk should not be considered to be serious. A risk to public safety shall be considered as part of the scope of the risk, while the likelihood that the harmful event may occur would be considered as part of the probability of risk.

The seriousness of the risk is to be determined after accommodation and on the assumption that suitable precautions have been taken to reduce the risk.

> *Example*: An ambulance dispatcher with a hearing impairment manages emergency calls over the telephone. Her capacity to do so safely

and reliably is properly assessed while using a prescribed hearing aid and a hearing aid-compatible telephone.

Consideration of Other Types of Risk

When assessing the seriousness of the risk posed by the obligation to modify or waive a health or safety requirement, consideration must be given to the other types of risks that are assumed within an organization. For example, many jobs have risks that are inherent to the nature of the work itself.

As well, job applicants may be denied employment on the basis of limitations related to their disabilities. Yet these same or similar limitations may be developed by employees who have been on the job for several years, with little or no effect on their ability to satisfactorily perform their duties and with no impact on their careers.

Everyday Risk

Many sources of risk exist in the workplace, aside from those risks that may result from accommodating an employee with a disability. All employees assume everyday risks that may be inherent in a work site, or in working conditions, or which may be caused by a co-worker's fatigue, temporary inattentiveness, or stress. Employers have recognized that not all employees are 100% productive every day, and many provide counselling programs or other means of coping with personal problems, emotional difficulties or other problems that may arise. Risks created by these situations are factored into the level of safety or risk that we all accept in our lives every day.

A potential risk that is created by accommodation should be assessed in light of those other, more common sources of risk in the workplace.

Risks in Society as a Whole

Risks that are present in comparable enterprises or in society as a whole should be considered. While maximizing safety is always desirable, as a society we constantly balance the degree of safety to be achieved against competing benefits. For example, we balance the risk of injury in contact sports against the benefits of participating in sports activities or because of the economic and entertainment benefits. We balance the risks involved in permitting higher speed limits against the benefits of increasing the efficient flow of traffic. We balance the risks involved in driving affordable cars against the costs that would be involved in making them even safer.

5.4 — Minimizing Undue Hardship

The following factors and strategies must be considered in order to avoid undue hardship and meet the duty to accommodate under the *Code*.

5.4.1 — Cost Recovery

Persons responsible for accommodation should take steps to recover the costs of accommodation. For example, by making reasonable changes to business practices or obtaining grants or subsidies, the expense of making accommodation can be offset. If the person responsible for accommodation believes that such measures will not be effective in avoiding undue hardship, s/he will have to demonstrate that such steps to recover costs are inadequate in the circumstances, are impossible, or will not yield the needed resources.

In other words, the person responsible for accommodation would be required to establish that the costs, which remain after steps are taken to recover costs, will alter the essential nature or substantially affect the viability of the enterprise.

5.4.2 — Distributing Costs

Costs of accommodation must be distributed as widely as possible within the organization responsible for accommodation so that no single department, employee, customer or subsidiary is burdened with the cost of an accommodation. The appropriate basis for evaluating the cost is based on the budget of the organization as a whole, not the branch or unit in which the person with disability works or to which the person has made an application. In the case of government, the term "whole operation" should refer to the programs and services offered or funded by the government. There may be accommodations that require substantial expenditure, which, if implemented immediately, would alter the essential nature of government programs or substantially affect their viability in whole or in part. In such instances, it may be necessary to implement the required accommodation incrementally.

5.4.3 — Reducing Financial Burden

Organizations should consider spreading the financing of accommodation over time by taking out loans, issuing shares or bonds, or other business methods of financing. Amortization or depreciation is another means that an organization might be expected to use to reduce the financial burden, where possible.

5.4.4 — Tax Deductions

Tax deductions or other government benefits flowing from the accommodation will also be taken into account as offsetting the cost of accommodation.

5.4.5 — Improvements to Productivity, Efficiency, or Effectiveness

The person responsible for accommodation is expected to consider whether accommodation of the needs of a person with a disability may improve productivity, efficiency or effectiveness, expand the business, or improve the value of the business or property.

> *Example*: An accommodation that affects a significant number of people with disabilities, such as persons requiring wheelchair access, could open up a new market for a storekeeper or a service provider. By building a ramp, several more persons will be able to access a store.

5.4.6 — Second Injury and Enhancement Fund[69]

The effects of the Second Injury and Enhancement Fund of the Workplace Safety and Insurance Board (the "WSIB") must be considered. In the event of an injury to a worker, where the injury is caused by the worker's disability, a claim may be made against this fund even if the employer did not have knowledge of the employee's pre-existing condition. The rates for the employer will not be increased as a result of making claims on the fund.

Approximately 90% of employees in the province of Ontario are under the protection of the WSIB. Since the fund is available to most employers, there will be few instances where increased liability insurance premiums for risk of injury to a person due to a pre-existing condition or disability will be a factor in creating undue hardship.

5.4.7 — Creative Design Solutions

Creative design solutions can often avoid expensive capital outlay. This may involve specifically tailoring design features to the individual's functional capabilities. Design solutions must be most respectful of dignity.

5.4.8 — A Less Expensive Alternative

Where undue hardship is claimed, cost and risk estimates should be carefully examined to ensure that they are not excessive in relation to the stated objective. If so, a determination should be made as to whether a less expensive or lower-risk alternative exists which could accomplish the accommodation (either as an interim measure to a phased-in solution or permanently) while still fully respecting the dignity of the person with a disability.

---

[69] *Supra*, note 65.

5.4.9 — Phasing in Accommodation

Some accommodations will be very important but will be difficult to accomplish in a short period of time.

> *Example*: A small municipality may be able to show that to make its community centre or transportation system accessible in a single year would cause undue hardship. Or, a small employer may find it impossible to make its entrance and washroom facilities accessible immediately without undue hardship.

In these situations, undue hardship should be avoided by phasing in the accessible features gradually.

Some accommodations will benefit large numbers of persons with disabilities, yet the cost may prevent them from being accomplished. One approach, which may reduce the hardship, is to spread the cost over several years by phasing in the accommodation gradually.

> *Example*: A commuter railroad might be required to make a certain number of stations accessible per year.

In many cases, while accommodation is being phased in over an extended period of time it may still be possible to provide interim accommodation for the individual. If both short- and long-term accommodation can be accomplished without causing undue hardship, then both should be considered simultaneously.

5.4.10 — Establishing a Reserve Fund

A second method of reducing the impact of the cost of an accommodation is to establish a reserve fund into which the person responsible for accommodation makes payment under specified conditions. One of the obvious conditions should be that the reserve fund is to be used only to pay for accommodation costs in the future. Accommodations could gradually be accomplished by expenditures out of the reserve fund or could eventually be accomplished once enough funds had been set aside.

A reserve fund should not be considered as an alternative to a loan where the accommodation could be made immediately and the cost paid back over time. Rather, the reserve fund is to be used in circumstances where it would create undue hardship for the person responsible for accommodation to obtain a loan and accomplish the accommodation immediately. The reserve fund is one of several financing options to be considered in assessing the feasibility of an accommodation. If a reserve fund is to be established, provision should be made for considering future changes in circumstances.

Both phasing in and the establishment of a reserve fund are to be considered only after the person responsible for accommodation has demonstrated that the most appropriate accommodation could not be accomplished immediately. Phasing in is to be preferred to the establishment of a reserve fund wherever possible.

5.4.11 — Assessing the Impact of Remaining Costs

After all costs, benefits deductions, outside sources of funding and other factors have been considered, the next step is to determine whether the remaining (net) cost will alter the essential nature or affect the viability of the organization responsible for making the accommodation.

The person responsible for accommodation would need to show how it would be altered or its viability affected. It will not be acceptable for the person responsible for accommodation to merely state, without evidence to support the statement, that the company operates on low margins and would go out of business if required to undertake the required accommodation.

Finally, if undue hardship can be shown, the person with a disability should be given the option of providing or paying for that portion of the accommodation that results in undue hardship.

5.4.12 — Expert Assessment

Where an undue hardship analysis anticipates assessing substantial capital or operating expenditures or procedural changes, for example, in making physical alterations to an apartment building, work site, vehicle or equipment or changing health and safety requirements, it might be advisable for the person responsible for accommodation to obtain a proposal and estimate from experts in barrier-free design and construction.

6. — Accommodation Planning and Implementation

The best defence against human rights complaints is to be fully informed and aware of the responsibilities and protections included in the *Code*. Organizations can achieve this by developing disability accommodation policy and procedures as well as by conducting an accessibility review.

6.1 — Organizational Policy

Organizations are responsible for dealing effectively, quickly and fairly with situations involving claims of harassment or discrimination. Organizations can be held liable by a court or tribunal if they or responsible staff members do not act to end discrimination or harassment in their workplaces.

When an act of harassment or discrimination or a need for accommodation is ignored, there are costs in terms of low morale, high stress, damaged professional reputations and employee absences.

Developing internal anti-discrimination policies and procedures to resolve complaints as part of a broad program to build a harassment-free and discrimination-free environment offers many benefits. Dealing promptly with these issues saves time and money. Letting people know the rules and defining unacceptable forms of behaviour makes it possible to avoid costly and upsetting hours in the courts or before specialized tribunals. In that way, strong policies and programs that prevent human rights complaints and help an organization effectively meet its duty to accommodate make good business sense.

The following should be part of any complete strategy to resolve human rights issues that arise in the workplace:

- anti-harassment or anti-discrimination policy
- disability accommodation policy
- a complaint resolution procedure
- ongoing education programs.

These elements should be developed in co-operation with the union or other workplace or organizational partners.

A disability accommodation policy should:

- outline rights and responsibilities
- require barrier analysis and prevention
- prepare and document accommodation plans
- monitor and evaluate implementation.

6.2 — Accessibility Review

Organizations should consider developing accessibility review plans, undertaking reviews and implementing the necessary changes to make facilities, procedures and services accessible to employees, members, tenants, clients or customers with disabilities.

Conducting the accessibility review will show to what extent an organization is accessible to persons with disabilities and what needs to be done.

An accessibility review plan should:

- state the purpose of the review plan along with a rationale, context and guidance for conducting a review

- acknowledge an organization's obligations under the *Code* to ensure accessibility for employees, clients or customers with disabilities
- identify internal and external resources that would provide guidance for conducting the review
- summarize current internal and external initiatives
- identify quality service measures
- outline the scope of the review and identify potential barriers as they may relate to procedures and practices, facilities, services and communications
- outline timeframes and responsibilities around conducting an accessibility review of the organization
- outline a communications plan for the accessibility review so that senior management, staff, members, clients, etc. are aware and supportive of the initiative and its purpose.

Results of the accessibility review should be documented in a Summary of Findings and Recommendations Report and submitted to senior management. Senior management should make the results available to all concerned along with a plan for undertaking barrier removal.

Accessibility review plans and barrier removal are up-front ways that an organization can address the needs of persons with disabilities. Developing and using a disability accommodation policy will also help an organization meet its duty to accommodate the individual needs of employees and customers with disabilities in accordance with the *Code*. Such a policy will make it clear to employees with disabilities, others who require accommodation, and managers responsible for providing accommodation what company procedures are in place to assist persons with disabilities effectively.

Policy and Guidelines on Discrimination Because of Family Status

Approved by the Commission: March 28, 2007

1. — Introduction

The Ontario *Human Rights Code* ("the *Code*") states that it is public policy in Ontario to recognize the inherent dignity and worth of every person and to provide for equal rights and opportunities without discrimination. The provisions of the *Code* are aimed at creating a climate of understanding and mutual respect for the dignity and worth of each person, so that each person feels a part of the community and feels able to contribute to the community.

Every person in Ontario has a right to be free from discrimination and harassment on the basis of family status, in the social areas of employment, services, goods, facilities, housing accommodation, contracts and membership in trade and vocational associations.

The ground of family status has been part of the *Code* since 1982, but has received relatively little analysis or attention, either in Ontario or in other Canadian jurisdictions. This is the first time the human rights issues related to family status have been explored in depth. It is to be expected that the understanding and public awareness of this ground of the *Code* will continue to develop over time.

The ground of family status, by its nature, raises complex and difficult issues related to the treatment of caregivers[1] in our society. The Supreme Court of Canada has stated, "That those who bear children and benefit society as a whole thereby should not be economically or socially disadvan-

[1]For the purposes of this *Policy*, the term "caregivers" refers to those persons who provide informal, unpaid assistance for the physical and emotional needs of another person who is reliant on them for that assistance. Generally, the recipient of care is a child, an older person, or a person with a disability. Caregiving can include a range of activities beyond direct physical care, such as advocacy on behalf of the care recipient, locating and organizing services, taking care recipients to appointments, carrying out errands and monitoring needs or well-being. Persons identified by family status (that is, persons in a parent-child relationship) will generally pass through stages where they are and are not caregivers to their parents or children. Persons not identified by family status (such as, for example, siblings) may also have caregiving responsibilities in some circumstances.

taged seems to bespeak the obvious."[2] The results of the Ontario Human Rights Commission's ("the Commission") research and consultation on family status indicate that, on the contrary, caregivers continue to face significant and ongoing disadvantage because of their role. It is the Commission's hope that this *Policy* will provide a meaningful step towards addressing this issue.

This *Policy* is based on extensive research and consultation on issues related to family status. In May 2005, the Commission published a Discussion Paper, *Human Rights and the Family in Ontario*, which outlined key issues and invited submissions from interested parties. At the same time, the Commission distributed a questionnaire and posted it on its website, inviting individual Ontarians to share their stories of how their family status had impacted on their access to housing, employment and services. The Commission heard from approximately 120 organizations and individuals, including employers, unions, housing providers, government, academics, community organizations, legal clinics, service providers, professional organizations and advocacy groups. During the fall of 2005, the Commission held four roundtables on specific issues of concern: issues affecting older Ontarians, the definition of family status, employment and housing. The Commission released a Consultation Report, *The Cost of Caring*, which examines the broad range of issues impacting on the ability of families with caregiving responsibilities to equally access and benefit from employment, housing and services, and outlines roles and responsibilities for government, institutions and the Commission itself.

Several themes emerged from this consultation, and have shaped this *Policy*:

- There is a profound lack of awareness among employers, housing providers, service providers, community advocates and the general public regarding rights and responsibilities under the *Code* with respect to family status.
- Persons providing care for family members face a range of serious systemic barriers to full participation in employment, housing and services, and experience ongoing disadvantage because of their family status. Employment, housing and services have often not been designed in ways that include persons with caregiving responsibilities.
- The existence and nature of these barriers are not widely understood, and issues related to family status are often viewed as "personal problems" rather than human rights concerns.

---

[2] *Brooks v. Canada Safeway Ltd*, [1989] 1 S.C.R. 1219 at para. 40.

- There are many different kinds of families in today's Ontario. Steps must be taken to ensure that all of these families are included and treated with respect and dignity.
- Each person's experience of his or her family status will be significantly affected by their race, sex, marital status, sexual orientation, age, creed, and whether that individual or a family member has a disability.
- Negative attitudes and stereotypes persist about the character and capabilities of persons based on certain types of family status, such as, for example, lone parents.
- Employers, housing providers, service providers, government and individuals must work together to remove existing barriers for persons identified by family status.

This *Policy* sets out the Commission's position on discrimination on the basis of family status as it relates to the provisions of the *Code*. It deals *only* with issues that fall within the *Code* and could be the subject of a human rights complaint. At the same time, the *Policy* interprets the protections of the *Code* in a broad and purposive manner, consistent with the principle that the quasi-constitutional status of the *Code* requires that it be given a liberal interpretation that best ensures its anti-discriminatory goals are attained. The Commission's Consultation Report contains a broader examination of social policy issues affecting persons disadvantaged by family status. In addition to this *Policy*, the Commission will continue to engage in promotion and advancement initiatives to address the broad systemic context of discrimination based on family status.

Commission policy statements contribute to creating a culture of human rights in Ontario. This *Policy* is intended to help the public understand the *Code* protections against discrimination and harassment because of family status. It is also meant to assist individuals, employers, organizations, providers of services and housing, and policy-makers in understanding their responsibilities and acting appropriately to ensure compliance with the *Code*.

The analysis and examples used in the *Policy* are based on the Commission's research on discrimination on the basis of family status, international standards, complaints that have come before the Commission, tribunal and court decisions, and the input of individuals and organizations in the Commission's consultation process.

2. — International Protections

The Supreme Court of Canada has indicated that the values and principles enshrined in international law constitute part of the legal context in which legislation is interpreted and applied.[3] Additionally, human rights commissions have been identified as key institutions in implementing and protecting international human rights standards. Accordingly, the Commission uses applicable international standards in its policy development and to inform its applications and interpretation of the *Code*.

The needs and rights of persons with familial responsibilities have been recognized in numerous international covenants to which Canada is a signatory, including the *Universal Declaration of Human Rights*,[4] the *International Covenant on Civil and Political Rights*,[5] the *International Covenant on Economic, Social and Cultural Rights*,[6] the *Convention on the Elimination of all Forms of Discrimination Against Women*,[7] and the *Convention on the Rights of the Child*.[8] As a signatory to these international human rights instruments, Canada has recognized that the family is a fundamental group unit of society, and has committed to provide the widest possible protection and assistance to the family.

Through these international human rights instruments, Canada has agreed to recognize the particular needs of families with young children, and to render appropriate assistance to parents and legal guardians in the performance of their child-rearing responsibilities and to ensure the development of institutions, facilities and services for the care of children.

As well, a number of these covenants recognize the unique role that women continue to play in providing care for families and require states parties to ensure a proper understanding of maternity as a social function, to promote recognition of the common responsibility of men and women in the upbringing and development of their children, and to take steps to ensure that women are not prevented from reaching their full potential, particularly in the workplace, because of caregiving responsibilities.

---

[3]See *Slaight Communications Inc. v. Davidson*, [1989] 1 S.C.R. 1038, and *Baker v. Canada (Minister of Citizenship and Immigration)*, [1999] 2 S.C.R. 817 at paras. 70-71.

[4]December 1948, General Assembly resolution 217A (III), UN Doc. A/810.

[5]19 December 1966, 999 U.N.T.S. 171, Can. T.S. 1976 No. 47 (entered into force 23 March 1976, accession by Canada 19 May 1976).

[6]16 December 1966, 993 U.N.T.S. 3, Can. T.S. 1976 No. 46 (entered into force 03 January 1976, accession by Canada 19 August 1976).

[7]18 December 1979, 1249 U.N.T.S. 13, Can. T.S. 1982 No. 31 (entered into force 03 September 1981, accession by Canada 09 January 1982).

[8]20 November 1989, GA Res. 44/25, Can. T.S. 1992 No. 3 (entered into force 02 September 1990, accession by Canada 12 January 1992, Article 18).

3. — *Code* Protections for Relationships

3.1 — *Code* Definitions

Contemporary families in Ontario are extremely diverse. There have always been families that did not fit the "traditional" family model, that is, a father in the paid workforce who is married to a mother who is a full-time caregiver for their children. However, demographic shifts over the past few decades mean that this model is no longer the norm. The Vanier Institute of the Family indicates that fewer than half of all Canadian families now consist of a married heterosexual couple with one or more children.[9] Some of the most important demographic shifts regarding families are noted below.[10]

- Almost one-quarter of families with children are now lone-parent families, in most cases headed by women.
- Increasing divorce rates have led to a rise in blended and dual custody families.
- There has been growing recognition of families headed by gay, lesbian, bisexual, and transgendered (LGBT) persons, whether as lone parents or part of a couple.[11]
- With the growing diversity of Ontario's population has come a broader range of cultural constructs of the family, often including increased emphasis on extended family networks.
- As Ontario's population continues to age, families are increasingly grappling with eldercare responsibilities.

---

[9]Vanier Institute of the Family, *Profiling Canada's Families III* (2004): 18, online: Vanier Institute of the Family, www.vifamily.ca.

[10]For a more detailed discussion of demographic trends relating to families, see the Ontario Human Rights Commission's Discussion Paper, *Human Rights & the Family in Ontario* (2005), online: Ontario Human Rights Commission www.ohrc.on.ca.

[11]See, for example, *M.D.R. v. Ontario (Deputy Registrar General)*, [2006] O.J. No. 2268 at paras. 111-115 (Ont. Sup. C.J.) in which the Court held that provisions of the *Vital Statistics Act* that prevented the inclusion of both lesbian parents on the Statement of Live Birth of a child conceived through artificial insemination violated the equality provisions of the *Charter* with respect to sex and sexual orientation. In a very recent decision by the Ontario Court of Appeal, *A.A. v. B.B.*, [2007] O.J. No. 2 at para. 7 (Ont. C.A.), the Court ruled that three legal parents could be recognized under the *Children's Law Reform Act*: a lesbian couple who were the child's guardians, and the child's biological father.

- The movement *en masse* of women into the paid labour force has led to shifts in gender roles and expectations within families.

These familial relationships of care and commitment are essential, both to individual well-being and to the effective functioning of society. Persons who are providing care to family members are benefiting society as a whole, and should not face discrimination, exclusion or disadvantage as a result.

The *Code* provides explicit protection against discrimination for specific relationships, through prohibitions on discrimination because of marital status and family status.

Section 10(1) of the *Code* broadly defines the ground of marital status as follows:

> "marital status" means the status of being married, single, widowed, divorced or separated and includes the status of living in a conjugal relationship with a person outside of marriage.

This definition includes both same-sex and opposite-sex relationships.

The ground of "family status" is more narrowly defined in section 10(1) as "the status of being in a parent and child relationship."

These two grounds intersect to cover a range of family forms, including lone-parent and blended families, and families where parents are in same-sex or "common-law" relationships.

These grounds do not, however, cover the full range of relationships that most would consider familial, including relationships with siblings, or with members of the extended family, such as grandparents, grandchildren, aunts, uncles, nieces, nephews and cousins. It excludes the kinds of "chosen families" often adopted by LGBT persons, as well as the diverse forms of support networks developed by persons with disabilities. Persons discriminated against because of these relationships cannot file complaints on the basis of "family status" unless they can demonstrate a parent-child type of relationship, as is further discussed below. While not all familial relationships attract negative stereotyping or disadvantage, a broad definition can ensure that the needs of caregivers in various familial relationships will be accommodated.

In its Consultation Report on Family Status, *The Cost of Caring*, the Commission states that the current *Code* definition excludes important familial relationships, and has an adverse impact on individuals identified by sexual orientation, gender identity, sex, disability, age, creed, and race and race-related grounds (ethnic origin, place of origin, ancestry, citizenship, and colour) of the *Code* and concludes that the *Code* should be amended to recognize the broad spectrum of family types in today's Ontario.

The Commission recommends that, as a best practice, employers and housing and service providers recognize and accommodate a broader range of familial relationships than those described by the grounds of marital and family status.

> *Example*: When drafting its policy on accommodating caregiving needs, an employer includes siblings, extended family, and other persons dependent on the employee for care and assistance.

3.2 — The Scope of the Ground of "Family Status"

In accordance with the principle that a broad and purposive approach must be taken to the interpretation of human rights protections, tribunals and courts have taken an expansive approach to the interpretation of the ground of family status, which is currently defined as the "status of being in a parent and child relationship."

The ground of family status protects non-biological parent and child relationships, such as families formed through adoption, step-parent relationships, foster families, and non-biological gay and lesbian parents.[12]

An Ontario Board of Inquiry has set out the principle that the definition of family status covers all those who are in a parent and child "type" of relationship:

> [S]omeone acting in the position of a parent to a child is, in our view, embraced by this definition; for example, a legal guardian or even an adult functioning in fact as parent. Occasionally, for example, due to death or illness of a relative or friend, someone will step in and act as parent to a child of the deceased or incapacitated adult. Thus, if a nephew were to reside with an aunt for an indefinite period, in our view their relationship would fall within the meaning of "family status" . . .[13]

---

[12]*Moffatt v. Kinark Child and Family Services (No. 4)* (1998), 35 C.H.R.R. D/205 at para. 12 (Ont. Bd. Inq.) dealt with discrimination against a gay foster parent. Discrimination against adoptive families was dealt with in *McKenna v. Canada (Secretary of State* (1993), 22 C.H.R.R. D/486 (C.H.R.T.) and *Pringle v. Alberta (Municipal Affairs)* (2003), 48 C.H.R.R. C/111 (Alta. H.R.P.).

[13]*York Condominium Corp. No. 216 v. Dudnik (No. 2)* (1990), 12 C.H.R.R. D/325, at para. 165 (Ont. Bd. Inq.); aff'd (1991), 14 C.H.R.R. D/406 (Ont. Div. Ct.).

The ground of family status may therefore embrace a range of circumstances where there are no blood or adoptive ties, but relationships of care, responsibility and commitment that resemble a parent-child relationship.

> *Example*: When a single mother has difficulty caring for her two young children because of her economic circumstances, her cousins offer to take them in until she is back on her feet. When that couple attempts to find rental housing that will accommodate these two young children, a landlord turns them away on the basis that this is an "adult-oriented building." The couple files a complaint of discrimination on the basis of family status.

The Commission has taken the position that the ground of family status includes care relationships between adult children and those who stand in parental relationship to them. For example, individuals providing eldercare for aging parents are protected from discrimination under the ground of family status. The protection extends to include anyone in a "parent type" of relationship with the caregiver. For example, a person providing eldercare to a grandparent who played a significant role in his or her upbringing may be protected under the ground of family status.

The ground of family status has been interpreted to prohibit differential treatment between various forms of families. For example, there is a lengthy history of differential treatment of families formed through adoption or fostering, compared to biological families. A Canadian Human Rights Tribunal found that citizenship rules that distinguished between biological and adoptive children discriminated on the basis of family status.[14]

Human rights protections for marital and family status include protection against discrimination based on the particular identity of a spouse or family member.[15] For example, it would be discriminatory for an employer to take negative actions towards an employee because of personal animosity towards that person's child or parent.

> *Example*: A man works in a family-run company with his brothers-in-law. When his daughter raises allegations of sexual abuse against one of her uncles, he is abruptly fired from his job. He successfully files a human rights complaint of discrimination based on family status.

---

[14] *Canada (Attorney General) v. McKenna* (1993), 22 C.H.R.R. D/486, at para. 58. (C.H.R.T.).

[15] *B. v. Ontario (Human Rights Commission)*, [2002] 3 S.C.R. 403 at para. 58.

It should be noted that, in some circumstances, *Code* protections related to the ground of family status overlap with those for the ground of sex, which includes pregnancy. Under this ground, a woman is protected against discrimination because she is, was or may become pregnant, or because she has had a baby. It includes the period following childbirth, including the post-delivery period and breastfeeding. Employers and service providers may, for example, have a duty to accommodate the needs of breastfeeding mothers. A full discussion of these issues is set out in the Commission's *Policy on Discrimination Because of Pregnancy and Breastfeeding*.

3.3 — Alternative Grounds

There may be situations where a person who believes he or she has faced negative treatment because of his or her role as a caregiver does not fall within the grounds of family or marital status, but may file complaints based on other *Code* grounds.

3.3.1 — Sex Discrimination

Caregiving has traditionally been regarded as a feminine role. Historically, it has been assumed that women are, and ought to be, primarily responsible for providing care for children, aging parents and relatives, and family members who are ill or have disabilities. Women and men who failed to conform to their assigned gender roles faced significant negativity and opposition.

Stereotypes and assumptions about caregiving roles, while less pervasive than in the past, remain powerful, to such an extent that issues about caregiving are frequently characterized as "women's issues." While gender roles are becoming more flexible, caregiving responsibilities remain highly gendered, with women providing the bulk of caregiving for children, aging parents or relatives, or family members with disabilities.[16] These caregiving responsibilities contribute significantly to women's ongoing inequality, and in particular to their ability to obtain, maintain, and advance in employment. The status of women in employment, housing and services is fundamentally linked to their roles as primary caregivers. Men may also in some circumstances find themselves disadvantaged by these gender roles, in that,

---

[16] N. Zukewich, "Unpaid Informal Caregiving" *Canadian Social Trends* (Autumn 2003) 14; J.A. Frederick and J.E. Fast, "Eldercare in Canada: Who Does How Much?," *Canadian Social Trends* (Autumn 1999) 26; D. Cheal, M. Luxton and F. Woolley, *How Families Cope and Why Policy-Makers Need to Know* (Canadian Policy Research Network, 1998) at 30.

where they do take on primary caregiving responsibilities, these responsibilities are less likely to be recognized and supported.

The failure to recognize and accommodate caregiving responsibilities, because it is related to long-standing gender roles and assumptions, has an adverse impact on women and in some cases men, and may in appropriate circumstances be considered discrimination on the basis of sex, as an alternative to, or in addition to discrimination on the basis of family status.

> *Example*: Because Eva is the only daughter in her family, her parents and brothers have always assumed that, as her parents age, Eva will take on the role of primary caregiver to one of her brothers, who has a significant cognitive disability. After Eva's parents die, she finds it very difficult to attend to her caregiving responsibilities as well as her demanding job. She asks her employer for temporarily reduced work hours while she puts supports in place. Her manager tells her that he can reduce her work hours, but since work will no longer be her top priority, he will demote her to an entry level position. Eva files a human rights complaint on the ground of sex discrimination.

3.3.2 — Discrimination Because of Association

Section 12 provides that the *Code* is violated where discrimination occurs because of a relationship, association, or dealings with a person or persons identified by a prohibited ground of discrimination. A person who is denied a service or housing, for example, because of his or her relationship with a person who is identified by a *Code* ground can file a complaint of discrimination on the basis of association. This ground may extend to protect persons who are providing care for persons identified by the ground of disability.

> *Example*: A man who lives with, and is providing care for, a relative with a mobility-related disability, is turned away by a landlord who fears that they might request accessibility-related upgrades to the apartment. The man files a complaint of discrimination on the basis of association with a person with a disability.

4. — Relationship Between Family Status and Other *Code* Grounds

The experience of discrimination based on family status may differ based on other aspects of a person's identity. Whenever an issue relating to family status is raised, it is important to take into account the intersecting impact of the person's sex, marital status, sexual orientation, race and age, as well as whether the person or his or her family member has a disability.

4.1 — Sex

As noted in section 3.3.1 above, because caregiving is at the heart of the ground of family status, and caregiving roles and responsibilities have historically been and largely remain closely tied to gender roles and stereotypes, the issues related to family status cannot be adequately understood without thoughtful consideration of the impact of gender.

As a result, systemic discrimination on the basis of family status will often have an adverse impact on the ground of sex as well. As well, the experience of being in a parent-child relationship will generally differ for men and women because of the different expectations, assumptions and stereotypes about mothering and fathering. Therefore, when considering complaints related to family status, gender issues should always be taken into account.

> *Example*: After the birth of his first child, a father tells his supervisor that he is considering requesting a reduced work week. When he ultimately tells his supervisor that he will not be making a request for reduced work hours, his supervisor tells him, "That's good. We tolerate this kind of thing from the women because we have to but we really don't expect it from the men. Really, it would be a career-limiting move for you." The employee feels that his work environment has been poisoned by this comment, and that it is now impossible for him to request any accommodations related to his family status.

4.2 — Marital Status

The experience of caregiving will vary widely depending on whether one is married or single, or part of a blended or dual-custody family.

The situation of female lone parents deserves special attention. Female-headed lone-parent families are the most economically vulnerable of all families,[17] as well as being the subject of persistent negative stereotypes; for example, that they are "failed families." These stereotypes are often particularly virulent for female-headed lone-parent families from racialized or

[17]In 1997, 56% of all female-headed lone-parent families were poor, compared to 14% of all families. As well, these families are more likely to experience persistent low income. Vanier Institute of the Family, *Family Facts* (2004), online: Vanier Institute of the Family www.vifamily.ca, R. Morisette, "On the Edge: Financially Vulnerable Families," *Canadian Social Trends* (Winter 2002).

Aboriginal communities. These families often face massive practical barriers in accessing housing, employment and services.

> *Example*: A Black lone mother asks to meet with her son's teacher because he seems to be struggling with a certain aspect of the curriculum. Based on stereotypes about Black lone mothers, the teacher assumes that the child is not being properly supported and supervised at home, and is not likely to succeed at school. The teacher tells the child's mother that, "All things considered, we really shouldn't set our sights too high."

Families shaped by divorce, such as dual-custody and blended families, may require complex arrangements for childcare, housing and services, and their needs may not be taken into consideration by those who design housing, employment and services.

> *Example*: A school bussing service has a mandate to provide transportation to all children who require it and who live within specified boundaries. It has a rule that it will only do pick-ups and drop-offs at a single location. A dual-custody family asks for an exemption. The child in question rotates on a weekly basis between his parents' homes, both of whom are within the bus services boundaries. The bus service refuses, stating that the parents must chose one or the other of their homes as the sole pick-up and drop-off point. The parents file a complaint of discrimination based on family status.

4.3 — Sexual Orientation and Gender Identity

Often, the families of lesbians, gays, bisexuals and transgendered persons are not recognized as valid families, and are therefore invisible to others. As well, these individuals may face negative stereotypes about their fitness or capacity to parent. Discrimination, homophobia and transphobia may make it difficult for LGBT persons to openly discuss their families and request appropriate services or accommodations. Family members of LGBT persons may find themselves harassed, bullied or ostracized because of their relationship.

> *Example*: The daughter of gay parents comes home crying from school because her classmates are ostracizing and teasing her about her parents. After unsuccessful attempts to have the school take steps to deal with the problem, the parents help their daughter to file a human rights complaint on the basis of family status.

4.4 — Disability

Persons with disabilities may rely on caregiving networks that include not only spouses, parents and children, but also extended family and a range of unique arrangements such as homesharing, supported decision-making networks and alternate family arrangements.[18] The lack of adequate social supports for persons with disabilities makes such caregiving relationships crucial. Those who are providing such support to persons with disabilities face challenges and barriers beyond those faced by others with caregiving responsibilities, and require accommodation and support in order to access employment, housing and services.[19]

> *Example*: A lone mother of a child with a disability is frequently asked to pick up her child from school because of behaviours associated with her child's disability. Eventually, her employer meets with her because of her "persistent absenteeism." When the employee explains her situation, the employer explores accommodation options, and puts into place a flexible work hours arrangement that meets her needs.

As well, persons with disabilities who are themselves caregivers may face stereotypes regarding their ability to parent, or may face difficulties in finding services for caregivers that are accessible.

---

[18]Homesharing involves two or three adults, at least one of whom has a disability, who chose to live together; one of the adults who does not have a disability is provided with some remuneration for being available to provide personal support to the adult with a disability. In a supported decision-making network, one or more individuals are included in a personal network to assist in making personal, financial and health care decisions. In an alternate family, a person with a disability lives with a non-birth family, and family members are paid to provide support, similar to foster care arrangements. (See the ARCH Submission to the OHRC's Consultation on Discrimination Based on Family Status, September 2005, available online at www.archlegalclinic.ca).

[19]For example, a study by the Canadian Union of Postal Workers found that workers who had children with disabilities were more likely to turn down overtime hours, reduce their work hours and refuse promotions: *Moving Mountains: Work, Family and Children with Special Needs* (November 2002). Children with disabilities are more likely to live in poverty, and their parents are twice as likely to have social assistance as their primary source of income, according to a paper by the Canadian Association for Community Living, *Developing a Family Supportive Policy Agenda to Advance the Citizenship and Inclusion of People with Disabilities* (2006).

4.5 — Age

Young parents, particularly young lone-parents, are frequently the subject of negative assumptions and stereotypes, such as that they are irresponsible, or lack parenting skills. This may make it difficult for them to access employment, housing or services. As well, young parents are disproportionately likely to be poor: in 2001, 48% of all families where the main income earner was under the age of 25 were low income.[20]

On the other end of the spectrum, aging parents of adult children with disabilities face many difficulties, as they find themselves less able to provide the extensive care their children need, but may be unable to access the necessary community supports to ensure their children's wellbeing.

As well, there are increasing numbers of grandparents providing primary care for their grandchildren. Many of these caregivers have significant health and mobility limitations, and their needs are often overlooked by those designing and providing services.

4.6 — Race and Race-related Grounds

The *Code* prohibits discrimination on the grounds of race, ethnic origin, place of origin, colour, ancestry, citizenship and creed (religion). These grounds intersect with family status in complex ways.

There continue to be common negative stereotypes about the parenting practices and abilities of various racialized communities, and these stereotypes can have a significant impact on how members of these communities access housing, as well as important services such as education.

As well, services, employment and housing are often designed around definitions of family that are not inclusive of cultural differences. For example, immigrant and refugee families arriving from countries where average family sizes are larger may face extreme difficulty locating adequate housing.

As well, ongoing marginalization of racialized communities, including disproportionate levels of poverty, and the continued existence of discrimination and systemic barriers, leave these families especially vulnerable to the effects of discrimination based on family status.

> *Example*: Upon arrival in Canada, a family of refugees attempts to find rental housing. Because they are new to Canada and from a racialized community, a landlord assumes that they are less likely to pay the rent,

[20]Vanier Institute of the Family, 2005 *Report on the Current State of Family Finances* (2005), online: Vanier Institute of the Family, www.vifamily.ca.

and more likely to be disruptive. The landlord insists that she can only rent to them if they can provide her with a security deposit of three months' rent paid in advance.

5. — Discrimination Based on Family Status

5.1 — Defining Discrimination

The *Code* provides that every person has the right to be treated equally without discrimination because of family status. The purpose of anti-discrimination laws is to prevent the violation of human dignity and freedom through the imposition of disadvantage, stereotyping, or political or social prejudice. In many cases, differential treatment because of family status will clearly be discriminatory. However, in other cases it may be necessary to consider whether the treatment can be said to constitute "discrimination" in the sense of being something protected by human rights law. Not every distinction may be considered discriminatory.

There are several ways of defining and identifying discrimination based on family status. Discrimination because of family status includes any distinction, including exclusion, restriction or preference based on family status, that results in the impairment of the recognition of human rights and fundamental freedoms.

In keeping with the decision of the Supreme Court of Canada in *Andrews v. Law Society of British Columbia*,[21] discrimination based on family status may be described as any distinction, conduct or action, whether intentional or not, but based on a person's family status, which has the effect of either imposing burdens on an individual or group that are not imposed upon others, or withholding or limiting access to opportunity, benefits and advantages available to other members of society.

In the context of equality claims under s. 15 of the Canadian *Charter of Rights and Freedoms* (the "*Charter*"), the Supreme Court of Canada has offered the following three inquiries as a tool for determining whether discrimination has occurred:[22]

1) *Differential Treatment*

   Was there substantively differential treatment, either because of a distinction, exclusion or preference, or because of a failure to take

[21] *Andrews v. Law Society of British Columbia*, [1989] 1 S.C.R. 143 at 174.

[22] *Law v. Canada (Minister of Employment and Immigration)*, [1999] 1 S.C.R. 497, at para. 88 [hereinafter "*Law*"]. Whether or not this test is appropriately applied to human rights legislation has not yet been settled in the caselaw. In *Vancouver Rape*

into account the individual's already disadvantaged position within Canadian society?

2) *An Enumerated Ground*

Was the differential treatment based on an enumerated ground, in this case family status?

3) *Discrimination in a Substantive Sense*

Finally, does the differential treatment discriminate by imposing a burden upon, or withholding a benefit from, an individual? The discrimination might be based on stereotypes of a presumed group or personal characteristics, or might perpetuate or promote the view that an individual is less capable or worthy of recognition or value as a human being or as a member of Canadian society who is equally deserving of concern, respect and consideration. Does the differential treatment amount to discrimination because it makes distinctions that are offensive to human dignity?

5.2 — Forms of Discrimination Based on Family Status

5.2.1 — Negative Attitudes, Stereotypes and Bias

Discrimination can take many forms. In some cases, discrimination may be direct and intentional, where an individual or organization deliberately treats an individual unequally or differently because of family status.

> *Example*: A landlord decides that she does not wish to rent apartments to families with young children, and designates her building as "adults-only."

Relief Society v. Nixon, [2005] B.C.J. No. 2647 (B.C.C.A.), the British Columbia Court of Appeal declined to apply the *Law* test in determining whether discrimination had taken place, stating at para. 41 that "If . . .the Legislature has said that certain behaviour is prohibited and has established the available defences . . . the Legislature, as law-maker, has set the balance of competing rights in a way that we may not ignore and which is presumptively fair." On the other hand, in a recent decision by the Alberta Court of Appeal, *Alberta (Minister of Human Resources and Employment) v. Alberta (Human Rights, Citizenship and Multiculturalism Commission)*, [2006] A.J. No. 988, at para. 67 (Alta. C.A.), the Court relied on the *Law* analysis in ruling that it was not discriminatory to deny shelter allowances to social assistance recipients who are living with their parents. The Ontario Divisional Court recently applied the *Law* analysis in *Ontario Secondary School Teachers' Federation v. Upper Canada District School Board*, 78 O.R.(3d) 194, at para. 28.

This type of deliberate discrimination generally arises from negative attitudes and biases related to family status.

Attitudes about caregiving and caregivers are deeply embedded in our society, and negative comments or assumptions about caregivers are often not perceived to be a serious human rights issue. It is a principle of human rights that persons should be judged on their individual attributes, skills and capacities, rather than on stereotypes and assumptions based on the groups to which they belong. Negative attitudes and stereotypes may lead to harassment and discrimination, and affect an individual's access to services, employment and housing. Individual assessment combats the effects of negative attitudes and stereotypes based on *Code* grounds such as family status.

Given that providing care for others is generally viewed as a positive attribute, it may seem strange that family status may be the source of negative attitudes and stereotypes. However, there are a number of ways in which attitudes and stereotypes related to family status may manifest.

Those who provide caregiving, or who are perceived to be caregivers, may be assumed to be less competent, committed, intelligent and ambitious than others. This is often influenced by gender stereotypes. For example, when female employees become parents or take on other significant caregiving responsibilities, they may find themselves shunted on to the "mommy track," and passed over for promotions, learning opportunities and recognition because of biases, conscious or unconscious, about the attributes of mothers.[23] On the other hand, men who take on significant caregiving responsibilities may be viewed as less "manly" because of their failure to conform to stereotypical gender roles.

There are also assumptions and stereotypes regarding who should and who should not be providing caregiving. Stereotypes about persons with disabilities or about individuals who are LGBT may dictate that these persons do not have the capacity to parent well, and should not be responsible for children. As well, it may be assumed that LGBT persons do not have "real"

---

[23]Some studies have indicated that individuals tend to perceive mothers as less competent and committed as employees than either fathers or childless persons of either sex, and that there is less interest in hiring, promoting and educating mothers, relative to fathers or childless employees. See Kathleen Fuegen et al, "Mothers and Fathers in the Workplace: How Gender and Parental Status Influence Judgments of Job-Related Competence," *Journal of Social Issues*, Volume 60, Issue 4, page 737, December 2004 and Cuddy et al, "When Professionals Become Mothers, Warmth Doesn't Cut the Ice," Journal of Social Issues, Volume 60, Issue 4, Page 701, December 2004.

families and that they have no caregiving responsibilities when in fact stereotypical notions of the family are effectively making these families and their caregiving needs "invisible." There are also stereotypes about the parenting capacities of members of various racialized groups, as well as about the responsibility and capabilities of lone parents and young parents.

Treatment of persons identified by family status may also be influenced by attitudes regarding various family forms. For example, disapproval of lone parent families, foster families, families with large numbers of children, or families headed by LGBT persons may result in negative treatment and discrimination. Families formed by adoption may be treated as if they are less "real" or valid than biological families.

As well, access to services and housing by persons identified by family status may be impeded by negative attitudes towards children — for example, that they are noisy and disruptive, and have a lesser right to public spaces or housing than do adults.

5.2.2 — Subtle Discrimination

In some instances, discrimination takes on more subtle or covert forms. Intent or motive to discriminate is not a necessary element for a finding of discrimination — it is sufficient if the conduct has a discriminatory effect.

Discrimination based on a *Code* ground need only be one of several reasons for the decision or treatment.[24]

Subtle forms of discrimination can usually only be detected upon examining all of the circumstances. Individual acts themselves may be ambiguous or explained away, but when viewed as part of a larger picture, may lead to an inference that discrimination based on family status was a factor in the treatment a person received.

> *Example*: When a woman returns to work after the birth of her first child, she notices that her career, which had seemed to be on a "fast-track," now appears to have stalled. She is given smaller and less important projects to manage, and is passed over for several training opportunities. When she asks about a promotional opportunity, her manager tries to discourage her, stating that the job requires "super-dedication" and "killer hours."

---

[24] *Gray v. A&W Food Service of Canada Ltd.* (1994), CHRR Doc 94-146 (Ont. Bd. Inq.); *Dominion Management v. Velenosi*, [1977] O.J. No. 1277, at para. 1 (Ont. C.A.); *Smith v. Mardana Ltd. (No. 1)* (2005), 52 C.H.R.R. D/89, at para. 22 (Ont. Div. Ct.).

It can be difficult to determine whether subtle discrimination is indeed a factor in such situations. They may therefore require investigation and analysis that examines the context, including the presence of comparative evidence contrasting how others were treated, or evidence that a pattern of behaviour exists. It is not necessary for language or comments related to family status to be present in the interactions between the parties to demonstrate that discrimination on the basis of family status has occurred. However, where such comments are made, they can be further evidence that family status has been a factor in an individual's treatment.

5.2.3 — Harassment

Section 5(2) of the *Code* provides that all employees have a right to freedom from harassment in the workplace by the employer, employer's agent, or by another employee because of, among other grounds, family status. This right to be free from harassment includes the workplace but also the "extended workplace," i.e., events that occur outside of the physical workplace or regular work hours but which have implications for the workplace such as business trips, company parties or other company related functions.

Section 2(2) of the *Code* provides that every person who occupies accommodation has a right to freedom from harassment by the landlord or agent of the landlord or by an occupant of the same building because of among other grounds, family status.

The *Code* contains no explicit provisions dealing with harassment in the areas of services, goods and facilities (section 1 of the *Code*), contracts (section 3 of the *Code*) or membership in trade and vocational associations (section 6 of the *Code*). However, it is the position of the Commission that harassment because of family status in such situations would constitute a violation of sections 1, 3 and 6 of the *Code*, which provide for a right to equal treatment without discrimination with respect to services, goods and facilities, contracts and membership in trade and vocational associations respectively.

Harassment is defined in section 10(1) of the *Code* as "engaging in a course of vexatious comment or conduct that is known or ought reasonably to be known to be unwelcome." The reference to comment or conduct "that is known or ought reasonably to be known to be unwelcome" establishes both a subjective and an objective test for harassment.

The subjective part of the test considers the harasser's own knowledge of how his or her behaviour is being received. This knowledge may arise in different ways. In some situations, it should be obvious that the conduct or comments will be offensive or unwelcome. Some conduct or comments relating to a person's family status may not, on their face, be offensive. However, they may still be "unwelcome" from the perspective of a particular individual. If similar behaviour is repeated despite indications from the individual that it is unwelcome, there may be a violation of the *Code*.

> *Example*: Many of the female employees at a particular business become pregnant within a relatively short period of time. Their male manager begins to make jokes that "there must be something in the water cooler." Other employees do not find this offensive or threatening, and there is no indication that pregnant employees are being penalized; however, one employee fears that the comments indicate that the manager is concerned about the number of pregnancies, and that he looks on her pregnancy with disfavour. She raises her concerns with her manager. If he continues to make such comments, the employee may have a basis for filing a complaint of harassment based on pregnancy or family status.

The objective component of the test considers, from the point of view of a "reasonable" third party, how such behaviour would generally be received. The determination of the point of view of a "reasonable" third party must take into account the perspective of the person who is harassed.[25]

It is important to note that there is no requirement that the individual objected to the harassment at the time, in order for a violation of the *Code* to exist or for a person to claim their rights under the *Code*. An individual who is the target of harassment may be in a vulnerable situation, and afraid of the consequences of speaking out. Employers, landlords and service providers have an obligation to maintain an environment that is free of discrimination and harassment, whether or not anyone objects. Each situation must be assessed on its own merits.

> *Example*: When a couple with a small child moves into a new apartment, one of their neighbours comments to them that she has raised her kids and now "has a right to peace and quiet." This neighbour repeatedly tells them that "children shouldn't be in apartments — they need yards to play in." No matter how hard they try to keep their child quiet, this neighbour constantly complains to their landlord about them. The landlord provides the neighbour with information about rights and responsibilities under the *Code*, and offers either to provide some further

---

[25] *Dhanjal v. Air Canada* (1996), 28 C.H.R.R. D/367, at para. 210 (C.H.R.T.).

soundproofing or to relocate the complaining neighbour to the first available vacant apartment.

Because stereotypes relating to family status differ according to race, sex, marital status, age, sexual orientation or disability, harassment on the basis of family status may take on different forms depending on whether the impacted individual is identified by other *Code* grounds. It is the Commission's position that where multiple grounds intersect to produce a unique experience of discrimination or harassment, this must be acknowledged to fully address the impact of discrimination or harassment on the person who experienced it.

Example: A lesbian mother brings her small child to an infant music class at her community centre. After her partner joins them for one of the sessions, the music teacher makes repeated comments referring to the child's lack of "proper role models" and a "real family."

5.2.4 — Poisoned Environment

The *Code* definition of harassment refers to more than one incident of comment or conduct. However, even a single statement or incident, if sufficiently serious or substantial, can have an impact by creating a poisoned environment.[26] A poisoned environment is based on the nature of the comments or conduct and the impact of these on the individual, rather than on the number of times the behaviour occurs. A consequence of creating a poisoned environment is that certain individuals are subjected to terms and conditions of employment, tenancy, services, etc. that are quite different from those experienced by individuals who are not subjected to those comments or conduct. Such instances give rise to a denial of equality under the *Code*.

In the employment context, tribunals have held that the atmosphere of a workplace is a condition of employment just as much as hours of work or rate of pay. A "term or condition of employment" includes the emotional and psychological circumstances of the workplace.[27] Management personnel who know or ought to know of the existence of a poisoned atmosphere but permit it to continue thereby discriminate against affected employees

---

[26]*Dhanjal v. Air Canada, ibid* at para. 209.

[27]*Dhillon v. F.W. Woolworth Co.* (1982), 3 C.H.R.R. D/743, at para. 6691 (Ont. Bd. Inq.); *Naraine v. Ford Motor Co. of Canada (No. 4)* (1996), at para. 50 (Ont. Bd. Inq.).

even if they themselves are not involved in the production of that atmosphere.[28]

While the notion of a poisoned environment has predominantly arisen in an employment context, it can apply equally where it results in unequal terms and conditions in occupancy of accommodation, the provision of services, contracting or membership in a vocational association.

5.2.5 — Systemic Discrimination and Societal Dimensions

Discrimination on the basis of family status may often take on systemic or institutional forms. Systemic or institutional discrimination consists of patterns of behaviour, policies or practices that are part of the social or administrative structures of an organization, and which create or perpetuate a position of relative disadvantage for persons identified by family status. These may appear neutral on the surface, but nevertheless have an exclusionary impact on the basis of family status. Systemic or institutional discrimination is a major barrier for persons identified by family status.

Systemic discrimination on the basis of family status may be linked to systemic issues related to gender roles and stereotypes. As well, systemic discrimination based on family status may be experienced differently based on intersection with other grounds of discrimination, such as age, disability, marital status, creed, receipt of social assistance, race, and race-related grounds. Systemic or institutional discrimination must be addressed in the context of the interacting impacts of multiple *Code* grounds.

Systemic discrimination may have its roots in broader societal structures and social attitudes. Conceptions of the family have historically centred around a set of assumptions about gender, marital status, and sexual orientation, with the "ideal" family being centred on heterosexual, marital relationships in which roles are defined according to strict gender norms. There have always been lone-parent and same-sex families, as well as those in which women and men do not conform to gender norms regarding caregiving roles; however, these families have frequently been denied recognition as families, and have been the subject, not only of negative attitudes, but also of outright discrimination and marginalization.

Institutional or systemic discrimination is tied to, and influenced by, wider societal patterns. In particular, the lack of adequate social supports for childcare, eldercare and for persons with disabilities places caregivers at significant disadvantage in accessing employment, housing and services.

---

[28] *Ghosh v. Domglas Inc. (No.2)* (1992), 17 C.H.R.R. D/216, at para. 76 (Ont. Bd. Inq.); *Naraine v. Ford Motor Co. of Canada (No. 4) ibid* at para. 54.

For example, where evening and weekend childcare services are difficult to access, caregivers may find themselves significantly disadvantaged in finding employment in sectors that require regular shift work, such as nursing or retail. Where caregivers for persons with disabilities must spend considerable time and advocacy to locate and maintain services for their loved ones, this will impact on their ability to find and maintain employment or pursue educational opportunities. Persons with caregiving responsibilities may find themselves having to make extremely difficult decisions in order to meet their caregiving responsibilities. For example, the lack of legal protections for those who must take time off work to care for aging relatives means that individuals may have to chose between losing their jobs or being unable to provide care for their loved ones when they most need it. The lack of social supports weighs most heavily on those who are already disadvantaged and cannot make up, through private funds, for gaps in social supports. These persons are disproportionately women, youth, older persons, lone parents, persons with disabilities and their caregivers, and persons from racialized communities.

The interaction between these societal realities and institutional policies and practices is complex. For example, the situation of a mother of small children who loses her job because of her inability to "balance" her work and familial responsibilities may be the result of the compounding effects of her employer's rigid and inflexible scheduling policies, the lack of adequate social supports for caregiving, and prevailing gender norms about the role of women as primary caregivers. Employers, housing providers and service providers must take into account the broader societal context in determining whether their programs, policies and services may be having a disproportionate impact on those identified by family status. Failure to take this broader context into account may perpetuate the disadvantage of persons identified by family status and lead to a violation of the *Code*.

Systemic discrimination may therefore arise when institutions fail to take into account the reality of contemporary family structures when designing their policies, programs and structures. Where organizations fail to design in a way that includes persons with caregiving responsibilities, persons identified by family status may find themselves disadvantaged and excluded.

As is discussed at greater length in the Commission's *Policy and Guidelines on Racism and Racial Discrimination*, the Commission employs the following three considerations in identifying and addressing systemic discrimination:

i. Organizational Culture

Organizational culture can be described as shared patterns of informal social behaviour, which are the evidence of deeply held and possibly unconscious values, assumptions and behavioural norms.

ii. Numerical Data

Numerical data that demonstrates that members of certain groups are disproportionately represented may be an indicator of systemic or institutional discrimination. For example, the under-representation of women with young children in senior positions in an organization, together with over-representation in entry-level positions, may indicate inequitable practices in hiring, training, promoting and accommodating persons identified by sex and family status. By itself, numerical data is usually not proof of systemic discrimination; however, it may form strong circumstantial evidence of the existence of inequitable practices.

iii. Policies, Practices and Decision-making Processes

Policies, practices and decision-making processes that do not take into account the realities of persons identified by family status may lead to exclusion for persons who are in a parent-child relationship, and result in systemic discrimination.

Specific policies and practices that may create systemic barriers for persons identified by family status are outlined in the sections on Employment, Housing, and Services.

5.3 — Special Programs and Special Interest Organizations

Section 14 of the *Code* permits the use of special programs in all social areas. This allows preferential treatment or programs aimed only at persons identified by family status, if the purpose of the program is to relieve hardship or economic disadvantage or to assist disadvantaged persons or groups to achieve equal opportunity.

Example: Based on research that indicates that female lone-parents often have difficulty finding and maintaining employment because of the lack of affordable childcare options, a community centre develops a childcare program specifically for low-income female-led lone-parent families.

It is important that special programs be designed so that restrictions within the program are rationally connected to the objective of the program. A failure to do so can lead to successful challenge of the program and a finding that it is discriminatory.[29]

The Commission's *Guidelines on Special Programs* provide detailed information on how a special program can be planned, implemented and monitored.

Section 18 of the *Code* allows certain types of organizations to limit participation or membership based on *Code* grounds, including family status:

> 18. The rights under Part I to equal treatment with respect to services and facilities, with or without accommodation, are not infringed where membership or participation in a religious, philanthropic, educational, fraternal or social institution or organization that is primarily engaged in serving the interests of persons identified by a prohibited ground of discrimination is restricted to persons who are similarly identified.

An organization that wishes to rely on this defence must show it meets all of the requirements of this section.

6. — The Duty to Accommodate

The duty to accommodate will only arise where a *prima facie* case of discrimination on the basis of family status has been demonstrated, as discussed above. Generally, the duty to accommodate will only become an issue in cases where rules, policies, practices, or institutional structures, assumptions or culture are perpetuating or leading to the disadvantage of persons identified by a particular family status.

In the context of family status, accommodation is usually associated with caregiving needs. Accommodation is central to overcoming the disadvantages experienced by caregivers, particularly in the areas of employment and services. Most of us will be both providers and recipients of care over the course of our lifetimes, so that accommodation of caregiving needs benefits us all.

An individual's caregiving needs will vary over the course of a lifetime. The nature of the needs associated with caring for children will be, for example, significantly different from the nature of the needs associated with caring for an aging parent. Some needs will remain stable over lengthy periods of time, while others may arise on an emergency basis.

---

[29] *Ontario (Human Rights Commission) and Roberts v. Ontario (Ministry of Health) (No. 1)* (1989), 10 C.H.R.R. D/6353 (Ont. Bd. Inq.); aff'd 14 C.H.R.R. D/1 (Ont. Div. Ct.); rev'd (1994), 21 C.H.R.R. D/259 (C.A.).

Most often, accommodation of caregiving needs is neither burdensome nor costly; rather, it is a matter of flexibility. A flexible and accommodating approach is ultimately a significant advantage to employers in attracting and maintaining good employees, and to service providers and landlords in expanding their potential markets.

The following sections set out the basic legal test that persons responsible for accommodation must meet, the principles of accommodation, and the shared responsibilities of all parties to the accommodation process.

6.1 — The Legal Test

Section 11 of the *Code*, combined with section 9, operates to prohibit discrimination that results from requirements, qualifications or factors that may appear neutral but which have an adverse effect on persons identified by family status. Section 11 allows the person responsible for accommodation to demonstrate that the requirement, qualification or factor is reasonable and *bona fide* by showing that the needs of the group to which the complainant belongs cannot be accommodated without undue hardship.

The Supreme Court of Canada sets out a framework for examining whether the duty to accommodate has been met.[30] If *prima facie* discrimination is found to exist, the person responsible for accommodation must establish on a balance of probabilities that the standard, factor, requirement or rule

1. was adopted for a purpose or goal that is rationally connected to the function being performed,
2. was adopted in good faith, in the belief that it is necessary for the fulfilment of the purpose or goal, and
3. is reasonably necessary to accomplish its purpose or goal, in the sense that it is impossible to accommodate the claimant without undue hardship.

As a result of this test, the rule or standard itself must be inclusive and must accommodate individual differences up to the point of undue hardship rather than maintaining discriminatory standards supplemented by accommodation for those who cannot meet them. This ensures that each person is assessed according to his or her own personal abilities instead of being judged against presumed group characteristics.[31]

---

[30] *British Columbia (Public Service Employee Relations Commission) v. BCGSEU*, [1999] 3 S.C.R. 3 [hereinafter "*Meoirin*"] at para. 54.

[31] *British Columbia (Superintendent of Motor Vehicles) v. British Columbia (Council of Human Rights)*, [1999] 3 S.C.R. 868 [hereinafter "*Grismer*"] at para. 20.

The ultimate issue is whether the person responsible for accommodation has shown that accommodation has been provided up to the point of undue hardship. In this analysis, the procedure to assess accommodation is as important as the substantive content of the accommodation.[32]

The following non-exhaustive factors should be considered in the course of the analysis:[33]

- whether the person responsible for accommodation investigated alternative approaches that do not have a discriminatory effect
- reasons why viable alternatives were not implemented
- ability to have differing standards that reflect group or individual differences and capabilities
- whether persons responsible for accommodation can meet their legitimate objectives in a less discriminatory manner
- whether the standard is properly designed to ensure the desired qualification is met without placing undue burden on those to whom it applies and
- whether other parties who are obliged to assist in the search for accommodation have fulfilled their roles.

6.2 — Inclusive Design

Many aspects of society have been designed around traditional notions of the "ideal family," and may exclude members of families that do not conform to these conceptions. For example, standard hours of work and overtime schedules reflect an era when it was common for families to have a member at home to provide full-time care for children and elders; policies for birth registration did not until very recently recognize the families created by gays and lesbians; school board policies on bussing may not acknowledge the needs of dual-custody families; and lack of access to part-time university programs excludes persons with significant caregiving requirements. The failure to design with the needs of persons disadvantaged by family status in mind may lead to the creation of barriers, and to discrimination against such persons.

The Supreme Court of Canada has made it clear that society must be designed to be inclusive of all persons, regardless of membership in a *Code* protected group.[34] It is no longer acceptable to structure systems in a way

---

[32] *Meoirin, supra*, note 30 at para. 66.

[33] *Meoirin, supra*, note 30, at para. 65.

[34] In *Meoirin, supra*, note 30, the Supreme Court said at para. 68:

that ignores needs related to family status; rather the systems should be designed in a way that does not create physical, attitudinal or systemic barriers for persons disadvantaged by family status.

As a corollary to this notion that barriers should be prevented at the design stage through inclusive design, where systems and structures already exist, organizations should be aware of the possibility of systemic barriers, and actively seek to identify and remove them. Where barriers have been identified, organizations must remove the barriers rather than making "one-off" accommodations, unless to do so would cause undue hardship.

Inclusive design is not only a principle of human rights, it makes good sense. Employers who fail to consider the needs of persons with caregiving responsibilities are likely to experience higher levels of absenteeism, burnout and turnover among employees. Flexible and inclusive practices can be a considerable draw in attracting and retaining highly skilled and motivated workers.[35] Similarly, service providers who do not take into account the needs of families may alienate a significant potential target market.

6.3 — Identifying Needs Related to Family Status

In most cases, accommodation needs related to family status will be connected to caregiving responsibilities. Human rights tribunals have found that the ground of family status must be interpreted to include the caregiving needs associated with the parent-child relationship.[36]

> Employers designing workplace standards owe an obligation to be aware of both the differences between individuals and differences that characterize groups of individuals. They must build conceptions of equality into workplace standards. By enacting human rights statutes and providing that they are applicable to the workplace, the legislatures have determined that the standards governing the performance of work should be designed to reflect all members of society, in so far as this is reasonably possible. [at 38]

[35]There are numerous studies on the business case for flexible work practices, and the costs to employers of lack of flexibility. See, for example, Catalyst, *Beyond a Reasonable Doubt: Building the Business Case fo Flexibility*, 2005; Aon Consulting, *Canada@Work Study*, 1999; Conference Board of Canada, *Survey of Canadian Workers on Work/Life Balance*, 1999; L. Duxbury et al., *An Examination of the Implications and Costs of Work-Life Conflict in Canada* (Ottawa: Health Canada, June 1999).

[36]In *Brown v. M.N.R., Customs and Excise* (1993), 19 C.H.R.R. D/39, the Canadian Human Rights Tribunal stated at para. 75 that:

Not every circumstance related to family status and caregiving will give rise to a duty to accommodate. As noted above, the duty to accommodate only arises where a *prima facie* case of discrimination has been shown. Where rules, requirements, standards or factors have the effect of disadvantaging persons who have significant caregiving responsibilities related to their family status, either by imposing burdens that are not placed on others or withholding or limiting access to opportunity, benefits or advantages available to others, a duty to accommodate caregiving needs related to family status may arise.[37] In most circumstances where there is a significant conflict between an important caregiving responsibility and an institutional rule, requirement, standard or factor, a duty to accommodate will arise.[38]

> It is this Tribunal's conclusion that the purposive interpretation to be affixed to s. 2 of the CHRA is a clear recognition within the context of "family status" of a parent's right and duty to strike that balance [between family needs and employment requirements] coupled with a clear duty on the part of an employer to facilitate and accommodate that balance within the criteria set out in the *Alberta Dairy Pool* case . . . To consider any lesser approach to the problems facing the modern family within the employment environment is to render meaningless the concept of "family status" as a ground of discrimination.

[37]In *Health Sciences Association of British Columbia v. Campbell River and North Island Transition Society*, [2004] B.C.J. No. 922 (B.C. C.A.) [hereinafter *"Health Sciences"*] the British Columbia Court of Appeal emphasized that prior to considering accommodation based on family status, a prima facie case of discrimination must be made out, stating at para. 38 that:

> [The parameters of the concept of family status] cannot be an open-ended concept . . . for that would have the potential to cause disruption and great mischief in the workplace; nor, in the context of the present case, can it be limited to "the status of being a parent *per se*" as found by the arbitrator . . . for that would not address serious negative impacts that some decisions of employers might have on the parental and other family obligations of all, some or one of the employees affected by such decisions.

[38]"[A] *prima facie* case of discrimination is made out when a change in a term or condition of employment imposed by an employer *results in a serious interference with a substantial parental or other family duty or obligation of the employee*," *Health Sciences*, *ibid*, at para. 39.

In considering whether a duty to accommodate has arisen, the following considerations may be of assistance:

1. The nature of the caregiving responsibility and of the conflict between that responsibility and the organization's rules, requirements, standards, processes or other factors

This factor must be assessed on a case-by-case basis. The more substantial the caregiving obligation at stake, and the more serious the interference of that rule, requirement or factor, the more likely it is that a duty to accommodate will arise. For example, it is more likely that a duty to accommodate will arise with respect to a serious illness on the part of a family member, than with respect to a desire to attend a child's recreational activity.[39] The assessment of the caregiving responsibility at stake should be grounded in the practical, lived reality of caring for children, elders or persons with disabilities. It should also take into account the range of family forms that exist, for example, stereotypical assumptions about LGBT people may make their families, and thereby their accommodation needs, "invisible" to employers.

2. The systemic barriers faced by caregivers, including intersectional impacts based on disability, age, gender, sexual orientation, race and race-related grounds, and marital status.

It is all too easy to consider individual caregiving needs as isolated personal issues. An employee seeking reduced work hours or a flexible schedule to attend to the needs of their children or their aging parents may easily be viewed as simply expressing their personal preferences regarding balancing their various responsibilities. Viewed in the broader light of the disadvantage faced by caregivers, particularly those who are vulnerable by virtue of being racialized, low-income, newcomer, female, disabled or lone-parent, these "one-off personal issues" may be seen in a different light.

In assessing requests for accommodation based on family status, organizations should consider whether systemic barriers may exist

---

[39]In a recent decision of the Saskatchewan Human Rights Tribunal, *Palik v. Lloydminster Public School Div. No. 99* (2006), CHRR Doc. 06-630 at para. 124, an employer's termination of an employee who attended her diabetic son's hockey tournament during the working day, without permission from her employer, was found not to constitute discrimination on the basis of family status, on the basis that there was no serious interference with a substantial parenting obligation.

within their own organization, including the representation of persons with significant caregiving responsibilities, the organizational culture, and the inclusiveness of its policies, procedures and decision-making practices. Specific systemic barriers facing caregivers in employment, housing and services are discussed in the relevant sections.

3. The availability and adequacy of social supports for caregiving needs

In determining whether a rule, factor or requirement significantly interferes with a caregiving responsibility, it is important to take into account whether adequate social supports and services are available for the individual to resolve their caregiving needs without accommodation. For example, workers who find that there simply are no adequate childcare or eldercare supports available in the evenings or the weekends may need accommodation from their employers in terms of shifts. Both the adequacy and availability of supports should be taken into account: caregivers should not be required to place their loved ones into situations of significant risk of physical, emotional or psychological harm in order to meet the needs of their employer, landlord or service provider.

6.4 — Appropriate Accommodation

Where an accommodation need related to family status has been identified, the organization must identify and implement the most appropriate accommodation, short of undue hardship. The determination of what is and is not an appropriate accommodation is a separate determination from an undue hardship analysis.

An accommodation will be considered appropriate if it will result in equal opportunity to attain the same level of performance or to enjoy the same level of benefits and privileges experienced by others, or it if is proposed or adopted for the purpose of achieving opportunity and meets the individual's needs related to family status.

Example: Rather than require employees with caregiving needs to use their vacation days in order to attend to caregiving needs, and therefore receive a lower level of benefits than other employees, an employer allows employees to use their standard sick days for both their own sicknesses and those of persons they are caring for.

Organizations need not provide more than the individual requires in order to meet the actual identified needs related to family status. For example, if rescheduling of work hours would enable an employee to attend to an important caregiving responsibility, the employer need not provide a paid day off.

The most appropriate accommodation will be that accommodation that most promotes inclusion and full participation, and effectively addresses any systemic issues.

> *Example*: Rather than making a one-time exemption for a student with substantial caregiving responsibilities to complete his degree on a part-time schedule, an educational institution re-examines whether the requirement that students complete their studies full-time is a *bona fide* requirement. When it determines that it is not, it alters the rule, and permits part-time studies.

It will be more difficult for an organization that has not taken steps to investigate and implement policies and practices that support and include caregivers to justify a failure to accommodate individual requests for flexibility.

It is a principle of human rights law that there is no set formula for accommodation: each person's needs are unique and must be considered afresh when an accommodation request is made. Accommodations must take into account individual situations and requirements. However, it is also the case that many accommodations will benefit large numbers of persons identified by the ground of family status.

Where the most appropriate accommodation would cause undue hardship, organizations should consider next-best, phased-in or interim accommodations.

Accommodations must acknowledge the practical realities of caregiving. An accommodation that is not in accordance with good caregiving practices, or that would place an undue burden on the family, will not be considered appropriate.

> *Example*: A parent of a child with a disability has found a centre that can provide expert programming and care for the child after school hours. However, the centre closes at 5:00 p.m. The alternative is to leave the child with a neighbouring teenager for the after-school hours; however, due to the nature of the child's complex medical needs, the parent is very concerned that any error or inattention on this teenager's part would place the child at risk. While the parent's employer would prefer the second option because its standard hours run from 9:00 a.m. until 5:30 p.m., it recognizes that this would not be an appropriate ac-

commodation, and instead allows the parent to work from 8:00 a.m. until 4:30 p.m.

Examples of potential accommodation strategies in the employment context are provided in section 9.3.

6.5 — Roles and Responsibilities

Accommodation is a multi-party process. Everyone in the accommodation process should work together cooperatively and respectfully to develop and implement appropriate accommodation solutions.

The person seeking accommodation has a responsibility to inform the accommodation provider that he or she has caregiving needs related to a parent-child relationship, and that there is a conflict between those needs and the organization's rules, requirements, standards, processes or procedures.

Persons seeking accommodation may be expected to make reasonable efforts to first avail themselves of outside resources available to them prior to making accommodation requests to an employer, landlord or service provider. However, such resources should:

- most appropriately meet the accommodation needs of the individual
- be consistent with good caregiving practices and
- not place an undue burden on the family.

Accommodation seekers are in the best position to identify and evaluate such outside resources. However, it is a best practice for employers and service providers to provide assistance to individuals in locating information regarding such resources; for example, through employee assistance programs.

Accommodation providers should accept requests in good faith, unless there are objective reasons not to do so. Where necessary, organizations may request documentation of the validity of the accommodation seeker's needs, such as medical documentation related to a family member's disability or illness.

Example: An employee has a lengthy history of absenteeism, and has in the past been disciplined for failing to provide valid reasons for absences. When this employee requests flexible start and finish times to address a new eldercare responsibility, the employer requests further information to verify that the need exists.

Organizations may make reasonable requests for information that is necessary to clarify the nature and extent of the accommodation need.

> *Example*: An employee requests a lengthy leave of absence to attend to a serious illness of a child. The employee provides the employer with medical documentation verifying the child's illness and setting out the length of time that the illness is expected to last.

The organization may also seek reasonable information regarding any available outside resources that the individual has enquired into.

> *Example*: An employee's father has had a serious fall and is no longer able to manage household tasks on his own. The employee asks for a temporarily reduced work week so that he can attend to the needs of his father. He indicates to his employer that he has looked into homecare services for his father, and that there is a waiting list of approximately six months. The employer provides him with a reduced workweek for six months.

However, organizations should not seek details of private family arrangements, unless there are objective reasons to believe that the accommodation seeker is not acting in good faith. For example, an employer may not be entitled to know why another sibling is not taking a greater role in caring for an aging parent. Accommodation providers should not make enquiries based on stereotypical assumptions (such as, "Why can't your wife do it?").

As information related to family needs and arrangements may be highly personal, organizations should take steps to ensure that information related to accommodation requests is kept confidential, and shared only with those who need it.

Organizations should act in a timely manner, take an active role in seeking accommodation solutions, and bear any required costs associated with the accommodation. Accommodation seekers should cooperate in the accommodation process, provide relevant information and meet any agreed-upon standards once accommodation has been provided.

6.6 — Undue Hardship

Accommodation providers are not required to implement accommodations that would amount to undue hardship. The test for undue hardship is set out fully in the Commission's *Policy and Guidelines on Disability and the Duty to Accommodate*. The same standard applies to all grounds of the *Code*, including family status.

The *Code* prescribes three considerations in assessing whether an accommodation would cause undue hardship. No other considerations, other than those that can be brought into these three, can properly be considered. These are:

- cost
- outside sources of funding, if any, and
- health and safety requirement, if any.

The onus of proving that an accommodation would cause undue hardship lies on the accommodation provider. The evidence required to demonstrate undue hardship must be real, direct, objective and, in the case of costs, quantifiable. A mere claim, without supporting evidence, that the cost or risk is "too high" based on impressionistic views or stereotypes will not be sufficient.

In most cases, accommodations for needs related to family status will not require significant expenditures; rather, they involve increasing the flexibility of policies, rules and requirements. This may involve some administrative inconvenience, but inconvenience by itself is not a factor for assessing undue hardship.

Accommodation for persons identified by family status may in some cases cause resentment among others, who perceive these individuals to be receiving unjustified "perks" and privileges. Using an inclusive design approach to accommodation will address some of these concerns, since all may benefit from approaches that increase flexibility and choice. Given that all of us will be either the recipients or the providers of care at some point during our lives, accommodation for needs related to family status ultimately benefits us all. In any case, accommodation providers should take positive steps to educate their organizations about the *Code*, and ensure that accommodation seekers are not subjected to a poisoned environment.

7. — Organizational Responsibility

The ultimate responsibility for a healthy and inclusive environment rests with employers, landlords, unions, vocational and professional organizations, service providers, and other organizations and institutions covered by the *Code*. There is an obligation to ensure that environments are free from discrimination and harassment. It is not acceptable from a human rights perspective to choose to remain unaware of the potential existence of discrimination or harassment, or to ignore or fail to act to address human rights matters, whether or not a complaint has been made.

An organization violates the *Code* where it directly or indirectly, intentionally or unintentionally, infringes the *Code*, or where it does not directly infringe the *Code* but rather authorizes, condones, adopts or ratifies behaviour that is contrary to the *Code*. Organizations should ensure that rules, policies, procedures, decision-making processes and organizational culture are non-discriminatory on their face, and do not have a discriminatory impact.

In addition, there is a human rights duty not to condone or further a discriminatory act that has already occurred. To do so would extend or continue the life of the initial discriminatory act. The obligation extends to those who, while not the main actors, are drawn into a discriminatory situation nevertheless, through contractual relations or otherwise.[40] An organization should also not punish a person because of how they responded to discrimination or harassment: persons who reasonably believe that they are being discriminated against can be expected to find the experience upsetting and might well react in an angry and verbally aggressive manner.

Unions and vocational professional organizations are responsible for ensuring that they are not engaging in, condoning or contributing to discrimination or harassment. They may be liable for discriminatory policies or actions to the same extent as an employer, and share the same obligation to take measures to address harassment or a poisoned environment. Where a union or vocational or professional organization obstructs an accommodation process, it may be the subject of a human rights complaint.

Human rights decisions frequently find organizations liable, and assess damages based on an organization's failure to respond appropriately to address discrimination and harassment. An organization may respond to complaints about individual instances of discrimination or harassment, but they may still be found to have failed to respond appropriately if the underlying problem is not resolved. There may be a poisoned environment, or an organizational culture that excludes or marginalizes persons based on family status, despite sanction of individual harassers. In these cases, the organiza-

---

[40] *Payne v. Otsuka Pharmaceutical Co. (No. 3)* (2002), 44 C.H.R.R. D/203, at para. 63 (Ont. Bd. Inq.):

> The nature of when a third party or collateral person would be drawn into the chain of discrimination is fact specific. However, general principles can be determined. The key is the control or power that the collateral or indirect respondent had over the complainant and the principal respondent. The greater the control or power over the situation and the parties, the greater the legal obligation not to condone or further the discriminatory action. The power or control is important because it implies an ability to correct the situation or do something to ameliorate the conditions.

tion should take further steps, such as training and education, in order to more appropriately address the problem.

The following factors have been suggested as considerations for determining whether an organization met its responsibilities to respond to a human rights complaint:

- procedures in place at the time to deal with discrimination and harassment
- the promptness of the institutional response to the complaint
- the seriousness with which the complaint was treated
- resources made available to deal with the complaint
- whether the organization provided a healthy work environment for the person who complained and
- the degree to which the action taken was communicated to the person who complained.[41]

Under section 46.3 of the *Code*, a corporation, trade union or occupational association, unincorporated association or employers' organization will be held responsible for discrimination, including acts or omissions, committed by employees or agents in the course of their employment. This is known as vicarious liability. It applies not only to human rights violations in the workplace, but also in housing accommodation, goods, services and facilities, contracting, and membership in unions and vocational associations.

Simply put, it is the Commission's position that vicarious liability automatically attributes responsibility for discrimination to an organization for the acts of its employees or agents, done in the normal course, whether or not it had any knowledge of, participation in, or control over these actions.

Vicarious liability does not apply to breaches of the sections of the *Code* dealing with harassment, although since the existence of a poisoned environment is a form of discrimination, when harassment amounts to or results in a poisoned environment, vicarious liability under section 46.3 of the *Code* is restored. Further, in these cases the "organic theory of corporate liability" may apply. That is, an organization may be liable for acts of harassment carried out by its employees if it can be proven that it was aware of

[41] *Wall v. University of Waterloo* (1995), 27 C.H.R.R. D/44, at para. 162-67 (Ont. Bd. Inq.). These factors assist in assessing the reasonableness of an organization's response to harassment. A reasonable response by the organization will not affect its liability but will be considered in determining the appropriate remedy. In other words, an employer that has reasonably responded to harassment is not absolved of liability but may face a reduction in the damages that flow from the harassment.

the harassment, or the harasser is shown to be part of the management or "directing mind" of the organization. In such cases, the decisions, acts or omissions of the employee will engage the liability of the organization where:

- The employee who is part of the "directing mind" engages in harassment or inappropriate behaviour that is contrary to the *Code* or
- The employee who is part of the "directing mind" does not respond adequately to harassment or inappropriate behaviour of which he or she is aware, or ought reasonably to be aware.

Generally speaking, managers and central decision-makers in an organization are part of the "directing mind." Employees with only supervisory authority may also be part of the "directing mind" if they function, or are seen to function, as representatives of the organization. Even non-supervisors may be considered to be part of the "directing mind" if they have *de facto* supervisory authority or have significant responsibility for the guidance of employees. For example, a member of the bargaining unit who is a lead hand may be considered to be part of the "directing mind" of an organization.

8. — Preventing and Responding to Discrimination Based on Family Status

Organizations and workplaces can take a number of steps to prevent and appropriately address human rights complaints. Important elements of an organization's strategy to address human rights issues related to family status include:

1. Anti-harassment and anti-discrimination policies and complaint procedures

Anti-discrimination and anti-harassment policies are valuable tools in promoting equity and diversity within an organization. Adoption, implementation and promotion of these policies can help to limit potential harm, and reduce the organization's liability in the event of a complaint. These policies should explicitly address discrimination based on all grounds of the *Code*, including family status.

These elements should be developed in co-operation with workplace or organization partners where they exist, such as unions. Unions are important partners in the creation of a non-discriminatory workplace. As part of a "best practices" initiative, they should work with employers in the development of internal policies and procedures.

A detailed description of best practices for developing and implementing such policies and procedures can be found in the Commission's publication, *Human Rights at Work*.[42]

2. *Barrier review and removal programs*

   Organizations should take proactive steps to ensure that policies, programs, rules and requirements are not having an adverse impact based on family status. Organizations should undertake regular reviews and, based on their findings, develop and implement barrier removal strategies. Examples of common barriers are found in the sections on Employment, Housing and Services.

   As well, organizations should ensure that whenever new policies, procedures, rules and requirements are developed, their possible impact on persons identified by family status is considered, and that the most inclusive options are selected, short of undue hardship.

3. *Education and training*

   Education and training are essential components of any organization's human rights strategy. Both management and staff should have a solid understanding, not only of the requirements of the *Code* and of the organization's own human rights policies and procedures, but also of the common barriers and stereotypes facing persons identified by *Code* grounds, including family status.

   Education and training are not a panacea for all human rights issues: they will work most effectively when partnered with strong and effective policies and procedures, and a proactive strategy for developing an inclusive organization.

9. — Employment

To a significant degree, the workplace is still built on the assumption that families are composed in a "traditional" fashion, of two married heterosexual parents, one of whom is providing full-time caregiving for children, aging relatives and other family members, as necessary. Work schedules, policies and benefits all too often reflect the assumption that employees do not have substantial caregiving obligations. The corollary to this assumption is

---

[42]Human Resources Professionals Association of Ontario and Ontario Human Rights Commission, 2004, at Chapter V. See also the Commission's publication, *Developing Procedures to Resolve Human Rights Complaints within Your Organization* (1996), available online at www.ohrc.on.ca.

the belief that workers who do have substantial caregiving obligations are in some way inferior and undesirable employees.

However, the reality is that all employees will, at some point in their careers, have to juggle the demands of work and caregiving. The recognition of employees' familial responsibilities is an important element of hiring, retaining, and getting the best possible performances from employees.

It is also the law. Section 5 of the *Code* requires employers to provide their employees with equal treatment without discrimination because of family status. Section 11 provides that requirements that have an adverse impact on employees who are identified by family status will be discriminatory, unless the requirement is reasonable and *bona fide*, and the employer has accommodated to the point of undue hardship. In *Brown v. M.N.R., Customs and Excise*, the Canadian Human Rights Tribunal ruled that employers have a duty to accommodate needs related to family status, including employees' needs to strike a "fine balance between family needs and employment requirements."[43] The British Columbia Court of Appeal has ruled that there will be a *prima facie* case of discrimination, and a resulting duty to accommodate, where a change in a term or condition of employment imposed by an employer results in a serious interference with a substantial parental or other family duty or obligation of the employee.[44]

9.1 — Negative Attitudes and Assumptions Related to Family Status

Because of stereotypes and negative attitudes associated with caregiving roles, employers may assume that persons with significant caregiving responsibilities will not be willing to work longer hours, do overtime or take on challenging or complex projects, and may consciously or unconsciously slot such individuals into workplace roles consistent with these assumptions. Because of continuing societal assumptions regarding gender roles, these stereotypes may have particularly significant impact on women in the workforce.

As well, the stigma that some continue to associate with being a lone-parent, a young parent, or an LGBT parent may result in significant disadvantage in the workplace. In *Moffat v. Kinark Child and Family Services (No. 4)*, a human rights board of inquiry found that a gay man had suffered discrimination based on family status and sexual orientation when he was sub-

[43](1993), 19 C.H.R.R. D/39, at para. 74 (C.H.R.T.).

[44]*Health Sciences*, *supra*, note 37 at para. 40 (B.C. C.A.).

jected to workplace rumours, harassment and false accusations because he was the foster parent to an adolescent boy.[45]

Decisions regarding hiring, promotion, training or dismissal should not be directly or indirectly based on assumptions related to family status. Family status need only be one of the reasons for a decision or treatment in order for it to be considered discriminatory. Employers should ensure that, rather than judging individuals against presumed group characteristics, they be considered and assessed as the unique individuals they are. For example, rather than assuming that an individual with caregiving responsibilities would not be interested in a relocation or a promotion, he or she should be offered the same opportunities to apply and qualify as other staff.

> *Example*: When interviewing applicants for a promotion, a manager repeatedly asks a candidate who has recently returned from maternity leave whether she is truly "committed" to her career, emphasizing, "this job is not for those who are nine-to-fivers." The candidate is ultimately passed over in favour of an employee who is childless.

Stereotypes may operate during the hiring process, as well as on the job. Employers should therefore be careful during the hiring process not to ask for information that may reveal the family status of applicants. For example, employers should not ask:

- Whether a person has or is planning to have children
- Whether a person has family responsibilities or
- Whether the person's family responsibilities may limit their availability.

Questions regarding irregular hours or ability to travel may reveal the family status of applicants and have the effect of screening out such persons. Questions about the ability of an applicant to undertake such hours or to travel may *only* be asked where irregular hours or regular travel are a *bona fide* occupational requirement. In order for a workplace rule to be a *bona fide* occupational requirement, it must meet the test set out at section 6.1; as part of that test, the employer must demonstrate that it would be impossible to accommodate without undue hardship.

The *Code* makes an exception for nepotism and anti-nepotism policies. Section 24(1)(d) of the *Code* specifically permits employers to grant or withhold employment or advancement in employment to someone who is the

---

[45](1998), 35 C.H.R.R. D/205, at para. 232 (Ont. Bd. Inq.).

spouse, child or parent of the employee. For example, an employer can have a policy that spouses, parents or children cannot be employed in positions where one would report to the other. An employer could also have a policy providing preferential treatment to children of current employees for summer employment. Where such policies are in place, an employer may make inquiries during the hiring process as to whether an applicant is the child or parent of a current employee.

Information about an employee's family status may be relevant to the provision of benefits. Where this is the case, such information should only be requested after the person has been hired. Information that may disclose an employee's family status should be kept confidential. All information should remain exclusively with designated personnel (such as human resources staff) in a secure filing system.

Co-workers as well as managers and supervisors may hold negative attitudes and stereotypes related to family status, and such attitudes may give rise to harassment or a poisoned work environment. Employers should take positive steps to ensure that their workplaces are free of discriminatory attitudes and stereotypes, and that they are welcoming to persons identified by family status.

9.2 — Workplace Policies, Practices and Culture

Described below are some workplace policies and practices that commonly form barriers for persons identified by family status. Employers should carefully consider their policies on these issues to determine whether they may be posing barriers based on *Code* grounds and, if so, whether they are *bona fide* requirements.

9.2.1 — Absenteeism Policies and Leaves of Absence

It is common for persons with family care responsibilities to find that their responsibility to provide care for family members requires absences from work. Such absences may be very short or much more lengthy. Absences may be planned or may arise as emergencies.

It is a legitimate goal for employers to ensure that employees are able to reliably and effectively perform their duties. Employers are entitled to manage absenteeism. However, rigid attendance management programs and absenteeism policies that do not take into account the needs of persons with caregiving responsibilities may discriminate on the basis of family status.

> *Example*: An employer's attendance policy states that any employee absence during a three-month probationary period is cause for termination. A new employee's mother has a serious fall. He takes two days

off from work to attend to her at the hospital and to arrange supports for her return home. Upon his return to work, he is dismissed because of his violation of the attendance policy.

As well, employers may fail to take into account the needs of persons identified by family status when designing their programs and policies. For example, it is not uncommon for employers to allow employees to take time off from work for their own sickness, but to make no provision at all for caring for the needs of sick family members or to require employees to use their vacation days to attend to the needs of their family members. Employees should not find themselves disadvantaged in the provision of benefits as compared to other employees because of their needs related to family status. Where employers provide paid leaves of absence to employees for needs related to disability, creed, pregnancy or for other reasons, employees with needs related to family status should receive comparable treatment.[46]

The Ontario *Employment Standards Act*[47] provides some minimum entitlements for caregivers:

- Employers of over 50 employees must provide up to 10 days of unpaid leave for employees to attend to urgent family matters, including a death, severe illness, injury or medical emergency. "Family" in this context includes spouses (including same-sex spouses), children (including step and foster children), grandparents, siblings, spouses of children and any other relatives that are dependent on the employee for care and assistance.[48]
- Employees are entitled to up to eight weeks of unpaid leave to provide care or support to family members who are at significant risk of death within the next six months.[49]

---

[46]In *Alberta Hospital Association v. Parcels* (1992), 17 C.H.R.R. D/167, at para. 23 (Alta. Q.B.), the Alberta Court of Queen's Bench found that, where an employer provided benefits to employees for health or disability-related absences, it was discriminatory not to provide similar benefits to employees who were absent for reasons related to pregnancy.

[47]*Employment Standards Act, 2000*, S.O. 2000, c. 41.

[48]*Ibid.* at s. 50.

[49]*Ibid.* at s. 49.1. Under the *Employment Insurance Act*, S.C. 1996, c. 23, ss. 12 and 23, employees who take caregiving, pregnancy or parental leaves may be entitled to employment insurance benefits.

- Pregnant employees are entitled to pregnancy leave if they meet certain qualifications, and their job security, seniority and benefits are protected during that leave.[50]
- Parental leaves are provided to employees who meet the requirements. Job security, seniority and benefits are protected during such leaves.[51]

The *Employment Standards Act* and the Ministry of Labour should be consulted for detailed information on these entitlements. It should be emphasized that these are minimum standards only and should be interpreted and implemented in the light of the *Code*. The *Code* duty to accommodate takes precedence over the requirements of the *Employment Standards Act*, and employers may be required by the *Code* to go beyond these minimum requirements.

9.2.2 — Hours of Work and Overtime

Inflexible, excessive or unpredictable work hours may pose barriers to persons with caregiving responsibilities. Court and tribunal decisions have found that employers may be required to consider modifications to work hours and schedules in order to accommodate needs related to family status.[52]

Inflexible schedules for work hours and breaks may pose barriers for employees attempting to meet their responsibilities both to their employers and to their loved ones. For example, given that few daycares operate prior to 8:00 a.m. or after 6:00 p.m., even the most dedicated employee with children may find it difficult to comply with a work schedule that requires them to start precisely at 8:00 a.m. Of course, there will be circumstances where the nature of the work demands specific start, finish and break times. Where such timetables are not a *bona fide* requirement, employers should consider designing schedules in a more flexible manner, and should at minimum provide adjustments to accommodate *Code*-related needs.

Some professions or workplaces have a "culture of hours" in which employees' value and dedication is judged by the number of hours they are visibly at work, regardless of their productivity or the quality of their work. Such workplace cultures are likely to exclude or undervalue persons with significant caregiving responsibilities, regardless of their skills and accomplishments.

---

[50] *Ibid.* ss. 46-47.

[51] *Ibid.* at ss. 48-49.

[52] See *Brown v. M.N.R., Customs and Excise, supra* note 37 at para. 75 and *Health Sciences, supra*, note 37.

Individuals who have multiple or very heavy caregiving responsibilities may find it impossible to work lengthy hours on a regular basis. Where such hours are not a *bona fide* requirement, employers should consider offering temporary or permanent reductions in work hours or other alternative work arrangements.

Similarly, employees with significant caregiving responsibilities may be unable to be consistently available for last-minute demands to stay late or work overtime.

Where social supports for childcare, eldercare or for persons with disabilities are limited, employees with significant caregiving responsibilities may require accommodations to shift scheduling.

> *Example*: An employee worked rotating night and day shifts. Her husband, a police officer, was required to do the same. After their first child was born, they looked for night-time childcare, but were unsuccessful in finding any in their community. The employee requested her employer to schedule her for straight day shifts. The employer refused. A human rights tribunal found that the employer was required to enter into the accommodation process with the employee, and that it had violated the employee's human rights.[53]

9.2.3 — Travel Requirements

Where employees have significant caregiving responsibilities, their ability to undertake regular or extensive travel may be limited. Of course, this is not the case for all employees with family responsibilities: employers should not make the assumption that, for example, a person with young children or other significant caregiving responsibilities will not be interested in work that involves travel. Some jobs require regular travel as an essential duty. Where it is not a *bona fide* requirement, employees should not be denied opportunities because their caregiving responsibilities prevent them from undertaking regular or extensive travel.

Even where travel is an essential duty of the job, employers can accommodate family status-related needs of employees by, for example, recognizing related dependent-care expenses or providing appropriate supports.

9.2.4 — Access to Benefits

Employee benefit plans or employment practices that result in disadvantage because of family status constitute discrimination under the *Code*.

---

[53]*Brown v. M.N.R., Customs and Excise*, *ibid.* at para. 78.

Persons with caregiving responsibilities are disproportionately likely to find themselves in part-time, casual or other non-standard work.[54] This is particularly true for women. Those in non-standard work are unlikely to have access to pensions and health-related benefits.[55] This has long-term consequences for the economic security of caregivers and has the effect of disadvantaging persons identified by family status, particularly as it intersects with the ground of sex.[56] Where discrepancies in the treatment of full-time and part-time workers have an adverse impact on persons identified by family status, this may be grounds for a complaint under the *Code*.

9.2.5 — Workplace Culture

Organizational culture may contribute to the marginalization of persons with caregiving responsibilities, either where it is not inclusive of persons with caregiving responsibilities, or where it supports negative attitudes towards persons disadvantaged by family status.

> *Example*: An employer that wishes to develop teamwork and camaraderie among employees sets up regular, non-mandatory after-hours social events for staff, at which colleagues often share information about training and promotion opportunities and workplace events. Employees with caregiving responsibilities, who are not able to regularly attend these events, begin to find themselves "out of the loop," and at a disadvantage in accessing workplace opportunities.
>
> *Example*: A mother of small children finds that, although she completes her work efficiently and her manager considers her a good per-

---

[54]Statistics Canada figures for 2004 found that 27.5 percent of all part-time workers aged 25–44 have chosen part-time work in order to care for children (CANSIM Table 282-0014 and 282-0001). This does not take into account caregiving for family members with disabilities or aging relatives. Over the past 30 years, women have consistently represented 70 percent of the part-time workforce.

[55]Derrick Comfort *et al.*, *Part-time Work and Family Friendly Practices in Canadian Workplaces* (Ottawa: Statistics Canada and Human Resources Development Canada, 2003).

[56]In other jurisdictions outside Canada, discrepancies between the treatment of part-time and full-time workers have been the subject of successful human rights complaints. For example, in a case decided by the European Court of Justice, the differential treatment of the mainly female part-time cleaning staff with respect to calculation of length of service and possibility of appointment to permanent staff was found to be sex discrimination: *Nikoloudi v. Organismos Tilepikinonion Ellados AE* OJ C-106, 30.04.2005, p. 1.

former, her co-workers assume that she is not "pulling her weight" because she does not regularly stay late at the office, and she is therefore the subject of gossip and resentful comments.

9.2.6 — Reprisal

It is common for employees who need accommodations related to their caregiving obligations to fear that requesting or using such accommodations will be detrimental to their position at work. Employees who seek accommodations related to their family status should not be treated as less valuable or less committed to their work as a result. Employers are responsible for ensuring an environment where caregivers are not afraid to seek and use strategies to accommodate their needs.

> *Example*: A teacher seeks and obtains part-time work in order to balance her caregiving responsibilities with her work. However, she finds that her employer will no longer approve her requests for training opportunities because the employer perceives her to be "on the parent track."

9.3 — Workplace Accommodations for Caregiving Needs

Employers should take steps to ensure that the workplace is "family friendly" and has a positive work-life culture. Steps to achieve such a culture include:

- A visible, senior-level statement of continuing support for an inclusive, family-friendly workplace
- Education and training programs for management and staff on the requirements of the *Code* respecting family status, and
- The development and implementation of an organizational strategy for ensuring the creation of an inclusive workplace.

Programs and policies should recognize and support the range and diversity of contemporary Canadian families. Recognition of only a narrow spectrum of families is not only not in harmony with the *Code*, but may create a negative reaction to the organization's policies and programs, with unintended negative consequences. As well, policies and programs should take into account the impacts of gender, sexual orientation, age, disability and race-related grounds on the experience of family status.

In many cases, the best approach to accommodating needs related to caregiving is by increasing the flexibility and options available to all workers. This approach is in harmony with the principle of inclusive design, contributes towards employee satisfaction, productivity and retention, aids in employee recruitment, and reduces the need to deal with multiple individual requests. The following is a non-exhaustive list of common policies and programs that address needs related to family status:

Flexible Hours Programs: With a flexible hours program, the employer sets core work hours (for example, from 10:00 a.m. to 3:00 p.m.) during which all employees must be at work, and sets the length of a standard work day. Employees can then choose to work from 7:00 a.m. until 3:00 p.m., for example or from 10:00 a.m. until 6:00 p.m.

Compressed Work Weeks: Under a compressed work week program, employees work a standard number of work hours but in fewer days — for example, by working 10 hours four days per week, rather than eight hours five days per week. There are many possible variations on this concept.

Reduced Work Hours: Employers may provide either permanent or temporary access to reduced work hours. Employees who work reduced hours should not be disadvantaged in terms of access to training, pro-rated benefits or quality of work.

Job Sharing: This is an innovative form of reduced work hours, in which two employees both reduce their hours and "share" a single position and set of responsibilities.

Leaves of Absence: Beyond the statutorily mandated maternity, parental and family medical leaves, employers may provide extended or additional caregiving leaves for employees, whether short or long-term. They may include employer-funded leaves, employer-subsidized leaves, unpaid leaves or self-funded leaves (where the employee pays in a portion of his or her salary over a period of time to fund the leave, and the employer administers the funds to provide salary continuance during the leave).

Childcare and/or Eldercare Services: This can include information and referral services, the provision of subsidies or vouchers, access to emergency dependent care services or the provision of on-site care. For example, some large employers who regularly require employees to be available for night shifts have made arrangement to provide night-time childcare for employees.

Employee Assistance Programs: EAPs can provide a wide range of services, including information and referral for a range of programs, counselling and other supports.

Telework: Under these arrangements, employees may work at least some of their regular scheduled hours at home.

10. — Housing

Section 2 of the *Code* prohibits discrimination in housing based on family status. This right applies to renting, being evicted, building rules and regulations, repairs, harassment and use of services and facilities.

There is a lengthy history of families with children being turned away from housing because of negative perceptions associated with family status. These negative perceptions are compounded for young families, lone-parent families, families from racialized and Aboriginal communities, and those in receipt of social assistance. The pattern of complaints received by the Commission, as well as social science evidence, indicates that this is a persistent, endemic problem in the rental housing market. The continued prevalence of "adult only" housing despite the clear prohibitions of the *Code* is a strong example of this.

As well, families face a range of systemic barriers to accessing housing. Families with young children, lone-parent families, parents with disabilities, parents of children with disabilities, families from racialized communities and Aboriginal and newcomer families are disproportionately likely to be low-income. The shelter allowance rates for families on social assistance are far below market levels. This, together with tight rental housing supply in many parts of the province, puts families at a significant disadvantage when seeking shelter.

Families identified by multiple *Code* grounds face a double disadvantage when seeking housing — for example, a family that includes a member with a disability must find shelter that is both accessible and accepting of children.

10.1 — Refusal to Rent to Families with Children

As noted above, families seeking shelter face a range of negative and discriminatory attitudes and stereotypes. Some landlords prefer not to rent to families with children because they believe that children are noisy, disruptive and will damage the property. As well, there are specific negative stereotypes about teenage children, especially if they are male or from Aboriginal or racialized communities. Female-headed lone-parent families face a range of negative attitudes, particularly if they are Aboriginal, racialized, young or in receipt of social assistance, including stereotypes that they are less responsible, less reliable, and more likely to default on their rent.[57] Foster families also face extra difficulties in accessing housing because of negative attitudes towards foster children and foster families.

The *Code* does permit age restrictions in housing under some circumstances.

- Section 15 of the *Code* permits preferential treatment of persons aged 65 and over, and therefore permits housing that is limited to persons over the age of 64.
- Section 14 of the *Code* permits special programs to alleviate hardship and disadvantage, such as specially designed barrier-free housing projects aimed at older persons with disabilities.
- Section 18 creates a defence for religious, philanthropic, educational, fraternal or social institutions or organizations that primarily serve the interests of older persons and that provide housing as part of their services.

However, there is no defence that permits "adult lifestyle" housing that results in the exclusion of children or persons under a certain age.[58]

In some cases, landlords directly refuse applications because of the presence of children. They also use a number of euphemisms to discourage or deny applications from families with children. Statements that a building is

- a "quiet building"
- an "adult lifestyle" building
- "not soundproof" or
- "geared to young professionals"

may, when coupled to a refusal to rent to a family with children, indicate that discriminatory attitudes related to family status played a role in the refusal. Section 13 of the *Code* prohibits the publication or display before the public of any notice, sign, symbol, emblem or other representation that indicates the intent to discriminate. Use of such phrases in advertisements may be considered such an announcement of an intent to discriminate.

Landlords should not require rental housing applicants to provide information that would reveal their family status. For example, application forms

[57]See, for example, *Flamand v. DGN Investments* (2005), 52 C.H.R.R. D/142 (H.R.T.O.). This case involved a landlord who denied housing to an Aboriginal woman who was a mother of one child, and subjected her to racial slurs.

[58]*York Condominium Corp. No. 216 v. Dudnik (No. 2)* (1990), 12 C.H.R.R. D/325, at paras. 165-66; aff'd (1991), 14 C.H.R.R. D/406, at para. 23 (Ont. Div. Ct.).

should not require applicants to reveal the age of co-occupants.[59] If landlords have a *bona fide* requirement for such information about tenants, they can request it after the housing application has been approved.

10.2 — Rental Criteria

There are a number of criteria commonly used by landlords in assessing prospective tenants that may create systemic barriers for families with children. The *Code*, in section 21(3), provides specific guidance to housing providers with respect to the use of certain criteria in assessing and selecting tenants. Landlords are permitted to use income information, credit checks, credit references, rental history and guarantees in assessing and selecting tenants. However, Regulation 290/98 restricts the manner in which these business practices may be used, and specifically reaffirms that landlords may not reject prospective tenants on the basis of *Code* grounds. None of these assessment tools may be used in an arbitrary manner to screen out prospective tenants based on *Code* grounds. The criteria must be used in a *bona fide* and non-discriminatory fashion. Where income information, credit checks, credit references, rental history or guarantees are being applied in a fashion that creates systemic barriers for persons identified by a *Code* ground, the landlord will be required to show that this is a *bona fide* requirement — that is, that the criteria could not be applied in a way that was more accommodating without creating undue hardship for the landlord.

10.2.1 — Use of Income Information

Section 21(3) and Regulation 290/98 permit landlords to seek and take into consideration income information from prospective tenants. "Income information" encompasses "information about the amount, source and steadiness of a potential tenant's income."[60] The prohibitions in the *Code* against discrimination on the basis of receipt of public assistance mean that landlords cannot discriminate against potential tenants on the basis that the source of their income is social assistance benefits. Nor can landlords refuse to consider income such as allowances that are provided to foster families.

Income information may be sought and considered *only* if the landlord also seeks and considers information about the prospective tenant's credit references and rental history. Only if the prospective tenant, when requested, provides no credit references or rental history information, can the landlord

---

[59] *St. Hill v. VRM Investments Ltd.* (2004), C.H.R.R. Doc. 04-023, at para. 32 (H.R.T.O.).

[60] *Vander Schaaf v. M & R Property Management Ltd.* (2000), 38 C.H.R.R. D/251, at para. 105 (Ont. Bd. Inq.).

consider income information in isolation. The assessment must be *bona fide*, meaningful and non-discriminatory.

It has in the past been a common practice for landlords to assess prospective tenants by applying income ratios (e.g., no more than 30% of a tenant's income should be required to pay the rent) or minimum income requirements. This practice was assessed in *Shelter Corp. v. Ontario*[61] and found to have a systemic impact on a range of groups protected by the *Code*, including those identified by family status.[62] The Board of Inquiry found that these practices were not *bona fide* requirements as they had no value in predicting whether a tenant would default on the rent. The subsequent addition of section 21(3) to the *Code* and the enactment of Regulation 290/98 do not permit landlords to use minimum income requirements or apply income ratios, as has been clarified in a subsequent decision of the Tribunal.[63]

Regulation 290/98 makes a specific exception for rent-geared-to-income housing. In assessing applicants for rent-geared-to-income (RGI) housing, landlords may request and consider income information on its own.

10.2.2 — Rental History

Regulation 290/98 permits landlords to request information regarding rental history and to consider it, either alone or in combination with other factors, in assessing a potential tenant.

Prospective tenants may lack a rental history for reasons related to *Code* grounds, for example, recent immigrants and refugees may have no rental history in Canada. Women attempting to re-establish themselves following a marital breakdown may find themselves in a similar situation.

Landlords should not treat the lack of a rental history as equivalent to a negative rental history.[64] Where a prospective tenant lacks a rental history for reasons related to a *Code* ground, landlords should look at other available information regarding the prospective tenant to make a *bona fide* assessment of the tenant.

---

[61] *Shelter Corp. v. Ontario* (1998), 34 C.H.R.R. D/1; aff'd (2001), 39 C.H.R.R. D/111 (Ont. Sup. Ct.).

[62] *Ibid.* at para. 137.

[63] *Vander Schaaf v. M & R Property Management Ltd., supra* note 60 at para. 110.

[64] *Ahmed v. 177061 Canada Ltd.* (2002), 43 C.H.R.R. D/379 (Ont. Bd. Inq.).

10.2.3 — Credit History

Regulation 290/98 permits landlords to request credit references and to conduct credit checks (with permission from the prospective tenant), and to consider this information in selecting or refusing a tenant.

Women returning to the workforce after lengthy periods of caregiving, young families and newcomer families may have little or no credit history. Human rights tribunals have found that the practice of refusing applicants with little or no credit history may have a disparate impact based on *Code* grounds. Landlords should not reject tenancy applications on the basis of a lack of credit history.[65]

In any case, credit history must only be considered in a *bona fide*attempt to validly assess potential tenants.

10.2.4 — Employment History

Some landlords require that potential tenants have "stable," long-term employment. This requirement can be problematic for caregivers returning to the workforce after lengthy periods as full-time caregivers. Requirements that applicants be employed on a permanent basis or satisfy a criterion of minimum tenure with an employer have been found to discriminate on *Code* grounds.[66]

10.2.5 — Guarantors and Security Deposits

Regulation 290/98 permits landlords to require guarantees for rent or to pay security deposits in accordance with the *Residential Tenancies Act, 2006* (formerly the *Tenant Protection Act*). While the use of co-signors or security deposits may be appropriate where a tenant has poor references or a history of default, it is impermissible to require guarantors or security deposits because the prospective tenant is a member of a *Code* protected group, such as being a lone-parent or in receipt of social assistance.

When landlords request a co-signor or guarantor, they cannot require that this person meet minimum income requirements or rent-to-income ratios that would be impermissible to impose on the prospective tenant him- or herself.

---

[65]*Ahmed v. 177061 Canada Ltd.*, *ibid.* at para. 85.

[66]*Sinclair v. Morris A. Hunter Investments Ltd.* (2001), 41 C.H.R.R. D/98 (Ont. Bd. Inq.) at paras. 36-37. This decision found discrimination on the basis of age, as younger persons are less likely to have permanent employment or lengthy job tenure. However, similar issues arise with respect to the ground of family status, particularly with respect to the situation of caregivers.

10.2.6 — Health and Safety Concerns

Landlords may not refuse to rent high-rise apartment units to families with young children on the basis of health and safety concerns. Landlords are required by the *Residential Tenancies Act, 2006* to maintain health and safety standards and ensure units are in a state of good repair. Moreover, the duty to accommodate needs relating to family status applies to landlords: where modifications are required to a housing unit to meet needs related to family status, the landlord must accommodate to the point of undue hardship.

> *Example*: A family with small children applies to rent an apartment that is on the 10th floor of the apartment building. The landlord is concerned about the safety of the children, because the apartment has a balcony. Rather than deny the apartment to the family, the landlord ensures that the balcony meets all appropriate safety standards.

10.3 — Occupancy of Accommodation

10.3.1 — Occupancy Policies

Occupancy policies must be based on *bona fide* requirements. Landlords are not obliged to permit overcrowding of their units. However, arbitrary rules regarding occupants per room or per bedroom may have an adverse impact on families with children. A human rights tribunal found a violation of the *Code* where a landlord denied a three bedroom apartment to a single mother of three children because the "Canadian standard" was that such apartments should be rented to couples with two children.[67] Similarly, landlords should not deny apartments to families on the basis of arbitrary rules regarding the sharing of bedrooms by children of the opposite sex.

10.3.2 — No Transfer Policies

As children join a family, its housing needs will change and additional space will be required. In such circumstances, families may request transfers between rental units in the same building. An Ontario Board of Inquiry held that rules prohibiting transfers between rental units discriminate on the basis of family status.[68]

---

[67] *Cunanan v. Boolean Developments Ltd.* (2003), 47 C.H.R.R. D/236, at paras. 65-66 (H.R.T.O.).

[68] *Ward v. Godina* (1994), C.H.R.R. Doc. 94-130, at para. 50 (Ont. Bd. Inq.).

10.3.3 — Access to Recreational Facilities and Common Areas

Age based restrictions on access to recreational facilities and common areas may discriminate on the basis of family status. For example, rules banning use of certain areas or facilities by children or restricting their use as compared to other occupants, have a negative effect on families.[69]

> *Example*: A condominium restricts use of its swimming pool and recreational facilities by persons under age 18 to the hours between 3:00 p.m. and 5:00 p.m. For families who do not have an adult at home during working hours, this essentially means that they cannot use the pool or recreational facilities with their children. This may constitute grounds for a human rights complaint.

There may be legitimate health and safety concerns regarding the use of certain facilities by children. Where a rule restricts or prohibits access to facilities or areas in a way that impacts on usage by families, the burden will be on the landlord to demonstrate that the rule is a *bona fide* requirement, and that a more inclusive rule could not be implemented without undue hardship.

10.4 — Children's Noise

Persons living in multi-residential housing live in close quarters and children, by their very nature, can be noisy. It is natural that children cry, run and play. Children's noise is frequently a source of conflict in apartment-type housing. It has been used as a reason for denial of housing, has been the source of evictions and has led to harassment and poisoned environments for families with children.

The normal noise associated with children should not be a reason for denial of housing, eviction or harassment of families. Parents are obliged to take steps in accordance with good parenting practices to manage the noise made by their children and to be good neighbours. However, it should be recognized that children will naturally make some noise.

Landlords should take steps to ensure that families with children are not harassed by neighbours because of the normal noise associated with children, just as they would with regard to harassment based on other *Code*

---

[69] In *Leonis v. Metropolitan Toronto Condominium Corp. No. 741* (1998), 33 C.H.R.R. D/479, at para. 62 (Ont. Bd. Inq.): rules banning those under 16 from accessing certain facilities, and severely restricting the use of others, were found to discriminate on the basis of family status.

grounds. Where necessary, landlords can explore options such as moving the complaining tenant or providing soundproofing where it is possible to do so without undue hardship.

11. — Services

Section 1 of the *Code* prohibits discrimination on the basis of family status in services, goods and facilities. This includes, but is not limited to, educational institutions, hospitals, public transit services, social services, public places like malls and parks, and stores and restaurants.

11.1 — Negative Attitudes and Stereotypes

Discrimination on the basis of family status in the area of services often arises because of negative perceptions regarding children or regarding specific types of families. For example, female-headed lone-parent families are heavily stigmatized, particularly when they are racialized or Aboriginal or are in receipt of social assistance. These families may find themselves subjected to unwarranted scrutiny, denied services or subjected to harassment when seeking services.

> *Example*: A social service provider tells an Aboriginal lone mother that she is just having babies to get money from the system, and subjects her to an extra audit of her compliance with program rules.

Similarly, some families may have difficulty in obtaining recognition from service providers that they are "real" families. This is particularly true for foster families and LGBT families. Services ordinarily available to families may be denied to them or only accessed with difficulty.

> *Example*: A gay man and his partner have cared for his mother for years. When she is in the final stages of her illness, she is admitted to the hospital. Due to the hospital rules, her son's partner can only visit her by pretending to be another of her sons.

11.2 — Inclusive Design and the Duty to Accommodate

One prevalent source of discrimination against families is the failure to design services in ways that include them.

> *Example*: A law school student's mother is diagnosed with cancer. The law school agrees to provide a short-term leave-of-absence; however,

when the leave is over, and the mother is still ill, the student is forced to drop out of school because part-time studies are not available.

Service providers can take steps to make their services more inclusive of families. Public facilities should install change tables in washrooms, both male and female, so that parents are not left in an awkward dilemma when taking their infants for an outing. Education providers can provide options for day or evening programs, leave-of-absence options, and quality distance education alternatives. Recreational facilities can provide family changerooms.

Inclusive design should take into account that families may include persons who have disabilities, are LGBT or are from various cultural communities.

Example: A parent with a disability is reliant on specialized transit services for transportation. Needing to visit a health care provider, she arranges to drop her child off at a childcare centre. However, because the specialized transit provider does not permit her to travel with her child, she finds she has no means of accessing either the childcare service or her healthcare appointment.

Families with young children, like persons with disabilities and older persons, face challenges from physically inaccessible buildings, and would benefit from barrier removal and inclusive design. Families with young children in strollers, for example, will have difficulty in accessing buildings with many stairs and heavy doors. Rules that ban or restrict stroller access pose barriers to families, particularly for parents who have disabilities and cannot carry their small children. Where, as a result of inaccessible design or stroller bans, persons with small children are not able to access a service, this may amount to a violation of the *Code*.

Like employers, service providers should take steps to provide accommodation for service recipients who have caregiving needs.

Example: When a student's child falls gravely ill just before a final examination, the education provider agrees to defer the examination until the child has recovered.

Governments have a significant role to play in ensuring the accessibility of their services, regardless of family status. The Supreme Court of Canada has stated that, when governments provide benefits to the general population, they have an obligation to take positive steps to ensure that members of disadvantaged groups benefit equally from those services, subject of course to the undue hardship standard.[70]

> *Example*: A government social assistance program requires recipients to work, study or do volunteer work. Many recipients are lone parents and have significant childcare responsibilities. The program providers are required to ensure that appropriate childcare supports are available or that work, study or volunteer requirements are compatible with the recipient's caregiving needs.

11.3 — Age-Based Restrictions and "Child-Free" Spaces

The *Code* prohibits discrimination in services on the basis of age only for persons aged 18 or older. In other words, service providers are entitled, under the *Code*, to restrict the services they provide to minors. However, a recent Tribunal decision has indicated that this provision of the *Code* can be an unjustifiable abridgement of the equality rights of children under the *Charter of Rights and Freedoms*.[71]

In any case, restrictions on services to children that have the effect of restricting the access to services for their parents may discriminate on the basis of family status. For example, in a British Columbia case, a restaurant that refused to allow customers with children to use its services, on the basis that other customers did not like being disturbed when children made a fuss, was found to have discriminated on the basis of family status.[72] Negative attitudes or intolerance towards children may lead to discriminatory behaviour towards families. It is the Commission's position that services that bar access to families with children under a certain age may be violating the *Code*.

There are, of course, valid reasons for treating minors differently than adults in some circumstances. It is legitimate to take steps to ensure that children do not have access to services or facilities that would compromise their safety or wellbeing. Where the health, safety or wellbeing of children would be put at risk, it is likely that a service-provider will have a *bona fide*

---

[70] *Eldridge v. British Columbia (Attorney General)*, [1997] 3 S.C.R. 624 at para. 79.

[71] *Arzem v. Ontario (Ministry of Community and Social Services) (No. 6)* (2006), 56 C.H.R.R. D/426, at para. 157 (H.R.T.O.).

[72] *Micallef v. Glacier Park Lodge Ltd.* (1998), 33 C.H.R.R. D/249, at para. 37 (B.C.H.R.T.).

reason for denying access to children. However, arbitrary age restrictions should not be used to enforce mere preferences for "child-free" spaces.

In some cases, behaviour that is typically associated with children may be incompatible with the nature of a particular service. For example, loud and persistent crying during a theatrical performance may substantially interfere with the ability of other patrons to hear and enjoy the performance. Children, like adults, vary in their behaviour, and judgements about children's behaviour cannot necessarily be made beforehand. Rather than using age-based restrictions, it may be more appropriate to specify the essential requirements for accessing the service in question: those who cannot meet those essential requirements may be excluded, regardless of their age.

> *Example*: A community swimming pool, rather than designating times for "adult swimming" and "family swimming," designates times for "lane swimming" and "free swimming." Children who are proficient swimmers, and adults who are boisterous, will each have access to the appropriate services.

The *Code* sets out specific exceptions where services may be denied on the basis of family status. Section 20(3) allows recreational facilities to restrict or qualify access to services or facilities and to give preference in membership dues or fees on the basis of marital and family status. This defence would likely protect a single's club, for example. As well, section 18 permits religious, philanthropic, educational, fraternal or social institutions or organizations that are primarily engaged in serving the interests of persons identified by a prohibited ground to restrict membership or participation to those who are similarly identified.

Policy and Guidelines on Racism and Racial Discrimination

Approved by the Commission: June 9, 2005

Part I — Setting the Context: Understanding Race, Racism and Racial Discrimination

1. — Introduction

1.1 — The *Code* Context

The Ontario *Human Rights Code* (the "*Code*") states that it is public policy in Ontario to recognize the inherent dignity and worth of every person and to provide for equal rights and opportunities without discrimination. The provisions of the *Code* are aimed at creating a climate of understanding and mutual respect for the dignity and worth of each person, so that each person feels a part of the community and feels able to contribute to the community.

Every person in Ontario has a right to be free from racial discrimination and harassment in the social areas of employment, services, goods, facilities, housing accommodation, contracts and membership in trade and vocational associations.

The *Code* evolved in part from the *Ontario Racial Discrimination Act* of 1944. But, despite laws to address racial discrimination having existed for over 60 years, racial discrimination and racism persist in Ontario. The Ontario Human Rights Commission (the "Commission") continues to receive a significant number of complaints of racial discrimination and harassment. Each year, about 30% to 40% of the complaints filed with the Commission cite race and related grounds. Many other instances of racial discrimination never come forward as complaints to the Commission and there are manifestations of racism that are beyond the jurisdiction of the Commission, for example hate crimes perpetuated by individuals.[1]

---

[1]Hate crimes continue to occur in Ontario and Canada and have an impact on the victim, his or her community and wider society that is disproportionate and longer lasting than that of most other crimes. Despite the fact that it is estimated by the police that hate crimes are reported in only 10–15% of cases, the Toronto Police recorded a total of 163 hate crime occurrences in 2004 against a variety of groups; see Toronto Police Service Hate Crime Unit, *2004 Annual Hate/Bias Crime Statistical Report*, online: www.torontopolice.on.ca/publications/files/reports/2004 hatecrimereport.pdf. B'nai Brith's League for Human Rights notes that anti-Semi-

There are numerous other indicators of the reality of racial discrimination in Canada. Racialized persons experience disproportionate poverty, over-representation in the prison population, under-representation in the middle and upper layers of political, administrative, economic and media institutions, and barriers to accessing employment, housing and health care to name just a few.[2] Courts have recognized that racism exists in Canada.[3]

It is all too easy for those who do not experience it to deny the reality of racism. This is counterproductive and damaging to our social fabric. Racial discrimination and racism must be acknowledged as a pervasive and continuing reality as a starting point to assessing how the *Code* applies and what can be done to address them.

While our province's statutes exclude racial discrimination from any legal acceptance, racism and racial discrimination remain widespread and even socially accepted among many people. The *Code* therefore compels the Commission to face this challenge and calls on our leaders and people to develop an unconditional culture of rights. Racism and racial discrimination must become a regretted part of Ontario's past, not a tolerated part of its present and future.

---

tism in Canada continues to escalate and that the year 2004 was characterized by a surge, for the fourth year in a row, in the number of reported anti-Semitic incidents; see League for Human Rights of B'nai Brith Canada, *Audit of Antisemitic Incidents: Patterns of Prejudice in Canada* (Toronto: League for Human Rights, 2005), online: www.bnaibrith.ca.

[2]See reports on racial inequality as well as the *Report of the United Nations Special Rapporteur on contemporary forms of racism, racial discrimination, xenophobia and related intolerance*, Commission on Human Rights, E/CN.4/2004/18/Add.2 (1 March 2004) [hereinafter *Report of the Special Rapporteur on Racism*].

[3]For example, in *R. v. Parks* (1993), 15 O.R. (3d) 324 at 342, the Ontario Court of Appeal stated:

> Racism, and in particular anti-black racism, is a part of our community's psyche. A significant segment of our community holds overtly racist views. A much larger segment subconsciously operates on the basis of negative racial stereotypes. Furthermore, our institutions, including the criminal justice system, reflect and perpetuate those negative stereotypes. These elements combine to infect our society as a whole with the evil of racism.

See also, *R. v. Williams*, [1998] 1 S.C.R. 1128, and *R. v. Hamilton*, [2004] O.J. No. 3252 (C.A.). For cases concerning racial profiling see *infra*, note 66.

1.2 — The Purpose and Scope of Human Rights Policy

This policy is based on extensive research and consultation. In 2003, the Commission conducted a province-wide inquiry into the effects of racial profiling, resulting in a report, *Paying the Price: The Human Cost of Racial Profiling*. In March 2004, the Commission began a process of consultation specifically geared to developing this policy. Numerous focus groups were held with stakeholders representing a diversity of interests and perspectives. In October 2004, in partnership with the Association of Canadian Studies,[4] the Commission held a three-day Policy Dialogue with experts and stakeholders to identify and discuss trends and developments relevant to a Commission policy on racial discrimination and racism.

In December 2004, papers generated by speakers at the Policy Dialogue were published in a dedicated issue of *Canadian Diversity* and posted on the Commission's Web site in January 2005. The public was invited to comment on the issues and ideas presented in the papers. In addition, respondent-oriented stakeholders were asked for input on specific issues that would be addressed in the policy.

This policy sets out the Commission's position on racism, racial discrimination and racial harassment, at the time of publication. It replaces the Commission's 1996 *Policy on Racial Slurs and Harassment and Racial Jokes*. It deals primarily with issues that fall within the Commission's jurisdiction and which can form the subject matter of a complaint to the Commission. The policy is therefore bounded by the provisions of the Ontario *Human Rights Code* and Canada's legal framework for analyzing discrimination. At the same time, the policy interprets the protections in the *Code* in a broad and purposive manner. This is consistent with the principle that the quasi-constitutional status of the *Code* requires that it be given a liberal interpretation that best ensures its anti-discriminatory goals are attained.

In the policy, discrimination and harassment due to race are analyzed with an understanding of the pernicious influence of the wider social fact of racism. The policy highlights some of the broader issues of racism to create appropriate context. However, a detailed discussion of all manifestations of racism in Canadian society is beyond the scope of this policy. Indeed, there are many lengthy documents and reports dedicated to specific issues of racism such as the *Report of the Commission on Systemic Racism in the On-*

---

[4]The Association for Canadian Studies is a voluntary non-profit organization. It seeks to expand and disseminate knowledge about Canada through teaching, research and publications.

tario Criminal Justice System,[5] *Unequal Access: A Canadian Profile of Racial Differences in Education, Employment and Income,*[6] the Commission's Report *Paying the Price: The Human Cost of Racial Profiling*[7] and the *Royal Commission on Aboriginal Peoples,*[8] to name just a few.

Several key themes have emerged from the Commission's research and consultation and form the basis of this policy:

- Racism and racial discrimination continue to exist and to affect the lives of not only racialized persons, but also all persons in Canada. The reality of racism and racial discrimination must be acknowledged to take effective measures to combat them.
- Race is a socially constructed way of judging, categorizing and creating difference among people. Despite the fact that there are no biological "races," the social construction of race is a powerful force with real consequences for individuals.
- Racism operates at several levels, including individual, systemic or institutional and societal.
- Racial discrimination can be impacted by related *Code* grounds such as colour, ethnic origin, place of origin, ancestry and creed. In addition, race can overlap or intersect with other grounds such as sex, disability, sexual orientation, age and family status to create unique or compounded experiences of discrimination.
- Racial discrimination can occur through stereotyping and overt prejudice or in more subconscious, subtle and subversive ways.
- Racial discrimination also occurs in significant measure on a systemic or institutional level. Policies, practices, decision-making processes and organizational culture can create or perpetuate a position of relative disadvantage for racialized persons.

---

[5] *Report of the Commission on Systemic Racism in the Ontario Criminal Justice System* (Toronto: Queen's Printer for Ontario, 1995) (Co-Chairs: D. Cole & M. Gittens).

[6] *Unequal Access: A Canadian Profile of Racial Differences in Education, Employment and Income*, Report Prepared for the Canadian Race Relations Foundation by the Canadian Council on Social Development (Toronto: Canadian Race Relations Foundation, 2000).

[7] Ontario Human Rights Commission, *Paying the Price: The Human Cost of Racial Profiling* (Toronto: Queen's Printer, 2003).

[8] *Report of the Royal Commission on Aboriginal Peoples* (Ottawa: Canada Communication Group Publishing, 1996) (Co-Chairs: R. Dussault & G. Erasmus).

- Organizations have a responsibility to take proactive steps to ensure that they are not engaging in, condoning or allowing racial discrimination or harassment to occur. Obligations in this regard range from collecting numerical data in appropriate circumstances, accounting for historical disadvantage, reviewing policies, practices and decision-making processes for adverse impact, and having in place and enforcing antidiscrimination and anti-harassment policies and education programs, to name just a few.

While the policy covers all of the social areas in the *Code*, it places a heavier emphasis on employment. This is due to the fact that the majority of complaints to the Commission allege employment-related discrimination. Employment is also integral to socio-economic well-being, which in turn impacts on health, access to education and access to services more broadly. There is therefore an interrelationship between discrimination in employment and discrimination in other social areas covered by the *Code*.

In addition to, and to supplement, this policy statement, the Commission is engaged in, and will continue to undertake, promotion and advancement initiatives to address broader human rights issues related to racial discrimination and racism.

Commission policy statements contribute to creating a culture of human rights in Ontario. They educate the public about human rights and set out standards for how individuals, employers, service providers and policy makers should act to ensure compliance with the *Code*. Commission policy statements must be understood in a wider context of Canada's global commitments.

1.3 — International Obligations

In 1948, the United Nations General Assembly adopted the landmark Universal Declaration of Human Rights, the foundation of international human rights law. The Universal Declaration established an international standard of non-discrimination on the basis of race, colour, language, national origin and a number of other grounds. The principles in the Universal Declaration were given force through various instruments[9] including the *International*

[9]For example, the *International Covenant on Civil and Political Rights*, 16 December 1966, 999 U.N.T.S. 171 (entered into force 23 March 1976, accession by Canada 19 May 1976) [hereinafter the *ICCPR*] and the *International Covenant on Economic Social and Cultural Rights*, 16 December 1966, 993 U.N.T.S. 3 (entered into force 03 January 1976, accession by Canada 19 August 1976) [hereinafter *ICESCR*].

Convention on the Elimination of All Forms of Racial Discrimination[10] (CERD). Canada ratified CERD in 1970 and in so doing accepted responsibility for respecting, protecting and fulfilling the rights contained therein.

Numerous other UN documents have addressed aspects of racial discrimination and racism.[11] In 2003, Canada hosted the UN Special Rapporteur on Racism, Racial Discrimination, Xenophobia and Related Intolerance who prepared a report on his visit.[12]

Some of the key highlights from the various UN documents and instruments include:

- Confirming that race is a social construct, related to geographic, historical, political, economic, social and cultural factors with no justification for notions of racial superiority or racial prejudice
- Urging public recognition that racism persists and of the continuing impact of the historical legacy of racism, such as the effect of colonialism and slavery, including the trans-Atlantic slave trade, on indigenous persons, persons of African descent and persons of Asian descent
- Creating a positive obligation on states to review policies, laws and regulations which create or perpetuate racial discrimination, to enact legislation to prohibit racial discrimination by any person, group or organization and to report on the realization of rights
- Affirming the importance of barrier removal and corrective measures to achieve equal participation in all aspects of society
- Recognizing the interrelationship between economic status, marginalization and social exclusion and racism and the intersectional nature of racial discrimination
- Promoting collecting, compiling and analyzing reliable statistical data, in accordance with privacy and human rights laws, to monitor the situa-

---

[10] 21 December 1965, 660 U.N.T.S. 195 (entered into force 04 January 1969, accession by Canada 14 October 1970) [hereinafter *CERD*].

[11] For the purposes of this policy, the most relevant are the *Vienna Declaration and Programme of Action*, adopted by the World Conference on Human Rights, UN Doc. A/CONF. 157/23 (1993), endorsed GA Res. 48/121, UN Doc. A/RES/48/121 (1993), the *Declaration on Race and Racial Prejudice*, adopted and proclaimed by the General Conference of the United Nations Educational, Scientific and Cultural Organization (UNESCO) 27 November 1978, E/CN.4/Sub.2/1982/2/Add.1, annex V, 1982 and most recently the World Conference Against Racism, Racial Discrimination, Xenophobia and Related Intolerance *Declaration and Programme of Action*, 25 January 2002, A/CONF.189/12.

[12] *Report of the Special Rapporteur on Racism, supra*, note 2.

tion of racialized groups and to assess whether legislation, policies, practices and other measures have an adverse impact on racialized groups and

- Emphasizing the particular and extreme marginalization of Aboriginal peoples, and the unique issues raised in relation to treaties and land disputes and the *Indian Act*.

The Supreme Court of Canada has indicated that the values and principles enshrined in international law constitute a part of the legal context in which legislation is interpreted and applied.[13]Additionally, human rights commissions have been identified as key institutions in implementing and protecting international human rights standards. Accordingly, the Commission uses applicable international standards in its policy development and to inform its application and interpretation of the *Code*. History shows, however, that while Canada has affirmed international instruments on racism and racial discrimination, many people have continued to tolerate both.

1.4 — Historical Context: The Legacy of Racism in Canada

A starting point of a policy on racial discrimination and racism is to provide a brief historical context of racial discrimination and racism in Canada. We must be aware of the events of the past in order to address contemporary manifestations of racial discrimination and racism. A review of the history of racism reveals that Canada has made progress. For example, laws such as the Canadian *Bill of Rights*, the Ontario *Human Rights Code* and the Canadian *Charter of Rights and Freedoms* have been enacted to provide protection against racism and racial discrimination.[14] However, much work remains to be done.

---

[13]See *Slaight Communications Inc. v. Davidson*, [1989] 1 S.C.R. 1038, and *Baker v. Canada (Minister of Citizenship and Immigration)*, [1999] 2 S.C.R. 817 at paras. 70-71.

[14]In 1960, Canada enacted a declaratory statement of human rights in the Canadian *Bill of Rights*, S.C. 1960, c. 44. While the bill was cast as a constitutional document, it was a statute that could be overridden by other laws. It did not apply to provincial legislation. Courts tended to interpret it narrowly and the bill was considered a disappointment by those who wanted to see a truly constitutional *Bill of Rights*; see *McLachlin, infra*, note 22 at paras. 37-38. In 1962, the Ontario Human Rights Commission, the first of its kind in Canada, was established to administer and enforce the Ontario *Human Rights Code*, which was enacted in 1962. The Canadian *Charter of Rights and Freedoms* came into force in April 1982, although the equality rights provisions in section 15 came into effect three years after the rest of the *Charter*. It is a constitutional document and federal and provincial laws and

It is no coincidence that communities which historically experienced racial discrimination continue to be placed on the lowest rungs of the social, economic, political and cultural ladder in Canada. The legacy of racism in Canada has profoundly and lastingly permeated our systems and structures.[15] As such, it must be acknowledged in any policy statement, particularly when considering such matters as institutional or systemic discrimination, inclusive design, barrier removal and methods to respond to racism. What follows is a brief, non-exhaustive historical overview to promote an understanding of the context of racism and racial discrimination in Canada.[16] Although many of the events described may appear to be in the distant past, it is important to note that there are many contemporary examples of racism.[17]

Historically, policies and practices towards Aboriginal persons[18] have been based on assumptions that they are inferior and incapable of governing

---

state actions are required to conform to it. The *Charter* is founded on the rule of law and entrenches in the *Constitution of Canada* the rights and freedoms, including equality rights, that Canadians believe are necessary in a free and democratic society.

[15]*Report of the Special Rapporteur on Racism*, *supra*, note 2 at paras. 68-9.

[16]This summary is intended to concisely outline and show the commonalities of some of the most significant events of racism in Canadian history. It is not, and cannot be, a detailed or exhaustive review of the experience of every racialized community nor should it be considered a basis for comparing the degree of racism suffered by various communities.

[17]See statistics on hate crimes, *supra*, note 1. A recent Ipsos-Reid survey commissioned by the Dominion Institute found that one in six Canadian adults report that they have personally been the victims of racism. Moreover, approximately one in ten Canadian adults would not welcome people from another race as next-door neighbours; see Ipsos-Reid, "March 21st, International Day for the Elimination of Racial Discrimination: One in Six Canadians Say They Have Been the Victim of Racism" (21 March 2005), online: www.dominion.ca/Downloads/IRracism Survey.pdf. See also the *Report of the Special Rapporteur on the situation of human rights and fundamental freedoms of Indigenous people*, Commission on Human Rights, E/CN.4/2005/88/Add.3 (02 December 2004) [hereinafter *Report of the Special Rapporteur on Indigenous People*].

[18]This brief history of the Aboriginal experience of racism is based on more detailed discussions in: F. Henry, C. Tator, W. Mattis & T. Rees, *The Colour of Democracy: Racism in Canadian Society*, 2d ed. (Toronto: Nelson, a division of Thomson Canada Ltd., 1998) at 119–142; M. Jacko, "The Experience of Aboriginal Peoples in Canada" Paper for the International Council on Human Rights Policy (2001).

themselves. Other patterns of interaction were characterized by a desire to assimilate, displace or segregate Aboriginal persons, or to suppress Aboriginal cultures.[19] While recent decades have seen progress in addressing Aboriginal rights in Canada, much remains to be done as illustrated by outstanding issues regarding land rights, residential schools restitution, self-governance as well as other issues identified in the *Report of the Royal Commission on Aboriginal Peoples*, and recently the *Report of the Special Rapporteur on the situation of human rights and fundamental freedoms of Indigenous people.*

The *Indian Act*, first enacted in 1876, gave the federal government control over "Indian" political structures, landholding patterns, resource and economic development and almost every important aspect of Aboriginal peoples' lives. Just a few of the racist features of the *Act* included prohibiting land ownership, rules on electing leaders, denial of the right to vote, prohibiting leaving reserves without a pass, preventing ceremonial festivals and events, and determining who was an "Indian."

Aboriginal children were forcibly removed from their homes and communities and sent to residential schools operated by missionary societies where they were forbidden to speak their language, to practice their traditions and customs and to learn about their history. They were often given an inferior education and many experienced malnutrition, overcrowding, illness, harsh discipline and sexual abuse. Many of these schools were closed in the 1960s, with the last one closing in 1988.

The enslavement of Africans, racial segregation and discrimination are also part of Canada's history. Black slavery was actively practiced in Canada. Between 1628 and the early 1800s, approximately 3000 people of African origin came to Canada and most were held as slaves. In 1793, the Parliament of Upper Canada (now Ontario) under Lieutenant Governor John Graves Simcoe passed an *An Act to prevent the further introduction of Slaves, and to limit the term of contracts for Servitude within this Province*, the first act to limit slavery in the British Empire.[20] Ontario became a destination for those fleeing slavery in the United States via the "underground

---

[19]For a detailed discussion of the various events that have had such a profound impact on Aboriginal culture that they have sometimes been described as "cultural genocide," see *Report of the Royal Commission on Aboriginal Peoples, supra*, note 8 at Part One, Chapter 6 "Stage Three: Displacement and Assimilation."

[20]See Archives of Ontario www.archives.gov.on.ca/english/exhibits/humnrits/slavery.htm and Ontario Heritage Foundation www.heritagefdn.on.ca/userfiles/HTML/nts_1_2724_1.html.

railroad."[21] In 1833 the British Parliament's *Emancipation Act* abolished slavery in all parts of the Empire, including Ontario, but its legacy remained.[22] Prejudice and discrimination would still constrict the opportunities of most Canadians of African ancestry.

African Canadians were excluded from schools, churches, restaurants, hospitals and public transportation. They were restricted to menial, low-paying and exhausting labour.[23] Many African Canadians lived in segregated communities in Nova Scotia, New Brunswick and Ontario. In addition, residential segregation was perpetuated through racially restrictive covenants attached to deeds and leases.[24] The Ontario legislature established segregated schools, and legal challenges to these failed.[25] The legislation remained on books as late as 1964.[26]

Prior to human rights statutes, court challenges to address racial discrimination were largely unsuccessful. In 1939, the Supreme Court of Canada rejected a lawsuit for humiliation brought by Fred Christie, a Black man who was refused service by a Montreal tavern. The Court declined to comment on the racial discrimination, instead concluding that freedom of commerce allowed a merchant to deal with the public in any way he may choose.[27]

---

[21]See Archives of Ontario, *ibid.*

[22]The Rt. Hon. Beverly McLachlin, "Racism and the Law: The Canadian Experience" (2002) 1 J.L. & Equality 7-24 at para. 18, online: QL (JOUR).

[23]*Ibid.*

[24]Henry, Tator, Mattis & Rees, *supra*, note 18 at 71-72.

[25]*Stewart and School Trustees of Sandwich* (1864), 23 U.C.Q.B. 634 at 638, (where no separate school was in existence, attendance at common school could not be denied); *Hutchinson and School Trustees of St. Catharines* (1871), 31 U.C.Q.B 274 at 277–279, (application to compel school trustees to admit Black student dismissed because common school over-crowded, but court held refusal to admit Black student on account of the child's colour was unjustified); *Re Hill v. School of Trustees of Camden and Zone* (1874), 11 U.C.Q.B. 573 at 578-579, (application to compel school trustees to admit Black students dismissed because establishment of a separate school for coloured students precluded their parents from choosing the common school); *Dunn v. Board of Education of Windsor* (1884), 6 O.R. 125 at 127-128 (Ch. Div.) (application to compel school trustees to admit Black student dismissed because no prior request had been made to school inspector and because common school was over-crowded).

[26]Henry, Tator, Mattis & Rees, *supra*, note 18 at 72 and C. Smith, "Tuition Fee Increases and the History of Racial Exclusion in Canadian Legal Education" (2004) 3:3 Canadian Diversity 32–35 at 33.

[27]McLachlin, *supra*, note 22 at para. 21.

The experience of Chinese Canadians is similarly tainted by a history of racism. In the 1880s, labourers were recruited from China to take on the dangerous work of building the railway through the mountains. After being subjected to deplorable working conditions, once their labour was no longer needed, they were seen as a threat to society and an "alien race" and subjected to intense racial discrimination.[28]

Laws were passed to limit Chinese immigration. The 1885 *Chinese Immigration Act* imposed a $50 "head tax" on all Chinese persons entering Canada. In 1903, this amount was raised to $500, a prohibitive amount of money.[29] In 1872, the right to vote in provincial and municipal elections was also taken away from Chinese Canadians in British Columbia (Japanese Canadians and South Asian Canadians were also disenfranchised in 1895 and 1907 respectively).[30] Chinese Canadians were also subjected to discriminatory laws and policies affecting their ability to own property, operate businesses, serve the public and enter certain professions. "In the interest of the morals of women and girls,"[31] laws were passed to prevent Chinese men from employing White women.[32]

Many are familiar with the experience of Japanese Canadians in World War II. Twenty-three thousand Japanese Canadians living on the west coast of British Columbia were sent to relocation and detention camps in isolated areas in the interior of British Columbia, Southern Alberta, Manitoba and Northern Ontario. In addition to other violations and deprivations, Japanese Canadians were stripped of their property, businesses and savings. Towards the end of the war, Japanese Canadians were threatened with further expulsion. They were given the option for "dispersal" to towns east of the Rocky Mountains, or outright "repatriation" to Japan (by 1947, 4,000 Japanese Canadians, half of whom were Canadian born, had left Canada). The Canadian government did not release them until 1947 and it took a further two years before they were able to resettle on the west coast. In 1988, twelve

---

[28]Henry, Tator, Mattis & Rees, *supra*, note 18 at 72-73.

[29]A class action lawsuit against the Canadian government to seek compensation for the effects of the head tax has been unsuccessful; *Mack v. Canada (Attorney General)* (2001), 55 O.R. (3d) 113 (Sup. Ct.); aff'd (2002), 60 O.R. (3d) 737 (C.A.); leave to appeal denied [2002] S.C.C.A. No. 476.

[30]McLachlin, *supra*, note 22 at para. 13.

[31]*Quong Wing v. The King* (1914), 49 S.C.R. 440 at 444, Sir Charles Fitzpatrick C.J.C.

[32]McLachlin, *supra*, note 22 at para. 14.

thousand surviving Japanese Canadians were paid $20 000 each as compensation and a formal apology was issued by Parliament.[33]

Other groups have suffered from racism in Canada's history. For example, South Asian Canadians[34] were viewed with the same racial bias, hostility and resentment as was directed at other racialized groups and they had similar experiences with discriminatory laws, such as legislation to control their economic and social mobility and to remove their right to vote.[35] Like others, they were adversely impacted by immigration laws that preferred immigrants from Northern and Western European countries. In 1914 a shipload of 400 would-be immigrants from India were denied entry at Vancouver. They were held aboard the ship for nearly three months before being forced to return to India.[36]

Islamophobia

A contemporary and emerging form of racism in Canada has been termed "Islamophobia." Islamophobia can be described as stereotypes, bias or acts of hostility towards individual Muslims or followers of Islam in general. In addition to individual acts of intolerance and racial profiling, Islamophobia leads to viewing Muslims as a greater security threat on an institutional, systemic and societal level.

Jewish Canadians have been subjected to anti-Semitism and legalized discrimination. "None is too many" was the response given by a high level Canadian government official when asked how many Jews should be accepted as immigrants, at the time of the Nazi persecution of Jews.[37] Signs posted along the Toronto beaches stated "No Dogs or Jews Allowed." Many hotels and resorts had policies prohibiting Jews as guests.[38] There were restrictions on where Jewish persons could live or buy property. In 1951, a Jewish man challenged one such restrictive covenant preventing

[33]Henry, Tator, Mattis & Rees, *supra*, note 18 at 76-77. See also Canadian Race Relations Foundation, "From Racism to Redress: The Japanese Canadian Experience," online: www.crr.ca/EN/MediaCentre/FactSheets/eMedCen_FacSht FromRacismToRedress.pdf.

[34]This term encompasses persons originating from India, Pakistan, Sri Lanka, Bhutan, Nepal and Bangladesh; Henry, Tator, Mattis & Rees, *supra*, note 18 at 76.

[35]*Ibid.* at 76-77.

[36]*Ibid.* at 79.

[37]For a detailed discussion see: I. Abella & H. Troper, *None Is Too Many: Canada and the Jews of Europe*, 1933 to 1948 (Toronto: Lester & Orpen Dennys, 1982).

[38]Henry, Tator, Mattis & Rees, *supra*, note 18 at 80.

property from being sold to anyone of "the Jewish, Hebrew, Semitic, Negro or coloured race or blood." The Supreme Court of Canada declared the covenant void on the basis it was overly broad.[39]

More recently, immigration policies and practices have been informed by and have contributed to racism in Canada. A discussion of immigration is beyond the scope of this policy;[40] however, at various times, Canada's immigration policies and practices have either directly or indirectly made it easier for some groups (such as Northern and Western Europeans), and more difficult for racialized groups, to gain entry.

The history of racism has had an enduring effect on racialized communities. For example, paternalistic and assimilationist policies and practices toward Aboriginal persons have had a devastating impact. Many Aboriginal persons experience profound disadvantage in all spheres of life including housing, employment, health and education. Aboriginal communities continue to struggle to assert their land and treaty rights. Racialized groups can all trace their continued experience of marginalization to the legacy of racism in Canada.

2. — "Race", Racism and Racial Discrimination

2.1 — "Race": A Social Construct

Race is a prohibited ground in the *Code* that is not specifically defined. As the term is commonly used in the human rights context and society in general, it is important to clarify its meaning.

In the past, race was defined as a natural or biological division of the human species based on physical distinctions including skin colour and other bodily features. This notion of race emerged in the context of European imperial domination of nations and peoples deemed "non-white" and was used to establish a classification of peoples.[41] Some of the greatest atrocities in human history have been associated with notions of racial superiority.

There is no legitimate scientific basis for racial classification. Genetic science now tells us that physical characteristics and genetic profiles correlate

---

[39]*Noble v. Alley*, [1951] S.C.R. 64.

[40]Such federal immigration policies are matters within the jurisdiction of the Canadian Parliament and consequently not subject to provincial human rights codes.

[41]F. Henry, "Concepts of Race and Racism and Implications for OHRC Policy" (2004) 3:3 Canadian Diversity 4.

more strongly between "races" than among them.[42] It is now recognized that notions of race are primarily centred on social processes that seek to construct differences among groups with the effect of marginalizing some in society.

While biological notions of race have been discredited, the social construction of race remains a potent force in society. The process of social construction of race is termed racialization. The *Report of the Commission on Systemic Racism in the Ontario Criminal Justice System* defined racialization "as the process by which societies construct races as real, different and unequal in ways that matter to economic, political and social life."[43] Even groups and people that have only marginal physical distinctions from Western European people have been racialized in Canada. For example, immigrants from Southern or Eastern Europe were deemed as "races" of less worth when they first came to Canada.

Racialization extends to people in general but also to specific traits and attributes, which are connected in some way to racialized people and are deemed to be "abnormal" and of less worth. Individuals may have prejudices related to various racialized characteristics. In addition to physical features, characteristics of people that are commonly racialized include:

- accent or manner of speech
- name
- clothing and grooming
- diet
- beliefs and practices
- leisure preferences
- places of origin
- citizenship

---

[42] Robert Miles & Rudy Torres, Does "Race" Matter? Transatlantic Perspectives on Racism after "Race Relations," in V. Amit-Talai and C. Knowles, eds., *Re-Situating Identities: The Politics of Race, Ethnicity and Culture* (Peterborough: Broadview Press, 1995) 24-46:

> . . .earlier this century, the biological and genetic sciences established conclusively in light of empirical evidence that the attempt to establish the existence of different types or "races" of human beings by scientific procedures had failed. [at 25]

[43] *Report of the Commission on Systemic Racism in the Ontario Criminal Justice System*, *supra*, note 5 at 40-41.

Despite the fact that we know there are no "races," the social construction of race is a powerful force in our society, with real consequences for individuals.[44] Therefore, the ground of "race" in the *Code* continues to be important to the discussion of racism and racial discrimination and to the receipt and processing of complaints by the Commission.

2.1.1 — A Word about Terminology

There are inherent challenges in finding ways in which to best describe people. Terminology is fluid and what is considered most appropriate will likely evolve over time. Moreover, people within a group may disagree on preference and may choose to use different terms to describe themselves. However, it is useful to provide some general guidelines on terminology that the Commission considers most inclusive at the present time.

When it is necessary to describe people collectively, the term "racialized person" or "racialized group" is preferred over "racial minority," "visible minority,"[45] "person of colour"[46] or "non-White" as it expresses race as a social construct rather than as a description based on perceived biological traits. Furthermore, these other terms treat "White" as the norm to which racialized persons are to be compared and have a tendency to group all racialized persons in one category, as if they are all the same.

Where identification of individuals is necessary, allowing people to self-identify is always a preferred approach. If this isn't possible, terms that are selected should be linked to the reason identification is required. For example, if intending to compare a group's representation within an organization to its representation in the general population, terms used in the Canadian census would be a logical choice. It is generally better to avoid a broad term (*e.g.*, Asian) where a specific term is available, such as one that refers to national origin (*e.g.*, Chinese Canadian). Terms that are clearly considered

---

[44]M. Castagna & G.J.S. Dei, "An Historical Overview of the Application of the Race Concept in Social Practice," in A. Calliste and G.J.S. Dei, eds., *Anti-Racist Feminism* (Halifax: Fernwood Publishing, 2000) 19–37 at 35.

[45]Words that describe racialized persons as a "minority" assume that White people are the predominant population group which is an inaccurate portrayal of most countries in the world and, increasingly, of many areas in Canada.

[46]A term which applies to all people who are not seen as White by the dominant group, generally used by racialized groups as an alternative to the term visible minority. It emphasizes that skin colour is a key consideration in the "everyday" experiences of their lives; Canadian Race Relations Foundation, Glossary of Terms (April 2005). However, the term is imprecise and not all racialized people would describe themselves in this way.

inappropriate must be avoided and if an individual objects to a term, it should not be used.

The terms "Black" and "White"[47] are widely used to describe individuals, and may even be the terms people prefer to use in describing themselves. While at this time, these terms are not viewed by most as inappropriate, nevertheless, it is important to remember that they refer to racialized characteristics.

2.2 — Understanding Racism

Racism is a wider phenomenon than racial discrimination. While the *Code* seeks to combat racism through public education and the advancement of human rights, not every manifestation of racism can be dealt with through the current human rights complaint mechanism and process. Rather, it is only racially discriminatory actions in specified social areas that are prohibited by the *Code* (see section *2.3. The Code and Racial Discrimination*). Nevertheless, racism plays a major role in the social processes that give rise to and entrench racial discrimination. As such, acknowledging and understanding racism as a historical and current reality in Canadian society is critical for a human rights policy.

Many different definitions of racism exist. They differ in complexity and emphasis and can often be very difficult to understand. Therefore, what follows is a general discussion of the key elements for understanding racism.

Definitions of racism all agree that it is an ideology that either explicitly or implicitly asserts that one racialized group is inherently superior to others. Racist ideology can be openly manifested in racial slurs, jokes or hate crimes. However, it can be more deeply rooted in attitudes, values and stereotypical beliefs. In some cases these beliefs are unconsciously maintained by individuals and have become deeply embedded in systems and institutions that have evolved over time.

---

[47]The Commission has chosen to capitalize the terms "Black" and "White" although with a recognition that whether these terms should be capitalized is a matter open to debate.

Consider this:

In discussing racism, it is necessary to consider the unearned privileges (*i.e.*, benefits, advantages, access and/or opportunities) that exist for members of the dominant group in society or in a given context. This notion is often termed "White privilege."

While this notion may be controversial to some, consider the following statements that are helpful in understanding how experiences differ based on privilege.

1. If I want or need to move, I can be pretty sure that I will not be told that an apartment has already been rented when the landlord sees me.
2. If I talk to "the person in charge," it is likely it will be a person of my "race."
3. I can go shopping alone and do not expect to be followed. I do not have to think about how well I am dressed before I go to a high-end store.
4. When I use cheques or credit cards, I can count on my skin colour not to work against the appearance of financial reliability.
5. If I choose to openly discuss or display my religious beliefs, I do not worry that people will think I should "go back to where I came from."

(Adapted from P. McIntosh, "White Privilege: Unpacking the Invisible Knapsack": online: www.utoronto.ca/acc/events/peggy1.htm)

Racism differs from simple prejudice in that it has also been tied to the aspect of power, *i.e.* the social, political, economic and institutional power that is held by the dominant group in society. In Canada and Ontario, the institutions that have the greatest degree of influence and power, including governments, the education system, banking and commerce, and the justice system are not, at this time, fully representative of racialized persons, particularly in their leadership.

Racism often manifests in negative beliefs, assumptions and actions. However, it is not just perpetuated by individuals. It may be evident in organizational or institutional structures and programs as well as in individual thought or behaviour patterns. Racism oppresses and subordinates people because of racialized characteristics. It has a profound impact on social, economic, political and cultural life.

2.2.1 — How Racism Operates

From the discussion above it is clear that racism exists at a number of levels[48], in particular (1) individual, (2) institutional or systemic, and (3) societal (also described as cultural/ideological).

At the individual level, racism may be expressed in an overt manner but also through everyday behaviour that involves many small events in the interaction between people. This is often described as "everyday racism" and is often very subtle in nature. Despite being plain to the person experiencing it, everyday racism by itself may be so subtle as to be difficult to address through human rights complaints. However, at other times, where it falls within a social area covered by the *Code*, there may be circumstances where everyday racism, as part of a broader context, may be sufficient to be considered racial discrimination (please refer to section *3.3, Subtle Racial Discrimination*, for a discussion of these situations). Either way, the cumulative effect of these everyday experiences is profound.

Everyday Experiences of Racism

Examples of everyday experiences of racism might include:

Speech: When dealing with customers who are African Canadian, a sales clerk uses an unfriendly, curt or sarcastic tone of voice.

Glances: Looks of contempt are given to a Muslim Canadian family post-9/11.

Actions: When a Chinese Canadian takes a seat on the bus, passengers vacate the adjacent seat.

Canada is a country founded upon colonization and immigration. It is known for having one of the most diverse populations in the world. This mosaic of individuals and cultures presents unique and evolving challenges for human relations. Some complaints to the Commission allege racism by, among or within racialized groups. The consequences of these situations, for example loss of a job, are every bit as serious as racism perpetuated by White persons against racialized persons and will be treated equally as seriously in complaints before the Commission.

At the institutional or systemic level, racism is evident in organizational and government policies, practices and procedures and "normal ways of doing things" which may directly or indirectly, consciously or unwittingly, pro-

[48]Please see for greater detail F. Henry, "Concepts of Race and Racism and Implications for OHRC Policy," *supra*, note 41.

mote, sustain, or entrench differential advantage for some people and disadvantage for others.

At a societal level, racism is evident in cultural and ideological expressions that underlie and sustain dominant values and beliefs. It is evident in a whole range of concepts, ideas, images and institutions that provide the framework of interpretation and meaning for racialized thought in society. It is communicated and reproduced through agencies of socialization and cultural transmission such as the mass media (in which racialized persons are portrayed as different from the norm or as problems), schools, universities, religious doctrines and practices, art, music and literature. It is reflected in everyday language; for example, "whiteness" is associated with overwhelmingly positive connotations, while "blackness" is associated with negative connotations.[49] This form of racism is maintained through socialization as children begin to absorb these beliefs and values at an early age.[50]

As mentioned above, any effective response to racism must clearly acknowledge that it persists in Ontario. However, as great stigma attaches to allegations of racism, there is a tendency to deny its existence generally or in a particular situation.

It is important to emphasize that racism in its more entrenched forms is often unconsciously applied and its operation is often unrecognized by even those practising it. In addition, as noted earlier in the Policy, while Canada has made much progress, racism remains a reality. It should not be treated as aberrant behaviour or a set of deviant attitudes on the part of a deviant individual — a so-called "rotten apple" within the system. Failing to recognize the complex, subtle and systemic nature of racism impedes effective action against it.

Finally, it is the Commission's view that, except in the most obvious circumstances, such as where individuals clearly intend to engage in racist behaviour, it is preferable that actions rather than individuals be described as racist.

---

[49]A review of a thesaurus or dictionary makes this clear. For example, consider the positive connotation of the terms "white lie" and "white knight" compared with the negative meanings of "blacklist," "black market" and "blackmail" and many other words beginning with "black."

[50]Henry, Tator, Mattis & Rees, *supra* note 18 at 56-7.

Did you know?

"The Canadian Government should add credibility, trust, and recognition to its undoubted political commitment to combating racism, discrimination and xenophobia by recognizing, at the highest level, that such evils still persist, despite the efforts accomplished."

(Report of the Special Rapporteur on Racism p. 24)

2.3 — The *Code* and Racial Discrimination

2.3.1 — Defining Racial Discrimination

The purpose of anti-discrimination laws, such as the *Code*, is to prevent the violation of human dignity and freedom through the imposition of disadvantage, stereotyping or political or social prejudice. While racism is a social phenomenon, it is racial discrimination that is a legally prohibited act.[51]

There is no fixed definition of racial discrimination and society's understanding of what constitutes racial discrimination will continue to evolve over time. Several descriptions of racial discrimination have been offered which can be helpful in understanding and explaining it.

For example, in the international human rights context, it has been described as any distinction, exclusion, restriction or preference based on race that nullifies or impairs the human rights or fundamental freedoms afforded citizens.[52] One approach in Canadian case law suggests that it may be described as any distinction, conduct or actions, whether intentional or not, but based on a person's race, which has the effect of imposing burdens on an individual or group, not imposed upon others or which withholds or limits access to benefits available to other members of society.[53] Moreover, the case law has clearly stated that race need only be *a factor* for there to be a finding of racial discrimination.

---

[51]This distinction was succinctly acknowledged by the Nova Scotia Board of Inquiry in *Johnson v. Halifax (Regional Municipality) Police Service* (2003), 48 C.H.R.R. D/307 (N.S. Bd. Inq.).

[52]Adapted from the definition in the *CERD*, *supra*, note 11 Article 1:

> any distinction, exclusion, restriction or preference based on race, colour, descent, or national or ethnic origin which has the purpose or effect of nullifying or impairing the recognition, enjoyment or exercise, on an equal footing, of human rights and fundamental freedoms in the political, economic, social cultural or any other field of public life.

[53]*Andrews v. Law Society of British Columbia*, [1989] 1 S.C.R. 143 at 174.

The *Code* offers every Ontarian protection from racial discrimination specifically in the realms of employment, services, contracts, housing and vocational associations.

2.3.2 — Racial Discrimination and Related Code Grounds

In addition to race, the *Code* prohibits discrimination on several related grounds. These include primarily the grounds of colour, ethnic origin, ancestry, place of origin, citizenship and creed (religion).

Depending on the circumstances, discrimination based on race may cite race alone or may include one or more related grounds. However, as a social construct, the ground of race is capable of encompassing the meaning of all of the related grounds, and any other characteristic that is racialized and used to discriminate.

In many instances of racial discrimination, the particular notion of race acted on is given specific meaning by related grounds. In such instances, it would be appropriate to cite these other grounds along with race. For example, when a man named Muhammad is screened from an employment competition on the basis of his name, it is appropriate to cite as grounds for discrimination race, ethnic origin, ancestry, place of origin and creed, as the name in question is racialized precisely because it is stereotypically connected to a specific origin and creed.

In other instances, indicators including the related grounds cited in the *Code* are employed as euphemisms or proxies for notions of race[54]. As most people have come to know that they cannot explicitly differentiate and judge people based on their race, racial discrimination often takes the shape of employing other less stigmatized notions and terms in the place of racial ones. Even those who experience racial discrimination often feel reluctant to employ explicitly racial notions and terms. For example, instances of racial discrimination may make reference to a person's accent or place of origin as a proxy for race. It is appropriate to cite related grounds of the *Code* together with race in instances where racial discrimination employs these descriptors as euphemisms or proxies for race.

In practice, it is often difficult to tell specifically what underlies racial discrimination. A First Nations woman may be discriminated against based on the colour of her skin or because of stereotypes associated with her ethnic origin or her ancestry, or with some distaste for the practices of her creed or by some combination of these factors. All are possibilities and it is often

[54]See for greater detail J. A. Rummens, "Operationalizing Race and Its Related Grounds in Ontario Human Rights Policy" (2004) 3:3 Canadian Diversity 7.

difficult to distinguish these in specific instances. In such situations, race, being a social construct, can encompass other related grounds within its meaning, but in practice it may be preferable to cite every ground which may have been a factor in an individual's experience.

2.3.3 — Intersectional and Overlapping Grounds

Several prohibited grounds stipulated by the *Code* have less direct relationship with the ground of race including for example the grounds of gender, disability, age, family status and sexual orientation. Nevertheless, a person's experience of discrimination can be impacted by these other grounds.

Acts of discrimination often accompany people in relationship to overlapping and intersecting[55] identifications as much as to any single identification. Individuals, based on their unique combination of identities, may be exposed to unique forms of discrimination and may uniquely experience the personal pain and social harm that accompanies acts of discrimination.

Correspondingly, instances of racial discrimination may occur in intersection with other grounds of the *Code* to form unique and meaningful combinations. For example a young Black man can be seen as a "Black person," or as a "young person," or as a "man." All these sources of identity overlap but in addition also intersect in a socially significant way. Such a person may be exposed to discrimination based on any of the grounds of race and/or colour, age and gender independently when these identifications do not mix in specific circumstances in any significant way. However, such a person may also be exposed to an intersectional form of discrimination on the basis of being identified as a "young Black man" based on the various assumptions and/or stereotypes that are uniquely associated with this socially significant intersection.

The Commission will look to all possible implications of intersecting and overlapping identities in its application of the *Code* and expects others in society to similarly recognize this diversity. Accordingly, it is important to consider possible intersections when allegations of racial discrimination are raised and, when circumstances indicate it, to cite the prohibited ground of race along with other grounds when intersections are apparent.

---

[55]The Commission has repeatedly recognized the importance of applying an intersectional approach to discrimination involving multiple grounds as well as the particular relevance of the intersectional approach for racial discrimination complaints. See Ontario Human Rights Commission, *An Intersectional Approach to Discrimination: Addressing Multiple Grounds in Human Rights Claims* (October 2001), online: www.ohrc.on.ca.

2.4 — Racism and Racial Discrimination — Common "Myths"

Discussions of racism and racial discrimination often evoke a different type of response than when other types of human rights concerns are raised. In fact, there is a set of common "myths" that frequently come into play when racism and racial discrimination are raised. These myths serve to silence persons who speak out against racism and racial discrimination, hamper efforts to combat racism and racial discrimination and even affect the ability of decision-makers to objectively deal with claims of racism and racial discrimination.[56]

Some of the most common myths and misconceptions about racism and racial discrimination include:

- racism is exaggerated and that, except for exceptional cases or the actions of a "few bad apples," racism does not exist in Canada
- people in Canada are "colour blind" and do not even notice race
- mentioning the existence of racism or racial discrimination or taking proactive measures to address racism or racial discrimination constitutes reverse racism towards White people
- racialized people are less credible and their assertions must be more carefully scrutinized and investigated or must be corroborated
- racialized people play the "race card" to manipulate people or systems to get what they want
- racialized people are too sensitive, tend to overreact or have a "chip on their shoulder"
- racialized people themselves, and not racism or racial discrimination, are at fault for their disadvantage or state of "otherness," commonly known as "blaming it on the victim"
- immigration is bad for Canada as immigrants take jobs away, commit more crime, are a drain on the system or do not fit into our society and
- if a racialized person has been treated acceptably in the past, then discriminatory treatment cannot take place in the future.[57]

---

[56]For a discussion of five assumptions that have played out in human rights tribunals' analysis of race cases, see R. Dhir, "Common Myths and Misconceptions about Racial Discrimination: A Case Study" (2nd Annual Human Rights Symposium: Focus on Racial Discrimination, May 2003).

[57]In particular, see *Smith v. Mardana*, *infra*, note 79. The Tribunal had reasoned, "[w]hy would the very people who hired him, who were impressed by him, who promoted him, and who accommodated his school schedule in terms of working hours, suddenly make a decision against him on his race?" at para. 23. However,

These myths create a climate that prevents any kind of effective response to racial inequality.[58]

Part II — The Policy Framework

3. — Types of Racial Discrimination

It is not possible to slot people's experiences of racial discrimination into clear categories. Manifestations of discrimination blur together and overlap to a large degree. However, for the purposes of this policy, it is necessary to describe the different ways in which racial discrimination can take place. Therefore, what follows is a discussion of the main ways in which racial discrimination can occur that are helpful in understanding and addressing the experience of racial discrimination.

3.1 — Stereotyping and Prejudice

Although racial discrimination has become more subtle and concealed, stereotyping, prejudice and bias remain a reality in a variety of areas including but not limited to workplaces, housing accommodation, stores, malls, restaurants, hospitals, schools and the justice system.

One of the most obvious ways in which people experience racial discrimination is through stereotyping. Stereotyping can be described as a process by which people use social categories such as race, colour, ethnic origin, place of origin, religion, *etc.*, in acquiring, processing and recalling information about others.[59] Stereotyping typically involves attributing the same characteristics to all members of a group, regardless of their individual differences. It is often based on misconceptions, incomplete information and/or false generalizations. Practical experience and psychology both confirm that anyone can stereotype, even those who are well meaning and not overtly biased. While it may be somewhat natural for humans to engage in racial stereotyping it is nevertheless unacceptable.

In most cases, stereotypes ascribe negative characteristics to a group. It is impossible to describe all the generalizations that people may reach about others. However, they tend to include assumptions that racialized persons as

---

the Divisional Court recognized this as a common myth and one that inappropriately focused on the motivation of the respondents, which does not properly form part of the analysis of whether racial discrimination occurred.

[58]See also Henry, Tator, Mattis & Rees, *supra*, note 18 at pp 384-5.

[59]*Paying the Price: The Human Cost of Racial Profiling*, *supra*, note 7 at 6.

a whole, or specific racialized groups, are unintelligent, lazy, unreliable, dirty, uncivilized, promiscuous, submissive, more likely to abuse drugs or alcohol, of questionable moral character, more likely to engage in criminal activity or alien (*i.e.*, do not fit into Canadian society).

In some cases, "positive stereotypes" may be at play, (*e.g.*, generalizations that members of a particular group are math whizzes, great athletes or dutiful employees). It is also important not to minimize the harmful effects of these types of "positive stereotypes" in that they can also result in unequal treatment. For example, an educator who encourages African Canadian students only towards sports and discourages academics, thinking that they will only go far in school as good athletes, may be, in fact, failing to support them in their educational interests and aspirations. The students may come to believe these stereotypes, thereby giving priorities to their athletic roles at the expense of their academic performance and educational achievements.[60]

Stereotypes are insidious both because they can be acted upon in a way that results in unequal treatment, but also because they may be internalized by their subjects who, as a result, believe or accept the stereotypes.

Many racial discrimination complaints allege that a respondent has relied, usually obliquely, on stereotypes.

> *Example*: A landlord didn't rent an apartment to a Black woman, in part, because of a stereotype that Black people are indigent and noisy. A Tribunal held[61] that where racial stereotyping is one of the factors in a decision not to rent a residential unit, this would constitute a violation of the *Code*.[62]
>
> *Example*: An Aboriginal woman was evicted from a hotel and denied service in the lounge. The tribunal found it particularly offensive that

[60] C. James, "Stereotyping and its consequence for racial minority youth" (2004) 3:3 Canadian Diversity 40 at 42.

[61] *Richards v. Waisglass* (1994), 24 C.H.R.R. D/51 (Ont. Bd. Inq.).

[62] See also *Fuller v. Daoud* (2001), 40 C.H.R.R. D/306 (Ont. Bd. Inq.) where the Tribunal found that the respondent, a White woman, falsely accused her Black male tenant of threatening to rape her. The Commission argued that this allegation had particularly serious consequences for the complainant because it "mobilized a history of racist views about White fear of Black men to White womanhood" at para. 78.

the hotel owner assumed that the woman was a prostitute because she was a single Aboriginal woman in a hotel by herself.[63]

Racial discrimination also occurs because of overt prejudice, an antipathy or negative feelings held by someone about another person or a group.

Example: An employer rejected a Black candidate for a job position after meeting her. He was visibly shocked and turned her down flat, without any inquiry regarding her credentials. When asked what was wrong he said something about maintaining the company image.[64]

Example: Two women of Aboriginal ancestry were seeking to rent a house. Upon learning that they were Aboriginal, the owner's wife stated she didn't rent to "Indians" and made further disparaging comments. She then asked what the women did and when one of the women said she was on social assistance, responded "That's just as bad."[65]

Racial stereotyping and prejudice can also lead to racial harassment (discussed below).

3.2 — Racial Profiling

The Commission has defined racial profiling as any action undertaken for reasons of safety, security or public protection that relies on stereotypes about race, colour, ethnicity, ancestry, religion or place of origin, rather than on reasonable suspicion, to single out an individual for greater scrutiny or different treatment. Its practice is not limited to any one group of people or particular institution.

The Commission has stated that racial profiling is, at its heart, a form of stereotyping based on preconceived ideas about a person's character. As

---

[63] *Frank v. A.J.R. Enterprises Ltd.* (1993), 23 C.H.R.R. D/228 (B.C.C.H.R.).

[64] In *Payne v. Otsuka Pharmaceutical Co. (No. 3)* (2002), 44 C.H.R.R. D/203 (Ont. Bd. Inq), a pharmaceutical company did not allow the complainant, after meeting her, to act as their receptionist at an exhibit booth during a conference for Canadian ophthalmologists. The Tribunal concluded the complainant was rejected because she was Black and accordingly held the company liable. The Tribunal, however, also held the conference organizers liable for assisting the pharmaceutical company in locating other individuals to act as the pharmaceutical company's receptionist without properly investigating Ms. Payne's allegations of racial discrimination.

[65] *DesRosiers v. Kaur* (2000), 37 C.H.R.R. D/204 (B.C.H.R.T.).

human rights are founded on the need to ensure individualized decision-making about individuals, instead of judgments based on presumed characteristics, racial profiling is a form of racial discrimination and can result in complaints to the Commission.

The Ontario Court of Appeal has recognized the inherent problem with evidence needed to prove a racial profiling case. The Court has noted that racial profiling can rarely be proven by direct evidence and therefore if racial profiling is to be proven, it must be done by inference drawn from circumstantial evidence.[66] Race only needs to be a factor in the conduct alleged to constitute profiling. It need not be the main or major cause of the adverse treatment and racial profiling can be found to have occurred even if race was mixed in with other legitimate factors.[67]

In order to prove an allegation of profiling, it must be shown that the person alleged to have profiled had some opportunity to observe or presume the race of the complainant.[68] If this is demonstrated, it is necessary to determine whether this knowledge led the person alleged to have profiled to act in a discriminatory way. The following considerations will be relevant to determining whether racial profiling was an element in a particular situation:

- Statements were made that indicate the existence of stereotyping or prejudice: racial slurs, statements suggesting that someone is viewed as "foreign" (*e.g.*, "In this country we don't. . .," "Do you speak English?") comments that are indicative of stereotypes (*e.g.*, "What are you doing in this neighbourhood?,"[69] "You have to pay for this cab ride upfront.")
- Actions corresponded to the phenomenon of racial profiling.[70]

---

[66] *R. v. Brown* (2003), 64 O.R. (3d) 161 (C.A.). See also, *R. v. Richards* (1999), 120 O.A.C. 344 (C.A.), *Peart v. Peel (Regional Municipality) Police Services Board*, [2003] O.J. No. 2669 (Sup. Ct.) and *R. v. Khan* (2004), 244 D.L.R. (4th) 443 (Ont. Sup. Ct.).

[67] *Johnson v. Halifax (Regional Municipality) Police Service*, *supra*, note 51 at para. 8.

[68] *Ibid.* at para. 10.

[69] For a discussion of stereotypes that have triggered heightened scrutiny of Black men, see D.M. Tanovich, "E-Racing Racial Profiling" (2004) 41 Alta. L. Rev. 905–933.

[70] *R. v. Brown*, *supra*, note 66 at 174 (C.A.).

- A non-existent, contradictory or changing explanation is given for why someone was subjected to greater scrutiny or differential treatment or an explanation is offered that does not accord with common sense.[71]
- The situation unfolded differently than if the person had been White.[72]
- There were deviations from the normal practice.[73]
- An unprofessional manner was used or the person was subjected to discourteous treatment.[74]

Example: Two Black men in a Texas-registered black Ford Mustang were pursued by a Halifax Police Constable and stopped. The Constable asked for proof of insurance and vehicle registration but did not accept the validity of the documents offered or the explanations given. He ticketed the driver, and ordered the car towed. In fact, the documentation was valid under Texas law. The seizure was erroneous and the car was released the following day. In finding racial discrimination, the

---

[71] In *R. v. Khan*, *supra*, note 66, the police officers' explanation for why they stopped Mr. Khan and searched his car was found to be inconsistent with the documentary evidence and to defy common sense. Accordingly, the Court concluded that the reasonable inference was that Mr. Khan was stopped because of racial profiling, because he was a young Black male driving an expensive Mercedes.

[72] "In order to consider if differential treatment has occurred, the board must necessarily hypothesize about how events would have unfolded if the driver and passenger of the vehicle had been White rather than Black. . . . I find it difficult to imagine that these events would have unfolded the same way if a White driver from Texas had been involved in this stop." *Johnson v. Halifax (Regional Municipality) Police Service*, *supra*, note 51 at para. 51 and 57.

See also *Hum v. Royal Canadian Mounted Police* (1986), 8 C.H.R.R. D/3748 (C.H.R.T.): "Although Mr. Hum was quite legitimately pulled over and asked for his license, registration and insurance slip, there was no warrant for asking him questions about his citizenship and place of birth in circumstances in which a Caucasian exhibiting the same conduct and speaking and dressed in the same way would not have been so challenged." [at para. 29697].

[73] In *Johnson v. Halifax Regional Police Service*, *ibid*. at para. 57, the Nova Scotia Board of Inquiry held that in deciding whether there has been a *prima facie* case of differential treatment, a board of inquiry must try to establish how events normally unfold in a given situation. Deviations from normal practice and evidence of discourtesy or intransigence are grounds for finding differential treatment.

[74] *Ibid*. The Board of Inquiry found that the unprofessional manner in which the complainant was treated during a traffic stop was based on the complainant's race and that it would be hard to imagine similar treatment of a White driver.

> Board of Inquiry concluded that the Constable's actions were influenced by a racial stereotype of Black male criminality. In addition to over $15,000 in monetary damages and costs, the Board ordered institutional remedies. The Halifax Regional Police Service was required to hire consultants to assess the effectiveness of the Service's anti-racism and diversity training policies, to make the report public and to publicly indicate what steps the Service has taken and will take in light of the report.[75]

Finally, it is important to note that persons who reasonably believe they are being racially profiled can be expected to find the experience upsetting and might well react in an angry and verbally aggressive manner. A citizen who honestly and reasonably believes that he or she is being treated unjustly is entitled to protest vigorously, as long as there is no resort to threatening gestures to accompany the words. A Tribunal has stated that a person's use of abusive language in these circumstances requires reasonable tolerance and tact and cannot form the basis for further differential treatment.[76]

3.3 — Subtle Racial Discrimination

While racial discrimination is sometimes displayed overtly, it is recognized that in many instances racial discrimination takes on more subtle and covert forms. Tribunals have frequently noted: "Discrimination is not a practice which one would expect to see displayed overtly"[77] and that it is "often subversive and subtle."[78] It has long been established in Canadian law that intent or motive to discriminate is not a necessary element for finding that a discriminatory act took place. It is sufficient if there is a discriminatory ef-

---

[75] *Ibid.*

[76] See *Johnson v. Halifax (Regional Municipality) Police Service*, *ibid.* at para. 41 and 60. Also, in *Hum*, *supra*, note 72 at para. 29696 and 29697, the Tribunal recognized the broader social and historical context that informed the complainant's feelings of concern, hurt and resentment when he was pulled over and asked questions about his citizenship and place of birth.

[77] From *Basi v. Canadian National Railway Co. (No. 1)* (1988), 9 C.H.R.R. D/5029 at para. 38481 (C.H.R.T.).

[78] *Raheja v. Newfoundland (Human Rights Commission)* (1997), 155 Nfld. & P.E.I.R. 38 at para. 32.

fect to the conduct.[79] Racial discrimination need only be one of several reasons for the decision or treatment received.[80]

Subtle forms of discrimination can often only be detected upon examining all of the circumstances.[81] Individual acts themselves may be ambiguous or explained away, but when viewed as part of the larger picture and with an appropriate understanding of how racial discrimination takes place, may lead to an inference that racial discrimination was a factor in the treatment an individual received.

Cases alleging subtle discrimination will therefore require an investigation and analysis that examines the total context of the behaviour, comment or conduct alleged, including the presence or absence of comparative evidence contrasting how others were treated in a comparable situation or evidence that a pattern of behaviour exists.

There are many examples of how subtle forms of racial discrimination may occur. It can be particularly difficult to determine whether racial discrimination was a factor in hiring. Where a racialized person is qualified and someone else, no better qualified, is selected, the organization will need to provide a non-discriminatory explanation for failing to hire the racialized person.[82] Discrimination in the hiring process may be established even if

---

[79] *Ontario Human Rights Commission and O'Malley v. Simpson-Sears Ltd.*, [1985] 2 S.C.R. 536. This was again confirmed in *Smith v. Mardana Ltd.* (2005), CHRR Doc. 05-094 (Ont. Div. Ct.); rev'g in part (2002), 44 C.H.R.R. D/142 (Ont. Bd. Inq.).

[80] *Gray v. A & W Food Service of Canada Ltd.* (1994), CHRR Doc. 94-146 (Ont. Bd. Inq.), *Dominion Management v. Velenosi* (1997), 148 D.L.R. (4th) 575 at 576 (Ont. C.A.), *Smith v. Mardana Ltd.* (Div. Ct.) *ibid.* at para. 22.

[81] In *Grover v. National Research Council of Canada (No. 1)* (1992), 18 C.H.R.R. D/1 (C.H.R.T.), the Tribunal recognized that in weighing the evidence, one often has to assess circumstantial evidence in order to identify "the subtle scent of discrimination" [at para. 158].

[82] The precise test is set out in *Lasani v. Ontario (Ministry of Community and Social Services) (No. 2)* (1993), 21 C.H.R.R. D/415 at para. 50 (Ont. Bd. Inq.). The Tribunal also stated:

> I entirely accept the view urged upon me by the Commission that where ethnic prejudice is a reality, but a secret, unadmitted reality, a board of inquiry should look very carefully at the proffered explanations for failure to hire or failure to promote members of ethnic communities who are otherwise qualified for a position, but are not hired or promoted. [at para. 54.]

the complainant would not have been the successful candidate in the absence of discrimination.[83]

On the job, the following types of treatment may be indicative of racial discrimination:

- Exclusion from formal or informal networks
- Denial of mentoring or developmental opportunities such as secondments and training which was made available to others
- Differential management practices such as excessive monitoring and documentation or deviation from written policies or standard practices when dealing with a racialized person
- Disproportionate blame for an incident[84]
- Assignment to less desirable positions or job duties[85]
- Treating normal differences of opinion as confrontational or insubordinate when involved with racialized persons
- Characterizing normal communication from racialized persons as rude or aggressive[86]

---

[83]*Abdolalipour v. Allied Chemical Canada Ltd.* (1996), C.H.R.R. Doc. 96-153 at para. 188 (Ont. Bd. Inq.).

[84]See *Smith v. Mardana Ltd.* (Div. Ct.) *supra*, note 79 at paras. 15-16. Also, in *McKinnon v. Ontario (Ministry of Correctional Services) (No. 3)* (1998), 32 C.H.R.R. D/1 (Ont. Bd. Inq.), the complainant was moved to a less desirable posting for making a mistake that was quite common. No one else had been reassigned after making the same type of mistake.

[85]In *Nelson v. Durham Board of Education (No. 3)* (1998), 33 C.H.R.R. D/504 (Ont. Bd. Inq.), the Tribunal found that taking away the complainant's "release time," time away from teaching to allow administrators to focus on administrative skills to prepare for non-classroom roles within the school board, constituted direct discrimination:

> The unfavourable proposals of release time appeared to have been an effective tool to stifle the ambitions of a dedicated qualified teacher who, because of his race, was unwelcome in the upper echelons of the Durham School Board. [at para. 136.]

[86]In *Nelson, ibid.* at para. 131, the Tribunal found that an interviewer's conduct during an interview was "egregious and created a climate of racial hostility, that was tolerated by other Durham Board officials." The interviewer had turned his back to the complainant throughout the interview except to admonish the complainant for being "aggressive" in response to an interviewer's oversight of his Masters degree.

- Penalizing a racialized person for failing to get along with someone else (*e.g.*, a coworker or manager), when one of the reasons for the tension is racially discriminatory attitudes or behaviour of the co-worker or manager.[87]

In some instances, a non-discriminatory explanation may be available for such treatment. However, subjective explanations such as "bad attitude" or undocumented "poor performance" will be received with caution. It is therefore in an organization's best interest to engage in good human resources practices, such as documented progressive performance management of all employees. It has also been established that an individual's behaviour may itself be a reaction to the experience of discrimination or the existence of a poisoned environment.[88]

In housing accommodation, subtle screening methods may be used to deny racialized applicants equal access to housing:

- Racialized persons may be advised that an apartment has already been rented only to have a White friend inquire about the availability of the accommodation and be told that it is still available.
- Tenants may not be granted equal access to housing related services because of race and related grounds. This may be in the form of substandard living conditions or failing to carry out repairs.[89]

---

[87] In *Smith v. Mardana Ltd.*, *supra*, note 79, the owner of the company had threatened to dismiss the complainant because of his strained relationship with an acting manager. However, this relationship was tainted by the acting manager's racist attitudes.

[88] *Naraine v. Ford Motor Co. of Canada (No. 4)* (1996), 27 C.H.R.R. D/230 (No. 4) (Ont. Bd. Inq.); aff'd (1999), 34 C.H.R.R. D/405 (Ont. Ct. (Gen. Div.)); Board of Inquiry's order upheld except with respect to the issue of reinstatement (2001), 41 C.H.R.R. D/349 (Ont. C.A.); leave to appeal denied [2002] S.C.C.A. No. 69.

[89] A landlord may discriminate by failing to carry out repairs for a single tenant or for failing to carry out repairs throughout a building that is predominantly rented to a racialized group:

> In my opinion, the utterances and conduct of Mr. Elieff as reported by Mr. Van Moorsel in the *London Free Press* created a poisoned environment. By implying that Cambodians did not deserve decent living conditions, he infringed the rights of Cambodians under s. 2(1) of the *Code* . . .because of race or place of origin, even though all other tenants who were not Cambodian were subject to the same deplorable conditions. [*Ontario (Human Rights Commission) v. Elieff* (1996), 37 C.H.R.R. D/248 at para. 16 (Ont. Gen. Div.)]

- Discrimination may occur as a result of issues being made about the cultural practices of tenants.[90]

  Example: A Black man responded to an ad for an apartment and was invited to view it. After the viewing he was told that another person was coming to view the suite and that he would be advised if it would be available. On phoning the landlord he was told that the suite had been rented. However, when his girlfriend's sister phoned back, she was told the suite was still available. The Tribunal rejected the landlord's evidence that the man's demeanour made her uncomfortable and the evidence of another tenant, a woman of Chinese origin, that the landlord could not have practised racial discrimination *vis-à-vis* the Black man, as she had rented a suite to her.[91]

In the context of education services, subtle forms of discrimination can manifest in a number of ways including:[92]

- how educators treat racialized students

---

[90]For example, cooking odours have been the subject of two Tribunal decisions. In one case, the Tribunal found that South Asian tenants were denied an apartment because of stereotypes regarding cooking odours; *Fancy v. J & M Apartments Ltd.* (1991), 14 C.H.R.R. D/389 (B.C.C.H.R.). In another, the complainant was found to have cooked foods in her home that were an expression of her ethnicity and ancestry which produced odours. She experienced differential treatment when she was ordered to cease producing these odours or face eviction. The right to express and enjoy one's ethnicity and ancestry was found to be central to one's dignity. Moreover, the landlord was not found to have a reasonable and *bona fide* justification for its conduct; see *Chauhan v. Norkam Seniors Housing Cooperative Association*, 2004 B.C.H.R.T. 262.

[91]*Wattley v. Quail* (1988), 9 C.H.R.R. D/5386 (B.C.C.H.R.); see also *Grant v. Wilcock* (1990), 13 C.H.R.R. D/22 (Ont. Bd. Inq.). In that case Mrs. Grant, who was White, went to view a cottage she and her husband were interested in purchasing. When Mr. Grant, who was Black, attended to view the cottage, the respondent said he was probably going to sell the cottage to his brother and that he would let the Grants know. Mrs. Grant phoned several times but did not receive a satisfactory answer regarding the cottage. Her mother phoned and was told that the cottage was still up for sale. The respondent told the mother that a man had been interested in purchasing it but he was Black and the respondent would not sell to him.

[92]For a discussion of racism in education see *Racism in our Schools: What to Know About It; How to Fight It*, Report prepared for the Canadian Race Relations Foundation (June 2000), online: www.crr.ca/en/Publications/ePubHome.htm. Also,

- whether racialized students are encouraged to pursue technical versus academic streams
- low teacher expectation of racialized students
- differential disciplinary action directed toward racialized students
- deviating from written policies or standard practices when it comes to dealing with racialized students
- failing to deal with racial incidents or bullying between children or downplaying the seriousness of such conduct and
- treating a racialized student's response to racial incidents or bullying as a disciplinary problem without dealing with the underlying incident or considering the underlying incident as a mitigating factor.

Issues can also arise in other service areas.

> *Example*: An Aboriginal man reserved a room at an inn and was given a dirty, substandard room. There was statistical evidence drawn from the hotel's records that certain rooms were more often assigned to Aboriginal clients and that better rooms were more often assigned to non-Native clients. In addition, a local police officer who phoned the hotel on behalf of people needing accommodation was asked whether the people were Native "because all the Native rooms were occupied."[93]

It is not necessary for language or comments related to race to be present in the interactions between the parties to demonstrate that racial discrimination has occurred. However, where such comments are made, they can be further evidence that race has been a factor in an individual's treatment. Similarly, negative comments made about an individual advocating for human rights or equitable practices will tend to support an inference that race is a factor in an individual's or organization's interaction with that individual.[94]

> *Example*: A Black Vice Principal repeatedly tried to secure a promo-

---

with regard to educational issues for Aboriginal students, see *Report of the Special Rapporteur on Indigenous People*, *supra*, note 17.

[93]*Angeconeb v. 517152 Ontario Ltd.* (1993), 19 C.H.R.R. D/452 (Ont. Bd. Inq.).

[94]Refusing to hire someone because they are perceived as a "troublemaker" as a result of having made a previous human rights complaint against the respondent or other organizations, has also been found to be discriminatory; see *Abouchar v. Toronto (Metro) School Board (No. 3)* (1998), 31 C.H.R.R. D/411 (Ont. Bd. Inq.). It could also constitute a reprisal under s. 8 of the *Code*.

> tion to the position of Principal. In looking at the totality of the evidence, the Tribunal found that irrelevant references to the race of the complainant and a Black teacher by management staff during interviews and/or discussions about transfer opportunities as well as admonishments to Black teachers who advocated for equitable practices "not to expect things to change overnight" supported an inference that transfer and promotion decisions were influenced by considerations of race.[95]

Where racial discrimination prohibited by the *Code* is alleged, "everyday racism" can form part of the context in assessing whether subtle racial discrimination is at play. Such cases will normally require an element of recurrence and repetitiveness[96] as well as an examination of how others in comparable situations were treated.[97]

> *Example*: A manager frequently rolls his eyes or interrupts when a racialized employee speaks during staff meetings, even though nothing

[95]*Nelson, supra,* note 85.

[96]See P. Essed, "Everyday Racism: A New Approach to the Study of Racism" in P. Essed & D.T. Goldberg, eds., *Race Critical Theories* (Malden: Blackwell Publishers Ltd., 2002) 176 at 177 and 190.

> "The fact that it concerns repetitive practices indicates that everyday racism consists of practices that can be generalized." at 177.

[97]It is important to note that it is very difficult to determine "objectively" the nature of everyday interactions between non-racialized and racialized persons. A variety of studies show that the perspectives of those who experience everyday racism are very different than that of White persons who have not themselves experienced these daily slights; see Henry, Tator, Mattis & Rees, *supra,* note 18 at 55 and 61. While the case law in this area is still in a state of development, it generally adopts an approach to discrimination that looks at the action or conduct from both a subjective and objective perspective. This analysis takes into account the claimants' or the groups' traits, history and circumstances to determine whether a reasonable person or people comparably situated would find the treatment demeaning; see *Pringle v. Alberta (Human Rights, Multiculturalism and Citizenship Commission)* (2004), CHRR Doc. 04-430, 2004 ABQB 821 at para. 46; *Gwinner v. Alberta (Minister of Human Resources and Employment)* (2002), 44 C.H.R.R. D/52, 2002 ABQB 685 at para. 112, affirmed (2004), CHRR Doc. 04-151, 2004 ABCA 210, leave to appeal denied [2004] S.C.C.A. No. 342. However, only in rare cases is differential treatment based on a *Code* ground not discriminatory; see *Pringle* at para. 49. This may be particularly so where the differential treatment is based on "race" and related grounds.

> untoward is being said. The manager is not observed to do this with other employees. When the relationship between the employee and manager becomes excessively tense, the racialized person's employment is terminated. The explanation provided is his failure to get along with his manager.

Similar fact evidence will be used to support an allegation of racial discrimination where appropriate.[98] In addition, recognizing that most racialized persons are more likely to see discrimination that remains invisible to others, it is the Commission's position that a perception of discrimination by others may have some relevance in a complaint.[99]

Evidence that an individual who shares the racialized characteristics of the complainant *has not* experienced discrimination may or may not have relevance, depending on the nature of the allegations of discrimination. General allegations of failing to promote "minorities" may call for an examination of whether an organization has promoted other "minorities." However, with regard to a specific allegation regarding the treatment of African Canadians, evidence regarding treatment of Chinese Canadians may be of little or no use. This is due to the fact that racial discrimination can manifest very differently based on each person's racialized characteristics. This is particularly so among racialized groups but it can also be the case within a group.

---

[98]Similar fact evidence has been used in a number of race cases. For example, in *Nelson*, *supra*, note 85, similar fact evidence concerning the treatment of a Black teacher was found to be supportive of the complainant's testimony as the details of his experiences mirrored those of the complainant. In *Dhillon v. F.W. Woolworth Ltd.* (1982), 3 C.H.R.R. D/743 (Ont. Bd. Inq.), a complainant of "East Indian" ancestry alleged racial name calling by White co-workers and racial discrimination in the allotment of holidays, the distribution of workload and rates of dismissal. He was permitted to introduce evidence of co-workers of "East Indian" background who had also experienced racial name-calling and of the demotion of another worker of "East Indian" ancestry.

[99]In finding that a co-worker's perception of racism provided some evidence of discrimination, a Tribunal noted:

> It is widely accepted that discrimination has an invisible face. Those who discriminate usually fail to see that they are discriminating. This does not mean that it is invisible to others. . .It would be a mistake to reduce the process of adjudication to a contest between the perceptions on either side of the case. I nevertheless think that impressions, even mere impressions, may have some probative value. [*Brooks v. Canada (Dept. of Fisheries and Oceans) (No. 2)* (2004), CHRR Doc. 04-384, 2004 CHRT 36 at paras. 109 to 111.]

For example, a person who speaks with a South Asian accent and wears South Asian cultural clothing may have a very different experience than someone who is seen to be more "assimilated," a light skinned person may have a different experience than someone with darker skin; and a person may be singled out for harsh treatment while others are not because the person refuses to fit a stereotype, or asserts his or her rights.

Since anyone can engage or participate in discrimination, asserting that racial discrimination could not have occurred because a person alleged to be involved is himself or herself a racialized person is also not necessarily a defence.

3.4 — Racial Harassment

3.4.1 — Code *Protections for Harassment*

Section 5(2) of the *Code* provides that all employees have a right to freedom from harassment in the workplace by the employer, employer's agent, or by another employee because of, among other grounds, race, colour, ancestry, place of origin, ethnic origin, citizenship and creed. This right to be free from harassment includes the workplace but also the "extended workplace" (*i.e.*, events that occur outside of the physical workplace or regular work hours but which have implications for the workplace such as business trips, company parties or other company related functions).

Section 2(2) of the *Code* provides that every person who occupies accommodation has a right to freedom from harassment by the landlord or agent of the landlord or by an occupant of the same building because of, among other grounds, race, colour, ancestry, place of origin, ethnic origin, citizenship and creed.

The *Code* contains no explicit provisions dealing with harassment in the areas of services, goods and facilities (section 1 of the *Code*), contracts (section 3 of the *Code*) or membership in trade and vocational associations (section 6 of the *Code*). However, it is the position of the Commission that racial harassment in such situations would constitute a violation of sections 1, 3 and 6 of the *Code*, which provide for a right to equal treatment without discrimination with respect to services, goods and facilities, contracts and membership in trade and vocational associations.

3.4.2 — What Constitutes Harassment

Harassment is defined in section 10(1) of the *Code* as "engaging in a course of vexatious comment or conduct that is known or ought reasonably to be known to be unwelcome."

The reference to comment or conduct "that is known or ought reasonably to be known to be unwelcome" establishes a subjective and objective test for harassment. The harasser's own knowledge of how his or her behaviour is being received is the subjective part of the test. The objective component considers, from the point of view of a "reasonable" third party, how such behaviour would generally be received. The determination of the point of view of a "reasonable" third party must take into account the perspective of the person who is harassed.[100]

Tribunals have accepted the particular impact that racial terms have on racialized persons. When White people in positions of power insult Black or other racialized individuals in racially abusive terms, their words reflect society's judgments about the superiority of White people and the inferiority of others. Racist language has this effect, whether or not it is intended, because these judgments are built into the meanings of the words.[101]

In many situations it should be obvious that the racially based conduct or comments will be offensive or unwelcome. While the Commission will assess each case on its merits, the following types of behaviours would in most instances be considered "a course of comment or conduct which ought reasonably to be known to be unwelcome":

- racial epithets, slurs or jokes
- being subjected to racial name-calling or nicknames[102]
- racial cartoons or graffiti
- comments ridiculing individuals because of race-related characteristics, religious dress, *etc.*
- singling out an individual for teasing or jokes related to race, ancestry, place of origin or ethnic origin
- being subjected to inappropriate references to racist organizations such as the Ku Klux Klan or
- circulating racially offensive jokes, pictures or cartoons by e-mail or having a racially offensive screensaver.

It is important to note that conduct or comments which involve a person's race may not, on their face, seem offensive. However, they may still be "unwelcome" from the perspective of a particular individual. If the indivi-

---

[100] *Dhanjal v. Air Canada* (1996), 28 C.H.R.R. D/367 (C.H.R.T.).

[101] *Fuller v. Daoud* (2001), 40 C.H.R.R. D/306 at para. 84 (Ont. Bd. Inq.).

[102] *McKinnon v. Ontario (Minister of Correctional Services), supra,* note 84, *Naraine v. Ford Motor Company, supra,* note 88, *Smith v. Mardana, supra,* note 79.

dual objects and if a similar behaviour is repeated, it may constitute a violation of the *Code*.

In addition, the comments or conduct need not be explicitly racial in order to constitute racial harassment:

> *Example*: In a workplace, only the Hispanic employees are made the brunt of demeaning practical jokes and teasing. An inference may be drawn from the particular circumstances that the treatment was racial harassment, even though the practical jokes and teasing contained no reference to race.

If an individual objects to behaviour, this will provide strong support for a conclusion that the behaviour was known or ought reasonably to have been known to be unwelcome. At the same time, however, it is important to recognize that persons experiencing racial harassment may not object and may even appear to be going along with or participating in the comments or conduct.

Tribunals have recognized that this type of response is understandable and does not defeat a complaint of harassment. Some persons who are experiencing harassment do not object because they are in a vulnerable situation, are afraid of the consequences of speaking out, or are internalizing the stress through quiet acceptance. Others can be expected to respond with outbursts, by becoming angry or emotional or by using strong language, including retaliating with racial comments.[103]

It is not possible for an individual to contract out of his or her human rights. As well, employers, landlords and service providers have an obligation to maintain an environment that is free of discrimination and harassment, whether or not anyone objects. Therefore, arguing that a racialized person accepted, condoned or participated in harassment or discrimination will not provide a defence.

3.4.3 — Harassment Based on Multiple Grounds

As with racial discrimination, people sometimes experience racial harassment in complex ways based on the intersection of multiple grounds. For example, the experience of racial harassment will often differ for men and women. This is because people often experience distinctive forms of stereotyping based on the combination of race and gender. Similarly, factors

---

[103] *Naraine v. Ford Motor Company* (1996), *ibid.*

such as sexual orientation, disability, age, language[104] and religion can give rise to a unique and complex experience of racial harassment.

Racial stereotypes about the sexuality of women have played a part in a number of sexual harassment complaints. Women may be targeted because of a belief that based on racialized characteristics, they are more sexually available, more likely to be submissive to male authority, more vulnerable, *etc*.

> *Example*: A woman of mixed Métis and Black ancestry was subjected to a serious course of sexual comments by her employer that repeatedly referenced his preference for Black women and the physical characteristics of Black and African women. She was also subjected to physical touching and pornography. The Tribunal found that her employer sexually and racially harassed her because she is a young Black woman over whom, as her employer, he could assert economic power and control. He repeatedly diminished her because of his racist assumptions about the sexuality of Black women. Separate monetary damages were awarded for each of the racial and sexual harassments. The tribunal also found that the intersectionality of the harassment and discrimination exacerbated her mental anguish.[105]

It is the Commission's position that where multiple grounds intersect to produce a unique experience of discrimination or harassment, this must be acknowledged to fully address the impact of discrimination or harassment on the person who experienced it. Where the evidence indicates that harassment occurred on the basis of multiple grounds, the Commission will apply the concept of intersectionality with respect to the issue of liability and the remedy available to the complainant.

3.5 — Poisoned Environment

The *Code* definition of harassment refers to more than one incident of comment or conduct. However, even a single statement or incident, if sufficiently serious or substantial, can have an impact on a racialized person by creating a poisoned environment.[106] A consequence of creating a poisoned environment is that certain individuals are subjected to terms and conditions

---

[104] *Etienne v. Westinghouse of Canada Ltd.* (1997), 34 C.H.R.R. D/45 (Ont. Bd. Inq.). The Board found that the complainant was repeatedly harassed by his co-workers because he is a francophone and a Black person of Haitian origin.

[105] *Baylis-Flannery v. Walter DeWilde c.o.b as Tri Community Physiotherapy (No. 2)* (2003), C.H.R.R. Doc. 03-296 (H.R.T.O.).

[106] *Dhanjal v. Air Canada, supra*, note 100.

of employment, tenancy, services, etc. that are quite different from those experienced by individuals who are not subjected to those comments or conduct. Such instances give rise to a denial of equality under the *Code*.

In the employment context, tribunals have held that the atmosphere of a workplace is a condition of employment just as much as hours of work or rate of pay. A "term or condition of employment" includes the emotional and psychological circumstances of the workplace.[107] Management personnel who know or ought to know of the existence of a poisoned atmosphere but permit it to continue thereby discriminate against affected employees even if they themselves are not involved in the production of that atmosphere.[108]

While the notion of a poisoned environment has predominantly arisen in an employment context, it can apply equally where it results in unequal terms and conditions in occupancy of accommodation, the provision of services, contracting or membership in a vocational association.

A poisoned environment can specifically arise in the context of educational services. Schools have a duty to maintain a positive non-discriminatory learning environment.[109] Students are entitled to be free from a poisoned

---

[107] *Dhillon v. F.W. Woolworth* (1982), *supra*, note 98; *Naraine v. Ford Motor Company of Canada* (Ont. Bd. Inq.), *supra* note 88 at paras. 50 & 54.

[108] *Ghosh v. Domglas Inc. (No.2)* (1992), 17 C.H.R.R. D/216 at para. 76 (Ont. Bd. Inq.).

[109] See *Ross v. New Brunswick School District No. 15*, [1996] 1 S.C.R. 825, 25 C.H.R.R. D/175; *Quebec (Comm. Des droits de la personne) c. Deux-Montagnes, Comm. Scolaire* (1993), 19 C.H.R.R. D/1 (T.D.P.Q.); *Jubran v. North Vancouver School District No. 44* (2002), 42 C.H.R.R. D/273, 2002 BCHRT 10. In *Jubran*, the Tribunal held that the School Board (i) had a duty to provide an educational environment that did not expose students to discriminatory harassment, (ii) knew that students were harassing another student, and (iii) was liable for failing to take adequate measures to stop that harassment. The B.C. Supreme Court quashed the Tribunal's decision on the basis that the harassment was not linked to a protected ground under the legislation, as the complainant did not identify as gay and his harassers did not perceive him to be gay. However, the B.C. Court of Appeal reversed the Divisional Court decision finding that the complainant was protected by B.C.'s human rights legislation regardless of whether he was gay, and regardless of whether his harassers perceived him to be gay. The Court stated that the focus of the inquiry ought to be on the effect of the harassment, rather than on the intent of the harassers. The Court of Appeal also held that the school board was liable for the discriminatory conduct of students and that the school board had failed to provide an educational environment free from discrimination: see *North Vancouver School District No. 44 v. Jubran*, [2005] B.C.J. No. 733 (C.A.).

educational environment created either by inappropriate behaviour of an education provider or by other students. Education providers have a responsibility to take immediate steps to intervene in situations where racial teasing, bullying or harassment may be taking place.

A poisoned environment is based on the nature of the comments or conduct and the impact of these on an individual rather than on the number of times the behaviour occurs. As mentioned earlier, even a single egregious incident can be sufficient to create a poisoned environment.[110]

A poisoned environment can be created by the comments or actions of any person, regardless of his or her position of authority or status in a given environment. Therefore, a co-worker, a supervisor, a co-tenant, a member of the Board of Directors, a service provider, *etc.* can all engage in conduct that poisons the environment of a racialized person.

Behaviour need not be directed at any one individual in order to create a poisoned environment. Moreover, a person can experience a poisoned environment even if he or she is not a member of the racialized group that is the target.

> *Example*: A Chinese Canadian woman worked in a bakery where racial slurs and stereotypical language were common in the kitchen. Although none of these remarks were directed specifically to her, but rather to her Black co-workers, a Board of Inquiry found that she had also been subjected to a racially poisoned environment.[111]

Examples of situations which could be viewed as a violation of the *Code* by creating a poisoned environment include the following:

- A supervisor or landlord saying to an employee or tenant "I don't know why you people don't go back where you came from because you don't belong here"
- Comments, signs, caricatures or cartoons displayed in a service environment such as a store or restaurant, or in a work or tenancy situation that shows racialized persons in a demeaning manner

---

[110] In *Dhanjal v. Air Canada*, *supra*, note 100 at para. 209, the Tribunal noted that the more serious the conduct, the less need there is for it to be repeated and, conversely, the less serious it is, the greater the need to demonstrate its persistence.

[111] *Lee v. T.J. Applebee's Food Conglomeration* (1987), 9 C.H.R.R. D/4781 (Ont. Bd. Inq.).

- Racial graffiti that is tolerated by an employer, a landlord or a service provider who does not act promptly to have the racial graffiti removed
- Racial remarks, jokes or innuendo about an employee, client, customer or tenant
- Racial remarks, jokes or innuendo made about other racialized persons or groups which may create an apprehension that similar views are held about the employee, client, customer or tenant

Where an employee is terminated within a poisoned work environment, a proper consideration of whether the termination was discriminatory requires that it be examined in the context of the poisoned work environment.[112]

Inappropriate comments or conduct not only poison the environment for racialized persons, they affect everyone's environment and are disruptive. It is the responsibility of every employer, landlord or service provider to ensure that its environment is free from this sort of behaviour, even if no one objects.

3.6 — Language-related Discrimination

While the *Code* does not include "language" as a prohibited ground of discrimination, language can be an element of a complaint based on the grounds of ancestry, ethnic origin, place of origin and race. As noted in the Commission's *Policy on Discrimination and Language*, a person's accent is related to his ancestry, ethnic origin or place of origin and as discussed earlier in this policy, accents or manners of speech can be racialized characteristics.

There can be situations where the issue of the fluency of language or a person's accent can be used to mask discrimination based on race.

> *Example*: An African Canadian woman who is involved in a disagreement with a co-worker over the phone is told by a manager that her accent can be interpreted to be "hard and rude" on the ears. The African Canadian woman is very offended by this characterization of her accent and the fact that her accent is being blamed for provoking the disagreement. When she insists on an apology from the manager, she is perceived by management to be "volatile," "difficult" and "aggressive" and singled out for performance management.

---

[112] *Smith v. Mardana Ltd.* (Ont. Div. Ct.), *supra*, note 79 at para. 24 and *Naraine v. Ford Motor Company of Canada* (Ont. Bd. Inq.), *supra*, note 88 at paras. 98 and 99.

Example: Workers from Ecuador and other Central and South American countries were treated differently and ridiculed for their use of the Spanish language, and for their inability to speak English consistent with their recent arrival in Canada.[113]

Example: A subsidized housing provider does not add an applicant to its waiting list because she is not fluent in English and will be hard to communicate with.

At the same time, it is recognized that in some circumstances proficiency in a certain language may be a reasonable and *bona fide* requirement.[114]

Example: An immigrant settlement agency that serves persons from South Asian countries requires support workers. Most of its clientele has recently arrived in Canada. Fluency in one or more South Asian languages in addition to English (or French) would likely be considered a *bona fide* requirement for the position.

3.7 — Association

The *Code* provides protection to persons who experience discrimination or harassment because of their association, relationship or dealings with a racialized person or persons.[115] This form of discrimination often arises in the context of inter-racial relationships and can manifest in several ways:

- Experiencing workplace harassment or a poisoned environment because of a relationship with a racialized person (*e.g.*, inappropriate sexual comments being made to a woman who is dating a racialized man)[116]

---

[113]See *Espinoza v. Coldmatic Refrigeration of Canada Inc.* (1995), 29 C.H.R.R. D/35 (Ont. Bd. Inq.).

[114]For a more detailed discussion please see the Commission's *Policy on Discrimination and Language* (June 1996), online: www.ohrc.on.ca.

[115]Section 12 of the *Code* states:

> A right under Part I is infringed where the discrimination is because of relationship, association or dealings with a person or persons identified by a prohibited ground of discrimination.

[116]Sexuality is sometimes intertwined with racism. Stereotypical and racist views may be held about people's sexuality based on their ethno-racial identity. See *Baylis-Flannery v. DeWilde*, *supra*, note 105. As mentioned in the section dealing with the history of racism in Canada, this form of discrimination was promoted by laws which prohibited Chinese and Japanese men from employing White women.

- Unsolicited warnings being offered to a woman that her racialized boyfriend will treat her badly because of a stereotypical assumption that "men from his part of the world are sexist"
- Experiencing differential treatment in services (*e.g.*, being stopped by police when in a car with a racialized man because of an assumption that a woman with a racialized man must be a prostitute)[117] and
- Being subjected to discrimination or harassment in housing because a landlord doesn't want a tenant's racialized friend visiting.

Racial discrimination because of association in the housing context can also arise where landlords prevent tenants from subletting to racialized persons.

> *Example*: A landlord was found to have discriminated against a tenant when he prevented him from subletting his apartment to a couple of Aboriginal ancestry.[118] In another case, a landlord was found liable for discrimination when he refused to allow assignment of a lease to persons of "East Indian" or Pakistani origin.[119]

Actions taken against persons who object to racist comments aimed at another group have been found to be discrimination because of association.

> *Example*: A woman who was a member of a club confronted other members about racist comments they made about "niggers" and "Indians." The Tribunal found that having spoken out against racism, the woman clearly associated herself with First Nations and racialized people, and that actions taken by the club because she stood up to racist comments amounted to a breach of the *Code*.[120]

For a detailed discussion, see C. Backhouse, *Colour-Coded: A Legal History of Racism in Canada, 1900–1950* (Toronto: University of Toronto Press, 1999) at 132–172.

[117]This experience was described to the Commission during its Racial Profiling Inquiry.

[118]*Québec (Comm. des droits de la personne) v. Thibodeau* (1993), 19 C.H.R.R. D/225 (Que. H.R.T.).

[119]*Tabar, Lee and Lee v. Scott and West End Construction Ltd.* (1984), 6 C.H.R.R. D/2471 (Ont. Bd. Inq.).

[120]*Barclay v. Royal Canadian Legion, Branch 12* (1997), 31 C.H.R.R. D/486 (Ont. Bd. Inq.).

3.8 — Special Interest Organizations

In certain circumstances, the *Code* permits certain types of organizations to limit participation or membership based on *Code* grounds including race and related grounds:

> 18. The rights under Part I to equal treatment with respect to services and facilities, with or without accommodation, are not infringed where membership or participation in a religious, philanthropic, educational, fraternal or social institution or organization that is primarily engaged in serving the interests of persons identified by a prohibited ground of discrimination is restricted to persons who are similarly identified.

> *Example*: A legal clinic that is primarily engaged in serving the interests of members of a specific racialized community only accepts members of that community as clients.

Similarly a religious, philanthropic, educational, fraternal or social institution that is primarily engaged in serving the interests of persons identified by their race and related grounds can give preference in employment to persons similarly identified if the qualification is reasonable and *bona fide* because of the nature of the employment (section 24(1)(a)).

An organization that wishes to rely on these defences must show it meets all of the requirements of the relevant section.

4. — Systemic or Institutional Dimensions

Racial discrimination exists not just in individual behaviour but can also be systemic or institutionalized. Systemic or institutional discrimination is one of the more complex ways in which racial discrimination occurs. Organizations and institutions have a positive obligation to ensure that they are not engaging in systemic or institutional racial discrimination.

Systemic or institutional discrimination consists of patterns of behaviour, policies or practices that are part of the social or administrative structures of an organization, and which create or perpetuate a position of relative disadvantage for racialized persons.[121] These appear neutral on the surface but,

[121]From C. Agocs, "Surfacing Racism in the Workplace: Qualitative and Quantitative Evidence of Systemic Discrimination" (2004) 3:3 Canadian Diversity 25 at 25. Other definitions have been offered; for example,

> . . .practices or attitudes that have, whether by design or impact, the effect of limiting an individual's or a group's right to the opportunities generally

nevertheless, have an exclusionary impact on racialized persons. However, systemic discrimination can overlap with other types of discrimination that are not neutral. For example, a discriminatory policy can be compounded by the discriminatory attitudes of the person who is administering it.

Systemic or institutional discrimination is a major barrier to racialized groups, particularly in the employment context, in education and in the criminal justice system. The impacts of systemic racial discrimination can be experienced differently based on intersection with other grounds of discrimination such as gender, disability, place of origin, *etc.* For example, in a workplace that relies heavily on culturally and gender-specific sporting activities to build informal networks which in turn lead to promotions, a racialized woman with a disability could find herself at a triple disadvantage. A man who has recently emigrated from Africa may face similar barriers in networking and ultimately advancing in this organization. Therefore, addressing systemic discrimination requires sensitivity to the interacting and cumulative effects of discrimination on multiple grounds.

As discussed in section 1.4, Historical Context: The Legacy of Racism in Canada, the history of racism in Canada continues to have a significant impact on affected communities. Disadvantage in many communities has accumulated as a result of past and present discrimination. For example the economic disadvantage apparent in First Nations and African Canadian communities may be related to discriminatory practices of the past that limited economic opportunities of members from these communities.

The combined impact of current and historical disadvantage is reflected in statistics regarding unemployment, underemployment, low wage jobs, low education, poverty and inadequate housing. For example, in the 2001 census, the median income of the total Canadian population 15 years and over was $22,120 compared with $17,610 of the total "visible minority" popula-

---

available because of attributed rather than actual characteristics. . .. [from *Action Travail des Femmes v. Canadian National* (1984), 5 C.H.R.R. D/2327 (C.H.R.T.); aff'd (1987), 8 C.H.R.R. D/4210 (S.C.C.) [hereinafter *Action Travail*] at para. 33248].

. . .systemic discrimination. . .results from the unintended consequences of established employment systems and practices. Its effect is to block employment opportunities and benefits for members of certain groups. Since the discrimination is not motivated by a conscious act, it is more subtle to detect and it is necessary to look at the consequences or the results of the particular employment system [from *National Capital Alliance on Race Relations v. Canada (Health and Welfare)* (1997), 28 C.H.R.R. D/179 (C.H.R.T.) [hereinafter *NCARR*] at para. 164].

tion. With regard to low-income families, the incidence of low income was 12.9% for the total population compared with 26.0% of the total "visible minority" population.[122] The situation is even more serious for Aboriginal persons.[123] For example, in 1996 Census data showed that Aboriginal peoples in urban areas were more than twice as likely to live in poverty as non-Aboriginal people and data from the 2001 census shows that the median income of all persons indicating Aboriginal identity is $13,526, or 61% of the median income for all Canadians.[124]

In some situations, the existence of historical disadvantage is a factor that gives rise or contributes to systemic discrimination. It is therefore necessary to consider an individual or group's already disadvantaged position in Canadian society as part of any analysis of whether systemic or institutional discrimination is taking place. For example, health services that are not as readily available to lower income individuals or in lower income areas, may result in a systemic barrier for racialized persons who, by virtue of historical disadvantage, are more likely to be poor.

4.1 — Identifying Systemic Discrimination

The following three considerations can be employed for identifying and addressing systemic discrimination:[125]

1. Numerical Data
2. Policies, Practices and Decision-making Processes

---

[122] See Statistics Canada, *Selected Income Characteristics* online: www.statcan.ca.

[123] See also the *Report of the Special Rapporteur on Indigenous People*, *supra*, note 17 for a more detailed discussion of the many indicators of historical and contemporary disadvantage among Aboriginal people in Canada:

> Economic, social and human indicators of well-being, quality of life and development are consistently lower among Aboriginal people than other Canadians. . . . Ever since early colonial settlement, Canada's indigenous peoples were progressively dispossessed of their lands, resources and culture, a process that led them into destitution, deprivation and dependency. . . [at 2].

[124] See *Statistics Canada, Selected Income Characteristics*, *supra*, note 122, and the Canadian Council on Social Development, *Aboriginal Children in Poverty in Urban Communities: Social exclusion and the growing racialization of poverty in Canada* (June 2003), online: www.ccsd.ca/pr/2003/aboriginal.htm.

[125] Adapted from C. Agocs, *supra*, note 121. Also, for a decision which considered numerical data, employment practices and organizational culture in finding systemic discrimination, see *NCARR*, *supra*, note 121.

3. Organizational Culture

The Commission expects organizations and institutions to use these three considerations as a basis for proactively monitoring for and, if found to exist, addressing systemic discrimination internally (*i.e.*, with regard to human resources and employment) or externally (in their service delivery). In addition, if a matter is brought to the attention of the Commission, these considerations will guide the Commission in its assessment of whether systemic discrimination exists within an organization or institution.

1. Numerical Data

Numerical data that demonstrate that members of racialized groups are disproportionately represented may be an indicator of systemic or institutional racism. Numerical data can be evidence of the consequences of a discriminatory system in the following ways:

- Under-representation in an organization relative to the availability of qualified individuals in the population or in the applicant pool suggests systemic discrimination in hiring practices or may be indicative of on-the-job discrimination resulting in a failure to retain racialized persons.
- Unequal distribution of racialized persons in an organization, for example, high concentration in entry-level positions and low representation in managerial positions, may demonstrate inequitable training and promotion practices.
- Over-representation of racialized persons in police stops, jails and in other areas of the justice system may be indicative of the practice of racial profiling or other forms of racial discrimination. Similarly, evidence of racialized children and youth being disproportionately disciplined, suspended or expelled under "zero tolerance" school safety policies may be suggestive of discriminatory effects of these policies.

Except in the most obvious circumstances, for example where the data shows gross disparities in treatment that are unlikely to be the result of random selection, numerical data alone will not be proof of systemic discrimination.[126] However, it will constitute strong circumstantial evidence of the existence of inequitable practices. An organization can challenge the statis-

[126] *Blake v. Mimico Correctional Institute* (1984), 5 C.H.R.R. D/2417 at para. 20100 (Ont. Bd. Inq.). The Tribunal went on to say that the less there is of other evidence of discrimination, the greater the statistical disparity must be in order to make out a *prima facie* case (at. paras. 20129-20130). For a very helpful summary of general propositions from the *Blake* case, see *Angeconeb*, *supra*, note 93 at paras. 28-29.

tics and their validity or can demonstrate a nondiscriminatory reason for disproportional representation.

It is important to note that numerical data can be evidence of both systemic discrimination and more overt forms of discrimination. For example, numerical data showing an under-representation of qualified racialized persons in management may be evidence of employment systems that have the effect of discriminating, and/or of decision-makers having an overt bias toward promoting White candidates into supervisory roles.

As discussed in detail in section 6. Collection and Analysis of Numerical Data, it is the Commission's position that data collection and analysis should be undertaken where an organization or institution has or ought to have reason to believe that discrimination, systemic barriers or the perpetuation of historical disadvantage may potentially exist. In addition, whether or not data collection has taken place, an organization or institution must be conscious of issues of representation and cannot choose to remain unaware of disparities that exist.

2. Policies, Practices and Decision-Making Processes

In addition to or apart from numerical data, evidence of systemic discrimination may be found in the policies, practices and decision-making processes. These may be either formal or informal in nature.

The Supreme Court of Canada has made it clear that systems must be designed to be inclusive of all persons.[127] It is no longer acceptable to structure systems in a way that assumes that everyone is a member of the dominant group and then try to accommodate those who do not fit this assumption. Rather, the racial diversity that exists in Ontario should be reflected in the design stages of programs so that barriers are not created.

As a corollary to the notion that inclusive design should be used from the outset, where barriers already exist within systems and structures, they should be actively identified and removed.

Therefore, an organization has a responsibility to ensure its practices create inclusiveness, and not merely to make exceptions to allow individuals to fit into an existing system. Barriers should be prevented at the design stage and

---

[127] See *British Columbia (Public Service Employee Relations Commission) v. B.C.G.S.E.U.*, [1999] 3 S.C.R. 3 at 38 (in the context of gender) and *British Columbia (Superintendent of Motor Vehicles) v. British Columbia (Council of Human Rights)*, [1999] 3 S.C.R. 868 at 880 (in the context of disability).

where systems already exist, organizations should be aware of the possibility of systemic barriers and actively seek to identify and remove them.

> *Example*: Employment systems reviews to identify barriers to recruitment, retention and advancement are a core requirement of federal employment equity legislation. These reviews involve looking at written policies and also informal practices which are in use in recruitment, selection and hiring of employees, the development and training of employees, the promotion of employees and the retention and termination of employees. The process of an employer self-monitoring its own practices and addressing any barriers identified is a best practice for any organization, whether or not it is governed by employment equity legislation in addition to human rights legislation.
>
> *Example*: The language and content of questions on a standardized test are based on mainstream White culture and have the effect of screening out racialized persons and recent immigrants. Recognizing this, an organization modifies the content of the test to reduce racial bias or adopts alternative means of academic assessment.

Several major types of barriers can lead to disadvantage for racialized persons. One of the most obvious ones is the use of informal or highly discretionary processes for decision-making. The less formal the process, the more likely that subjective considerations or differing standards will be applied and the more opportunity there is for unconscious or conscious biases to come into play.[128] In some situations, formal policies exist but are not always applied or are applied unevenly, thus leading to barriers for some. Another pitfall is failing to account for difference in standardized procedures and evaluating people using the dominant culture as the norm. For example, testing or evaluation that fails to account for cultural difference can be a barrier to racialized persons or immigrants. Historical disadvantage poses a major barrier in many contexts.

---

[128] *NCARR*, *supra*, note 121 at para. 142.

Issues in Education

Numerous studies and reports have identified systemic barriers in educational services affecting racialized children, particularly African Canadian and Aboriginal children. Concerns that have been identified include streaming, bias in testing and evaluation, a monocultural and exclusionary curriculum, unfair and unusual discipline, low expectations, failing to deal with racial incidents and bullying, lack of role models, negative attitudes and stereotypes and a lack of programs that support the needs and concerns of racialized students.

See *Racism in our Schools: What to Know About It; How to Fight It* report prepared for the Canadian Race Relations Foundation (June 2000).

For guidance on workplace policies, practices and decision-making processes that can lead to systemic discrimination, see the Appendix at the end of this policy.

3. Organizational Culture

Organizational culture can be described as shared patterns of informal social behaviour, such as communication, decision-making and interpersonal relationships, which are the evidence of deeply held and largely unconscious values, assumptions and behavioural norms. An organizational culture that is not inclusive can marginalize or exclude racialized persons.

Specific aspects of an organizational culture which tend to be socially constructed by dominant groups include communication styles, interpersonal skills and leadership abilities. These are highly subjective qualities which are influenced by cultural differences as well as the process of racialization. As such, racialized persons can run into difficulties when assessed against these dominant norms.

> *Example*: A White woman's straightforward communication style leads coworkers to appreciate her as a "straight talker." An African Canadian woman's similar style results in her being characterized as "abrupt."
>
> *Example*: A Pakistani Canadian man was not given a teaching job for which he was the most qualified candidate because a White woman was perceived to be more enthusiastic and to have greater potential to motivate students. In fact, the Pakistani Canadian man was extremely enthusiastic about teaching and had great potential to motivate students but demonstrated this in a different manner. The Tribunal found dis-

crimination because of the employer's failure to take cultural differences into account.[129]

Example: A senior manager in an organization noted in a memo that cultural differences were minimized in technical positions but that "soft skills" such as communicating, influencing and negotiating were impacted by cultural differences. The Tribunal found that "visible minorities" were viewed by senior management as culturally different and not considered suitable for managerial positions.[130]

A related issue can be an organization's tendency to undervalue the strengths and contributions of racialized employees.

Example: A Chinese Canadian teacher was placed on a surplus list because the school principal took a narrow view of what types of activities qualified as "extracurricular." Activities that for cultural reasons Chinese immigrants would be unlikely to undertake were included while legitimate activities in which they would be more disposed to engage were excluded.[131]

Social relationships and networks are also an important part of organizational culture. These networks can allow some people to know what is required for success in an organization, with others being excluded from this critical knowledge. In addition, social relationships can result in perceptions about whether a person "fits" within an organization or is seen as an outsider.

Example: A company emphasizes evening social events outside of the workplace as an important part of team building. Racialized employees who do not participate for cultural or religious reasons are seen as not being team players and miss out on significant networking opportunities.[132]

---

[129] *Quereshi v. Central High School of Commerce (No. 3)* (1989), 12 C.H.R.R. D/394 (Ont. Bd. Inq.).

[130] *NCARR*, *supra*, note 121 at paras. 153–158 and 162.

[131] *Wong v. Ottawa Board of Education (No. 3)* (1994), 23 C.H.R.R. D/37 (Ont. Bd. Inq.).

[132] See for example, *Wong v. Ottawa Board of Education*, *ibid.* at para. 103-104.

4.1.1 — Establishing a Link Between the System and the Individual

One of the challenges in addressing systemic discrimination is that there may be little or no evidence of individual discrimination. In other words, it is a system that may on its face appear completely neutral, but that is conveying certain privileges for some groups and having an adverse impact on others. There may be nothing to suggest that the individual was singled out for adverse treatment. In fact, it may seem as though the individual was treated in a fair manner and failed due to his or her own shortcomings.[133]

> *Example*: A racialized person is not awarded a promotion due to poor performance during the interview. Nothing is said or done to suggest that her race was a factor in the assessment. However, on closer examination, it becomes apparent that a significant component of the interview process involved assessing "presence" and "confidence." Moreover, the successful candidate had been coached on what to expect during the interview by a manager who really wanted to see her get the job, while the racialized person was not offered the same opportunity.

It can be very difficult for an individual to demonstrate that a discriminatory system had a discriminatory adverse effect on him or herself. This is particularly so as the individual will not likely have access to all of the information regarding how the system operates.

> *Example*: An independent school whose student population is predominantly White selects prospective students based, in part, on a "trial day" which involves a child attending the school for a day to see if the child "fits in." Parents of a racialized child who doesn't get offered a spot are simply told that there is a long waiting list and they choose the students who are "most suitable." There is no way for the parents to know why their child was not "suitable."

Accordingly, it is the Commission's position that if evidence of systemic discrimination is found to exist, the organization or entity responsible for the system will be required by the Commission to produce information to

---

[133] In *Action Travail*, *supra*, note 121 the Supreme Court of Canada noted that systemic discrimination fosters the belief that the exclusion is the result of "natural forces;" for example, that women "just can't do the job" (at para. 33249).

show that this system did not contribute to an individual's experience of discrimination.

4.2 — Reasonable and *Bona Fide* Requirements

There may be some instances where a policy, practice or decision-making process is neutral on its face but leads to systemic discrimination against racialized persons or groups. The organization or institution may nevertheless seek to justify or maintain the policy, practice or decision-making process by demonstrating that it is reasonable and *bona fide* in the circumstances.

In the context of claims of racial discrimination, it is the Commission's position that it will be rare that a policy, practice or decision-making process will be found to be *bona fide*. To date, this defence has been arisen primarily in three situations: (1) income requirements in housing accommodation, (2) language requirements (see section 3.6 Language-related Discrimination), and (3) access to professions and trades.

With respect to income requirements, there have been several decisions in Ontario, beginning with the landmark decision in *Kearney v. Bramalea Ltd. (No. 2)*[134] that have confirmed that the use of minimum income requirements and rent-to-income ratios results in discrimination on the basis of a number of grounds in the *Code*, including race.

Statistical evidence showed that the landlords' use of such criteria had a disparate impact on individuals based on their sex, race, marital status, family status, citizenship, place of origin, age and the receipt of public assistance. The landlords could not establish a defence, as they could not demonstrate that the use of the criteria was reasonable and *bona fide* or that stopping the use of the criteria would cause undue hardship.[135]

---

[134]*Kearney v. Bramalea Ltd. (No. 2)* (1998), 34 C.H.R.R. D/1 (Ont. Bd. Inq.); *Shelter Corp. v. Ontario (Human Rights Comm.)* (2001), 39 C.H.R.R. D/111 (Ont. Sup. Ct.).

[135]Subsequent to the initial decision in *Kearney, ibid.*, the Ontario government added section 21(3) and Regulation 290/98 to the *Code* which permit the use of income information in some circumstances. In subsequent decisions, tribunals have grappled with the effect of these regulations. While income information can be used along with other considerations such as rental history and credit, the Regulation does not allow the use of rent-to-income ratios as the sole basis for refusing a tenant; See *Vander Schaaf v. M&R Property Management Ltd.* (2000), 38 C.H.R.R. D/251 (Ont. Bd. Inq.) and *Sinclair v. Morris A. Hunter Investments Ltd.* (2001), 41 C.H.R.R. D/98 (Ont. Bd. Inq.).

The significance of these decisions from a racial discrimination perspective lies mainly in their recognition of the link between socio-economic status and race. They represent a successful challenge of a policy that impacted on low-income individuals because of the relationship between poverty and historical disadvantage experienced by racialized groups.

The issue of access to professions and trades is of significant concern to foreign-educated and -trained persons who seek to practice their profession or trade after their arrival in Ontario.[136] While it is an issue that is based primarily on the ground of "place of origin," it also has intersectional implications for racialized persons. The intersection of "place of origin," with race, colour or ethnic origin appears to compound the barriers to employment integration and intensify economic and social vulnerability for foreign-educated and -trained persons.[137]

4.2.1 — The Three-step Test

The Supreme Court of Canada has set out a three-step test for determining whether a standard, factor, requirement or rule can be justified as a *bona fide* one. The organization or institution must establish on a balance of probabilities that the standard, factor, requirement or rule:

1. was adopted for a purpose or goal that is rationally connected to the function being performed

2. was adopted in good faith, in the belief that it is necessary for the fulfilment of the purpose or goal and

---

[136]There have been legal challenges to qualification rules for foreign trained doctors. In *Jamorski v. Ontario (Attorney General)* (1988), 64 O.R. (2d) 161 (C.A.), different internship requirements for graduates of unaccredited medical schools were found not to be an infringement of s. 15 of the Canadian *Charter of Rights and Freedoms*. However, in *Bitonti v. British Columbia (Ministry of Health) (No. 3)* (1999), 36 C.H.R.R. D/263 (B.C.C.H.R.) a tribunal found that foreign-trained doctors were discriminated against on the basis of place of origin by a requirement of the College of Physicians and Surgeons of British Columbia that they have an additional year of post-graduate training in order to be eligible for registration.

[137]A report by the Canadian Race Relations Foundation indicates that barriers are especially persistent for racial minorities who are foreign-born. They face extensive inequities in income, employment and education within Canada. See Jean Lock Kuntz for Canadian Council on Social Development, *Unequal Access: A Canadian Profile of Racial Differences in Education, Employment and Income*, Toronto: Canadian Race Relations Foundation, 2000 p. 13, 17, 19, 22, 24–26.

3. is reasonably necessary to accomplish its purpose or goal, in the sense that it is impossible to accommodate the claimant without undue hardship.[138]

The ultimate issue is whether the person who seeks to justify the discriminatory standard, factor, requirement or rule has shown that accommodation has been incorporated into the standard up to the point of undue hardship.

In this analysis, the procedure used to assess and achieve accommodation is as important as the substantive content of accommodation. The following non-exhaustive factors should be considered in the course of the analysis:

- whether the person responsible for accommodation investigated alternative approaches that do not have a discriminatory effect
- reasons why viable alternatives were not implemented
- ability to have differing standards that reflect group or individual differences and capabilities
- whether persons responsible for accommodation can meet their legitimate objectives in a less discriminatory manner
- whether the standard is properly designed to ensure the desired qualification is met without placing undue burden on those to whom it applies and
- whether other parties who are obliged to assist in the search for accommodation have fulfilled their roles.[139]

5. — Organizational Responsibility

The ultimate responsibility for a healthy and inclusive environment rests with employers, landlords, unions, service providers and other organizations and institutions covered by the *Code*. There is an obligation to ensure that environments are free from discrimination and harassment.

As discussed earlier in this policy, organizations and institutions have an obligation to be aware of whether their practices, policies and programs are having an adverse impact or resulting in systemic discrimination *vis-à-vis* racialized persons or groups. It is not acceptable from a human rights perspective to choose to remain unaware of the potential existence of discrimination or harassment, to ignore or to fail to act to address human rights matters, whether or not a complaint has been made.

---

[138] *British Columbia (Public Service Employee Relations Commission) v. BCGSEU*, *supra*, note 127.

[139] *Ibid.*

An organization violates the *Code* where it directly or indirectly, intentionally or unintentionally infringes the *Code* or does not directly infringe the *Code* but rather authorizes, condones, adopts or ratifies behaviour that is contrary to the *Code*.

Consider this:
Strong policies and programs that prevent human rights violations make good business sense. A positive work environment contributes to workplace productivity. Taking proactive measures to avoid human rights issues, and having policies and programs in place that allow issues that may arise to be dealt with promptly and effectively save time and money. Letting people know the rules and defining acceptable forms of behaviour make it possible to avoid costly and disruptive hours in the courts or before specialized administrative bodies. Persons outside of an organization, such as the general public or prospective clients appreciate an organization's commitment to equity.

In addition, there is a human rights duty not to condone or further a discriminatory act that has already occurred. To do so would extend or continue the life of the initial discriminatory act. The obligation extends to those who become involved in a situation that involves a discriminatory act and, who, while not the main actors, are drawn into the matter nevertheless, through contractual relations or otherwise.[140]

> *Example*: A pharmaceutical company refused a Black woman employment in an exhibit booth at an International Congress of Ophthalmology. The woman informed the company that was organizing the Congress and had nominated her for the job. This company was found to have a relationship with the woman with respect to employment. As such, it had a duty to investigate the refusal of employment and arrive at a reasonable (although not necessarily correct) conclusion as to whether discrimination occurred. However, the Tribunal found that the

[140] *Payne v. Otsuka Pharmaceutical Co. (No. 3)* (2002), 44 C.H.R.R. D/203 (Ont. Bd. Inq.). The nature of when a third party or collateral person would be drawn into the chain of discrimination is fact-specific. However, general principles can be determined. The key is the control or power that the collateral or indirect respondent had over the complainant and the principal respondent. The greater the control or power over the situation and the parties, the greater the legal obligation not to condone or further the discriminatory action. The power or control is important because it implies an ability to correct the situation or do something to ameliorate the conditions; at para. 63.

investigation was "barebones" and the conclusion that there was a "misunderstanding" unreasonable. The company's assistance to the pharmaceutical company in finding other candidates for the booth condoned or furthered the pharmaceutical company's discriminatory act.[141]

Unions and vocational and professional organizations are responsible for ensuring that they are not engaging in discrimination or harassment *vis-à-vis* their membership. They are also responsible for ensuring that they are not causing or contributing to discriminatory actions in a workplace. A union can be held liable for discriminatory policies or actions to the same extent as an employer. This will include negotiating a term in a collective agreement that results in racial discrimination or failing to take reasonable measures to address workplace harassment or a poisoned environment.[142]

Failing to fulfill the duty to ensure that an organization is not engaging in or condoning discrimination or harassment has serious repercussions. Human rights decisions are full of findings of liability and assessments of damages that are based on, or aggravated by, an organization's failure to appropriately address discrimination and harassment.[143] A few examples include:

- A company was found to have discriminated against an "East Indian" Canadian by permitting a racially poisoned environment to develop and persist at the facility where he worked and by disciplining and eventually discharging him without taking into account the racially hostile environment in which he worked. The company should have undertaken systemic efforts to develop and advocate company policies against ra-

---

[141] *Ibid.*

[142] *Central Okanagan School District No. 23 v. Renaud*, [1992] 2 S.C.R. 970, *Mayo v. Iron Ore Co. of Canada* (2002), 43 C.H.R.R. D/65 (Nfld. Bd. Inq.).

[143] Tribunals have also dealt with failures to implement remedial orders from prior human rights complaints. In *Ontario (Ministry of Correctional Services) v. Ontario (Human Rights Comm.) (No. 7)* (2002), 45 C.H.R.R. D/61 (Ont. Bd. Inq.), the Tribunal found that the poisoned environment, which the remedial orders in its prior decision were intended to address, persisted. The respondent, at the highest levels, failed to stop the harassment of Michael McKinnon, an Aboriginal man, both before the prior decision and after it. When he complained about continuing harassment, he was met with refusals, delays, bias and unjustified findings against him. The Board of Inquiry found the handling of his complaints to have been in itself retaliatory and a further infringement of the complainant's rights under the *Code*. The Board issued new, or extensively rewritten, orders, including systemic remedies.

cist language, to root out offenders and to implement serious and effective measures of deterrence.[144]

- The owner of a company threatened to dismiss an African Canadian employee because of his strained relationship with his manager. The triggering event for this threat was the manager's report to the owner of the employee's reaction to being called "Kunta Kinte" (a slave name). The Court did not accept the company's argument that the owner was oblivious to the racial poison in the workplace. The company, through its "directing mind," was *at least* reckless in failing to do anything. Based on the poisoned environment, race was found to be a factor in the African Canadian man's dismissal.[145]
- An organization that disciplined an employee for reacting to racial harassment by a customer was found liable for how it responded to the customer's discriminatory conduct. The employer had no control over the customer's conduct but, by disciplining the employee in such circumstances, an employer is condoning the discriminatory conduct and allowing such conduct to invade the workplace.[146]

The following factors have been suggested as considerations for determining whether an organization met its responsibilities to respond to a human rights complaint:

- procedures in place at the time to deal with discrimination and harassment
- the promptness of the institutional response to the complaint
- the seriousness with which the complaint was treated
- resources made available to deal with the complaint
- whether the organization provided a healthy work environment for the person who complained and

---

[144] *Naraine v. Ford Motor Co. of Canada* (Ont. Bd. Inq.), *supra*, note 88.

[145] *Smith v. Mardana Ltd.* (Ont. Div. Ct.), *supra*, note 79.

[146] *Mohammed v. Mariposa Stores Ltd.* (1990), 14 C.H.R.R. D/215 (B.C.C.H.R.). See also Labour Arbitration decisions which have concluded that an employer must have procedures in place to deal with racial harassment of its staff by patrons. These procedures should indicate how staff are expected to respond to the harassment, ensure that serious and/or ongoing problems are brought to the attention of management and also that management takes appropriate steps to assess the situation and take remedial action; *C.U.P.E., Local 79 v. Toronto (City)* (1995), 1995 Carswell Ont 1840 (Ont. Arb. Bd.); *Clarendon Foundation v. O.P.S.E.U., Local 593*, [2000] L.V.I. 3104-6, 2000 Carswell Ont 1906, 91 L.A.C. (4th) 105 (Ont. Arb. Bd.).

- the degree to which the action taken was communicated to the person who complained.[147]

5.1 — Vicarious Liability

Section 45 of the *Code* provides for vicarious liability for breaches of the sections of the *Code* dealing with discrimination. This means that a corporation, trade union or occupational association, unincorporated association or employers' organization will be held responsible for any act or omission done in the course of his or her employment by an officer, official, employee or agent. This applies not only to human rights violations in the workplace but also in housing accommodation, goods, services and facilities, contracting and membership in unions and vocational associations.

Simply put, it is the Commission's position that vicarious liability automatically attributes responsibility for discrimination to an organization for the acts of its employees or agents, done in the normal course, whether or not it had any knowledge of, participation in, or control over these actions.

Vicarious liability does not apply to breaches of the sections of the *Code* dealing with harassment. However, in these cases the "organic theory of corporate liability" may apply. In addition, since the existence of a poisoned environment is a form of discrimination, it is the Commission's position that when harassment amounts to or results in a poisoned environment, vicarious liability under section 45(1) of the *Code* is restored.

5.2 — "Organic Theory" of Corporate Liability

While section 45(1) of the *Code* exempts an organization from liability for harassment, courts and tribunals have recognized that there are additional circumstances in which an organization will be held liable for the acts or omissions of its employees. The acts or omissions of an employee who is part of the "directing mind" of an organization will engage the liability of the organization where:

(a) the employee who is part of the "directing mind" engages in harassment or inappropriate behaviour that is contrary to the *Code*; or

[147] *Wall v. University of Waterloo* (1995), 27 C.H.R.R. D/44 (Ont. Bd. Inq.). These factors assist in assessing the reasonableness of an organization's response to harassment. A reasonable response by the organization will not affect its liability but will be considered in determining the appropriate remedy. In other words, an employer that has reasonably responded to harassment is not absolved of liability but may face a reduction in the damages that flow from the harassment.

(b) the employee who is part of the "directing mind" doesn't respond adequately to harassment or inappropriate behaviour of which the employee is aware, or ought reasonably to be aware.

Generally speaking, an employee who performs management duties is part of the "directing mind" of an organization. Employees with only supervisory authority may be viewed as part of an organization's "directing mind" if they function, or are seen to function, as representatives of the organization. Even non-supervisors may be considered part of the "directing mind" if they have *de facto* supervisory authority or have significant responsibility for the guidance of employees. For example, a member of the bargaining unit who is a lead hand may be considered to be part of the "directing mind" of an organization.

Finally, persons who are central decision-makers in an organization, such as members of the Board of Directors, may be seen as part of the "directing mind."

5.3 — Accounting for Historical Disadvantage

We all have a shared responsibility for addressing historical disadvantage. Therefore, it is the Commission's position that all organizations, institutions and levels of government should take steps to address historical disadvantage. This expectation is even higher for public bodies as they are more likely to have contributed to the causes of historical disadvantage in the first place[148] and because government has an enhanced responsibility to ensure

[148]For example, recognizing the significant disadvantage that was created by wartime measures targeting Japanese Canadians, on September 22, 1988 the Japanese Canadian Redress Agreement was signed. In the House of Commons, Prime Minister Brian Mulroney acknowledged the government's wrongful actions, pledged to ensure that the events would never recur and recognized the loyalty of the Japanese Canadians to Canada. As a symbolic redress for those injustices, the government offered individual and community monetary compensation to Japanese Canadians. The government also committed to create a national organization that would foster racial harmony and help to eliminate racism, the Canadian Race Relations Foundation. However, efforts by other communities to obtain redress for government laws and policies that have created historical disadvantage have not been successful, see *Mack v. Canada (Attorney General), supra*, note 29.

that everyone can benefit equally from its services. This was discussed by the Supreme Court of Canada in a disability accommodation case:

> . . .to promote the objective of a more equal society, s. 15(1) acts as a bar to the executive enacting provisions without taking into account their possible impact on already disadvantaged classes of persons.[149]

There are several approaches to addressing historical disadvantage which can be implemented, alone or in combination. These are discussed in section 7. Preventing and Responding to Racism and Racial Discrimination.

"Reverse Discrimination"

Unfortunately, measures to address historical disadvantage, such as through special programs under s. 14 of the *Code*, may sometimes be characterized as "reverse discrimination" or "tokenism." Persons who receive the benefit of the measures are thereby stigmatized as being undeserving or receiving special treatment.

It is important to emphasize that the purpose of these measures is not to give racialized persons an advantage but to place them on the same footing as persons who have not experienced historical disadvantage. These measures can open the doors of education, employment, housing and business development that would otherwise be shut to racialized persons. And while remedying past acts of discrimination, these measures also contribute to the prevention of future acts of discrimination, for example by increasing diversity which, in turn, promotes organizational change. Therefore, society as a whole benefits from removing barriers preventing each member from achieving his or her full potential.

As is the case with human rights-related accommodations, organizations and institutions that are implementing measures to address historical disadvantage should foster a positive environment and deal with negative responses that may arise.

5.4 — Public Interest Remedies

In addition to the ability to award monetary remedies, human rights tribunals are granted broad remedial powers to direct a party found responsible for discrimination to do anything that, in the opinion of the tribunal, the party ought to do to achieve compliance with human rights codes, both in

[149] *Eldridge v. British Columbia (Attorney General)*, [1997] 3 S.C.R. 624 at para. 64.

respect of the complaint and in respect of future practices (section 41(1) of the *Code*). Public interest remedies that have been ordered by tribunals are wide-ranging and have included requiring an organization to cease or change practices that have resulted in discrimination, to conduct internal or third-party monitoring, to implement comprehensive anti-discrimination and anti-harassment policies and to engage in widespread training of staff and management, to name a few.

In addition, there are several decisions in which human rights tribunals have sought to use their remedial authority to require measures that will account for historical disadvantage. In such cases, the decision maker has ordered corrective measures designed to remove barriers to full participation and redress the effects of past discrimination.

One of the most significant corrective programs ordered by a tribunal was in a gender discrimination case. A major Canadian employer that was found to have systemically discriminated against women was ordered to hire one woman for every four new hires into unskilled and blue-collar jobs until the representation of women reached the national percentage for women working in equivalent jobs.[150]

This type of program was more recently ordered in a racial discrimination case. The tribunal imposed a "special corrective measures program" to prevent future systemic discrimination and to eliminate past barriers arising out of the discriminatory practices that were identified. The program entailed seven permanent corrective measures targeted at changing aspects of the systems and organizational culture that were found to pose barriers to racialized persons. As well, 18 temporary corrective measures were identified, including hiring "visible minorities" into various levels of the organization at a particular rate (*e.g.*, 18% per year) for a certain number of years, outreach measures, mentoring programs and setting aside a percentage of positions in training programs for "visible minorities."[151]

Other tribunal decisions have ordered an organization to provide the Commission with sufficient information on employment practices and statistics to permit the Commission to monitor the employment practices of the organization for a period of time.[152]

---

[150] *Action Travail*, *supra*, note 121.

[151] *NCARR*, *supra*, note 121.

[152] See for example the remedial decisions in *McKinnon v. Ontario (Ministry of Correctional Services (No. 3)* (1998), 32 C.H.R.R. D/1 (Ont. Bd. Inq.) and *Ontario (Ministry of Correctional Services) v. Ontario (Human Rights Comm.) (No. 7)*

Organizations and institutions should proactively adopt measures to address disadvantage. However, where they fail to do so, in appropriate cases, the Commission will pursue public interest remedies aimed at correcting systemic discrimination and historical disadvantage in settlements and in decisions before the Tribunal.

Part III — Guidelines for Implementation: Monitoring and Combatting Racism and Racial Discrimination

6. — Collection and Analysis of Numerical Data

It is a common misperception that the *Code* prohibits the collection and analysis of data identifying people based on race and other *Code* grounds. Many individuals, organizations and institutions mistakenly believe that collecting this data is automatically antithetical to human rights.

In fact, the Commission has stated that not only does the *Code* permit the collection and analysis of identity data based on enumerated grounds for *Code*-legitimate purposes, appropriate data collection is necessary for effectively monitoring discrimination, identifying and removing systemic barriers, ameliorating historical disadvantage and promoting substantive equality.[153] It is the collection or use of data for improper purposes that further contributes to discrimination or stereotyping that is antithetical to human rights.

(2002), 45 C.H.R.R. D/61 (Ont. Bd. Inq.), *NCARR*, *supra*, note 121 and *Hendry v. Ontario (Liquor Control Board)* (1980), 1 C.H.R.R. D/160 (Ont. Bd. Inq.).

[153]See *Paying the Price: The Human Cost of Racial Profiling*, *supra*, note 7 at 70-71, Ontario Human Rights Commission, *Guidelines on Accessible Education*, (September 2004) at 33, and Ontario Human Rights Commission, *Guidelines for Collecting Data on Enumerated Grounds Under the* Code (September 2003), online: www.ohrc.on.ca.

Did you know?

Since 1989 the Law Society of Upper Canada has undertaken and reviewed studies that are indicative of inequality within the legal profession. Among other initiatives, in 2001 the Law Society commissioned Michael Ornstein, the Director of the Institute of Social Research of York University, to prepare a demographic study of the legal profession in Ontario. Using the 1996 census, the report showed that 7.3% of lawyers in Ontario are "non-White" compared to 17.5% of the population. The report also notes that the mean earnings of "non-White" lawyers are generally much lower than that of White lawyers.

In light of this and other studies, the Law Society has undertaken initiatives to promote equality within the legal profession.

See Law Society of Upper Canada www.lsuc.on.ca/about/b/equity/promoting-equity-and-diversity/.

All individuals, organizations and institutions in Ontario are responsible for upholding human rights within their respective environments. Individuals, organizations and institutions can be held liable for actions that are discriminatory or harassing but also for failing in their duties to take appropriate action to address human rights issues of which they are aware, or ought to be aware. In other words, in keeping with the preventative and remedial purpose of the *Code*, there is a positive duty to take corrective action to ensure that the *Code* is not being, and will not in future be, breached. Just as organizations and institutions have an obligation to conduct an investigation once aware of an allegation of racial harassment, awareness that racial discrimination may exist may call for an investigation that involves the collection of data.

In the context of racial discrimination, data collection is a necessary and in some cases, essential, tool for assessing whether rights under Part I of the *Code* are being or might potentially be infringed, and for taking corrective action. It is therefore the Commission's position that data collection and analysis should be undertaken where an organization or institution has or ought to have reason to believe that discrimination, systemic barriers or the perpetuation of historical disadvantage may potentially exist.

Whether an organization or institution has or ought to have reason to believe data collection is necessary will be assessed on a subjective and objective basis. First, the organization or institution's actual knowledge of a problem will be considered. Second, from the point of view of a reasonable third party, whether the organization or institution should have been aware of a problem necessitating data collection will be considered. The concept of the reasonable third party will take into consideration both the perspective of the organization or institution and racialized communities.

Some situations in which there will be a reasonable basis to believe that rights under Part I of the *Code* are being or might potentially be infringed and that a determination can best be made through data collection and analysis include:

- Persistent allegations or complaints of discrimination or systemic barriers; for example, an organization that receives multiple complaints under an internal human rights policy, through complaints to the Commission or using another process that deals with human rights issues such as labour arbitration
- A widespread public perception of discrimination or systemic barriers; for example, public concern with the phenomenon of racial profiling
- Observed unequal distribution of racialized persons; for example, a clear discrepancy in the number of racialized persons holding low-level positions as compared with those in senior positions
- Objective data or research studies demonstrating the existence of discrimination or systemic barriers; for example, studies that show increased drop-out rates in education
- Evidence from other organizations or jurisdictions that a substantially similar policy, program or practice has had a disproportionate effect on racialized persons; for example, evidence that "zero tolerance" school discipline policies have adversely affected racialized students in the United States and United Kingdom.

There are other situations where an organization or institution may not have reason to believe that a problem exists within its own area of responsibility but may nevertheless wish to voluntarily collect data for the purposes of advancing the objectives of the *Code*.

- Census data demonstrating under-representation of Aboriginal persons in a profession is used as the basis of a special program to encourage Aboriginal persons to pursue the profession.
- A survey of its clientele allows an organization to better ensure that its needs are being met, for example by issuing brochures in multiple languages, providing cross-cultural training to staff and tailoring its services to recognize the diversity of needs of its clientele.
- An organization that is instituting a new policy or program or embarking on significant organizational change wants to monitor the impact of this initiative on racialized persons to ensure that no adverse effects occur.

6.1 — Consequences of a Failure to Collect and Analyze Data

A failure to collect and analyze data does not, in and of itself, form the basis for complaint to the Commission. Rather, the collection and analysis of data may be a component of the duty to take action to prevent violation of the *Code*. Therefore, where a *prima facie* complaint of discrimination is made out, the Commission will consider the failure to collect and analyze data as part of its analysis of whether the respondent has met its duty to ensure it is not in violation of the *Code*.

> *Example*: School discipline policies appear to be having a disproportionate impact on racialized students and students with disabilities and to be further exacerbating their already disadvantaged position in society. Empirical research from the United States and United Kingdom demonstrates that racialized students and students with disabilities are disproportionately impacted by the application of suspensions and expulsions. The responsible authorities' failure to take this into account and to take steps to monitor for and prevent a disproportionate impact forms, in part, the basis of a human rights complaint.

Moreover, in cases where the collection of data was clearly warranted, the failure to collect accurate and reliable data may foreclose a respondent from making a credible defence that it did not discriminate. In addition, where systemic discrimination is alleged and the organization or institution has chosen not to collect data, the Commission may need to rely on qualitative evidence of disproportionate representation to determine whether racialized groups are experiencing disadvantage. Finally, the Commission will seek data collection and analysis as a public interest remedy in litigation and settlements.

Conversely, if an organization or institution collects and analyzes data it may also show that discrimination or systemic barriers do not exist. As well, efforts to monitor for discrimination or systemic barriers will assist an organization or institution to show that it has met its duty to protect and uphold human rights.

> *Example*: A perception exists that a program is having a disproportionate effect on racialized persons. However, data reveals that racialized persons are impacted at the same rate as others.
>
> *Example*: An organization is concerned that its workforce is not representative of the population it serves. It collects data to monitor whether its policies could be having a discriminatory effect as well as con-

ducting an employment systems review to remove any barriers that may exist.

6.2 — Data Collection and Analysis Methodology

In order to fulfill its purpose, data collection should be done in good faith with the purpose of producing accurate, good-quality data rather than attempting to achieve a particular outcome. Efforts should be made to collect data that will shed meaningful light on the issues and to gather it in a way that is consistent with accepted data collection techniques.

How data collection and analysis should be conducted is dependant on the context, including the issue that requires monitoring, the purpose of the data collection and the nature and size of the organization. Effective data collection and analysis in complex situations will generally require the use of proper research and design methodologies as well as training of staff who are collecting the data. Unless an organization has the relevant internal expertise, it is likely to require assistance from an expert such as a social scientist.

> *Example*: A police force concerned about the perception that racial profiling is a problem initiates a project to collect data about police stops. Through consultation with an expert who has a background in research methodologies and data analysis, a data collection program is designed. Officers are required to record all stops on a standard form, including the reason for the stop, the outcome and the perceived ethno-racial identity of the person stopped. A copy of the form is given to the person stopped and he is asked to verify the information recorded.

Conversely, a small organization that has basic data collection needs may be able to rely on existing resources.

> *Example*: A non-federally regulated company sees a problem in its staffing and decides to use existing employment equity resources as a resource to implement its data collection and analysis program.[154]

It is important to note that special studies where data is only collected for a limited period of time may be less accurate. Firstly, the data may only provide a snapshot of a situation and not assess changes over time. Moreover,

---

[154] For example, Human Resources Development Canada has numerous resources on workplace equity, online: www.hrsdc.gc.ca/en/gateways/topics/wzpgxr. shtml.

short-term studies may be affected by the normal human tendency to modify behaviour while under scrutiny. Data gathered in a time-limited study will, therefore, have to be considered with this in mind.

As stated earlier, data should only be used for *Code*-legitimate purposes and should not be used to perpetuate discrimination or stereotyping about a group. Public disclosure of the data should be carefully considered to ensure that adverse consequences will not result.

The individuals involved in the collection of data must be informed why such information is being collected and the use to which it will be put. The reason for data collection as well as how the collection and use of such data will assist to relieve disadvantage or discrimination and achieve equal opportunity should be explained. This will help alleviate the concern that may exist about being asked to self-identify. Privacy of individuals must be assured and data collection, storage, access and disclosure must be carefully controlled.

As stated earlier, numerical data can be a strong indicator of inequitable practices. Therefore, if the data reveal that there is a problem, an organization or institution must be prepared to act.

Please consult the Commission's publication *Guidelines for Collecting Data on Enumerated Grounds Under the Code* for further information about data collection and analysis methodologies.

7. — Preventing and Responding to Racism and Racial Discrimination

Organizations and institutions operating in Ontario have an obligation to have in place measures to prevent and respond to breaches of the *Code*. They have a duty to take steps to foster environments that are respectful of human rights. This takes commitment and work. However, this is part of the cost of doing business in a jurisdiction that is committed to the goal of equality, as a matter of public policy expressed through the *Code*.

Measures to respond to racism and racial discrimination have been referenced throughout this policy. To summarize, a solid organizational anti-racism[155] program will contain the following components:

(1) a comprehensive anti-racism vision statement and policy

---

[155]Anti-racism is an action-oriented approach to identifying and countering the production and reproduction of all forms of racism. It addresses the issues of racism and the interlocking systems of social oppression. Anti-racism implies a goal of producing an understanding of what racism is and how it can be challenged; C.

(2) proactive, ongoing monitoring
(3) implementation strategies and
(4) evaluation.

7.1 — Anti-racism Vision Statement and Policy

In addition to addressing obligations under the *Human Rights Code*, the adoption and implementation of an effective anti-racism vision statement and policy has the potential of limiting harm and reducing liability. It also promotes the equity and diversity goals of organizations and institutions and makes good business sense.

A clear, concrete and comprehensive anti-racism vision statement and policy is critical to the success of any anti-racism program. The Commission's publications *Developing Procedures to Resolve Human Rights Complaints within Your Organization* and *Human Rights at Work* discuss what should be contained in a general anti-discrimination and anti-harassment policy which covers all the grounds in the *Code*. However, there are some additional measures that are important to address the specific complexities of racism and racial discrimination.

It is essential that all key stakeholders in an organization be involved in and committed to the development of a strong anti-racism vision statement and policy. In addition, strong support from key leadership, such as senior management, the head of a union, *etc.*, is essential for the policy to be successful. The membership of the team responsible for developing the policy should be diverse. Ideally, a consultative process involving all persons within an organization should be used; for example surveying all staff, holding staff discussion groups or circulating a draft policy to staff for comment.

Tator, "Advancing the Ontario Human Rights Commission's Policy and Education Function" (2004) 3:3 *Canadian Diversity* 29 at 30.

An Anti-racism Model of Social Change

An anti-racist organization, institution or system is not one in which racism is absent. Rather, it takes a proactive stand against racism in all its forms. Commitment in anti-racist organizations is based on an acknowledgement that racism exists, that it manifests itself in various forms at the individual, institutional and systemic levels and that it is embedded in the mass culture of the dominant group. An anti-racist approach begins by acknowledging that the perceptions and experiences of racialized persons are real and that there may be a multiplicity of realities in one event.

Anti-racism emphasizes a holistic approach to the development of anti-racist ideologies, goals, policies and practices. It calls for the formation of new organizational structures; the introduction of new cultural norms and value systems; changes in power dynamics; the implementation of new employment systems; substantive changes in services delivered; support for new roles and relationships at all levels of the organization; new patterns and more inclusive styles of leadership and decision-making; and the reallocation of resources.

From C. Tator "Advancing the Ontario Human Rights Commission's Policy and Education Function" in (2004) 3:3 *Canadian Diversity* 29–31.

A strong anti-racism policy should have a strong vision statement. The absence of a vision statement shaped by anti-racism principles and goals can result in an inadequate framework for an anti-racism program. Vision statements should be concrete, address racism specifically and demonstrate the organization's leadership in and commitment to addressing racism.

Sample Vision Statement

We endorse the following anti-racism principles:

(1) We recognize that racism exists in Canadian society and in its institutions, and therefore affects .... itself.

(2) We recognize our role in combating racism in .... itself.

(3) We assert our commitment to implement specific measures to combat racism, and to engage in actions to eliminate it.

(4) We recognize and value the racial diversity of Ontario and of our own workplace.

(5) We strive for equality of results in our employment practices and delivery of services.

(6) We recognize and respect the unique identities of Aboriginal peoples and the need for a distinct approach to anti-racism measures for Aboriginal peoples.

Therefore, we will:

(1) Actively identify and challenge individual or systemic acts of racial discrimination in our workplace and service delivery.

(2) Ensure that management and all employees are responsible for challenging racial discrimination in our workplace and service delivery.

(3) Equip management and all employees with knowledge and skills to recognize and challenge racial discrimination in our workplace and service delivery.

(4) Foster respect on a daily basis amongst management and all employees.

(5) Ensure that any employee's or client's report of discriminatory treatment will be investigated and the employee or client will be protected against reprisals.

(6) Ensure that management staff members understand their legal responsibilities as "directing minds" to act immediately to deal with situations of potential harassment or discrimination.

(7) Continually monitor and assess progress in challenging racial discrimination in our workplace and service delivery.

In addition to a list of prohibited grounds of discrimination under the *Code*, an explanation of racism and racial discrimination will assist everyone within an organization understand what constitutes racism and racial discrimination and how they manifest and operate. In addition, definitions of harassment and a poisoned environment should be provided.

Examples of racial discrimination, harassment and a poisoned environment that are meaningful in an organization's particular context will be helpful in illustrating the types of behaviour that will not be tolerated. The consequences for engaging in harassing or discriminatory behaviour, up to and including termination, should be clearly indicated.

The policy should contain an effective internal complaint resolution procedure. It should indicate how internal complaints will be handled with details regarding:

- to whom a complaint is made
- confidentiality and protection from reprisal
- assistance that is available for parties to a complaint
- the availability of Alternative Dispute Resolution, such as mediation to resolve a complaint
- how the complaint will be investigated
- how long the process will take

- disciplinary measures that will be applied if the complaint is substantiated
- remedies that will be available to the person who complained and
- the right to file a complaint with the Commission, along with an explanation of the six month time requirement under the *Code*.

In practice, it is very important that all complaints be taken seriously, the complaint mechanism be applied, and that persons making complaints not be subjected to discipline or reprisal for raising the issue of racial discrimination.[156] It is often the experience of persons raising complaints of racial discrimination, in particular, to be told that the allegation is inappropriate and unfounded without any investigation taking place. There may be a tendency to want to protect persons against such allegations because of their perceived seriousness, rather than to consider the perspective of the complainant.[157] Persons alleging racial discrimination may even be accused of "reverse discrimination."

> *Example*: A group of racialized employees nominates a spokesperson to raise concerns that they have that a particular manager is treating them in a discriminatory fashion. When she speaks to the head of human resources, she is told not to "go there" and that what she is raising is going to "damage the reputation of a good man."

---

[156]Section 8 of the *Code* prohibits reprisal for asserting a human rights claim:

> 8. Every person has a right to claim and enforce his or her rights under this Act, to institute and participate in proceedings under this *Act* and to refuse to infringe a right of another person under this *Act*, without reprisal or threat of reprisal for so doing.

[157]Decision-makers have sometimes even tended to place a greater emphasis on the effect of a finding of discrimination on a respondent's reputation than on the effect of racism on an individual. See *Gaba v. Lincoln County Human Society* (1991), 15 C.H.R.R. D/311 at para. 37 (Ont. Bd. Inq.), *Smith v. Mardana Ltd.* (Ont. Bd. Inq.), *supra*, note 79 at para. 39 and *R. v. Brown* in which the trial judge in a criminal case in which racial profiling had been raised as a defence stated that the defence raised "very serious allegations" that he found "a little troubling." The Court of Appeal noted that the allegation of racial profiling was serious but just as serious as the impact of the racial profiling in question on the accused, if such were the case. The proper judicial attitude should have been one of detachment rather than one which appeared to show only concern respecting the impact of the defence allegations on the police officer; *R. v. Brown* (Ont. C.A.), *supra*, note 66 at para. 60.

7.2 — Proactive, Ongoing Monitoring

An important measure in addressing discrimination relates to simple awareness and monitoring. All too often, policies and programs are put into place without due consideration of the effect that they may have on racialized persons. Even where information comes to the attention of the responsible organization or institution that would suggest that the program is perpetuating disadvantage or causing discrimination, the organization may choose not to act, instead adopting a "head in the sand" approach. This is neither productive nor acceptable from a human rights perspective. It is therefore the Commission's expectation that where there is concern expressed that policies or practices are having a discriminatory effect on racialized persons or groups, the responsible organization or institution will take steps to assess whether this is in fact the case.

Monitoring will often involve the collection of data and production of statistics. However, other measures such as consulting with affected communities, systems reviews and research, including reviewing research available in other jurisdictions, are also important aspects of monitoring. Monitoring will consider the effects of the past, *i.e.*, historical disadvantage, the effect of systems currently in place and the potential impact of new initiatives.

Of course, monitoring alone is not sufficient. Steps must be taken to change policies and practices that are perpetuating historical disadvantage. Therefore, if a problem is revealed through monitoring or otherwise comes to the attention of an institution or organization, steps should be taken to remove systemic barriers, ameliorate disadvantage and promote substantive equality.

> *Example*: A school board recognizes that its discipline policies are having an adverse impact on racialized students. It revises its policies so that there is more room for an assessment of the individual circumstances of each student. In addition, it assigns support persons who can assist racialized youth at risk, establishes programs that emphasize conflict resolution and peer mediation and takes steps to ensure there is no loss of education where there is no alternative to suspension.

7.3 — Implementation Strategies

Anti-racism requires fundamental changes to the structures and systems of organizations. Therefore, for an anti-racism policy and program to be effective, attention, priority and resources must be given to implementation strategies.[158] A variety of measures may be needed, such as:

- organizational change initiatives such as the formation of new organizational structures, the introduction of new cultural norms, implementation of new systems, removal of old practices or policies that give rise to human rights concerns, use of more formal, less discretionary processes, focus on more inclusive styles of leadership and decision-making;
- special programs, corrective measures or outreach initiatives to address inequity or disadvantage
- internal and external surveying to receive feedback on issues of racism and racial discrimination; for example, exit interviews or surveys help determine whether racial discrimination or harassment was a factor in a person's decision to leave; employee or client satisfaction surveys can help assess whether employees or clients believe they are receiving equal treatment
- empowerment of racialized persons within an organization or institution and outside it; for example, through formal mentoring arrangements, internal committees to address equality issues, community consultation, *etc.*
- anticipating resistance to change and developing strategies to overcome any opposition that may arise
- seeking partnerships with others, including other institutions of a similar nature, to identify best practices
- mandatory education, training and development initiatives, including effective training of all staff on the anti-racism vision statement and policy and developing specific skills and knowledge of those with additional responsibilities for human rights including any part of the "directing mind" of the organization, human resources staff and human rights advisors. Additional training should also be made available to those in the organization responsible for proactive, ongoing monitoring or implementing organizational change
- dissemination of information about the anti-racism vision statement and policy, human rights decisions and new Commission publications to existing and new staff and

[158]For a discussion of some of the barriers to anti-racism change initiatives see C. Tator, "Advancing the Ontario Human Rights Commission's Policy and Education Function," *supra*, note 155.

- retaining outside expertise to assist with any of the above.

"Tokenism"

Tokenism can be described as the practice of hiring a few members of racialized groups for relatively powerless positions in order to create an appearance of having an inclusive and equitable organization. In reality, these individuals have little voice in the organization. At the same time, they are seen as representative of the group to which they belong and, as a result, their thoughts, beliefs, and actions are likely to be taken as typical of all in their group. Token measures to promote organizational diversity do not work and circumvent substantive change.

It is important to set specific timelines and identify an individual within the organization with accountability and responsibility for each measure as well as for the overall anti-racism goals of the organization. This person should have full powers, backing and resources to make sure that the measures can be effectively carried out. Progress in implementation should be tracked and reported back to senior management.

7.3.1 — A Word about Training

Training is often seen as a panacea to all human rights problems. However, training in isolation from other initiatives is unlikely to succeed in fostering a non-discriminatory environment. Similarly, inadequate training is not likely to be effective in bringing about a change in attitudes or behaviour. Training that emphasizes "cultural sensitivity," "race awareness" or "tolerance" or that only seeks to deal with issues through promoting the value of "multiculturalism," such as through potluck lunches, does not lead to meaningful change as it fails to address the dynamics of racism and reduces racial discrimination to cultural misunderstandings.

Effective training should not avoid the use of anti-racism terminology. Anti-racism training implies a goal of producing an understanding of what racism is and how it can be challenged. Anti-racism training aims to achieve not only a change in individual attitudes, but also a transformation of individual and collective practices.

It is, therefore, important to take steps to ensure that training will be effective, appropriate and timely. It helps to engage experts, do research into effective anti-racism training techniques, set goals for the training and then evaluate people's learning against those goals. For example, a training program for an organization that is seeking to address the phenomenon of racial profiling might include the following specific goals:

- that local racialized communities be involved in the design and delivery of the training
- that training is conducted by trainers with sufficient expertise in the subject area
- that training will develop a full understanding that good community relations are essential to the organization's mandate
- that training will develop a full understanding of what racism is and how it can be challenged
- that training will develop a full understanding of what constitutes racial profiling, racial discrimination and harassment or any other violations of the Ontario *Human Rights Code*
- that training will develop a full understanding that racial profiling, racial discrimination and harassment or any other violations of the Ontario *Human Rights Code* are unacceptable and will be dealt with seriously by the organization
- that training will develop a full understanding that a respect for human rights is aligned with and not contrary to the organization's objectives and
- that negative reactions to perceived racial profiling by racialized persons are contextualized so that employees of the organization understand why racialized persons may react negatively and how to respond to such reactions in a manner that is professional and not contrary to the *Human Rights Code*.

Ideally, the organization would also engage in regular, independent monitoring to assess whether the training program is adequate, effective, appropriate and timely to meet the objectives described above. The monitoring could include consultation with local racialized communities as well as a survey of the attitudes of staff receiving the training to assess whether the training has been effective in increasing understanding or changing attitudes about racial profiling, racial discrimination and racial harassment.

7.3.2 — Special Programs

The *Code* recognizes the importance of addressing pre-existing hardship and disadvantage in the section dealing with special programs. Section 14 of the *Code* allows for programs to alleviate hardship or economic disadvantage or to assist disadvantaged persons or groups to achieve, or attempt to achieve, equal opportunity.[159]

Therefore, it is the Commission's position that organizations and institutions should endeavour to undertake special programs where hardship or disadvantage exist. To clarify how section 14 of the *Code* works, the Commission has adopted *Guidelines on Special Programs.*

Some examples of the types of special programs that alleviate historical disadvantage for racialized persons include:

- Hiring — special programs that address under-representation of racialized persons in an organization, profession, or job category
- Housing — programs that assist communities which have historically had difficultly finding housing, such as Aboriginal persons and new immigrants
- Health — special strategies to improve mental health outcomes for racialized and Aboriginal communities[160]
- Education — initiatives which support racialized persons in school or in gaining admittance to programs from which they have been historically excluded[161] and
- Contracting — schemes which assist community businesses and businesses run by racialized persons to have access to business opportunities, contracts and procurement by governments.

7.4 — Evaluation

Ongoing evaluation of an organization's or institution's anti-racism program is important to ensure its effectiveness. As with the other aspects of an

---

[159]For a discussion of the purposes of section 14 of the *Code* see *Ontario (Human Rights Commission) v. Ontario (Ministry of Health)*, 21 C.H.R.R. D/259 (Ont. C.A.). The majority of the Court stated that s. 14(1) has two purposes. One is to protect affirmative action programs from being challenged as violating the formal equality provisions contained in Part I of the *Code*. The second purpose is the promotion of substantive or concrete equality. Affirmative action programs are aimed at achieving substantive equality by assisting disadvantaged persons to compete equally with those who do not have the disadvantage. Section 14(1) is also an interpretive aid that clarifies the full meaning of equal rights by promoting substantive equality.

[160]See K. Kafele, "Racial Discrimination and Mental Health: Racialized and Aboriginal Communities" (2004) 3:3 *Canadian Diversity* 43.

[161]See for example, C.C. Smith, "Tuition Fee Increases and the History of Racial Exclusion in Canadian Legal Education" (2004) 3:3 *Canadian Diversity* 32.

anti-racism program it is important to devote resources to ongoing assessment. An internal review committee can be appointed for the purposes of conducting ongoing evaluation. However, the use of independent consultants or outside expertise can be particularly helpful in conducting this type of review and reporting back to senior management.

A review, evaluation and revision of an organization or institution's vision statement and policy should occur on a periodic basis, with input from those affected by it. It is also prudent to conduct a review of situations in which complaints have been raised under the policy, how they were handled and where improvements can be made.

APPENDIX — WORKPLACE POLICIES, PRACTICES AND DECISION-MAKING PROCESSES AND SYSTEMIC DISCRIMINATION

There are many tools available to assist employers in engaging in employment systems reviews to identify systemic barriers to racialized persons as well as others identified by *Code* grounds such as women and employees with disabilities. The following is a non-exhaustive summary of workplace policies, practices and decision-making processes that can lead to systemic discrimination:[1]
Recruitment, Selection and Hiring
In a best-case scenario, racialized persons would be hired at a rate that reflects their representation in the qualified external workforce. However, in many situations, this is not the reality. Employers who do not have a representative workforce may cite the failure of racialized persons to apply for the jobs, or the fact that the jobs were given to the most qualified candidate who happened not to be a racialized individual. In some cases the above explanations will hold true. However, in others, it is the recruitment, selection and hiring process itself that is impeding access to employment opportunities. Recruitment methods have a strong influence on the pool of candidates available to the employer. Moreover, some policies and practices tend to inappropriately screen out racialized persons, making them seem unqualified for the job. The following is a list of common barriers that can result in systemic discrimination and best practices to avoid systemic racial discrimination.

Barriers	*Best Practices*
Use of personal networks (*e.g.*, the recruiter's hockey team), social relationships (*e.g.*, friendships) and word-of-mouth referrals to recruit for vacancies. These types of informal processes tend to exclude those who do not share the same ethno/racial characteristics as the recruiter.	Formal job postings, which clearly describe the position and qualifications, are widely circulated (*e.g.*, through ads placed in newspapers, internet web sites and through the use of employment agencies) so that they can readily come to the attention of racialized persons.
	Some employers who are actively seeking to increase their diversity specifically advertise in ethno/racial newspapers. Others undertake outreach initiatives and go to places with a high representation of racialized persons to encourage applications from these individuals.

Barriers	*Best Practices*
Staffing decisions based on informal processes are much more likely to lead to subconsciously biased decision-making. For example, conducting an interview by chatting with the applicant to see if he or she shares similar interests and will "fit" into the organizational culture may present a barrier for persons who are or appear different than the dominant norm in the workplace.	Use of formal interviews conducted by multiple-person interview panels that use preset questions and score the answers against a pre-determined answer guide is a fair process that focuses on the ability to perform the essential duties of the job. Ideally, an interview panel should reflect the diversity available in the organization. The questions asked should be tailored to the objective requirements of the job, and not be based on subjective considerations such as whether the person exhibits "confidence" or is "suitable." The employer should be prepared to explain why a particular candidate was chosen. Written records from the interview and the entire job competition should be kept for at least six months if no complaint about the process is made, and longer if a complaint is made (until final resolution of the complaint).
Inflated job requirements (*e.g.*, a Masters degree when a Bachelors is all that is really required for the job, "Canadian experience" and specifying desirable personality traits as such "aggressiveness") can screen out or discourage racialized persons.	Job requirements should be reasonable and *bona fide* (see discussion of *bona fide* requirements). All prior experience should be assessed, regardless of where it was obtained. Culturally neutral qualifications (*e.g.*, the ability to plan a project and, complete it to required timelines) should be sought.

Barriers	*Best Practices*
Testing and simulations should be reasonable and *bona fide* so as to be reliable indicators of job performance. For example, psychometric and psychological testing may favour the dominant culture. A written test for a job that does not require written skills may screen out persons for whom English or French are a second language.	Testing should only be administered after a conditional offer of employment is made. It should only be used where the test can be shown by the employer to be a reasonable and *bona fide* method of assessing an applicant's ability to do the job. Testing that assesses personal interests, attitudes and values should be avoided altogether or, if legitimately required for assessing ability to perform a job, should be used with great care to ensure it does not favour certain cultures.

Training and Development
Training and development is integral to an employee's performance in the current job as well as to qualify an employee for future opportunities. The ability to engage in continuous learning is also a significant factor for employee morale.
Some training and development practices may exclude racialized employees. This has a direct impact on their careers, especially their upward mobility within the organization. It is prudent for organizations to monitor whether racialized persons are participating in training and development opportunities at the same rate as other employees and to address any differences.

Barriers	*Best Practices*
Training opportunities that are limited to senior employees may exclude racialized persons who may tend to be concentrated in lower level positions. In other cases, training for those at lower levels may be focused on current job skills, while training for more senior level employees may prepare them for promotion.	Organizations should make appropriate training available to all employees. Training should enhance current job skills as well as prepare employees for different or more advanced jobs.
Informing employees of training opportunities in an informal manner such as word of mouth or selecting employees for training based on the discretion of supervisors can result in discrimination.[2]	Training information needs to be widely disseminated through formal means such as e-mails, memos and posting on bulletin boards so it can reach all staff. Employers should allow employees to nominate themselves for training or should encourage all employees to seek out training, instead of selecting some for these opportunities. Fair, objective and clearly articulated criteria for deciding who receives the training should be used.
Lack of appropriate mentoring has been identified as a major barrier to training and development on the job. Informal mentoring that has managers selecting employees to "take under their wing" can result in racialized persons being left out.	Formal mentoring programs can ensure that all employees receive mentorship. In addition, participation of senior racialized persons in mentoring programs should be encouraged to provide role models.

Barriers	*Best Practices*
In an organization that does not provide training in anti-racism and human rights, managers may be unaware of what constitutes discrimination or harassment and how barriers operate to exclude people.	Ongoing training in human rights and anti-racism should be an integral part of training for all employees, but particularly those who act in a supervisory capacity. It should be made clear that human rights are part of the organization's culture and goals and that the training is not simply "window dressing" to comply with human rights laws.

Promotion and Advancement
Studies on employment equity consistently show that racialized persons are still largely concentrated in lower level positions within organizations and that upward mobility continues to be a problem. This is reflected in the number of human rights complaints that relate to promotion and advancement.
It is therefore important for organizations to be aware of how systems for promotion and advancement may result in obstacles for career progression. Some of the barriers and best practices in hiring, for example, in the interview process, are also applicable to promotions. And, as with all other decision making, the use of informal guidelines rather than written or circulated policies is likely to attract concerns, even more so if informal approaches are applied inconsistently.[3]

Barriers	*Best Practices*
Acting assignments as a stepping-stone to promotion can result in significant barriers if the process for awarding acting positions is informal, as is often the case. Even where there is a formal process for awarding acting assignments, an employer must be careful to ensure that all employees are equally aware of these opportunities.[4]	Acting assignments are awarded through a formal process that includes circulating information about acting opportunities to all eligible staff, using a clearly set out process for selection that is based on objective criteria such as a written test, a formal interview and written performance appraisals.
Organizations that rely on management identifying people who are "promotable," approaching certain employees to encourage them to bid for higher-level jobs, or assisting a favourite employee prepare for the selection process run the risk of human rights complaints.	Opportunities to move up in an organization should be openly publicized with the pre-requisites for eligibility and the process that will be used to select the successful candidate clearly identified. Moreover, as employees tend to watch for signals from management that if they bid for a higher-level position, they will be given fair consideration, it is therefore prudent not to encourage only certain employees to apply. Of course, any assistance with the process, for example, mock interviews, background reading materials, *etc.* should be provided on an equal basis to all candidates.

Barriers	*Best Practices*
Performance appraisals and progressive performance management are important tools in avoiding issues of discrimination. However, it is also a good idea for organizations to be aware that in some instances they can pose a barrier. For example, some performance evaluation systems have the employee rate him or herself and then discuss this with the manager. This may impact on some racialized persons, due to past experiences of discrimination or to cultural differences in selling oneself. As well, certain appraisals can inadvertently have an impact on an employee later seeking promotion. For example, emphasizing an employee's "ability to follow instructions" may pose a barrier to a promotion where "ability to take initiative" is being sought.	All employees should be measured against the same criteria. Managers should be sensitive to whether the performance appraisal methodology or the specific evaluation given could be having an unintentional adverse impact.
The clustering or concentration of racialized persons in certain jobs or categories, such as technical positions, can result in dead-ends to advancement, particularly into management. This can be compounded where subjective criteria, such as "communication skills" are emphasized in assessing suitability for a promotion.	Persons with strong technical skills should have the same opportunity to demonstrate the skills for other jobs. If necessary, training should be made available to bridge between technical and other jobs. An organization should acknowledge that there is more than one way to perform a job successfully and that requirements like "communication skills" may result in culturally non-neutral criteria being applied.

Retention and Termination
A barrier-free workplace will help reduce the turnover rate for racialized employees. In addition, appropriate procedures contribute to fewer human rights complaints arising from layoff, disciplinary action and termination.

Barriers	*Best Practices*
Racialized employees may leave an organization for reasons related to discrimination, harassment or perceived unfairness.	Organizations should have in place anti-discrimination and anti-harassment policies, including a mechanism to address any complaints. In addition, exit interviews can assist in determining whether human rights considerations are a factor in employees leaving.
Undefined policies for discipline or uneven application of discipline are a common basis for human rights complaints. Similarly, layoff and termination decisions that are not based on clearly defined, job-related, objective criteria are problematic.	An organization that has a well-documented progressive performance management process in place and that applies it evenly to all staff is engaging in good human resources practices as well as avoiding human rights concerns. If termination becomes necessary, this organization is better placed to demonstrate a legitimate basis for the termination.

Notes:

1 See also the Commission's publication *Human Rights at Work* which explains the types of questions that are and are not permitted at various stages in the recruitment process, Human Resources Professionals of Ontario & Ontario Human Rights Commission, *Human Rights at Work* (Toronto: Government of Ontario, 2004) at 40–50.

2 In *NCARR*, *supra*, note 121 a workplace questionnaire revealed that racial minorities had career development training experiences less often than White persons. There was also a difference as to how employees became aware of a training opportunity. White persons were more often informed of these opportunities by managers, whereas minorities tended to find out about these opportunities by using their own initiative [at paras. 55 and 56]. In *Nelson*, *supra*, note 85 the Tribunal found that officials of the Board of Education subjectively decided which teacher would be approved to take principal's courses. The complainant had to ask permission to take these courses and he was discriminated against because of the Board's refusal to let him take these courses, telling him that only those with an expectation of succeeding were being approved.

3 In *NCARR*, *ibid.* the Tribunal explained: Staffing decisions based on an informal process can present a barrier for promotion because, according to D. Weiner, the less formal the process, the less likely job qualifications will be set out in advance, will be assessed in a standard manner for all candidates and will allow for their recognition in candidates who are different from those who typically perform the job. [at para. 142]

4 Human rights decisions have identified informal practices with regard to providing acting assignments as a barrier for racialized employees who may be less likely to be approached with these opportunities. See for example, *NCARR*, *ibid*:

> This informality can create barriers in that not all potentially qualified staff can seek the acting position. Further, the acting assignment provides valuable managerial experience and gives the person who is acting the appearance of being "right" for the jobs. [at para. 147]

Policy on Creed and the Accommodation of Religious Observances

Approved by the Commission: October 20, 1996

The Ontario *Human Rights Code* (the *"Code"*) states that it is public policy in Ontario to recognize the inherent dignity and worth of every person and to provide for equal rights and opportunities without discrimination. The *Code* aims at creating a climate of understanding and mutual respect for the dignity and worth of each person so that each person feels a part of the community and feels able to contribute to the community.

Creed is a prohibited ground of discrimination under the *Code*. Every person has the right to equal treatment with respect to services, goods, facilities, employment, the occupancy of accommodation, the right to enter into contracts and the right to join trade unions or other vocational associations without discrimination because of creed.

These policy guidelines set out the position of the Ontario Human Rights Commission with respect to creed and the accommodation of religious observances related to a person's creed.

1. — Application of this Policy

The *Human Rights Code* applies to:

i) the workplace (including recruiting, application forms, interviews, promotions, office dress codes and shift schedules)

ii) services, goods and facilities (schools, school boards, shops, restaurants, hospitals, schools, correctional facilities and insurance services)

iii) the occupancy of accommodation (including rental accommodation such as apartments, college residences, hotel/motel facilities and condominium housing)

iv) contracts (verbal or written agreements), and

v) membership in occupational associations and trade unions.

2. — Creed[1]

Creed is not a defined term in the *Code*. The Ontario Human Rights Commission has adopted the following definition of creed:

> Creed is interpreted to mean "religious creed" or "religion." It is defined as a professed system and confession of faith, including both beliefs and observances or worship. A belief in a God or gods, or a single supreme being or deity is not a requisite.
>
> Religion is broadly accepted by the Commission to include, for example, non-deistic bodies of faith, such as the spiritual faiths/practices of Aboriginal cultures, as well as *bona fide* newer religions (assessed on a case-by-case basis).
>
> The existence of religious beliefs and practices are both necessary and sufficient to the meaning of creed, if the beliefs and practices are sincerely held and/or observed.

"Creed" is defined subjectively. The *Code* protects personal religious beliefs, practices or observances, even if they are not essential elements of the creed,[2] provided they are sincerely held.

It is the Commission's position that every person has the right to be free from discriminatory or harassing behaviour that is based on religion or which arises because the person who is the target of the behaviour does not share the same faith. This principle extends to situations where the person who is the target of such behaviour has no religious beliefs whatsoever, including atheists and agnostics who may, in these circumstances, benefit from the protection set out in the *Code*.[3]

In either situation, creed must be involved — either because the person who is the subject of the discrimination is seeking to practice his or her own religion, or because the person who is harassing or discriminating is trying to impose their creed on someone else. In both cases, creed must be involved.

---

[1]Human rights laws in other Canadian jurisdictions use terms such as "religion" as prohibited grounds of discrimination. For a review of decisions dealing with "creed" and "religion" see Tarnopolsky, *Discrimination and the Law* (Toronto: Richard De Boo, 1985) at 6-1 to 6-6.

[2]See *Singh v. Workmen's Compensation Board Hospital & Rehabilitation Centre* (1981), 2 C.H.R.R. D/549 (Ontario Board of Inquiry); *Bhinder v. Canadian National Railway Co.* (1981), 2 C.H.R.R. D/546 (Cdn. Human Rights Tribunal); reversed [1983] 2 F.C. 531; affirmed [1985] 2 S.C.R. 561.

[3]Atheists deny the existence of God; agnostics are of the view that nothing is known or likely to be known about the existence of God.

Creed does *not* include secular, moral or ethical beliefs or political convictions.[4] This policy does not extend to religions that incite hatred or violence against other individuals or groups,[5] or to practices and observances that purport to have a religious basis but which contravene international human rights standards or criminal law.[6]

3. — Equal Treatment on the Ground of Creed

Freedom of religion is the basic principle that informs the right to equal treatment under the *Code* on the ground of creed.[7] First, this implies that the law can require measures to facilitate the practice of religious observances.[8] Second, it also means that no person can force another to accept or comply with religious beliefs or practices.

This dual aspect of equality is emphasized by case law that has consistently protected freedom of religion and expressions of religious beliefs *as well as* non-beliefs and refusals to participate in religious practices.[9] According to a 1989 Board of Inquiry, no matter how convinced a person may be that he or she has a religious message that others should hear and heed, the *Code* prohibits the imposition of that message onto others. "In the workplace, a religiously militant employer is no more entitled to impose his or her version of

---

[4]But see *Obdeyn v. Walbar Machine Products of Canada Ltd.* (1982), 3 C.H.R.R. D/712 (Ont. Bd. of Inquiry) at D/716 - D/717.

[5]Not only are such groups not protected under the *Code*, but they may also be subject to provisions of the *Criminal Code*. Any reports of activities involving such groups should be immediately reported to the police.

[6]For example, female genital mutilation is a violation of women's human rights and is not protected on the ground of creed. See the Commission's *Policy on Female Genital Mutilation*.

[7]This is reflected in the Preamble of the *Code* which recognizes that the

> recognition of the inherent dignity and the equal and inalienable rights of all members of the human family is the foundation of freedom, justice and peace . . . [and that has as its aim] the creation of a climate of understanding and mutual respect for the dignity and worth of each person so that each person feels a part of the community and able to contribute fully to the development and well-being of the community and the Province.

[8]The notion of "accommodation" is dealt with in the section entitled "Duty to Accommodate."

[9]The principle was established in the Charter context in *R. v. Big M Drug Mart Ltd.*, [1985] 1 S.C.R. 295 and in *Ontario Human Rights Commission and O'Malley v. Simpsons-Sears Ltd.* (1985), 7 C.H.R.R. D/3102 (S.C.C.) at para. 24775.

religious enlightenment on employees than a sexually militant employer is entitled to impose his or her sexual ideas or wishes."[10]

4. — "Discrimination"

4.1 — Discrimination and Harassment

In *Dufour v. J. Roger Deschamps Comptable Agréé*, the Ontario Board of Inquiry stated that:

> [h]arassment or discrimination against someone because of religion is a severe affront to that person's dignity, and a denial of the equal respect that is essential to a liberal democratic society.[11]

Discrimination because of creed includes any distinction, exclusion, restriction or preference based on religion or belief and having as its purpose or as its effect the nullification or impairment of the recognition of human rights and fundamental freedoms on an equal basis.[12]

Harassment on the ground of creed is a form of discrimination. It involves conduct or comments concerning religious beliefs or practices which are known or ought to be known to be offensive. A single incident may constitute "harassment" and may create a poisoned environment if it is substantial or significant enough.

> *Example*: Management makes an employee's religious practices or beliefs the subject of jokes or derogatory comments or by other employees. This conduct is a form of harassment and the employee has the right to complain to the Commission.

4.2 — Direct and Indirect Discrimination

Discriminatory practices that fail to meet any statutory justification test[13] are illegal and will be struck down.

> *Example*: Unless the client-employer is a "special interest organiza-

---

[10] *Dufour v. J. Roger Deschamps Comptable Agréé* (1989), 10 C.H.R.R. D/6153 (Ont. Bd. of Inquiry) at 6170.

[11] *Ibid.*

[12] See the *International Declaration on the Elimination of All Forms of Intolerance and of Discrimination Based on Religion or Belief* (1981).

[13] S. 24(1)(a) of the *Code*, for example, allows an institution which primarily serves the interests of an identifiable religious group to prefer job applicants who are also members of that group.

tion,"[14] an employment agency that screens out all persons who do not share the employer-client's religion is acting illegally. Such practices cannot be justified on the grounds of customer preference.[15]

Example: A public school that gives priority to the Lord's Prayer as part of opening and closing exercises fails to treat non-Christians equally.[16]

Discrimination can also be indirect.

Example: A landlord prefers renting to tenants whose religion is the same as the landlord's. If a tenant refuses to sublet the apartment based on the landlord's "rule," then the landlord may be also be named as a respondent to a human rights complaint.[17]

4.3 — Constructive Discrimination

Constructive discrimination arises when a neutral requirement, qualification or factor has an adverse impact on members of a group of persons who are identified by a prohibited ground of discrimination under the *Code*. Because of its adverse impact, this is said to result in "constructive discrimination." Section 11(1) of the *Code* provides that discrimination occurs:

> Where a requirement, qualification or factor exists that is not discrimination on a prohibited ground but that results in the exclusion, restriction or preference of a group of persons who are identified by a prohibited ground of discrimination and of whom the person is a member.

Unless an exception is provided by law, constructive discrimination cannot be tolerated unless the employer takes reasonable steps to accommodate the affected person. A *prima facie* case of constructive discrimination is established if it can be shown that an individual has been subject to an exclusion, restriction or preference that has had an adverse impact on members of a group protected by the *Code*.

Typically, in the context of creed, issues arise in the areas of:

i) dress codes

---

[14] *Ibid.*

[15] S. 23(4) of the *Code*.

[16] See *Opening and Closing Exercises for Public Schools in Ontario* (Ministry of Education and Training, 1993). See also *Zylberberg v. Sudbury Board of Education (Director)* (1988), 65 O.R. (2d) 641 (Ont. C.A.).

[17] S. 9 of the *Code* deals with indirect discrimination.

ii) break policies

iii) recruitment and job applications

iv) flexible scheduling

v) rescheduling

vi) religious leave.

We will deal each of these special cases in Part 7.

4.4 — "Needs of the Group"

The term "needs of the group" means the needs of the religious group to which an individual belongs. The group's needs must be assessed in order to accommodate the individual.[18] Courts have looked to the accepted religious practices and observances that are part of a given religion or creed in order to assess those needs.

> *Example*: School teachers of the Jewish faith request a paid day of leave in order to observe Yom Kippur. In order to assess the needs of the group, the employer should seek information about the tenets of the Jewish faith, which establish that observant Jews cannot work on Yom Kippur.[19]

5. — The Duty to Accommodate

The *Code* provides the right to be free from discrimination, and there is a general corresponding duty to protect the right: the "duty to accommodate." The duty arises when a person's religious beliefs conflict with a requirement, qualification or practice. The *Code* imposes a duty to accommodate based on the needs of the group of which the person making the request is a member. Accommodation may modify a rule or make an exception to all or part of it for the person requesting accommodation.

Subsection 11(2) of the *Code* imposes the duty to accommodate in cases of constructive discrimination:

> 11. (2) The Commission, the board of inquiry or a court shall not find that a requirement, qualification or factor is reasonable and *bona fide* in the circumstances unless it is satisfied that the needs of the group of which the person is a member cannot be accommodated without undue hardship on

---

[18]S. 11(2) of the *Code*.

[19]*Commission scolaire régionale de Chambly v. Bergevin* (1994), 22 C.H.R.R. D/1 (S.C.C.).

the person responsible for accommodating those needs, considering the cost, outside sources of funding, if any, and health and safety requirements, if any.

5.1 — Rights and Duties

Both the people responsible for providing the accommodation and the person requesting it have rights and responsibilities during accommodation. We list some of these below by way of example:

For the Person Requesting Accommodation (person requesting)

For the Person or Organization Responsible for Providing Accommodation (Person responsible)

Person requesting: Take the initiative to request accommodation.

Person responsible: Respect the dignity of the person seeking accommodation.

Person requesting: Explain why accommodation is required.

Person responsible: Assess the need for accommodation based on the needs of the group of which the person is a member.[20]

Person requesting: Provide notice of request in writing, and allow a reasonable time for reply.

Person responsible: Reply to the request within a reasonable time.

Person requesting: Explain what measures of accommodation are required.

Person responsible: Grant requests related to the observance of religious practices.

Person requesting: Deal in good faith.

Person responsible: Deal in good faith.

---

[20] S. 11 of the *Code*. Individuals may seek accommodation for religious practices or observances that do not conform to established dogma, or they may seek to observe a practice which is not shared by all members of the creed. Dress codes, dietary laws, *etc.* are good examples of religious practices that are sincerely observed but may not be followed by all practitioners of a creed.

Person requesting: Be flexible and realistic.

Person responsible: Consider alternatives.

Person requesting: The individual may request details of the cost of accommodation if undue hardship may be a factor.

Person responsible: If accommodation is not possible because of undue hardship, explain this clearly to the person concerned and be prepared to demonstrate why this is so.

Sometimes, it may not be possible to completely resolve the conflict without causing undue hardship to the person responsible for providing the accommodation. A measure of accommodation may be acceptable if it meets the needs of the person, to the greatest extent possible short of undue hardship, and if it respects the dignity of the person requiring the accommodation.

5.2 — Unions and the Duty to Accommodate

In the case of discrimination in the workplace, both management and the union have a duty to accommodate. In *Central Okanagan School District No. 23 v. Renaud*,[21] the Court noted that although the principle of equal liability applies, the employer has charge of the workplace and will be in a better position to formulate measures of accommodation. The employer, therefore, can be expected to initiate the process of taking measures to accommodate an employee. Nevertheless, the Court also noted that they will not absolve a union of its duty if it fails to put forward alternative measures that are available. In short, when a union is a co-discriminator with an employer, it shares the obligation to remove or alleviate the source of the discriminatory effect.[22]

Example: Mr. Renaud, a school custodian, complained that the school board and the union had failed to agree on how to modify Mr. Re-

[21]*Central Okanagan School District No. 23 v. Renaud* (1992), 16 C.H.R.R. D/425, Supreme Court of Canada. The British Columbia *Human Rights Act* which was in force at the time did not mention the duty to accommodate explicitly. The principle reached by the Supreme Court of Canada in *Renaud*; namely, that the union as well as the employer has a duty to accommodate short of undue hardship, applies a *fortiori* to the Ontario *Human Rights Code* which explicitly imposes a duty to accommodate, short of undue hardship.

[22]*Ibid.* at D/438.

naud's shift hours. As a Seventh Day Adventist, he was unable to work Friday afternoons. It was decided that the union, together with the employer, had a duty to accommodate Mr. Renaud, short of undue hardship. Mr. Justice Sopinka wrote that the union may be liable in two situations:

> . . .first, [the union] may cause or contribute to the discrimination by participating in the formulation of the work rule that has a discriminatory effect on the complainant. This will generally be the case if the rule is a provision in the collective agreement;
>
> second, a union may be liable if it impedes the reasonable efforts of an employer to accommodate.[23]

In *Gohm v. Domtar*[24] the employer agreed to accommodate Mrs. Gohm by rescheduling her to work Sunday instead of Saturday, if she would not receive premium pay as provided by the collective agreement. The employer's attempt was blocked by the union. In finding that the union had discriminated against the complainant, the Ontario Divisional Court set out the concept of "equal partnership":

> Discrimination in the workplace is everybody's business. There can be no hierarchy of responsibility . . . companies, unions and persons are all in a primary and equal position in a single line of defence against all types of discrimination. To conclude otherwise would fail to afford to the *Human Rights Code* the broad purposive intent that is mandated. Any interpretation short of this would . . . be inconsistent with the philosophy and policy enunciated by the Supreme Court of Canada in *O'Malley v. Simpson-Sears*.[25]

6. — The Standard of "Undue Hardship"

The duty to accommodate is limited to those steps that may be required to accommodate, short of undue hardship. The burden of proving undue hardship lies with the person responsible for providing the accommodation. Each option should be examined to decide whether undue hardship will result. In determining whether or not an accommodation measure creates undue hardship, the following factors should be considered.

Cost: This includes the actual, present financial cost of carrying out an accommodation measure, as well as any reasonably foreseeable costs

[23]*Supra*, note 21 at D/436-D/437.

[24](1982), 89 D.L.R. (4th) 305 (Ont. Div. Ct.).

[25]*Ibid.* at 312.

which may arise. The cost to the person responsible for providing the accommodation may include operational costs which may be significant enough to constitute undue hardship.

Health and Safety Risks: Health and safety risks to the person requesting the accommodation, as well as to other employees and/or the general public are to be taken into consideration.

The assessment of these factors should be undertaken having regard to the size of the organization and its operations, the nature of its business, and its financial capabilities. In no circumstances should discriminatory customer preferences or those of co-workers be considered valid factors when evaluating whether or not an accommodation measure will create undue hardship.

Undue hardship is a relative concept. Accommodation may cause undue hardship to one employer but not to another. It is also possible that a method of accommodation which does not cause undue hardship to an employer now may cause undue hardship in the future. This may happen as circumstances change; for example, the number of employees requesting accommodation may increase significantly. Therefore, it is important to take into consideration all the relevant factors when attempting to determine when the standard of undue hardship is met.

7. — Specific Cases

Dress codes, work schedules or shift work sometimes impact adversely on individuals because of religious requirements. When this happens, the obligation to accommodate the individual, based on the needs of the *group*, is triggered under the *Code*.

7.1 — Dress Codes

Workplaces, services and facilities frequently have rules about dress. These may take the form of having to wear a particular uniform, having to wear protective gear, or a requirement that no person may wear a head covering. These rules may come into direct conflict with religious dress requirements. When they do, there is a duty to accommodate the person, short of undue hardship.

Example: A school requires its students to wear a particular uniform which prohibits any head covering. A Muslim girl wears a head covering as part of her religious observance. The school authorities have a duty to accommodate such a student and to permit her to wear the head covering.

Example: Certain creeds do not permit men to cut their hair. Workplaces that prefer to employ men with short hair are acting in a discriminatory manner, unless they fall under a legal exception under the *Code*. It should be noted that for health and safety reasons, an employer may ask employees to contain their hair with a net or other appropriate head covering.

Example: A school principal tells the parents of a Sikh child that wearing a turban or kirpan to school is not allowed. However, the "five K's" and related religious rules that include the wearing of a turban by Sikh men are part of the Sikh faith. In similar cases, boards of inquiry have rejected arguments by schools based on safety, on the grounds that wearing a ceremonial kirpan does not raise sufficiently compelling safety concerns. Schools must modify their policies to accommodate children seeking to modify the application of the rule for religious reasons.[26]

Considerations when dealing with dress codes:

i) What is the exact nature of the religious observance?

ii) What is the reason for the uniform or dress code?

iii) What measures can be taken to accommodate the person? Are there alternatives?

iv) Are there health or safety factors involved?

v) If so, do they involve the health or safety of the employee alone or are there consequences for other employees?

vi) If so, has the employer shown that to accommodate the employee would create a health or safety hazard that would amount to undue hardship for the employer?

As a rule, uniforms such as school uniforms and work uniforms that have no health or safety rationale can be modified easily to permit the person concerned to wear the required item(s) of clothing. Clothing or gear with a health or safety rationale may constitute a reasonable occupational requirement. Nevertheless, the employer is obliged to accommodate the employee; for example, by seeing whether the gear can be modified to permit the per-

---

[26] *Sehdev v. Bayview Glen Junior Schools Ltd.* (1988), 9 C.H.R.R. D/4881 (Ont. Bd. of Inquiry); *Pandori v. Peel Board of Education* (1990), 12 C.H.R.R. D/364; aff'd (1991), 14 C.H.R.R. D/403 (Ont. Div. Ct.) leave to Ont. C.A. refused.

son to wear the religious dress safely (subject to the undue hardship test), or by examining whether the employee can be transferred to another job that may be available in the company that does not require the clothing or gear.

7.2 — Break Policies

Some religions require that their members observe periods of prayer at particular times during a day. This practice may conflict with an employer's regular work hours or daily routines in the workplace. The employer has a duty to accommodate the employee's needs, short of undue hardship.

Possible forms of accommodation:

i) a modified break policy

ii) flexible hours, and/or

iii) providing a private area for devotions.

7.3 — Recruitment Procedures

A job applicant's religion cannot be used as a selection criterion for employment. There is an exception if the workplace qualifies as a "special interest" organization under the *Code*; that is, one that is a religious, educational or other social institution or organization that is primarily engaged in serving the interests of persons who are identified by their creed (s. 24(1)(a) of the *Code*). Subject to this exception, attempting to obtain information concerning the applicant's creed at the pre-interview stage of a recruitment process is not acceptable.

Consequently, invitations to apply for employment and job application forms cannot contain:

i) questions about availability for work that are asked in a manner that reveals the applicant's creed

ii) questions designed to reveal that religious requirements may conflict with the prospective employer's work schedules or workplace routines, or

iii) inquiries as to religious affiliation, places of worship that are attended or customs observed.

However, nothing prevents the employer from asking questions about creed at a personal employment interview, if the questions are otherwise permitted by the *Code*. A list of questions that can and cannot be asked during the employment application process can be found in the Commission's publication, *Employment Applications: Forms, Interviews*.

Example: It is permitted at an employment interview to ask religious membership for a teaching position in a denominational school if the job involves communicating religious values to students.

If a person has been offered employment, the person has the obligation to notify the employer of any religious requirements that are relevant to the performance of his or her duties, and to request accommodation.

7.4 — Religious Leave

When an employee requests time off to observe a holy day, the employer has an obligation to accommodate the employee. The extent of the accommodation required is an issue that comes up frequently: does the person have to be paid? Until what point? What about unpaid leave?

Two Christian holidays (Christmas Day and Good Friday) are also statutory holidays in Ontario. This is sometimes held up as evidence of the "non-discriminatory" nature of these holidays. Some employers have argued that because these holidays are now statutory, the employer has no obligation to accommodate employees by paying for other religious holidays. The Supreme Court of Canada has stated that this approach is incorrect.

In *Chambly*,[27] the Court examined the issue of whether the "secularized" nature of Good Friday and Christmas can excuse a policy alleged to be discriminatory based on religion because it is based on the Christian calendar. The Court wrote:

> Here the schedule of work is based upon the Catholic calendar of holidays. Nonetheless, I think the calendar should be taken to be secular in nature and thus neutral or non-discriminatory on its face. It will be remembered that the majority of the Court of Appeal determined that since the calendar did not have any religious aims, it was not discriminatory. With respect, I think this was an erroneous conclusion. It is true that this approach can properly serve to determine that there has been no direct discrimination. However, the analysis cannot stop there. Consideration must still be given to the *effect* of the calendar in order to determine if there is indirect or adverse effect discrimination.[28] [Emphasis in original.]

[27] *Commission scolaire régionale de Chambly v. Bergevin* (1994), 22 C.H.R.R. D/1 (S.C.C.).

[28] *Ibid.* at D/11.

In other words, the secularized nature of traditional Christian holidays may remove the taint of direct discrimination but not of constructive discrimination.

> *Example*: In *Chambly*, three Jewish teachers employed by a Catholic school board were denied access to the special purpose paid-leave provisions in the collective agreement so that they could observe Yom Kippur. They were told instead that they could take the day off, but unpaid. The Court held that the school board's leave policy had an adverse effect on Jewish teachers despite the secularized nature of Good Friday and Christmas. The analysis which led to the Court's finding of adverse effect is set out by Mr. Justice Cory.
>
>> . . . Christian holy days of Christmas and Good Friday are specifically provided for in the calendar. Yet, members of the Jewish religion must take a day off work in order to celebrate Yom Kippur. It thus inevitably follows that the effect of the calendar is different for Jewish teachers . . . [t]hey . . . must take a day off work while the majority of their colleagues have their religious holy days recognized as holidays from work. In the absence of some accommodation by their employer the Jewish teachers must lose a day's pay to observe their holy day. It follows that the effect of the calendar is to discriminate against members of an identifiable group because of their religious beliefs. The calendar or work schedule is thus discriminatory in its effect.[29]

The Court then examined the nature of the accommodation which would be required to alleviate the adverse effect. It rejected the view that the school board's offer of unpaid leave to the Jewish teachers was sufficient accommodation. Mr. Justice Cory wrote:

> If a condition of work existed which denied all Asian teachers one day's pay, it would amount to direct discrimination . . . The loss of one day's pay resulting from direct discrimination would not be tolerated . . . and would fly in the face of human rights legislation. Similarly adverse-effect discrimination resulting in the same loss cannot be tolerated *unless the employer takes reasonable steps to accommodate the affected employees*[30] [emphasis added].

The Court concluded religious leave should have been available under the special purpose paid-leave provision in the collective agreement. This did not cause undue hardship to the school board.

---

[29] *Ibid.* at D/11-D/12.

[30] *Ibid.* at D/12.

A number of general principles emerge from this case that are not limited in their application to the particular terms of the collective agreement examined in *Chambly*.

i) The employer has a duty to consider and grant requests for religious leave, including paid religious leave, unless to do so will cause undue hardship.

ii) Equality of treatment requires at a minimum that employees receive paid religious days off, to the extent of the number of religious Christian days that are also statutory holidays, namely two days (Christmas and Good Friday).

iii) The number of paid days may be three under some collective agreements which also make Easter Monday a holiday.

iv) Beyond this point (*i.e.*, two or three days) individuals may still seek accommodation. For example, measures might include additional paid leave days such as floating days or compassionate leave days, if such exist under company policy or collective agreements, or through unpaid leave.

v) The standard for *all* accommodation requests is undue hardship, which places a specific burden on the employer to produce evidence to the standard of undueness of the hardship and of its effect.

7.5 — Flexible Scheduling

The purpose of this measure is to allow a flexible work schedule for employees, or to allow for substitution or rescheduling of days when an employee's religious beliefs do not permit him or her to work certain hours. For example, Seventh Day Adventists and members of the Jewish faith observe a Sabbath from sundown Friday to sundown Saturday. Observant members of these religions cannot work at these times.

Flexible scheduling may include: alternative arrival and departure times on the days when the person cannot work for the entire period, or use of lunch times in exchange for early departure or staggered work hours. Where the person has already used up paid holy days to which he or she is entitled, the employer should also consider permitting the employee to make up time lost or use floating days off.

7.6 — Rescheduling and the *Employment Standards Act*

In some workplaces, rescheduling is a practicable accommodation measure but it poses a financial difficulty because of the requirement of paying wages at a premium rate, typically at one and a half times the regular rate, to individuals who work on Good Friday and Christmas. In Ontario, the *Employment Standards Act*, R.S.O. 1990, c. E-14 provides that:

> 26. (1) . . .where an employee works on a public holiday,[31] the employer shall pay to the employee for each hour worked a premium rate of not less than one and one-half times the employee's regular rate and, where the employee is entitled to the holiday with pay, his or her regular wages in addition thereto.

The requirement of premium pay for work done on public holidays may present a financial obstacle to accommodation in that it may constitute undue hardship. However, subsection 25(3) of the *Employment Standards Act* allows for another alternative, namely the substitution of public holidays:

> 25. (3) . . .where a public holiday falls upon a working day for an employee, an employer may with the agreement of the employee or the employee's agent substitute another working day for the public holiday which day shall not be later than the next annual vacation of the employee, and the day so substituted shall be deemed to be the public holiday.

If a person seeks accommodation and if s. 25(3) of the *Employment Standards Act* presents an alternative, rescheduling would constitute an acceptable form of accommodation.

Since the employer and the union have a joint legal obligation to accommodate employees as established in *Renaud*[32] and other cases, the employer and the union should be free to enter into agreements that are more generous than the minimum standards set by the *Employment Standards Act*, according to s. 4 of that *Act* such that a:

> 4. . . . right, benefit, term or condition of employment under a contract . . . that provides in favour of an employee a higher remuneration in money, a greater right or benefit or lesser hours of work than the requirement imposed by an employment standard shall prevail over an employment standard.

8. — Exceptions

Discrimination or unequal treatment may be legally defensible in certain circumstances.

---

[31] "Public holiday" is defined in s. 1 of the ESA as including "New Year's Day, Christmas Day and the 26th day of December."

[32] *Supra*, note 21.

8.1 — Participating in Special Interest Organizations

First, s. 18 of the *Code* provides that religious, philanthropic, educational, fraternal or social institutions which are primarily engaged in serving the interests of persons who are identified by their creed, may give priority to persons of the same creed with regard to participation or membership.

8.2 — Employment in Special Interest Organizations

Second, s. 24(1)(a) of the *Code* provides that religious, philanthropic, educational, fraternal or social institutions that are primarily engaged in serving the interests of persons identified by their creed may employ or give preference in employment to persons similarly identified, if the qualification is *reasonable and in good faith* in relation to the nature of the employment.

> *Example*: An educational institution such as a denominational school may prefer to employ teachers of the same denomination or faith. This hiring policy would be permitted if the teacher's own faith is related to the professional functions that teachers are expected to perform in denominational schools. However, this same defence is not available to the school with respect to the hiring of maintenance staff. The school must show that the requirement of belonging to a particular faith has a rational connection to the essential duties of a job.

8.3 — Reasonable and *Bona Fide* Occupational Requirements, Qualifications or Factors

If a requirement, qualification or factor is neutral or nondiscriminatory on its face, it may nonetheless have an adverse impact effect and may be discriminatory under s. 11 of the *Code*. However, the *Code* provides a defence if the requirement, qualification or factor is *reasonable and in good faith*, and if the needs of the persons affected cannot be accommodated without undue hardship to the person responsible for accommodating those needs.

> *Example*: A policy that requires all employees to work on a day which coincides with the holy day of a particular creed may be defensible, despite its adverse impact on some employees, because the nature of the business is such that a certain day of the week is critical to the operations of the establishment. However, the employer has a duty to accommodate an employee, if this can be accomplished short of undue hardship to the employer. Administrative inconvenience does not constitute undue hardship.

i) The requirement in question must be established in good faith with the *intention* of achieving its stated business objective, and not as a means to avoid the purpose of the *Code*.

ii) The requirement must be objectively connected to its stated business purpose.

iii) The requirement should be the least discriminatory alternative available, other things being equal.

9. — Conclusion

Religious pluralism poses a challenge in any multicultural society, especially one as diverse as ours. Although the law is developing rapidly in this area, an informed spirit of tolerance and compromise is indispensable to any civil society, as well as to its capacity to make opportunities available to everyone, on equal terms, regardless of creed.

Policy on Discrimination Against Older Persons Because of Age

Approved by the Commission: March 26, 2002
Revised by Commission: February 1, 2007

1. — Introduction

The Ontario *Human Rights Code* (the "*Code*") states that it is public policy in Ontario to recognize the inherent dignity and worth of every person and to provide for equal rights and opportunities without discrimination. The provisions of the *Code* are aimed at creating a climate of understanding and mutual respect for the dignity and worth of each person, so that each person feels a part of the community and feels able to contribute to the community.

The *Code* prohibits discrimination because of age in the social areas of employment, services, goods, facilities, housing accommodation, contracts and membership in trade and vocational associations. The *Code*'s protection against age discrimination extends to all persons over the age of 18.

Most of the complaints filed with the Ontario Human Rights Commission (the "Commission") regarding age discrimination are in the area of employment with services constituting the next largest area. Complaints in which age is cited as a ground of discrimination account for approximately 7–9% of the Commission's case load.[1] However, it is likely that incidents of age discrimination, particularly in job seeking and in services such as health care, remain unreported.[2]

This policy is the outcome of extensive research and consultation on issues of discrimination faced by older persons in Ontario.[3] In 2000, the Commis-

[1] In 2004-2005, age was cited in 184 out of 2,399 (7.7%) complaints filed with the Commission; Ontario Human Rights Commission, *Annual Report 2004-2005* (Toronto: Queen's Printer, 2005). In 2005-2006, it was listed as a ground in 211 of 2.399 complaints (8.8%) filed; Ontario Human Rights Commission, *Annual Report 2005-2006* (Toronto: Queen's Printer, 2006). Please note that complaints can cite multiple grounds; for example, age could be cited with sex or race.

[2] This observation is based on information received from individuals and organizations during the Commission's consultation on age discrimination and on data gathered in the Commission's research (*e.g.*, unemployment rates for older workers).

[3] Age discrimination experienced by younger persons was not included as it raises separate issues requiring their own study.

sion published a Discussion Paper, *Discrimination and Age: Human Rights Issues Facing Older Persons in Ontario* which set the stage for a province-wide public consultation. In June 2001, the Commission released its Consultation Report, *Time For Action: Advancing Human Rights for Older Ontarians* ("*Time for Action*"). The Report was intended to be a broad examination of all issues that may have an impact on the dignity and worth of older adults and may affect the enjoyment of equal rights and opportunities. As such, it contained a number of recommendations for government and community action. The Commission also outlined several measures that it would take to address age discrimination, including developing this public policy statement.

Several conclusions resulted from the Commission's research and consultation and form the basis of this Policy:

- Age discrimination is not seen as something that is as serious as other forms of discrimination, despite the fact that it can have the same economic, social and psychological impact as any other form of discrimination.
- Society has accepted age-based criteria as a way in which to structure policies and programs and to make decisions about people in areas such as employment and services.
- Despite the fact that the population is aging, many aspects of society have been designed in a way that is not inclusive of older persons.
- Preconceived notions, myths and stereotypes about the aging process and older persons persist and give rise to discriminatory treatment.
- Age often works in "intersection" or combination with other grounds of discrimination to produce unique forms of disadvantage. For example, women experience aging differently than men and older persons with disabilities face compounded disadvantage.
- Employers, service providers and others with responsibilities under the *Code* are looking for more information and guidance on meeting their human rights obligations *vis-à-vis* older persons. A shortage of skilled workers in certain fields means creative strategies are being sought by employers to attract and retain older workers.

This policy sets out the Commission's position on discrimination against older persons as it relates to the provisions of the *Code*. It deals *only* with issues that fall within Parts I and II of the *Code* and can be addressed under Part IV of the *Code*. *Time for Action* contains a broader examination of social policy and other issues which must be addressed through positive action by government and community partners. In addition, the Commission is engaged in, and will continue to undertake, initiatives to address broader human rights issues related to age. The purpose of this policy is to:

- help the public understand how the *Code* protects persons against discrimination as they age
- make older persons aware of their right to equal treatment in employment, housing accommodation, goods, services, and facilities, contracts and membership in trade unions, without discrimination
- assist employers and providers of services and housing accommodation, to understand their responsibilities under the *Code*
- set out how the Commission and its staff will deal with complaints based on age
- provide a resource for educational initiatives and development of internal policies and procedures.

The analysis and examples used in this policy are based on the Commission's research on age discrimination, principles and recommendations developed by the United Nations to guide countries in the promotion of the rights of older persons,[4] cases that have come before the Commission, tribunal and court decisions and the input of individuals and organizations in the Commission's consultation process.

2. — "Age", "Older" Person and Human Rights Concepts

2.1 — The Definition of "Age" in the *Human Rights Code*

Subsection 10(1) of the *Code* defines age as:

> an age that is eighteen years or more.

Older persons an bring a complaint of age discrimination in all social areas including:

- employment

[4]This includes the *Vienna International Plan of Action on Ageing*, Report of the World Assembly on Ageing, Vienna, 26 July–6 August 1982 (United Nations publication, Sales No. E.82.I.16), the *United Nations Principles for Older Persons*, General Assembly Resolution 48/91 of 16 December 1991, online: UN Programme on Ageing www.un.org/esa/socdev/ageing/index.html and *General Comment No. 6: The Economic, Social and Cultural Rights of Older Persons*, United Nations Committee on Economic, Social and Cultural Rights, E/C.12/1995/16/Rev.1 (1995), online: www.unhchr.ch/tbs/doc.nsf.

- services, goods and facilities (health care, social services, transit services, shops, restaurants, education, etc.)
- housing accommodation (such as rental accommodation, condominium facilities, hotels and motels, residential care facilities and social housing)
- contracts
- membership in occupational associations, trade unions and self-governing professions.

2.2 — The Terms "Older" and "Ageism" as Used in this Policy

Persons may experience age discrimination at any time in their lives. However, persons who belong to, or are perceived to belong to, certain age groups tend to be more vulnerable to certain forms of discrimination. For example, younger persons may be more likely than middle-aged or older persons to be turned away from housing because of stereotypes around the desirability of younger tenants. As this policy focuses on the forms of age discrimination most commonly experienced by persons *as they age*, it has become necessary for the Commission to adopt some terminology to describe the cohort who is at risk for experiencing these forms of age discrimination. It has chosen to do so by using the term "older" persons or workers. However, discrimination on the basis of age can be experienced by persons beginning as early as 40 to 45, particularly in employment. The term "older" is not meant to denote "old age" or stigmatize persons in any way. Rather it is simply being used as a relative concept, meaning older than those who are less likely to face the particular types of discrimination being discussed.

It is important to remember that the concept of who is an "older" person may be a contextual one. For example, while older workers are generally those over age 45, if the average age in a workplace is 25, a 37-year-old job applicant may be turned away because of a perception that she is unable to fit in with the workplace culture. Therefore in some situations, for example where the allegation pertains to negative attitudes and stereotypes about aging, it may be necessary to think not in terms of absolute, but rather relative age. In other contexts, actual age may be relevant; for example, where a person's age is used to determine eligibility for a program or service.

The terms ageism and age discrimination are both used in the Commission's work. Ageism refers to a socially constructed way of thinking about older persons based on negative stereotypes about aging as well as a tendency to structure society as though everyone is young. Ageism refers primarily to attitudinal barriers while age discrimination encompasses actions, namely treating someone in an unequal fashion due to age. Moreover, discrimination is a legal concept that has been defined in the *Code* and in court decisions and not every manifestation of ageism is age discrimination within the meaning of human rights law and policy. Ageism, however, is often the cause of age discrimination. It is therefore important from a human rights perspective to address both acts of age discrimination and also ageist attitudes that exist in society.

2.3 — Other Human Rights Concepts Referenced in this Policy

The *Code* and human rights case law contain a number of complex concepts and legal standards. For those who are not familiar with the terminology, it can be very difficult to understand a discussion of rights issues when these terms are used. Please see the Glossary at the end of this policy for a summary of the meaning of some of the key concepts that are referenced throughout this policy.

3. — The Intersection of Age with Other Grounds of Discrimination

The experience of age discrimination may differ based on other components of a person's identity. For example, certain groups of older persons may experience unique barriers as a result of the intersection of age with gender, disability, sexual orientation, race, ethnicity, religion, culture and language. Please see *Time for Action* for a more detailed discussion of "age and intersectionality" and the particular barriers faced by certain groups.

This understanding of the complexity of how people experience age discrimination means that, where appropriate to the circumstances of the alleged discrimination, all relevant grounds must be considered along with age.

> *Example*: A 55-year-old woman alleges that she was refused a job as a waitress because she didn't fit the image that the restaurant is trying to promote. The evidence reveals that the restaurant employs many younger women as waitresses as well as older men as waiters and maître d's. The fact that older persons (men) are employed and younger women are employed does not necessarily defeat her claim of discrimination as there may be unique stereotypes attributed to older women with regard to image or attractiveness.

It may be necessary to examine any stereotypes as well as the historical, social and political context associated with the particular combination of grounds.

> *Example*: A 72-year-old man has recently immigrated to Canada. He has difficulty finding a physician in his community as there is already a shortage of doctors and he is perceived as a patient who will require a lot of time due to his age and the fact that he is not conversant in English or French. He finds he must attend drop-in clinics and when he complains of feeling depressed, he is told that it is to be expected considering his age and the fact that he has recently moved to Canada. He is not sent for further assessment.[5]

In some cases persons may be put at a "double disadvantage" as a result of age combined with other grounds of discrimination.

> *Example*: Empirical evidence confirms that older persons and persons with disabilities all face higher unemployment rates. As well, members of racialized groups are more likely to be underemployed. Therefore, an older African Canadian person who is developing a disability will likely face compounded disadvantage in a job search.[6]

---

[5]This example is based on information received during the age consultation about the difficulty that older patients face in accessing medical services, which can be compounded by language barriers. In addition, empirical evidence suggests that many family doctors fail to treat older patients for depression, anxiety disorders and dementia and tend to "normalize" these conditions; see Ontario Human Rights Commission, *Discrimination and Age: Human Rights Issues Facing Older Persons in Ontario* (May 2000), online: Ontario Human Rights Commission homepage www.ohrc.on.ca. Studies on immigration and health have found that serious communication problems lead ethnic elderly populations to receive deficient treatment, extended hospital stays, unnecessary testing, premature discharge and problematic follow-up. (D. Kinnon, *Canadian Research on Immigration and Health* (Ottawa: Health Canada, 1999)).

[6]See Ontario Human Rights Commission, *Time for Action: Advancing Human Rights for Older Ontarians* (Toronto: Queen's Printer, June 2001) at 24, also available online: www.ohrc.on.ca and also *In Unison: A Canadian Approach to Disability Issues: A Vision Paper* (Federal/Provincial/Territorial Ministers Responsible for Social Services, 1998) which notes, "persons with disabilities have a lower rate of employment as well as a lower participation rate in the labour force than those without disabilities" (at 36). Similarly, Canadian Race Relations Foundation, *Unequal Access: A Canadian Profile of Racial Differences in Education, Employment and Income* (Prepared for the Canadian Race Relations Foundation by the Canadian

As a society, we must be aware of the unique ways in which people may experience disadvantage. In seeking to understand rights and responsibilities, in addition to this policy dealing with age discrimination, where other grounds of discrimination may be at play, other Commission policies such as the *Policy and Guidelines on Disability and the Duty to Accommodate* may be relevant.

4. — General Principles

4.1 — When is Differential Treatment Discriminatory?

The purpose of anti-discrimination laws is to prevent the violation of human dignity and freedom through the imposition of disadvantage, stereotyping, or political or social prejudice. In many cases, differential treatment because of age will clearly be discriminatory. However, in other cases, it may be necessary to consider whether the treatment can be said to constitute "discrimination" in the sense of being something that is protected by human rights law.

Some age-based criteria or qualifications are not based on stereotypes, are not offensive to human dignity and do not target a historically disadvantaged age group. For example, discounts on services for persons under 25 or over 55, retirement schemes that are based on a minimum age combined with years of service and measures aimed at facilitating the transition from full-time employment to retirement[7] would not likely be considered discrimination within the meaning of human rights law and policy.

In the context of equality claims under s. 15 of the Canadian *Charter of Rights and Freedoms* (the *"Charter"*), the Supreme Court of Canada has

---

Council on Social Development, 2000) describes barriers to employment faced by "visible minorities."

[7]In *Broadley v. Steel Co. of Canada Inc.* (1991), 15 C.H.R.R. D/408 (Ont. Bd. Inq.) [hereinafter *"Broadley"*], a provision in a collective agreement that granted employees with 25 years of service extended vacation benefits beginning at age 61 was challenged on the basis that it discriminated against employees under age 61. The Board found that this benefit was a special program designed to alleviate the difficulty older workers often experience in the transition from full employment to full retirement. The tribunal used a very broad definition of hardship: hardship covers a range of problems stretching from something "more than mere inconvenience" through "adversity, suffering, or humiliation" to "extreme privation or difficulty" (at D/411). However, this case was decided prior to the *Law* decision, *infra*, note 8. Today, a similar scheme could be dealt with by considering whether it discriminates by making distinctions which are offensive to human dignity.

offered the following three broad inquiries as a tool for determining whether discrimination has occurred:

> (1) **Differential Treatment** — Was there substantively differential treatment, either because of a distinction, exclusion or preference, or because of a failure to take into account the individual's already disadvantaged position within Canadian society?
>
> (2) **An Enumerated Ground** — Was the differential treatment based on an enumerated ground, in this case age?
>
> (3) **Discrimination in a Substantive Sense** — Finally, does the differential treatment discriminate by imposing a burden upon, or withholding a benefit from, an individual? The discrimination might be based on stereotypes of a presumed group or personal characteristics, or might perpetuate or promote the view that an individual is less capable or worthy of recognition or value as a human being or as a member of Canadian society who is equally deserving of concern, respect and consideration. Does the differential treatment amount to discrimination because it makes distinctions that are offensive to human dignity?

In *Law v. Canada (Minister of Employment and Immigration)*[8] the Supreme Court of Canada applied these three inquiries to conclude that even though the claimant was not entitled to a survivor's pension when her spouse died simply because of her age (she was 30), it was not discrimination under s. 15 of the Charter. Under the pension scheme, full benefits were paid to surviving spouses over the age of 45, partial benefits were paid to those between 35 and 45 and no benefits were available to surviving spouses under age 35. The Court found that persons under age 45 have not historically been subjected to discrimination and that younger persons do not face the same barriers to long-term labour force participation that the benefit was designed to address. The law did not stereotype, exclude, devalue or demean adults of the claimant's age.

4.2 — Age 65 Benefits, Special Programs and Special Interest Organizations

In certain circumstances, the *Code* permits programs and benefits aimed at a specific age group.

---

[8] *Law v. Canada (Minister of Employment and Immigration)*, [1999] 1 S.C.R. 497, [hereinafter *"Law"*].

The *Code* expressly provides for the preference of persons over 65 years of age:

> 15. A right under Part I to non-discrimination because of age is not infringed where an age of sixty-five years or over is a requirement, qualification or consideration for preferential treatment.

This permits seniors' discounts, seniors-only housing and other benefits aimed only at persons over 65.

As well, section 14 of the *Code* permits the use of special programs in all social areas. This allows preferential treatment or programs aimed only at older persons, even if they have not yet reached the age of 65, if the purpose of the program is to relieve hardship or economic disadvantage or to assist disadvantaged persons or groups to achieve equal opportunity.

It is important that special programs be designed so that restrictions within the program, for example with regard to the age of those eligible to participate, are rationally connected to the objective of the program. A failure to do so, can lead to successful challenge of the program and a finding that it is discriminatory.[9]

The Commission's *Guidelines on Special Programs* provide detailed information on how a special program can be planned, implemented and monitored.[10]

Section 18 of the *Code* allows certain types of organizations to limit participation or membership based on *Code* grounds including age:

> 18. The rights under Part I to equal treatment with respect to services and facilities, with or without accommodation, are not infringed where membership or participation in a religious, philanthropic, educational, fraternal or social institution or organization that is primarily engaged in serving the

---

[9]*Ontario (Human Rights Commission) v. Ontario (Ministry of Health)* (1989), 10 C.H.R.R. D/6353 (Ont. Bd. Inq.); affd 14 C.H.R.R. D/1 (Ont. Div. Ct.); revd (1994), 21 C.H.R.R. D/259 (C.A.) [hereinafter *"Roberts"*].

[10]Ontario Human Rights Commission, *Guidelines on Special Programs*, published in *Human Rights Policy in Ontario*, 3rd ed. (Toronto: CCH, 2001) at 241, also available online: www.ohrc.on.ca. The *Guidelines* provide valuable interpretation of section 14 of the *Code*; however, some of the requirements identified may not fit well with special programs designed to alleviate hardship or disadvantage associated with age. In particular, the *Guidelines* state that a special program should indicate that it is for a specific time and should be temporary in nature. However, this may not be appropriate in all cases; for example, where housing is specially designed to meet the special needs of older persons as, in all likelihood, those special needs will always exist.

interests of persons identified by a prohibited ground of discrimination is restricted to persons who are similarly identified.

Example: A charitable organization that is primarily engaged in serving the interests of women over the age of 55 through researching issues of interest to this group and lobbying government to make changes to law and policy limits its membership to persons similarly identified.

An organization that wishes to rely on this defence must show it meets all of the requirements of this section.

4.3 — When are Standards, Factors, Requirements or Rules that Discriminate on the Basis of Age Justifiable?

A person who wishes to assert a human rights complaint (a "complainant") has the burden of making out a *prima facie* case of discrimination. After that, the legal burden shifts to the party complained about (often known as the "respondent") to justify that its action is reasonable and *bona fide* in the circumstances (rules that can be justified as *bona fide* are often referred to as *bona fide* requirements or BFRs.).

Section 11 of the *Code* allows a respondent to justify a standard, factor, requirement or rule that has an adverse effect because of age by showing that it is a BFR. For example, a requirement that job applicants be "recent graduates" of a program may have the effect of excluding older candidates who are less likely to have completed their studies recently. However, the employer has the opportunity to show a justifiable reason for this requirement.

Section 24 allows direct discrimination in employment for reasons of age if the age of the applicant is a BFR because of the nature of the employment. For example, if an employer has a policy of hiring persons under a certain age only, it can attempt to show that this is reasonable in the circumstances.

Whether the discrimination is direct or by adverse effect, the Supreme Court of Canada has set out the same *three-step test* for determining whether discriminatory standard, factor, requirement or rule can be justified as a BFR. The respondent must establish on a balance of probabilities that the standard, factor, requirement or rule:

1. was adopted for a purpose or goal that is rationally connected to the function being performed
2. was adopted in good faith, in the belief that it is necessary for the fulfilment of the purpose or goal

3. is reasonably necessary to accomplish its purpose or goal, in the sense that it is impossible to accommodate the claimant without undue hardship.

The ultimate issue is whether the person who seeks to justify the discriminatory standard, factor, requirement or rule has shown that accommodation has been incorporated into the standard up to the point of undue hardship.

In this analysis, the procedure used to assess and achieve accommodation is as important as the substantive content of accommodation. The following non-exhaustive factors should be considered in the course of the analysis:

- whether the person responsible for accommodation investigated alternative approaches that do not have a discriminatory effect
- reasons why viable alternatives were not implemented
- ability to have differing standards that reflect group or individual differences and capabilities
- whether persons responsible for accommodation can meet their legitimate objectives in a less discriminatory manner
- whether the standard is properly designed to ensure the desired qualification is met without placing undue burden on those to whom it applies
- whether other parties who are obliged to assist in the search for accommodation have fulfilled their roles.

4.4 — Combating "Ageism" Through Inclusive Design

The Commission has defined "ageism" to mean, in part, "a tendency to structure society based on an assumption that everyone is young, thereby failing to respond appropriately to the real needs of older persons."[11] Ageism occurs when planning and design choices do not reflect the circumstances of all age groups to the greatest extent possible.

The Supreme Court of Canada has recently made it clear that society must be designed to be inclusive of all persons. It is no longer acceptable to structure systems in a way that assumes that everyone is young and then to try to accommodate those who do not fit this assumption. Rather, the age diversity that exists in society should be reflected in the design stages so that physical, attitudinal and systemic barriers are not created.[12]

---

[11] *Time for Action*, *supra*, note 6 at 13.

[12] In *British Columbia (Public Service Employee Relations Commission) v. BCGSEU*, [1999] 3 S.C.R. 3, [hereinafter *"Meiorin"*], the Supreme Court said:

> Employers designing workplace standards owe an obligation to be aware of both the differences between individuals, and differences that characterize

As a corollary to the notion that barriers should be prevented at the design stage through inclusive design, where systems and structures already exist, organizations should be aware of the possibility of systemic barriers and actively seek to identify and remove them.

4.5 — Individualization vs. Assumption

Another emerging human rights principle that has particular significance for age discrimination is the notion of individualized assessment and accommodation.

In the past, many standards, factors, requirements and qualifications that discriminate on the basis of age have been justified on the basis of *presumed characteristics* associated with aging.

> *Example*: Mandatory retirement of police officers and firefighters at age 60 has been accepted where an employer has provided evidence of cardiovascular disease and decline of aerobic capacity associated with aging and has shown that individualized testing is "impractical."[13]

However, in light of recent decisions from the Supreme Court of Canada, the Ontario Court of Appeal and the British Columbia Court of Appeal it does not appear that this type of approach is sufficient.[14] Rather, those seeking to justify age based policies must show that individualized assess-

---

> groups of individuals. They must build conceptions of equality into workplace standards. By enacting human rights statutes and providing that they are applicable to the workplace, the legislatures have determined that the standards governing the performance of work should be designed to reflect all members of society, in so far as this is reasonably possible. [at 38]

And in *British Columbia (Superintendent of Motor Vehicles) v. British Columbia (Council of Human Rights)*, [1999] 3 S.C.R. 868, [hereinafter *"Grismer"*] this principle was extended to all social areas covered by human rights legislation:

> Employers and others governed by human rights legislation are now required in all cases to accommodate the characteristics of affected groups within their standards, rather than maintaining discriminatory standards supplemented by accommodation for those who cannot meet them. [at 880]

[13] *Large v. Stratford (City)*, [1995] 3 S.C.R. 733.

[14] See *Meiorin, supra*, note 12, *Grismer, supra*, note 12, *Entrop v. Imperial Oil Limited* (2000), 37 C.H.R.R. D/481 (Ont. C.A.) and most recently *Greater Vancouver Regional District Employees' Union v. Greater Vancouver Regional District*, [2001] B.C.C.A. 435, a case dealing with mandatory retirement at age 65 in the public sector.

ment as a form of accommodation is impossible, *i.e.*, there is no method to do so, or that it represents an undue hardship.

The onus is on those seeking to justify a discriminatory standard to show they have provided individualized assessment and accommodation that recognizes the "unique capabilities" of every individual, unless to do so would cause undue hardship. Specifically, rather than judging individuals against *presumed group characteristics*, individualized assessment or testing to determine whether a person has the necessary aptitude or qualifications should be used, subject to the undue hardship standard.[15]

5. — Employment

Assumptions and stereotypes about older workers are unfortunately all too prevalent in our workplaces. Older workers are often unfairly perceived as less productive, less committed to their jobs, not dynamic or innovative, unreceptive to change, unable to be trained or costly to the organization due to health problems and higher salaries. These ideas about older workers are simply myths that are not borne out by evidence. In fact, there is significant evidence that older workers:

- are highly-productive, offering considerable on-the-job experience[16]
- do as well or better than younger workers on creativity, flexibility, information processing, accident rates, absenteeism and turnover[17]
- can learn as well as younger workers with appropriate training methods and environments[18]
- do not fear change but rather fear discrimination.[19]

Aging is a highly individual experience and it is not possible to generalize about the skills and abilities of a person based on his or her chronological

---

[15]*Grismer*, *supra*, note 12 at 880.

[16]TD Economics, *Canada's Talent Deficit* (September 6, 2001), online: TD Bank Financial Group homepage www.td.com/economics/index.html.

[17]N.C. Agarwal, *Mandatory Retirement and the Canadian Human Rights Act* (Prepared for the Canadian Human Rights Act Review Panel, October 1999) as cited in *Time for Action*, *supra*, note 6 at 39.

[18]*Ibid.* See also S. Imel, *Older Workers: Myths and Realities* (Eric Clearinghouse on Adult, Career and Vocational Education, 1999), online: Eric Clearinghouse on Adult, Career and Vocational Education, Ohio State University homepage http://ericacve.org.

[19]*Older Workers: Myths and Realities*, *ibid.*

age, any more than it is possible to make assumptions about someone based on any *Code* ground.

As a general principle, older workers should be treated as individuals, assessed on their own merits instead of presumed group characteristics, and offered the same opportunities as everyone else in hiring, training and promotion. They should be subjected to the same performance management practices as every other worker. Age, including assumptions based on stereotypes about age, should not be a factor in decisions about lay-off or termination.

In fact, underestimating the capabilities of older workers and treating them differently as a result can actually hinder them from maintaining their productivity and value. On the other hand, treating older workers equally allows employers to utilize a valuable resource, especially given that there are current and projected labour shortages.

> *Example*: An employer assumes that an older worker is too difficult to train and, in any event, is "riding it out to retirement." She is not sent for training and is given performance reviews that do not meaningfully identify strengths and areas where there is room for improvement. Her skills do not remain current, she cannot work on improving in her weaker areas and she is less motivated to work hard because she feels she is not a valued worker, is not expected to perform and will never be recognized for her contribution.

5.1 — Hiring

Older workers face significant barriers in finding employment. These can take the form of overt discrimination, such as not hiring someone simply because of his or her age, or more subtle or systemic discrimination, such as eliminating someone because of a perception he or she lacks "career potential." Such barriers can be compounded for persons who belong to groups that face their own barriers in accessing employment such as racialized persons, newcomers to Canada and persons with disabilities.

Whether the discrimination is overt or systemic, the *Code* protects individuals against discrimination on the basis of age in the hiring process. The *Code* prohibits a job advertisement that directly or indirectly classifies or indicates qualifications by age (subsection 23(1)). Similarly, application forms and oral questions must not directly or indirectly classify or indicate qualifications on the basis of age (subsection 23(2)). However, during an employment interview, questions may be asked about age provided that drawing a distinction on the basis of age is permitted under the *Code*.

This means that:

- *In an advertisement*: Statements that directly or indirectly relate to age should be avoided. Nothing should unfairly prevent or discourage an older worker from applying for a job. Requirements or duties for employment should be reasonable, genuine and directly related to the performance of the job.
- *On an application form*: While a form may ask "Are you 18 years or older?", it should not ask any other questions about or relating to age or date of birth. The form should not request copies of documents that indicate age. Some employers may even choose not to ask when schooling was completed as this may often indicate age.
- *During an interview*: Questions relating to age should only be asked if a *Code* defence applies such as where a special program is in place (section 14), employment is aimed specifically at persons 65 or over (section 15), the employer is a special interest organization serving a particular age group (section 18), or age is a BFR.

Where age or date of birth is relevant to company pension and benefit plans, this information should be collected after making an offer of employment and should be kept confidential.

Demonstrating that age was directly or indirectly a factor in a hiring decision can be challenging. Employers rarely state that age was the reason for not giving an applicant the job. However, the following considerations may suggest that age was a factor in not hiring an applicant:

- The employer indicated qualifications at any stage of the recruitment process which can reasonably be interpreted as a euphemism for age: *e.g.*, "Do you think you can handle this job? It takes a person who is full of vim and vigour." "We are looking to rejuvenate the workforce."
- There is evidence the assessor made an issue about the age of the applicant such as by commenting on the applicant's appearance and/or health or suggesting that the applicant may not fit into a youthful work culture.
- There is evidence that the employer considered age to be relevant when determining whether a person might adapt to certain job conditions such as menial tasks, minimal responsibility, low pay, shift work, being supervised by a younger person or that the employer felt that the candidate would not be trainable.[20]

---

[20]See *O'Brien v. Ontario Hydro* (1981), 2 C.H.R.R. D/504 (Ont. Bd. Inq.) where a 40-year-old man was refused an apprenticeship and the board of inquiry concluded that age stereotyping was the proximate cause and therefore discrimination had oc-

- There is evidence that the employer felt that person would be too costly to the organization because of his or her age: *e.g.*, there was an assumption that there will be less time to recoup training costs, the applicant will expect a higher salary, or an older person will cost more in benefits, especially related to disability.
- There is a pattern in the past hiring or employment practices of the employer suggesting a preference for, or an institutional bias toward, younger workers. Statistical evidence can be relevant in this regard (see discussion of statistical evidence in section 5.2 On the Job].
- The applicant's qualifications for the job were as good or better than those of the person hired and the person hired was significantly younger than the applicant. This will be compounded if any of the above factors are also present, such as a pattern of preferring younger applicants or commentary related to age. Also, the intersection of other disadvantaging factors such as race, ethnic origin, gender and disability may be important to consider if there is evidence of other patterns of discrimination in the workplace.

Some of the reasons that may be given for not selecting an older candidate are neutral on their face and yet may have a disproportionate impact on older persons. Some non-exhaustive examples include:

- *Turning away someone due to a perceived lack of "career potential"*: This requirement tends to adversely affect older applicants, especially where they are applying for "entry-level" type jobs. Given the high rates of turnover in today's labour force and the fact that it is rare for someone to remain with the same organization for their entire career, it may be difficult to justify turning away an otherwise qualified person on the basis that they will not stay and grow within the organization solely because of their age.
- *Refusing an applicant who has "too much experience" or who is "overqualified"*: Sometimes this is simply used as a pretext for direct discrimination. However, most often this is a neutral factor that is not intended to discriminate. Nevertheless, turning away candidates who are "overqualified" may sometimes have an adverse effect on older persons, as they are more likely to have significant work experience and at the same time be changing careers due to a period of unemploy-

---

curred. Although the employer did hire persons in the 40 to 65 age range, it did not hire them for the apprenticeship program. The employer considered that age had relevancy when determining whether a person might adapt to certain job conditions such as menial tasks, minimal responsibility, low pay and shift work.

ment or a desire to transition into retirement. This can be compounded for others such as newcomers to Canada who may have no choice but to apply to positions they may seem overqualified for in order to get "Canadian experience"[21] or to "get their foot in the door." Human rights law is based on the principle that employment decisions should be based on the applicant's ability to do the job. Therefore, the potential for human rights claims can arise where a qualified person is willing to take a job at the rank and salary offered but is refused simply because he or she has additional experience or skills.

- *Eliminating an applicant because the applicant's background is too diversified or contains gaps, the applicant is too specialized and will have trouble learning or the applicant's experience is too remote*: All of these factors can serve to disproportionately screen out older workers. Persons with longer work careers may appear more diversified and less "focused." This can be a particular problem for older women who have re-entered the workforce after childrearing and have had to retrain. Older workers may seem too specialized if they have been doing a job for a long period of time. Of course, if someone's experience is not relevant to the job, they may not be qualified and will not have to be hired. However, an older applicant should be attributed with just as much potential for redevelopment in a new area as a younger one. Finally, because older persons on average take longer to find a job and may have to accept alternative employment, it will not be unusual for an older applicant not to have worked in his preferred occupation for some time. This should not be an automatic disqualifying factor. Rather, consideration should be given to whether the time lapse has devalued his credentials.

An employer can always demonstrate a non-discriminatory reason for not hiring a candidate or preferring another candidate. Therefore, it is a sound practice, both from a human resources and human rights perspective, to develop up-front, objective and job-related screening criteria for job competitions, to score candidates relative to these criteria and to retain all records related to job competitions for at least one year after the competition has been completed.[22] As well, as discussed earlier in this policy an employer

---

[21]Requiring Canadian experience has been identified as a discriminatory barrier for newcomers to Canada; see Ontario Human Rights Commission, *Hiring? A Human Rights Guide and Human Rights at Work* (Toronto: Queen's Printer, 1999), available online: www.ohrc.on.ca.

[22]Persons who wish to file a human rights complaint are generally required to do so within six months of the last alleged incident of discrimination, unless the delay

can disqualify someone because of age, either directly or through a neutral rule that has an adverse impact, if it can justify the requirement as reasonable and *bona fide* using the *three-step test* set out above. However, it should be borne in mind that the decisions to date where employers have tried to justify turning someone away solely because of their age have shown that it can be very hard to do so, especially if the concern for the employee's capacity is largely based on cost rather than on health and safety.[23]

5.2 — On the Job

Due to current and anticipated labour shortages, many employers, economists and labour market specialists are beginning to stress the importance of promoting retention of older workers. Of course, ensuring an equal opportunity and discrimination-free work environment is one of the best ways to ensure that older workers will remain in the workforce longer.

Subject to *bona fide* requirements, denying or restricting employment opportunities or treating a worker differently because of age is a violation of the *Code*. Examples of unequal treatment because of age include but are not limited to:

- Limiting or withholding employment opportunities including transfer, promotion and training opportunities.

---

in filing the complaint has been incurred in good faith and has not caused substantial prejudice to any person affected by the delay (subsection 34(1)(d)). Under the amendments to the *Code* in Bill 107, which received Royal Assent on December 20, 2006 but has not yet come into force, applicants will be able to file applications with the Human Rights Tribunal up to one year after the last alleged incident of discrimination; the Tribunal may accept applications after that period if the delay was incurred in good faith and no substantial prejudice will result from the delay (section 35).

[23]In *Canada (Human Rights Commission) v. Greyhound Bus Lines of Canada Ltd.* (1984), 6 C.H.R.R. D/2512 (Can. Trib.); affd 7 C.H.R.R. D/3250 (Can. Rev. Trib.); affd 8 C.H.R.R. D/4184 (F.C.A.) the employer was unable to establish that its policy of only hiring new bus drivers under the age of 34 was a *bona fide* requirement. The evidence of a relationship between age and inability to cope with stress was rejected. Air Canada did not succeed in justifying a similar requirement that pilot applicants over age 27 have greater qualifications than younger applicants. Air Canada sought to do so on the basis of public safety and economic factors; *Air Canada v. Carson* (1985), 6 C.H.R.R. D/2848 (Fed. C.A.).

- Not assigning an older worker to certain tasks or projects or subjecting an older worker to an unwanted transfer because of age.[24]
- Performance managing older workers in a different way than other workers. This includes subjecting an older worker's performance to a higher level of scrutiny but also failing to performance manage because of a perception that the older worker's performance is linked to age or because of a belief that performance management is not necessary as the person will soon be retiring.
- Not recalling someone from lay-off because of age.[25]
- Terminating someone's employment because of age.[26] Of course, employers are not precluded from terminating older workers, using the same performance management criteria as for any other worker, where there are legitimate performance concerns that are based on objective evidence about the employee's ability to perform the duties of the job.

Statistical evidence regarding systemic issues in the workplace can constitute circumstantial evidence from which it may be possible to infer that discrimination probably occurred in an individual case.[27]

> *Example*: An organization was concerned about the aging of its employees and the fact that there would be a number of managers retiring within a 15-year period. Accordingly, recruitment practices were modi-

---

[24]See *Andronik v. Guildford Golf and Country Ltd.* (1993), 21 C.H.R.R. D/400 (B.C.C.H.R.) [hereinafter *"Andronik"*].

[25]In *Silzer v. Chaparral Industries (86) Inc.* (1993), 20 C.H.R.R. D/155 (B.C.C.H.R.), the tribunal found that the 64-year-old complaint was discriminated against on the basis of age and a perceived physical or mental disability when he was not recalled to work after a layoff. The complainant's history of medical problems was found to be a factor in his not being recalled and the employer suggested early retirement as a possible solution to the complainant's perceived health problems. This possibility existed because of the complainant's age, therefore age, in combination with perceived disability, was a factor in failing to recall the complainant.

[26]In *Kearns v. Dickson Trucking Ltd.* (1988), 10 C.H.R.R. D/5700 (Can. Trib.) a 69-year-old salesman was terminated despite excellent performance. The first time the alleged reason for termination was raised was in the termination letter. The reason given suggested that there would no longer be a need for his position, however it was not declared redundant and was filled by a younger person. A case of age discrimination was successfully made out.

[27]*Chopra v. Department of National Health and Welfare* (1998), 32 C.H.R.R. D/168 (F.C.J.).

fied to meet the "long-term professional needs of the department." Statistical evidence dealing with age distribution of employees showed a disproportionate number of employees under 40 and the vast majority of recruits under 30. The tribunal found that the organization had set about recruiting a younger work force and that the 43-year-old complainant who had been with the organization seven years was not offered a promotion into a particular position, in part, because he did not fit the profile for the organization's recruits into that position. There was "compelling circumstantial evidence of an organizational predisposition against promoting older internal candidates into ES positions."[28]

Older workers tend to experience disproportionate displacement or disadvantage as a result of workplace reorganization and downsizing. This can occur for a number of reasons such as an assumption that due to their age, or the fact that they have been doing their job a certain way for a period of time, they will have more trouble learning new technology or procedures, a perception that they will not be willing to accept changes to terms and conditions of work such as reduced pay or different work hours, or a belief that it is more equitable to displace them as they can take early retirement. As well, reorganization and downsizing may simply be used as a means to "rejuvenate" the workforce by getting rid of older workers.

Example: Due to an economic downturn, a company was forced to lay off staff. The complainant, a foreman, had worked for the company for over 32 years and was 57 at the time he was selected for termination along with another foreman who was aged 56. Both were offered a generous retirement package. The two foremen who remained were younger than the two released. The vice-president had prepared a note indicating that the two older workers who were terminated were told of the need to reduce people and that they "hoped to keep people with career potential." The tribunal found age discrimination on the basis of the good employment record of the complainant, the ages of those selected for lay-off compared to those retained and this statement which was found to be a "euphemism; its meaning concerns age."[29]

---

[28] *Singh v. Canada (Statistics Canada)* (1998), 34 C.H.R.R. D/203 at para. 226 (Can. Trib.) [hereinafter "*Singh v. Statistics Canada*"].

[29] *McKee v. Hayes-Dana Inc.* (1992), 17 C.H.R.R. D/79 (Ont. Bd. Inq.) [hereinafter "*McKee*"].

Example: A business that served the public opened a larger facility designed to handle a greater volume of clients and introduced a new computer system. Two female staff persons in their 50s were transferred to positions which represented a demotion. Younger workers staffed the positions that they previously held. In finding age discrimination, the tribunal noted that the employer had not provided the complainants a meaningful opportunity to demonstrate they were able to perform the new duties, failed to provide even a minimal training and didn't give the complainants notice of the alleged performance concerns that were raised as a defence at the hearing. The tribunal noted that the employer's belief about older workers' capacity to learn and adapt to technological change was impressionistic and not a valid reason for changing the complainants' duties.[30]

The following factors will help guide any consideration of whether age discrimination has occurred in a workplace reorganization or downsizing:

- Comparison of the performance of those who were selected for termination versus those who remained with the organization.
- Statistical evidence indicating a disproportionate number of younger workers can suggest an organizational bias for younger workers. As well, an analysis of the ages of those who were selected for adverse treatment in a reorganization as well as an analysis of the ages of those who were not can be relevant circumstantial evidence that age was a factor in the company's decision making.[31]
- Criteria that can be applied in a way that disproportionately impacts on older workers such as: flexibility, rate of pay, ability to adapt to change, ability to be trained, being a generalist vs. a specialist. An assessment of personal suitability that is based on subjective considerations is always vulnerable to scrutiny as it can result in stereotyping or unconscious biases being brought into play.[32]
- Indications that workers were selected for termination because of a perceived propensity to retire or because they are pension-eligible.[33]

---

[30]*Andronik*, *supra*, note 24.

[31]See *Salter*, *infra*, note 33 and *McKee*, *supra*, note 29.

[32]*Singh v. Statistics Canada*, *supra*, note 28 at para. 245.

[33]In *Salter v. Newfoundland* (2001), 41 C.H.R.R. D/68 (Nfld. Bd. Inq.) [hereinafter "*Salter*"], the tribunal found that the factor of being a pension-eligible employee was considered in making the determination to declare the complainant redundant

- A determination that the organization deviated from a previous approach, such as using seniority.
- Evidence of statements that can be interpreted as euphemisms for age such as "career potential," "rejuvenate," "renewal," *etc*.

On the other hand, there are ways in which employers can ensure that the decisions made in a workplace reorganization will be fair and non-discriminatory. Criteria should be objective and not based on subjective impressions about the particular worker's enthusiasm, flexibility or willingness to adapt. They should be demonstrably related to the goals of the reorganization or the needs that have been identified by the company. Ideally, positions rather than people should be selected for elimination and those positions should not subsequently be refilled.[34]

> *Example*: A company decides that due to decreased profits and the need to be more competitive in the marketplace, it will introduce a new, more automated production system. It identifies the number of positions that will be required to be staffed and what the duties of each will be. It also identifies the current positions that will no longer be required and why. It advises each person whose position has been determined redundant of this fact and how this decision was reached. It then invites all of these persons to compete for the new positions. It runs the competition using objective, age-neutral criteria and a scoring system which measures each candidate against the stated criteria. Past performance reviews are taken into account. The candidates with the best scores are selected and sent for training.

---

and that this was synonymous with considering his age. Age discrimination was found in the case.

[34]In *Salter*, *ibid*. one of the factors that contributed to a finding of age discrimination was that the complainant's position, though declared redundant, had been modified and then filled by a younger co-worker:

> . . .the Board finds that William Clarke occupies either Eric Salter's previous position . . . or a modification of [his] previous position . . . This brings into question the propriety of the selection process for this position and the decision to declare Mr. Salter redundant. The fact that Eric Salter was told his position was abolished when it was not is a very significant factor in allowing this Board to conclude that his redundancy has more than a "subtle scent of discrimination." [at para. 155.]

5.3 — Retirement

Prior to December 12, 2006, the *Code* did not prohibit age discrimination in employment against persons aged 65 or older. As a result, policies requiring mandatory retirement at age 65 could not be challenged under the *Code*. This is now no longer the case. Persons aged 65 and older who believe that they have been discriminated against on the basis of age, including through mandatory retirement policies, may file a complaint of discrimination on the basis of age.

This does not mean that employers cannot have retirement programs based on a certain age. Rather, it means that such programs cannot be mandatory, except for judges, masters, and justices of the peace under the *Courts of Justice Act*, for whom there is a specific exemption under the *Code*.

In some occupations, employers may wish to impose mandatory retirement on workers who reach a certain age on the basis that being less than that age is a BFR.[35] For example, policies that require police officers and fire fighters to retire at age 60 are frequently used. In the past, before the new *three-step test*, such policies were found justifiable on the basis of evidence of a correlation between age and physical decline that could impact upon the ability to perform the essential duties of the job safely, combined with evidence that individualized testing is impractical. However, it should be noted that in light of the new *three-step test* articulated by the Supreme Court of Canada, it is no longer acceptable to rely on presumed group characteristics associated with aging. An employer seeking to justify mandatory retirement must show that individualized assessment, as a form of accommodation, is impossible, in the sense that there is no method to do so, or that individualized assessment represents an undue hardship. Moreover, the British Columbia Court of Appeal has recently confirmed that mandatory retirement policies should be approached on a case-by-case basis with the employer bearing the onus of establishing that its policy is justifiable in the circumstances of its workplace.

---

[35]Mandatory retirement at age 60 for police officers, fire fighters and a Chief Fire Prevention officer have been found to be a BFR; *Large v. Stratford (City), supra*, note 13 (Police Officers), *Saskatchewan (Human Rights Commission) v. Saskatoon (City)*, [1989] 2 S.C.R. 1297, (Chief Fire Prevention Officer), *Hope v. St. Catharines (City)* (1998), 9 C.H.R.R. D/4635 (Ont. Bd. Inq.) (Firefighters). Mandatory retirement of school bus drivers at age 65 has been found to be a BFR as expert medical evidence indicated that, as a group, those over 65 are more likely to have accidents, and that it is impossible to test individually to determine who is likely to have health problems or create risks for others; *MacDonald v. Regional Administrative School Unit No. 1* (1992), 16 C.H.R.R. D/409 (P.E.I. Bd. Inq.).

Except in circumstances where mandatory retirement can be shown to be a *bona fide* requirement, collective agreements containing mandatory retirement provisions can no longer be enforced.

Early retirement packages are often offered as an incentive to promote voluntary exit from the workforce. This can have many benefits to all workers: older workers may be offered a lucrative incentive which will allow them to pursue other interests or ambitions while at the same time ensuring that fewer workers will involuntarily lose their jobs. When designed properly, early retirement schemes are appropriate and will not raise human rights concerns. Also, if an employer has a non-discriminatory reason for terminating an older worker and wishes to offer the option of early retirement, there is nothing to prevent it from doing so. However, as early retirement schemes by definition target older workers, great care must be employed in using them as a means to achieve downsizing objectives.

In some situations using early retirement to encourage older workers to leave the organization can raise concerns from a human rights perspective. This will occur if there is direct or implicit pressure being applied to accept retirement. Furthermore, if the older worker does not accept retirement, is subsequently selected for termination and the reason for selecting him or her for termination is related to age, an organization may face a human rights complaint.

> *Example*: A company decides that it needs to reduce its workforce by 10%. Human resources reviews the files of all workers and identifies all workers over the age of 60. Each one of them is called in for a meeting with management and told that they are nearing retirement age and should accept an early retirement package so that younger persons won't lose their jobs. They are warned that if they do not do so, their position may be selected for elimination in which case they will simply receive severance and lose the opportunity to receive the early retirement package. Under these circumstances, some older workers feel compelled to accept the offer despite the fact that they were planning to work longer.

The fact that a generous retirement package is offered does not defeat a claim of age discrimination if the early retirement option was not truly voluntary.[36]

---

[36]See *McKee*, *supra*, note 29.

Employers can take steps to ensure that an offer of early retirement is not coercive:

- Define the eligibility criteria for the voluntary retirement program and share them with all staff, irrespective of age, through a neutral medium such as a written document. A response deadline and contact who can provide information should be provided so that those who qualify and are interested in the option can then decide if they wish to follow up on the offer, without any pressure from management. Some employers even choose to offer similar voluntary exit incentive packages to persons who are not near retirement age.
- Do not make any link between acceptance of the package and job loss. If the workforce is being downsized, indicate what the criteria will be for selecting the jobs that will be eliminated. Employees can even be assured that eligibility for the voluntary exit program will in no way influence decisions about job loss.

Conversely, an employee cannot claim age discrimination if the employer does not offer him or her access to the voluntary exit program because the employer still requires his or her services.[37]

5.4 — Pensions, Benefits and Seniority

The protections in the *Code* extend to pension and benefit plans. As well, other grounds of discrimination such as disability, marital status and same-sex partnership status are often relevant when considering pension benefits.

Section 25(2) of the *Code* states that rights are not infringed by pension and benefit plans that comply with the *Employment Standards Act* and regulations. O. Reg. 286/01 under the *Employment Standards Act* regulates employment-related disability, medical, dental, drug, life insurance and pension plans. This regulation defines "age" as "any age of 18 years or more and less than 65 years." This means that pension and benefit plans that differentiate based on age 65 cannot be challenged under the *Code*. The Commission has publicly expressed its concerns regarding these provisions and recommended legislative change.[38] The Commission would encourage employers and unions to nevertheless develop and maintain pension and bene-

---

[37]See for example *Boeing Toronto Ltd. v. CAW-CLC, Local 673*, Arbitrator Kevin M. Burkett, Grievance No. W18/01, July 5, 2001.

[38]See the Commission's *Submission to the Standing Committee on Justice Policy on Bill 211*, the *Ending Mandatory Retirement Amendment Act*, dated November 23, 2005, available online at www.ohrc.on.ca.

fit policies and programs that comply with the spirit of the *Code*, do not use age-based criteria, and are based on *bona fide* requirements.

The Regulation also permits other age-related distinctions in the provision of pension and benefit plans, for example where age-related distinctions in contribution rates are made on an actuarial basis.

Sick leave plans that make benefits available based on age have been found to be discriminatory.[39] Reduced pension benefits for early retirees have been found not to be discriminatory where the actuarial present value of reduced pensions for early retirees is at least equal to the present value of the deferred pension for those who wait until the age of eligibility for full pensions.[40] Similarly, basing eligibility for pension benefits on reaching a certain age will not likely be considered discriminatory.[41]

It is not permissible to use age to assign seniority when more than one employee is hired on the same day.[42]

5.5 — Accommodating the Older Worker

Older workers may require accommodation for reasons such as disability and the need to care for an ailing spouse. The Commission's *Policy and Guidelines on Disability and the Duty to Accommodate* outlines rights and responsibilities with regard to accommodating workers with disabilities. In addition, the Commission's publication *Human Rights at Work* explains that an employer's duty to accommodate on the basis of family and marital status extends to employees who have work absences due to family-related responsibilities and encourages flexible work arrangements to help employ-

[39] *Heidt v. Saskatoon (City)* (1988), 9 C.H.R.R. D/5380 (Sask. Bd. Inq.); affd 10 C.H.R.R. D/5808 (Sask. Q.B.); revd 12 C.H.R.R. D/387 (C.A.); leave to appeal refused 74 D.L.R. (4th) vii (S.C.C.). The Saskatchewan *Human Rights Code* contained a provision that the prohibition on age discrimination in employment does not prevent the operation of any term of a *bona fide* group or employee insurance plan. The Court of Appeal held that the defence had not been made out as no evidence was led to establish that the discrimination was reasonably necessary to allow the employer to put into place a viable and cost-effective sick plan.

[40] *Younger v. Gulf Canada Resources Ltd.* (1988), 10 C.H.R.R. D/6114 (Alta. H.R. Comm.).

[41] For example, a Factor 80 retirement scheme.

[42] *Dalton v. Canadian Human Rights Commission* (1985), 15 D.L.R. (4th) 548 (T.D.); rev'd in part 25 D.L.R. (4th) 260 (C.A.); leave to appeal refused 67 N.R. 158n (S.C.C.).

ees balance work and personal life.[43] These obligations exist regardless of the age of the employee; however, due to a relationship between age and disability, these needs may become more apparent as workers, and members of their family, age.

Flexible work arrangements also benefit older workers who may be experiencing a decline in capacity and provide for an easier transition into retirement. Traditionally, workforce participation has been seen as an "all or nothing proposition;" people either work full-time or are retired. However, moving from fulltime work, spanning a lifetime, to the complete absence of work is a major change carrying with it social, psychological and financial implications.[44]

In order to facilitate the transition from employment to retirement and to encourage older workers to remain in the workforce longer, there is currently a trend towards more flexibility and phased in retirement. Therefore, employers may want to consider measures such as:

- flexible hours and conditions of work such as compressed work weeks (working longer days in exchange for a shorter work week), flex-time (flexibility in start, end and break times as long as an agreed upon number of hours are worked), tele-working (working from home)
- part-time arrangements and job sharing, which allow for a transition into retirement while at the same time providing opportunities for other workers, e.g., a new parent who wishes to work part-time as well
- employing workers who have chosen to retire on short-term contracts or as consultants.

As discussed earlier, the duty to accommodate requires designing a workplace that is inclusive of older workers. It also requires individualized assessment and accommodation to meet the changing needs and capacities of older workers. For example, if an older worker finds a physically demanding task challenging, the employer should either assign it to someone else if it is not one of the essential duties of the position, or seek other ways in which to accommodate the worker.

6. — Housing Accommodation

Section 2 of the *Code* protects older persons against discrimination in housing. This right applies to renting, being evicted, building rules and regula-

---

[43]Ontario Human Rights Commission, *Human Rights at Work*, *supra*, note 21 at 71-72.

[44]*Broadley v. Steel Co. of Canada Ltd.*, *supra*, note 7 at D/412.

tions, repairs and use of services and facilities. Housing includes a range of accommodation options including rental accommodation, condominiums, retirement homes and care facilities. There can be some overlap between housing and services, for example seniors' residences in which services such as housekeeping, meals or medical assistance are provided.

The *Code* prohibits either direct or adverse effect discrimination in housing. For example, a housing provider should not turn away older persons because it wishes to attract more youthful residents. Similarly, older persons who may be paying lower rents due to longer tenure in their rental unit should not be targeted for eviction by landlords who wish to attract new tenants at a higher rent.

While there are some exceptions, older persons tend not to be turned away from housing due to discriminatory perceptions about age. Rather the main barrier to housing experienced by older persons is a lack of housing to meet their needs both in terms of affordability and also in terms of accessibility.

It is the Commission's view that older persons benefit from the support, community, and income security offered by seniors' housing projects. As well, the concept of "aging in place" has been recognized by the Commission as a central consideration so that in some cases it may be appropriate to offer "seniors' housing" to those under the age of 65 who may have special needs that will remain as they age.

Therefore, the Commission would encourage housing aimed at older persons, including those less than 65 years of age, which will foster the objectives of the *Code*. However, those responsible for such housing must be aware that age restrictions are *prima facie* discriminatory and that they must be able to justify them using one of the defences in the *Code*. Possible options include:

- Section 15: provides a defence to preferential treatment of persons 65 and over. This insulates housing that is limited to persons over age 64 from challenge by those too young to qualify.
- Section 14: permits special programs to alleviate hardship and disadvantage. This may allow social housing aimed at older low-income persons over a certain age, but starting at less than 65, if it can be shown that this group experiences particular disadvantage associated with their socio-economic status that younger persons do not experience. This might also permit specially designed barrier-free housing projects offered exclusively to older persons with disabilities.
- Section 18: religious, philanthropic, educational, fraternal or social institutions or organizations which primarily serve the interests of older persons, or older persons who belong to a particular religious or ethnic community, and which provide housing accommodation as part of their

services may be able to restrict that accommodation to persons who are similarly identified. However, in order to rely on this defence, the provision of accommodation alone is not sufficient, some other "service or facility" must be provided.[45]

Example: A synagogue runs a seniors' residence the purpose of which is to foster the religion and culture of its residents. Prayer services are provided and kosher food is served. It restricts membership to persons of the Jewish faith who are over the age of 60.

There is no defence, however, that will permit "adult lifestyle" housing that results in the exclusion of children or persons under a certain age.[46]

Older persons may require accommodation in order to enjoy housing on an equal basis with other residents. The person responsible for the housing, such as the landlord in the case of rental accommodation or the condominium corporation in the case of condominium units, has a duty to accommodate the needs and capabilities of older residents, subject to the undue hardship standard:[47]

Example: A tenant in a rental unit develops arthritis and requests that doorknobs in her suite as well as to common areas such as the laundry room be changed from round knobs which are difficult to grip to handles that are suitable for persons with arthritis. The landlord willingly

---

[45]See *Gregory v. Donauschwaben Park Waldheim Inc.* (1990), 13 C.H.R.R. D/505 at para. 29 (Ont. Bd. Inq.). In that case, this defence was successfully relied upon by a non-profit society whose objectives were to foster and preserve the culture and heritage of Danube Swabians. The sale of property within the Park would only be approved by the respondent if the purchaser were German-speaking.

[46]A condominium corporation was found to be in breach of the *Code* because of by-laws which barred families with children younger than 14 or 16 from occupying the condominium units; *York Condominium v. Dudnik* (1991), 14 C.H.R.R. D/406 (Ont. Div. Ct.).

[47]In *Julie Ramsey v. S.W.M. Investments* (August 22, 1994), #642 [unreported] (Ont. Bd. Inq.), a tenant alleged discrimination because of disability due to the landlord's lack of designated "handicapped" parking. Under a settlement, the landlord agreed to provide two designed parking spots for tenants, one designated spot for visitors and further designated spots for tenants as required so that each tenant entitled to a spot would have one. The landlord also agreed to maintain the parking spots by clearing snow, sanding or salting the parking spots and the route to the door of the building.

makes this change as it is not an undue hardship to do so. Moreover, it will benefit other tenants in the building who are also aging.

The duty to take steps to address special needs might include changes to an older person's apartment (except where owned by the person him or herself), building entrance, sidewalks, parking facilities and common areas. This might include physical modifications such as installing elevators, ramps, visual fire alarms and doorbells for the hearing impaired, different door handles, lower counters etc. It can also require other forms of accommodation such as waiving or changing a rule, allowing transfer to another unit without penalty,[48] providing better maintenance such as more frequent snow removal and so on.

7. — Goods, Services and Facilities

Section 1 of the *Code* prohibits age discrimination in "services, goods and facilities." This includes but is not limited to educational institutions, hospitals and other health services, community care access centres, long-term care facilities, insurance providers, public places like malls and parks, public transit services, and stores and restaurants.

Older persons have a right to the same level and quality of services as everyone else and service providers have a legal responsibility to ensure accessibility, subject to the undue hardship standard.

Age discrimination in services can arise as a result of direct discrimination, for example through programs with age requirements that are discriminatory.

> *Example*: An Ontario Ministry of Health assistive devices program provided closed circuit television magnifiers only to persons under age 25. A 71 year old who was refused the visual aid successfully challenged the age limitation on the basis that it was an under- inclusive special program. The Court noted that special programs should be designed so that restrictions within the program are rationally connected to the objective of the program. In this case the connection was not established,

---

[48]For example, during its consultations, the Commission heard that older persons who become widowed face particular hardship when they seek to move to a smaller unit that they can better maintain but face significant rent increases. A possible accommodation in this situation may mean facilitating transfer to another unit in the building without treating the situation as a new lease to which higher rents would apply.

> rather the program had age restrictions to have a small pool of clients and to conserve financial resources and not because younger persons had a greater need for such aids and less access to them.[49]

Age discrimination in goods, services and facilities often results from a lack of access to services that meet the needs of older adults. As well, ageism persists as a problem with regard to provision of services and facilities to older persons. The social construction of age, which involves incorrect assumptions and stereotypes, results in perceptions that older persons are a drain on services such as health care and home care or leads to undue attention being given to age when an issue, such as driving accidents, arises. At the same time, the other manifestation of ageism in services and facilities is the failure to take the real needs of older persons into account. For example, buildings may not be designed in a manner that promotes full accessibility, appropriate transit services may not exist that will allow older persons to participate in their communities and services may be structured around how quickly and "efficiently" clients can be served with the result that insufficient time may be allotted for older clients.

The relationship between age and other *Code* grounds becomes particularly apparent when services are involved.

> *Example*: A residential care facility does not allow a resident's same-sex partner the same visiting privileges as opposite-sex spouses.
>
> *Example*: A transit service provider offers a conventional service and a paratransit system. Many older persons who have disabilities do not qualify for the paratransit system and must struggle to use the conventional transit system. Therefore, the extent to which it is accessible (e.g., contains elevators, uses low floor buses, provides access to TTY phones and so forth) has a direct impact on older persons, particularly if they also have a disability.
>
> *Example*: A hospital recognizes the need for food that is culturally appropriate for patients on its geriatric ward. It therefore makes arrangements for special meals to be brought in several times a week.[50]

---

[49] *Roberts*, *supra*, note 11.

[50] Services that are not culturally sensitive have been identified as a particular problem for older persons; see Kinnon, *supra* note 5 and J.A. Auger, "Ethnic Seniors: Accessing Health Services" in R. Masi, L. Menash and K.A. McLeod, eds. *Health and Cultures: Exploring the Relationships,* Vol. II (Oakville: Mosaic Press, 1993) at 155–167.

The right to be free from age discrimination in goods, services and facilities covers direct discrimination based on age and also policies, rules and requirements that appear neutral on their face but which have an adverse impact on older persons. The *three-step test* to justify requirements that discriminate on the basis of age (described in section 4.3 of this Policy) also applies to complaints of discrimination with respect to goods, services and facilities.

As well, consistent with the Supreme Court of Canada's decision in *Eldridge v. British Columbia (Attorney General)*, those who are responsible for the provision of services to the public must take positive steps to ensure that disadvantaged persons benefit equally from those services.[51] Once again, this requires providing services in a manner that is inclusive and accessible from the start and also providing accommodation, subject to the undue hardship standard.

With respect to insurance services, section 22 of the *Code* provides that automobile, life, accident, sickness or disability insurance, group insurance or life annuity policies that are outside of the employment context may make distinctions based on age and other grounds but these must be made on reasonable and *bona fide* grounds.[52] In *Bates v. Zurich*,[53] the Supreme Court of Canada stated that a discriminatory practice in the insurance industry is "reasonable" if a) it is based on a sound and accepted insurance practice; and b) there is no practical alternative.

8. — Harassment/Poisoned Environment

The *Code* prohibits harassment on the basis of age. Harassment means a course of vexatious comment or conduct that is known, or ought reasonably to be known to be unwelcome. The phrase "ought to have known" introduces an objective element to the test.

In addition, the *Code* prohibits creation of a poisoned environment. A poisoned environment is a form of discrimination and can arise from even a

---

[51] *Eldridge v. British Columbia (Attorney General)*, [1997] 3 S.C.R. 624. In *Eldridge* the Supreme Court of Canada found that hospitals must provide sign-language interpreters for Deaf patients in order for them to access health care services on equal terms.

[52] For further information, see the Commission's Discussion Paper and Consultation Report on *Human Rights Issues in Insurance*, online: www.ohrc.on.ca.

[53] *Zurich Insurance Co. v. Ontario (Human Rights Commission)*, [1992] 2 S.C.R. 321.

single incident. It may be created by the comments or actions of any person, regardless of his or her status. The comments or conduct do not have to be directed at a particular individual.

Ongoing jokes and comments or derogatory statements made about older persons in a workplace or service setting, may constitute harassment or create a "poisoned environment" for older persons by making them feel uncomfortable, threatened or unwelcome.

> *Example*: A worker is referred to as the "old fart" and teased by his co-workers about his age and perceived health problems associated with aging. He walks away from any conversation in which this occurs and from time to time tells people that he doesn't find these comments funny. When he mentions it to his manager, he is told not to worry about it as "it is all in fun since everyone gets old eventually anyway."

Even though comments and conduct on the basis of age may be perceived by some to be less offensive than if based on other *Code* grounds, there may be situations where it has the same negative effect on the recipient. It is important to remember that for harassment to occur, behaviour must be known or ought reasonably to be known to be unwelcome, but that this determination will be made based on the perspective of a "reasonable person" which includes the perspective of the person who is being harassed.

Appendix — Glossary of Concepts in Human Rights

Prima facie Case of Discrimination

The phrase '*prima facie* case of discrimination' is often used in human rights cases. The Supreme Court of Canada has described the test for such a case as follows:

The complainant in proceedings before human rights tribunals must show a prima facie case of discrimination. A *prima facie* case in this context is one which covers the allegations made and which, if they are believed, is complete and sufficient to justify a verdict in the complainant's favour in the absence of an answer from the respondent-employer.[54]

Forms of Discrimination

Discrimination can take many forms. It can occur when a service provider adopts a rule that, on its face, discriminates against persons on the basis of age.

Discrimination can also take place through another person or other means.

Rules, policies, procedures, requirements, eligibility criteria or qualifications may appear neutral but may nonetheless amount to constructive, or "adverse effect" discrimination.

Bona Fide and Reasonable Requirements or Qualifications (BFORs or BFOQs)

Where the complainant makes out a *prima facie* case of discrimination because a standard or requirement has had an adverse impact based on a prohibited ground of discrimination,the respondent may avoid liability by establishing that the standard or requirement in question is a 'BFOR' or 'BFOQ'.

[54]*O.H.R.C. and O'Malley v. Simpsons-Sears. Ltd.*, [1985] 2 S.C.R. 526 at 558. There is current debate as to whether the approach in O'Malley is still appropriate in human rights cases in light of the more recent approach to discrimination cases set out by the Supreme Court of Canada in *Law v. Canada (Minister of Employment and Immigration)*, *supra*, note 49. Nevertheless, an approach that first asks whether the complainant has made out a "prima facie case" continues to be used by many human right tribunals.

The Supreme Court of Canada has held in that in such cases, a *three-step test* should be adopted to assess the standard or requirement in question. In the context of an employment case, the Court described the test as follows:

> (1) The employer must show the standard is adopted for a purpose rationally connected to the performance of the job
>
> (2) The employer must establish it adopted the standard in an honest and good faith belief that it was necessary to the fulfillment of that legitimate work-related purpose
>
> (3) The employer must show that the standard is reasonably necessary to the accomplishment of that purpose. To demonstrate this, the employer must show that it is impossible to accommodate individual employees sharing the characteristics of the complainant without imposing undue hardship upon the employer.[55]

Undue Hardship

The duty to accommodate exists up to the point of undue hardship. It is the Commission's position that the *Code* prescribes only three considerations in assessing whether an accommodation would cause an undue hardship:

Cost: Both the *Code* and the courts have set the cost standard as a high one. Costs will amount to an undue hardship if they are: quantifiable; shown to be related to the accommodation; and so substantial that they would alter the essential nature of the enterprise, or so significant that they would substantially affect its viability.

Outside Sources of Funding: Outside sources of funding may be available to alleviate accommodation costs. Organizations should avail themselves of such resources in order to meet their duty to accommodate and must do so before claiming undue hardship.

Health and Safety Risks: Whether a health and safety risk is sufficient to constitute an undue hardship must be evaluated using the *three-step test* described in this policy. The nature, probability, severity and scope of the risk must be determined based on objective, cogent evidence and not on assumptions or impressionistic evidence. It is also necessary to consider the fact that, in most things, perfect safety is not possible and that a reasonable level of safety is the goal.

---

[55] *Supra*, note 13.

Policy on Discrimination and Harassment Because of Gender Identity

Approved by the Commission: March 30, 2000

1. — Introduction

The *Human Rights Code*[1] (the *"Code"*) states that it is public policy in Ontario to recognize the inherent dignity and worth of every person and to provide for equal rights and opportunities without discrimination. The *Code* aims at creating a climate of understanding and mutual respect for the dignity and worth of each person so that each person feels a part of the community and feels able to contribute to the community.

The Ontario Human Rights Commission (the "Commission") has developed policy statements and guidelines that cover many human rights issues. However, issues related to gender identity remain largely unresolved in policy, procedures, and law.

Gender identity is not an enumerated ground in the *Code*. However, the existing legal structure in the *Code* can support a progressive understanding of the ground of "sex" to include "gender identity" and protect individuals who are subject to discrimination or harassment because of gender identity. This approach toward the application of the *Code* has been accepted for some time and is well demonstrated by Mr. Justice McIntyre who said:

> It is not, in my view, a sound approach to say that according to established rules of construction no broader meaning can be given to the *Code* than the narrowest interpretation of the words employed. *The accepted rules of construction are flexible enough to enable the Court to recognize in the construction of a human rights code the special nature and purpose of the enactment . . . and give to it an interpretation which will advance its broad purposes* [Emphasis added]. Legislation of this type is of a special nature, not quite constitutional, but certainly more than the ordinary[2] . . .

The right to equal treatment without discrimination or harassment because of sex extends to all persons. The Commission has taken the policy position that this protection extends to persons because of gender identity. However,

---

[1] *Human Rights Code*, R.S.O. 1990, c. H.19, as amended.

[2] *Ontario Human Rights Commission v. Simpsons-Sears Ltd.* (1985), 7 C.H.R.R. D/3102 at D/3105 (S.C.C.).

this policy focuses on persons whose gender identity diverges from their birth-assigned identity.

Complaints related to gender identity are made almost exclusively by transgenderists and transsexuals. There are, arguably, few groups in our society today who are as disadvantaged and disenfranchised as transgenderists and transsexuals. Fear and hatred of transgenderists and transsexuals[3] combined with hostility toward their very existence are fundamental human rights issues. As the organization responsible for the administration and enforcement of the *Code*, the Commission is in a unique position to forward the policy that the dignity and worth of every person be recognized and that equal rights and opportunities be provided without discrimination because of gender identity. Mr. Justice Sopinka once noted:

> Human rights legislation is amongst the most pre-eminent category of legislation. It has been described as having a "special nature, not quite constitutional but certainly more than the ordinary . . ." (*Ontario Human Rights Commission v. Simpsons-Sears Ltd.*, [1985] 2 S.C.R. 536 at p. 547. *One of the reasons such legislation has been so described is that it is often the final refuge of the disadvantaged and the disenfranchised.*[4] [Emphasis added.]

2. — Purpose

This policy sets out the position of the Commission with respect to gender identity and is intended to help the public understand how the *Code* protects against discrimination and harassment because of gender identity and to assist employers and providers of services and accommodation to understand their responsibilities under the *Code*. The policy also can be used for educational initiatives such as the development of training materials and the revision of anti-discrimination and harassment policies so that they include gender identity.

By developing this policy the Commission is:

- promoting the dignity and equality of those whose gender identity does not conform to traditional social norms
- ensuring that all people are protected by the *Code*
- promoting awareness of gender identity and preventing discrimination and harassment

---

[3] Referred to as "transphobia."

[4] See *Zurich Insurance Co. v. Ontario (Human Rights Commission)*, [1992] 2 S.C.R. 321.

- dispelling stereotypes and myths that foster discrimination and harassment against individuals because of their gender identity.

3. — Background

Over the last two decades, there has been a growing awareness of people whose gender identity is different from their birth-assigned genders and from social norms of "male" and "female." These people may include pre- and post-operative transsexuals, transgenderists, intersexed people, cross-dressers and others.[5] Along with the emerging visibility of these individuals is a growing appreciation and understanding of the problems that they face in their daily lives. There are numerous community organizations, newspapers, magazines and websites dedicated to gender identity issues that have chronicled these problems which include employment discrimination, harassment, denial of services, violence, high suicide rates, substance abuse and poverty.

This increased awareness of gender identity led the British Columbia Human Rights Commission to propose including "gender identity" as a formal ground for protection in their human rights law.[6] However, at this time, this proposal has not been adopted. Other jurisdictions are moving toward recognition of "gender identity" as a protected ground in their laws. Australian discrimination laws as well as several American municipalities and states recognize transgendered people and have included the ground of gender identity or similar concepts in their human rights laws.[7]

In 1998, the Commission developed a discussion paper on gender identity. The discussion paper was based on research, community consultations and

---

[5]A glossary containing definitions used in this policy can be found at the end of the document.

[6]See B.C. Human Rights Commission, *Human Rights for the Next Millennium*, (January 1998), recommendation 6.

[7]Two examples are the Australian province New South Wales' *Anti-Discrimination Act 1977* which prohibits discrimination *inter alia* because of transgender; and the City of Pittsburgh, Pennsylvania which covers discrimination under its *Pittsburgh Code of Ordinances, Title Six — Conduct\Article V: Chapter 651(Ord. 20-1992)* which seeks to assure equal opportunity for all persons because of 'sex' among other grounds, and defines 'sex' as "the gender of a person, as perceived, presumed or assumed by others, including those who are changing or have changed their gender identification." For more information see Appendix 1, *Toward a Commission Policy on Gender Identity, Discussion Paper,* from www.ohrc.on.ca/english/Discussion/genderid.htm.

interviews with selected officials and health professionals. The paper canvassed jurisprudence, domestic and international legislation, literature, and other human rights organizations' policies. The discussion paper *Toward a Commission Policy on Gender Identity* was publicly released in October 1999.[8] This policy is based on the work done to date and reflects the Commission's formal position on gender identity.

4. — What is "Gender Identity"?

Gender identity is linked to an individual's intrinsic sense of self, and particularly the sense of being male or female. Gender identity may or may not conform to a person's birth assigned sex. The personal characteristics that are associated with gender identity include self-image, physical and biological appearance, expression, behaviour and conduct, as they relate to gender.

At birth, a child is assigned a gender by a health care professional based on observation of the child's genitalia. Society makes the assumption that based on this medical assessment a child will grow up to exhibit correspondingly masculine or feminine behaviours and appearances. However, this is not always the case. A person's felt identity or core identity may differ in part or in whole from their birth assigned sex.[9] Individuals whose birth-assigned sex does not conform to their gender identity include transsexuals, transgenderists, intersexed persons and cross-dressers.

A person's gender identity is fundamentally different from and not determinative of their sexual orientation.

5. — Application of this Policy

Based on a purposive and liberal interpretation of the ground of sex, it is the Commission's position that the protection of the *Code* extends to all individuals who are denied equal treatment because of gender identity. The Commission will accept complaints related to gender identity on the ground of sex where it is the person's gender identity that is the reason for the

---

[8] *Ibid.*

[9] The incident rate in relation to transsexual adults is 1 in 24,000 to 37,000 men and 1 in 103,000 to 150,000 women, according to the American Psychiatric Association. The Gender Identity Clinic at the Clark Institute of Psychiatry in Toronto uses data from the United Kingdom, Sweden and Australia which estimates the prevalence of transsexualism at about 1 case per 50,000 adults. It is important to note that transsexualism is a subgroup and the statistical information does not include transgenderists, the inter-sexed, or cross-dressers.

discrimination. The Commission deals with complaints on a case by case basis regardless of which grounds are identified.

This policy applies to:

i) The workplace (including recruiting, application forms, interviews, promotions, and access to and receipt of employee benefits)

ii) Services, goods and facilities (private businesses, municipal governments, shops, restaurants, hospitals, correctional facilities, insurance services, etc.)

iii) The occupancy of accommodation (including rental accommodation such as apartments, college residences, hotel/motel facilities, condominium housing as well as commercial premises)

iv) Contracts (verbal or written agreements)

v) Membership in vocational associations and trade unions.

6. — Discrimination

Every person has the right to equal treatment without discrimination because of sex, which includes gender identity. Discrimination because of gender identity includes distinctions such as exclusions, restrictions or preferences based on gender identity, or those that result in the impairment of the recognition of human rights and fundamental freedoms on an equal basis. In *Andrews v. Law Society of British Columbia*,[10] Mr. Justice McIntyre defined discrimination as:

> . . . a distinction, whether intentional or not but based on grounds relating to personal characteristics of the individual or group, which has the effect of imposing burdens, obligations, or disadvantages on such individual or group not imposed upon others, or which withholds or limits access to opportunity, benefits, and advantages available to other members of society.[11]

6.1 — Direct Discrimination

A person discriminates directly when he or she treats another person unequally or differently because of his or her gender identity.

> *Example*: An employee advised her employer that she was taking time off work to undergo sex-reassignment surgery. The employer granted the employee the time off but when the employee returned to work af-

[10] *Andrews v. Law Society of British Columbia*, [1989] 1 S.C.R. 143.

[11] *Ibid.* at 174.

ter the surgery, she was terminated. In this case, the tribunal considered the meaning of the protected ground of sex contained in section 10 of Québec's *Charter of Human Rights and Freedoms* and concluded that sex does not include just the state of a person but also the very process of transformation that is part of transsexualism.[12]

6.2 — Indirect Discrimination

Discrimination can also be indirect and may occur when one person causes another to act on his or her behalf and to discriminate against a person because of his or her gender identity.

> *Example*: A landlord advises the superintendent that she does not want any apartments rented to transsexuals. A person who is a transsexual responds to an advertisement for the apartment and is advised by the superintendent that there are no units available, even though there are units available. The landlord may also be named as a respondent in a human rights complaint because the landlord indirectly discriminated by requiring the superintendent to follow a discriminatory instruction.

6.3 — Constructive Discrimination

Constructive discrimination arises when a neutral requirement, qualification or factor has an adverse impact on members of a group of persons who are identified by a prohibited ground of discrimination under the *Code*. Constructive discrimination results from this adverse impact. Section 11(1) of the *Code* provides that constructive discrimination occurs:

> Where a requirement, qualification or factor exists that is not discrimination on a prohibited ground but that results in the exclusion, restriction or preference of a group of persons who are identified by a prohibited ground of discrimination and of whom the person is a member.

In such a case, the person responsible for the discrimination must establish if the rule is reasonable and *bona fide* and then take steps to accommodate the affected person to the point of undue hardship.

> *Example*: A nightclub patron who is a pre-operative male to female transsexual was denied access to the women's washroom even though she was presenting herself as a woman. The nightclub's policy on the use of washrooms was that transsexuals were not permitted to use the

[12] See *M.L. and Commission des droits de la personne et des droits de la jeunesse du Québec v. Maison des jeunes* (1998) (Trib. Qué.).

women's washroom. She filed a human rights complaint and the tribunal found that while this policy was neutral, it had an adverse effect on transsexuals. The tribunal concluded its decision, which was in the complainant's favour, by stating that discrimination against a transsexual constitutes discrimination because of sex.[13]

Example: The *Vital Statistics Act*[14] requires that all birth certificates in the province identity individuals as male or female. This requirement is neutral on its face since it requires all people to be identified as male or female. However, for an individual whose gender identity does not conform to the designation on his or her birth certificate, this may have an adverse impact. The person who shows this identification or relies on it to obtain a permit or official document may be refused because the service provider observes an inconsistency between the way the person presents him/herself and the designation on the birth certificate.

6.4 — Discrimination Because of Association

Persons who are subject to discrimination because of their association with a person protected under the *Code* may file a complaint based on section 12, which protects against discrimination because of association.

Example: A female tenant of an apartment asks for maintenance on her unit. This request is denied because the superintendent says he does not like her friend who is a cross-dresser. Although the tenant was not subjected to discrimination because of her own gender identity, she was subjected to discrimination because of her relationship with a person who is a cross-dresser.

7. — Employment

Section 5(1) of the *Code* provides that every person has a right to equal treatment in employment without discrimination because of sex, which includes gender identity. Denying or restricting employment opportunities in hiring, training, promotion, transfers, etc. because of gender identity is a violation of the *Code*. This is based on the notion that individuals who are the targets of the discriminatory behaviour are being judged on stereotypes

---

[13] *Sheridan v. Sanctuary Investments Ltd. et al.*, January 8, 1999 (B.C. Human Rights Tribunal) from www.bchrt.gov.bc.ca/sheridan2.

[14] *Vital Statistics Act*, R.S.O. 1990, c. V.4.

about how men and women should behave and look and not on the basis of merit.

Example: A woman working on a temporary basis is offered a full-time position as a customer service associate by her supervisor on the condition that she wear dresses and change her hairstyle to a more feminine one. The employer believes this is necessary because the customers will not like the woman's overly masculine appearance.

Example: An employee discloses to his manager that he cross-dresses. The manager subsequently tells the employee that he will no longer qualify for promotions or further career training because customers and co-workers will be uncomfortable with him.

8. — Services

Section 1 of the *Code* provides that every person has a right to equal treatment with respect to services, goods, and facilities, without discrimination because of sex, which includes gender identity. This includes refusal of a service or other differential treatment.

Example: A transsexual woman volunteered as a librarian at a community organization for lesbians and also became a member of the organization. In an article that appeared in a community newspaper, she identified herself as a lesbian but not a woman. Two board members of the organization disapproved of her remarks in the newspaper article. The woman subsequently received a letter advising that her services as a librarian were no longer required and that she was no longer welcome in the organization. The woman filed a human rights complaint, and while the tribunal did not find that the individual was an employee of the organization, they did find that she was discriminated against in the provision of a service because of sex.[15]

Example: A municipality that provides the service of issuing proclamations must do so in a non-discriminatory manner. A transgender support group asks for a proclamation for "Transgender Pride Week" and the Mayor and City Council reject the request. The basis for the refusal is that the Mayor and City Council morally oppose the goals and activi-

[15]*Mamela v. Vancouver Lesbian Connection*, September 8, 1999 (B.C. Human Rights Tribunal) from www.bchrt.gov.bc.ca/mamelav.htm.

ties of the group, while they routinely approve proclamations from other groups whom they support.[16]

Example: A restaurant owner who refuses service to a customer who is a transsexual and throws her out of the restaurant infringes the person's right to receive a service without discrimination.[17]

9. — Accommodation (Housing)

Section 2(1) of the *Code* provides that every person has a right to equal treatment with respect to the occupancy of accommodation (housing) without discrimination because of sex which includes gender identity.

Example: A student responds to an advertisement for a house that is for rent and arranges to view the house and meet with the owner. A few days later, she contacts the owner and advises him that she wishes to rent the house. At the second meeting with the owner of the house, he asks her if she is really a woman and proceeds to tell her that he does not rent to transvestites.

10. — Membership in Vocational Associations

Section 6 of the *Code* provides that every person has a right to equal treatment with respect to membership in any trade union, trade or occupational association or self-governing profession without discrimination because of sex which includes gender identity.

Example: A transsexual employee was involved with in a dispute with her employer. The individual did not feel that her union's actions on her behalf regarding this dispute were adequate. She alleged that the union discriminated against her in its response to the incident, both initially and with respect to the events that followed the initial dispute, and in the way it responded to the employer's handling of the complaint made against her. The tribunal found that the union had treated her worse than it would have treated other union members in similar

---

[16]For example see generally *Oliver v. Hamilton (City)* (1994), 24 C.H.R.R. D/293 (Ont. Bd. Inq.); *Hudler v. London (City)* (1997), 31 C.H.R.R. D/500 (Ont. Bd. Inq.); *Hill v. Woodside* (1998), 33 C.H.R.R. D/349 (N.B. Bd. Inq.).

[17]*Commission des droits de la personne du Québec v. Anglsberger* (1982), 3 C.H.R.R. D/892 (P.C.).

circumstances and that her status as a transsexual was a factor in her treatment. The tribunal ordered the union to cease its contravention of the human rights law and to pay her damages for lost wages and the injury it had done to her dignity, feelings and self-respect.[18]

11. — Harassment

Harassment because of gender identity is covered by the *Code* under the ground of sex.

a) — *Definition of Harassment*

Harassment is defined in subsection 10(1) of the *Code* as "engaging in a course of vexatious comment or conduct that is known or ought reasonably to be known to be unwelcome." This definition guides the Commission in determining what forms of behaviour are inappropriate under the *Code*.

The reference to comment or conduct that is known or ought reasonably to be known to be unwelcome establishes an objective test for harassment:

i) In some situations, it should be obvious that the conduct or comments will be offensive or unwelcome.

ii) Since the individual may be in a vulnerable situation, there is no requirement that the individual object to the behaviour in order for there to be a violation of the *Code*. It may be unrealistic to require an individual who is the target of harassment to object to the offensive treatment as a condition of being able to claim a right to be free from such treatment.

iii) Conduct or comments which relate to a person's gender identity may not, on their face, be offensive. However, they may still be unwelcome from the perspective of the particular individual. If the individual objects and if similar behaviour is repeated, it may constitute a violation of the *Code*.

Each situation that is brought to the attention of the Commission through a human rights complaint will be assessed on its own merits. However, transphobic epithets, comments ridiculing individuals because of their gender identity, or singling out an individual for humiliating or demeaning teasing or jokes related to, or because of, gender identity may be conduct which ought reasonably to be known to be unwelcome.

---

[18] *Ferris v. Office and Technical Employees Union, Local 15*, October 15, 1999 (B.C. Human Rights Tribunal) from www.bchrt.gov.bc.ca/ferrisv.htm.

Examples of situations that might be considered harassment include the following:

i) A landlord says to a tenant, who is a member of a cross-dresser organization, "I don't know why you people don't go live with your own kind, because you sure don't belong here."

ii) Demeaning sexual remarks, jokes or innuendo about an employee, client or customer, or tenant told to others might deny the right of those persons who are the subject of the comments to be viewed as equals.

iii) Demeaning comments, signs, caricatures, or cartoons displayed in a service environment such as a store, restaurant, or in a workplace or rental apartment building may create a poisoned environment in violation of the *Code*.

iv) The display of transphobic, derogatory or offensive pictures, graffiti or materials is humiliating and also impairs the right of those persons who are members of the targeted group to be viewed as equals. An employer, service provider or landlord that tolerates inappropriate pictures, graffiti or materials and does not take any steps to remove them may create a poisoned environment. Depending on the particular circumstances, some persons may be humiliated or may experience feelings of hurt, anger and resentment because of their gender identity.

b) — *Comments or Conduct Need Not be Explicit*

Comments or conduct do not need to be explicit to infringe a person's right to equal treatment without discrimination or harassment. Where a person is singled out and treated differently because of gender identity, even where the differential treatment does not include explicit reference to gender identity, there may still be a violation of the *Code*.

Example: In a warehouse, a transgendered female employee is repeatedly made the brunt of practical jokes and called a "freak" by her co-workers.

c) — *Poisoned Environment*

A single instance of harassment because of gender identity may not fall within the definition of harassment under the *Code*. However, there could be circumstances in which a single incident of inappropriate behaviour may be significant or substantial enough to constitute a breach of the *Code* by creating a poisoned environment for individuals because of their gender identity. In other words, there could be circumstances in which unequal treatment does not have to occur continually or repeatedly in order for a violation of the *Code* to occur.

A consequence of creating a poisoned environment is that certain individuals are subjected to terms and conditions of employment, tenancy, services, etc. that are quite different from those experienced by individuals who are not subjected to these comments or conduct. In such instances, the right to equal treatment may be violated. Demeaning remarks, jokes or innuendo based on gender identity not only poison the environment for transgenderists and transsexuals but affect everyone's environment.

The conduct at issue must be objectively evaluated. It must be of such a nature and degree so as to amount to a denial of equality through the creation of a poisoned environment.

12. — Confidentiality of Information

Gender identity is a personal characteristic that may or may not be known to others. While most people are not concerned about others knowing their gender identity, this may not be the case for transsexuals and transgenderists. Despite the protections set out in the *Code*, individuals who identify or are identified as transsexual or transgendered face the very real possibility of being subjected to overt or subtle discrimination and/or harassment. This can be particularly detrimental in the workplace.

An employer or service provider who legitimately requires and collects personal information that either directly or indirectly identifies a person's sex which may be different from his or her gender identity must ensure the maximum degree of privacy and confidentiality of the information. This applies in all situations and circumstances including employment records and files, insurance company records, medical information, etc. The information might be required to enable an employee or individual to claim or register for benefits, to apply for an apartment, or other purposes. All information should remain exclusively with designated personnel (such as the human resources person) in a secure filing system in order to protect the individual's confidentiality.

Confidential information that might be collected includes:

- birth certificate
- driver's licence
- identification of next of kin
- identification of beneficiary for insurance purposes
- a claim for health benefits.

An employer or service provider who fails to properly safeguard personal information about an individual's sex or gender identity may infringe the *Code*. A complaint could be made where this results in a person being subject to discrimination and/or harassment because of his or her gender identity.

13. — Liability of Employers for the Actions of Their Employees/Agents

13.1 — Employer's Liability

a) — Common Law: The Organic Theory of Corporate Responsibility

Generally, an employer is not liable for acts of harassment carried out by its employees unless it can be proven that it was aware of the harassment. The corporation may also be held responsible for the actions of that employee if it can be shown the employee was part of the management or "directing mind" of the organization. In such cases, the decisions and acts of the employee are so closely identified with the employer that they are treated as one and the same. In other words, the acts or omissions of supervisors, managers, etc. are considered to be the acts of the employer, giving rise to corporate responsibility.

b) — Vicarious Liability

Under section 45 of the *Code*, a corporation, union, trade or occupational association will be held responsible for discrimination committed by employees or agents as though the corporation, union, trade or occupational association had committed the breaches itself. This is known as vicarious liability. The corporation, union, etc. is vicariously liable for the acts of its employees or agents. The doctrine of vicarious liability does not apply to harassment as defined in subsection 10(1)(f) of the *Code*. Rather, it applies to breaches of the equality rights provisions of the *Code*.

14. — The Role of the Commission

14.1 — Remedies under the *Code*

The purpose of human rights legislation is not to find fault but to eliminate discrimination and to provide redress. It is meant to be preventative and remedial, rather than punitive. A remedy to a complaint might include restoring the complainant to a position the individual would have held had the *Code* not been violated. It may consist of compensation for loss of earnings or job opportunities, or damages for mental anguish suffered as a result of the violation.

Human rights remedies also address issues of public interest. This may include requiring changes to an organization's policies, the implementation of training initiatives, the establishment of internal human rights complaint resolution mechanisms, introduction of anti-harassment policies, a written apology, etc.

Appendix — Glossary

This glossary was developed based on the Commission's research for this policy and for the discussion paper, *Toward a Commission Policy on Gender Identity*. The glossary is intended to provide general information on the terminology related to gender identity and is not intended to be an exhaustive or authoritative guide on the subject.

- *Cross-dresser* refers to people who dress in the clothes of the opposite sex for emotional satisfaction and psychological well being. Cross-dresser is preferred over the term "transvestite" which is seen as a diagnostic term associated with medical identity.
- *Gender* may be defined in various ways and could include any or all of the following categories: physical anatomy (or sex organs), secondary sex characteristics that develop at and after puberty, behaviour and conduct, the mind, and fashion choices.
- *Intersexed* means being born with the (full or partial) sex organs of both genders, or with underdeveloped or ambiguous sex organs. About four per cent of all births may be intersexed to some degree. This word replaces the inappropriate term "hermaphrodite."
- *Sexual orientation* is more than simply a status that an individual possesses; it is an immutable personal characteristic that forms part of an individual's core identity. Sexual orientation encompasses the range of human sexuality from gay and lesbian to bisexual and heterosexual orientations.
- *Sex-reassignment surgery (SRS)* is the medical procedure by which an individual is surgically altered to create the physical appearance of the opposite sex.
- *Transgendered* describes individuals who are not comfortable with, or who reject, in whole or in part, their birth assigned gender identities. The word transgendered is generally viewed as an umbrella term that unifies people who identify as transsexual, transgenderist, intersexed, transvestite or as a cross-dresser.
- *Transgenderists* self-identify and live as the opposite gender but have decided not to undergo sex reassignment surgery.
- *Transition* is the process of changing sex, including hormones, cross living, and surgery. A practical minimum duration for this process is about two years but it is not unusual for it to take longer.
- *Transphobia* is the unrealistic or irrational fear and hatred of cross-dressers, transsexuals and transgenderists. Like all prejudices, it is

based on negative stereotypes and misconceptions that are then used to justify and support hatred, discrimination, harassment, and violence toward people who are transgendered.

- *Transsexuals* are individuals who have a strong and persistent feeling that they are living in the wrong sex. This term is normally used to describe individuals who have undergone sex-reassignment surgery. A male transsexual has a need to live as a woman and a female transsexual has a need to live as a man.

Policy on Discrimination and Harassment Because of Sexual Orientation

Approved by the Commission: January 11, 2000
Update confirmed by the Commission: January 25, 2006

Part I — The Context: Sexual Orientation, Human Rights Protections, Case Law and Legislation

1. — Introduction

The Ontario *Human Rights Code* (the "*Code*") states that it is public policy in Ontario to recognize the inherent dignity and worth of every person and to provide for equal rights and opportunities without discrimination. The provisions of the *Code* are aimed at creating a climate of understanding and mutual respect for the dignity and worth of each person, so that each person feels a part of the community and feels able to contribute to the community.

Every person in Ontario has a right to be free from discrimination and harassment relating to sexual orientation in the all the social areas protected by the *Code*. These include employment, services, goods and facilities, housing accommodation, contracts, and membership in trade unions and vocational associations.

1.1 — Sexual Orientation

"Sexual orientation" is not specifically defined in the *Code*. However, the Commission recognizes that sexual orientation is more than simply a "status" that an individual possesses; it is an immutable personal characteristic that forms part of an individual's core identity. Sexual orientation encompasses the range of human sexuality from gay and lesbian to bisexual and heterosexual orientations, including intimate emotional and romantic attachments and relationships. It is most commonly gay and lesbian people who make complaints to the Commission on the basis of sexual orientation. However, the protection of the *Code* extends to all individuals who are denied equal treatment because of sexual orientation. The *Code* also prohibits discrimination because of gender identity, such as that faced by transsexual, transgendered and intersex persons. These protections are extended on the basis of sex, rather than sexual orientation, and are discussed in the Commission's *Policy on Discrimination and Harassment Because of Gender Identity*.

Courts at all levels have recognized the past and ongoing disadvantage suffered by lesbian, bisexual and gay people.[1] In *Egan v. Canada*, the Supreme Court noted:

> The historic disadvantage suffered by homosexual persons has been widely recognized and documented. Public harassment and verbal abuse of homosexual individuals is not uncommon. Homosexual women and men have been the victims of crimes of violence directed at them specifically because of their sexual orientation. They have been discriminated against in their employment and their access to services.
>
> They have been excluded from some aspects of public life solely because of their sexual orientation. The stigmatization of homosexual persons and the hatred which some members of the public have expressed towards them has forced many homosexuals to conceal their orientation. This imposes its own associated costs in the work place, the community and in private life.[2]

While our province's statutes prohibit discrimination and harassment on the basis of sexual orientation, unfair treatment based in homophobia and heterosexism is widespread and even socially accepted among many people. The *Code* requires that the Commission and all organizations under its mandate take steps to prevent and appropriately respond to this unfair treatment, and develop a culture of rights that is inclusive of lesbian, bisexual and gay people.

1.2 — Homophobia and Heterosexism

"Homophobia" and "heterosexism" are terms used to describe prejudice relating to sexual orientation. They refer to the assumption that heterosexuality is superior and preferable, and is the only right, normal or moral expression of sexuality. Both may also be the basis for negative treatment of gay, lesbian or bisexual people based on sexual orientation. Although these terms are closely related and overlapping, they also can emphasize different aspects and expressions of prejudice, and can therefore be helpful in identifying and addressing different aspects of the discrimination and harassment experienced by lesbian, bisexual or gay people.

"Homophobia" is often defined as the irrational aversion to, or fear or hatred of gay, lesbian or bisexual people and communities, or to behaviours stereotyped as "homosexual." It is commonly used to signify a hostile psy-

---

[1] For example, *Egan v. Canada*, [1995] 2 S.C.R. 513; *Vriend v. Alberta*, [1998] 1 S.C.R. 493; *Attorney General of Ontario v. M. and H.*, [1999] 2 S.C.R.; *Halpern v. Canada (Attorney General)* (2003), 65 O.R. (3d) 161 (C.A.).

[2] *Egan v. Canada*, [1995] 2 S.C.R. 513 at para. 173, per Cory, J.

chological state in the context of overt discrimination, harassment or violence against gay, lesbian or bisexual people.

"Heterosexism" is used to refer to the assumption that everyone is heterosexual. This definition is often used in the context of discrimination against bisexual, lesbian and gay people that is less overt, and which may be unintentional and unrecognized by the person or organization responsible for the discrimination. It can also be useful in understanding and identifying some kinds of institutional or societal bias, although homophobia may also be at play.

1.3 — A Further Word about Terminology

Terminology is fluid, and what is considered appropriate tends to evolve over time. Moreover, people within a group may prefer different terms to describe themselves. However, it is useful to identify terms that are considered most appropriate in order to avoid compounding a person's experience of prejudice, harassment or discrimination. It is generally best to use terms by which individuals self-identify, such as "bisexual," "gay," "lesbian" and "two-spirit."

In contemporary usage, "gay" usually refers to men, although it is also used as a general term instead of "homosexual." Some women may identify as "gay," but may prefer the term "lesbian," which refers specifically to women. Aboriginal lesbian, bisexual or gay people may describe themselves as "two-spirit" or "two-spirited."[3] Individuals may use other terms to describe their sexual orientation; however, "gay," "lesbian," and "bisexual" are usually accepted as neutral, general terms.

The term "homosexual" was popularized through medical usage, and has often been used to denigrate and stereotype lesbian and gay people, as well as a range of behaviours and practices ascribed to them. It is sometimes used as a general term, such as in legal documents and medical texts, and some individuals may identify as "homosexual." However, many lesbian and gay people may perceive the term to be clinical or offensive, and bisexual people may also perceive it as exclusionary. It is therefore often better to avoid using the term "homosexual," particularly to refer to an individual, and to use instead the terms by which people self-identify, such as "bisexual," "lesbian" and "gay."

---

[3] Aboriginal people who are transsexual or transgendered or intersex may also refer to themselves and their gender identity as "two-spirited."

1.4 — The Purpose and Scope of the Policy

This policy sets out the position of the Commission with respect to sexual orientation at the time of publication, and replaces the Commission's earlier policy, approved in January 2000. The policy was developed based on extensive research and community consultations, and was updated in 2006 to reflect the significant legal and legislative changes that took place after the initial document was approved.

This policy deals primarily with issues that fall within the Commission's jurisdiction and which can form the subject matter of a complaint to the Commission. The policy is therefore bounded by the provisions of the Ontario *Human Rights Code* and Canada's legal framework for analyzing discrimination. At the same time, the policy interprets the protections in the *Code* in a broad and purposive manner. This is consistent with the principle that the quasi-constitutional status of the *Code* requires that it be given a liberal interpretation that best ensures its anti-discriminatory goals are attained.

Commission policy statements contribute to creating a culture of human rights in Ontario. This policy is intended to help the public understand *Code* protections against discrimination and harassment because of sexual orientation. It is also meant to assist individuals, employers, organizations, providers of services and housing accommodation, and policy makers in understanding their responsibilities, and acting appropriately to ensure compliance with the *Code*.

2. — International Protections

Several international bodies and covenants recognize the rights of gay, lesbian and bisexual people, and the need for protection against discrimination and violence based on sexual orientation.

The United Nations *International Covenant on Civil and Political Rights* (1966) (the "*Covenant*") is monitored by the United Nations Human Rights Committee (UNHRC). The *Covenant* does not specifically list sexual orientation as a protected ground; however, in 1994, the UNHRC held that laws criminalizing consensual homosexual conduct violate protections for privacy (article 17) and against discrimination (articles 2 and 26),[4] and have

[4]*Toonen v. Australia* (1994): *Views of the Human Rights Committee under article 5, paragraph 4, of the optional Protocol to the International Covenant on Civil and Political Rights*, UNHRCOR, 50th Sess., Communication No. 488 (1994).

since affirmed the rights of same-sex couples.[5] A number of UN bodies and documents explicitly list sexual orientation in non-discrimination and protections clauses.[6]

The *European Convention for the Protection of Human Rights and Fundamental Freedoms* (*ECHR*) has been interpreted to extend protections on the basis of sexual orientation. Although the *ECHR* does not explicitly include sexual orientation in its prohibition on discrimination (Article 14), the European Court of Human Rights has ruled that discrimination and privacy (Article 8) protections extend to sexual orientation and the family relationships

---

[5] *Young v. Australia* (2003): *Views of the Human Rights Committee under the optional Protocol to the International Covenant on Civil and Political Rights*, UNHRCOR, 78th Sess., Communication No. 941 (2003).

[6] The United Nations Committee on Economic, Social and Cultural Rights has specified that, as it threatens health, discrimination on the basis of sexual orientation is a violation of rights under Article 2.2 of the *International Covenant on Economic, Social and Cultural Rights* (General Comment No. 14 (2000).

United Nations Commission on Human Rights adopted a resolution on extrajudicial, summary or arbitrary executions in April, 2002, calling on governments to investigate "promptly and thoroughly cases of . . . all killings committed for any discriminatory reason, including sexual orientation . . . and to bring those responsible to justice before a competent, independent and impartial judiciary, and to ensure that such killings are neither condoned nor sanctioned by government officials or personnel."

United Nations High Commissioner for Refugees (UNHCR) also extends protection based on sexual orientation, indicating that gay and lesbian persons facing attack, inhumane treatment or serious discrimination, and whose governments are unable or unwilling to protect them, should be recognized as refugees: UNHCR, *Protecting Refugees: Questions & Answers* (Geneva, UNHCR, 1996).

Other United Nations conventions may provide protections to gay, lesbian or bisexual persons, although sexual orientation may not be specifically mentioned. For example, *Convention against Torture and Other Cruel, Inhuman or Degrading Punishment* (1984), *Convention on the Elimination of All Forms of Discrimination Against Women* (1981), and *Convention on the Rights of the Child* (1989) (article 2).

of lesbian and gay people.[7] The European Union (EU) has also established important protections based on sexual orientation.[8]

3. — The Canadian Context

3.1 — Sexual Orientation in Provincial and Federal Human Rights Protections

The Commission first recommended in 1977 that the *Code* should extend protection from discrimination on the basis of sexual orientation.[9] The Ontario legislature amended the *Code* to add the ground of sexual orientation in 1986. In 1996, the Commission initiated a community consultation process, resulting in an options paper[10] and increased efforts in education, enforcement, complaint processing and litigation relating to sexual orienta-

---

[7]Criminal laws against consensual sexual relations violate the right to privacy under Article 8 (*Dudgeon v. United Kingdom* (1981), 3 E.H.R.R. 40; *Norris v. Ireland* (1991), 13 E.H.R.R. 186, and that such laws must be fully repealed (*Modinos v. Cyprus* (1993), 16 E.H.R.R. 485. The Court has similarly found that bans on military service (*Lustig-Prean and Beckett v. UK: Lustig-Prean and Beckett v. United Kingdom* (1999), [2000] 29 E.H.R.R. 548) and denial of custody (*Salgueiro da Silva Mouta v. Portugal* (1999), [2001] 31 E.H.R.R. 47) based on sexual orientation violate Article 8. In the latter case, the Court also affirmed that Article 14 protection against discrimination is to be interpreted as including sexual orientation. Article 14 has subsequently been used to affirm the family rights of same-sex couples (*Karner v. Austria* (2003), [2004] 38 E.H.R.R. 24), and to find that differing ages of consent for heterosexual and homosexual relations are discriminatory (*L. v. Austria* (2003), 36 E.H.R.R. 55; *S.L. v. Austria* (2003), 37 E.H.R.R. 39).

[8]The *Treaty of Amsterdam*, which came into effect on May 1, 1999, establishes human rights provisions on a number of grounds, and empowers the EU to take appropriate action to combat discrimination.

In December, 2000, the Council of the European Union issued a directive on equal treatment in employment and occupation, barring employment discrimination based on sexual orientation and other grounds. The directive is binding on member states, and national implementation is a condition for states wishing to join the EU.

The *Charter of Fundamental Rights of the European Union*, signed in December 2000 by the Presidents of the European Parliament, the Council of the European Union and the European Commission, explicitly prohibits discrimination based on sexual orientation (Article 21(1)).

[9]*Life Together*, A Report on Human Rights in Ontario (Ontario Human Rights Commission, 1977).

[10]*Sexual Orientation Strategies*, Options Paper (December 1996: Ontario Human Rights Commission, unpublished).

tion. Out of this process, the Commission developed the *Policy on Discrimination and Harassment Because of Sexual Orientation*, approved in January 2000.

On June 20, 1996, section 3(1) of the *Canadian Human Rights Act* (CHRA), was amended to include sexual orientation as a protected ground. Administered by the Canadian Human Rights Commission, the CHRA guarantees the right to equality, equal opportunity, fair treatment and an environment free from discrimination in employment and the provision of goods, services, facilities or accommodation within federal jurisdiction.

The ground of sexual orientation is not named in the anti-discrimination section of the *Canadian Charter of Rights and Freedoms* (the *"Charter"*: section 15).[11] However, the courts have accepted that section 15 is to be interpreted broadly, and that "analogous" grounds, i.e., personal characteristics other than those specifically listed, may also form the basis for discrimination against a group or individual.[12] In 1995, in *Egan v. Canada*,[13] noting the significant historical and ongoing disadvantage faced by gay and lesbian people, the Supreme Court unanimously found that sexual orientation was an analogous ground similar to the other grounds in section 15.

The Supreme Court subsequently found, in *Vriend v. Alberta* (1998),[14] that the Alberta government's assertion that human rights protection was being introduced incrementally did not justify the failure to include protection for lesbians and gay men in the province's human rights legislation, and that the omission of this protection is not reasonable within the meaning of section 1 of the *Charter*. The Court therefore required that sexual orientation be "read into" into the offending legislation, and that Alberta extend protection from discrimination based on sexual orientation. All jurisdictions in Canada now offer protections from discrimination on the basis of sexual orientation in their human rights legislation.

3.2 — Recognition of Same-sex Relationships

Despite legal protections on the basis of sexual orientation, same-sex couples have been subject to specific kinds of discrimination because their relationships were not recognized under the law. Statutes have traditionally used the concept of "spouse" as the basis for allocating rights, powers, benefits and responsibilities to partners, and "spouse" has been implicitly or

---

[11] *Constitution Act*, 1982, Part I.

[12] *Andrews v. Law Society of British Columbia*, [1989] 1 S.C.R 143.

[13] *Egan v. Canada*, [1995] 2 S.C.R. 513.

[14] *Vriend v. Alberta*, [1998] 1 S.C.R. 493.

explicitly defined in heterosexual terms. This was reflected in many Ontario statutes, including the *Code*; however, there have been significant changes in legislation and case law on these matters in recent years.

Same-sex relationships began to gain important recognition through cases involving family law, and denial of spousal survivor, pension, health and employment benefits. In these cases, definitions of spouse and marital status that were limited to opposite-sex couples were found by human rights tribunals to be discriminatory[15] and to constitute denial of the equality rights in section 15 of the *Charter*.[16] In *M. v. H* (1999),[17] the Supreme Court of Canada found that opposite-sex definition of "spouse" in section 29 of Ontario's *Family Law Act*[18] (FLA), which precluded "M" from making an application for support from her former same-sex partner of 12 years, violated section 15 of the *Charter*:

> The societal significance of the benefit conferred by the statute cannot be overemphasized. The exclusion of same-sex partners from the benefits of s. 29 of the FLA promotes the view that M., and individuals in same-sex relationships generally, are less worthy of recognition and protection. It implies that they are judged to be incapable of forming intimate relationships of

---

[15]*Leshner v. Ontario (No. 2)* (1992), 16 C.H.R.R. D/184 (Ont. Bd. Inq.), *Dwyer and Simms v. Municipality of Metropolitan Toronto & Attorney General of Ontario*, Unreported decision, September 27, 1996, Ont. Bd. Inq.

[16]In *Leshner v. Ontario (No. 2)* (1992), 16 C.H.R.R. D/184 (Ont. Bd. Inq.), the Board of Inquiry ordered the provincial government to "read down" the opposite-sex definition of marital status in the *Code* and to provide equivalent survivor benefits to its gay and lesbian employees through an arrangement outside of the existing pension plan.

In *Attorney General of Ontario v. M. and H.*, [1999] 2 S.C.R. 3, (*"M. v. H"*), the Supreme Court of Canada found that that the opposite-sex definition of "spouse" in section 29 of Ontario's *Family Law Act*, R.S.O. 1990, c. F.3 ("*FLA*"), which precluded "M" from making an application for support from her former same-sex partner of 12 years, constituted a denial of the equality rights in section 15 of the *Charter*. Writing for the majority, Cory J. stated:

> The societal significance of the benefit conferred by the statute cannot be overemphasized. The exclusion of same-sex partners from the benefits of s. 29 of the FLA promotes the view that M., and individuals in same-sex relationships generally, are less worthy of recognition and protection. It implies that they are judged to be incapable of forming intimate relationships of economic interdependence as compared to opposite-sex couples, without regard to their actual circumstances (at para. 73).

[17]*Attorney General of Ontario v. M. and H.*, [1999] 2 S.C.R. 3.

[18]*Family Law Act*, R.S.O. 1990, c. F.3.

economic interdependence as compared to opposite-sex couples, without regard to their actual circumstances.[19]

In response, the Ontario legislature amended the *FLA* and a number of other statutes so that they applied to same-sex partners, adding "same-sex partnership status" as a prohibited ground of discrimination under the *Code*.

While these measures were important in extending greater equality rights, there were still many distinctions in law that had discriminatory effects on gay, lesbian and bisexual people, and their families. Some of these distinctions related to access to the actual status of marriage. While opposite-sex couples continued to have the choice to live "common-law" or to become married, those in same-sex couples were still denied this choice. Furthermore, the insistence on a separate category of same-sex partnership, instead of inclusive definitions of terms such as "marital status," "family," "spouse," and "relative" reaffirmed discriminatory views and reinforced the stereotypes held by some, that same sex couples are not "real" families.[20]

This situation shifted significantly on June 10, 2003, when the Ontario Court of Appeal released its decision in *Halpern v. Attorney General of Canada* (*"Halpern"*).[21] In its decision, the Ontario Court of Appeal found that the common law definition limiting marriage to persons of the opposite sex breached the equality rights of same-sex couples under the Canadian *Charter of Rights and Freedoms* (the *"Charter"*). The Court reformulated the definition of marriage as "the voluntary union for life of two persons to the exclusion of all others," effective immediately. Following this decision, the Government of Canada announced that it would not pursue appeals in

---

[19]*Attorney General of Ontario v. M. and H.*, [1999] 2 S.C.R. 3 at para. 73, per Cory J.

[20]Letter from Chief Commissioner Keith C. Norton, Q.C., B.A., LL.B to Hon. James Michael Flaherty, Attorney General of Ontario (Feb. 8, 2000) Toronto.

[21]*Halpern v. Canada (Attorney General)* (2003), 65 O.R. (3d) 161 (C.A.). This case combined two applications brought to the courts by several couples in Toronto, and directly addressed the exclusion of same-sex couples from the institution of marriage. One application was brought in August, 2000, by seven gay and lesbian couples whose requests for marriage licences had been held in abeyance by the clerk of the City of Toronto, while she applied to the Court for directions. The other application was made by two couples who were issued marriage certificates by their minister in January 2001. Their marriages were solemnized by an ancient Christian tradition, called the publication of banns, which was lawful in Ontario; however, the Registrar general refused to register the documents, citing an alleged federal prohibition against same-sex marriage.

Halpern and similar cases in other provinces.[22] As a result of *Halpern*, Ontario became the first jurisdiction in Canada in which same-sex couples could legally marry. Many other jurisdictions followed suit,[23] and the federal government began a process of addressing the matter.[24]

On March 9, 2005, the Ontario Legislature passed legislation amending a broad range of provincial statutes, changing definitions of spouse and marriage, and removing other heterosexist bias.[25] Changes to the *Code* included removal of the ground of "same-sex partnership," which was no longer required due to the newly inclusive, gender-neutral definitions of "marital status" and "spouse."

On July 20, 2005, the federal *Civil Marriage Act* was signed into law, legalizing same-sex marriage across Canada by defining civil marriage as "the

---

[22]In an earlier decision, (*EGALE Canada Inc. v. Canada (Attorney General)* (2003), 225 D.L.R. (4th) 472 (B.C. C.A.)), the British Columbia Court of Appeal had also found the definition of marriage unconstitutional and had amended the definition but had suspended the remedy until July 2004 to allow a legislative response. However, in light of the immediate effect of the Ontario decision and the fact that the federal government chose not to appeal it, on July 8, 2003, the BC Court changed its order to allow the reformulated definition of marriage to apply immediately.

Similarly, on March 19, 2004, the Quebec Court of Appeal upheld a lower court decision that declared the opposite-sex definition of marriage unconstitutional, and lifted the delayed effect of the ruling so same-sex couples had the immediate right to marry in Quebec (*Hendricks v. Canada (Attorney General)* (2004), 238 D.L.R. (4th) 577 (Que. C.A.)).

[23]For example: *Dunbar v. Yukon Territory*, [2004] Y.J. No. 61, 2004 YKSC 54; *Vogel v. Canada (Attorney General)*, [2004] M.J. No. 418; *Boutilier v. Nova Scotia (Attorney General)*, [2004] N.S.J. No. 357; *N.W. v. Canada (Attorney General)*, [2004] S.J. No. 669, 2004 SKQB 434.

[24]In response to *Halpern*, in July of 2003, the federal Minister of Justice submitted a draft Bill to the Supreme Court of Canada for an opinion, in a process known as a reference. The Bill defined civil marriage as "the lawful union of two persons to the exclusion of all others." The Supreme Court rendered its opinion on December 9, 2004, indicating that extension of marriage rights to same-sex couples is consistent with s. 15(1) of the *Charter*. Bill C-38, known as the *Civil Marriage Act*, S.C. 2005, c. 33 was then introduced into Parliament.

[25]The Ontario *Spousal Relationships Statute Law Amendment Act, 2005*, S.O. 2005, c. 5 (Bill 171).

lawful union of two persons to the exclusion of all others."[26] Amendments were made to federal legislation most directly affected by the *Civil Marriage Act*, replacing opposite-sex definitions of "spouse" and other language with gender-neutral terms. Additional barriers were removed by changing legislative references to "natural" parents and "blood" or adoptive relationships, to focus instead on "legal" parent-child and familial relationships.[27]

3.3 — A Note on Balancing Rights

A question that has arisen in a number of cases alleging discrimination based on sexual orientation is that of when parties make competing rights claims.[28] It should be noted that the extension of rights to one group does

---

[26]This codified the definition of marriage for the first time in Canadian law, and made Canada the fourth nation in the world to legalize same-sex marriage, following Belgium, the Netherlands and Spain.

[27]During the legal and legislative proceedings that culminated in the *Civil Marriage Act*, the question of protection of religious freedoms with regard to performing same-sex marriages has became the subject of significant political, legal and social debate. Amendments to both the *Code* and Ontario's *Marriage Act* clarified existing protections of religious belief to address the specific matter of solemnization of same-sex marriages. Section 18(1) of the *Code*, and 20(6) of the *Marriage Act* clarify that religious officials (those registered under s. 20 of the *Marriage Act*) may refuse to solemnize or assist in solemnizing same-sex marriages, and to refuse to allow a sacred place to be used for this purpose, due to religious belief.

[28]*Trinity Western University v. British Columbia College of Teachers*, [2001] 1 S.C.R. 772. Trinity Western University ("TWU") had been denied approval of a teacher education program by the British Columbia College of Teachers on the basis that it was contrary to the public interest because TWU appears to follow discriminatory practices. TWU offers education within a "Christian context" and requires students to sign a document outlining "Community Standards" containing a prohibition of "homosexual behaviour." The Court concluded that, due to the absence of concrete evidence that the training teachers would receive at TWU would foster discrimination in the public schools of British Columbia, the freedom of individuals to adhere to certain religious beliefs while at TWU should be respected. However, the Court held that the freedom to hold these beliefs is broader than the freedom to act on them, and acknowledged that teachers must understand the pluralistic and diverse nature of Canadian society. A teacher in a public school who acts on these beliefs in a discriminatory manner would still be subject to disciplinary proceedings.

In *Hall v. Powers* (2002), 213 D.L.R (4th) 308 (Ont. S.C.J.), the Ontario Superior Court granted an interlocutory injunction restraining the Durham Catholic District School Board from preventing Marc Hall's attendance at his high school prom with not itself diminish the rights of another group, and it must be established whether there is indeed a genuine conflict. If so, rights claims have been balanced based on the particulars of each case, and the understanding that no right is absolute.[29] Case law has indicated that services normally offered to the public must be offered in a non-discriminatory manner,[30] and that human rights protections are to be interpreted broadly, while defences for discrimination are interpreted narrowly.

---

his boyfriend. The Court was called upon to balance Hall's s. 15 *Charter* right to be free from discrimination on the basis of his sexual orientation with the right to freedom of religion in s. 2(a) of the *Charter* and the protection of denominational school rights in s. 93(1) of the *Constitution Act, 1867*. The Court recognized a diversity of opinion within the Catholic community with regard to homosexuality, and found that the restrictions imposed on Mr. Hall's rights were not defensible under section 1 of the *Charter*.

In *Brockie v. Brillinger (No. 2)* (2002), 222 D.L.R. (4th) 174 (Ont. Sup. Ct. Div. Ct.), the Ontario Divisional Court considered whether a Board of Inquiry decision on the complaint of discrimination in a service because of sexual orientation infringed Scott Brockie's right to freedom of religion under s. 2 of the *Charter*. The Board of Inquiry had found that Brockie and Imaging Excellence Inc. denied services to Ray Brillinger and the Canadian Lesbian and Gay Archives contrary to the *Code*, and ordered Brockie and Imaging to provide the same printing services to lesbian and gay people, and to organizations in existence for their benefit, that they provide to other members of the public. The Divisional Court cited *R. v. Big M Drug Mart Limited* (1985), 18 D.L.R. (4th) 321, Dixon C.J.C, noting that service of the public in a commercial service must be considered at the periphery of activities protected by freedom of religion. However, the Court held (at para. 56) that the objectives of the *Code* must be balanced against Mr. Brockie's right to freedom of religion and conscience. The Court narrowed the Tribunal's order to clarify that Mr. Brockie would not be required to print material which could reasonably be considered to be in direct conflict with the core elements of his religious belief [at para. 58].

[29]*Trinity Western University v. British Columbia College of Teachers*, [2001] 1 S.C.R. 772 at para. 29.

[30]*Ontario Human Rights Commission v. Brockie*, [2002] O.J. No. 2375 (Ont. Sup. Ct.).

Part II — The Policy Framework

4. — Discrimination Based on Sexual Orientation

The *Code* provides that every person has the right to be treated equally without discrimination because of sexual orientation. The purpose of anti-discrimination laws is to prevent the violation of human dignity and freedom through the imposition of disadvantage, stereotyping, or political or social prejudice.

There are several ways of defining and identifying discrimination based on sexual orientation. Discrimination because of sexual orientation includes any distinction, including exclusion, restriction or preference based on sexual orientation, that results in the impairment of the recognition of human rights and fundamental freedoms.

In *Andrews v. Law Society of British Columbia*,[31] the Supreme Court of Canada suggests that discrimination may be described as any distinction, conduct or action, whether intentional or not, but based on a person's sexual orientation, which has the effect of either imposing burdens on an individual or group that are not imposed upon others, or withholding or limiting access to opportunity, benefits, and advantages available to other members of society.

In the context of equality claims under s. 15 of the *Canadian Charter of Rights and Freedoms* (the "*Charter*"), the Supreme Court of Canada has offered the following three inquiries as a tool for determining whether discrimination has occurred[32]:

1) Differential Treatment

Was there substantively differential treatment, either because of a distinction, exclusion or preference, or because of a failure to take into account the individual's already disadvantaged position within Canadian society?

2) An Enumerated Ground

Was the differential treatment based on an enumerated ground, in this case sexual orientation?

---

[31] *Andrews v. Law Society of British Columbia*, [1989] 1 S.C.R. 143 at 174.

[32] *Law v. Canada (Minister of Employment and Immigration)*, [1999] 1 S.C.R. 497 [hereinafter "*Law*"].

3) Discrimination in a Substantive Sense

Finally, does the differential treatment discriminate by imposing a burden upon, or withholding a benefit from, an individual? The discrimination might be based on stereotypes of a presumed group or personal characteristics, or might perpetuate or promote the view that an individual is less capable or worthy of recognition or value as a human being or as a member of Canadian society who is equally deserving of concern, respect and consideration. Does the differential treatment amount to discrimination because it makes distinctions that are offensive to human dignity?

5. — Forms of Discrimination Based on Sexual Orientation

Discrimination can take many forms. In many cases it may be direct and intentional, in which an individual or organization treats another person unequally or differently because of sexual orientation.

Example: An employer terminates an employee because of her sexual orientation and her decision to "come out" at the workplace as a lesbian.[33]

Discrimination can also take place in more subtle and less direct ways. For example, business may wish to refuse employment to gay or lesbian applicants because they think their clients will disapprove. However, it is a clearly established principle in human rights law that customer preference can not be used to justify a discriminatory act.[34] If a person or organization causes or requires another to act on his or her behalf and to discriminate against someone because of their sexual orientation, both parties may be liable.

Example: A landlord has a rule that same-sex couples must rent a two-bedroom unit in her apartment building, while opposite-sex couples can rent one-bedroom apartments. If a tenant refuses to sublet the apartment to a same-sex couple based on the landlord's "rule," then both the

---

[33] *Waterman v. National Life Assurance Co. of Canada (No. 2)* (1993), 18 C.H.R.R. D/176 (Ont. Bd. Inq.).

[34] *Berry v. Manor Inn* (1980), 1 C.H.R.R. D/152.

landlord and the tenant may be named as a respondents to a human rights complaint.

Similarly, a placement agency may not refuse work to a bisexual, lesbian or gay person on the instruction of the company contracting their services.

Subtle forms of discrimination can often only be detected upon examining all of the circumstances. Individual acts themselves may be unambiguous or explained away, but when viewed as part of the larger picture, may lead to an inference that discrimination based on sexual orientation was a factor in the treatment a person received.

> *Example*: A woman is one of four people granted job interviews, from a pool of several dozen applicants who sent resumes by mail. When she appears in person, the interviewer seems surprised and uncomfortable, does not make eye contact, and seems to hurry through the interview. The woman feels that the interviewer assumed that she was a lesbian based on aspects of her gender presentation, such as her hairstyle and clothing. She later learns that she did not get the position, but the company does not explain their decision.

It can be difficult to determine whether subtle discrimination is indeed a factor in such situations. They may therefore require investigation and analysis that examines the context, including the presence of comparative evidence contrasting how others were treated, or evidence that a pattern of behaviour exists. An organization should be able to provide a non-discriminatory reason for failing to hire a person.

5.1 — Harassment

Harassment because of sexual orientation is not explicitly covered by the *Code*. However, in *Crozier*,[35] the Commission referred a complaint to a Board of Inquiry that dealt in part with harassment based on sexual orientation, based on the notion that harassing behaviour can become a condition of the person's employment and therefore would be a violation of the *Code* for the purposes of making a complaint. The Board of Inquiry, applying principles articulated by the Supreme Court of Canada in *Janzen*,[36] stated that harassment because of sexual orientation is also a form of discrimination based on sexual orientation and is a violation of the *Code*.

---

[35] *Crozier v. Asseltine* (1994), 22 C.H.R.R. D/244 at para. 9 (Ont. Bd. Inq.).

[36] *Janzen v. Platy Enterprises Ltd.*, [1989] 1 S.C.R. 1252.

Harassment is defined in section 10(1) of the *Code* as "engaging in a course of vexatious comment or conduct that is known or ought reasonably to be known to be unwelcome." The reference to comment or conduct "that is known or ought reasonably to be known to be unwelcome" establishes both a subjective and an objective test for harassment.

The subjective part of the test considers the harasser's own knowledge of how his or her behaviour is being received:

- In some situations, it should be obvious that the conduct or comments will be offensive or unwelcome.
- Some conduct or comments relating to a person's sexual orientation or same-sex marital status may not, on their face, be offensive. However, they may still be "unwelcome" from the perspective of a particular individual. If similar behaviour is repeated despite indications from the individual that it is unwelcome, there may be a violation of the *Code*.

The objective component of the test considers, from the point of view of a "reasonable" third party, how such behaviour would generally be received:

> The determination of the point of view of a "reasonable" third party must take into account the perspective of the person who is harassed.[37]

It is important to note that there is no requirement that the individual object to the harassment in order for there to be a violation of the *Code*, or for a person to claim their rights under the *Code*. An individual who is the target of harassment may be in a vulnerable situation, and afraid of the consequences of speaking out. Employers, landlords and service providers have an obligation to maintain an environment that is free of discrimination and harassment, whether or not anyone objects.

Each situation brought to the attention of the Commission through a human rights complaint will be assessed on its own merits. However, the following types of behaviours are examples that would in most instances be viewed as conduct or comments that "ought reasonably to be known to be unwelcome":

- use of homophobic epithets, slurs, or jokes
- comments ridiculing individuals because of their sexual orientation, or their same-sex partner or spouse
- homophobic name calling, "nicknames," or remarks
- singling out an individual for "teasing" or jokes related to sexual orientation
- hints being made about a person's sexual orientation

---

[37] *Dhanjal v. Air Canada* (1996), 28 C.H.R.R. D/367 (C.H.R.T.).

- circulating or posting of homophobic, derogatory or offensive signs, caricatures, graffiti, pictures or other materials.

Examples of situations that might be considered harassment include the following:

- A landlord says to a tenant, who is a member of the gay and lesbian community, "I don't know why you people don't go live with people like yourself, because you sure don't belong here."
- Graffiti that is tolerated by a service provider, employer, or landlord who does nothing to remove it may be creating a "poisoned environment."

5.2 — Poisoned Environment

The *Code* definition of harassment refers to more than once incident or comment or conduct. However, even a single statement or incident may be significant or substantial enough to constitute a breach of the *Code* by creating a "poisoned environment" for individuals because of their sexual orientation. A consequence of creating a poisoned environment is that certain individuals are subjected to terms and conditions of employment, tenancy, services, etc. that are quite different from those experienced by individuals who are not subjected to these comments or conduct. In such instances, the right to equal treatment may have been violated.

Heterosexist assumptions may lead employers, landlords, service providers and others to believe that there are no gay, lesbian or bisexual people present, and that homophobic behaviour is therefore not problematic. This is not the case. Homophobic remarks, jokes and innuendo poison the environment for individuals who are, or are perceived to be, bisexual, gay and lesbian, their friends and families, and others.

In the employment context, tribunals have held that the atmosphere of a workplace is a condition of employment just as much as hours of work or rates of pay. The notion of a poisoned environment can also apply in housing, the provision of services, contracting, or membership in a vocational association. Inappropriate comments and conduct are exclusionary and unprofessional, and have a negative and disruptive effect on everyone's environment. It is the responsibility of every service provider, landlord and employer to ensure that its environment is free from this sort of behaviour, even if no one objects. See section 7. Organizational Responsibility.

5.3 — Confidentiality and Sexual Orientation

An individual's sexual orientation and marital status are personal characteristics that may or may not be known to others. While individuals who are heterosexual may not be concerned about others knowing their sexual orientation or marital status, this may not be the case for individuals who are bisexual, gay or lesbian. Despite the protections set out in the *Code*, and the *Charter*, courts have recognized that individuals and couples who identify themselves as, or are identified by others as gay, lesbian or bisexual have faced historical disadvantage, and continue to face the very real possibility of being subjected to overt or subtle discrimination or harassment, verbal abuse and physical violence. As a result, they may wish to conceal their sexual orientation, or share the information only with certain individuals.

Comments and questions about an individual's personal or romantic life, such as questions or statements about marital status, whether they will have children, who they are dating, where they go out on weekend evenings, or who they find attractive, may be inappropriate, particularly if the person has voiced or shown discomfort, or avoided responding. Repeated or ongoing comments of this nature may amount to sexual harassment, or make people uncomfortable for reasons relating to other grounds under the *Code*. For gay, lesbian and bisexual people, this may also amount to harassment or create a poisoned environment relating to sexual orientation. For example:

- If they have not disclosed their sexual orientation, this behaviour pressures them to either disclose or to deny their sexual orientation. This is intrusive, and may seem threatening: it may be the instigator's way of signalling that they know or suspect the person's sexual orientation, and that they may disclose this to others. This plays on the genuine fears of discrimination, harassment, or violence that may have led the person to conceal his or her sexual orientation in the first place.
- Lesbian, bisexual and gay people, like some other groups, have been targeted by dehumanizing stereotypes that represent them not as whole people, but only in terms of sex, distorting and overemphasizing the sexual aspect of their lives.[38] This pattern of comment or question may therefore be received as a prurient interest in their sexual lives, relating to stereotypes about their sexual orientation.

Individuals and organizations responding to complaints of discrimination and harassment relating to sexual orientation should take into account the disadvantage that forms part of the perspective of the individual. In order to make a human rights complaint based on sexual orientation, it is not necessary for the person to identify him or herself as gay, lesbian or bisexual, but to establish discriminatory or harassing treatment relating to sexual orientation. Furthermore, the needs of many lesbian, bisexual or gay people for

---

[38] *Schnell v. Machiavelli and Associates Emprize Inc (No. 2)* (2002), 43 C.H.R.R. D/453 at paras. 59-63 (C.H.R.T.).

confidentiality regarding their sexual orientation should come into play in an analysis of whether discrimination or harassment has occurred. See section 9.1 Protecting Confidentiality of Information for related information about organizational best practices.

5.4 — Systemic Discrimination

Discrimination may also be institutional or systemic. Policies, practices, rules or requirements, decision-making processes, and organizational culture may all have discriminatory effects on individuals based on sexual orientation.

5.4.1 — Organizational Culture

Organizational culture can be described as shared patterns of informal social behaviour, which are the evidence of deeply held and possibly unconscious values, assumptions, and behavioural norms. An organizational culture that is not inclusive can marginalize lesbian, bisexual or gay people and contribute to homophobia or heterosexism.

Examples may include informal social interactions and subjective assessments of employee skills, such as:

- jokes or gossip about gay, lesbian and bisexual people
- questions or comments presuming that employees have or seek (or should have or want) opposite-sex partners or spouses
- exclusion of lesbian or gay employees from social or informational networks
- negative employer valuation of the work, skills, or "fit" of employees who are, or are perceived to be, gay or lesbian, or who do not conform to gender roles
- employer bias toward employees who conform to a heterosexual nuclear model of family and marital status, such as in evaluation of employee dedication or reliability
- lack of workplace training in non-discrimination, or training that excludes mention of sexual orientation.

> *In Practice*: An employer holds regular holiday parties and picnics as "team-building" events, expecting staff to bring their families. A lesbian employee, aware of the assumption that she is heterosexual, feels uncomfortable attending or bringing her female partner. However, she is concerned that her employer will decide that she is not a "team player" if she does not attend.

Workplace culture has influenced the employee's discomfort in this situation. She is forced to make a choice between three options, all of which are unsatisfactory to her:

1. She may attend alone, but would be misrepresenting herself as single.
2. She may avoid the event altogether, but risks being assessed as a poor "team player."
3. She may also attend with her partner, but this would amount to publicly disclosing her sexual orientation, in a workplace environment that she experiences as heterosexist.

Linking work goals or performance evaluations with social events or with employee's non-work lives, such as expecting family involvement, may lead to exclusion or discrimination based on sexual orientation or other *Code* grounds. Assessment of worker skills should be based on employee performance, and should avoid subjective evaluations that may relate to sexual orientation and other *Code* grounds.

An organization may have genuinely good intentions and wish to foster a positive social environment by hosting or organizing social events, including those involving family. However, it must be clear that any such events are optional, and organizations must take care to avoid creating expectations or requirements that may have exclusionary or discriminatory effects. Prudent employers and organizations may encourage inclusive organizational culture by ensuring that anti-discrimination policies and training are in place. They may thereby be able to prevent exclusion or discrimination, and will be better prepared to address any problems that do arise.

5.4.2 — Policies, Procedures and Rules

Policies, procedures and rules may be non-discriminatory on their face, yet may be applied in a discriminatory way, so that they disproportionately affect members of gay, bisexual or lesbian communities.

> *Example*: A bookstore which serves a largely lesbian, gay, bisexual and transgendered clientele finds that Customs officials regularly delay, confiscate, destroy, damage, prohibit or misclassify as "obscene" materials which they import from their main suppliers in the U.S., while the same or comparable materials imported by other businesses are not similarly treated. The Supreme Court of Canada found that Canada Customs had discriminated against the store on the basis of sexual orientation, engaged in "systemic targeting" of the bookstore's

imports, stigmatized and harassed the appellants, and had violated their legitimate sense of self-worth and dignity.[39]

Rules, policies, procedures, requirements, eligibility criteria or qualifications may appear neutral and be equally applied, but may nonetheless be discriminatory. This is because they may have an adverse impact based on sexual orientation, due to an exclusionary assumption or other bias.

Example: A "birth registration" form contains spaces for "mother" and "father." Lesbians whose female partners have conceived through donor insemination are not allowed to list themselves on the form, and are told that they are required to go through the process of second-parent adoption. This results in increased costs, delay, inconvenience and ongoing difficulties in proving the relationship because of the special position of birth registration in documenting the child's familial relationships. This has been found to be discriminatory, and to amount to denial of their status as parents.[40]

5.4.3 — Reasonable and Bona Fide *Requirements*

An organization or institution may seek to justify or maintain a discriminatory policy, practice or decision-making process by demonstrating that it is reasonable and *bona fide* in the circumstances. While such claims are not uncommon, the standard for establishing that a requirement is *bona fide* is high, and there are limited criteria through which it can be met. It is therefore rare for a discriminatory requirement to be found to be *bona fide*.

The Supreme Court of Canada has set out a three-step test for determining whether a discriminatory standard, factor, requirement or rule can be justified as a *bona fide* one. The organization or institution must establish on a balance of probabilities that the standard, factor, requirement or rule:

1. was adopted for a purpose or goal that is rationally connected to the function being performed
2. was adopted in good faith, in the belief that it is necessary for the fulfilment of the purpose or goal

[39]*Little Sisters Book and Art Emporium v. Canada (Minister of Justice)*, [2000] 2 S.C.R. 1120 at para. 123.

[40]*Gill v. British Columbia (Ministry of Health) (No. 1)* (2001), 40 C.H.R.R. D/321 (B.C.H.R.T.).

3. is reasonably necessary to accomplish its purpose or goal, in the sense that it is impossible to accommodate the claimant without undue hardship.[41]

   In Practice: In the previous example involving birth registration, the agency argued that the form must list the child's biological parents. However, there was a regulation that allowed male partners of women who have just given birth to list themselves as the father of the child, without any requirement that they establish biological parentage. In fact, men whose partners had conceived through donor insemination ("DI") were protected from having to disclose this fact. The agency's justification was found not to be *bona fide*.[42]

The ultimate issue is whether the person who seeks to justify the discriminatory standard, factor, requirement or rule has shown that accommodation has been incorporated into the standard up to the point of undue hardship. In this analysis, the procedure used to assess and achieve accommodation is as important as the substantive content of accommodation. The following non-exhaustive factors should be considered in the course of the analysis:

- whether the person responsible for accommodation investigated alternative approaches that do not have a discriminatory effect
- reasons why viable alternatives were not implemented
- ability to have differing standards that reflect group or individual differences and capabilities
- whether persons responsible for accommodation can meet their legitimate objectives in a less discriminatory manner
- whether the standard is properly designed to ensure the desired qualification is met without placing undue burden on those to whom it applies
- whether other parties who are obliged to assist in the search for accommodation have fulfilled their roles.[43]

---

[41] *British Columbia (Public Service Employee Relations Commission) v. B.C.G.S.E.U.*, [1999] 3 S.C.R. 3.

[42] *Gill v. British Columbia (Ministry of Health) (No. 1)* (2001), 40 C.H.R.R. D/321 (B.C.H.R.T.).

[43] *British Columbia (Public Service Employee Relations Commission) v. B.C.G.S.E.U.*, [1999] 3 S.C.R. 3.

In Practice: The agency responsible for birth registration could have accommodated those negatively affected by changing the form to make it more inclusive. They could have accommodated by allowing the same-sex spouse of the birth mother to list herself on the form, whether under "father" or, crossing out that term, as "co-parent," as the complainants attempted to do. Instead, the agency discriminated on the basis of a heterosexist view of family and spousal relationships, reinforced by a standardized form that did not account for the realities of gay and lesbian-headed families.[44]

5.5 — Discrimination Because of Association

Persons who are subject to discrimination because of their association with a person protected under the *Code* may file a complaint based on s.12, which protects against "discrimination because of association."

Example: A female tenant of an apartment makes a request for maintenance on her unit. The superintendent denies her request, making negative comments about the tenant's close friend, who is an African-Canadian lesbian.

Example: Several employees of a retail store wear a pin in support of an organization for parents and friends of lesbian, gay, bisexual and transgendered people. Despite the fact that other employees are permitted to wear buttons, pins or other jewellery identifying their affiliation with volunteer and interest groups, the employer insists that employees must remove this particular pin. The employer confiscates some of the pins, stating that they violate the dress code, and threatens to sanction employees who wear them.

Although these individuals were not subjected to discrimination because of their own sexual orientation, they were subjected to discrimination because of their relationship or association with someone identified by a prohibited ground of discrimination.

5.6 — Discrimination Because of Perceived Sexual Orientation

The right to equal treatment means that if you have been discriminated against because of bias about sexual orientation, you are entitled to the

---

[44] *Gill v. British Columbia (Ministry of Health) (No. 1)* (2001), 40 C.H.R.R. D/321 (B.C.H.R.T.).

Code's protection. A person does not actually have to be of a particular sexual orientation, but can make a complaint as long as it can be shown that there was unequal treatment based on perceived sexual orientation.

> *Example*: Two women who are not lesbians are dancing together in a bar when the owner interrupts them and asks them to leave. This happens after one of the women overheard the owner say, "I don't want people thinking this is a lesbian bar." Even though the women are not lesbians, they can file a complaint with the Commission because they believe they were subjected to unequal treatment because of perceived sexual orientation.
>
> *Example*: A male student is subjected to years of homophobic harassment and bullying in school. The student is not gay, and his harassers deny believing that he is gay. However, he is still found to be entitled to protections based on sexual orientation.

Even if the perpetrators deny that they actually believe a person to be gay, lesbian or bisexual, that person may make a human rights complaint if she or he is subject to discrimination or harassment that is homophobic in nature. This is because the treatment is based in prejudice about sexual orientation, and it is the effect of the discrimination or harassment, rather than the intent or belief of the harassers, that is the basis for determining that discrimination has occurred.[45] In this case, a "reasonable person" would also likely conclude that the perpetrators perceived the person to be gay, lesbian or bisexual, based on the nature of the harassment.

5.7 — Comments or Conduct Need Not be Explicit

Comments or conduct do not need to be explicit to infringe a person's right to equal treatment without discrimination or harassment. Where a person is singled out and treated differently because of sexual orientation, even where the differential treatment does not include explicit reference to sexual orientation or same-sex partnership status, there may still be a violation of the *Code*.

> *Example*: In a workplace, the only gay employee is repeatedly made the brunt of practical jokes and is ridiculed by his co-workers for no

---

[45] *North Vancouver School District No. 44 v. Jubran* (2005), 39 B.C.L.R. (4th) 153 (B.C. C.A.); *Ontario Human Rights Commission v. Simpson-Sears Ltd.*, [1985] 2 S.C.R. 536.

apparent reason. The workplace has a history of homophobic attitudes. It may be inferred from the particular circumstances that the treatment is based on sexual orientation although the practical jokes or ridicule may not have contained any direct reference to the employee's sexual orientation.

6. — Relationships Between Sexual Orientation and Other *Code* Grounds

Discrimination based on sexual orientation may involve any other ground of discrimination listed in the *Code*. The grounds of sex, marital status and family status in particular can have unique relationships to the ground of sexual orientation.

6.1 — Sex

Discrimination and harassment on the ground of sexual orientation can involve the ground of sex in a number of ways. Discrimination against people because they are gay, lesbian or bisexual may take the form of sexual harassment.[46]

> *Example*: After she had worked for about a year in her job, a woman's male co-worker asked her about her sexual orientation. When she indicated that she liked women, he began harassing her, using homophobic epithets, and directing sexually explicit questions, comments and gestures to her. He also made negative, stereotypical comments to her female colleagues about her sexual orientation and practices.[47]

Even if the harassment does not explicitly mention or refer to the person's sexual orientation, if he or she is targeted because of actual or perceived sexual orientation, the complaint may use the ground of sexual orientation.

Gender expression and gender identity are both also addressed in Commission complaints under the ground of sex. In cases of discrimination or har-

---

[46] It is important to note that sexual harassment and inappropriate gender-related comments or conduct are prohibited regardless of the gender or sexual orientation of the parties involved. For more information, see the Commission's *Policy on Sexual Harassment and Inappropriate Gender-Related Comments and Conduct.*

[47] *Baczkowski v. Suffesick* (2000), 43 C.H.R.R. D/240 (Y.T. Bd. Adj.).

assment, these grounds are sometimes confused with, or serve as a proxy for sexual orientation. For example:

- a co-worker assumes that a transgendered person is gay, and makes homophobic comments in the workplace
- a woman does not dress or wear her hair in a "feminine" style. Her manager makes jokes about sexual orientation and gender identity in her presence and to coworkers
- a landlord believes that a male tenant is gay because his clothing and manner of expression do not seem "masculine." He calls the tenant homophobic names, and refuses to do repairs and maintenance in the apartment.

6.2 — Marital Status and Family Status

Marital status is defined under section 10(1) of the *Code* as "the status of being married, single, widowed, divorced or separated and includes the status of living with a person in a conjugal relationship outside marriage." This definition is inclusive of same-sex couples, whether married or "common-law." Therefore, the separate ground of "same-sex partnership" has been removed. Complaints brought by persons regarding discrimination on the basis of a conjugal relationship with a person of the same sex will be addressed as discrimination based on the grounds of sexual orientation and marital status, in addition to any other grounds that may be involved.

Family status is a protected ground in the *Code*, and is defined under section 10(1) as the "status of being in a parent and child relationship". Lesbian, gay and bisexual people may have children through previous heterosexual unions, same-sex relationships with biological parents, adoption, or assistive reproductive technologies. Homophobic stereotypes and lack of legal recognition have both contributed to discrimination faced by these individuals and families. Gay, bisexual and lesbian people may also form important dependency and caregiving relationships that are not currently recognized under this ground of the *Code* or other provincial and federal legislation.

6.3 — Intersectionality and Overlapping Grounds

Persons who are bisexual, gay or lesbian may experience various forms of discrimination, depending on what other characteristics form part of their personal identity or status in a society. A combination of *Code*-related grounds may compound the person's experience of discrimination.

Individuals may experience discrimination or harassment based on one ground in certain contexts, and on another ground in other contexts. For example, a gay man accessing services geared toward persons of his race, ancestry, ethnic origin or place of origin may be subjected to comment by a service worker that gay people "don't belong in our culture." At another time, he may experience discrimination based on race or culture-related grounds in his volunteer work with a gay community organization. Or, he may experience discrimination based on all of these grounds at once.

A complaint involving sexual orientation may involve any other ground under the *Code*, and a person may experience discrimination based on several characteristics or aspects of their identity at the same time. For example, a lesbian with a disability may be seen as a lesbian, a woman, or a person with a disability, and thus be exposed to discrimination or harassment based on her sexual orientation, sex or disability, or on a combination of these (and other) grounds. Discrimination or harassment relating to one ground may have a greater negative impact on persons due to the vulnerability they experience stemming from the other grounds.

Different aspects of a person's identity may intersect in such a way that the person may be exposed to stereotyping and discrimination that is unique and distinct to that combination of grounds. For example, a gay man may be seen as a man, and as a gay or homosexual person generally. However, he may be exposed to an intersectional form of discrimination on the basis of being identified as a "gay man," because of unique stereotypes about gay men that are distinct from those about lesbian or bisexual people, or about men in general.

> *Example*: When a gay man working at a family services agency took sick leave, rumours circulated in his workplace that he had AIDS. Later, he was falsely rumoured to be sexually abusing his adolescent male foster child. He complained to the employer about the rumours, but was terminated for reasons relating to the unfounded allegations. The Board found that the man had been subjected to harassment, a poisoned work environment, discrimination and reprisal.[48]

In this case, the individual suffered discrimination based on specific stereotypes about sex, sexual orientation, family status and disability.

---

[48] *Moffat v. Kinark Child and Family Services* (1998), 35 C.H.R.R. D/205 (Ont. Bd. of Inq.).

7. — Organizational Responsibility

The ultimate responsibility for a healthy and inclusive environment rests with employers, landlords, unions, vocational and professional organizations, service providers, and other organizations and institutions covered by the *Code*. There is an obligation to ensure that environments are free from discrimination and harassment. It is not acceptable from a human rights perspective to choose to remain unaware of the potential existence of discrimination or harassment, or to ignore or fail to act to address human rights matters, whether or not a complaint has been made.

An organization violates the *Code* where it directly or indirectly, intentionally or unintentionally infringes the *Code*, or where it does not directly infringe the *Code* but rather authorizes, condones, adopts or ratifies behaviour that is contrary to the *Code*. Organizations should ensure that rules, policies, procedures, decision-making processes and organizational culture are non-discriminatory on their face, and do not have a discriminatory impact.

In addition, there is a human rights duty not to condone or further a discriminatory act that has already occurred. To do so would extend or continue the life of the initial discriminatory act. The obligation extends to those who, while not the main actors, are drawn into a discriminatory situation nevertheless, through contractual relations or otherwise.[49] An organization should also not punish a person because of how they responded to harassment:

> *Example*: A woman's co-worker verbally harassed her because of sex and sexual orientation. After a couple of months, she complained to her manager, who told them to stay away from each other. However, the co-worker continued to make negative comments to other staff about her. When she reported this again to her manager, he told her she should figure out how to resolve the problem. When he found out that she had complained to the police, the employer terminated her. The

---

[49] *Payne v. Otsuka Pharmaceutical Co. (No. 3)* (2002), 44 C.H.R.R. D/203 (Ont. Bd. Inq.) at para. 63. The nature of when a third party or collateral person would be drawn into the chain of discrimination is fact specific. However, general principles can be determined. The key is the control or power that the collateral or indirect respondent had over the complainant and the principal respondent. The greater the control or power over the situation and the parties, the greater the legal obligation not to condone or further the discriminatory action. The power or control is important because it implies an ability to correct the situation or do something to ameliorate the conditions.

court found the employer liable for the offensive conduct, his failure to respond appropriately to her complaints, and for the role her police complaint played in his decision to terminate her.[50]

Unions, vocational and professional organizations are responsible for ensuring that they are not engaging in, condoning or contributing to discrimination or harassment. They may be liable for discriminatory policies or actions to the same extent as an employer, and share the same obligation to take measures to address harassment or a poisoned environment.

Human rights decisions frequently find organizations liable, and assess damages, based on an organization's failure to respond appropriately to address discrimination and harassment. An organization may respond to complaints about individual instances of discrimination or harassment, but they may still be found to have failed to respond appropriately if the problem is not resolved. There may be a poisoned environment, an organizational culture that excludes or marginalizes persons based on sexual orientation, or an ongoing pattern of homophobic comments or incidents, despite sanction of individual harassers. In these cases, the organization should take further steps, such as training and education, in order to more appropriately address the problem.

The following factors have been suggested as considerations for determining whether an organization met its responsibilities to respond to a human rights complaint:

- procedures in place at the time to deal with discrimination and harassment
- the promptness of the institutional response to the complaint
- the seriousness with which the complaint was treated
- resources made available to deal with the complaint
- whether the organization provided a healthy work environment for the person who complained
- the degree to which the action taken was communicated to the person who complained.[51]

---

[50] *Baczkowski v. Suffesick* (2000), 43 C.H.R.R. D/240 (Y.T. Bd. Adj.).

[51] *Wall v. University of Waterloo* (1995), 27 C.H.R.R. D/44 (Ont. Bd. Inq.). These factors assist in assessing the reasonableness of an organization's response to harassment. A reasonable response by the organization will not affect its liability but will be considered in determining the appropriate remedy. In other words, an em-

For more information, see also section *9. Preventing and Responding to Homophobia and Discrimination Based on Sexual Orientation.*

7.1 — Vicarious Liability

Under section 45 of the *Code*, a corporation, trade union or occupational association, unincorporated association or employers' organization will be held responsible for discrimination, including acts or omissions, committed by employees or agents in the course of their employment. This is known as vicarious liability. It applies not only to human rights violations in the workplace, but also in housing accommodation, goods, services and facilities, contracting, and membership in unions and vocational associations.

Simply put, it is the Commission's position that vicarious liability automatically attributes responsibility for discrimination to an organization for the acts of its employees or agents, done in the normal course, whether or not it had any knowledge of, participation in, or control over these actions.

Vicarious liability does not apply to breaches of the sections of the *Code* dealing with harassment. However, in these cases the "organic theory of corporate liability" may apply. In addition, since the existence of a poisoned environment is a form of discrimination, it is the Commission's position that when harassment amounts to or results in a poisoned environment, vicarious liability under section 45(1) of the *Code* is restored.

7.2 — The "Organic Theory" of Corporate Responsibility

An organization may be liable for acts of harassment carried out by its employees if it can be proven that it was aware of the harassment, or the harasser is shown to be part of the management or "directing mind" of the organization. In such cases, the decisions, acts, or omissions of the employee will engage the liability of the organization where:

- the employee who is part of the "directing mind" engages in harassment or inappropriate behaviour that is contrary to the *Code*; or
- the employee who is part of the "directing mind" does not respond adequately to harassment or inappropriate behaviour of which he or she is aware, or ought reasonably to be aware.

Example: An employee informed his manager that he was being subjected to discriminatory rumours in the workplace related to his sexual orientation. The manager failed to take appropriate steps to investigate

---

ployer that has reasonably responded to harassment is not absolved of liability but may face a reduction in the damages that flow from the harassment.

> the rumours or to advise senior management, and subsequently filed a misleading report leading to the employee's termination. The board found the organization vicariously liable for the discriminatory gossip, the manager's failure to investigate and address it, and the manager's misleading report. The board also held the organization to be directly liable for the failure to deal with the discriminatory rumours and for the manager's misleading report, on the basis of the "organic theory" of corporate liability.[52]

Generally speaking, managers and central decision-makers in an organization are part of the "directing mind." Employees with only supervisory authority may also be part of the "directing mind" if they function, or are seen to function, as representatives of the organization. Even non-supervisors may be considered to be part of the "directing mind" if they have *de facto* supervisory authority or have significant responsibility for the guidance of employees. For example, a member of the bargaining unit who is a lead hand may be considered to be part of the "directing mind" of an organization.

8. — Employment, Services and Housing

Employment, services and housing are the grounds most commonly cited in complaints of discrimination based on sexual orientation. As in all social areas, employers, service providers and landlords should be aware of their obligations under the *Code*, and understand their corporate responsibility as described in section *7. Organizational Responsibility*. There are many steps that prudent organizations can take to prevent and appropriately respond to complaints. For further guidance, see section *9. Preventing and Responding to Homophobia and Discrimination Based on Sexual Orientation*.

8.1 — Employment

Section 5(1) of the *Code* provides that every person has a right to equal treatment in employment without discrimination because of sexual orientation and marital status. The majority of complaints of discrimination based on sexual orientation relate to employment. Denying or restricting employ-

---

[52] *Moffat v. Kinark Child and Family Services* (1998), 35 C.H.R.R. D/205 (Ont. Bd. of Inq.).

ment opportunities in hiring, training, promotion, transfers, etc. because of sexual orientation or same-sex marital status is a violation of the *Code*.

> *Example*: An employee discloses that he is gay to his manager. The manager subsequently tells the employee that he will no longer qualify for promotions, postings, or further career training.[53]
>
> *Example*: A woman works for a company on a temporary contract in the same department as her same-sex partner. An "out" lesbian, she has been subject to homophobic comment from management. Her supervisor offers her a full-time position, but stipulates that to protect company security, her partner will be transferred to another department in the company. He claims that the same requirement would be imposed were she heterosexual. She questions the company's consistency in applying this rule to heterosexual workers and suggests alternatives, but the company terminates her without further discussion.[54]

In this case, the Board of Inquiry found that the company had discriminated against the employee and, specifically, that employer discomfort with her sexual orientation and her openness about it was a factor in her termination.

Individuals with same-sex spouses, as defined under "marital status" in section 10(1) of the *Code*, are entitled to the same employment-related benefits as individuals with opposite-sex spouses. This may include benefits such as employee superannuation or pension plans or funds, or a contract of group health insurance between an insurer and an employer, even if it complies with other relevant legislation and regulations.

Employers must ensure that they are not discriminating in extending opportunities, such as in hiring, promoting, providing training or mentoring, or in other decision-making, including termination or discipline.

> *Example*: When a gay man's co-worker finds out that he is HIV-positive, she complains to management, who terminates him. When he files a human rights complaint, the employer claims not to have known his HIV status, but states that it would present a health and safety risk. They allege that he was terminated for inappropriate sexualized comments in the workplace. However, there was no evidence that they had investigated or substantiated these allegations prior to the termination,

---

[53] *Haig v. Canada* (1991), 5 O.R. (3d) 245 (Gen. Div.).

[54] *Waterman v. National Life Assurance Co. of Canada (No. 2)* (1993), 18 C.H.R.R. D/176 (Ont. Bd. Inq.).

and they did not establish that being HIV-negative was a bona fide requirement for the position.

Employers should be able to provide non-discriminatory reasons for decisions and assessments affecting employees, and ensure that they are not causing or condoning discrimination or harassment in the workplace. See section *9. Preventing and Responding to Homophobia and Discrimination Based on Sexual Orientation*, and the Commission's publication *Human Rights at Work* for more information about preventing and responding to human rights complaints in employment.[55]

8.2 — Services

Section 1 of the *Code* provides that every person has a right to equal treatment with respect to services, goods and facilities, without discrimination because of sexual orientation.

> *Example*: A municipality that provides the service of issuing proclamations must do so in a non-discriminatory manner. Refusal to proclaim "Gay and Lesbian Pride" events has been found to be discriminatory in several cases.[56] In one instance, the event was proclaimed, but the proclamation was altered and the word "Pride" eliminated. This was also found to be discriminatory.[57]
>
> *Example*: A representative of a gay community organization went to a printing company to have some of its business materials printed. The owner of the company, upon discovering that the job was for a gay organization, refused to print the materials citing his religious beliefs on sexual orientation.[58]
>
> *Example*: An all-male team of police officers entered a "women only" night at a bathhouse for investigation of alleged liquor license infractions. The committee organizing the event filed a complaint alleging

---

[55] Human Resources Professionals of Ontario & Ontario Human Rights Commission, *Human Rights at Work* (Toronto: Government of Ontario, 2004).

[56] *Hudler v. London (City)* (1997), 31 C.H.H.R. D/500 (Ont. Bd. Inq), *Hill v. Woodside* (1998), 33 C.H.R.R. D/349 (N.B. Bd. Inq.), *Oliver v. Hamilton (City)* (1994), 24 C.H.H.R. D/293 (Ont. Bd. Inq.), *Rainbow Committee of Terrace v. Terrace (City)* (2002), 43 C.H.R.R. D/413 (B.C.H.R.T.).

[57] *Hughson v. Kelowna (City)* (2000), 37 C.H.R.R. D/122 (B.C.H.R.T.).

[58] *Brockie v. Brillinger (No. 2)* (2002), 222 D.L.R. (4th) 174 (Ont. Sup. Ct. Div. Ct.).

discrimination of the basis of sex and sexual orientation. They alleged that despite having advance knowledge of the nature of the event, the police service scheduled male officers to investigate, although female officers were available. They also alleged that the officers remained much longer than the investigation required, observing numerous women in various states of undress. The negotiated settlement included a comprehensive training program for all officers, involving consultation with the complainants and the community, and clear objectives and reporting requirements.[59]

Service providers must respond appropriately to complaints of discrimination and harassment. They should investigate individual incidents and sanction the persons responsible, but may also need to take other measures to effectively address the problem.

Example: A student was subjected to years of homophobic harassment by other students in his secondary school. Although the school board reacted to specific instances of harassment by sanctioning the individual harassers, it did not take further measures to address the ongoing pattern of harassment. The school board was found responsible for discrimination, having failed to provide an educational environment free from discriminatory harassment.[60]

The Commission has addressed similar situations in Ontario, mediating settlements with broad systemic remedies designed to curb further discrimination and harassment on the grounds of sexual orientation.[61]

---

[59]Ontario Human Rights Commission, *Annual Report 2004-2005*, p. 57.

[60]*North Vancouver School District No. 44 v. Jubran* (2005), 39 B.C.L.R. (4th) 153 (B.C. C.A.). The Supreme Court of Canada denied the school board's application for leave to appeal (*North Vancouver School District No. 44 v. Jubran*, [2005] S.C.C.A. No. 260).

[61]For example, the Lakehead District School Board agreed to a number of measures, including adopting and promoting an equity statement, developing a document on prevention of homophobic harassment, drafting a diversity plan and providing training and education for staff and students on understanding sexual diversity issues (Ontario Human Rights Commission News Release, "Commission mediates settlement with school board in sexual orientation complaint" (8 September 2005)).

8.3 — Accommodation (Housing)

Section 2(1) of the *Code* provides that every person has a right to equal treatment with respect to the occupancy of accommodation (housing) without discrimination because of sexual orientation.

Landlords must ensure that they are not denying housing to individuals based on sexual orientation or other *Code* grounds. They must likewise ensure that their treatment of current tenants and decisions about termination of tenancy are non-discriminatory and not influenced by subjective judgements relating to sexual orientation.

> *Example*: Two gay students respond to an advertisement for a house that is for rent and arrange to view the house and meet with the owner. A few days later, they contact the owner and advise him that they wish to rent the house. At their second meeting with the owner of the house he asks them if they are gay and proceeds to tell them that he does not rent to gays.[62]

Landlords must also address any discrimination or harassment relating to sexual orientation that may arise within their rental housing environment, whether between tenants, or involving agents of the landlord, or others who are part of the housing environment, such as contracted maintenance workers.

> *Example*: A tenant complains that the superintendent and another tenant are verbally harassing him and making false accusations against him because of his sexual orientation and religion.
>
> *Example*: A landlord discovers homophobic and racist graffiti on a wall in a public area of her apartment building.
>
> *Example*: A woman complains to a landlord that the building manager stopped doing maintenance in her unit and responding to her phone calls after her same-sex partner moved in.

If landlords become aware of discrimination or harassment, either through a complaint or other means, they must respond appropriately. Landlords who fail to take steps to address a poisoned environment or a complaint of discrimination or harassment may be found liable.

---

[62]*Quebec c. Martin* (1997), 33 C.H.R.R. D/487 (Trib. Qué.).

9. — Preventing and Responding to Homophobia and Discrimination Based on Sexual Orientation

Organizations and workplaces can take a number of steps to prevent and appropriately address human rights complaints. The following are particularly important elements of an organization's strategy to address human rights issues as they may arise with respect to sexual orientation:

- protection of confidentiality of information
- barrier review
- development and promotion of anti-harassment and anti-discrimination policies that address homophobia
- a complaint resolution procedure.

9.1 — Protecting Confidentiality of Information

Confidentiality can be particularly important for bisexual, lesbian and gay individuals. An employer or service provider who legitimately requires and collects personal information that either directly or indirectly identifies an individual's sexual orientation must ensure the maximum degree of privacy and confidentiality of the information. This applies in all situations and circumstances including employment records and files, insurance company records, medical information, etc. The information might be required to enable an employee or individual to claim or register for benefits, to apply for an apartment, or for other purposes.

Confidential Information that might be collected could include:

- identification of next of kin
- identification of beneficiary for insurance purposes
- a claim for benefits for a same-sex spouse.

All information should remain exclusively with designated personnel (such as the human resources person) in a secure filing system in order to protect the individual's confidentiality. An employer or service provider who fails to properly safeguard personal information about an individual's sexual orientation may infringe the *Code*, and a complaint can be made where this results in a person being subjected to discrimination and/or harassment because of their sexual orientation or same-sex partnership status.

9.2 — Barrier Review and Removal

Organizations may have rules, criteria or internal policies, practices and decision-making processes that perpetuate systemic discrimination and create barriers for gay, lesbian and bisexual people, as well as individuals identified by other *Code* grounds.[63] In general, informal processes are much more likely to lead to subconsciously biased decision-making, and may allow biased decisions and behaviours (whether intentional or not) to go unnoticed and uncorrected by the organization or company.

Some examples include:[64]

> *Barrier*: Relying on personal networks, social relationships, supervisor discretion or word-of-mouth referrals to recruit for vacancies or to extend opportunities such as training or career advancement. These types of informal processes often exclude those who do not share the same characteristics as the recruiter, management, or other organization members.
>
> *Best practices*: Formal announcements or postings should list requirements or criteria related to the essential requirements for the position or opportunity, and be widely distributed so that they can readily come to the attention of a diverse applicant pool. Information about internal opportunities should be shared with all employees or organizational members.
>
> *Barrier*: Staffing or membership decisions based on informal processes. For example, conducting an interview by chatting with the applicant to see if he or she shares similar interests and will "fit" into the organizational culture may present a barrier for persons who are or appear different than the dominant norm in the organization.
>
> *Best practices*: Formal interviews or reviews, conducted by multiple-person panels, using preset questions and scoring the answers against a pre-determined answer guide, help to eliminate bias. Criteria and questions must relate to ability to perform the essential duties of the job or meet objective, non-discriminatory organizational requirements, rather than focusing on subjective, unclear considerations such as whether the person exhibits "confidence" or is "suitable."

---

[63]Physical and technological barriers should also be identified and removed, to eliminate discrimination and increase access for older persons and persons with disabilities.

[64]For more information see Ontario Human Rights Commission, *Human Rights at Work*, which explains the types of questions that are and are not permitted at various stages in the recruitment process: Human Resources Professionals of Ontario & Ontario Human Rights Commission, *Human Rights at Work* (Toronto: Government of Ontario, 2004) at 40–50. The Appendix to the Commission's *Policy and Guidelines on Racism and Racial Discrimination* also provides numerous examples of systemic barriers and best practices in a workplace setting.

Barrier: Undefined policies for sanction, discipline or termination, or uneven application of such policies. These are a common basis for human rights complaints.

Best practices: Decisions to sanction an individual should be based in clearly defined, objective criteria, and related to identified job or organizational requirements. Well-documented, evenly applied progressive discipline, sanction, or performance management practices help organizations prevent or respond to human rights complaints. Information about policies and criteria should be shared with all persons to whom they are applicable.

In hiring, extending opportunities, assessing performance, and in other decision-making, employers, landlords, service providers and other organizations should establish non-discriminatory criteria and processes, and follow them consistently. They must ensure that they are not treating individuals differently because of factors that may relate to a ground under the *Code*, and that their processes do not have a discriminatory effect, even if unintentional. Assessments should be made based on the requirements of the job, service or organization, not on external factors.

If there is a human rights complaint, organizations, landlords and employers may be asked to provide evidence of how a decision was made, and that it was not based, even in part, on discriminatory criteria.

9.3 — Anti-Harassment and Anti-Discrimination Policies

Organizations should be pro-active in creating fair and equitable environments. Anti-discrimination and anti-harassment policies are valuable tools in promoting equity and diversity within an organization. Adoption and implementation of these policies can also help to limit potential harm, and reduce the organization's liability in the event of a complaint. These policies should explicitly address discrimination based on sexual orientation.

These elements should be developed in co-operation with workplace or organization partners where they exist, such as unions. Unions are important partners in the creation of a non-discriminatory workplace. As part of a "best practices" initiative, they should work with employers in the development of internal policies and procedures. Unions should also take a proactive role in human rights training and education for their members specifically, and for the entire workplace in general.

9.3.1 — Developing Anti-Discrimination and Anti-Harassment Policies

The following are suggested contents for an organization's anti-discrimination and anti-harassment policy:

- a statement setting out the organization's commitment to a fair and equitable environment free of discrimination and harassment, clarifying that discrimination and harassment will not be tolerated by the organization
- a statement of rights and obligations, including:
  - The rights of organization members, employees, or other associated personnel
  - rights of clients, tenants, or customers
  - organizational, employer, and/or management obligations
  - union or other workplace partner obligations
  - an explanation of corporate liability for the behaviour of officers, managers, employees, *etc.*
  - a statement indicating that no reprisals are permitted or will be taken against an individual making a complaint
- a list of the prohibited grounds of discrimination in the *Code*
- the *Code* definitions of "harassment" and "sexual harassment"
- an explanation of the concept of a "poisoned environment" as a violation of the *Code*
- description/examples of unacceptable behaviour, such as:
  - refusal to hire, promote, or provide service or accommodation based on a ground listed in the *Code*
  - examples of harassment based on a ground listed in the *Code*
  - examples of what would constitute discrimination or harassment based on sexual orientation, sex, marital status, etc.
- how internal complaints will be handled, including:
  - to whom is the complaint made
  - confidentiality
  - length of time for complaint to be investigated
- disciplinary measures that will be applied if a claim of harassment or discrimination is proven

- remedies that will be available if the claim of harassment or discrimination is proven, such as:
  - an oral or written apology from the harasser/person who discriminated and the organization or company
  - recovery of losses, such as wages, benefits, promotion or services that were denied
  - compensation for injury to dignity
- a statement reinforcing the right of individuals to go to the Commission at any time during the internal process
- an explanation of the six-month time requirement in the *Code*.

9.3.2 — Promoting Anti-Discrimination and Anti-Harassment policies

All employees or organization members should be aware of internal policies and any procedures in place for resolving complaints. This can be done by:

- distributing policies to all employees or organization members;
- providing an overview and copies of the policies in any orientation process for new employees, management or members
- training the management team on the contents of the policies
- posting information about the policies where staff and/or clients can see it
- where a problem has been identified, providing ongoing education on human rights issues.

In an organization that does not provide training in anti-discrimination and human rights, managers may be unaware of what constitutes discrimination or harassment and how barriers operate to exclude people. Ongoing training in human rights and anti-discrimination, including anti-homophobia, should be an integral part of training for all employees, and particularly for those who act in a supervisory capacity. It should be made clear that human rights are part of the organization's culture and goals and that the training is not simply "window dressing" to comply with human rights laws.

For more information see the Commission documents *Human Rights at Work*, and *Developing Procedures to Resolve Human Rights Complaints Within Your Organization*.[65]

---

[65]Human Resources Professionals of Ontario & Ontario Human Rights Commission, *Human Rights at Work* (Toronto: Government of Ontario, 2004); and Ontario Human Rights Commission, *Developing Procedures to Resolve Human Rights Complaints Within Your Organization* (Toronto: Queen's Printer, 1996)

Policy on Discrimination and Language

Approved by the Commission: June 19, 1996

1. — Introduction

The Ontario *Human Rights Code* (the *"Code"*) states that it is public policy in Ontario to recognize the inherent dignity and worth of every person and to provide for equal rights and opportunities without discrimination. The provisions of the *Code* are aimed at creating a climate of understanding and mutual respect for the dignity and worth of each person, so that each person feels a part of the community and feels able to contribute to the community.

This policy statement sets out the Ontario Human Rights Commission's (the "Commission") position on language-based discrimination in the areas of employment, accommodation, services, contracts and membership in unions.

The *Code*, like most other provincial human rights legislation in Canada, does not include "language" as a prohibited ground of discrimination.[1] For the Commission to have jurisdiction, the discriminatory action or behaviour must be in relation to a prohibited ground of discrimination in the *Code*.

Although the *Code* does not explicitly identify "language" as a prohibited ground of discrimination, the Commission does accept complaints under a number of related grounds, such as ancestry, ethnic origin, place of origin and in some circumstances, race.[2] In the Commission's experience, language can be an element of a complaint based on any of these grounds.[3]

---

[1]At present, Quebec and the Yukon Territory are the only Canadian jurisdictions which specifically state that language is a prohibited ground of discrimination in the area of employment.

[2]Sign language is not included in this policy as it is directly related to the ground of "handicap" which is protected under the *Code*. Issues relating to persons who sign are addressed in the Commission's *Guidelines for Assessing Accommodation Requirements for Persons with Disabilities*.

[3]In accordance with s. 10 of the *Interpretation Act*, R.S.O. 1990, c. I.11, the *Code* is to be given a fair, large and liberal interpretation. See also *Cousens v. Canadian Nurses Association* (1981), 2 C.H.R.R. D/365 (Ont. Bd. of Inq.).

2. — Language-Related Grounds of Discimination: Ancestry, Ethnic Origin, Place of Origin, Race

The first language we learn is frequently the language spoken by our parents or guardians and others who take care of us as children. There is almost inevitably a link between the language we speak or the accent with which we speak a particular language on the one hand, and our ancestry, ethnic origin or place of origin on the other.[4]

A person's accent is also often associated with her or his "mother tongue" or place of origin. Because a person's accent is usually related to her or his ancestry, ethnic origin or place of origin, the *Code* can be infringed when someone is denied employment, service, housing, or is otherwise discriminated against because of an accent. In these kinds of situations, the underlying discrimination is often actually based on ancestry, place of origin and/or ethnic origin.

> *Example*: After an interview for a job as a school bus driver, a woman from Quebec, whose first language is French, was told she would not be hired for the position because she does not speak English fluently. She believed that she did have adequate command of English, but that she was turned down because her first language is French. Fluency in English was not identified as an essential feature of the job. Since one's "mother tongue" is closely associated with ancestry,[5] to deny a person employment because she is French-speaking could constitute a violation of the *Code* on the ground of "ancestry." Also, as she is from Quebec, "place of origin" could be cited as a secondary ground in the complaint.[6]

---

[4]*Espinoza v. Coldmatic Refrigeration of Canada Inc. et al.* (March 31, 1995), unreported, Harman, R. (Ont. Bd. of Inq.).

[5]"Mother tongue": see further *supra, note 3, Cousens*. It should also be noted that there maybe a violation of the *Code*, based on "place of origin," when English as a "mother tongue" is a job requirement.

[6]Discrimination against a regional accent may also constitute an infringement of the *Code* on the basis of "place of origin." "Place of origin" may cover situations where the characteristics of a person are, to the respondent, strongly associated with a particular region, that trigger discrimination. For example, an Aboriginal man from Northern Ontario and a woman from Newfoundland may both speak with an accent typical of the regions where they live. If they are denied employment because of their accent, they may file a complaint with the Commission on

Example: A teacher, originally from Poland, was on a school board's substitute teacher's list from which individuals are selected for short-term assignments. A period of time went by when he was not selected from this list for temporary assignments. The teacher learned that a note had been attached to his file which said that he did not speak English. The teacher filed a human rights complaint, and at a hearing before a board of inquiry, the respondent indicated that the note should have stated that the complainant spoke English with an "accent" and therefore should not be assigned to substitute for teachers in English or Social Studies classes. The board of inquiry ruled that the teacher was discriminated against because of his accent which is directly related to his ancestry or place of origin.[7]

There can also be situations in which the issue of fluency in a language or a person's accent in speaking a particular language, can be used to mask discrimination based on race.

Example: An African Canadian woman grew up in North Africa, speaking Italian. She had also studied in Italy. She applied for a position as a social worker with a community organization. The job description stated that, in addition to the technical skills and experience as a social worker that would be required for the job, competence in speaking "Italian, Portuguese or Chinese would be an asset." Although she was the best qualified applicant, she was denied the position because the agency felt that its client group would not be able to relate to "how" she spoke Italian, that is, her accent. She felt that her race was the real reason she was not hired and subsequently filed a complaint with the Commission. Her complaint was investigated and referred to a board of inquiry.

3. — Harassment and "Poisoned Environment"

3.1 — Harassment

Harassment is defined in s. 10(1) of the *Code* as "engaging in a course of vexatious comment or conduct that is known or ought reasonably to be

---

the basis of "place of origin" (see further Judith Keene, *Human Rights in Ontario* (2d) (Toronto: Carswell, 1992) at 53).

[7]*Gajecki v. Surrey School District (No. 36)* (1989), 11 C.H.R.R. D/326 (B.C. Council of H.R.). See also *Segula v. Ferrant, Ball Packaging Products Inc.* (March 3, 1995), (unreported), Leighton, D. (Ont. Bd. of Inq.).

known to be unwelcome."[8] Harassment because of language or accent may be a form of discrimination on the grounds of ancestry, ethnic origin, place of origin or in some situations race, contrary to the *Code*.

> *Example*: A manager supervises a group of workers whose first language is Arabic. He gets angry when they speak among themselves in Arabic during their breaks. The manager orders these employees to speak "Canadian" while they are at work, and threatens to terminate their employment if they continue speaking Arabic. Unless the manager can demonstrate that speaking English at all times at the workplace is a reasonable and *bona fide* requirement in the circumstances, his behaviour could constitute harassment under s. 5 of the *Code*.

3.2 — "Poisoned Environment"

There are situations in which a single incident may be significant or substantial enough to constitute a breach of the *Code* by creating a "poisoned environment" for some individuals. Unequal treatment, in the form of offensive behaviour, does not have to occur continuously or repeatedly for there to be a violation of the *Code*.

Sections 1, 2, 3, 5, 6 and 9 of the *Code* provide protection from discrimination because of race, ancestry, place of origin or ethnic origin. Any one of these sections can be the basis for a claim that a single incident was substantial enough to create a "poisoned environment."

In determining whether a "poisoned environment" has been created for persons identified by a prohibited ground of discrimination, the Commission looks at the impact of the behaviour rather than the number of times the behaviour occurs. A "poisoned environment" can arise when a person or a group of people are treated differently for reasons related to the language they speak. Language is often a pretext for indirectly discriminating against someone because of her or his ancestry, place of origin or ethnic origin.[9]

---

[8]The subjective element of this definition assumes that the person responsible for the behaviour knows that his/her comments or actions are unwelcome. the objective element is based on the assumption that the person should reasonably know that his/her behaviour is unwelcome.

[9]The Supreme Court of Canada upheld the concept of "poisoned environment" in *Attis v. The Board of School Trustees, District No. 15 and The Human Rights Commission of New Brunswick et al.* (April 3, 1996) (S.C.C.) [unreported].

Example: A law professor tells his class that those who speak English with a "foreign" accent do not make "good lawyers," and should not be admitted to law schools in Ontario to occupy spaces that should be held by Canadians. This remark in itself may be sufficient to poison the environment for those students in the class whose first language is not English, or those whose first language may be English but come from a country other than Canada and speak English with an accent. It may also have an impact on students whose ancestors came from, for example, Asia or Africa, because the comment targets new Canadians, many of whom now immigrate from these regions of the world.

4. — Constructive Discrimination

Under s. 11 of the *Code*, constructive discrimination may occur where there is a requirement, qualification or factor that is not discriminatory on its face, but when applied, results in the exclusion, restriction or preference of a group of persons identified by a prohibited ground of discrimination in the *Code*.[10]

Section 11(1)(a) further provides that a requirement, qualification or factor will not be found to be discriminatory if it can be established that it is reasonable and *bona fide* in the circumstances. In order to do so, the requirement must be reasonable and *bona fide* in the circumstances unless it can be shown that the needs of the group adversely affected "cannot be accommodated without undue hardship on the person responsible for accommodating those needs . . ." Factors that would determine whether a required accommodation poses an undue hardship include the cost of the accommodation, outside sources of funding, if any, and health and safety requirements, if any.

If an employer refuses to hire or promote an employee, if a sales clerk chooses to serve only particular customers, or a building manager is consistently rude to certain tenants because of a characteristic that is closely related to grounds under the *Code*, these actions may give rise to a complaint. Language is a characteristic that is often closely associated with ancestry, ethnic origin or place of origin. Thus, the *Code* may be breached

---

[10]*R. v. Bushnell Communications Ltd. et al.* (1974), 1 O.R. (2d) 442; aff'd (1974), O.R. (2d) 288.

where a language requirement, such as "proficiency" in English,[11] excludes, gives preference to, or restricts persons because of their ancestry, ethnic origin or place of origin.

4.1 — *Bona Fide* Occupational Requirement

The Commission recognizes that proficiency in a certain language may be a reasonable and legitimate requirement for employment. For example, if English-language proficiency is required for a position, it should be established as a *bona fide* occupational requirement. The test for determining if a qualification is *bona fide* must be an objective one. The requirement for English proficiency, and the degree of proficiency required,[12] must bear an objective relationship to the essential requirements of the job, and be a *bona fide* occupational requirement that is imposed in good faith.[13]

> *Example*: A supervisor in British Columbia refused to hire a South Asian man for an entry level position in a lumber mill. According to the supervisor, the applicant "could not speak English." A board of inquiry found that the requirement of proficiency in English was not a

---

[11]Studies have shown that there is a significant relationship between English-language proficiency and discriminatory experiences, and that these experiences are not limited to employment (see further *Racism and Chinese-Canadian Business Participation*, prepared for the Chinese Information and Community Services, Toronto, March 1996). That is, persons with low levels of language skills are more likely to experience discrimination in employment, services and housing accommodation.

[12]The degree of proficiency required must be objectively determined. There may also be situations where a certain level of language requirement is justifiable for a particular position.

> *Example*: A store clerk should have sufficient language skills to be able to communicate with customers. Other occupations may require only a basic understanding of English and if there is no contact with the public limited communication skills may be adequate for the position. In these situations, requiring a high level of English-language proficiency would not be a *bona fide* occupational requirement.

On the other hand, a politician may need to hire an executive who is fluent in several Chinese dialects in order to serve her large Chinese-speaking constituency. In which case, fluency in particular Chinese dialects may be a *bona fide* occupational requirement.

[13]*Ontario (Human Rights Commission) v. Etobicoke (Borough)*, [1982] 1 S.C.R. 202.

> *bona fide* occupational requirement for the position, and that the complainant's level of English was good enough to allow him to complete a course on lumber grading in English and obtain high marks. The board of inquiry went on to find that the supervisor's refusal to hire the complainant was in fact motivated by race and place of origin, not lack of proficiency in English, and therefore constituted an infringement of his rights under the British Columbia *Human Rights Act*.[14]

Fluency in a particular language could be a *bona fide* requirement in some employment or service situations.

> *Example*: An agency that serves persons from Central America requires support workers who can also act as refugee advocates. The functions of the position include providing support to clients at refugee board hearings. Fluency in Spanish in addition to English (or French) would likely be considered a *bona fide* requirement for the position.

In these circumstances, the requirement for the position must focus on the particular language needed to function in the job, and not on the place of origin, ancestry, ethnic origin or race of candidates for the position. In the above example, if an applicant is qualified and speaks fluently in Spanish and English, but does not come from a Central America country, she could not be denied the position unless the agency could justify a defence under s. 24(1)(a) of the *Code*.

5. — Relevant Ontario *Human Rights Code* Provisions

The Ontario *Human Rights Code* (Part II of this book) includes provisions relevant to this policy in the following sections: 1, 2(1)(2), 3, 5(1)(2), 6, 8, 9, 11(1) and 24(1).

---

[14]*Dhaliwal v. B.C. Timber Ltd.* (1983), 4 C.H.R.R. D/1520 (B.C. Bd. of Inq.).

Policy on Discrimination Because of Pregnancy and Breastfeeding

Approved by the Commission: September 11, 1996
Revised by the Commission: May 26, 1999, October 9, 2001

1. — Introduction

The Ontario *Human Rights Code* (the "*Code*") states that it is public policy in Ontario to recognize the inherent dignity and worth of every person and to provide for equal rights and opportunities without discrimination. The provisions of the *Code* are aimed at creating a climate of understanding and mutual respect for the dignity and worth of each person, so that each person feels a part of the community and feels able to contribute to the community.

The *Code* prohibits discrimination because of sex. Section 10(2) of the *Code* establishes that the right to equal treatment without discrimination because of sex includes the right to equal treatment without discrimination because a woman is, was or may become pregnant or because she has had a baby.

In addition, section 11 of the *Code* provides that it is also discriminatory if a workplace rule or requirement results in an adverse impact on persons who are identified by a prohibited ground of discrimination, except where the requirement, qualification or factor is reasonable and *bona fide* in the circumstances. In other words, rules and requirements that are neutral on their face may have a discriminatory impact.

Most of the complaints filed with the Ontario Human Rights Commission (the "Commission") by women alleging discrimination because of pregnancy, including breastfeeding, are related to the workplace. Nevertheless, the right to equal treatment without discrimination because of sex or pregnancy extends to accommodation (housing, etc.), services, goods and facilities, contracts and membership in trade unions.

This policy has several purposes:

- to help the public understand how the *Code* protects women against discrimination because of pregnancy or because they are breastfeeding
- to make women aware of their right to equal treatment in employment, accommodation, services, goods and facilities, contracts and membership in trade unions, without discrimination because they are, or may become, pregnant, or because they are breastfeeding

- to assist employers and providers of services and accommodation, to understand that they also have responsibilities under the *Code* to accommodate the needs of women who are, or may become, pregnant or are breastfeeding.

2. — Background

Anti-discrimination legislation seeks to address and remove unfair disadvantages that result from the fact that a person belongs to a group identified under the *Code*. Child-bearing benefits society as a whole, and therefore women should not be disadvantaged as a result of being pregnant.[1] The Supreme Court of Canada has recognized that the financial and social burdens and the cost associated with having children should not rest entirely on women.[2]

Several international agreements and conventions to which Canada is a party contain provisions with respect to the pre-natal and post-natal periods. Article 10(2) of the *International Covenant on Economic, Social and Cultural Rights* provides that special protection should be accorded to mothers during a reasonable period before and after childbirth. During such a period, working mothers should be accorded paid leave or leave with adequate social security benefits. *The Convention on the Elimination of All Forms of Discrimination Against Women* states that women shall have appropriate services in connection with pregnancy and breastfeeding.

Unfortunately, discrimination against women because of pregnancy continues to be a common practice in society, particularly in employment. Many women who are, or may become, pregnant do not know how their employers will respond to their pregnancy. This often results in these women experiencing considerable stress and even fear that they may lose their job.

As well, women who are breastfeeding often face negative attitudes from employers, and when using services or facilities. They may experience difficulty in securing appropriate accommodation that will allow them to nurse their children.

Women who are pregnant may experience varying forms and degrees of discrimination, depending on what other characteristics form part of their personal identity or status in society. For example, pregnant women who receive social assistance, or who are young, single, involved in a same-sex relationship, or who have a disability, are often more vulnerable and there-

---

[1] *Brooks v. Canada Safeway Ltd.*, [1989] 1 S.C.R. 1219.

[2] *Ibid.*

fore more likely to be subject to discriminatory behaviour than pregnant women who are in a traditional family structure.

3. — Meaning of Pregnancy

The right to equal treatment without discrimination because of sex includes the right to equal treatment without discrimination because a woman is, was or may become pregnant or because she has had a baby. "Pregnancy" therefore includes the process of pregnancy from conception up to the period following childbirth and includes the post-delivery period and breastfeeding.[3] The term "pregnancy" takes into account all the special needs and circumstances of a pregnant woman and recognizes that the experiences of women will differ.

Special needs can be related to circumstances arising from:

- miscarriage[4]
- abortion
- complications because of pregnancy or childbirth
- conditions which result directly or indirectly from an abortion/miscarriage
- recovery from childbirth[5]
- breastfeeding.

---

[3]The length of the post-delivery period covered by human rights protections is dependent on the circumstances of the mother: *Alberta Hospital Association v. Parcels* (1992), 17 C.H.R.R. D/167 (Alta. Q.B.); *Parcels v. Red Deer General & Auxiliary Hospital Nursing Home (Dist. No. 15)* (1991), 15 C.H.R.R. D/257 (Alta. Bd. of Inq.).

[4]In a recent British Columbia Human Rights Tribunal decision, *Tilsley v. Subway Sandwiches* (2001), 39 C.H.R.R. D/102 (B.C.H.R.T.), a woman was fired for not showing up at work when she was in hospital because of a miscarriage. The Tribunal ruled that discrimination because of a miscarriage is one form of discrimination because of sex, and that the employer had a duty to accommodate the employee's pregnancy, which included her miscarriage, to the point of undue hardship.

[5]"Pregnancy" is understood to extend beyond the date of delivery and post-delivery recovery, which is included in the definition of "pregnancy." The length of time is dependent on the circumstances of the mother. See further *Parcels, supra*, note 4.

4. — Discrimination "Because of Pregnancy" is Discrimination Based on Sex

Only a woman can become pregnant, so pregnancy is a characteristic that is necessarily linked to a woman's sex.[6] Section 10(2) of the *Code* states that:

> The right to equal treatment without discrimination because of sex includes the right to equal treatment without discrimination because a woman is or may become pregnant.

5. — Breastfeeding and Discrimination

As noted above, pregnancy includes the post-natal period, which includes breastfeeding. Breastfeeding is a natural part of child-rearing, and so is integrally related to the ground of sex, as well as to family status. Numerous studies have demonstrated the benefits of breastfeeding for mothers, children and their communities, in terms of physical and emotional health and development. Women should not be disadvantaged in services, accommodation or employment because they have chosen to breastfeed their children.

Breastfeeding includes pumping or expressing milk, as well as nursing directly from the breast.

Sometimes women are discouraged by others from breastfeeding in public places because of concerns that it is indecent. Breastfeeding is really a health issue, and not one of public decency. Women should have the choice to feed their baby in the way that they feel is most dignified, comfortable, and healthy.

6. — Other Relevant Grounds of Discrimination under the *Code*

6.1 — Family status

In addition to sex, discrimination can occur because of one's family status. "Family status" is defined in section 10(1) of the *Code* and refers to:

> . . . the status of being in a parent and child relationship.

There are numerous stereotypes about a mother with a young child, particularly about her ability to continue working. For example, some believe that a mother who has an infant at home may miss work more often than employees who do not have a young family, or may be less committed to their

---

[6]*Supra*, note 1.

employer or to their career. Others may feel that hiring or keeping an employee who may become pregnant or who is on maternity leave costs the company too much. However, Boards of Inquiry have rejected the argument that the cost of upgrading or retraining a woman after she returns from maternity leave is a defence to discriminating against a woman because of her family status.

7. — Other Relevant Sections of the *Code*

The *Code* protects women against discrimination in the workplace (section 5); in services (section 1); in accommodation (*e.g.* housing) (section 2); contracts (section 3); and membership in trade unions (section 6). The *Code* also specifically prohibits harassment because of sex in accommodation (section 7(1)) and employment (section 7(2)).

Section 11 of the *Code* provides protection from constructive discrimination for women who are, were or may become pregnant, or who have had a baby, when there is a rule, requirement or factor which may not be discriminatory on the surface, but when applied may have an adverse impact on women because of pregnancy or breastfeeding.

8. — Employment (Section 5)

8.1 — *Hiring, Promotions, Transfers, Termination*

Subject to *bona fide* requirements, denying or restricting employment opportunities in hiring, or transferring, etc., a woman because she is, was or may become pregnant or because she has had a baby, is a violation of the *Code*. Certain work-related practices or behaviours may also constitute discrimination such as:

- limiting or withholding employment opportunities, or withholding training, regardless of work performance or years of service. This may include failing to inform women who are away on pregnancy leave about major developments and workplace opportunities
- not assigning a pregnant woman to a major project or team project
- being overly critical of a pregnant woman's work
- docking a pregnant woman's time for using the washroom more frequently
- making a pregnant woman the subject of inappropriate comments or jokes
- terminating her with or without notice, because of her pregnancy
- subjecting her to unwanted transfers

- denying sick leave benefits
- refusing to cooperatively engage in a process to find appropriate arrangements to permit a woman to continue breastfeeding her child (see footnote for detailed examples).[7]

---

[7]The following are examples of situations where Boards of Inquiry have found that a woman's right to be free from discrimination in employment because she is or may become pregnant has been violated:

Hiring: A pregnant woman was offered a position as a clerk, but when the employer learned that she was pregnant, the offer was withdrawn. A Board of Inquiry found that she was denied employment because she was pregnant and this constituted discrimination. It also found that the woman was entitled to compensation for lost employment insurance benefits for which she would have qualified had she not been denied the opportunity to work. If the employer had hired her as agreed, she would have received wages. "But for the discrimination," her employer would have made the appropriate deductions and therefore she would have been entitled to employment insurance benefits. *McAlpine v. Canada (Canadian Forces)* (1988), 9 C.H.R.R. D/5190 (C.H.R.T.). See also *Jenner v. Point West Development Corp.* (1990), 21 C.H.R.R. D/336 (Ont. Bd. of Inq.). In the *Jenner* decision, the Board of Inquiry found that the question of the complainant being available to work was so clearly linked with pregnancy and being a woman that the employer's decision not to hire her because she would not be available for the whole season amounts to deciding not to hire because she was pregnant.

Promotion: The B.C. Human Rights Council (B.C.H.R.C.) found that the employer discriminated against a pregnant employee when the employer failed to consider her for a promotion. Instead, she was *demoted* immediately before she was scheduled to go on maternity leave. The Board of Inquiry reviewed evidence that the employee was not provided with a written evaluation of her performance and that less than a standard period of time was allowed for the employee to meet performance objectives. It concluded that these also constituted discrimination on the basis of pregnancy. See further *Magee v. Warner Lambert Canada* (1990), 12 C.H.R.R. D/208 (B.C.H.R.C.).

Termination: The B.C. Human Rights Council found that a complainant was discriminated against when she was dismissed from her job as a cocktail waitress because she was pregnant. The employer had argued that it was not appropriate for a cocktail waitress to be pregnant. The Board of Inquiry did not accept the employer's argument that not being pregnant was a *bona fide* occupational requirement. In another situation, the Board of Inquiry found that the employer discriminated against the employee by refusing her a transfer from the employer's Saskatoon office to the Edmonton office and then terminating her, because she was pregnant. The employer did not want to replace the pregnant employee during her absence on maternity leave. *Infra*, note 8,

Even if pregnancy or being of child-bearing age is only one of the factors in a decision to deny a woman employment-related opportunities, this could nevertheless constitute a violation of a woman's right to freedom from discrimination under the *Code*.[8] A woman loses more than just a job or a promotion when she is discriminated against because of pregnancy. She experiences a "missed opportunity" which has far greater consequences for her employment prospects.

If an employee is terminated for any reason related to pregnancy, the employer may be found to have violated her rights under the *Code* and the *Employment Standards Act* (*"ESA"*).

Bona Fide *Occupational Requirement*

In some circumstances, differential treatment of a woman because she is, was or may become, pregnant may be legitimate if it can be demonstrated that *not* being pregnant is a *bona fide* occupational requirement.

> *Example*: A woman who was seven months pregnant was denied a position as kitchen help in a restaurant. The Board of Inquiry heard evidence that the position would be physically demanding. As the woman had never performed these kitchen duties she would not know the extent of the duties and physical requirements expected for this job. The Board of Inquiry was satisfied in this particular instance that it was

---

Stefanyshyn; Wormsbecker v. SuperValu and Westfair Foods Ltd. (1983), 4 C.H.R.R. D/1443.

Breastfeeding: A labour arbitrator found that a woman had been discriminated against when her employer did not accommodate her breastfeeding needs to the point of undue hardship. The grievor, who was on maternity leave, requested an extension of her leave in order to meet her breastfeeding needs. The employer was willing to have the grievor express or pump her milk during her scheduled breaks or lunch hour; however this was not practical for the grievor because of her particular breastfeeding history. The arbitrator ruled that the employer had failed to make a sufficient effort to seek solutions to accommodate the grievor, and that it had not accommodated her to the point of undue hardship. See *Carewest v. Health Sciences Association of Alberta (Degagne Grievance)* (8 January 2001), [2001] A.G.A.A. No. 2 (J.C. Moreau).

[8]*Riggio v. Sheppard Coiffures Ltd.* (1988), 9 C.H.R.R. D/4520 (Ont. Bd. of Inq.); *Stefanyshyn v. 4 Seasons Management Ltd. (4 Seasons Racquet Club)* (1987), 8 C.H.R.R. (B.C.H.R.C).

likely that not being in the later stages of pregnancy was a reasonable occupational requirement.[9]

To be considered a *bona fide* occupational requirement under human rights legislation, the requirement, qualification or factor must be imposed in good faith and be reasonable from an objective viewpoint.[10] Case law and Boards of Inquiry apply a very high standard before accepting the defence of a *bona fide* occupational requirement. In other words, certain restrictions may have a rational or reasonable connection to the occupation and are therefore acceptable defences. Without such a connection to the occupation the employer will not have a defence of a *bona fide* occupational requirement.

Example: A Board of Inquiry found that an employer had discriminated against a female employee when it refused to employ her in a section of the company that processed certain gases. The employer defended its action on the basis that, from time to time, there are accidental emissions of a gas which may be harmful to women of child-bearing age or to a fetus. The Board of Inquiry found that the risk of harm to a fetus from the accidental emission of the gas was minimal. As well, the scientific research did not support the company's concerns. The Board of Inquiry noted that any woman who knows she is pregnant or who intends to become pregnant, could be transferred from this section until after she has given birth.[11]

8.2 — *Duty to Accommodate*

In order for a requirement to be reasonable and *bona fide* in the circumstances, it must be shown that the needs of the particular group protected under the *Code* cannot be accommodated "short of undue hardship." "Short of undue hardship" is a standard that applies to the person required to make the accommodation, and takes into consideration costs, outside sources of funding, and health and safety factors. Customer complaints, business inconvenience, or collective agreement provisions do not justify discriminatory actions against women who are pregnant or breastfeeding.

Assessment of undue hardship must be based on evidence that is objective, real and direct.

---

[9] *Mack v. Marivtsan* (1989), 10 C.H.R.R. D/5892 (Sask. Bd. of Inq.).

[10] *Ontario (Human Rights Commission) v. Etobicoke (Borough)*, [1982] 1 S.C.R. 202.

[11] *Wiens v. Inco Metals Co.* (1988), 9 C.H.R.R. D/4795 (Ont. Bd. of Inq.).

The Supreme Court of Canada in *Brooks v. Canada Safeway* established that discrimination against women because of pregnancy includes not only discriminatory action, but also the failure to accommodate the special needs of persons who fall into this category.

Special needs during the pre-natal and post-natal period can be accommodated, short of undue hardship, in a variety of ways. Some examples are provided below.

- An employee may be temporarily relocated to another work station or location or reassigned to alternative duties.
- A flexible work schedule can be provided to accommodate medical appointments, including treatment for infertility.
- Breaks can be allowed as necessary. It is a general human rights principle that persons should not experience disadvantage owing to needs related to prohibited grounds of discrimination. Therefore, employees who require breaks, such as for pumping or breastfeeding, should normally be accorded those breaks, and not be asked to forgo normal meal breaks as a result, or work additional time to make up for the breaks, unless the employer can show undue hardship.
- A supportive environment can be provided for a woman who is breastfeeding. Accommodation may mean allowing the care-giver to bring the baby into the workplace to be breastfed, making scheduling changes to permit time to express milk or breastfeed at work, and providing a comfortable, dignified and appropriate area so that a woman can breastfeed, or express and store breast milk at work. In some special cases, it may involve permitting a leave of absence.[12] A supportive environment can be created with minimum disruption.

When the application of a rule has an adverse impact on women who are, were or may become pregnant or those who have had a baby, the rule may violate their rights under the *Code*. Consideration must be given to introducing an appropriate accommodation measure, short of undue hardship.

> *Example*: A police officer requested light duties for the last stages of her pregnancy. The Police Service had a policy that did not provide a modified work program and her request for light duties was denied. Instead, she was told that she could take a part-time civilian position at a much lower salary. This meant that the officer would have to resign from the force. The Board of Inquiry stated that the rule of "no modified duties" was applied to all officers but it clearly excluded "pregnant

---

[12] See *Carewest v. Health Sciences Association of Alberta, supra*, note 7.

> women from consideration of the fact they are at higher risk during the latter stages of their pregnancy." It found that the accommodation offered was unreasonable because other male officers who were injured were given lighter duties. The Board of Inquiry concluded that the Police Service discriminated against the police officer because of her sex.[13]

In this example, the policy was applied equally to all police officers and, on its face, did not discriminate. However, because the rule adversely affected those who became pregnant, it constituted "constructive discrimination" in relation to pregnant women. The uniform application of the policy of not providing modified duties resulted in pregnant police officers being negatively affected.

It is important to note that an employer cannot arbitrarily decide that a pregnant employee should take a leave of absence as an accommodation measure, without considering other options for dealing with a situation requiring accommodation, in consultation with the affected employee.

Employee's and Employer's Responsibility

Both the employee and the employer share the responsibility for determining the most appropriate form of accommodation that a given set of circumstances may require. There is a duty to enter into a cooperative and respectful dialogue in order to develop, implement and maintain appropriate accommodation.

- If a pregnant employee is advised by her doctor that she can no longer work in a particular job, she is responsible for clearly informing the employer of her need for accommodation and of the accommodation required.
- Employers should accept requests for accommodation in good faith, unless there are legitimate reasons for acting otherwise. The employer is entitled to request sufficient information from the employee in order to make the accommodation, and may seek expert advice or opinion where required.

---

[13] *Julie Lord v. Haldimand-Norfolk Police Services Board* (June 14, 1995), unreported, Mikus, L. (Ont. Bd. of Inq.). See also, *Emrick Plastics v. Ontario (Human Rights Commission)* (1992), 16 C.H.R.R. 300 (Div. Ct.), *Hienke v. Brownell* (1991), 14 C.H.R.R. D/68 (Ont. Bd. of Inq.); *Re Orangeville Police Services Board and Orangeville Police Assn* (1994), 40 L.A.C. (4th) 269.

- Once the employer is aware of what accommodation is required, the employer has a duty to take the necessary steps to accommodate the special needs and circumstances of the pregnant employee, short of undue hardship.[14]
- The employer cannot insist that the employee take an unpaid leave of absence as an accommodation measure. Accommodation should be provided in a way that most nominally affects the employee's rights.

Under the *Code*, employers must demonstrate that a particular form of accommodation would lead to excessive costs or health and safety concerns, in order to justify a claim of undue hardship.

8.3 — *Benefit Plans*

As discussed below, employee benefit plans or employment practices that result in disadvantage because of pregnancy constitute discrimination under the *Code* on the basis of sex and pregnancy.

A Divisional Court decision, *Crook v. Ontario Cancer Treatment and Research Foundation*, confirmed a Board of Inquiry's decision that sick leave benefits should be available, for health-related reasons, to a woman who has recently given birth when she has chosen not to go on maternity leave under the *ESA*.[15]

8.4 — *Health-Related Absences*[16]

In the *Brooks* decision, the Supreme Court of Canada said that pregnancy leave should be included in employee benefit plans without having to be

---

[14]In an unreported decision, *Tammy Turnbull v. 539821 Ontario Ltd.–Andre's Restaurant* (June 21, 1996), McKellar, M.A. (Ont. Bd. of Inq.), the Board of Inquiry decided that because the employer knew the employee was pregnant, the employer was responsible for accommodating her even if she did not specifically request accommodation.

[15]*Ontario Cancer Treatment & Research Foundation v. Ontario (Human Rights Commission)* (1998), 34 C.C.E.L. (2d) 56, 108 O.A.C. 289 (Ont. Div. Ct.); upholding *Crook v. Ontario Cancer Treatment & Research Foundation (No.3)* (1996), 30 C.H.R.R. D/104 (Ont. Bd. Of Inquiry).

[16]While pregnancy is an entirely normal condition, serious medical complications can arise involving some period of time during which the woman is unable to work. Pregnancy itself cannot be classified as an illness; it is a unique condition which does not fit appropriately into any other category for compensating time lost from work.

After several years of debating whether or not pregnancy is "akin" to sickness or disability, the courts and provincial legislatures have acknowledged that the special categorized as an illness, accident or a disability. Under the *Brooks* doctrine, if a pregnant employee produces proof that she must be absent from work for health-related reasons, at whatever stage this might be during the pregnancy, she cannot be treated differently or adversely from other employees who are also absent from work for other "health-related reasons."

"Health" was broadly defined in the *Brooks* decision to include:

- the physical and psychological health of the woman
- the health, well-being, growth and development of the fetus
- a woman's ability to function as a social being, interacting with her family, employer and significant others.

A "health-related absence from work" can therefore mean any absence that is related to a woman's health, or the health and well-being of the fetus.

Pregnancy leave is used for bonding and nurturing. As well, different women have different medical and physiological needs following childbirth depending on their circumstances, and the time required to recover from childbirth varies. Because women respond differently to pregnancy, requests for health-related absences are usually assessed and granted on an individual basis. Pregnant employees who require leave for health-related pregnancy concerns should follow the proof-of-claim procedures of the employer's benefit plan to establish that the health-related absence is valid.

An Alberta court decision in *Alberta Hospital Association v. Parcels* endorsed the *Brooks* principle that a health-related reason for absence from the workplace by a pregnant employee is not to be treated differently from other health-related absences.[17] This applies generally where the woman is pregnant and where the condition which requires time off is associated with pregnancy.

The court in *Parcels* concluded that:

- Where an employer has a benefit plan that compensates health-related absences or provides disability benefits to its employees, a woman should be entitled to disability benefits during that portion of the pregnancy or parental leave that she is unable to work for health reasons related to the pregnancy and childbirth. Payment must begin as soon as the pregnant woman is away from the workplace for a health-related reason.

---

needs associated with pregnancy do not correspond to any other health-related condition. This recognition was crucial to advancing the development of pregnancy-related benefits.

[17] *Alberta Hospital Association v. Parcels* (1992), 17 C.H.R.R. D/167 (Alta. Q.B.).

- Any health-related portion of maternity leave is to be treated the same as other health-related leaves such as a sick leave or disability leave. The employee should be compensated at substantially the same level and should be subject to the same conditions as an employee who becomes ill, such as the requirement to provide a medical confirmation for the absence.[18]
- Pregnant employees are to be compensated for the full period of their health-related absence, whether it occurs during the pre-natal or post-natal period, and including recovery from childbirth.

These principles are consistent with the general tenet in *Brooks* that women who are absent for health reasons related to their pregnancy should not be treated differently from employees absent for other health-related reasons.

Section 25(2) of the *Code* states that contracts of group insurance between employers and insurers do not violate the equal treatment provisions of the *Code* with respect to age, sex, marital status, same-sex partnership status or family status, so long as they comply with the *ESA* and regulations.

Prior to the proclamation of a new *ESA* in 2001,[19] Regulation 321 under the previous *ESA* permitted health-related absences because of pregnancy during maternity leave to be treated differently from other health-related absences where a workplace disability plan was based on a contract of group insurance. Such a plan was defined in that regulation[20] to include any plan, fund or arrangement that insures against loss of income because of sickness, accident or disability and includes short- and long-term income insurance or benefit plans. Practically speaking, this meant that the right to receive benefits under disability plans ended when a woman chose to go on pregnancy or parental leave under the *ESA*. But if an employer offered disability benefits to other employees who were off on other kinds of leave such as educational leaves or sabbaticals, then the *ESA* provided that benefits should also be paid to women on pregnancy leave and parental leave. No provisions permitting differential treatment of health-related absences because of pregnancy during maternity leave have been included in the Regulations under the new *ESA*. Regulations under the new Act require employers to provide the same benefit entitlements to employees on pregnancy leave or parental leave as are provided to employees who are on other types of leave.[21]

---

[18]See further *Stagg v. Intercontinental Packers Ltd.* (1992), 18 C.H.R.R. D/392 (Sask. Bd. of Inq.).

[19]S.O. 2000, c. 41, in force September 4, 2001.

[20]Regulation 321 to the *Employment Standards Act*, section 1.

[21]O. Reg. 286/01 under the *Employment Standards Act, 2000*, s. 10.

Finally, a woman may have health problems related to her pregnancy that force her to be away from work *before or after* her pregnancy leave or parental leave. She can access health benefits under a workplace sick or disability plan in this situation. However, she should check her dates of leave with the Employment Standards Branch at the Ministry of Labour since her decision to take short- or long-term disability leave may affect her right to take pregnancy and/or parental leave. There are strict rules about when she is entitled to take pregnancy or parental leave and when she must notify her employer.

Women on maternity leave continue to be entitled to other benefits under employment-related benefit plans including pension plans, life insurance plans, accidental death plans, extended health plans and dental plans.[22] Employers are also required to continue to make contributions to such plans.[23]

8.5 — *Special Programs: Section 14*

Section 14 of the *Code*, which deals with "special programs," allows for differential treatment of persons protected under the *Code* if that program is designed to relieve hardship or economic disadvantage or to assist disadvantaged persons or groups to achieve equality of opportunity. The purpose of maternity leave (both health-related and voluntary portions) is to address the circumstances related to pregnancy. Women have experienced, and continue to experience, considerable disadvantage in employment, housing, etc. because of pregnancy. As previously noted, the Supreme Court of Canada has acknowledged that the cost associated with bearing children rests disproportionately on women.

Section 14 recognizes that:

- "special programs" which are designed to relieve hardship or economic disadvantage or to achieve equality are necessary and legitimate
- the equality rights provisions of the *Code* are not infringed by the implementation of a special program.

For further information on the application of section 14 please refer to the Commission's *Guidelines on Special Programs*.

8.6 — *Harassment/Poisoned Environment*

Actual intention to harass is not required to establish evidence of a poisoned environment. If the comment or conduct is known or ought reasonably to be known to be unwelcome, it may be considered as "harassment." The phrase

---

[22]Subsections 51(1) and (2) of the *Employment Standards Act*.

[23]Subsection 51(3) of the *Employment Standards Act*.

"ought to have known" introduces an objective element to the test.[24] Ongoing jokes and comments or derogatory statements made about pregnant women in a workplace or service setting, may create a "poisoned environment" for women by making them feel harassed, threatened or unwelcome.

9. — Accommodation (e.g. Housing) (Section 2)

Section 2 of the *Code* protects a woman who is, was or may become pregnant, or has had a baby against discrimination in housing.

> *Example*: A young woman shared a two-bedroom apartment with various roommates. The owners were aware of the arrangement, and she received their approval for each new co-tenant. She was later involved with one of these co-tenants and became pregnant. When the superintendent found out she was pregnant, he asked her if she was "intending to give up the baby for adoption" and said that the owners "didn't want kids in the building." The Board of Inquiry found that the complainant had been discriminated against because of her sex and family status. In the Board's view, one of the main reasons she was evicted "was her pending motherhood."[25]

A Board of Inquiry has also decided that "Adult Only" rules in condominiums discriminate on the grounds of "family status."[26]

10. — Services, Goods and Facilities (Section 1)

The *Code* prohibits discrimination in "services, goods and facilities" against women who are pregnant. This includes educational institutions, hospitals and health services, insurance providers, public places like malls and parks, public transit, and stores and restaurants. This means that women who are pregnant, or who are accompanied by their newborn babies to a restaurant or a theatre, cannot be denied service or access unless there is a *bona fide* reason for doing so.

---

[24]See section 10 of the *Code* for the definition of "harassment."

[25]*Peterson v. Anderson* (1992), 15 C.H.R.R. D/1 (Ont. Bd. of Inq.).

[26]See further *Dudnik v. York Condominium Corp. No. 216* (1990), 12 C.H.R.R. D/325 (Ont. Bd. of Inq.); reversed in part (1991), (sub nom. *York Condominium Corp. No. 216 v. Dudnik)* 79 D.L.R. (4th) 161 (Div. Ct.).

The *Code* prohibits discrimination in "services, goods and facilities" against women who are breastfeeding. This means that women have a right to nurse undisturbed, and cannot be prevented from breastfeeding a child in, for example, a public area or restaurant. They also cannot be asked to move to a more "discreet" area to breastfeed a child, or to "cover up." Complaints from other persons will not justify interfering with a woman's right to breastfeed.

Education providers have the same type of obligation as employers to accommodate women who are breastfeeding, including the obligation to co-operatively discuss options and create a supportive environment.

The *Code* allows for an exception for certain types of insurance policies, under section 22. This section permits individual and group insurance policies, which are offered as a service, to make distinctions based on sex if the distinctions are made on reasonable and *bona fide* grounds. In *Bates v. Zurich*,[27] the Supreme Court of Canada stated that a discriminatory practice in the insurance industry is "reasonable" if:

a) it is based on a sound and accepted insurance practice

b) there is no practical alternative.

Example: A professional association offers as a service to its members an optional insurance policy. The policy has a specific provision requiring a 30-day pre-existing condition restriction that applies only to women who are pregnant. This means that a woman who is pregnant at the time she applies for the policy is not eligible for coverage. If a pregnant woman challenges this requirement, the insurance provider, and possibly the professional association, would have to show that this requirement meets the test of a sound and accepted insurance practice and that there is no practical alternative, according to *Bates v. Zurich*.

[27] *Zurich Insurance Co. v. Ontario (Human Rights Commission)*, (sub nom. *Bates v. Zurich Insurance Co. of Canada)* 6 C.H.R.R. D/2948(1985) (Ont. Bd. of Inq.); reversed 8 C.H.R.R. D/4069, (sub nom. *Ontario (Human Rights Commission) v. Zurich Insurance Co.)* 10 O.A.C. 220 (Div. Ct.); affirmed (1989), 70 O.R. (2d) 639; leave to appeal granted (1990), 73 O.R. (2d) x (note) (S.C.C.); affirmed [1992] 2 S.C.R. 321.

11. — Collective Agreements and Company Policies

Employers and labour representatives are recognizing their obligations under the *Code*, as well as their shared responsibility to maintain workplace environments that are free from discrimination.

Collective agreements or other contractual arrangements cannot act as a bar to providing accommodation, subject of course to the undue hardship standard. Unions and employers are jointly responsible for negotiating collective agreements that comply with human rights laws, and should build conceptions of equality into collective agreements.

A woman who is pregnant or breastfeeding may have rights that can be pursued by a grievance under a collective agreement. Provincial labour laws allow arbitrators to apply and interpret the *Code* to grievances that involve human rights violations.[28] Some issues that may be more appropriately dealt with through the grievance process include:

- whether a pregnant woman can use sick leave and annual vacation leave for maternity leave[29]
- whether sick-leave days and vacation leave can be accumulated while a woman is on maternity leave[30]
- seniority issues relating to maternity leave.[31]

---

[28]*Bill 7* amended the *Labour Relations Act* (section 48 (12)(j)) to permit arbitrators to interpret and apply human rights and other employment-related statutes, despite any conflict between those statutes and the terms of the collective agreement.

[29]See *Ontario Secondary School Teachers' Federation (District 34) v. Essex County Board of Education* (April 4, 1996), unreported, Adams, J. (Ont. Div. Ct.).

[30]Where the sick leave or vacation leave or pay is calculated based on the period of time that a person has been "in service" or "continuously employed," most arbitrators have held that employees who were off work because of maternity leave were entitled to include the period of time that they were not at work. If the collective agreement clearly excludes women who are on maternity leave from accruing sick leave or vacation leave/pay, the grievor should consider filing a human rights complaint with the Commission.

[31]Section 52 of the *ESA* states that seniority and service lengths accrue during pregnancy and parental leave. Section 5 of the *ESA* states that no one can contract out of an employment standard. This includes collective agreements. Employees may therefore have protection under the *ESA* if their collective agreement says that seniority will not accrue while a woman is off on maternity leave.

Persons are not obligated to exhaust an internal complaint resolution mechanism before considering other avenues of complaint such as approaching the Commission or filing a grievance. An individual may elect to file two complaints at the same time — one under the employer's internal policy and one with the Commission. However, if there is a grievance procedure in place under a collective agreement, the Commission may elect to exercise its discretion under section 34 of the *Code*, and decide to not deal with a complaint. This is because section 48(11)(j) of the *Labour Relations Act* allows labour arbitrators to interpret and apply human rights legislation.

Internal anti-harassment and anti-discrimination policies are not governed by provincial legislation and the Commission does not consider them in the same way as the grievance procedure under a collective agreement. This means that if the complainant is not satisfied with the resolution, s/he can contact the Commission. If this is the case, the complaint *should* be filed within the six-month limitation period which begins from the time of the alleged harassment. If a complaint is not filed within the time frame, the Commission may decide not to deal with the complaint, subject to section 34 (1)(d) of the *Code*.

12. — Other Pregnancy-Related Legislation

The *Code* protects women's right to equal treatment in employment without discrimination because they are, were, or intend to become pregnant. The federal *Employment Insurance Act* and the provincial *ESA* also have provisions that relate to pregnancy, but with different purposes.

The *ESA* identifies employees' and employers' rights and responsibilities concerning pregnancy leave and job security. The *ESA* provides for the following:

- employees' and employers' responsibilities concerning pregnancy and parental leave and job security
- requirements for qualification for pregnancy and parental leave
- entitlement of women to return to the job held prior to the leave
- the employer's responsibility to maintain certain benefits on the woman's behalf while she is absent on leave
- a prohibition on intimidating, dismissing, or otherwise penalizing a woman, or threatening to do so, because that woman is or will become entitled to take pregnancy leave, intends to take a leave, or actually takes a leave.

For detailed information on the ESA, please contact the Employment Standards Branch of the Ministry of Labour.

Under the *Employment Insurance Act*, a woman who has worked the required number of hours during the qualification period can receive employment insurance benefits for up to 15 weeks while she is off work due to her pregnancy. The benefit period can begin up to eight weeks before her child is expected to be born, and ends at the latest 17 weeks after the child was expected to be delivered, or was delivered. The *Act* also provides for parental employment insurance benefits for up to 35 weeks, for a combined potential total of 50 weeks of employment insurance benefits for women who give birth.

For detailed information on employment insurance, please contact Human Resources Development Canada.

There are areas of overlap between the *Code* and the *ESA* with respect to pregnancy and the workplace. Generally speaking, the Ontario Human Rights Commission deals with the following situations:

- harassment because of pregnancy or breastfeeding
- accommodation needs arising from pregnancy or breastfeeding
- reprisal against pregnant employees, including withholding of employment opportunities or training because of pregnancy or breastfeeding
- employee benefit plans that discriminate because of pregnancy.

The Ministry of Labour's Employment Standards Branch deals with the following situations:

- disputes with the employer regarding the commencement or duration of maternity or parental leave, or reinstatement following leave
- disputes regarding the continuation of benefits during maternity or parental leave
- reprisal because of pregnancy or parental leave, including situations where women who are eligible for pregnancy leave are reprised against after they have informed their employers that they are pregnant, but before a formal request for leave has been made under the *ESA*.

12.1 — Related Provisions under the *Employment Standards Act*

- A pregnant employee is entitled to take a leave of absence without pay, so long as she has been employed for at least 13 weeks prior to her due date. The leave may commence as early as 17 weeks prior to her due date, or as late as the day she gives birth (s. 46(2)).
- An employee is responsible for notifying her employer that she wishes to take pregnancy leave, and her employer may require her to provide a certificate from a legally qualified medical practitioner stating her due date (s. 46(4)).

- The pregnancy leave may last for up to 17 weeks; the employee may then begin parental leave, which may last for up to 35 weeks (s. 47(1)).
- Women who experience a still-birth or miscarriage are entitled to take at least six weeks off after their still-birth or miscarriage, or to complete their 17-week pregnancy leave, whichever ends later (s. 47(1)).
- Women who are away on pregnancy leave continue to participate in their employers' pension, life insurance, accidental death, extended health, or dental plans, unless they elect in writing not to do so. Employers must continue to make their contributions to these plans during the leave, unless they are notified in writing that the employee does not intend to continue making her contribution (s. 51).
- The period of the leave is included in the calculation of the employee's length of employment, length of service and seniority, for the purpose of determining employment rights. However, it is not included in the calculation of whether a probationary period has been completed (s. 52).
- When the pregnancy leave ends, the employer must reinstate the employee to the position she most recently held, if it still exists. If it does not, she must be reinstated to a comparable position, unless her employment has been terminated for reasons unrelated to her pregnancy (s. 53).
- Upon reinstatement, the employee must be paid the greater of the wage she was most recently earning with the employer, or the wage she would have been earning had she worked through the leave (s. 54).
- Employers may not reprise against women for exercising, or attempting to exercise, their rights regarding pregnancy leave (s. 74). Employers who violate these provisions of the *ESA* may be required to reinstate the employee, financially compensate her, or both.

13. — Relevant *Code* Provisions

The Ontario *Human Rights Code* (Part II of this book) includes provisions relevant to this policy in the following sections: 1, 2(1)(2), 3, 5(1)(2), 6, 7(1)(2), 8, 10(2), 11(1)(2) and 22.

Policy on Drug and Alcohol Testing

Revised Version Approved by the Commission: September 27, 2000

1. — Introduction

The Ontario *Human Rights Code* (the *"Code"*) states that it is public policy in Ontario to recognize the inherent dignity and worth of every person and to provide for equal rights and opportunities without discrimination. The provisions of the *Code* are aimed at creating a climate of understanding and mutual respect for the dignity and worth of each person so that each person feels a part of the community and feels able to contribute to the community.

The Commission recognizes that it is a legitimate goal for employers to have a safe workplace. One method sometimes used by employers to achieve that goal is drug and alcohol testing. However, such testing is controversial and, especially in the area of drug testing, of limited effectiveness as an indicator of impairment. It is not used to a significant degree anywhere in the world except in the United States (the "U.S.").[1]

It is the Commission's view that such testing is *prima facie* discriminatory and can only be used in limited circumstances. The primary reason for conducting such testing should be to measure impairment.[2] Even testing that measures impairment can be justified only if it is demonstrably connected to the performance of the job, for example, if an employee occupies a safety-sensitive position, or after significant accidents or "near-misses," or if there is reasonable cause to believe that a person is abusing alcohol or drugs and only then as part of a larger assessment of drug and alcohol abuse. It is the Commission's view that by focusing on testing that actually measures impairment, especially in jobs that are safety sensitive, an appropriate balance can be struck between human rights and safety requirements, both for employees and for the public.

---

[1]See *Drug and Alcohol Testing in the Workplace*, Report of the ILO Tripartite Experts Meeting (May 1993, Oslo, Norway), cited in Butler *et al.*, *The Drug Testing Controversy: Imperial Oil and Other Lessons* (Carswell, Toronto: 1997) at 5.

[2]As distinct from deterrent value, for which there is no reliable study showing successful outcomes, or for the purposes of monitoring moral values among employees.

2. — Scope of the Policy

Persons with disabilities, who have had disabilities, or who are perceived to have or have had disabilities are protected against discrimination in all of the social areas of the *Code*.

Drug and alcohol testing are of particular concern in the workplace, notably for those Ontario employers who have safety sensitive operations, and/or that are subject to U.S. regulatory requirements (e.g., the trucking industry)[3] or to the policies of U.S. affiliates with "zero tolerance" for the consumption of drugs or alcohol. For this reason, this Policy focuses on the workplace. However, it applies to other social areas as well.[4] For example, the Commission has taken the position that drug or alcohol testing as a prerequisite to eligibility for basic income support programs is also *prima facie* discriminatory.[5]

It should be noted that international and interprovincial transportation companies are under federal jurisdiction.[6] Thus airlines, interprovincial trucking and bus services are subject to the federal *Canadian Human Rights Act*[7] and not provincial human rights laws.

3. — Drug or Alcohol Dependency and Abuse as a Disability

Section 5(1) of the *Code* prohibits discrimination in employment on several grounds including "handicap" (the *Code* uses the term "handicap" but the more currently accepted term is "disability" and it is therefore used in this

---

[3]Most employers who are subject to U.S. commercial motor vehicle regulations are likely to be under federal jurisdiction under the *Canadian Human Rights Act*. However, even provincially regulated companies that may have only the occasional driver seeking to enter the U.S. are also subject to regulatory requirements for drug and alcohol testing in order to enter the U.S.

[4]There are five social areas covered in the *Code*. These are employment, accommodation (housing), goods, services and facilities, membership in vocational associations and contracts.

[5]Letter from Chief Commissioner Keith C. Norton to the Hon. John Baird, Minister of Community and Social Services (unpublished, July 1999). The Commission expressed concern about the Government's announced plans to test welfare recipients for drugs or alcohol.

[6]Section 91 of the *Constitution Act, 1867*.

[7]R.S.C. 1985, c. H-6.

and other Commission documents). The *Code* adopts an expansive definition of the term "handicap" which encompasses physical, psychological and mental conditions. Severe substance abuse is classified as a form of substance dependence,[8] which has been recognized as a form of disability. Examples include alcoholism and the abuse of legal drugs (e.g., over-the-counter drugs) or illicit drugs. These types of abuse and dependence therefore constitute a disability within the meaning of the *Code*.

The following examples represent situations in which the use of legal or illicit drugs or alcohol may fall within the *Code*:[9]

a) Where an individual's use of drugs or alcohol has reached the stage that it constitutes severe substance abuse, addiction or dependency, e.g., maladaptive patterns of substance use leading to significant impairment or distress, including:

i) recurrent substance abuse resulting in a failure to fulfil major obligations at work

ii) recurrent substance abuse in situations which are physically hazardous

iii) continued substance abuse despite persistent social, legal or interpersonal problems caused or aggravated by the effects of the substance.[10]

b) Where an individual is *perceived* as having an addiction or dependency due to drug or alcohol use, the *Code* will protect that individual.

Example: An employer refuses to promote a particular employee because of the perception that the employee has an alcohol dependency. As a result of this perception and consequent action on the part of the employer, the individual's right to equal treatment under the *Code* may have been infringed.

c) An individual who has had a drug or alcohol dependency in the past,

---

[8]"Drug abuse and drug dependence are diseases, illnesses, malfunctions and mental disorders, which can create mental impairment and result in mental disorder and physical disability." *Entrop v. Imperial Oil Ltd.*, Interim Decision #8 Sept. 12, 1996, Decision No. 96-030-I. This aspect of the ruling was not challenged on appeal to the Court of Appeal. See *Entrop*, *infra* at note 14.

[9]*Ibid.*

[10]Adapted from the definition of "substance abuse" in the *Diagnostics and Statistical Manual of Mental Disorders* (American Psychiatric Association, 4th ed., 1994) cited in *Entrop* #8, *supra* note 9.

but who no longer suffers from an ongoing disability, is still protected by the *Code*.

4. — Drug and Alcohol Testing: Direct or Constructive Discrimination?

Although the *Code* distinguishes between direct and constructive discrimination,[11] the distinction is less important than it used to be, particularly in the area of disability. This is a result of the combined impact of two factors. First, the Supreme Court of Canada has blurred the distinction between the two for practical purposes and has developed a single three-step test.[12] The Ontario Court of Appeal has applied similar reasoning in the Ontario context, specifically in the area of disability and drug and alcohol testing.[13]

Second, s. 17 of the *Code* provides a defence where a person with a disability is unable to perform an essential requirement. However, the defence is only available if the requirement is *bona fide* and reasonable, and only after the person has been accommodated to the point of undue hardship. Since employers usually argue that the requirement for impairment-free performance is essential, s. 17 of the *Code* will be an important part of a respondent's defence.

In either event, the Ontario Court of Appeal has indicated that except in the most obvious cases of direct discrimination, the focus should be on determining whether the employer can justify the policy or standard using the new three-step test set out by the Supreme Court of Canada.[14] Applying this approach, company-wide policies such as drug and alcohol testing polices will attract the need to accommodate employees and, most importantly, on an individual basis.[15] The Commission supports this position. Individualization is central to the notion of dignity for persons with disabilities and to the concept of accommodation on the ground of disability, regardless of whether a particular form of drug testing or alcohol testing is

---

[11]See, *e.g.* ss. 5 and 11 of the *Code*.

[12]*British Columbia (Public Service Employee Relations Commission) v. B.C.G.S.E.U.* (1999), 176 D.L.R. (4th) 1 (S.C.C.) [hereinafter *Meiorin*].

[13]*Entrop v. Imperial Oil Ltd.* (unreported decision of the Ontario Court of Appeal, 21 July 2000).

[14]*Ibid.* at para. 79-82.

[15]*Ibid.*

likely to be considered to be "direct" or "constructive."[16] "Blanket" rules that make no allowances for individual circumstances are necessarily unable to meet individual requirements and are therefore likely to be struck down.

5. — Drug and Alcohol Testing: Basic Principles

Drug and alcohol testing is *prima facie* discriminatory under Canadian human rights law. Employers can nevertheless justify discriminatory rules if they can meet a three-part test:[17]

- the employer has adopted the standard or test for a purpose that is rationally connected to the performance of the job
- the employer adopted the particular standard or test in an honest and good faith belief that it was necessary to the fulfilment of that legitimate work-related purpose
- the standard or test is reasonably necessary to the accomplishment of that legitimate work-related purpose. To show that the standard is reasonably necessary, it must be demonstrated that it is impossible to accommodate individual employees sharing the characteristics of the claimant without imposing undue hardship upon the employer.

Drug and alcohol testing policies are part of workplace rules and standards. Therefore, standards governing the performance of work should be inclusive. Employers must build conceptions of equality into workplace policies.

Drug and alcohol testing should be limited to determining actual impairment of an employee's ability to perform or fulfil the essential duties or requirements of the job. It should not be directed towards simply identifying the presence of drugs or alcohol in the body.

Drug and alcohol testing that has no demonstrable relationship to job safety and performance has been found to be a violation of employee rights.[18] A relationship or rational connection between drug or alcohol testing and job performance is an important component of any lawful drug or alcohol testing policy. In this regard, the policy must not be arbitrary in terms of which groups of employees are subject to testing. For example, to test only new or returning employees but not other employees may not be justifiable having

---

[16]See generally the Commission's *Guidelines for Assessing Accommodation Requirements for Persons with Disabilities*, in Ontario Human Rights Commission, *Human Rights Policy in Ontario* (Queen's Printer, Toronto: 1999).

[17]See *Entrop*, *supra* note 14, citing *Meiorin*, *supra* note 13.

[18]See *Entrop*, *supra* note 14.

regard to the stated objectives of a company's testing policy. At the same time, testing employees in safety sensitive positions only may be justifiable.

Applying the three-part test to drug and alcohol testing, the following questions should be considered by employers, where applicable:

i) Is there an objective basis for believing that job performance would be impaired by drug or alcohol dependency? In other words, is there a rational connection between testing and job performance?

ii) In respect of a specific employee, is there an objective basis for believing that unscheduled or recurring absences from work, or habitual lateness to work, or inappropriate or erratic behaviour at work are related to alcoholism or drug addiction/dependency? These factors could demonstrate a basis for "for cause" or "post incident" testing provided there is a reasonable basis for the conclusions drawn.

iii) Is there an objective basis to believe that the degree, nature, scope and probability of risk caused by alcohol or drug abuse or dependency will adversely affect the safety of co-workers or members of the public?

6. — Pre-Employment Testing for Drug and Alcohol Use as Part of an Employment-Related Medical Examination

Testing for alcohol or drug use is a form of medical examination. Therefore, an employer considering such testing should be guided by the three-part test cited above, by the Commission's *Policy on Employment-Related Medical Information*[19] and by the Ontario Court of Appeal's recent decision in the *Entrop* case. The following are the main principles that should be borne in mind:

i) Employment-related medical examinations or inquiries, conducted as part of the applicant screening process, are prohibited under s. 23(2) of the *Code*.

ii) Pre-employment medical examinations or inquiries at the interview stage should be limited to determining an individual's ability to perform the essential duties of a job.

---

[19]A copy of the Ontario Human Rights Commission *Policy on Employment-Related Medical Information* (1996) is available on the Web at www.ohrc.on.ca, through the Commission offices and printed in *Human Rights Policy in Ontario*, *supra* note 17.

iii) In order to implement a testing program prior to hiring, the employer must therefore be able to demonstrate that pre-employment testing provides an effective assessment of the applicant. Since drug testing cannot be shown to actually measure impairment, pre-employment drug testing should not be conducted. Although there has been no clear indication from the courts, it is the Commission's view that, in the absence of clear medical research, pre-employment alcohol testing does not appear to predict an employee's ability to perform the essential requirements of a safety-sensitive position. All it can do is assess impairment *before* the person is actually on the job. It is therefore difficult to see how an employer could justify pre-employment alcohol testing.

iv) Medical examinations to determine an individual's ability to perform the essential duties of a job should only be administered after a conditional offer of employment has been made, preferably in writing.

v) Where drug or alcohol testing will be a valid requirement on the job, the employer should notify job applicants of the requirement at the time that an offer of employment is made. The circumstances under which such testing might be required should be made clear to the applicant.

vi) If the applicant or employee requests accommodation in order to enable him or her to perform the essential duties of the job, the employer is required to provide individual accommodation unless it is impossible to do so without causing undue hardship.

7. — On the Job Testing

On-the-job testing should be administered only where a link has been established between impairment and performance of job functions, such as in the case of employees who are in safety sensitive positions. Once again, because drug tests do not actually measure impairment, random drug testing is an unjustifiable intrusion into the rights of employees. With respect to random alcohol testing, the use of breathalysers is a minimally intrusive yet highly accurate measure of both consumption and actual impairment. Consequently, the Commission supports the view that random alcohol testing *is acceptable in safety sensitive positions, especially where the supervision of staff is minimal or non-existent, but only if the employer meets its duty to accommodate the needs of those who test positive* (see below).

"For cause" and "post incident" testing for either alcohol or drugs may be acceptable in specific circumstances. Following accidents or reports of dangerous behaviour, for example, an employer will have a legitimate interest in assessing whether the employee in question had consumed substances that are psychoactive and which may have contributed to the incident. The results of the assessment may provide an explanation of the cause of the accident. Such testing should only be conducted as part of a larger assessment of drug or alcohol abuse. This larger assessment could include a broader medical assessment under a physician's care where there are reasonable grounds to believe that there is an underlying problem of substance abuse. Additional components of a larger assessment may include employee assistance programs ("EAPs"), peer reviews and supervisory reviews.

Employers should also have regard to the following criteria and considerations when developing on-the-job testing criteria:

7.1 — Competent Handling of Test Samples

Qualified professionals must perform drug and alcohol testing and the results must be analyzed in a competent laboratory. Further, it is the responsibility of the employer to ensure that the samples taken are properly labelled and protected at all times.

7.2 — Confidentiality of Test Results

In order to protect the confidentiality of test results, all health assessment information should remain exclusively with the examining physician and away from the employee's personnel file.

7.3 — Review of Results with the Employee

Procedures should be instituted for the physician to review the test results with the employee concerned.

7.4 — Mandatory Self-Disclosure

Where mandatory self-disclosure is a part of a workplace drug or alcohol policy, there must be a reasonable time period within which previous substance abuse will be considered relevant to assessment of current ability to perform the essential duties. The reasonable time period is based on whether the risk of relapse or recurrence is greater than the risk that a member of the general population will suffer a substance abuse problem. Mandatory self-disclosure of all previous substance dependencies, without any reasonable limitation on how long ago these conditions occurred, has been found to be a *prima facie* violation of employee rights.[20]

---

[20]*Entrop*, *supra* note 14.

7.5 — Alternative Methods

The Commission supports the use of methods other than drug and alcohol testing (e.g., functional performance testing) where such methods exist, or the development of such tests, where feasible, to assess impairment. The Commission also encourages the development and implementation of EAPs and peer monitoring.

8. — Consequence of a Positive Test

Section 17 of the *Code* requires individualized or personalized accommodation measures. Therefore, policies that result in automatic loss of employment, reassignment or that impose inflexible reinstatement conditions, without regard for personal and individual circumstances, are unlikely to meet this requirement.[21]

Although the emphasis in the *Code* is on ensuring that persons with disabilities are not treated in a discriminatory manner because of their disability, it is recognized that in some circumstances, the nature and/or degree of a person's disability may preclude that individual from performing the essential duties of a job. Section 17(1) of the *Code* states that the right to equal treatment in respect of employment is not infringed where an individual is treated differently because she or he is incapable of performing or fulfilling the essential duties of the position because of a disability. Assessment of incapacity must be both fair and accurate.

9. — Duty to Accommodate

9.1 — Section 17(2)

Section 17(2) provides that an employee shall not be found incapable of performing the essential duties of a job unless it would cause undue hardship to accommodate the individual employee's needs, taking into account the cost of the accommodation and health and safety concerns.[22]

Sections 17(1) and 17(2) provide a two-stage test for the validity of a workplace drug and alcohol testing policy.

> *Example*: An employer is concerned about fairness and decides to extend an existing alcohol testing policy originally designed for employees in safety-sensitive positions to cover all other employees. Although

[21] *Ibid.*

[22] *Ibid.*

the policy's generous rehabilitation programs may satisfy the accommodation requirement set out in s. 17(2), this defence is not available to the employer unless it can be shown that employees in non-safety-sensitive positions who fail the test are incapable of performing their essential duties.

9.2 — Onus on the Employee to Co-operate with the Employer

A person who requires accommodation in order to perform the essential duties of a job has a responsibility to communicate the need for accommodation in sufficient detail and to co-operate in consultations to enable the person responsible for accommodation to respond to the request. It should be noted that this obligation does not interfere with the employer's obligation to treat the person equally even if the employer believes or perceives (even with good reason) that the employee has substance abuse problem.

> *Example*: An employee in a clerical position appears to be inebriated frequently during work hours, and the employer has a conversation to address the problem. The employee refuses to acknowledge the problem or seek counselling at the employer's expense. Shortly after, the employee is fired without formal warning.
>
> In this case, the employer clearly "perceived" the person to have a substance abuse problem and therefore the protection of the *Code* is engaged. The fact that a person refuses treatment or accommodation does not in and of itself justify immediate dismissal. The employer has to demonstrate, through progressive discipline, that the employee has been warned and is unable to perform the essential duties of the position. If the employee refuses offered accommodation and if progressive discipline and performance management have been implemented, then disciplinary steps can be taken.

If an employee's drug or alcohol addiction/dependency is interfering with that person's ability to perform the essential duties of the job, the employer must first provide the support necessary to enable that person to undertake a rehabilitation program unless it can be shown that such accommodation would cause undue hardship.

9.3 — Undue Hardship

The employer will be relieved of the duty to accommodate the individual needs of the alcohol or drug addicted/dependent employee if the employer can show, for example, that:

i) the cost of the accommodation would alter the nature or affect the viability of the enterprise

ii) notwithstanding accommodation efforts, health or safety risks to workers or members of the public are so serious that they outweigh the benefits of providing equal treatment to the worker with an addiction or dependency.

9.4 — Alternative Mechanisms

The Commission supports the use of the least intrusive means of assessing impairment or fitness for work. All workplaces should consider using comprehensive workplace health policies that may include such programs as EAPs and drug education and health promotion programs.

When considering how best to address the needs of employees with substance dependencies, employers are encouraged to consider the establishment of alternatives such as EAPs. EAPs are personal assistance programs that help employees who have substance abuse or other problems. Such programs can assist not only individuals with a drug or alcohol addiction/dependency, but can also help workers deal with the stress which may lead to such an addiction or dependency. Off-site counselling and referral services are examples of EAPs that are used successfully in the workplace. In addition, health promotion and drug education programs can prevent problems before they start by getting at the causes. Other alternative mechanisms include performance tests for safety-sensitive positions, where physical and/or mental coordination are integral parts of the job, peer or supervisory monitoring.

10. — Relevant Ontario *Human Rights Code* Provisions

The Ontario *Human Rights Code* (Part II of this book) includes provisions relevant to this policy in the following sections: 5(1), 10(1), 11(1)(2), 17(1)(2) and 23(2).

Policy on Employment-Related Medical Information

Approved by the Commission: June 19, 1996

1. — Introduction

The Ontario *Human Rights Code* (the "*Code*") states that it is public policy in Ontario to recognize the inherent dignity and worth of every person and to provide for equal rights and opportunities without discrimination. The provisions of the *Code* are aimed at creating a climate of understanding and mutual respect for the dignity and worth of each person so that each person feels a part of the community and feels able to contribute to the community.

The guidelines contained in this policy are intended to help applicants, employees and employers to understand their rights and responsibilities regarding employment-related medical information.

2. — Employment-Related Medical Information

2.1 — Employment Applications

In the past employers often screened out applicants with disabilities based on medical information requested on application forms or obtained through pre-employment medical examinations. The Commission believes that such questions, asked as part of the application screening process, violate subsection 23(2) of the *Code*.

Any medical assessment to verify or determine an individual's ability to perform the essential duties of a job, should only take place after a conditional offer of employment is made, preferably in writing. This allows an applicant with a disability the right to be considered exclusively on her or his merits during the selection process.

The Commission recognizes the fact that it would be advantageous to both the employer and prospective job applicants, if the employer were to disclose information on any specific medically related requirements of a position at an early stage of the recruitment process.

> *Example*: A Police Services Board may stipulate in a recruitment advertisement that applicants must meet a minimum vision standard without corrective lenses to qualify for selection.

2.2 — The Personal Interview

The prohibition contained in subsection 23(1) of the *Code* is qualified by subsection 23(3), which allows an employer to ask at a personal interview, whether an applicant has any disability-related needs that would require accommodation to enable her or him to do the essential duties of the job. The duty to provide such accommodation is discussed in more detail in the following section.

It is not unusual for an employer to ask about, or for a job applicant or an employee to volunteer information about her/his specific medical condition. However, an employer or supervisor may be placed in a vulnerable position if he or she directly receives any information about the particular medical condition of an applicant or employee. This information leaves the way open for an allegation to be made that subsequent decisions relating to the hiring of the applicant, or the promotion or termination of the employee were based on that information.

It is the view of the Commission that to protect the employer from allegations of discrimination, as well as the applicant or employee, medical related information should remain exclusively with the examining physician and away from an employee's personnel file.

2.3 — Duty to Accommodate

In some circumstances, the nature or degree of a person's disability may preclude that individual from performing the essential duties of a job. Subsection 17(1) provides that the right to equal treatment in employment is not infringed if the individual is *incapable of performing or fulfilling the essential duties* of the position because of a handicap.

However, subsection 17(2) provides that a job applicant or employee shall not be found incapable of performing the essential duties of a job, unless it can be demonstrated that it would cause undue hardship to accommodate her or his needs. The standard of undue hardship considers the cost of the required accommodation and any health and safety concerns that may be involved (see further the Commission's *Guidelines for Assessing Accommodation Requirements for Persons with Disabilities*).

> A person who requires accommodation in order to perform the essential duties of a job has a responsibility to communicate her or his needs in sufficient detail and to cooperate in consultations to enable the person responsible for accommodation to respond to the request.

The duty to provide accommodation extends to all facets of the employment process: hiring, employment testing, on-the-job training, working conditions, transfer, promotions, *etc*.

3. — Relevant Ontario *Human Rights Code* Provisions

The Ontario *Human Rights Code* (Part II of this book) includes provisions relevant to this policy in the following sections: 17(1)(2) and 23(1)(2)(3).

Policy on Female Genital Mutilation

Approved by the Commission: April 9, 1996
Revised by the Commission: November 22, 2000

1. — Overview

Female genital mutilation ("FGM") refers to the cutting and removal of the female genitalia. FGM is a traditional practice rooted in the political, social, cultural and economic structures of the societies in which it is practised.

FGM is a gender-specific violation of the rights of girls and women to physical integrity.[1] This traditional practice is conducted in many cultures and in many countries. FGM has become recognized not only as a health hazard and a form of violence against women and girls, but also as a human rights issue under international law. Efforts at the international level, particularly by United Nations agencies, have placed FGM on women's health and human rights agendas.

For most Canadians, FGM is a vaguely understood practice usually associated with "distant" and "tradition bound" cultures. Most people know very little about what is involved in the procedure or about the health and sociological implications for the women and girls who are subjected to it.

The Ontario Human Rights Commission (the "Commission") acknowledges that FGM is an internationally recognized violation against women and girls' human rights. The Commission has developed this policy to ensure the effective protection and promotion of human rights of women and girls.

The purpose of this document is to outline the policy position of the Ontario Human Rights Commission with respect to the practice of FGM. This position has been developed within the framework of:

(i) female genital mutilation as an internationally recognized human rights issue

---

[1] "Female genital mutilation involves the use of dangerous and frightening weapons, causes permanent physical damage and sometimes death, and is targeted in the most gender specific way possible at the female genitalia." Fitzpatrick, "International Norms and Violence Against Women" in Rebecca J. Cook, ed., *Human Rights of Women: National and International Perspectives*, (Philadelphia: University of Pennsylvania Press, 1994) at 11.

(ii) the domestic implications of Canada's obligations as a signatory to international conventions and treaties which recognize FGM as a human rights violation

(iii) the mandate and jurisdiction of the Ontario Human Rights Commission under the Ontario *Human Rights Code* (the *"Code"*).

2. — What is Female Genital Mutilation?

2.1 — The Practice of FGM

In 1991, the term "Female Genital Mutilation" was adopted at the Inter-African Committee Regional Conference on Traditional Practices Affecting the Health of Women and Children held in Burkina-Faso.[2] Female genital mutilation (FGM) is the collective term given to several different procedures that involve the cutting of female genitalia and permanently mutilating the sexual organs of young females for non-medical reasons. For the purpose of this paper, FGM refers to the ritualistic or traditional practices involving the cutting and removal of the female sexual organs.

Over centuries, FGM has been conducted as a ritual intended to prepare a girl for womanhood. Most commonly, girls are subjected to FGM between the ages of four and eight.

The practice is common in certain traditional Islamic communities although some religious experts note that there is no religious basis in the Quran for the practice.[3] While it is true that the practice has its roots in some countries in Africa, the Arabian Peninsula, Asia and South America, global migration patterns have brought the practice to Canada.

Women and girls who undergo FGM routinely experience pain, physical and emotional trauma and health complications as a result of infection to their genitalia and other reproductive organs. In some cases, severe bleeding and infection result in chronic disability or even death.[4] Substantial psychological effects on the self-image and sexual lives of women are also a

---

[2]UN Doc. E/CN.4/Sub.2/1991/48 para. 136 (5)(1001).

[3]See, Gloria Jacobs, *Female Genital Mutilation: A Call for Global Action* (New York: Women, Ink., 1993) at 5.

[4]The physical effects on women and children include immediate complications such as haemorrhaging, acute infections, bleeding of adjacent organs and violent pain, and may sometimes lead to death. Later complications include so-called vicious or keloid scars which considerably shrink the genital apertures with attendant consequences; chronic infections which can lead to infertility; haematic complications (inability of menstrual blood to exit) and obstetric complications. Cutting and restitching performed on infibulated women can result in subsequent health risks.

documented consequence of the practice. The most severe form of FGM, infibulation, which involves removal of the clitoris, results in trauma that is repeated after each childbirth.

Since the sole function of the clitoris is sexual stimulation, the main purpose of the practice is to control female sexuality, ensure chastity until marriage and to render young women more desirable for marriage purposes. Background information for this document, derived from the Commission's participation on the Ontario Female Genital Mutilation Prevention Task Force, lists a number of reasons for the practice, including: (a) preservation of virginity; (b) control over women's sexuality; (c) cosmetic reasons; (d) class distinction; and (e) cultural identity. "Hygienic" reasons have also been cited for continuing the practice.

In 1996, the World Health Organization estimated that between 100 and 132 million girls and women have been mutilated, and approximately 2 million girls and young women are at risk globally.[5] Because of the nature of FGM, reliable statistics on the incidence of the practice here in Canada are not available. However, there is sufficient information obtained through discussions with members of at-risk communities to indicate that there is a significant population of women in Ontario and other provinces in Canada who have been subjected to the practice, and whose girl children may be at risk. Although the practice is often referred to as "female circumcision," the term belies the severity of what is actually involved.

2.2 — Degrees of FGM

FGM includes any or all of the following: the removal of the hood of the clitoris; the complete removal of the clitoris along with labia minora excisions; the complete removal of the clitoris and surrounding tissues, and suturing of the vaginal opening (infibulation). An opening as small as 3-4 millimetres or as large as 1.8 centimetres is maintained to permit urination, menstruation and intercourse. The instruments that are often used include scissors, shards of glass, cactus spines or other rigid plant materials, and razor blades. In most instances it is performed outside of proper health care facilities, and without anaesthesia.[6]

As well, psychological complications often develop, including functional psychiatric manifestations.

[5] *Female Genital Mutilation*: *PREVALENCE AND DISTRIBUTION*, World Health Organization, August 1996, www.who.int/frh-whd/FGM/infopack/English/fgm_infopack.htm#PREVALENCE AND DISTRIBUTION (8 December 2000).

[6] See further *Working Group on Traditional Practices Affecting the Health of Women and Children*, Report of the UN Economic and Social Council, Commission

FGM can be broadly classified into the following two categories:

Clitoridectomy (sometimes known as "Sunna circumcision"[7]): In this set of operations, one or more parts of the external genitals are removed. The prepuce, or hood of the clitoris, is cut and there is partial or complete removal of the clitoris. Approximately 85% of all women who undergo FGM have clitoridectomies.

Infibulation ("Pharaonic mutilation"): This is the most severe FGM procedure and it is practised widely in countries in the Horn of Africa. The clitoris is removed, some or all of the labia minora are cut off and incisions are made in the labia majora to create raw surfaces. The raw surfaces are either stitched together, or kept in contact by pressure until they heal as a "hood of skin" which covers the urethra and most of the vagina, leaving only a very small opening. This obstruction may lead to urinary and menstrual flow retention, dysmenorrhoea, and infections of the reproductive and urinary systems. An estimated 15% of all women who experience FGM have been infibulated. In some countries, however, 80 to 90% of all FGM cases involve infibulation.[8]

2.3 — FGM and Male Circumcision

FGM is often referred to as "female circumcision." This term implies a comparable practice to male circumcision. However, the degree of excision and trauma involved in FGM is generally much more extensive, including the actual removal of genital organs.

Male circumcision involves excision of the foreskin from the tip of the penis. The Canadian Paediatric Society conducted a literature review and concluded that "the overall evidence of the benefits and harms of male circumcision is so evenly balanced," that "the benefits have not been shown to clearly outweigh the risks and costs" and that male "circumcision for

---

on Human Rights, First Session, March 18–22, 1985; *Female Genital Mutilation: Information Kit*, Division of Family Health World Health Organization, Geneva, July 31, 1994; *Human Rights are Women's Rights* (London: Amnesty International), 1995.

[7]"Sunna" refers to any practice required of Muslims. Yet, there are no direct references to FGM in the Quran and religious leaders generally remain silent on the practice. See further note 32.

[8]Nahid Toubia, *Female Genital Mutilation* in Julie Peters and Andrea Wolper, eds., *Women's Rights Human Rights* (New York: Routledge, 1995) at 227.

newborns should not be routinely performed."[9] The Canadian Paediatric Society advises that when parents are making a decision about circumcision, they should be informed with respect to the present state of medical knowledge about its reported benefits and risks.

3. — FGM: An Internationally Recognized Human Rights Issue

3.1 — International Policy and Law

FGM has been condemned by numerous international and regional bodies including: the United Nations Commission on Human Rights, the United Nations International Children Emergency Fund (UNICEF), the Organization of African Unity and the World Medical Association. In addition to the broader issues of health and human rights of the child, FGM is gender-specific discrimination related to the historical suppression and subjugation of women that is unique to women and female children.

In various African countries where the procedure is performed, comprehensive action plans were developed by women's groups to attempt to eliminate the practice, but overall, progress has been slow. FGM has been outlawed in Sudan since 1946, but it continues to be widely practised. In Burkina-Faso and Egypt, resolutions were signed by the respective Ministers of Health in 1959, recommending that only partial clitoridectomy be allowed, and decreeing that it be performed only by doctors. In 1978, as a direct result of the efforts of the Somali women's movement, Somalia established a Commission to abolish infibulation.

The issue of FGM was raised at the United Nations for the first time in 1952. However, it took some 20 years before the United Nations began official discussion of the issue. It was not until the 1970s, at the instigation of non-governmental organizations, that United Nations agencies were pushed to address the multitude of problems related to the practice. In July 1980, the World Conference of the United Nations' Decade for Women was held in Copenhagen on the sub-themes of health, education and employment. In 1984, participants from 20 African countries, as well as representatives of international organizations attending a seminar in Dakkar on "Traditional Practices Affecting the Health of Women and Children," recommended that the practice be abolished. States acknowledged that there was a need to es-

---

[9]Neonatal Circumcision Revisited. Fetus and Newborn Committee, Canadian Paediatric Society (CPS). Approved by the CPS Board of Directors in 1996, *Canadian Medical Association Journal* 1996; 154(6): 769-780. Reference No. FN96-01.

tablish strong, on-going education programs for meaningful progress towards elimination of the practice.

FGM was again addressed by the 1993 United Nations World Conference on Human Rights. A Conference declaration stated:

> The World Conference supports all measures by the United Nations and its specialized agencies to ensure the effective protection and promotion of human rights of the girl-child. The World Conference urges States to repeal existing laws and regulations and remove customs and practices which discriminate against and cause harm to the girl-child.[10]

In 1995, the Platform for Action of the World Conference on Women in Beijing included a section on the girl child and urges governments, international organizations and nongovernmental groups to develop policies and programs to eliminate all forms of discrimination against the girl child including FGM.[11]

Canada plays a prominent role in the international arena as a supporter and promoter of women's human rights. In 1995, at the 9th United Nations Congress on the "Prevention of Crime and the Treatment of Offenders," Canada introduced a resolution on the "Elimination of Violence Against Women" (Agenda Item 6: Cairo Egypt, April 29–May 8, 1995). The resolution, which was passed by the Congress, strongly urged States, *inter alia*, to take measures to:

> . . . prevent, prohibit, eliminate and impose effective sanctions against rape or sexual assault, sex abuse and all practices harmful to women and girl children, including *female genital mutilation* (emphasis added).

International conventions, covenants and declarations which Canada has signed recognize that human beings have the inherent right to life,[12]equality,[13] freedom and security,[14] the right not to suffer discrimina-

---

[10]*Declaration and Program of Action* adopted in Vienna on June 25, 1993, the World Conference on Human Rights, quoted in *Human Rights Are Women's Rights* (London: Amnesty International, 1995) at 132.

[11]*Female Genital Mutilation*: *UNITED NATIONS ACTION*, World Health Organization, August 1996, www.who.int/frh-whd/FGM/infopack/English/fgm_infopack.htm#PREVALENCE AND DISTRIBUTION (8 December 2000).

[12]*International Covenant on Civil and Political Rights*, Art. 6; *International Convention on the Elimination of all Forms of Racial Discrimination*, Art. 2.

[13]*International Covenant on Civil and Political Rights*, Art. 26.

[14]*Universal Declaration of Human Rights*, Art. 3; *International Covenant on Civil and Political Rights*, Art. 9; *International Convention on the Elimination of all Forms of Racial Discrimination*, Art. 5(b).

tion,[15] the right to the best possible state of physical and mental health,[16] and the right not to be subjected to torture or to cruel and degrading punishment or treatment.[17]

3.2 — FGM and Gender Discrimination

FGM has implications for the human rights of women as directly reflected in several international instruments, including the *United Nations Convention on the Elimination of All Forms of Discrimination against Women.*

The *United Nations Declaration on the Elimination of Violence Against Women* defines "violence against women" as encompassing, *inter alia*, "female genital mutilation and other traditional practices harmful to women."[18] In Europe, legislation prohibiting the practice of FGM exists in Sweden, France and Great Britain where the procedure carries a penalty of imprisonment.

The legal obligation to eliminate all forms of discrimination against women is described as a "fundamental tenet of international human rights law."[19] Sex is a prohibited ground of discrimination under the *Universal Declaration of Human Rights*, the *International Covenant on Civil and Political Rights*, the *International Covenant on Economic, Social, and Cultural Rights*, and three regional human rights conventions: the *European Convention for the Protection of Human Rights and Fundamental Freedoms*, the *American Convention on Human Rights* and the *African Charter on Human and People's Rights.* The most comprehensive instrument, the *Convention on the Elimination of All Forms of Discrimination against Women,*[20] con-

---

[15]*International Covenant on Civil and Political Rights*, Art. 26.

[16]*International Covenant on Economic, Social and Cultural Rights*, Art. 12.

[17]*Universal Declaration of Human Rights*, Art. 5; *International Covenant on Civil and Political Rights*, Art. 7; *Convention Against Torture and Other Cruel, Inhuman and Degrading Treatment or Punishment.*

[18]*Declaration of the United Nations General Assembly on the Elimination of Violence Against Women*, Plenary Session A/Res./48/104, December 20, 1993.

[19]Cook, *Introduction: The Way Forward*, in Cook, ed., *supra*, note 1 at 10.

[20]Ratified by Canada on December 10, 1981; date of entry into force in Canada was January 10, 1992.

There are several provisions of the *Convention* which require States parties to take action against such practices as FGM, namely:

i) to take all appropriate measures, including legislation, to modify or abolish existing laws, regulations, customs and practices which constitute discrimination against women (Art. 2.f.)

stitutes an international "bill of rights" for women, and sets out an agenda for nations to take action to end discrimination based on sex.

Article 5 of the *Universal Declaration of Human Rights* provides that no one shall be subjected to torture, nor to cruel, inhuman or degrading treatment. However, many signatory countries continue to violate that article through tolerance of the practice of FGM. Renée Bridel, of the Fédération Internationale des Femmes de Carrières Juridiques, noted:

> One cannot but consider Member States which tolerate these practices as infringing their obligations as assumed under the terms of the *Charter* [of the UN].[21]

3.3 — FGM and the Rights of the Child

FGM is a violation of the rights of the child guaranteed in treaties adopted by the United Nations and the Organization of African Unity. *The Convention on the Rights of the Child* has direct implications for the human rights of the child. The *Convention* was adopted by the UN General Assembly in 1989 and ratified by Canada in 1990.

That *Convention* asserts that children should have the possibility to develop physically in a healthy and normal way, with adequate medical attention and be protected from all forms of cruelty. The *Convention* establishes the rights of children to gender equality (Art. 2), to freedom from all forms of mental and physical violence and maltreatment (Art. 19.1) and to the highest attainable standard of health (Art. 24.1). Article 24.3 of the *Convention* explicitly requires States to take all effective and appropriate measures to abolish traditional practices prejudicial to the health of children.

3.4 — FGM and Health Rights

The physical and psychological health complications resulting from genital mutilation of women have been extensively documented. The partial or

---

ii) to modify the social and cultural patterns of conduct of men and women, with a view to achieving the elimination of prejudices and customary and all other practices which are based on the idea of the inferiority or the superiority of either of the sexes or on stereotyped roles for men and women (Art. 5.a.)

iii) States parties shall take all appropriate measures to eliminate discrimination against women in the field of health care in order to ensure, on a basis of equality of men and women, access to health care services including those related to family planning (Art. 12).

[21]See E. Dorkenoo, *Female Genital Mutilation: Proposals for Change* (1992) *Minority Rights Group Report* at 16, Renée Bridel, *L'enfant Mutilé*, presented on behalf of the F.I.F.C.J. to the U.N., Geneva, 1978.

complete loss of sexual function constitutes a violation of a woman's right to physical integrity and mental health. Health rights are guaranteed by the *International Covenant on Economic, Social and Cultural Rights* (Art. 12), the *Convention on the Rights of the Child* (Art. 2.4) and the *African Charter on Human and People's Rights* (Art. 16). The equal right to health care is further guaranteed by the Convention on the *Elimination of All Forms of Discrimination Against Women* (Art. 12).

4. — FGM in Canada

For some time now, Canada has experienced immigrant and refugee movements from countries in which FGM is commonly practised. In Toronto, community groups have estimated that there are 70,000 immigrants and refugees from Somalia and 10,000 from Nigeria, both of which are countries in which FGM is commonly practised.[22] As already noted, because of the nature of FGM, reliable statistics on the incidence of its practice are not available. However, based on discussions with members of the communities that are at risk, there is some evidence to indicate that FGM is practised in Ontario and across Canada. There is also evidence that suggests that in some cases, families from those communities send their daughters out of Canada to have the operation performed.[23]

There is a growing recognition of FGM as a violation of human rights. Immigrant and refugee movements, governments and advocacy organizations in Canada have acknowledged the need to deal with FGM as an internationally recognized health and human rights concern.

4.1 — Domestic Implications of International Human Rights Law

Canada is a signatory to over 20 major international conventions and treaties. A significant number of these are based on fundamental human rights principles. Canada's commitment to the development and maintenance of fundamental human rights in the international community and in Canada is therefore a matter of law. Domestic or national courts are required to interpret implementing legislation in conformity with international convention insofar as the domestic legislation permits.[24] In Canada, like other common

---

[22]Omayma Gutbi, *Preliminary Report on Female Genital Mutilation (FGM)* (Ontario Violence Against Women Prevention Section of the Ontario Women's Directorate, 10 April 1995) [unpublished].

[23]*Ibid.* at 8.

[24]*Op. cit.* note 1, *General Approaches to Domestic Application of International Law*, Cook, ed., at 364.

law countries, the presumption that the State does not intend to breach its international obligations also applies to conventional law. States should implement international laws where there is no obvious inconsistency between the domestic law and the international law.

Canada's treaty obligations under international instruments can bind the domestic courts if: (i) international law is specifically incorporated in domestic legislation or is incorporated by necessary implication, and (ii) where such legislation is itself enacted by the legislature with jurisdiction over the subject matter of the treaty.[25]

In 1976, Canada and the provinces acceded to the *International Covenant on Civil and Political Rights*. It has been argued that this and other instruments to which Canada is a party are incorporated into Canadian law by implication through the Canadian *Charter of Rights and Freedoms* (the "*Charter*").[26] The *Charter* is described as implementing legislation that is *supremely authoritative and binding on all Canadian tribunals and institutions*, with governing phrases that are derived from the principles and instruments of the international legal system.[27]

In 1983, Chief Justice Dickson, in his dissenting opinion in *Reference Re Public Service Employee Relations Act*, [1987] 1 S.C.R. 313 at pages 348–50, positioned the role of international law in *Charter* litigation in the following way.

> . . . Canada is a party to a number of international human rights Conventions which contain provisions similar or identical to those in the *Charter*. Canada has thus obliged itself internationally to ensure within its borders the protection of certain fundamental rights and freedoms which are also contained in the *Charter*. The general principles of constitutional interpretation require that these international obligations be a relevant and persuasive factor in *Charter* interpretations.

Chief Justice Dickson reaffirmed this position in a majority decision in *Slaight Communications Inc. v. Davidson*, [1989] 1 S.C.R. at page 1041, in which he reiterated the importance of Canada upholding its obligations under international treaties to protect rights enshrined therein. He noted that where legislation is interpreted with the same status as an international instrument, either under customary international law or under a treaty to

---

[25]Maxwell Cohen and Ann F. Bayefsky, "The Canadian *Charter of Rights and Freedoms* and Public International Law" (1983) 61 *Canadian Bar Review* 265 at 288.

[26]*Ibid.* at 267. Part I of the *Constitution Act*, 1982, being Schedule B of the *Canada Act* 1982 (U.K.), 1982, c.11 [1985, Appendix II, No. 44].

[27]*Ibid.*

which Canada is a State Party, the objective of the legislation should generally be indicative of a high degree of importance attached to the right at international law.

Because FGM is gender-specific discrimination, internationally condemned and proscribed in international instruments to which Canada is a party, the Province of Ontario would be in compliance with its obligations by taking steps to eradicate this practice. Any such initiatives taken by the Government of Ontario would be reflected in reports to international bodies in compliance with international conventions to which Canada is a signatory.

4.2 — Criminal Law

The *Criminal Code* of Canada continues to be used as a means to address the issue of FGM. For example, it can be used to control the transportation of female children outside the country for the purposes of obtaining FGM.[28] Canada has recognized fear of gender persecution as a ground for claiming refugee status since the early 1990s. In May 1994, the Immigration and Refugee Board granted refugee status to a woman whose 10-year-old daughter would have been subjected to FGM if she had been forced to return to her country of origin.[29]

As a result of the growing recognition of FGM as a violation of human rights, in October 1994, the then Ministry of the Solicitor General and Correctional Services[30] issued a memorandum to all Chiefs of Police and the Commissioner of the Ontario Provincial Police, explaining that FGM is a criminal offence, and informing them of the investigative and charging procedures for offences related to FGM. The Ministry of the Attorney General also sent a memorandum to all Crown Attorneys on the prosecution of charges related to FGM.

In May 1997, the federal government amended the *Criminal Code* and included the performance of FGM as aggravated assault under section 268(3).[31] Under the *Criminal Code*, any person who commits an aggravated assault is guilty of an indictable offence and liable to imprisonment for a

---

[28]Section 273, *Criminal Code*, R.S.C. 1985, c. C-46, as am. S.C. 1993, c. 45, s. 3, as am. S.C. 1997, c. 18, s. 13.

[29]*Minister of Employment and Immigration v. Farah* (May 10, 1994), Doc. 93-2198 (I.R.B. Toronto).

[30]In June 1999, the Ministry of the Solicitor General and Correctional Services was divided to form two ministries: the Ministry of the Solicitor General, and the Ministry of Correctional Services.

[31]*Criminal Code*, R.S.C. 1985, c. C-46, s. 268, as am. S.C. 1997, c. 16, s. 5:

term not exceeding 14 years.[32] A parent who performs FGM on their child may be charged with aggravated assault. Where the parent does not commit the act but agrees to have it performed by another party, the parent can be convicted as a party to the offence under section 21(1) of the *Criminal Code*.[33]

4.3 — The Quebec *Charter of Human Rights and Freedoms*[34]

In December 1994, the Quebec *Commission* released a paper in which it states that it considers FGM to be a practice that jeopardizes "the right of women to personal inviolability, equality and non-discrimination."[35] The Quebec *Charter* sets out that the obligation of each person is to respect the rights of others and "any unlawful interference with any right or freedom recognized by this *Charter* entitles the victim to obtain the cessation of such interference and compensation for the moral or material prejudice resulting therefrom."[36]

---

(3) For greater certainty, in this section, "wounds" or "maims" includes to excise, infibulate or mutilate, in whole or in part, the labia majora, labia minora or clitoris of a person, except where

(a) surgical procedure is performed, by a person duly qualified by provincial law to practise medicine, for the benefit of the physical health of the person or for the purpose of that person having normal reproductive functions or normal sexual appearance or function; or

(b) the person is at least eighteen years of age and there is no resulting bodily harm.

[32] *Ibid.* s. 268(2).

[33] *Ibid.* s. 21.

[34] R.S.Q., c. C-12. In Quebec, no social area is required to file a complaint. The Quebec *Charter* protects fundamental rights, political rights and judicial rights. FGM would be framed as a complaint under "the right to integrity" under fundamental rights. Note that under section 136 of the Quebec *Charter*, civil and criminal proceedings may be instituted by the Commission against any person who contravenes the Quebec *Charter*. To date, no complaints based on FGM have been filed.

[35] Maurice Drapeau and Hailou Wolde-Giorghis, *Sexual Mutilation: Unlawful Interference with Personal Inviolability* (The Quebec Commission des droits de la personne, December 21, 1994). Adopted in resolution COM-388-6.1.5. The Quebec *Charter of Human Rights and Freedoms*, section 1, "Every human being has a right to life, and to personal security, inviolability and freedom."

[36] *Ibid.*

The report goes on to note that:

> This type of (genital) mutilation is performed exclusively on women, and *is unquestionably a discriminatory interference* with their physical and mental inviolability. The Commission des droits de la personne would therefore have competence to investigate complaints of sexual mutilation and, with the consent of the victim, to take legal action for discriminatory violation of personal inviolability with a view to obtaining civil redress and having the person found guilty condemned to exemplary damages.[37](Emphasis added)

The Quebec Commission took the position that it has the jurisdiction to investigate a complaint filed by a woman who has been subjected to FGM, and to institute both civil and criminal proceedings where investigation findings support the allegation that a woman's right has been violated as a result of FGM. The report concludes by indicating that preventative measures, via education and awareness-raising, must be given priority.

4.4 — Ontario

4.4.1 — FGM Prevention Task Force

In the early 1990s, an increasing number of women who had been subjected to FGM began seeking medical assistance.[38] The Canadian Centre for Victims of Torture, working with women from at-risk communities, family physicians and the Department of Health established the first mutual support outreach group for women who had been subjected to FGM. Since then, a number of other initiatives have been developed.

As there were no co-ordinated efforts between various professionals and institutions, and no consistent policy in Canada regarding FGM, members of affected communities requested that the Minister Responsible for Women's Issues establish an Ontario FGM Prevention Task Force. The Task Force, an inter-ministerial/agency/community initiative, was mandated to develop and recommend strategies and policies designed to provide support for girls and women who have been subjected to FGM, to prevent the practice, and to support community work by, and for women affected by genital mutilation.[39]

---

[37]*Supra*, note 34 at 6.

[38]*Female Genital Mutilation Prevention/Eradication Strategies*, Draft Paper (Ontario FGM Prevention Task Force for Ontario Women's Directorate, Violence Against Women Prevention Unit, June 1995) at 4.

[39]*Ibid.*

4.4.2 — FGM and the Duty to Report

In Ontario, a duty to report FGM exists under the policy of the College of Physicians and Surgeons of Ontario (CPSO) and under the *Child and Family Services Act.*

Under the CPSO policy, the performance of female circumcision, excision, infibulation and/or reinfibulation by a physician licensed in Ontario, unless medically indicated, would be regarded as professional misconduct.[40] The CPSO also requires that:

> Any physician who becomes aware of a procedure of this nature being performed by another physician should, in accordance with the Code of Ethics, bring this information to the attention of the College at the earliest opportunity. Since the performance of circumcision, excision and/or infibulation on any female child by any person may constitute child abuse, the Children's Aid Society and appropriate police agencies must be notified.[41]

Under Ontario's *Child and Family Services Act*,[42] there is a duty to report information with respect to a child who is in need of protection. This duty exists despite the provisions of any other *Act*. If a person has reasonable grounds to suspect that a child is or may be in need of protection, (*e.g.*, from physical harm such as FGM), the person is obliged to report the suspicion to appropriate authorities. The duty to report under this *Act* applies to all members of the public and those who perform professional or official duties with respect to children.[43]

5. — The Ontario *Human Rights Code*

The Ontario *Human Rights Code* recognizes the inherent worth and dignity of every person in Ontario. The Preamble makes particular reference to the *Universal Declaration of Human Rights* and the inherent principles of dignity and equal and inalienable rights of the person. The creation of a society

---

[40] *The Regulated Health Professions Act, 1991*, S.O. 1991, c. 18. s. 85, as am. S.O. 1993, c. 37, s. 23.

[41] The College of Physicians and Surgeons of Ontario, College Notice No.25 published in March 1992.

[42] *The Child and Family Services Act*, R.S.O. 1990, c. C.11. s. 72, as am. S.O. 1999, c. 2, ss. 22(1), 38.

[43] The Ontario Association of Children's Aid Societies has a policy that supports the duty to report and the protection of the rights of children. In March 1992, the Ontario Association of Children's Aid Societies issued the following statement on FGM. The performance of female circumcision, excision or infibulation on a child meets the definition of child abuse in the *Child and Family Services Act* of 1984.

in which all persons can live and work in an environment that is free from discrimination is central to the policy objectives of the Ontario Human Rights Commission in virtue of the *Code*. The Commission thus recognizes that FGM violates the basic human rights and human dignity of women and girl children.

In Ontario, evidence indicates that FGM is practised within certain immigrant groups.[44] There are new immigrants to Canada who may not be aware that some of their traditional or culturally rooted attitudes and values may result in practices that are clearly in conflict with Canadian law, including the Ontario *Human Rights Code*. The Ontario Children's Aid Society, in its Policy on Female Genital Mutilation (April 1995) notes that most families who seek out this procedure do not consider the mutilation of female genitalia as a form of physical or sexual abuse. The Society also stresses the need to understand the sociocultural context in the development of strategies to stop the practice.

The Commission recognizes the need for public sensitivity, awareness and understanding in dealing with culturally rooted practices which may conflict with the principles and provisions of the *Code*. At the same time, the Commission has a dual responsibility under its mandate to enforce the provisions of the *Code* and educate the public on human rights issues.

5.1 — Interpretation

The practice of FGM in Canada raises human rights issues as well as health, social and criminal law concerns. The international community, including Canada, has condemned FGM as a human rights violation. This has implications for the *Code* with respect to matters within provincial jurisdiction.

The Commission acknowledges the complex social and cultural roots of FGM and the need for dialogue and education initiatives within the at-risk communities in Ontario and across Canada. However, it is the Commission's view that arguments based on a defence of cultural or religious values should not be accepted as justification for the practice, nor for discriminating against women who have been subjected to, or perceived to have been subjected to, genital mutilation.

The Commission has a responsibility to ensure that the fundamental human rights principles enshrined in the international conventions and treaties to which Canada is a signatory, and which are protected in the *Code*, are respected and upheld in Ontario.

---

[44] *Supra*, note 21.

It is the Commission's position that the practice of FGM is contrary to the *Criminal Code* and public policy in Ontario. The practice offends the inherent dignity of women and infringes their rights as set out in the Ontario *Human Rights Code*. The Commission will therefore, accept, investigate and make a determination on complaints involving FGM filed by victims of the practice or their legal guardian.

Under the *Code*, an allegation of discrimination must be based on a prohibited ground of discrimination in relation to an identified social area.

a) — Primary Prohibited Ground — Sex

International law and human rights law in particular have identified FGM as a gender issue. A complaint filed with the Commission would most likely fall under the prohibited ground of "sex." Genital mutilation is reported to be used as a means of social control over women in affected communities.[45] The Commission's *Policy on Sexual Harassment and Inappropriate Gender-Related Comment and Conduct* refers, at page 2, to the imbalance of power and authority as a policy consideration in reviewing behaviours that result in discrimination based on sex. The Policy reads in part:

> . . . unequal treatment based on gender typically involves the abuse of male power and authority over women, resulting in the reinforcement of a woman's subordinate status in relation to the dominant male group.

b) — Other Prohibited Grounds

Although the most likely prohibited ground of discrimination on which a complaint might be based is sex, particular facts relating to a specific complaint could also involve other prohibited grounds of discrimination. For example, the facts relating to a particular allegation of discrimination could lead to "place of origin" being cited as a ground in the complaint, if the alleged discriminatory treatment is clearly linked to FGM as a practice that only occurs in immigrant communities from specific countries.

"Handicap" or "perceived handicap" may be relevant in situations in which women who have been subjected to the procedure are treated differentially in respect of services or employment, subject to health considerations.[46]

---

[45] *Ibid.*

[46] FGM would appear to fall under the ground of "handicap" under section 10. As previously noted, the health complications arising from FGM are many and can manifest themselves at different times.

c) — Social Areas

Services, Goods and Facilities (section 1):

Women who have been subjected to the procedure visit health care practitioners who have rarely treated FGM patients. The *Code* protections may be applied to prevent discrimination against women (and girls, where applicable) who:

1. have undergone FGM, to ensure that they receive adequate and appropriate medical treatment without differential treatment, except as required for health reasons; or
2. refuse to be reinfibulated, but whose wishes are opposed by another family member.

The performance of FGM, including infibulation or reinfibulation by a physician licensed in Ontario, would also be regarded as professional misconduct according to the CPSO's policy, and may give rise to criminal charges of assault.

Employment (section 5):

Women who have been subjected to FGM, or who may be perceived to have been subjected to FGM because of their creed or place of origin, may experience discrimination in employment. The Commission is aware through the Ontario FGM Prevention Task Force, that employment-related discrimination involving FGM and perceptions relating to the practice has occurred.[47]

Discrimination may take the form of harassment by co-workers or management about the practice, or denial of employment because of the perception that women who have been subjected to FGM will have health complications resulting in high absenteeism rates.

5.2 — Public Education

The Commission is mandated to undertake public education activities directed at promoting a greater understanding of human rights principles and voluntary compliance with the provisions of the *Code*.

The Commission recognizes the benefits to be gained towards the eradication of the practice of FGM through public education. Therefore, the Com-

[47] Such a situation involved an employment interview where, during the course of the interview, a human resources representative who was aware of the practice of FGM allegedly inquired as to the applicant's place of origin with a view to eliciting information about the applicant's long-term health as potentially unpredictable and her eventual reliability as an employee.

mission is committed to working with members and organizations of the at-risk communities, as well as with other agencies in the public sector, within the boundaries of its mandate and resources, in developing public education initiatives around FGM. The efforts of the Commission, together with those of the affected communities and concerned organizations, can help to create an environment in which people are encouraged to eradicate the practice, without imposing a threat to the dignity and cultural identity of the affected communities.[48]

The Commission has prepared a pamphlet version of this policy in six languages, including French, Arabic, Somalian, Swahili, Amharic and English and in various formats: IBM compatible disk, audio tape and large print.

---

[48] At the June 1995 CASHRA (Canadian Association of Statutory Human Rights Associations) Conference, the Commission tabled the following resolution which was unanimously passed:

> INTERNATIONAL HUMAN RIGHTS AND THE PROTECTION OF WOMEN
>
> WHEREAS Canada is a party to international instruments that provide for the respect and protection of the fundamental human rights of women and children; and
>
> WHEREAS Canada is participating in an international initiative to eradicate the practice of female genital mutilation; and
>
> WHEREAS Canadians are concerned that women and girls who are ordinarily resident in Canada are being subjected to the practice of female genital mutilation;
>
> BE IT RESOLVED that CASHRA recommend to the Minister of Employment and Immigration that all prospective immigrants be provided with information setting out Canada's commitment to upholding international human rights instruments; emphasizing that the protection and respect of human rights is a cornerstone of Canadian society and extends to the protection of women and children against any acts which would cause grave interference with their personal inviolability, including female genital mutilation; and advising that practices such as female genital mutilation are deemed to be a criminal activity under the Canadian *Criminal Code*.

Policy on Height and Weight Requirements

Approved by the Commission: June 19, 1996

1. — Introduction

The Ontario *Human Rights Code* (the *"Code"*) states that it is public policy in Ontario to recognize the inherent dignity and worth of every person and to provide for equal rights and opportunities without discrimination. The provisions of the *Code* are aimed at creating a climate of understanding and mutual respect for the dignity and worth of each person, so that each person feels a part of the community and feels able to contribute to the community.

Standards for height and weight are sometimes used to screen or evaluate job applicants. In the Commission's experience, this tends to occur in recruitment for occupations that traditionally have been male dominated. These standards or selection criteria are based on the average physical stature of men in the majority population group. Women and members of racial minority population groups are, on the average, physically smaller than members of the majority population group. Consequently, these groups tend to be disadvantaged by height and weight criteria.

The policy of the Ontario Human Rights Commission (the "Commission") with regard to such recruitment practices is set out below. This policy applies to all height and weight criteria used in the context of employment.

2. — Background

Having two separate sets of height and weight criteria for men and women may reduce the discriminatory impact on women. However, individuals from racial minority groups who are on average of smaller build may still be excluded. For example, persons of Asian descent or persons belonging to indigenous population groups from Latin America are, on average, of smaller physical stature than the majority population group in Ontario.

3. — Constructive or Indirect Discrimination

Human rights complaints arising from the use of height and weight criteria tend to raise issues of constructive or indirect discrimination. Constructive or indirect discrimination is defined as a disadvantage or adverse impact that may result from the uniform application of a requirement, factor or rule. It is the Commission's opinion that height and weight criteria in employment, which on their face appear to be neutral, may in some circumstances contravene section 11 of the *Code* which states:

> (1) A right of a person [under Part I] is infringed where a requirement, qualification or factor exists that is not discrimination on prohibited ground but that results in the exclusion, restriction or preference of a group of persons who are identified by a prohibited ground of discrimination and of whom the person is a member, except where,
>
> > (a) the requirement, qualification or factor is reasonable and *bona fide* in the circumstances[.]

4. — Height and Weight as *Bona Fide* Occupational Requirement

The test for determining whether an occupational requirement is *bona fide* was established by the Supreme Court of *Canada in Ontario (Human Rights Commission) v. Etobicoke (Borough)*, [1982] 1 S.C.R. 202. The Court established that for a requirement to be considered as *bona fide*, two conditions must be met. First, there must be an objective relationship between the standards required and the job in question. Second, the standards must have been imposed in good faith.

Except in limited circumstances, there is little evidence to demonstrate that height and weight criteria are a *bona fide* occupational requirement, according to decisions from human rights tribunals in Ontario and other Canadian provinces.[1] Empirical research indicates that physical stature alone is not determinative of an individual's ability to perform the essential duties of a job, even if significant physical exertion is required. As a result, minimum standards for height and weight will not necessarily meet the reasonable and *bona fide* standard. If so, the defence provided by section 11(1) of the *Code* cannot be used to justify the requirement, qualification or factor.

5. — Duty to Accommodate

It should be noted that section 11 of the *Code* states that a requirement, qualification or factor will not be considered to be a reasonable and *bona fide* requirement unless the employer has tried to accommodate persons who are adversely affected. If height and weight criteria are used to recruit

---

[1] *Colfer v. Ottawa Board of Commissioners of Police* (1979), unreported (Ont. Bd. of Inquiry); *Hartling v. Timmins (Municipality) Commissioners of Police* (1981), 2 C.H.R.R. D/487 (Ont. Bd. of Inquiry). See also *Lewington, Moran and Leuszler v. Vancouver Fire Department*, 6 C.H.R.R. D/2599 (B.C. Board of Inquiry).

for a particular job, the employer must attempt to accommodate women and members of ethnic or racial groups who are adversely affected by the requirement, qualification or factor. The employer can, however, demonstrate that such an attempt to accommodate these applicants would cause undue hardship[2] or would substantially change the essential nature of the job. In those circumstances, the employer is not required to provide accommodation.

6. — The Commission's Position

The Commission urges employers who still use height and weight criteria in the employment recruitment process to discontinue the practice. However, if such criteria are maintained on the basis of demonstrated necessity for the performance of essential duties, accommodation of women and members of protected groups, short of undue hardship, is a requirement under the *Code*.

7. — Relevant Ontario *Human Rights Code* Provisions

The Ontario *Human Rights Code* (Part II of this book) includes provisions relevant to this policy in the following sections: 5(1) and 11(1)(2)(3).

---

[2]In assessing undue hardship, consideration will be given to the cost, any outside sources of funding and any health and safety requirements. The Commission's *Guidelines for Assessing Accommodation Requirements for Persons with Disabilities* are available at any Commission office.

Policy on HIV/AIDS-Related Discrimination

Approved by the Commission: November 27, 1996

> A society is judged by how it responds to those in greatest need. A tragedy such as the HIV epidemic brings a society face to face with the core of its established values, and offers an opportunity for the reaffirmation of compassion, justice and dignity.
>
> James D. Watkins, Chair
> Presidential Committee on the
> Human Immunodeficiency Virus Epidemic Report
> Report of June 24, 1988

1. — Introduction

The Ontario *Human Rights Code* (the "*Code*") states that it is public policy in Ontario to recognize the inherent dignity and worth of every person and to provide for equal rights and opportunities without discrimination. The provisions of the *Code* are aimed at creating a climate of understanding and mutual respect for the dignity and worth of each person, so that each person feels a part of the community and feels able to contribute to the community.

The *Code* provides for equal treatment without discrimination because of handicap. AIDS (Acquired Immunodeficiency Syndrome) and other medical conditions related to infection by the Human Immunodeficiency Virus (HIV) are recognized as handicaps within the meaning of the *Code*. All persons who have or have had, or who are believed to have or have had, or are perceived to have, AIDS or HIV-related medical conditions, including those who do not show symptoms of AIDS or AIDS-related illnesses, are entitled to the protection of the *Code* in employment, services, housing, contracts and membership in trade unions.

HIV is transmitted through very limited ways. It is most commonly transmitted through unprotected sexual activity and through contact with infected blood and other body fluids. A person may become infected with HIV by receiving blood transfusions or using blood contaminated needles. It is important to recognize that today, the risk of transmitting HIV through blood transfusions has been minimized in North America. Since 1985, blood banks across Canada and the United States have implemented routine procedures for comprehensive HIV antibody screening.

AIDS is much more than just a medical/scientific phenomenon. It challenges our fundamental values such as a commitment to a compassionate society, to justice and to the elimination of all aspects of discrimination that undermines these values.

2. — Purpose of this Policy

This policy clarifies the scope of the *Code*'s protection for persons who are or are perceived to be infected with HIV or who have contracted HIV-related illnesses. The guidelines contained in this policy are based on extensive consultations between the Commission and a wide-ranging number of interest and advocacy groups, employer groups, services providers, and members of the medical community, including hospital administrators.

3. — Relevant Sections of the *Code*

3.1 — AIDS as a Handicap (Section 10)

The Commission recognizes that AIDS and other HIV-related medical conditions are handicaps under the *Code*. "Handicap" is defined under s. 10 of the *Code*. All persons infected with HIV or with HIV-related illness, or who are believed to have the virus, including those who are asymptomatic, are fully protected against discrimination in services s. 1; housing s. 2; contracts s. 3; employment s. 5; and membership in trade unions s. 6.

Protection under the *Code* is also extended to persons on the ground of "sexual orientation." Persons identified by this prohibited ground of discrimination are often believed to be at high risk of contracting AIDS or to be carriers of HIV. The erroneous perception of AIDS as a "gay disease" is a form of stereotyping that the *Code* prohibits. Discrimination on the grounds of sexual orientation is unlawful.

3.2 — Protection Against Discrimination and Harassment (s. 10)

Persons who have or have had, or are believed to have or have had, AIDS or HIV-related medical conditions are protected from discrimination and harassment in employment, housing, services, contracts and membership in trade unions. Harassment is defined under s. 10 of the *Code* and means:

> engaging in a course of vexatious comment or conduct that is known or ought reasonably to be known to be unwelcome.

3.3 — Discrimination Because of Association (s. 12)

The *Code* also protects against discrimination on the basis of "association." Section 12 of the *Code* states that:

> A right under Part I (of the *Code*) is infringed where the discrimination is because of a relationship, association or dealings with a person or persons identified by a prohibited ground of discrimination.

This means that a person who is associated with anyone who is identified by a prohibited ground of discrimination, such as a co-worker, a friend or a relative of the person who is HIV positive, cannot be discriminated against because of this association.

> *Example*: A rental property manager would be in breach of the *Code* if she refuses to rent a house to a representative of an AIDS advocacy organization because of the organization's association with persons identified by their disability.

3.4 — Duty to Accommodate

In addition to the specific grounds of prohibited discrimination mentioned above, s. 17 of the *Code* sets out a broad duty to accommodate the needs of persons with handicaps, short of undue hardship.

> *Example*: An employer is obliged to accommodate the needs of a person with AIDS in order to assist the person in "performing or fulfilling the essential duties or requirements" of the job. This might involve taking steps to redefine work duties and providing temporary work assignments to accommodate health-related absences.

"Short of undue hardship" is a standard that is applied to the person required to make the accommodation. It takes into consideration costs, available sources of funding, as well as health and safety factors (see further the Commission's *Guidelines for Accommodating Persons with Disabilities*).

It is well established in human rights case law that customer or third-party preferences are not to be considered in assessing undue hardship.

> *Example*: It is discriminatory for an employer to claim that customers and/or other employees would object to hiring a person who is HIV positive.

4. — Application of the *Code*

This policy is intended to provide particular guidance to those responsible for formulating and implementing infection control procedures in health-care settings and anti-harassment discriminatory policies in the workplace, in housing and in services.

Keeping with the spirit of *Code*, any health protection and promotion policies should be introduced in a manner that respects the individual's privacy. Treating persons with HIV-related illness in an arbitrary or discriminatory manner that is not supported by current medical or scientific knowledge may be a violation of the *Code*.

4.1 — Spirit of the *Code*

The spirit of the *Code* requires that persons who are HIV positive and those with HIV-related illness are to be given the opportunity to remain integral members of society and to maintain their social, employment and other relationships. This implies that any assessment of a person's illness must be based on his or her current abilities and on the situation's current risks, rather than on abilities or risks which may arise in the future. The *Code*'s accommodation requirements are designed to ensure integration and sensitivity to the needs of persons with disabilities as they may change over time.

4.2 — Respecting the Dignity of the Person

The *Code* prohibits, in all but exceptional circumstances, infection control techniques where the person with an HIV-related illness is isolated or quarantined. Current scientific knowledge on the transmission of the AIDS virus indicates that such measures do not prevent the spread of infection and are also inappropriate except in rare cases. Moreover, the fear of isolation may simply deter persons who have participated in high-risk activities from seeking voluntary testing and counselling.

4.3 — Universal Precautions

"Universal precautions" are a set of risk reduction measures employed at all times by medical and health-care professionals and workers whenever they encounter blood or other identified body fluids. The concept of universal precautions relates to the proper handling of sharp items, and the use of barriers, such as gloves and masks, to protect the person handling the blood or body fluids. It can be adapted to different medical settings depending on the medical procedure required.[1]

> *Example*: Dentists are expected to use the appropriate eye-wear, masks and gloves, etc. when dealing with *all* patients.

---

[1]Royal College of Dental Surgeons of Ontario, *Guidelines Respecting Infection Control in the Dental Office*, June 1995. The College notes that its guidelines can be used by other health professional bodies in determining whether appropriate standards of practice and professional responsibilities have been maintained.

With universal blood and body-fluid precautions widely in place, there is no need for using additional precautions for patients who are known or believed to have illnesses that can be transferred by blood.

4.4 — Testing

Testing for HIV infection would constitute a medical examination. It is the Commission's position that any medical examination carried out for employment purposes should focus on verifying whether or not an individual is able to perform the essential duties of a particular job.

Employers considering any form of employment-related medical testing should refer to the Commission's *Policy on Employment-Related Medical Information.*

The following are the main principles of that policy:

i) Employment-related medical examinations or inquiries, conducted as part of the applicant screening process, are prohibited under subsection 23 (2) of the *Code.*

ii) Any employment-related medical examinations or inquiries are to be limited to determining the individual's ability to perform the essential duties of a job.

iii) Medical examinations, if determined to be necessary to assess an individual's ability to perform the essential duties of a job should only be undertaken after a conditional offer of employment has been made, preferably in writing.

iv) If the applicant or employee requires accommodation in order to enable him or her to perform the essential duties of the job, the employer is required to provide such accommodation unless to do so would cause undue hardship.

The *Policy on Employment-Related Medical Information* does not allow employers to subject job applicants to any type of medical examination before a conditional offer of employment is made. After the person is hired, medical tests designed to identify employees with disabilities may constitute a breach of the *Code* if the disability being tested for is not a reasonable and *bona fide* concern with regard to the job performed.

In most work settings, it is unlikely that testing for HIV infection or other protective measures would be necessary or justifiable. Several studies have conclusively demonstrated that persons with HIV infection or HIV-related medical conditions pose virtually no risk to those with whom they interact.[2]

The U.S. Public Health Service guidelines state that workers infected with HIV should not be restricted from using telephones, office equipment, toilets, eating facilities or water fountains. There are no documented instances of HIV transmission from the serving or preparation of food or beverages. For non-sexual household contact, of 30,000 cases of AIDS reported to the U.S. Centre for Disease Control, none has occurred in family members of patients with AIDS, unless the members have partaken in other recognized risk-related behaviour.[3]

5. — Ensuring Privacy and Confidentiality

It is essential to ensure the maximum degree of privacy and confidentiality when medical information is legitimately required for health protection and promotion or other purposes. This applies in all situations and circumstances including hospitals, health clinics, insurance company records, employee's files, etc.

In employment settings, all health assessment information, including HIV testing results, should remain exclusively with the examining physician and away from an employee's personnel file in order to protect the confidentiality of the information.

6. — The Role of the Commission

6.1 — Remedies

The Commission has a broad statutory mandate, not only to provide a remedy when discrimination has taken place, but also to prevent it (see s. 29 of the *Code*). In seeking a remedy in situations where there is evidence to sup-

---

[2]The Canadian Medical Association released its policy on HIV in the workplace in May 1993, which includes the following statement:

> There have been no instances in Canada of HIV infections in patients resulting from exposure to infected health care workers . . . Health care workers with HIV infection should be afforded the opportunity to compete for jobs and continue to work at their usual occupation as long as they meet acceptable performance standards and are mentally and physically able to perform the essential components of work safely, efficiently and reliably.

[3]*Biggs v. Hudson* (1988), 9 C.H.R.R. D/834 (B.C. Human Rights Council).

port allegations of discrimination, the Commission may, in addition to monetary compensation, seek remedies such as the following:

i) implementation of a formal institutional policy expressing a commitment to the equal treatment of persons that have or have tested positive for HIV infection

ii) educational programs for others in the environment

iii) other accommodation required by the person with HIV infection.

6.2 — Priority Handling of Complaints Filed by Persons with HIV or HIV-related Illnesses

Once a person self-identifies as HIV positive, it is the Commission's policy is to expedite HIV/AIDS-related discrimination complaints because of the shortened life expectancy of persons with HIV or HIV-related illnesses. The Commission may also use its authority to initiate complaints to address HIV/AIDS-related policies or actions that may be discriminatory when such information comes to the Commission's attention.

6.3 — Preventing HIV/AIDS-related Discrimination

The most effective way to combat HIV/AIDS-related discrimination is through public education. The Commission is committed to working with community, public and private sector organizations in promoting greater understanding of the nature of HIV infection and HIV-related illness, and the rights of person with AIDS or HIV-related illnesses to be free from discrimination.

7. — Relevant Ontario *Human Rights Code* Provisions

The Ontario *Human Rights Code* (Part II of this book) includes provisions relevant to this policy in the following sections: 1, 2(1)(2), 3, 5(1)(2), 6, 10, 12, 17(1)(2), 23(1)(2) and 29.

Policy on Requiring a Driver's Licence as a Condition of Employment

Approved by the Commission: June 19, 1996

1. — Introduction

The Ontario *Human Rights Code* (the "*Code*") states that it is public policy in Ontario to recognize the inherent dignity and worth of every person and to provide for equal rights and opportunities without discrimination. The provisions of the *Code* are aimed at creating a climate of understanding and mutual respect for the dignity and worth of each person, so that each person feels a part of the community and feels able to contribute to the community.

Subsection 5(1) of the *Code* prohibits discrimination in employment on the grounds of race, ancestry, place of origin, colour, ethnic origin, citizenship, creed, sex, sexual orientation, age, record of offences, marital status, family status and handicap.

In addition, subsection 11(1) of the *Code* establishes that the right of a person is infringed where a requirement, qualification or factor exists that is not a prohibited ground of discrimination, but results in the exclusion or restriction of a group of persons who are identified by a prohibited ground of discrimination, unless the requirement or factor is reasonable and *bona fide* (in good faith).

Subsection 23(2) of *Code*, prohibits the use of application forms, or written or oral inquiries, which directly or indirectly classify or indicates qualifications of an applicant as being a member of a group that is protected from discrimination.

2. — Where Driving is not an Essential Duty of a Job

A driver's licence contains personal information about an individual which could lead to the classification of a job applicant according to a prohibited ground of discrimination, contrary to subsection 23(2) of the *Code*. Therefore, unless a driver's licence is required to enable a person to perform the essential duties of a job, it should not be requested in an application form or during an employment interview.

> *Example*: A driver's licence contains information about a person's date of birth. Requesting a job applicant to provide a photocopy of his/her

> driver's licence would yield information about the applicant's age, which would be contrary to subsection 23(2) of the *Code*.

Similarly, information on a driver's licence could yield information about whether or not an applicant has a handicap. This in turn could lead to the classification of applicants as members of a group identified by a prohibited ground of discrimination.

3. — Where Driving is an Essential Duty of a Job

For positions where driving is an essential duty of the job, a question relating to whether or not an applicant is licenced to drive, and/or the type of vehicle the applicant is licenced to drive, would be appropriate. The legitimate needs of the employer and the concerns of the applicant might be served by including the following statement on an application form or in a job advertisement:

> This position requires the successful candidate to have a valid driver's licence. The successful candidate would have to provide proof that s/he has a valid driver's licence upon being hired.

Employers should determine which jobs within their organization involve driving as an essential duty. Applications for these positions should include a statement relating to the need for successful candidates to provide proof that they possess a valid driver's licence.

Subsection 23(3) allows for employers to ask applicants if they have a valid driver's licence during a personal interview for positions in which driving is an essential duty.

3.1 — Duty to Accommodate (Section 17)

Subsection 17(2) of the *Code* requires an employer to accommodate the needs of a person with a disability in the performance of the essential features of a job, unless it could be demonstrated that the needs of the person cannot be accommodated short of undue hardship on the person responsible for accommodating those needs.

In some cases, an individual may be licenced to drive a vehicle with modified driving apparata, because of a particular disability. For positions that involve driving as an essential duty, an employer would have a duty to accommodate the needs of a person with a licence to drive a modified vehicle only, short of undue hardship, to enable that person to perform the essential duties of the position. Undue hardship would include consideration of any costs or health and safety factors related to the accommodation.

> *Example*: An employer may be able to accommodate the needs of a travelling salesperson with a mobility-related disability by purchasing and installing a set of hand-controls into a company car.

In some circumstances, the nature or degree of a person's disability might be such that the employer cannot accommodate the individual without incurring undue hardship.

3.2 — Record of Offences

Where driving is an essential duty of the job, an employer may refuse to consider an applicant who has a poor driving record even though the *Code* protects persons who have committed a violation under the *Highway Traffic Act*.

> *Example*: A company can refuse to hire a school bus driver who has accumulated too many demerit points.

At the same time, the *Code* does not protect persons who were convicted for careless driving under the *Criminal Code* and who have not been pardoned.

4. — Relevant Ontario *Human Rights Code* Provisions

The Ontario *Human Rights Code* (Part II of this book) includes provisions relevant to this policy in the following sections: 5(1), 10(1), 11(1)(2), 17(1)(2) and 23(1)(2)(3).

Policy on Scholarships and Awards

Approved by the Commission: July 8, 1997

1. — Introduction

The Ontario *Human Rights Code* (the *"Code"*) states that it is public policy in Ontario to recognize the inherent dignity and worth of every person and to provide for equal rights and opportunities without discrimination. The provisions of the *Code* are aimed at creating a climate of understanding and mutual respect for the dignity and worth of each person, so that each person feels a part of the community and feels able to contribute to the community.

This policy deals with scholarships or other forms of awards or grants that are available only on a limited basis to individuals who are identified by a ground set out in the *Code*. These grounds include race, sex, colour, religion, age and ethnic origin, to name a few. These types of scholarships or awards are called "exclusionary" because only certain individuals can apply for them, while others, who do not share the same characteristics, are excluded.

This policy provides information to potential applicants, sponsoring organizations and educational institutions about how the *Code* applies to exclusionary scholarships and awards. It should be noted that this policy applies whether the organization or body conferring the scholarship or award is public or private. It also applies to trusts and other entities that may be required to act on the instructions or directions of a third party, such as a trust settlor or other benefactor.

2. — Equality

Section 1 of the *Code* provides that every person has a right to equal treatment with respect to services, goods and facilities, without discrimination because of race, ancestry, place of origin, colour, ethnic origin, citizenship, creed, sex, sexual orientation, age, marital status, family status or handicap. Education and access to educational facilities are "services" under the *Code*. Obviously, the means to access those services are directly or indirectly related to education.[1] As well, scholarships and awards are signifi-

[1]Section 9 provides that no person shall infringe or do, directly or indirectly, anything that infringes a right to equal treatment.

cant for reasons other than monetary value alone. Recipients of scholarships or awards have benefits in employment and access to post-graduate training. If a person is unable even to compete for the assistance that leads to these benefits, he or she is placed at a significant disadvantage.

Criteria such as race, ancestry, place of origin, colour, ethnic origin, citizenship, creed, sex, sexual orientation, age, marital status, family status, handicap, etc. should not be the basis for deciding who gets a scholarship, unless particular exceptions apply. As late as 1990, the Ontario Court of Appeal examined a scholarship based on explicitly racist criteria.

The *Canada Trust* case involved a scholarship that was restricted to Protestant "Christians of the White race." According to the trust document, the person who had set up the trust believed that "the White race is, as a whole, best qualified by nature to be entrusted with the development of civilization and the general progress of the world . . ." The Court of Appeal's response to this trust is worth reproducing:

> To say that a trust premised on these notions of racism and religious superiority contravenes contemporary public policy is to [state] the obvious. The concept that any one race or any one religion is intrinsically better than any other is patently at variance with the democratic principles governing our pluralistic society, in which equality rights are constitutionally guaranteed, and in which the multicultural heritage of Canadians is preserved and enhanced.[2]

Public awareness of human rights issues and sensitivity to their social impact have developed considerably in recent years: legitimate concerns are raised when one group is promoted at the expense of another, or when advantages for some simply reinforce disadvantages for others. Many universities and colleges refuse to administer awards that are restricted to persons of a particular ethnic origin. Benefactors have, in some cases, changed their eligibility criteria so that awards are now granted according to merit, ability or potential. For example, it is preferable for a scholarship or other award to be restricted to persons wishing to pursue Italian studies rather than to a person of Italian origin.

For these reasons, the Ontario Human Rights Commission takes the position that scholarships and awards should be based on factors such as merit, personal financial need, course specialization, or recognition for special contributions to academic or extracurricular life. Exclusionary scholarships or awards, on the other hand, use discriminatory criteria to assess eligibility. These criteria affect access to educational opportunities, directly or indi-

---

[2]*Canada Trust Co. v. Ontario (Human Rights Commission)* (1987), 12 C.H.R.R. D/184 at D/191.

rectly. Scholarships or awards that designate a specific minority or ethnic group infringe the *Code*, unless they qualify as a "special program" that is designed to relieve economic hardship or disadvantage, or designed to achieve equality of opportunity. Section 14 of the *Code* is discussed below.

3. — Exceptions

"Discrimination" in human rights law does not simply mean treating someone differently. In human rights law, it means treating someone differently because of personal characteristics that are based on the grounds set out in the *Code*. The *Code* will apply, therefore, where the treatment is based on these characteristics and has the effect of imposing burdens or disadvantages on one group that are not imposed on others, or that limits or withholds opportunities and benefits.[3] Seen from this standpoint, equality of opportunity operates to permit certain forms of differential treatment if the impact and intent is to remove those burdens or disadvantages. Temporary measures therefore may be necessary or desirable to assist persons that have been subjected to disadvantage or hardship. These measures are called "special programs."

3.1 — *Special Programs*

The *Code* allows for a special program that creates a preference or advantage, even though it is based on grounds that are set out in the *Code*. Section 14 allows programs designed to:

- relieve hardship or economic disadvantage
- assist disadvantaged persons or groups to achieve or attempt to achieve equal opportunity
- help eliminate the infringement of rights that are protected under the *Code*.

The Commission is of the view that for section 14 to apply, the underlying basis for the program should be related to a ground set out in the *Code*.[4] For example, section 14 will not apply to members of a group who share a political affiliation, even if they have been subject to hardship, because political views are not covered by the *Code*.

[3] See generally *Andrews v. Law Society of British Columbia*, [1989] 1 S.C.R. 143.

[4] Race, ancestry, colour, place of origin, ethnic origin, citizenship, nationality, creed, sex, family status, marital status, age, disability, receipt of public assistance (in accommodation only), record of offences (in employment only).

Scholarships or awards should only be exclusionary if hardship or economic disadvantage is linked to the ground selected as a criterion for eligibility. It should also be clear that the special program is designed to relieve that hardship or disadvantage. Some scholarships are restricted to members of particular groups on the erroneous assumption that the group's members are disadvantaged. For example, scholarships awarded to "mature students" are sometimes awarded to persons more than 25 years of age, a group that does not share a pattern of economic hardship or historical disadvantage. Different levels of financial needs may exist across a group that may not be demonstrably linked to age, marital status or other grounds that are assumed to apply.

The Commission has *Guidelines on Special Programs*, that should be referred to in the event that a person wishes to set up or administer a scholarship or award on an exclusionary basis. In brief, the special program should state clearly:

- why the identified persons or groups are considered to be experiencing hardship, economic disadvantage or discrimination
- how the proposed measures will relieve the hardship, economic disadvantage, or discrimination, that is, how the target groups will be assisted
- that the program is for a specific period of time and is of a temporary nature.

If a scholarship or award is a valid special program, that is, if it meets the criteria set out in the *Code* and in the Commission's *Guidelines on Special Programs*, it will not be found to be contrary to the *Code*. Scholarships and awards are assessed on a case by case basis.

In the light of the direction from the Court of Appeal in the *Canada Trust* case, educational institutions may prefer to consider the impact of scholarship restrictions on overall equality. Universities that offer a number of scholarships are encouraged to attempt to achieve an overall balance so that disadvantaged groups have reasonable access to educational services.

> *Example*: If a particular program has a number of scholarships for women, and none for persons with a disability, the university may wish to try to attract a benefactor for the latter group, or may establish an award from its own resources.

3.2 — *Canadian Citizenship or Permanent Residence Status*

Subsection 16(2) provides an exception to the *Code* by permitting a requirement, qualification or consideration to be adopted for the purpose of fostering and developing participation in cultural, educational, trade union or athletic activities by Canadian citizens or persons lawfully admitted to Canada for permanent residence. This means that citizenship or permanent residence may be a requirement for a scholarship or award. However, it must be adopted for the purpose of "fostering and developing participation" in educational and other activities that are set out in the *Code* (see the *Code* sections listed at the end of this document).

3.3 — *Special Interest Organizations (Section 18)*

This section is in response to inquiries from universities as to whether section 18 of the *Code* applies and whether it allows exclusionary scholarships or awards.

Section 18 of the *Code* allows a religious, philanthropic, educational, fraternal or social institution or organization, which primarily serves the interests of a particular group, to restrict membership or participation to members of that group. Provided that an organization comes within section 18, it will be able to restrict eligibility for scholarships and awards only if the recipient is a member or a participant. Simply being awarded a scholarship does not mean that the recipient is necessarily a member of the special interest organization.

> *Example*: A fraternal association that offers an open scholarship for boys would only be protected from a challenge under the *Code*, if the fraternity primarily serves the interests of boys and if membership and participation in the fraternity is linked to receipt of the scholarship.
>
> *Example*: A Roman Catholic institution may seek to restrict awards for divinity studies to Roman Catholics who intend to study for the priesthood. Similarly, a Jewish Hebrew school may declare that only Jewish students are eligible for enrolment in that school which may also may designate scholarships or other financial awards strictly for Jewish applicants.

3.4 — *Scholarships as an Employment Benefit (Subsection 24(1)(d))*

Financial assistance in the form of scholarships or awards offered by employers to employees and their families are a form of assistance that provides advancement or benefits to eligible individuals. The *Code* allows this form of assistance, although it is limited to persons who are identified by their family or marital status. It is the Commission's view that educational subsidies offered to employees and their families are acceptable as a legitimate form of exclusionary benefit related to employment.

4. — Summary

A scholarship or award is an advantage or benefit to persons seeking employment or access to further education and training. For this reason, scholarships and other academic awards result in a benefit to some students, while excluding others who may be historically disadvantaged. Therefore, scholarships that restrict eligibility on the basis of prohibited grounds in the *Code* are not permissible unless the award:

- qualifies as a special program pursuant to subsection 14(1); or
- is restricted to Canadian citizens or permanent residents if the scholarship is for the purpose of fostering and developing participating in educational or other activities set out in subsection 16(2) of the *Code*, or
- is awarded by a religious, philanthropic, educational, fraternal or social institution or organization, to a member (section 18); or
- is an employment benefit to employees and their families (section 24(1)(d)).

5. — Relevant Sections of the *Code*

The Ontario *Human Rights Code* (Part II of this book) includes provisions relevant to this policy in the following sections: 1, 9, 14(1), 16(2), 18 and 24(1).

Policy on Sexual Harassment and Inappropriate Gender-Related Comments and Conduct

Approved by the Commission: September 10, 1996

1. — Introduction

The Ontario *Human Rights Code* (the "*Code*") states that it is public policy in Ontario to recognize the inherent dignity and worth of every person and to provide for equal rights and opportunities without discrimination. The provisions of the *Code* are aimed at creating a climate of understanding and mutual respect for the dignity and worth of each person, so that each person feels a part of the community and feels able to contribute to the community.

Inherent in this objective is the goal of ensuring that everyone can live and work in an environment which is free from harassment based on a prohibited ground of discrimination under the *Code*. The *Code* establishes the right to equal treatment without discrimination based on sex. Freedom from sexual harassment and other forms of unequal treatment expressed through demeaning comments and actions based on gender[1] is, therefore, a fundamental human right.[2]

Discrimination based on sex includes what is commonly referred to as sexual harassment or inappropriate comments and actions of a sexual nature.[3] The protection provided by the *Code* covers five areas of social interaction, namely, services, goods and facilities, occupancy of accommodation, contracts, employment, and membership in vocational associations such as trade unions.

---

[1]Gender is a cluster of social characteristics that are attributed to each sex. Based on stereotypes about what constitutes femaleness or maleness gender discrimination can take many forms. For example, calling a woman a "fat cow" may, in some circumstances, imply sexual unattractiveness.

[2]*Re Canada Post Corp. and Canadian Union of Postal Workers* (1988), 34 L.A.C. (3d) 27.

[3]*Bell v. Ladas* (1980), 1 C.H.R.R. D/158 (Ont. Bd. of Inq.).

Harassment and discrimination based on sex may not always be of a sexual nature. Sex discrimination may also include harassing comments or conduct made to a person because of his or her gender.[4]

> *Example*: A supervisor may continuously interrupt a female employee during meetings or comment on her physical appearance in a way that sets her apart from male employees as not being a fully participating equal in the organization, or by making such statements as "women don't belong in the boardroom."

The comments or conduct do not have to be made with the intention to discriminate to be in violation of the *Code*.

2. — Purpose of the Guidelines

The purpose of these guidelines is to assist individuals, community organizations and business establishments to understand the scope of the protection provided by the *Code* with regard to sexual harassment and inappropriate gender-related comments and conduct. This policy makes a clear distinction between accepted social interaction or consensual relations, and behaviour which is known or ought reasonably to be known to be unwelcome.

The policy also provides a framework for educational initiatives such as the development of training materials, anti-harassment policies and internal human rights complaint resolution mechanisms by employers and other establishments.

3. — The Ontario *Human Rights Code* and Sexual Harassment

Sexual harassment and inappropriate gender-related comments and conduct are complex issues which often involve one person's attempt to assert power over another. Sexual harassment and unequal treatment based on gender typically, but not exclusively, involves the exercise of power and authority over women, resulting in the reinforcement of a woman's subordinate status in relation to men.[5] It is important to note that sexual harassment and inappropriate gender-related comments and conduct are

---

[4] *Shaw v. Levac Supply Ltd.* (1990), 14 C.H.R.R. D/36 (Ont. Bd. of Inq.).

[5] *Cuff v. Gypsy Restaurant* (1987), 8 C.H.R.R. D/3972 (Ont. Bd. of Inq.).

prohibited regardless of the gender of the persons involved. The Commission has received complaints by men against women, as well as complaints involving persons of the same sex.

This power relationship can be particularly evident in employment situations. However, women tend to be more vulnerable to harassment by men, because relative to men, more women hold lower-paying, lower-authority and lower-status positions in the workplace. At the same time, even women in positions of authority are not free from sexual harassment or inappropriate gender-related behaviour.

Regardless of her position, this type of behaviour can diminish a woman's status and image in the eyes of other employees. Inappropriate gender-related comments or conduct can also endanger the continued employment of the harassed individual by negatively affecting her or his work performance, or undermining her or his sense of personal dignity, or in some cases causing physical and emotional illness.

4. — The *Code*

Sections 1, 2, 3, 5, 6 and 9 of the *Code* set out the basic right to equal treatment without discrimination because of sex in the areas of services, goods and facilities, occupancy of accommodation, contracts, employment, and vocational associations.

As stated earlier, sex discrimination includes inappropriate comments or conduct that are not, narrowly speaking, entirely sexual in nature.

The *Code* also includes provisions that specifically address sexual harassment in employment and accommodation, as well as sexual solicitation and reprisal for refusing a sexual advance.

4.1 — The Definition of "Harassment" under the *Code*

Section 10(1)(f) of the *Code* defines "harassment" as meaning:

> engaging in a course of vexatious comment or conduct that is known or ought reasonably to be known to be unwelcome.

a) — A Course of Vexatious Comment or Conduct

According to the definition of harassment in subsection 10(1)(f) of the *Code*, more than one event, or a "*course* of vexatious[6] comment or conduct" [emphasis added], must take place for there to be a violation of the

---

[6]"Vexatious conduct or comment" refers to actions or words that provoke, irritate, threaten, annoy, insult or demean, or result in some other form of discomfort.

Code. However, one incident could be significant or substantial enough to be interpreted by the Commission as constituting a breach of sections 1, 2, 3, 5 or 6 of the *Code*. Such an incident could be interpreted by the Commission as having an impact that is substantial enough to create a "poisoned environment" for some individuals because of their sex.

b) — Ought Reasonably to be Known to be Unwelcome

Comment or conduct "that is known or *ought reasonably to be known to be unwelcome*" [emphasis added] contains a subjective and an objective element. First, the harasser's own knowledge of how his or her behaviour is being received is part of the test. Second, from the point of view of a reasonable third party as well, i.e., how such behaviour might generally be received. In other words, the Commission or the board of inquiry can conclude on the basis of the evidence before it, that an individual knew, or should have known that his or her actions were unwelcome.[7]

Traditionally, the standard for judging such knowledge was based on the perspective of a "reasonable person," with "reasonable person" being drawn primarily from a male perspective. It included stereotypical notions of what forms of behaviour are, or are not, acceptable.

The proper objective standard should reflect full substantive equality.[8] The standard used to determine what the harasser ought to know is still gauged from the perspective of the "reasonable person."[9] However, the concept of the "reasonable person" has evolved to take into account the specific perspective of the *person who is harassed*: this means considering factors that ought reasonably to be known about the harassed person and his or her perspective as a member of a group protected under the *Code*.

> *Example*: A supervisor's ongoing questions to a woman about when she is going to marry and start having children may make this employee feel uncomfortable for a number of reasons. Her discomfort may be related to her own cultural background, a fear of losing her job,

---

[7] *Reed v. Cattolica Investments Ltd. and Salvatore Ragusa* (March 26, 1996), McNeilly, G., unreported (Ont. Bd. of Inq.).

[8] The substantive model of equality looks to the effect or result of the differential treatment rather than treating everyone in the same manner.

[9] The question to be asked is: "Would a person on the street, who is a member of the protected group (such as an Asian woman or a lesbian), and who experiences the behaviour in question, share the view that the behaviour was inappropriate?" Note that not all members of a group have to agree that the behaviour was inappropriate.

or to reasons related to other prohibited grounds of discrimination under the *Code*, such as creed, sexual orientation, or age.

As noted above, other prohibited grounds of discrimination such as race, creed, marital status or disability, may be intertwined with issues of gender. For persons who are members of more than one protected group certain forms of behaviour could have a particularly adverse impact.[10]

Example: Women with disabilities may feel particularly vulnerable to harassment and sexual assault. Inappropriate comments or conduct related to gender which may not necessarily be considered by some as problematic, may be viewed as particularly offensive or threatening by a woman with a disability.

It can reasonably be understood that some types of comments or behaviour are unwelcome based on the response of the person subjected to the behaviour, even when the person does not explicitly object. An example could be a person walking away in disgust after a coworker has asked questions of a sexual nature.

As previously noted, a person does not have to make explicit reference to another person's gender or be explicitly sexual for the behaviour to be contrary to the *Code*. Someone could indirectly harass a female employee in his area, with the intent of discouraging or driving her away from continuing her employment in a particular position, because she is a woman.[11]

4.2 — Harassment in Accommodation and Employment

Subsections 7(1) and (2) of the *Code* establishes a person's right to be free from sexual harassment and inappropriate gender-related comments and conduct in occupancy of accommodation and employment. Section 7(1) states:

> Every person who occupies accommodation has a right to freedom from harassment because of sex by the landlord or an agent of the landlord or by an occupant of the same building.

Section 7(2) states:

> Every person who is an employee has a right to freedom from harassment in the workplace because of sex by his or her employer or agent of the employer or by another employee.

---

[10]See further *Cuff. v. Gypsy Restaurant* at note 5.

[11]See further *Shaw v. Levac* at note 4.

4.3 — Sexual Solicitation or Advance

Subsection 7(3)(a) of the *Code* sets out a person's right to be free from unwelcome sexual advance or solicitation from an individual who is in a position to grant or deny a benefit to the person. The subsection states that:

> Every person has a right to be free from a sexual solicitation or advance made by a person in a position to confer, grant or deny a benefit or advancement to the person where the person making the solicitation or advance knows or ought reasonably to know that it is unwelcome.

This provision of the *Code* is violated when the person making the solicitation or advance knows, or should reasonably know, that such behaviour is unwelcome.

> *Example*: A professor or teacher makes an unwelcome sexual advance to a student and implies or explicitly makes it known that if s/he does not accept, she or he would likely not obtain passing grades. In a rental accommodation situation, a building superintendent makes granting a tenant's request for a transfer to a larger unit conditional upon receipt of sexual favours.

Sexual solicitation or advances covered by subsection 7(3)(a), can also occur between co-workers where one person is in a position to grant or deny an employment-related benefit to the other.

> *Example*: A situation could develop in which one worker makes the sharing of important job-related information with a colleague conditional upon the receipt of sexual favours from that colleague.

4.4 — Reprisal

Subsection 7(3)(b) of the *Code* sets out a person's right to be free from reprisal or threats of reprisal for rejecting a sexual solicitation or advance by someone who is in a position to grant or deny a benefit. Subsection 7(3)(b) states that:

> Every person has a right to be free from a reprisal or a threat of reprisal for the rejection of a sexual solicitation or advance where the reprisal is made or threatened by a person in a position to confer, grant or deny a benefit or advancement to the person.

> *Example*: A manager who fires an employee, or denies her or him a promotion because the employee refused a sexual proposition would be violating the employee's rights under subsection 7(3)(b). Similarly, a social worker who threatens to prepare a negative report which would

disqualify a welfare recipient who has refused a sexual advance by the worker would also be in violation of subsection 7(3)(b) of the *Code*.

Section 8 of the *Code* provides additional protection against reprisal for claiming and enforcing one's rights under the *Code*. Section 8 states that:

> Every person has a right to claim and enforce his or her rights under this *Act*, to institute and participate in proceedings under this *Act*, and to refuse to infringe a right of another person under this *Act*, without reprisal or threat of reprisal for so doing.

4.5 — Association

Section 12 of the *Code* protects the rights of a person who is associated with a person who is member of a group identified by the *Code*. It states that:

> A right under Part I is infringed where the discrimination is because of relationship, association or dealings with a person or persons identified by a prohibited ground of discrimination.

4.6 — Poisoned Environment

As noted above, a specific instance of sexual harassment or inappropriate gender-related comments or conduct might not meet the literal definition of harassment under the *Code*. However, there could be circumstances in which a single incident of inappropriate behaviour may be significant or substantial enough to constitute a breach of the *Code*, by creating a "poisoned environment" for some individuals because of their sex. In other words, there could be circumstances in which unequal treatment does not have to occur continually or repeatedly for there to be a violation of the *Code*.

Sections 1, 2, 3, 5 and 6 of the *Code*, which provide protection from sex discrimination in general, can be the basis for a claim that the inappropriate behaviour was substantial enough to create a "poisoned environment," resulting in unequal terms and conditions in employment, occupancy of accommodation, the provision of services, contracting, or membership in a vocational association. In an employment situation, for example, a poisoned environment can cause emotional or psychological stress for some persons in a particular environment because of their sex. Such stress could have a significant negative impact on the person's overall health and/or performance on the job.

The concept of a poisoned environment as a form of harassment or discrimination is based on the impact of the comments or conduct on an individual because of her or his sex, rather than the number of times the behaviour occurs. A poisoned environment can be created by the comments or actions of any person regardless of his or her position of authority or status in a given environment, including a co-worker, supervisor, manager, co-tenant, etc.

> *Example*: A single action giving rise to a poisoned environment could be a statement made by a union representative, expressing the belief that women in general, or women of a certain race or ethnic background, are not suitable as union representatives. Similarly, a poisoned environment may be created by the distribution or publishing of written materials on a college campus by male students about women which are seen to have a threatening or intimidating content.[12]

Even if the comments or conduct are not directed at one person, another individual may still experience a poisoned environment because she or he is also a member of the group targeted. A person whose co-worker receives this unequal treatment or who hears someone tell an offensive joke to another may view the behaviour as poisoning the environment.[13]

As earlier indicated, sexual harassment is often interpreted as objectionable comments or conduct of a "sexual" nature. However, sexual harassment, in the broader context of unequal treatment based on gender, may refer to instances where the behaviour is not overtly sexual in nature, but is related to the person's gender, and demeans or causes personal humiliation or embarrassment to the recipient.

Examples of sexual harassment and inappropriate gender-related behaviour within the meaning of the *Code* include, but are not limited to, comments, gestures and non-verbal behaviour, visual materials, and physical contact. The following is not an exhaustive list but should assist in identifying what may constitute sexual harassment or inappropriate gender-related comments and conduct:

i) gender-related comments about an individual's physical characteristics or mannerisms

---

[12]*Saskatchewan (Human Rights Commission) v. Engineering Society* (1989), 10 C.H.R.R. D/5636 (Sask. Bd of Inq.).

[13]Depending on the fact situation, a human rights complaint may be filed under Part I of the *Code*, or be based on discrimination because of association (section 12).

See further, Judith Keene, *Human Rights in Ontario* (Toronto: Carswell, 1992) at 145.

ii) unwelcome physical contact

iii) suggestive or offensive remarks or innuendoes about members of a specific gender

iv) propositions of physical intimacy

v) gender-related verbal abuse, threats, or taunting

vi) leering or inappropriate staring

vii) bragging about sexual prowess

viii) demands for dates or sexual favours

ix) offensive jokes or comments of a sexual nature about an employee, client or tenant

x) display of sexually offensive pictures, graffiti or other materials

xi) questions or discussions about sexual activities

xii) paternalism based on gender which a person feels undermines his or her self-respect or position of responsibility

xiii) rough and vulgar humour or language related to gender.

A situation could arise in which particular comments or actions might not be intended to offend another person, but result in a violation of that person's rights under the *Code*. The reason for this is that intent is not a prerequisite to establishing that the treatment is discriminatory.[14] Rather, the Commission looks to the effect or the result of the comments or actions on the recipient.

> *Example*: Even the best intentioned "compliments" regarding a woman's appearance, hair, clothes etc., if made on a repeated basis in the work environment, or during a formal business meeting, can set a woman apart as different. Such comments also undermine her credibility as a professional.

5. — Burden of Proof: Evidentiary Issues

Sexual harassment and inappropriate gender-related comments and conduct do not frequently occur in full public view. Since there are often no witnesses or material evidence to these comments or conduct, issues of evi-

[14]W.S. Tarnopolsky, *Discrimination and the Law in Canada* (Toronto: De Boo, 1982), at 109-122.

dence and credibility often arise in complaints alleging sexual harassment.[15]

Under the *Code*, the onus of proving an allegation of sexual harassment or inappropriate gender-related behaviour rests with the complainant. After a matter is referred to a board of inquiry the Commission has to demonstrate before the board that, on a "balance of probabilities," there was a contravention of the *Code*. The burden of proof for demonstrating harassment under the *Code* is not as onerous as the proof required for establishing guilt in criminal cases.

Proving a case on a "balance of probabilities" is a civil burden of proof, meaning that there is evidence to support the allegation that the comments or conduct "more likely than not" took place, and that the behaviour constituted sexual harassment or inappropriate gender-related comments or conduct within the meaning of the *Code*.

> *Example*: An investigation into a complaint may reveal that the complainant did not welcome or consent to the behaviour alleged to have occurred. It is then up to the respondent to demonstrate that the behaviour did not occur or did not constitute a violation of the *Code*. The respondent may introduce evidence that the complainant is mistaken, or misinterpreted the comments or conduct.

In the absence of independent witnesses or corroborating evidentiary material, complaints alleging sexual harassment often turn on the credibility of the parties. Boards of inquiry have accepted that it is difficult sometimes to make a finding based on credibility only, but acknowledge that boards often have to rely on subjective evidence presented.

Where credibility is at issue, similar fact evidence[16] may be introduced to show that a pattern of behaviour might have occurred.

> *Example:* Similar fact evidence could include testimony from others who indicate that they have been treated similarly, based on their gen-

---

[15] *Phillips v. Hermiz* (1985), 5 C.H.R.R. D/2450 (Sask. Bd. of Inq.).

[16] "Similar fact evidence" is evidence of past similar conduct by the alleged harasser which may be relied upon to support an allegation of harassment. The usefulness of this kind of evidence in supporting a claim of harassment depends mostly on whether the past incidents of misconduct are sufficiently similar to the kind of harassment alleged by the complainant. For example, were other female employees in receipt of similar comments or treatment by the respondent?

der, by the alleged harasser. It may also show intent or wilfulness, which could call into question the credibility of a respondent whose defence is that the conduct was intended to be a joke, or was a mistake or the result of a misunderstanding.

6. — Corporate Liability

Section 45 of the *Code* establishes that a corporation is liable for the actions of an officer, official, employee or agent of the corporation, when such actions are done in the course of their employment. Section 45 also provides an exception to this corporate liability with regard to the harassment provisions of subsections 2(2) and 5(2), and s. 7. In instances of harassment within the framework of subsections 2(2) or 5(2), or s. 7 of the *Code*, the corporate respondent[17] may not necessarily be liable where it can be established that the respondent was unaware of, or had no reason to believe that there was a problem relating to sexual harassment.

However, the liability of the corporation with regard to subsections 2(2) or 5(2), or s. 7 is restored, if the offending party is a part of or is the actual "directing mind" of the corporation.[18] In such a situation, a "directing mind" represents the persona of the corporation itself, as if the two were the same, and the latter becomes liable because it is deemed to have breached the *Code*.

Therefore, corporate liability may be found:

a) where the employer's personal action, either directly, or indirectly infringes a protected right, or authorizes or condones, the inappropriate behaviour

b) where an employee responsible for the harassment or inappropriate behaviour, or who knew of the sexual harassment or inappropriate gender-related behaviour, or that a poisoned environment existed, but did not attempt to remedy the situation is part of the "directing mind" of the corporation.[19]

---

[17] "Corporate respondent" is the business entity which may be held responsible for conduct of persons who are associated with the business and who are alleged to have contravened the *Code*.

[18] *Edilma Olarte et al. v. Rafael deFilippis and Commodore Business Machines Ltd.* (1983), 4 C.H.R.R. D/1744 [4] and [5]; affirmed (1984), 14 D.L.R. (4th) 118 (Div. Ct.).

[19] *Kerryann Henwood v. Gerry Van Wart Sales Inc. and Claudio Saggese* (February 21, 1995), Anand, R., unreported (Ont. Bd. of Inq.).

6.1 — "Directing Mind": An Employer or its Agents

Employees with supervisory authority may be viewed as part of a corporation's "directing mind," if they function, or are seen to function as a representative of the organization itself. Generally speaking, an employee who performs management duties is part of the "directing mind" of the corporation.[20] If an employee is part of the "directing mind" of the corporation and a violation of the *Code* occurs while this person is carrying out corporate duties, the act of the employee becomes an act of the corporation.

A person who is a central decision-maker in a service provision or accommodation-related situation may also be liable if she or he knew of the harassment or inappropriate gender-related comment or conduct and did not address it. A community centre supervisor or a superintendent of a rental accommodation facility are examples of persons who may be seen as part of the "directing mind" of an organization.

Persons who are not identified as supervisors *per se*, including members of the bargaining unit, may also be "directing mind" if they have supervisory authority or have significant responsibility for the guidance of employees.

> *Example*: A head chef has the responsibility to address such problems if they arise among the kitchen staff.
>
> *Example*: A lead-hand who is part of the bargaining unit would have "directing mind" authority with regard to union members.

A corporate employer may also be responsible for a supervisor's actions where the employer had, or should have had, knowledge of the harassment and failed to take immediate and appropriate action to correct the situation.

On being made aware of such inappropriate comments or conduct, an employer is required to take immediate action to remedy the situation. In particular, where the employer is satisfied that the allegation has been substantiated, the employer should consider both disciplinary action and preventative steps including the development and introduction of policy statements and educational initiatives. Depending on the fact situation, disciplinary measures could range from a verbal warning or a letter of reprimand to termination of employment.

It should be noted that an employer may also be held liable for incidents of sexual harassment or inappropriate behaviour in situations involving activi-

---

[20] *Michael Naraine v. Ford Motor Company of Canada Ltd., et al.* (July 25, 1996), Backhouse, C., unreported (Ont. Bd. of Inq.).

ties or events which occur outside of normal business hours or off business premises, but are linked to the workplace and employment.

> *Example*: An employer may be held liable for incidents that take place during business trips, company parties, or other company-related functions.

6.2 — Obligation to Maintain a Harassment-Free Environment

Employers, rental accommodation providers, service providers, professional associations, and unions all have an obligation to ensure that their respective environments are free from behaviour that could constitute sexual harassment. An employer may be responsible for harassment by supervisors, managers, co-workers, and in some cases non-employees, who are present in the workplace, particularly if the employer knew or should have known about the alleged harassment and failed to take remedial action.

Liability on the part of an organization for harassment of its employees by non-employees, such as customers, will depend on the facts of a particular situation, including the employer's knowledge of and control over the situation, and what corrective measures might be available.

> *Example*: A fitness club owner, on learning of female or male staff being sexually harassed by a patron or someone who is a member of the club, has an obligation to address this problem. If the allegations can be substantiated the owner may decide to suspend or not renew the harasser's membership. Membership agreements usually contain clauses permitting the club to deal with members in such circumstances.
>
> *Example*: The superintendent or manager of a building, on becoming aware that female tenants are being harassed by non-residents in the unlocked laundry, is under an obligation to take steps to correct the situation, such as securing the laundry room from non-tenants.

7. — Remedies under the *Code*

The purpose of human rights legislation is not to find fault but to eliminate discrimination and to provide redress. It is meant to be preventative and remedial, rather than punitive.[21] A remedy to a complaint might include restoring the complainant to a position the individual would have held had the *Code* not been violated. It may consist of compensation for loss of earn-

[21] *Robichaud v. Canada (Treasury)*, [1987] 8 C.H.R.R. D/4326 (C.H.R.T.).

ings or job opportunities, or damages for mental anguish suffered as a result of the violation.

Human rights remedies also address issues of public interest. This may include requiring changes to an organization's policies, the implementation of training initiatives, the establishment of internal human rights complaint resolution mechanisms, introduction of anti-harassment policies, a written apology, etc.

8. — Filing a Complaint

When a person believes that she or he has been subjected to sexual harassment or other forms of inappropriate gender-related comments or conduct, the individual should seek to resolve the problem through any internal policies or resolution mechanisms the organization may have in place. However, while many companies now have internal human rights complaint resolution mechanisms, these procedures do not replace an individual's right to file a complaint with the Commission. A complaint filed with the Commission may be withdrawn at any time during the complaint process. Under section 34 of the *Code*, the Commission has the discretion to refuse to deal with certain complaints, where the matter: (1) can be more appropriately dealt with under another provincial statute; (2) is "trivial, frivolous, vexatious or made in bad faith;" (3) is not within the Commission's jurisdiction or (4) is based on facts which are more than six months old.

> *Example*: The Commission may exercise its discretion to not deal with a complaint if it appears to the Commission that the person is bringing the complaint in order to embarrass an organization or another person, or if the allegations relate to events that occurred more than six months before the person files a complaint with the Commission, or where there is a grievance procedure in place under a collective agreement to address complaints of discrimination in the workplace.

9. — Collective Agreements and Company Policies

As many sexual harassment complaints arise in the context of employment, the Commission encourages employers and organizations to take responsibility for preventing and remedying incidents of sexual harassment and inappropriate gender-related comments and conduct. The Commission encourages organizations to develop and adopt in-house anti-harassment policies and to ensure that the workplace is properly informed and educated about the nature, effects, and cost of this type of behaviour.

9.1 — Collective Agreements

An increasing number of collective agreements and company policies include specific clauses relating to the prevention and resolution of incidents of discrimination and sexual harassment in the workplace. Employers and labour representatives are recognizing their liabilities under the *Code*, as well as their shared responsibility to maintain workplace environments that are free from sexual harassment.

Persons are not obligated to exhaust an internal complaint resolution mechanism before considering other avenues of complaint such as approaching the Commission or filing a grievance. An individual may elect to file two complaints at the same time — one under the employer's internal policy and one with the Commission. However, if there is a grievance procedure in place under a collective agreement, the Commission may elect to exercise its discretion under s. 34 of the *Code*, and decide to not deal with a complaint. This is because section 48(12)(j) of the *Labour Relations Act* allows labour arbitrators to interpret and apply human rights legislation.

9.2 — Internal Policies

Internal anti-harassment and anti-discrimination policies do not fall under provincial legislation and therefore the Commission does not consider them in the same way as the grievance procedure under a collective agreement. This means that there is the option of contacting the Commission if the resolution obtained through the in-house process is not satisfactory. In which case, the complaint *should* be filed within the six-month limitation period which begins from the time of the alleged harassment. Failure to do so could result in the Commission deciding not to deal with the complaint, subject to section 34(1)(d) of the *Code*.

10. — Relevant *Human Rights Code* Provisions

The Ontario *Human Rights Code* (Part II of this book) includes provisions relevant to this policy in the following sections: 1, 2(1)(2), 3, 5(1)(2), 6, 7(1)(2)(3), 8, 12, 34(1) and 45(1)(2).

Developing Procedures to Resolve Human Rights Complaints within Your Organization

Approved by the Commission: June 19, 1996

1. — Introduction

The Ontario *Human Rights Code* (the "*Code*") states that it is public policy in Ontario to recognize the inherent dignity and worth of every person and to provide for equal rights and opportunities without discrimination. The provisions of the *Code* are aimed at creating a climate of understanding and mutual respect for the dignity and worth of each person, so that each person feels a part of the community and feels able to contribute to the community.

The purpose of this guide is to help organizations develop effective and fair ways to deal with claims of harassment or discrimination that may arise in the workplace. Since most of the questions that the Commission receives deal with human rights issues arising in employment, these guidelines focus on the workplace. However, the principles in these guidelines may also apply in some circumstances to other areas covered by the *Code*, such as a rental accommodation situation.

Ignoring acts of harassment and discrimination has a bad effect on the workplace. Low employee morale, high stress, damaged professional reputations and employee absences are a few of the results of not paying attention to discrimination and harassment.

Dealing promptly with these issues will save you time and money. By letting everyone know what the rules are and what forms of behaviour are not acceptable, you may avoid costly and upsetting procedures in the courts or before special tribunals. In other words, strong policies and programs prevent human rights complaints and make good business sense.

The Commission suggests that employers develop internal anti-discrimination policies and procedures to solve complaints that may arise as part of a broad program to build an environment that is free from discrimination and harassment. Such a program should be:

i) based on a strong message against discrimination and harassment

ii) effective in investigating and settling specific complaints

iii) communicated clearly to all staff or members of the organization

iv) respectful of the privacy of all the individuals taking part in the process and

v) wherever possible, part of an ongoing educational program in the workplace.

2. — Who is Responsible?

2.1 — Employer Responsibility

Employers have a responsibility to:

i) provide a working environment that is free from harassment and discrimination and

ii) deal effectively, quickly and fairly with any situations involving claims of harassment or discrimination that come to their attention.

Employers could be held liable by a court or tribunal if they or their managers do not act to put an end to discrimination or harassment in their workplaces.

2.2 — The Role of the Ontario Human Rights Commission

Internal policies and procedures sometimes fail to resolve a problem of harassment and discrimination. If such a problem is brought to the attention of the Commission, it may be necessary for the Commission to intervene to try to settle the complaint.

3. — Guidelines for Developing Internal Processes in Your Organization

Several factors, including how complex or how large your organization might be, could determine the kind of procedures you use. These guidelines should provide a useful framework for any organization to use. The following elements should be part of any complete strategy to resolve human rights issues that may arise in the workplace:

i) an anti-harassment or anti-discrimination policy

ii) a complaint resolution procedure and

iii) on-going education programs.

These elements should be developed together with the union or other employees' organizations where they may exist in any given workplace.

3.1 — Policy

A policy statement should make it clear that discrimination and harassment are violations of the *Code* and will not be tolerated. The policy should describe the types of behaviour that are discriminatory, and should send the message that management takes this issue seriously. The policy should spell out what disciplinary measure would be applied, including the possibility of the loss of employment, if a claim of harassment or discrimination is proven.

It is important to make it clear to employees that having an internal complaint resolution procedure in place does not in any way stop an individual from going to the Commission, if she or he wants to.[1] Some employees may also have rights under employee collective agreements that will give them other choices for dealing with a problem.

Policies should include:

i) a list of the prohibited grounds of discrimination listed in the *Code* (see Appendix "A")

(ii) a definition of "harassment" as defined by the *Code* (subsection 10(1); see Appendix "B")

(iii) an explanation of the notion of a "poisoned environment"[2] as a violation of the *Code* (see Appendix "C") and

(iv) an explanation of the liability of corporations for the behaviour of their officers, managers, employees, *etc.* (see Appendix "B").

All employees should be aware of this internal policy and of any procedures in place for resolving complaints. You can do this by:

i) distributing the policy to everyone when it is introduced

ii) sharing it with new employees when they are hired and

iii) training any employee who becomes a member of management on the contents of the policy.

---

[1]*Ontario Human Rights Commission v. Etobicoke (Borough)*, [1982] 1 S.C.R. 202 states that one cannot contract out of the rights under the *Code*.

[2]A "poisoned environment" is a form of discrimination. It may be created by comments or actions of any person regardless of her/his position or status. These offensive comments or actions spoil the work, housing or other environment. The poisoned environment forms an unequal term or condition of employment, accommodation, *etc.* and is therefore a violation of the right to be free from discrimination. See *Wei Fu v. Ontario Government Protective Services* (1985), 6 C.H.R.R. D/2797 (Ont. Bd. of Inquiry); *Dhillon v. F.W. Woolworth Co.* (1982), 3 C.H.R.R. D/743 (Ont. Bd. of Inquiry); *Lee v. T.J. Applebee's Food Conglomeration* (1987), 9 C.H.R.R. D/4781 (Ont. Bd. of Inquiry).

3.2 — Complaint Resolution Procedures

a) — Appoint an Advisor

Anyone who feels that she or he has been discriminated against or harassed in the workplace may want to discuss the situation with someone in the company who is familiar with the policy. This person is called an "advisor," and should be able to provide advice on how to deal with the problem, including information on how to file an internal complaint with management. A person who has been accused of harassment or discrimination should also have the right to meet with an advisor.

The advisor is supposed to be neutral, objective and knowledgeable about human rights issues. The person should be able to provide information and explain choices for dealing with a problem, including the option to approach the Commission for help. The advisor should also know about grievance procedures under collective agreements or other internal complaint procedures that may apply to the situation. The advisor should be professional and experienced. He or she also has to make sure that all issues are kept strictly confidential.

b) — Documentation

For everyone involved in the process, it is important to make and keep written notes about the events leading to the complaint. These details should include:

i) what happened — a description of the events or situation

ii) when it happened — dates and times of the events or incidents

iii) where did it happen and

iv) who saw it happen — the names of any witnesses, if any.

As well, any other documents or materials, such as letters, notes, offensive pictures, *etc.*, that may have something to do with the complaint should be kept.

c) — Protection from Reprisal

Persons who make a complaint, as well as anyone else who is involved, should not be penalized for doing so. This is called "reprisal." Protection from reprisal covers:

i) complainants

ii) witnesses

iii) advisors

iv) representatives of complainants and witnesses

v) investigators and

vi) decision makers/management.

d) — Representation

The people involved in an internal complaint resolution process should be allowed to have someone represent them if they wish. Representatives may include union stewards or a colleague.

e) — Investigators

Investigators are responsible for examining the circumstances of a complaint. They should therefore be, and be seen to be, as independent and objective as possible. Wherever possible, an investigator should not be in a position of direct authority over any of the people involved in a complaint, but should report to someone with the authority to make decisions and have them enforced. If not, the process will be seen to be weak and without "teeth."

An investigation should not be carried out by anyone who is seen as taking sides with either party. For example, it is not very likely that a lawyer who often represents management in labour disputes will be seen as being objective by non-management employees. Also, the investigator should not be someone in a position to have any power or influence over the career progress of either of the parties.

Investigators must:

i) know about human rights in general, and what the *Code* says, in particular and

ii) make sure that the investigation process is confidential.

In most cases, investigations should start immediately after an investigator is chosen, and finish within 90 days.

f) — Resolution

If a complaint cannot be settled through the internal procedure, the employee should be told that a complaint may be filed with the Commission or a grievance filed with the union if one exists in the particular workplace.

3.3 — Education Programs

Education is an important part of preventing harassment in the workplace. Training programs for all staff ensure that everyone knows what the rules are and how they will be applied.

Everyone responsible for enforcing the policy or advising on procedures should be thoroughly aware of the policies and procedures that are part of the workplace rules. The organization can:

i) provide up-to-date information about human rights issues and important court decisions or board of inquiry decisions in this area of the law

ii) make sure that all staff are trained on how to deal with discrimination and harassment in the workplace

iii) measure the effectiveness of the policies and procedures, and change them if necessary and

iv) respond immediately to any claim of discrimination or harassment.

Both the person making a complaint and the person against whom it is made should know how the internal procedure works. This includes information like:

i) who will investigate

ii) how long the process is likely to take

iii) what you will receive at the end of the investigation

iv) who will decide what action the employer will take and

v) what solutions or results are possible.

The person making the complaint should also be told about the time limits that apply with the other choices available for the enforcement of human rights, such as filing a grievance with the union or a complaint with the Commission.

For example, complaints under the *Code must* be filed within six months from the date the last act of alleged discrimination occurred. The Commission has the choice, under section 34(1)(d) of the *Code*, as to whether or not to deal with complaints which are filed past this time limit. For a grievance under a collective agreement, employees should be aware that a much shorter time limit (days or weeks) may apply.

4. — The Ontario Human Rights Commission

A person who wishes to complain directly to the Commission may do so, even if she or he has used, or has chosen not to use, the company's internal procedures.

If a person believes that he or she has been harassed or discriminated against, the Commission will try to settle the dispute, if possible. If that fails, the complaint will then be investigated by the Commission.

5. — Will the Commission Deal with All Complaints?

According to the *Code*, the Commission does not have to deal with all complaints. The *Code* allows the Commission to decide not to deal with a complaint in certain situations:

i) if another provincial law, such as the *Employment Standards Act* or the grievance procedure under the *Labour Relations Act*, would be a better law for dealing with the complaint

ii) if the complaint is trivial, petty, bothersome or made in bad faith

iii) if the employer is outside provincial law and therefore the *Code* does not apply (*e.g.*, if someone has a complaint against a bank or an airline, that complaint would be dealt with under federal jurisdiction) or

iv) if an individual files a complaint more than six months after the events upon which the complaint is based. The Commission will decide not to deal with complaints of this kind if the complainant's delay was in bad faith (*e.g.*, if a person delays the filing of a complaint on purpose), or if the delay causes significant prejudice to the employer (*e.g.*, if after six months, important documents are destroyed or witnesses are no longer available).

Only the Commissioners have the right to make a decision not to deal with a complaint. In such situations, the Commission will decide each case on its own merit or value. The Commission by law has to provide reasons to the parties when a decision is made not to deal with a case under section 34. If a decision is made not to deal with a complaint, this does not mean the complaint has been dismissed or evaluated on its merits. It simply means that the complaint is outside of the Commission's control, or that it would be unfair to the parties to go ahead with the complaint for the reasons outlined above.

6. — The Commission and the Board of Inquiry

The Commission is required by the *Code* to try to settle complaints and to conduct investigations. If the Commission cannot settle a complaint and if there is enough evidence, the Commission may refer the complaint to a board of inquiry.

Boards of inquiry are separate decision-making bodies or tribunals that are completely independent from the Commission. The board of inquiry has a wide range of powers to make orders against the employer, organization or individual who is named as a respondent to the complaint. Orders may include offers of employment or job reinstatement, financial compensation for lost wages, mental anguish, *etc*. A board of inquiry can also order an employer to adapt the workplace to accommodate the needs of a person with a disability.

APPENDIX A — RELEVANT ONTARIO HUMAN RIGHTS CODE PROVISIONS

The Ontario *Human Rights Code* (Part II of this book) includes provisions relevant to this policy in the following sections: 10(1), 34(1) and 45(1).

Guide to Releases with Respect to Human Rights Complaints

Approved by the Commission: May 30, 2006

1. — Introduction

The issue of how to deal with releases has been a matter of concern to the Commission.

Under section 34(1)(b) of the *Human Rights Code* [the "*Code*"] the Ontario Human Rights Commission [the "Commission"] can exercise its discretion to not deal with a complaint where the complaint has been brought in bad faith. The Commission often receives requests from employers to exercise this power in cases where an employee has either been terminated, dismissed, or resigned from his or her position and has then signed a "release."

Many standard form releases will often contain a broadly worded clause simply indicating that the person agrees that he or she "will not bring any proceedings or claims" or "waives all rights" under, amongst other things, the *Code*.

Employers take the position that in the face of such a release, to permit the complaint to proceed would constitute bad faith. When confronted with such a claim, complainants usually take the position that they were not aware of what they were signing, or that they did not know about the discrimination at the time the release was signed, or that they did not have enough time to think about what to do, or that they felt pressured into signing the release because they believed that if they did not they would not receive any severance pay at all, or simply that they needed the money right away.

Ontario courts and the Supreme Court of Canada have set out important principles that have assisted the Commission in dealing with these often-difficult release cases. Accordingly, the Commission has formed the view that the time is ripe for the development of a guide to releases with respect to human rights complaints. It is hoped that this Guide will serve to assist both employers and employees and will help them to structure termination agreements and releases that reflect appropriate human rights principles.

In addition, the Commission offers a sample proposed text for a release of a human rights claim. The text is intended to address a number of these important principles. Mere use of the words in this text alone, however, is not enough. Parties to a release should also deal with each other in a manner consistent with the principles and procedures set out in this Guide. It is important, therefore, to review the content of this Guide, including the tips for employers and employees in the Appendix in negotiating and concluding a release of a human rights complaint.

The Commission has identified that the standard form release that is often used is problematic for a number of reasons. Accordingly, the Commission proposes the following text as being preferable:

1. The parties agree that they have discussed or otherwise canvassed any and all human rights complaints, concerns or issues arising out of or in respect to the employee's employment at Company "A."
2. The parties agree that this agreement constitutes a full and final settlement of any existing, planned or possible complaint or complaints against the employer under the *Human Rights Code* up to the date of this agreement, arising out of or in respect to the employee's employment at Company "A."
3. The parties agree that the employee has received a separate sum in the amount of $X as compensation for settling and resolving the outstanding human rights complaint, concern or issue.

3a. [Where the employee agrees that that there are no human rights issues or concerns, the following can be included instead of paragraphs 2 and 3]: The employee agrees that he or she is aware of his or her rights under the *Human Rights Code*, and confirms that he or she is not asserting such rights or advancing a human rights claim or complaint.

4. The parties further agree that signing this agreement is not a condition for the employee to first receiving money to which he would otherwise be entitled to by operation of law. Such monies include the separate sum of $X for wages, $Y for statutory severance pay, and $Z for statutory termination pay.
5. The employee agrees that he [or she] has been given sufficient time and opportunity to obtain independent legal advice before signing this settlement agreement and

   (a) He [or she] has done so, or

   (b) He [or she] has freely chosen not to do so.

2. — Section 34(1)(b)

A precondition for the operation of s. 34(1)(b) of the *Code* is a finding by the Commission that a complainant has acted in "bad faith." The mere existence of the signed release is not, without more information, sufficient to conclude that the human rights complaint was brought in bad faith. Rather, the Commission is required to look into the circumstances surrounding the signing of the release.

In legal terms, the Commission must satisfy itself that the complainant should be estopped (i.e., prohibited) from proceeding with the complaint. To meet the test of bad faith, the Commission must find that the evidence reveals not an honest or negligent mistake on the complainant's part but an *intention* to mislead — the conscious doing of a wrong because of "dishonest purpose" or "ill will."[1]

Where a complainant has fully agreed to settle a human rights complaint, has received or was provided with adequate time to receive legal advice has signed the release form and has received sufficient consideration, only the filing of a human rights complaint may well constitute such a dishonest purpose or ill will. This would prohibit him or her from proceeding with the human rights complaint because to proceed with a complaint that has already been settled would be bad faith.

3. — Common Law Principles

A release is a contract. Under that contract, one party agrees not to take any proceedings, or further proceedings, against the other. The purpose of a release is to prohibit person A from proceeding with a subsequent claim against person B.

As a first step, for a contract to exist, a court must be satisfied that there was an "accord," which consists of "agreement" and "consideration" and "satisfaction."

3.1 — Agreement

Agreement is "a mutual assent to do a thing" — a common understanding.

A court must be satisfied either that the parties had a meeting of the minds, or that the party accepting the funds acted in such a way as to cause the other party to believe and act upon the belief that the settlement was deemed satisfactory, and that no further claim would be advanced.

3.2 — Consideration

Consideration is the *quid pro quo* of a contract — the giving of one valuable thing for another, without which a contract is not valid and binding. An individual who signs a release gives up something valuable — a right — in

[1] Black's Law Dictionary, 5th Edition (West Publishing Company, St. Paul Minnesota, 1979) p. 127, definition of "bad faith."

exchange for something else of value — usually (but not always) financial compensation. For example, in some cases adequate compensation may be an apology, or the removal of a negative reference in an employee's file.

3.3 — Satisfaction

Satisfaction is the "carrying into effect of an accord;" that is, the carrying out of the agreed-upon obligation, such as the payment of the money, or the giving of the apology.

4. — The Special Status of Human Rights Legislation: "Settlement vs. Contracting Out"

A person cannot be required to "contract out" of the protection of the *Human Rights Code*.[2] This means that a person cannot agree to relinquish his or her right to file a human rights complaint, since such a right is guaranteed by section 32 of the *Code* to any person that believes that their rights have been infringed.

However, one can agree to settle a human rights complaint. A settlement is not a promise to relinquish a right, but a promise not to proceed with a claim because it has been resolved. The *quid pro quo* need not be a substantial sum of money; indeed, it may be a letter of reference, or an apology. But there must be evidence that the complainant received some consideration as vindication or recognition of a right.

This distinction between "contracting out," which is prohibited, and settling a complaint, which is permitted, may appear complex at first. However, the

---

[2]Human rights legislation sets out a floor beneath which the parties cannot contract out. Given its public and fundamental nature, "no one, unless clearly authorized by law to do so, may contractually agree to suspend its operation and thereby put oneself beyond the reach of its protection," (Insurance Corporation of *British Columbia v. Heerspink*, [1982] 2 S.C.R. 145 at 158). Any contract having that effect is void, as contrary to public policy (*Ontario Human Rights Commission v. Etobicoke (City)*, [1982] 1 S.C.R. 202 at 213-14). Human rights legislation frequently deals with situations where the parties may not possess equal bargaining power. By prohibiting the ability to contract out of the statute, the courts have prevented the exploitation of inequality of bargaining power. If contracting out were allowed, those without bargaining power might be coerced or forced to give up their rights under human rights legislation (*Newfoundland Association of Public Employees v. Newfoundland (Green Bay Health Care Centre)*, [1996] 2 S.C.R. 3 at para. 21). See also: *Leisure World Nursing Homes Ltd. and Director of Employment Standards* (1980), 29 O.R. (2d) 144 (Div. Ct.).

difference can usually be determined by the answer to one straightforward question: Did both the employer and employee know of the existence of a human rights complaint or, if not, a formal complaint at least of the existence of a human rights concern or issue, prior to the release being signed? If there was no knowledge at all of the presence of a human rights issue between the parties, it cannot be said that a human rights complaint was settled. One cannot settle an issue of which one is not even aware. There is not "a meeting of minds." The very first of the common law requirements for a contract, an agreement or accord is not present. (This can be contrasted with the situation where the complainant positively asserts that he has no human rights issues or concerns and the employer relies on this assertion, which is further discussed below).

When a standard release containing a clause purporting to prohibit the bringing of a human rights complaint is presented to the Commission by an employer in support of a s. 34(1)(b) application, the Commission must be satisfied that the agreement in question is not a case of contracting-out in advance, but is a settlement after the fact. Proof that the parties raised a human rights concern or issue will be required.

Accordingly, as a very first step, the Commission requires some evidence that the parties to a release were aware of the human rights issue. Otherwise, a statement in the release that the complainant agrees not to file a complaint or commence a proceeding under the *Code* will constitute contracting out, and the release will not be evidence of "bad faith" under s. 34. It will not be a bar to proceeding.

Where the human rights issue was discussed or raised in writing between the parties, then the first of the common law requirements will be present. So long as the requirements for consideration and satisfaction are met, the release will likely constitute a valid settlement of the complaint.

This approach is supported by cases that have recognized the unequal bargaining power between employers and employees.[3] When one side has a

---

[3]In *Slaight Communications Inc. v. Davidson*, [1989] 1 S.C.R. 1038 at 1051-1052, the Court quoted with approval the following description of the employment relationship:

> The relation between an employer and an isolated employee or worker is typically a relation between a bearer of power and one who is not a bearer of power. In its inception it is an act of submission, in its operation it is a condition of subordination. The main object of labour law has always been, and we venture to say will always be, a countervailing force to counteract the inequality of bargaining power which is inherent and must be inherent in the employment relationship.

strong bargaining advantage, it is not unfair to ask it to provide proof that a release, in fact, constitutes a settlement.

Determining whether or not a human rights issue was discussed or raised during the negotiations leading up to the signing of the release may be contentious. The parties may disagree, after the fact, as to whether or not this occurred. In this regard, the conduct of the parties and the terms of the release itself will be important. Where, for example, the respondent can show that it sought details of the human rights issue from the complainant prior to drawing up the release, this will be strong evidence that the issue was raised. Similarly, where the resolution involves an apology from the respondent for the alleged misconduct, this is an indicator that the human rights issue was resolved. Finally, in those cases in which the terms of the resolution separately demarcate a sum of money to compensate for "any alleged violations of the human rights of the complainant," this will be a very strong indication that the case involved a settlement of an outstanding human rights issue.

The settlement of a human rights complaint should be explicit. In *Syndicat Northcrest v. Amselem*, [2004] 2 S.C.R. 551 at para. 100, the Supreme Court of Canada has stated, in the context of foregoing a right under the *Charter of Rights and Freedoms*:

> [A]t a minimum, waiver of a fundamental right such as freedom of religion, if possible at all, presumably need not only be voluntary; it must also be explicit, stated in express, specific and clear terms. Not only would a general prohibition on constructions, such as the one in the declaration of co-ownership, be insufficient to ground a finding of waiver, but arguably so would any document lacking an explicit reference to the affected *Charter* right.

There is, however, at least one instance where the failure on the part of the parties to raise a human rights concern at the time of the release could still lead to a finding of bad faith. In order to calculate a fair settlement, an employer may canvass with the employee all outstanding claims, such as any wrongful dismissal claims, benefit claims, and any outstanding human rights complaints or issues. If the employee, having been given a fair opportunity to consult with a legal or other advisor, expressly says that there are

---

Similarly, in *Milne v. Ocean Express Ltd.* (1989), 26 C.C.E.L. 187 at 189-190 (B.C. C.A.), in which the Court adopted a "fairness and reasonableness" approach:

> Courts have generally implied concepts of reasonableness, or found some way of protecting employees even in the face of written contracts of employment, as the employer or master is usually in a dominant position at the time that the master and servant relationship is created.

"no" human rights concerns, but later turns around and files a human rights complaint, this may constitute bad faith. This is not because the complaint has been settled. Indeed, if the parties proceeded on the basis that there was no human rights issue it cannot be said that a human rights complaint was settled. Rather, this will be because the employer has relied in good faith on the representations of the employee in an attempt to obtain finality and closure on the issue. The employee's deliberate dishonesty in the face of an explicit request may well disentitle him or her to proceed with a complaint. Such dishonesty would normally amount to the "intention to mislead" or "ill will" that constitutes bad faith. In such a case, the complainant should be required to provide a good explanation as to why he or she expressly stated that there were no human rights issues against the employer. If, for example, the human rights issue did not become known until after the release was signed, or if the employee can demonstrate that he or she truly did not understand or appreciate the content of his or her representation, then there could be a conclusion that no bad faith was present.

Where the evidence is clear that human rights issues did not form a part of the discussions of the parties prior to the signing of the release, that will be sufficient to end the inquiry. The release will be an impermissible contracting out of the protections of the *Code*. It will not be necessary to go further and consider the four implied factors set out in the *Pritchard* case, below.

On this issue of contracting out versus settlement, the Commission provides the following tips for parties involved in preparing and signing a release of a human rights complaint.

- An employer should, at the time of termination, ask the employee orally or in writing whether there are any outstanding human rights issues or concerns.
- It is important to give the employee a reasonable opportunity to consult with independent counsel or an advisor before being required to answer this question.
- Where the answer is "yes," the employer should ask for details, in order to be able to fairly assess what would be a reasonable offer for settling the human rights issues.
- Where the answer is "yes," it is optimum to also prepare Minutes of Settlement, in addition to the release, which will expressly deal with the human rights issue.
- In addition, where the answer is "yes," the text of the standard form of release should be altered to include a clause that separately recognizes that there is a human rights issue or complaint that has been fully and finally resolved between the parties.

- An employee should seek outside independent advice prior to signing a release or answering a question concerning the existence of a human rights issue.
- Where the answer is "no," and the employee has obtained or had the opportunity to obtain independent advice, it is appropriate for the release to state that the employee has obtained independent legal advice, is aware of his or her rights under the *Human Rights Code*, and warrants that he or she is not asserting such rights or advancing any human rights claim or complaint.

5. — The Four *Pritchard* Factors

There will be cases where the parties tell diametrically opposing stories on the issue of whether or not a human rights issue was discussed prior to the signing of the release. In addition, even where the parties may have discussed human rights issues there may still be disagreement as to whether or not the release constituted a binding, legal settlement of the human rights complaint. In a leading case, the Divisional Court in *Pritchard v. OHRC*[4] set out four implied factors that must be examined to determine whether or not the release actually reflects a settlement of a human rights complaint. If it does, then permitting the complainant to proceed with the complaint would be bad faith. These factors are designed to help infer or imply whether a settlement actually occurred. They are:

1) Did the complainant understand the significance of the release? This will usually turn on whether or not they were given sufficient time, and a sufficient opportunity to obtain advice.
2) Did the complainant receive compensation for the alleged breach of the human rights issue? If, for example, the complainant only received an amount akin to what they would have been entitled to under statute (e.g., severance and termination pay under the *Employment Standards Act*) then it may be inferred that they did not also receive compensation for the human rights violation.
3) Was the complainant subject to such significant economic pressure that his or her consent was negated due to duress?

---

[4] *Pritchard v Ontario Human Rights Commission* (1999), 45 O.R. (3d) 97 (Div. Ct.). It is important to emphasize that a number of cases prior to *Pritchard* have also recognized these factors as being sufficient to negate the employee's consent to a release. *Lloyd's Bank v. Bundy*, [1975] Q.B. 326, per Lord Denning (U.K. C.A); *McKenzie v. Bank of Montreal* (1977), 70 D.L.R. (3d) 113 (Ont. C.A.); *Blackmore v. Cablenet Ltd.*, [1994] A.J. No. 938 (Alta. Q.B.).

4) Was the complainant subject to such significant psychological or emotional pressure that his or her consent was negated due to duress?[5]

5.1 — Did the complainant misunderstand the significance of the release?

This will require a consideration of the extent to which the complainant is sophisticated. For example, a human resources manager with years of experience dealing with terminations will rarely be able to claim that he or she was unaware of the significance of the release and settlement documents. An unsophisticated complainant may be in a stronger position to do so. Special consideration should be given to complainants who are experiencing a mental disability such as depression or bi-polar disorder that may impair their ability to understand the significance of the document.

In addition, whether or not the employer explicitly provided the complainant with an opportunity to obtain legal or other advice prior to signing a release will also be significant. Normally, an employer should permit a person a reasonable amount of time to obtain advice. What is reasonable will vary depending on the sophistication of the complainant and the circumstances of each case. Special consideration should be given to complainants with a disability, who may, for example, require additional time to physically meet with and retain counsel.

Further, where the complainant has difficulty finding counsel within a short period of time and requests an extension, an unreasonable refusal by the employer will be taken into account. (See *Pritchard*, *supra*).

A requirement to sign the release on the same day as the termination strongly suggests that the complainant did not have sufficient time to consult. His or her claim to not understand the significance of the release will have greater weight.

---

[5]In *Pritchard*, *supra* at para. 17, the Divisional Court stated as follows:

> [T]he facts may show that the employee misunderstood the significance of the release, or received little or no consideration for it beyond statutory entitlements under employment standards legislation, or was in such serious financial need that she or he felt there was not choice but to accept the package offered. To take the approach that there is bad faith whenever a human rights complaint is brought after signing a release risks ignoring the context within which a particular complainant has signed the release and denying access to the investigative procedure under the *Human Rights Code* without assessing the complainant's individual moral blameworthiness in pursuing the complaint.

Often a complainant will state that the employer gave them some time to retain counsel for the purpose of reviewing the settlement package but he or she declined to do so. This does not mean that the complainant necessarily understood the significance of the release. The reasons why the complainant rejected the offer of time to review the documents must be considered. For example, if the complainants reasonably believe that they will not get any money at all until the release is signed, and decline the offer of time to consult because of a fear of not being able to make imminent rent payments, this may constitute sufficient duress to support a claim that they did not understand the consequences of what they were signing. As the Court noted in *Clarke v. Optyl (Can)*:[6]

> [W]hen they signed the dismissal letters each one of them had been accustomed to fulltime employment; when they were abruptly dismissed they could not help but be concerned as to how they were going to meet their commitments to their families and to their creditors. Each was facing an uncertain future. Each knew, as did their employer, that they had been dismissed in difficult economic times.

In *Deacon v. Macmillan Bloedel*[7] an employee was asked to sign a release on the same day as his termination. He asked for more money than was initially offered. This was agreed to by the employer. The employer argued that this negotiation was proof that Deacon understood the significance of what he was signing. The Court disagreed. The Court held:

> Having regard to the circumstances that I have described as to the loss of the job, I do not think that an employee who suddenly, unexpectedly, without notice, without expectation, loses his job can be said to be acting as a reasonable and rational individual. I do not imply that the amount suggested by Mr. Deacon constitutes a legal bar to this action he had instituted.
>
> In order for such estoppel or defence to be valid, it would be necessary that Mr. Deacon have independent advice and that he clearly indicate that knowing his rights, he was nevertheless satisfied with the amount and then agreed. He was under economic duress, he was under emotional duress and strain.

On the other hand, a complainant who formed the opinion that they did not need legal advice or did not want to pay for a lawyer may be stuck with that decision. This is not because he or she necessarily understood the conse-

---

[6]*Clarke v. Optyl (Can)* (1985), 7 C.C.E.L. 1 (N.B.C.A.). See also: *Blackmore v. Cablenet Ltd.*, [1994] A.J. No. 938 at paras. 36 to 38 (Alta. Q.B.).

[7]*Deacon v. MacMillan Bloedel Ltd.* (1982), 3 C.C.E.L. 166 at para. 25 (Ont. Dist. Ct.); See also: *Gordon v. Aklavik (Hamlet)* (1995), 10 C.C.E.L. (2d) 249 (N.W.T. S.C.).

quences of what was being signed. They may well have not. Rather, where he or she has been specifically advised that they have sufficient time to respond and there is no pressure or duress, it can separately amount to bad faith for a person to freely elect not to retain counsel and to then use the fact that they consciously chose not to do so in an attempt to get out of a signed agreement.

On this issue of understanding the significance of the release, the Commission provides the following tips for parties involved in preparing and signing a release of a human rights complaint:

- An employer should always give an employee a reasonable period of time to retain and instruct counsel or a legal advisor.
- Reasonable requests for an extension of time should be granted.
- To avoid claims of unwarranted pressure or duress, it is optimum that an employer not accept a signed release on the same day as termination (even where the employee offers to sign it on that day).
- An employee should always seek separate and independent legal or expert advice before signing a release.
- The employee should also canvass with their advisor the full range of remedies that may be available at common law, under the *Employment Standards Act*, the *Human Rights Code*, or other statutes.

5.2 — Did the complainant receive compensation for the alleged breach of the human rights issue?

As noted, one of the common law principles is that a person receive consideration in exchange for settling their issue or complaint. Accordingly, if the complainant received a sum of money that appears to compensate him or her for the alleged breach of human rights, then it can be implied that the human rights complaint was settled. If he or she did not, then it is more likely that the human rights issue was not resolved through the signing of the release.

In this regard, attention should be paid to whether or not the complainant received anything other than the statutory entitlement in exchange for a promise not to proceed. Where the amount is around, or just slightly more, than what could have been received, for example, as severance or termination pay under the *Employment Standards Act*, then it is reasonable to infer that the human rights issue was not resolved. The Divisional Court noted in *Pritchard*, for example, that the additional amount received was only two weeks' salary. In addition, the Court commented on the lack of demarcation in the release noting, "the quantum beyond the statutory minimum was not clearly spelled out in the documentation provided to her."

There will be rare cases where it can be demonstrated that the parties never considered the human rights issue at all. The signed release would constitute "contracting out" and not a settlement. In these instances, the case cannot be disposed of under section 34 since it is not "bad faith" to continue with a claim that has not been settled. However, if an examination of the amount of money received demonstrates that the complainant received a sum that would have compensated him or her for the loss of human rights, and the respondent has offered to provide suitable public interest remedies, then this may be a case in which Commission staff may recommend that the procedure of referral is not appropriate pursuant to section 36 of the *Code*, in a manner similar to cases involving a reasonable settlement offer[8].

On this issue of adequate compensation, the Commission provides the following tips for parties involved in preparing and signing a release of a human rights complaint:

- Employers wishing to guard against a claim that they have not compensated a complainant for the human rights issue should consider demarcating in the settlement specific sums for each "head" of damages, such as severance, termination, vacation pay and wages, as well as a set amount in compensation for any alleged human rights concern.
- The demarcation can be in separate Minutes of Settlement.
- An employee, after consulting with independent counsel or an advisor, should separately negotiate each head of damages or remedy when negotiating the terms of the settlement.

5.3 — Was the complainant subject to undue economic duress in the signing of the release?

If one party is pressured by another party or by circumstance into signing a release, a court may find it "unconscionable" to uphold the agreement. The underlying theory is that the state of duress deprives the contracting individual of the exercise of her or his free will.

For example, in *Adamson v. Watts & Henderson (Atlantic) Ltd.*, [1987] 16 C.C.E.L. 74 (H.C.J.), the Court found that the defendant knew that the plaintiff was under undue financial pressure because his house in Halifax had not been sold, he had rented a home in the Ottawa area and he was out

---

[8]See *Losenno v. Ontario Human Rights Commission* (2005), 78 O.R. (3d) 161 (C.A.); leave to appeal denied [2005] S.C.C.A. No. 531.

of work with no immediate prospect of employment. The Court found that there was an:

> inequality of bargaining position between the plaintiff and the defendant because of the plaintiff's distress, lack of sophistication in business matters and the genuinely felt need of the plaintiff to have his pay continued that put him in a position that he was not thinking as clearly as he should have been at the time when he was discussing his termination with the defendant.

In this context the question of statutory entitlements also arises. Case law has indicated that where an employer states, or strongly suggests, that the complainant will not receive the amount that they are legally entitled to by statute (such as severance and termination payments under the *Employment Standards Act*) unless he or she first signs a release barring all other claims (including proceedings under the *Human Rights Code*), then this will be found to constitute economic duress.

Case law strongly supports the requirement that the employer cannot withhold, or even imply to the employee that there will be a withholding of, statutory entitlements until the release is first signed.

Lord Denning, in the leading case of *Lloyd's Bank Ltd. v. Bundy*, [1975] 1 Q.B. 326 at 339 (U.K. C.A.), made it clear that the employer need not have committed any wrongdoing and may indeed be "unconscious of the distress he is bringing to the other." In addition, the stress need not rise to the level of being "undue" to the point that the employee's reason is "overcome." Indeed, the Court recognized that "[o]ne who is in extreme need may knowingly consent to a most improvident bargain, solely to relieve the straits in which he finds himself."

In *Adamson v. Watts & Henderson (Atlantic) Ltd., supra* the Ontario High Court of Justice, following the principles enunciated in *Lloyd's Bank*, held that the plaintiff should be granted relief from the wording of a release. The Court noted that the release had been presented to the employee prior to the employee receiving the cheque in circumstances in which it would have been reasonable for the employee to infer that, if he failed to sign the release, the corporation would not release the cheque.

Similarly, in *Augustine v. Nadrofsky Corporation* (1986), 17 O.A.C. 297 (Div. Ct.), the Divisional Court found that the refusal of an employer to forward the funds unless the fired employee signed the release, negated the consent:

> The plaintiff was told that he must sign the document if he was to receive his pay cheque, to which he was entitled. The employer here had absolutely no right to insist that the plaintiff employee sign the agreement or go without the pay he had earned and for which he had a real need. In our view, this unreasonable demand of the employer, having regard to age and education

of the plaintiff and the imbalance of bargaining power between the parties, constituted sufficient coercion to vitiate the legal effect of the document signed.[9]

Accordingly, where a former employer stipulates that severance payments or other monies owed will not be provided if the employee does not sign a release, a state of duress for the employee is created such that the release is of no effect.

On this issue of economic duress, the Commission provides the following tips for parties involved in preparing and signing a release of a human rights complaint:

- The employer should state that the employee will receive his or her statutory entitlements (wages owed, vacation pay, statutory termination or severance payments) regardless of whether he or she signs the release.
- The release itself should contain a clause which makes it clear that the signing of the release was not a precondition for the payment of these statutory entitlements.
- An employee should first request a calculation or breakdown of his or her statutory entitlements and other entitlements prior to negotiating the terms and conditions of any settlement of an outstanding human rights issue or complaint.
- Notwithstanding that he or she may feel that they "need the money right away," an employee should request their statutory entitlements first, and always take time to consult with his or her legal counsel or advisor second, in order to negotiate an appropriate settlement. If the employer refuses to provide the statutory entitlements as required by law, the employee should address this issue with the Ministry of Labour.

5.4 — Was the complainant experiencing undue psychological or emotional duress when signing of the release?

Canadian courts have recognized that duress can also be psychological, where there has been an "improper use by one party to a contract of any kind of coercion, oppression, abuse of power or authority, or compulsion in order to make the other party consent."[10] Relevant questions to consider are

---

[9]See also *Blackmore v. Cablenet Ltd.*, *supra* at para. 45; *Deacon v. MacMillan Bloedel Ltd.*, *supra.*

[10]*Re Chow* (1999), 37 C.H.R.R. D/442 at para. 104 (Alta. Q.B.); *Thompson v. Providence Health Care* (2003), 47 C.H.R.R. D/368 at para. 44 (B.C.H.R.T.).

whether the complainant was pressured, humiliated, demeaned, or browbeaten before signing the release.

In addition, the inquiry can examine whether the employer improperly threatened the complainant with sanctions should he or she not sign the release; for example, suggesting that a criminal investigation into alleged impropriety would otherwise be called unless the release was signed. However, discussions concerning whether or not a positive letter of reference would be provided or withheld would not normally constitute untoward pressure as such letters are often a term and condition of a settlement.

Even where the employer did not behave inappropriately at all, the mere act of termination can also create psychological stress amounting to duress. In *Pilon v. Peugeot* (1980), 114 D.L.R. (3d) 378 (Ont. H.C.J.), Galligan, J. applied this reasoning to the wrongful dismissal context and on the facts of that case, concluded at p. 383:

> In my opinion, it cannot fail to have been in the contemplation of the defendant that if he suddenly, without warning, unlawfully discharged a man whom it had led to believe was secure in his job for his working life, there would be the gravest likelihood that such a man would suffer vexation, frustration, distress and anxiety.

The shock of being terminated is likely in most cases to create emotional stress. For this reason as well the Commission recommends that an employee not be asked to sign his or her release on the same day as the termination and, indeed, not be permitted to do so even where he or she offers. Requiring a minimum period of time to study and examine the offer will help to provide the employee with a reasonable chance to get over the shock of termination, to retain outside assistance, and to fairly assess his or her financial situation.

Finally, there may be instances where separate and apart from the employer's conduct or the shock of termination, an employee is experiencing psychological problems which may impair his or her capacity to freely enter into a release. If the employee at the time of his or her termination was experiencing psychological problems, such as depression or mental illness, this can impact on his or her ability to consent.

On this issue of and emotional duress, the Commission provides the following tips for parties involved in preparing and signing a release of a human rights complaint:

- Termination meetings should be conducted with dignity, ensuring privacy, and with the employer exhibiting professionalism.
- Employers should never require an employee to sign a release on the same day as termination.

- If an employee has allegedly engaged in criminal wrongdoing, such as theft or fraud, the employer should not promise to refrain from contacting the police in exchange for a release.
- Employees should always take sufficient time to study the terms and conditions of a proposed release and obtain independent legal advice before signing.
- Where the employer has a reasonable basis to believe that an employee is experiencing a mental disability that could impair his or her judgment, he or she should request the employee obtain medical clearance before signing the release.

6. — Binding Releases

There will certainly be cases where the employee has bargaining power. He or she may also have a potentially significant claim for wrongful dismissal, or access to a grievance procedure under a strong collective agreement. Such an employee will have retained a lawyer, and engaged in extended negotiations. The human rights issues will have been discussed and negotiated. In such cases, the employer is willing to pay an amount that more than moderately exceeds the statutory requirements, and where the parties have discussed the fact that all claims will be extinguished through an agreement, it may be argued that the parties have considered the cost and likely merit of a future claim, attached a price tag to it, and reached a final settlement. The more the evidence suggests negotiations and settlement, the less likely will it be unconscionable to enforce the release.

On the other hand, if the release is an all-purpose, broadly-worded release, then, in the absence of evidence that the issues of human rights were specifically addressed, the release will not bar a human rights proceeding. Furthermore, if there is no consideration provided other than the statutory entitlement, one can infer that the matter of human rights could not have been specifically addressed. It is unlikely that an employee, given proper legal advice, or understanding the nature of the claims being settled, would give them away for nothing in return.

To avoid uncertainty and to assist all parties, the Commission has put forward this Guide with proposed wording for appropriate releases, as well as tips regarding the appropriate conduct of the parties that indicate that human rights complaints have been fully and finally settled by the parties.

APPENDIX — TIPS FOR PARTIES TO A RELEASE

For Employers

- An employer should, at the time of termination, ask the employee orally or in writing whether there are any outstanding human rights issues or concerns.
- It is important to give the employee a reasonable opportunity to consult with independent counsel or an advisor before being required to answer the above question or to sign a legal release.
- Reasonable requests for an extension of time should be granted.
- Where the answer is "yes," the employer should ask for details, in order to be able to fairly assess what would be a reasonable offer for settling the human rights issues.
- Where the answer is "yes," it is optimal to also prepare Minutes of Settlement, in addition to the release, which will expressly deal with the human rights issue.
- In addition, where the answer is "yes," the text of the standard form of release should be altered to include a clause that separately recognizes that there is a human rights issue or complaint that has been fully and finally resolved between the parties.
- Where the answer is "no," and the employee has obtained, or had the opportunity to obtain, independent advice, it is appropriate for the release to state that the employee has obtained independent legal advice, is cognizant of his or her rights under the *Human Rights Code*, and warrants that he or she is not asserting such rights or advancing any human rights claim or complaint.
- To avoid claims of unwarranted pressure or duress, it is optimal that an employer not accept a signed release on the same day as termination (even where the employee offers to sign it on that day).
- Employers wishing to guard against a claim that they have not compensated a complainant for the human rights issue should consider demarcating in the settlement specific sums for each "head" of damages, such as severance, termination, vacation pay and wages, as well as a set amount in compensation for any alleged human rights concern.
- The employer should state that the employee will receive his or her statutory entitlements (wages owed, vacation pay, statutory termination or severance payments) regardless of whether he or she signs the release.

- The release itself should contain a clause which makes it clear that the signing of the release was not a precondition for the payment of these statutory entitlements.
- Termination meetings should be conducted with dignity, ensuring privacy, and with the employer exhibiting professionalism.
- If an employee has allegedly engaged in criminal wrongdoing, such as theft or fraud, the employer should not promise to refrain from contacting the police in exchange for a release.
- Where the employer has a reasonable basis to believe that an employee is experiencing a mental disability that could impair his or her judgment, he or she should request the employee to obtain medical clearance before signing the release.

For Employees

- An employee should seek outside independent advice prior to signing a release, or answering a question concerning the existence of a human rights issue.
- The employee should also canvass with their advisor the full range of remedies that may be available at common law, under the *Employment Standards Act*, the *Human Rights Code*, or other statutes.
- To avoid unwarranted pressure or duress, it is optimal that an employee never accept or sign a release on the same day as termination.
- An employee, after consulting with independent counsel or an advisor, should separately negotiate each head of damages or remedy when negotiating the terms of the settlement.
- An employee should first request a calculation or breakdown of his or her statutory entitlements and other entitlements prior to negotiating the terms and conditions of any settlement of an outstanding human rights issue or complaint.
- Employees should ask that the settlement set out specific sums for each "head" of damages, such as severance, termination, vacation pay and wages, as well as a set amount in compensation for any alleged human rights concern.
- The employee should ask that he or she receive his or her statutory entitlements regardless of whether he or she signs the release.
- The release itself should contain a clause which makes it clear that the signing of the release was not a precondition for the payment of these statutory entitlements.

- Notwithstanding that he or she may feel that they "need the money right away," an employee should request his or her statutory entitlements first, and always take time to consult with his or her legal counsel or advisor second, in order to negotiate an appropriate settlement. If the employer refuses to provide the statutory entitlements as required by law, the employee should address this issue with the Ministry of Labour.

Part II — Ontario Human Rights Code and Regulations

Human Rights Code

R.S.O. 1990, c. H.19, as am. S.O. 1993, c. 27, Sched.; 1993, c. 35, s. 56; 1994, c. 10, s. 22; 1994, c. 27, s. 65 [s. 65(7) not in force at date of publication.]; 1995, c. 4, s. 3; 1997, c. 16, s. 8; 1997, c. 24, s. 212; 1999, c. 6, s. 28; 2001, c. 13, s. 19; 2001, c. 32, s. 27; 2002, c. 18, Sched. C; 2005, c. 5, s. 32; 2005, c. 18, s. 17; 2005, c. 29, s. 1; 2006, c. 19, Sched. B, s. 10 (Fr.); 2006, c. 21, Sched. F, ss. 136(2), Table 2, 137; 2006, c. 30 [ss. 1–5, 7–9 to come into force June 30, 2008; s. 11 conditions not yet satisfied.]; 2006, c. 35, Sched. C, ss. 54(1), 132 [s. 132(5), (6) conditions not yet satisfied.].

Preamble

WHEREAS recognition of the inherent dignity and the equal and inalienable rights of all members of the human family is the foundation of freedom, justice and peace in the world and is in accord with the Universal Declaration of Human Rights as proclaimed by the United Nations;

AND WHEREAS it is public policy in Ontario to recognize the dignity and worth of every person and to provide for equal rights and opportunities without discrimination that is contrary to law, and having as its aim the creation of a climate of understanding and mutual respect for the dignity and worth of each person so that each person feels a part of the community and able to contribute fully to the development and well-being of the community and the Province;

AND WHEREAS these principles have been confirmed in Ontario by a number of enactments of the Legislature and it is desirable to revise and extend the protection of human rights in Ontario;

Therefore, Her Majesty, by and with the advice and consent of the Legislative Assembly of the Province of Ontario, enacts as follows:

PART I — FREEDOM FROM DISCRIMINATION

1. **Services** — Every person has a right to equal treatment with respect to services, goods and facilities, without discrimination because of race, ancestry, place of origin, colour, ethnic origin, citizenship, creed, sex, sexual orientation, age, marital status, family status or disability.

1999, c. 6, s. 28(1); 2001, c. 32, s. 27(1), item 1; 2005, c. 5, s. 32(1)

2. (1) **Accommodation** — Every person has a right to equal treatment with respect to the occupancy of accommodation, without discrimination because of race, ancestry, place of origin, colour, ethnic origin, citizenship, creed, sex, sexual orientation, age, marital status, family status, disability or the receipt of public assistance.

(2) **Harassment in accommodation** — Every person who occupies accommodation has a right to freedom from harassment by the landlord or agent of the landlord or by an occupant of the same building because of race, ancestry, place of origin, colour, ethnic origin, citizenship, creed, age, marital status, family status, disability or the receipt of public assistance.

1999, c. 6, s. 28(2), (3); 2001, c. 32, s. 27(1), item 2; 2005, c. 5, s. 32(2), (3)

3. **Contracts** — Every person having legal capacity has a right to contract on equal terms without discrimination because of race, ancestry, place of origin, colour, ethnic origin, citizenship, creed, sex, sexual orientation, age, marital status, family status or disability.

1999, c. 6, s. 28(4); 2001, c. 32, s. 27(1), item 3; 2005, c. 5, s. 32(4)

4. (1) **Accommodation of person under eighteen** — Every sixteen or seventeen year old person who has withdrawn from parental control has a right to equal treatment with respect to occupancy of and contracting for accommodation without discrimination because the person is less than eighteen years old.

(2) **Idem** — A contract for accommodation entered into by a sixteen or seventeen year old person who has withdrawn from parental control is enforceable against that person as if the person were eighteen years old.

5. (1) **Employment** — Every person has a right to equal treatment with respect to employment without discrimination because of race, ancestry, place of origin, colour, ethnic origin, citizenship, creed, sex, sexual orientation, age, record of offences, marital status, family status or disability.

(2) **Harassment in employment** — Every person who is an employee has a right to freedom from harassment in the workplace by the employer or

agent of the employer or by another employee because of race, ancestry, place of origin, colour, ethnic origin, citizenship, creed, age, record of offences, marital status, family status or disability.

1999, c. 6, s. 28(5), (6); 2001, c. 32, s. 27(1), item 4; 2005, c. 5, s. 32(5), (6)

6. Vocational associations — Every person has a right to equal treatment with respect to membership in any trade union, trade or occupational association or self-governing profession without discrimination because of race, ancestry, place of origin, colour, ethnic origin, citizenship, creed, sex, sexual orientation, age, marital status, family status or disability.

1999, c. 6, s. 28(7); 2001, c. 32, s. 27(1), item 5; 2005, c. 5, s. 32(7)

7. (1) Harassment because of sex in accommodation — Every person who occupies accommodation has a right to freedom from harassment because of sex by the landlord or agent of the landlord or by an occupant of the same building.

(2) Harassment because of sex in workplace — Every person who is an employee has a right to freedom from harassment in the workplace because of sex by his or her employer or agent of the employer or by another employee.

(3) Sexual solicitation by a person in position to confer benefit, etc. — Every person has a right to be free from,

(a) a sexual solicitation or advance made by a person in a position to confer, grant or deny a benefit or advancement to the person where the person making the solicitation or advance knows or ought reasonably to know that it is unwelcome; or

(b) a reprisal or a threat of reprisal for the rejection of a sexual solicitation or advance where the reprisal is made or threatened by a person in a position to confer, grant or deny a benefit or advancement to the person.

8. Reprisals — Every person has a right to claim and enforce his or her rights under this Act, to institute and participate in proceedings under this Act and to refuse to infringe a right of another person under this Act, without reprisal or threat of reprisal for so doing.

9. Infringement prohibited — No person shall infringe or do, directly or indirectly, anything that infringes a right under this Part.

PART II — INTERPRETATION AND APPLICATION

10. (1) Definitions — In Part I and in this Part,

"age" means an age that is 18 years or more;

"because of handicap" [Repealed 2001, c. 32, s. 27(2).]

"disability" means,

(a) any degree of physical disability, infirmity, malformation or disfigurement that is caused by bodily injury, birth defect or illness and, without limiting the generality of the foregoing, includes diabetes mellitus, epilepsy, a brain injury, any degree of paralysis, amputation, lack of physical co-ordination, blindness or visual impediment, deafness or hearing impediment, muteness or speech impediment, or physical reliance on a guide dog or other animal or on a wheelchair or other remedial appliance or device,

(b) a condition of mental impairment or a developmental disability,

(c) a learning disability, or a dysfunction in one or more of the processes involved in understanding or using symbols or spoken language,

(d) a mental disorder, or

(e) an injury or disability for which benefits were claimed or received under the insurance plan established under the *Workplace Safety and Insurance Act, 1997*;

"equal" means subject to all requirements, qualifications and considerations that are not a prohibited ground of discrimination;

"family status" means the status of being in a parent and child relationship;

"group insurance" means insurance whereby the lives or well-being or the lives and well-being of a number of persons are insured severally under a single contract between an insurer and an association or an employer or other person;

"harassment" means engaging in a course of vexatious comment or conduct that is known or ought reasonably to be known to be unwelcome;

"marital status" means the status of being married, single, widowed, divorced or separated and includes the status of living with a person in a conjugal relationship outside marriage;

"record of offences" means a conviction for,

(a) an offence in respect of which a pardon has been granted under the *Criminal Records Act* (Canada) and has not been revoked, or

(b) an offence in respect of any provincial enactment;

"same-sex partner" [Repealed 2005, c. 5, s. 32(9).]

"same-sex partnership status" [Repealed 2005, c. 5, s. 32(9).]

"services" does not include a levy, fee, tax or periodic payment imposed by law;

"spouse" means the person to whom a person is married or with whom the person is living in a conjugal relationship outside marriage.

(2) **Pregnancy** — The right to equal treatment without discrimination because of sex includes the right to equal treatment without discrimination because a woman is or may become pregnant.

(3) **Past and presumed disabilities** — The right to equal treatment without discrimination because of disability includes the right to equal treatment without discrimination because a person has or has had a disability or is believed to have or to have had a disability.

1997, c. 16, s. 8; 1999, c. 6, s. 28(8); 2001, c. 13, s. 19; 2001, c. 32, s. 27(2)–(4); 2005, c. 5, s. 32(8)–(10); 2005, c. 29, s. 1(1)

11. (1) **Constructive discrimination** — A right of a person under Part I is infringed where a requirement, qualification or factor exists that is not discrimination on a prohibited ground but that results in the exclusion, restriction or preference of a group of persons who are identified by a prohibited ground of discrimination and of whom the person is a member, except where,

(a) the requirement, qualification or factor is reasonable and *bona fide* in the circumstances; or

(b) it is declared in this Act, other than in section 17, that to discriminate because of such ground is not an infringement of a right.

(2) **Idem** — The Commission, the Tribunal or a court shall not find that a requirement, qualification or factor is reasonable and *bona fide* in the circumstances unless it is satisfied that the needs of the group of which the person is a member cannot be accommodated without undue hardship on the person responsible for accommodating those needs, considering the cost, outside sources of funding, if any, and health and safety requirements, if any.

(3) **Idem** — The Commission, the Tribunal or a court shall consider any standards prescribed by the regulations for assessing what is undue hardship.

1994, c. 27, s. 65(1), (2); 2002, c. 18, Sched. C, s. 2

12. **Discrimination because of association** — A right under Part I is infringed where the discrimination is because of relationship, association or dealings with a person or persons identified by a prohibited ground of discrimination.

13. (1) **Announced intention to discriminate** — A right under Part I is infringed by a person who publishes or displays before the public or causes the publication or display before the public of any notice, sign, symbol, emblem, or other similar representation that indicates the intention of the person to infringe a right under Part I or that is intended by the person to incite the infringement of a right under Part I.

(2) **Opinion** — Subsection (1) shall not interfere with freedom of expression of opinion.

14. (1) **Special programs** — A right under Part I is not infringed by the implementation of a special program designed to relieve hardship or economic disadvantage or to assist disadvantaged persons or groups to achieve or attempt to achieve equal opportunity or that is likely to contribute to the elimination of the infringement of rights under Part I.

(2) **Review by Commission** — The Commission may,

(a) upon its own initiative;

(b) upon application by a person seeking to implement a special program under the protection of subsection (1); or

(c) upon a complaint in respect of which the protection of subsection (1) is claimed,

inquire into the special program and, in the discretion of the Commission, may by order declare,

(d) that the special program, as defined in the order, does not satisfy the requirements of subsection (1); or

(e) that the special program as defined in the order, with such modifications, if any, as the Commission considers advisable, satisfies the requirements of subsection (1).

Proposed Amendment — 14(2)

(2) **Application to Commission** — A person may apply to the Commission for a designation of a program as a special program for the purposes of subsection (1).

2006, c. 30, s. 1 [To come into force June 30, 2008.]

(3) **Reconsideration** — A person aggrieved by the making of an order under subsection (2) may request the Commission to reconsider its order and section 37, with necessary modifications, applies.

Proposed Amendment — 14(3)

(3) **Designation by Commission** — Upon receipt of an application, the Commission may,

(a) designate the program as a special program if, in its opinion, the program meets the requirements of subsection (1); or

(b) designate the program as a special program on the condition that the program make such modifications as are specified in the designation in order to meet the requirements of subsection (1).

2006, c. 30, s. 1 [To come into force June 30, 2008.]

(4) **Effect of order** — Subsection (1) does not apply to a special program where an order is made under clause (2) (d) or where an order is made under clause (2) (e) with modifications of the special program that are not implemented.

Proposed Amendment — 14(4)

(4) **Inquiries initiated by Commission** — The Commission may, on its own initiative, inquire into one or more programs to determine whether the programs are special programs for the purposes of subsection (1).

2006, c. 30, s. 1 [To come into force June 30, 2008.]

(5) **Subs. (2) does not apply to Crown** — Subsection (2) does not apply to a special program implemented by the Crown or an agency of the Crown.

Proposed Amendment — 14(5)

(5) **End of inquiry** — At the conclusion of an inquiry under subsection (4), the Commission may designate as a special program any of the programs under inquiry if, in its opinion, the programs meet the requirements of subsection (1).

2006, c. 30, s. 1 [To come into force June 30, 2008.]

Proposed Addition — 14(6)–(10)

(6) **Expiry of designation** — A designation under subsection (3) or (5) expires five years after the day it is issued or at such earlier time as may be specified by the Commission.

(7) **Renewal of designation** — If an application for renewal of a designation of a program as a special program is made to the Commission before its expiry under subsection (6), the Commission may,

(a) renew the designation if, in its opinion, the program continues to meet the requirements of subsection (1); or

(b) renew the designation on the condition that the program make such modifications as are specified in the designation in order to meet the requirements of subsection (1).

(8) **Effect of designation, etc.** — In a proceeding,

(a) evidence that a program has been designated as a special program under this section is proof, in the absence of evidence to the contrary, that the program is a special program for the purposes of subsection (1); and

(b) evidence that the Commission has considered and refused to designate a program as a special program under this section is proof, in the absence of evidence to the contrary, that the program is not a special program for the purposes of subsection (1).

(9) **Crown programs** — Subsections (2) to (8) do not apply to a program implemented by the Crown or an agency of the Crown.

(10) **Tribunal finding** — For the purposes of a proceeding before the Tribunal, the Tribunal may make a finding that a program meets the requirements of a special program under subsection (1), even though the program has not been designated as a special program by the Commission under this section, subject to clause (8)(b).

2006, c. 30, s. 1 [To come into force June 30, 2008.]

14.1 [Repealed 1995, c. 4, s. 3(1).]

15. Age sixty-five or over — A right under Part I to non-discrimination because of age is not infringed where an age of sixty-five years or over is a requirement, qualification or consideration for preferential treatment.

16. (1) Canadian Citizenship — A right under Part I to non-discrimination because of citizenship is not infringed where Canadian citizenship is a requirement, qualification or consideration imposed or authorized by law.

(2) Idem — A right under Part I to non-discrimination because of citizenship is not infringed where Canadian citizenship or lawful admission to Canada for permanent residence is a requirement, qualification or consideration adopted for the purpose of fostering and developing participation in cultural, educational, trade union or athletic activities by Canadian citizens or persons lawfully admitted to Canada for permanent residence.

(3) Idem — A right under Part I to non-discrimination because of citizenship is not infringed where Canadian citizenship or domicile in Canada with the intention to obtain Canadian citizenship is a requirement, qualification or consideration adopted by an organization or enterprise for the holder of chief or senior executive positions.

17. (1) Disability — A right of a person under this Act is not infringed for the reason only that the person is incapable of performing or fulfilling the essential duties or requirements attending the exercise of the right because of disability.

(2) Accommodation — The Commission, the Tribunal or a court shall not find a person incapable unless it is satisfied that the needs of the person cannot be accommodated without undue hardship on the person responsible for accommodating those needs, considering the cost, outside sources of funding, if any, and health and safety requirements, if any.

Proposed Amendment — 17(2)

(2) Accommodation — No tribunal or court shall find a person incapable unless it is satisfied that the needs of the person cannot be accommodated without undue hardship on the person responsible for accommodating those needs, considering the cost, outside sources of funding, if any, and health and safety requirements, if any.

2006, c. 30, s. 2(1) [To come into force June 30, 2008.]

(3) Idem — The Commission, the Tribunal or a court shall consider any standards prescribed by the regulations for assessing what is undue hardship.

Proposed Amendment — 17(3)

(3) Determining if undue hardship — In determining for the purposes of subsection (2) whether there would be undue hardship, a tribunal or court shall consider any standards prescribed by the regulations.

2006, c. 30, s. 2(2) [To come into force June 30, 2008.]

(4) Powers of Commission — Where, after the investigation of a complaint, the Commission determines that the evidence does not warrant the subject-matter of the complaint being referred to the Tribunal because of the application of subsection (1), the Commission may nevertheless use its best endeavours to effect a settlement as to the duties or requirements.

Proposed Repeal — 17(4)

(4) [Repealed 2006, c. 30, s. 2(3). To come into force June 30, 2008.]

1994, c. 27, s. 65(2), (3); 2001, c. 32, s. 27(5), item 1; 2002, c. 18, Sched. C, ss. 1 (item 1), 3

18. Special interest organizations — The rights under Part I to equal treatment with respect to services and facilities, with or without accommodation, are not infringed where membership or participation in a religious, philanthropic, educational, fraternal or social institution or organization that is primarily engaged in serving the interests of persons identified by a prohibited ground of discrimination is restricted to persons who are similarly identified.

18.1 (1) Solemnization of marriage by religious officials — The rights under Part I to equal treatment with respect to services and facilities are not infringed where a person registered under section 20 of the *Marriage Act* refuses to solemnize a marriage, to allow a sacred place to be used for solemnizing a marriage or for an event related to the solemnization of a marriage, or to otherwise assist in the solemnization of a marriage, if to solemnize the marriage, allow the sacred place to be used or otherwise assist would be contrary to,

(a) the person's religious beliefs; or

(b) the doctrines, rites, usages or customs of the religious body to which the person belongs.

(2) Same — Nothing in subsection (1) limits the application of section 18.

(3) Definition — In this section,

"sacred place" includes a place of worship and any ancillary or accessory facilities.

2005, c. 5, s. 32(11)

19. (1) Separate school rights preserved — This Act shall not be construed to adversely affect any right or privilege respecting separate schools enjoyed by separate school boards or their supporters under the *Constitution Act, 1867* and the *Education Act*.

(2) Duties of teachers — This Act does not apply to affect the application of the *Education Act* with respect to the duties of teachers.

20. (1) Restriction of facilities by sex — The right under section 1 to equal treatment with respect to services and facilities without discrimination because of sex is not infringed where the use of the services or facilities is restricted to persons of the same sex on the ground of public decency.

(2) Minimum drinking age — The right under section 1 to equal treatment with respect to services, goods and facilities without discrimination because of age is not infringed by the provisions of the *Liquor Licence Act* and the regulations under it relating to providing for and enforcing a minimum drinking age of nineteen years.

(3) Recreational clubs — The right under section 1 to equal treatment with respect to services and facilities is not infringed where a recreational club restricts or qualifies access to its services or facilities or gives preferences with respect to membership dues and other fees because of age, sex, marital status, or family status.

(4) Tobacco and young persons — The right under section 1 to equal treatment with respect to goods without discrimination because of age is not infringed by the provisions of the *Smoke-Free Ontario Act* and the regulations under it relating to selling or supplying tobacco to persons who are, or who appear to be, under the age of 19 years or 25 years, as the case may be.
1994, c. 10, s. 22; 1999, c. 6, s. 28(9); 2005, c. 5, s. 32(12); 2005, c. 18, s. 17

21. (1) Shared accommodation — The right under section 2 to equal treatment with respect to the occupancy of residential accommodation without discrimination is not infringed by discrimination where the residential accommodation is in a dwelling in which the owner or his or her family reside if the occupant or occupants of the residential accommodation are required to share a bathroom or kitchen facility with the owner or family of the owner.

(2) Restrictions on accommodation, sex — The right under section 2 to equal treatment with respect to the occupancy of residential accommodation without discrimination because of sex is not infringed by discrimination on that ground where the occupancy of all the residential accommodation in the building, other than the accommodation, if any, of the owner or family of the owner, is restricted to persons who are of the same sex.

(3) Prescribing business practices — The right under section 2 to equal treatment with respect to the occupancy of residential accommodation without discrimination is not infringed if a landlord uses in the manner prescribed under this Act income information, credit checks, credit references, rental history, guarantees or other similar business practices which are prescribed in the regulations made under this Act in selecting prospective tenants.

1997, c. 24, s. 212

22. Restrictions for insurance contracts, etc. — The right under sections 1 and 3 to equal treatment with respect to services and to contract on equal terms, without discrimination because of age, sex, marital status, family status or disability, is not infringed where a contract of automobile, life, accident or sickness or disability insurance or a contract of group insurance between an insurer and an association or person other than an employer, or a life annuity, differentiates or makes a distinction, exclusion or preference on reasonable and *bona fide* grounds because of age, sex, marital status, family status or disability.

1999, c. 6, s. 28(10); 2001, c. 32, s. 27(5), item 2; 2005, c. 5, s. 32(13)

23. (1) Discriminatory employment advertising — The right under section 5 to equal treatment with respect to employment is infringed where an invitation to apply for employment or an advertisement in connection with employment is published or displayed that directly or indirectly classifies or indicates qualifications by a prohibited ground of discrimination.

(2) Application for employment — The right under section 5 to equal treatment with respect to employment is infringed where a form of application for employment is used or a written or oral inquiry is made of an applicant that directly or indirectly classifies or indicates qualifications by a prohibited ground of discrimination.

(3) Questions at interview — Nothing in subsection (2) precludes the asking of questions at a personal employment interview concerning a prohibited ground of discrimination where discrimination on such ground is permitted under this Act.

(4) Employment agencies — The right under section 5 to equal treatment with respect to employment is infringed where an employment agency discriminates against a person because of a prohibited ground of discrimination in receiving, classifying, disposing of or otherwise acting upon applications for its services or in referring an applicant or applicants to an employer or agent of an employer.

24. (1) Special employment — The right under section 5 to equal treatment with respect to employment is not infringed where,

(a) a religious, philanthropic, educational, fraternal or social institution or organization that is primarily engaged in serving the interests of persons identified by their race, ancestry, place of origin, colour, ethnic origin, creed, sex, age, marital status or disability employs only, or gives preference in employment to, persons similarly identified if the qualification is a reasonable and *bona fide* qualification because of the nature of the employment;

(b) the discrimination in employment is for reasons of age, sex, record of offences or marital status if the age, sex, record of offences or marital status of the applicant is a reasonable and *bona fide* qualification because of the nature of the employment;

(c) an individual person refuses to employ another for reasons of any prohibited ground of discrimination in section 5, where the primary duty of the employment is attending to the medical or personal needs of the person or of an ill child or an aged, infirm or ill spouse or other relative of the person;

(d) an employer grants or withholds employment or advancement in employment to a person who is the spouse, child or parent of the employer or an employee.

(e) a judge or master is required to retire or cease to continue in office on reaching a specified age under the *Courts of Justice Act*;

(f) a case management master is required to retire on reaching a specified age under the *Courts of Justice Act*;

(g) the term of reappointment of a case management master expires on the case management master reaching a specified age under the *Courts of Justice Act*; or

(h) a justice of the peace is required to retire on reaching a specified age under the *Justices of the Peace Act*.

(2) Reasonable accommodation — The Commission, the Tribunal or a court shall not find that a qualification under clause (1)(b) is reasonable and *bona fide* unless it is satisfied that the circumstances of the person cannot be accommodated without undue hardship on the person responsible for accommodating those circumstances considering the cost, outside sources of funding, if any, and health and safety requirements, if any.

Proposed Amendment — 24(2)

(2) Reasonable accommodation — No tribunal or court shall find that a qualification under clause (1)(b) is reasonable and *bona fide* unless it is satisfied that the circumstances of the person cannot be accommodated without undue hardship on the person responsible for accommodating those circumstances considering the cost, outside sources of funding, if any, and health and safety requirements, if any.

2006, c. 30, s. 3(1) [To come into force June 30, 2008.]

(3) Idem — The Commission, the Tribunal or a court shall consider any standards prescribed by the regulations for assessing what is undue hardship.

Proposed Amendment — 24(3)

(3) Determining if undue hardship — In determining for the purposes of subsection (2) whether there would be undue hardship, a tribunal or court shall consider any standards prescribed by the regulations.
2006, c. 30, s. 3(2) [To come into force June 30, 2008.]

(4) Same — Clauses 24(1)(e), (f), (g) and (h) shall not be interpreted to suggest that a judge, master, case management master or justice of the peace is an employee for the purposes of this Act or any other Act or law.
1994, c. 27, s. 65(4); 1999, c. 6, s. 28(11); 2001, c. 32, s. 27(5), item 3; 2002, c. 18, Sched. C, s. 4; 2005, c. 5, s. 32(14); 2005, c. 29, s. 1(2), (3)

24.1 [Repealed 1995, c. 4, s. 3(2).]

25. (1) Employment conditional on membership in pension plan — The right under section 5 to equal treatment with respect to employment is infringed where employment is denied or made conditional because a term or condition of employment requires enrolment in an employee benefit, pension or superannuation plan or fund or a contract of group insurance between an insurer and an employer, that makes a distinction, preference or exclusion on a prohibited ground of discrimination.

(2) Pension or disability plan — The right under section 5 to equal treatment with respect to employment without discrimination because of sex, marital status or family status is not infringed by an employee superannuation or pension plan or fund or a contract of group insurance between an insurer and an employer that complies with the *Employment Standards Act, 2000* and the regulations thereunder.

(2.1) Same — The right under section 5 to equal treatment with respect to employment without discrimination because of age is not infringed by an employee benefit, pension, superannuation or group insurance plan or fund that complies with the *Employment Standards Act, 2000* and the regulations thereunder.

(2.2) Same — Subsection (2.1) applies whether or not a plan or fund is the subject of a contract of insurance between an insurer and an employer.

(2.3) Same — For greater certainty, subsections (2) and (2.1) apply whether or not "age", "sex" or "marital status" in the *Employment Stan-*

dards Act, 2000 or the regulations under it have the same meaning as those terms have in this Act.

(3) **Employee disability and pension plans: disability** — The right under section 5 to equal treatment with respect to employment without discrimination because of disability is not infringed,

(a) where a reasonable and *bona fide* distinction, exclusion or preference is made in an employee disability or life insurance plan or benefit because of a pre-existing disability that substantially increases the risk;

(b) where a reasonable and *bona fide* distinction, exclusion or preference is made on the ground of a pre-existing disability in respect of an employee, pay-all or participant-pay-all benefit in an employee benefit, pension or superannuation plan or fund or a contract of group insurance between an insurer and an employer or in respect of a plan, fund or policy that is offered by an employer to employees if they are fewer than twenty-five in number.

(4) **Compensation** — An employer shall pay to an employee who is excluded because of a disability from an employee benefit, pension or superannuation plan or fund or a contract of group insurance between an insurer and the employer compensation equivalent to the contribution that the employer would make thereto on behalf of an employee who does not have a disability.

1999, c. 6, s. 28(12); 2001, c. 32, s. 27(5), item 4; 2005, c. 5, s. 32(15); 2005, c. 29, s. 1(4), (5)

26. (1) **Discrimination in employment under government contracts** — It shall be deemed to be a condition of every contract entered into by or on behalf of the Crown or any agency thereof and of every subcontract entered into in the performance thereof that no right under section 5 will be infringed in the course of performing the contract.

(2) **Idem: government grants and loans** — It shall be deemed to be a condition of every grant, contribution, loan or guarantee made by or on behalf of the Crown or any agency thereof that no right under section 5 will be infringed in the course of carrying out the purposes for which the grant, contribution, loan or guarantee was made.

(3) **Sanction** — Where an infringement of a right under section 5 is found by the Tribunal upon a complaint and constitutes a breach of a condition under this section, the breach of condition is sufficient grounds for cancellation of the contract, grant, contribution, loan or guarantee and refusal to

enter into any further contract with or make any further grant, contribution, loan or guarantee to the same person.

2002, c. 18, Sched. C, s. 5

PART III — THE ONTARIO HUMAN RIGHTS COMMISSION

27. (1) Commission continued — The Ontario Human Rights Commission is continued under the name Ontario Human Rights Commission in English and Commission ontarienne des droits de la personne in French and shall be composed of such persons, being not fewer than seven, as are appointed by the Lieutenant Governor in Council.

(2) Responsible to Minister — The Commission is responsible to the Minister for the administration of this Act.

(3) Chair — The Lieutenant Governor in Council shall designate a member of the Commission as chair, and a member as vice-chair.

(4) Remuneration — The Lieutenant Governor in Council may fix the remuneration and allowance for expenses of the chair, vice-chair and members of the Commission.

(5) Employees — Such employees as are considered necessary for the proper conduct of the affairs of the Commission shall be appointed under Part III of the *Public Service of Ontario Act, 2006*.

(6) Divisions — The Commission may authorize any function of the Commission to be performed by a division of the Commission composed of at least three members of the Commission.

Proposed Amendment — 27

27. (1) The Commission — The Ontario Human Rights Commission is continued under the name Ontario Human Rights Commission in English and Commission ontarienne des droits de la personne in French.

(2) Composition — The Commission shall be composed of such persons as are appointed by the Lieutenant Governor in Council.

(3) Appointment — Every person appointed to the Commission shall have knowledge, experience or training with respect to human rights law and issues.

(4) Criteria — In the appointment of persons to the Commission under subsection (2), the importance of reflecting, in the composition of the

Commission as a whole, the diversity of Ontario's population shall be recognized.

(5) **Chief Commissioner** — The Lieutenant Governor in Council shall designate a member of the Commission as Chief Commissioner.

(6) **Powers and duties of Chief Commissioner** — The Chief Commissioner shall direct the Commission and exercise the powers and perform the duties assigned to the Chief Commissioner by or under this Act.

(7) **Term of office** — The Chief Commissioner and other members of the Commission shall hold office for such term as may be specified by the Lieutenant Governor in Council.

(8) **Remuneration** — The Chief Commissioner and other members of the Commission shall be paid such remuneration and allowance for expenses as are fixed by the Lieutenant Governor in Council.

(9) **Employees** — The Commission may appoint such employees as it considers necessary for the proper conduct of its affairs and the employees shall be appointed under the *Public Service Act.*

Proposed Amendment — Conditional Amendment — 27(9)

On the later of the coming into force of S.O. 2006, c. 35, Sched. C, s. 132 [In force August 20, 2007.] and S.O. 2006, c. 30, s. 4 (Bill 107, s. 5) [To come into force June 30, 2008.], subsection 27(9) is replaced by the following:

> (9) Employees — The Commission may appoint such employees as it considers necessary for the proper conduct of its affairs and the employees shall be appointed under Part III of the *Public Service of Ontario Act, 2006.*
>
> 2006, c. 35, Sched. C, s. 132(5) [Conditions not yet satisfied.]

(10) **Evidence obtained in performance of duties** — A member of the Commission shall not be required to give testimony in a civil suit or any proceeding as to information obtained in the performance of duties under this Act.

(11) **Same, employees** — An employee of the Commission shall not be required to give testimony in a civil suit or any proceeding other than a proceeding under this Act as to information obtained in the performance of duties under this Act.

(12) **Delegation** — The Chief Commissioner may in writing delegate any of his or her powers, duties or functions under this Act to any member of the Anti-Racism Secretariat, the Disability Rights Secretariat or an

advisory group or to any other member of the Commission, subject to such conditions as the Chief Commissioner may set out in the delegation.

(13) **Divisions** — The Commission may authorize any function of the Commission to be performed by a division of the Commission composed of at least three members of the Commission.

2006, c. 30, s. 4 [To come into force June 30, 2008.]

2006, c. 35, Sched. C, s. 54(1)

28. (1) **Race relations division** — The Lieutenant Governor in Council shall designate at least three members of the Commission to constitute a race relations division of the Commission and shall designate one member of the race relations division as Commissioner for Race Relations.

(2) **Functions** — It is the function of the race relations division of the Commission to perform any of the functions of the Commission under clause 29(f), (g) or (h) relating to race, ancestry, place of origin, colour, ethnic origin or creed that are referred to it by the Commission and any other function referred to it by the Commission.

Proposed Amendment — 28

28. (1) **Acting Chief Commissioner** — If the Chief Commissioner dies, resigns or is unable or neglects to perform his or her duties, the Lieutenant Governor in Council may appoint an Acting Chief Commissioner to hold office for such period as may be specified in the appointment.

(2) **Same** — An Acting Chief Commissioner shall perform the duties and have the powers of the Chief Commissioner and shall be paid such remuneration and allowance for expenses as are fixed by the Lieutenant Governor in Council.

2006, c. 30, s. 4 [To come into force June 30, 2008.]

29. **Function of Commission** — It is the function of the Commission,

(a) to forward the policy that the dignity and worth of every person be recognized and that equal rights and opportunities be provided without discrimination that is contrary to law;

(b) to promote an understanding and acceptance of and compliance with this Act;

(c) to recommend for consideration a special plan or program designed to meet the requirements of subsection 14(1), subject to the right of a person aggrieved by the implementation of the plan or program to request the Commission to reconsider its recommendation and section 37 applies with necessary modifications;

(d) to develop and conduct programs of public information and education and undertake, direct and encourage research designed to eliminate discriminatory practices that infringe rights under this Act;

(e) to examine and review any statute or regulation, and any program or policy made by or under a statute and make recommendations on any provision, program or policy, that in its opinion is inconsistent with the intent of this Act;

(f) to inquire into incidents of and conditions leading or tending to lead to tension or conflict based upon identification by a prohibited ground of discrimination and take appropriate action to eliminate the source of tension or conflict;

(g) to initiate investigations into problems based upon identification by a prohibited ground of discrimination that may arise in a community, and encourage and co-ordinate plans, programs and activities to reduce or prevent such problems;

(h) to promote, assist and encourage public, municipal or private agencies, organizations, groups or persons to engage in programs to alleviate tensions and conflicts based upon identification by a prohibited ground of discrimination;

(i) to enforce this Act and orders of the Tribunal; and

(j) to perform the functions assigned to it by this or any other Act.

Proposed Amendment — 29

29. Functions of Commission — The functions of the Commission are to promote and advance respect for human rights in Ontario, to protect human rights in Ontario and, recognizing that it is in the public interest to do so and that it is the Commission's duty to protect the public interest, to identify and promote the elimination of discriminatory practices and, more specifically,

(a) to forward the policy that the dignity and worth of every person be recognized and that equal rights and opportunities be provided without discrimination that is contrary to law;

(b) to develop and conduct programs of public information and education to,

(i) promote awareness and understanding of, respect for and compliance with this Act, and

(ii) prevent and eliminate discriminatory practices that infringe rights under Part I;

(c) to undertake, direct and encourage research into discriminatory practices and to make recommendations designed to prevent and eliminate such discriminatory practices;

(d) to examine and review any statute or regulation, and any program or policy made by or under a statute, and make recommendations on any provision, program or policy that in his or her opinion is inconsistent with the intent of this Act;

(e) to initiate reviews and inquiries into incidents of tension or conflict, or conditions that lead or may lead to incidents of tension or conflict, in a community, institution, industry or sector of the economy, and to make recommendations, and encourage and co-ordinate plans, programs and activities, to reduce or prevent such incidents or sources of tension or conflict;

(f) to promote, assist and encourage public, municipal or private agencies, organizations, groups or persons to engage in programs to alleviate tensions and conflicts based upon identification by a prohibited ground of discrimination;

(g) to designate programs as special programs in accordance with section 14;

(h) to approve policies under section 30;

(i) to make applications to the Tribunal under section 35;

(j) to report to the people of Ontario on the state of human rights in Ontario and on its affairs;

(k) to perform the functions assigned to the Commission under this or any other Act.

2006, c. 30, s. 4 [To come into force June 30, 2008.]

1994, c. 27, s. 65(6); 2002, c. 18, Sched. C, s. 1, item 2

30. (1) Evidence obtained in course of investigation — No person who is a member of the Commission shall be required to give testimony in a civil suit or any proceeding as to information obtained in the course of an investigation under this Act.

(2) Idem — No person who is employed in the administration of this Act shall be required to give testimony in a civil suit or any proceeding other than a proceeding under this Act as to information obtained in the course of an investigation under this Act.

Proposed Amendment — 30

30. Commission policies — The Commission may approve policies prepared and published by the Commission to provide guidance in the application of Parts I and II.

2006, c. 30, s. 4 [To come into force June 30, 2008.]

31. (1) Annual report — The Commission shall make a report to the Minister not later than the 30th day of June in each year upon the affairs of the Commission during the year ending on the 31st day of March of that year.

(2) Idem — The Minister shall submit the report to the Lieutenant Governor in Council who shall cause the report to be laid before the Assembly if it is in session, or, if not, at the next session.

Proposed Amendment — 31

31. (1) Inquiries — The Commission may conduct an inquiry under this section for the purpose of carrying out its functions under this Act if the Commission believes it is in the public interest to do so.

(2) Conduct of inquiry — An inquiry may be conducted under this section by any person who is appointed by the Commission to carry out inquiries under this section.

(3) Production of certificate — A person conducting an inquiry under this section shall produce proof of their appointment upon request.

(4) Entry — A person conducting an inquiry under this section may, without warrant, enter any lands or any building, structure or premises where the person has reason to believe there may be documents, things or information relevant to the inquiry.

(5) Time of entry — The power to enter a place under subsection (4) may be exercised only during the place's regular business hours or, if it does not have regular business hours, during daylight hours.

(6) Dwellings — A person conducting an inquiry under this section shall not enter into a place or part of a place that is a dwelling without the consent of the occupant.

(7) Powers on inquiry — A person conducting an inquiry may,

(a) request the production for inspection and examination of documents or things that are or may be relevant to the inquiry;

(b) upon giving a receipt for it, remove from a place documents produced in response to a request under clause (a) for the purpose of making copies or extracts;

(c) question a person on matters that are or may be relevant to the inquiry, subject to the person's right to have counsel or a personal representative present during such questioning and exclude from the questioning any person who may be adverse in interest to the inquiry;

(d) use any data storage, processing or retrieval device or system used in carrying on business in the place in order to produce a document in readable form;

(e) take measurements or record by any means the physical dimensions of a place;

(f) take photographs, video recordings or other visual or audio recordings of the interior or exterior of a place; and

(g) require that a place or part thereof not be disturbed for a reasonable period of time for the purposes of carrying out an examination, inquiry or test.

(8) Written demand — A demand that a document or thing be produced must be in writing and must include a statement of the nature of the document or thing required.

(9) Assistance — A person conducting an inquiry may be accompanied by any person who has special, expert or professional knowledge and who may be of assistance in carrying out the inquiry.

(10) Use of force prohibited — A person conducting an inquiry shall not use force to enter and search premises under this section.

(11) Obligation to produce and assist — A person who is requested to produce a document or thing under clause (7)(a) shall produce it and shall, on request by the person conducting the inquiry, provide any assistance that is reasonably necessary, including assistance in using any data storage, processing or retrieval device or system, to produce a document in readable form.

(12) Return of removed things — A person conducting an inquiry who removes any document or thing from a place under clause (7)(b) shall,

(a) make it available to the person from whom it was removed, on request, at a time and place convenient for both that person and the person conducting the inquiry; and

(b) return it to the person from whom it was removed within a reasonable time.

(13) Admissibility of copies — A copy of a document certified by a person conducting an inquiry to be a true copy of the original is admissible in evidence to the same extent as the original and has the same evidentiary value.

(14) Obstruction — No person shall obstruct or interfere with a person conducting an inquiry under this section.

2006, c. 30, s. 4 [To come into force June 30, 2008.]

Proposed Addition — 31.1–31.7

31.1 (1) Search warrant — The Commission may authorize a person to apply to a justice of the peace for a warrant to enter a place and conduct a search of the place if,

(a) a person conducting an inquiry under section 31 has been denied entry to any place or asked to leave a place before concluding a search;

(b) a person conducting an inquiry under section 31 made a request for documents or things and the request was refused; or

(c) an inquiry under section 31 is otherwise obstructed or prevented.

(2) Same — Upon application by a person authorized under subsection (1) to do so, a justice of the peace may issue a warrant under this section if he or she is satisfied on information under oath or affirmation that the warrant is necessary for the purposes of carrying out the inquiry under section 31.

(3) Powers — A warrant obtained under subsection (2) may authorize a person named in the warrant, upon producing proof of his or her appointment,

(a) to enter any place specified in the warrant, including a dwelling; and

(b) to do any of the things specified in the warrant.

(4) Conditions on search warrant — A warrant obtained under subsection (2) shall contain such conditions as the justice of the peace considers advisable to ensure that any search authorized by the warrant is reasonable in the circumstances.

(5) Time of execution — An entry under a warrant issued under this section shall be made at such reasonable times as may be specified in the warrant.

(6) Expiry of warrant — A warrant issued under this section shall name a date of expiry, which shall be no later than 15 days after the warrant is issued, but a justice of the peace may extend the date of expiry for an additional period of no more than 15 days, upon application without notice by the person named in the warrant.

(7) Use of force — The person authorized to execute the warrant may call upon police officers for assistance in executing the warrant and the person may use whatever force is reasonably necessary to execute the warrant.

(8) Obstruction prohibited — No person shall obstruct or hinder a person in the execution of a warrant issued under this section.

(9) Application — Subsections 31(11), (12) and (13) apply with necessary modifications to an inquiry carried out pursuant to a warrant issued under this section.

2006, c. 30, s. 4 [To come into force June 30, 2008.]

31.2 Evidence used in Tribunal proceedings — Despite any other Act, evidence obtained on an inquiry under section 31 or 31.1 may be received into evidence in a proceeding before the Tribunal.

2006, c. 30, s. 4 [To come into force June 30, 2008.]

31.3 (1) Anti-Racism Secretariat — The Chief Commissioner directs the Anti-Racism Secretariat which shall be established in accordance with subsection (2).

(2) Composition — The Anti-Racism Secretariat shall be composed of not more than six persons appointed by the Lieutenant Governor in Council on the advice of the Chief Commissioner.

(3) Remuneration — The Lieutenant Governor in Council may fix the remuneration and allowance for expenses of the members of the Anti-Racism Secretariat.

(4) Functions of the Secretariat — At the direction of the Chief Commissioner, the Anti-Racism Secretariat shall,

(a) undertake, direct and encourage research into discriminatory practices that infringe rights under Part I on the basis of racism or a related ground and make recommendations to the Commission designed to prevent and eliminate such discriminatory practices;

(b) facilitate the development and provision of programs of public information and education relating to the elimination of racism; and

(c) undertake such tasks and responsibilities as may be assigned by the Chief Commissioner.

2006, c. 30, s. 4 [To come into force June 30, 2008.]

31.4 (1) Disability Rights Secretariat — The Chief Commissioner directs the Disability Rights Secretariat which shall be established in accordance with subsection (2).

(2) Composition — The Disability Rights Secretariat shall be composed of not more than six persons appointed by the Lieutenant Governor in Council on the advice of the Chief Commissioner.

(3) Remuneration — The Lieutenant Governor in Council may fix the remuneration and allowance for expenses of the members of the Disability Rights Secretariat.

(4) Functions of the Secretariat — At the direction of the Chief Commissioner, the Disability Rights Secretariat shall,

(a) undertake, direct and encourage research into discriminatory practices that infringe rights under Part I on the basis of disability and make recommendations to the Commission designed to prevent and eliminate such discriminatory practices;

(b) facilitate the development and provision of programs of public information and education intended to promote the elimination of discriminatory practices that infringe rights under Part I on the basis of disability; and

(c) undertake such tasks and responsibilities as may be assigned by the Chief Commissioner.

2006, c. 30, s. 4 [To come into force June 30, 2008.]

31.5 Advisory groups — The Chief Commissioner may establish such advisory groups as he or she considers appropriate to advise the Commission about the elimination of discriminatory practices that infringe rights under this Act.

2006, c. 30, s. 4 [To come into force June 30, 2008.]

31.6 (1) Annual report — Every year, the Commission shall prepare an annual report on the affairs of the Commission that occurred during the 12-month period ending on March 31 of each year.

(2) Report to Speaker — The Commission shall submit the report to the Speaker of the Assembly no later than on June 30 in each year who shall cause the report to be laid before the Assembly if it is in session or, if not, at the next session.

(3) Copy to Minister — The Commission shall give a copy of the report to the Minister at least 30 days before it is submitted to the Speaker under subsection (2).

2006, c. 30, s. 4 [To come into force June 30, 2008.]

31.7 Other reports — In addition to the annual report, the Commission may make any other reports respecting the state of human rights in Ontario and the affairs of the Commission as it considers appropriate, and may present such reports to the public or any other person it considers appropriate.

2006, c. 30, s. 4 [To come into force June 30, 2008.]

PART IV — ENFORCEMENT

[Heading amended to "Human Rights Tribunal of Ontario", 2006, c. 30, s. 5. To come into force June 30, 2008.]

32. (1) Complaints — Where a person believes that a right of the person under this Act has been infringed, the person may file with the Commission a complaint in a form approved by the Commission.

(2) Idem — The Commission may initiate a complaint by itself or at the request of any person.

(3) Combining of complaints — Where two or more complaints,

(a) bring into question a practice of infringement engaged in by the same person; or

(b) have questions of law or fact in common,

the Commission may combine the complaints and deal with them in the same proceeding.

Proposed Amendment — 32

32. (1) Tribunal — The Tribunal known as the Human Rights Tribunal of Ontario in English and Tribunal des droits de la personne de l'Ontario in French is continued.

(2) Composition — The Tribunal shall be composed of such members as are appointed by the Lieutenant Governor in Council in accordance with the selection process described in subsection (3).

(3) **Selection process** — The selection process for the appointment of members of the Tribunal shall be a competitive process and the criteria to be applied in assessing candidates shall include the following:

1. Experience, knowledge or training with respect to human rights law and issues.
2. Aptitude for impartial adjudication.
3. Aptitude for applying the alternative adjudicative practices and procedures that may be set out in the Tribunal rules.

(4) **Remuneration** — The members of the Tribunal shall be paid such remuneration and allowance for expenses as are fixed by the Lieutenant Governor in Council.

(5) **Term of office** — A member of the Tribunal shall be appointed for such term as may be specified by the Lieutenant Governor in Council.

(6) **Chair, vice-chair** — The Lieutenant Governor in Council shall appoint a chair and may appoint one or more vice-chairs of the Tribunal from among the members of the Tribunal.

(7) **Alternate chair** — The Lieutenant Governor in Council shall designate one of the vice-chairs to be the alternate chair.

(8) **Same** — If the chair is unable to act, the alternate chair shall perform the duties of the chair and, for this purpose, has all the powers of the chair.

(9) **Employees** — The Tribunal may appoint such employees as it considers necessary for the proper conduct of its affairs and the employees shall be appointed under the *Public Service Act*.

Proposed Amendment — Conditional Amendment — 32(9)

On the later of the coming into force of S.O. 2006, c. 35, Sched. C, s. 132 [In force August 20, 2007.] and S.O. 2006, c. 30, s. 5 (Bill 107, s. 6) [To come into force June 30, 2008.], subsection 32(9) is replaced by the following:

> (9) Employees — The Tribunal may appoint such employees as it considers necessary for the proper conduct of its affairs and the employees shall be appointed under Part III of the *Public Service of Ontario Act, 2006*.
>
> 2006, c. 35, Sched. C, s. 132(6) [Conditions not yet satisfied.]

(10) **Evidence obtained in course of proceeding** — A member or employee of the Tribunal shall not be required to give testimony in a civil suit or any proceeding as to information obtained in the course of a proceeding before the Tribunal.

(11) Same — Despite subsection (10), an employee of the Tribunal may be required to give testimony in a proceeding before the Tribunal in the circumstances prescribed by the Tribunal rules.

2006, c. 30, s. 5 [To come into force June 30, 2008.]

33. (1) Investigation of complaints — Subject to section 34, the Commission shall investigate a complaint and endeavour to effect a settlement.

Proposed Amendment — 33(1)

(1) Investigation of complaints — Subject to section 34, the Commission shall investigate a complaint and may endeavour to effect a settlement.

1994, c. 27, s. 65(7) [Not in force at date of publication.]

(2) Investigation — An investigation by the Commission may be made by a member or employee of the Commission who is authorized by the Commission for the purpose.

(3) Powers on investigation — A person authorized to investigate a complaint may,

(a) enter any place, other than a place that is being used as a dwelling, at any reasonable time, for the purpose of investigating the complaint;

(b) request the production for inspection and examination of documents or things that are or may be relevant to the investigation;

(c) upon giving a receipt therefor, remove from a place documents produced in response to a request under clause (b) for the purpose of making copies thereof or extracts therefrom and shall promptly return them to the person who produced or furnished them; and

(d) question a person on matters that are or may be relevant to the complaint subject to the person's right to have counsel or a personal representative present during such questioning, and may exclude from the questioning any person who may be adverse in interest to the complainant.

(4) Entry into dwellings — A person investigating a complaint shall not enter a place that is being used as a dwelling without the consent of the occupier except under the authority of a warrant issued under subsection (8).

(5) Denial of entry — Subject to subsection (4), if a person who is or may be a party to a complaint denies entry to any place, or instructs the person investigating to leave the place, or impedes or prevents an investigation therein, the Commission may refer the matter to the Tribunal or may authorize an employee or member to apply to a justice of the peace for a warrant to enter under subsection (8).

(6) **Refusal to produce** — If a person refuses to comply with a request for production of documents or things, the Commission may refer the matter to the Tribunal, or may authorize an employee or member to apply to a justice of the peace for a search warrant under subsection (7).

(7) **Warrant for search** — Where a justice of the peace is satisfied on evidence upon oath or affirmation that there are in a place documents that there is reasonable ground to believe will afford evidence relevant to the complaint, he or she may issue a warrant in the prescribed form authorizing a person named in the warrant to search a place for any such documents, and to remove them for the purposes of making copies thereof or extracts therefrom, and the documents shall be returned promptly to the place from which they were removed.

(8) **Warrant for entry** — Where a justice of the peace is satisfied by evidence upon oath or affirmation that there is reasonable ground to believe it is necessary that a place being used as a dwelling or to which entry has been denied be entered to investigate a complaint, he or she may issue a warrant in the prescribed form authorizing such entry by a person named in the warrant.

(9) **Execution of warrant** — A warrant issued under subsection (7) or (8) shall be executed at reasonable times as specified in the warrant.

(10) **Expiration of warrant** — Every warrant shall name a date on which it expires, which shall be a date not later than fifteen days after it is issued.

(11) **Obstruction** — No person shall hinder, obstruct or interfere with a person in the execution of a warrant or otherwise impede an investigation under this Act.

(12) **Idem** — Subsection (11) is not contravened by a refusal to comply with a request for the production of documents or things made under clause (3)(b).

(13) **Admissibility of copies** — Copies of, or extracts from, documents removed from premises under clause (3)(c) or subsection (7) certified as being true copies of the originals by the person who made them, are admissible in evidence to the same extent as, and have the same evidentiary value as, the documents of which they are copies or extracts.

Proposed Amendment — 33

33. (1) Panels — The chair of the Tribunal may appoint panels composed of one or more members of the Tribunal to exercise and perform the powers and duties of the Tribunal.

(2) Person designated to preside over panel — If a panel of the Tribunal holds a hearing, the chair of the Tribunal shall designate one member of the panel to preside over the hearing.

(3) Reassignment of panel — If a panel of the Tribunal is unable for any reason to exercise or perform the powers or duties of the Tribunal, the chair of the Tribunal may assign another panel in its place.

(4) [Repealed 2006, c. 30, s. 5. To come into force June 30, 2008.]

(5) [Repealed 2006, c. 30, s. 5. To come into force June 30, 2008.]

(6) [Repealed 2006, c. 30, s. 5. To come into force June 30, 2008.]

(7) [Repealed 2006, c. 30, s. 5. To come into force June 30, 2008.]

(8) [Repealed 2006, c. 30, s. 5. To come into force June 30, 2008.]

(9) [Repealed 2006, c. 30, s. 5. To come into force June 30, 2008.]

(10) [Repealed 2006, c. 30, s. 5. To come into force June 30, 2008.]

(11) [Repealed 2006, c. 30, s. 5. To come into force June 30, 2008.]

(12) [Repealed 2006, c. 30, s. 5. To come into force June 30, 2008.]

(13) [Repealed 2006, c. 30, s. 5. To come into force June 30, 2008.]

2006, c. 30, s. 5 [To come into force June 30, 2008.]

1994, c. 27, s. 65(8), (9); 2002, c. 18, Sched. C, s. 1, item 3

34. (1) Decision to not deal with complaint — Where it appears to the Commission that,

(a) the complaint is one that could or should be more appropriately dealt with under an Act other than this Act;

(b) the subject-matter of the complaint is trivial, frivolous, vexatious or made in bad faith;

(c) the complaint is not within the jurisdiction of the Commission; or

(d) the facts upon which the complaint is based occurred more than six months before the complaint was filed, unless the Commission is satisfied that the delay was incurred in good faith and no substantial prejudice will result to any person affected by the delay, the Commission may, in its discretion, decide to not deal with the complaint.

(2) **Notice of decision and reasons** — Where the Commission decides to not deal with a complaint, it shall advise the complainant in writing of the decision and the reasons therefor and of the procedure under section 37 for having the decision reconsidered.

Proposed Amendment — 34

34. (1) **Application by person** — If a person believes that any of his or her rights under Part I have been infringed, the person may apply to the Tribunal for an order under section 45.2,

(a) within one year after the incident to which the application relates; or

(b) if there was a series of incidents, within one year after the last incident in the series.

(2) **Late applications** — A person may apply under subsection (1) after the expiry of the time limit under that subsection if the Tribunal is satisfied that the delay was incurred in good faith and no substantial prejudice will result to any person affected by the delay.

(3) **Form** — An application under subsection (1) shall be in a form approved by the Tribunal.

(4) **Two or more persons** — Two or more persons who are each entitled to make an application under subsection (1) may file the applications jointly, subject to any provision in the Tribunal rules that authorizes the Tribunal to direct that one or more of the applications be considered in a separate proceeding.

(5) **Application on behalf of another** — A person or organization, other than the Commission, may apply on behalf of another person to the Tribunal for an order under section 45.2 if the other person,

(a) would have been entitled to bring an application under subsection (1); and

(b) consents to the application.

(6) **Participation in proceedings** — If a person or organization makes an application on behalf of another person, the person or organization may participate in the proceeding in accordance with the Tribunal rules.

(7) Consent form — A consent under clause (5)(b) shall be in a form specified in the Tribunal rules.

(8) Time of application — An application under subsection (5) shall be made within the time period required for making an application under subsection (1).

(9) Application — Subsections (2) and (3) apply to an application made under subsection (5).

(10) Withdrawal of application — An application under subsection (5) may be withdrawn by the person on behalf of whom the application is made in accordance with the Tribunal rules.

(11) Where application barred — A person who believes that one of his or her rights under Part I has been infringed may not make an application under subsection (1) with respect to that right if,

(a) a civil proceeding has been commenced in a court in which the person is seeking an order under section 46.1 with respect to the alleged infringement and the proceeding has not been finally determined or withdrawn; or

(b) a court has finally determined the issue of whether the right has been infringed or the matter has been settled.

(12) Final determination — For the purpose of subsection (11), a proceeding or issue has not been finally determined if a right of appeal exists and the time for appealing has not expired.

2006, c. 30, s. 5 [To come into force June 30, 2008.]

35. (1) Human Rights Tribunal of Ontario — The board of inquiry established under this section as it read immediately before the day the *Government Efficiency Act, 2002* receives Royal Assent is continued under the name Human Rights Tribunal of Ontario in English and Tribunal des droits de la personne de l'Ontario in French and shall be composed of such members as are appointed by the Lieutenant Governor in Council.

(2) Remuneration — The members of the Tribunal shall be paid such allowances and expenses as are fixed by the Lieutenant Governor in Council.

(3) Chair, vice-chair — The Lieutenant Governor in Council shall appoint a chair and may appoint one or more vice-chairs of the Tribunal from among the members of the Tribunal.

(4) Employees — Such employees as are considered necessary for the proper conduct of the Tribunal may be appointed under the *Public Service Act*.

(5) **Rules** — The Tribunal may make rules regulating its practice and procedure and generally for the conduct and management of its affairs and such rules are not regulations within the meaning of the *Regulations Act.*

(6) **Panels** — The chair of the Tribunal may appoint panels composed of one or more members of the Tribunal to hold hearings in the place of the full Tribunal wherever the Tribunal is required to hold a hearing under this Act and, where a panel holds a hearing, the panel has all the powers and duties, except the power in subsection (5), given to the Tribunal under this Act.

(7) **Person designated to preside over panel** — The chair of the Tribunal shall designate one member of each panel to preside over the panel's hearings.

(8) **Reassignment of panel** — Where a panel of the Tribunal is unable for any reason to exercise the powers under section 39 or 41, the chair of the Tribunal may assign another panel in its place.

Proposed Amendment — 35

35. (1) **Application by Commission** — The Commission may apply to the Tribunal for an order under section 45.3 if the Commission is of the opinion that,

(a) it is in the public interest to make an application; and

(b) an order under section 45.3 could provide an appropriate remedy.

(2) **Form** — An application under subsection (1) shall be in a form approved by the Tribunal.

(3) **Effect of application** — An application made by the Commission does not affect the right of a person to make an application under section 34 in respect of the same matter.

(4) **Applications dealt with together** — If a person or organization makes an application under section 34 and the Commission makes an application under this section in respect of the same matter, the two applications shall be dealt with together in the same proceeding unless the Tribunal determines otherwise.

(5) [Repealed 2006, c. 30, s. 5. To come into force June 30, 2008.]

(6) [Repealed 2006, c. 30, s. 5. To come into force June 30, 2008.]

(7) [Repealed 2006, c. 30, s. 5. To come into force June 30, 2008.]

(8) [Repealed 2006, c. 30, s. 5. To come into force June 30, 2008.]
2006, c. 30, s. 5 [To come into force June 30, 2008.]

1994, c. 27, s. 65(10); 2002, c. 18, Sched. C, ss. 1 (items 4, 5), 6

36. (1) Referred to Tribunal — Where the Commission does not effect a settlement of the complaint and it appears to the Commission that the procedure is appropriate and the evidence warrants an inquiry, the Commission may refer the subject-matter of the complaint to the Tribunal.

(2) Notice of decision not to appoint inquiry — Where the Commission decides not to refer the subject-matter of a complaint to the Tribunal, it shall advise the complainant and the person complained against in writing of the decision and the reasons therefor and inform the complainant of the procedure under section 37 for having the decision reconsidered.

Proposed Amendment — 36

36. Parties — The parties to an application under section 34 or 35 are the following:

1. In the case of an application under subsection 34(1), the person who made the application.
2. In the case of an application under subsection 34(5), the person on behalf of whom the application is made.
3. In the case of an application under section 35, the Commission.
4. Any person against whom an order is sought in the application.
5. Any other person or the Commission, if they are added as a party by the Tribunal.

2006, c. 30, s. 5 [To come into force June 30, 2008.]

1994, c. 27, s. 65(12), (13); 2002, c. 18, Sched. C, s. 1, items 6, 7

37. (1) Reconsideration — Within a period of fifteen days of the date of mailing the decision and reasons therefor mentioned in subsection 34(2) or subsection 36(2), or such longer period as the Commission may for special reasons allow, a complainant may request the Commission to reconsider its decision by filing an application for reconsideration containing a concise statement of the material facts upon which the application is based.

(2) Notice of application — Upon receipt of an application for reconsideration the Commission shall as soon as is practicable notify the person complained against of the application and afford the person an opportunity to make written submissions with respect thereto within such time as the Commission specifies.

(3) **Decision** — Every decision of the Commission on reconsideration together with the reasons therefor shall be recorded in writing and promptly communicated to the complainant and the person complained against and the decision shall be final.

Proposed Amendment — 37

37. (1) **Intervention by Commission** — The Commission may intervene in an application under section 34 on such terms as the Tribunal may determine having regard to the role and mandate of the Commission under this Act.

(2) **Intervention as a party** — The Commission may intervene as a party to an application under section 34 if the person or organization who made the application consents to the intervention as a party.

(3) [Repealed 2006, c. 30, s. 5. To come into force June 30, 2008.]

2006, c. 30, s. 5 [To come into force June 30, 2008.]

38. [Repealed 1994, c. 27, s. 65(14).]

Proposed Amendment — 38

38. **Disclosure of information to Commission** — Despite anything in the *Freedom of Information and Protection of Privacy Act*, at the request of the Commission, the Tribunal shall disclose to the Commission copies of applications and responses filed with the Tribunal and may disclose to the Commission other documents in its custody or in its control.

2006, c. 30, s. 5 [To come into force June 30, 2008.]

39. (1) **Hearing** — The Tribunal shall hold a hearing,

(a) to determine whether a right of the complainant under this Act has been infringed;

(b) to determine who infringed the right; and

(c) to decide upon an appropriate order under section 41,

and the hearing shall be commenced within thirty days after the date on which the subject-matter of the complaint was referred to the Tribunal.

(2) **Parties** — The parties to a proceeding before the Tribunal are,

(a) the Commission, which shall have the carriage of the complaint;

(b) the complainant;

(c) any person who the Commission alleges has infringed the right;

(d) any person appearing to the Tribunal to have infringed the right;

(e) where the complaint is of alleged conduct constituting harassment under subsection 2(2) or subsection 5(2) or of alleged conduct under section 7, any person who, in the opinion of the Tribunal, knew or was in possession of facts from which the person ought reasonably to have known of the conduct and who had authority to penalize or prevent the conduct.

(3) **Adding parties** — A party may be added by the Tribunal under clause (2)(d) or clause (2)(e) at any stage of the proceeding upon such terms as the Tribunal considers proper.

(4) **Adjournment on production** — Where the Tribunal exercises its power under clause 12(1)(b) of the *Statutory Powers Procedure Act* to issue a summons requiring the production in evidence of documents or things, it may, upon the production of the documents or things before it, adjourn the proceedings to permit the parties to examine the documents or things.

(5) **Adjournment for view** — The Tribunal may, where it appears to be in the interests of justice, direct that the Tribunal and the parties and their counsel or representatives shall have a view of any place or thing, and may adjourn the proceedings for that purpose.

(6) **Members at hearing not to have taken part in investigation, etc.** — A member of the Tribunal hearing a complaint must not have taken part in any investigation or consideration of the subject-matter of the inquiry before the hearing and shall not communicate directly or indirectly in relation to the subject-matter of the inquiry with any person or with any party or any party's representative except upon notice to and opportunity for all parties to participate, but the Tribunal may seek legal advice from an adviser independent of the parties and in such case the nature of the advice shall be made known to the parties in order that they may make submissions as to the law.

Proposed Amendment — 39

39. Powers of Tribunal — The Tribunal has the jurisdiction to exercise the powers conferred on it by or under this Act and to determine all questions of fact or law that arise in any application before it.

2006, c. 30, s. 5 [To come into force June 30, 2008.]

1994, c. 27, s. 65(15)–(18); 2002, c. 18, Sched. C, s. 1, items 8–12

40. [Repealed 1994, c. 27, s. 65(19).]

Proposed Amendment — 40

40. Disposition of applications — The Tribunal shall dispose of applications made under this Part by adopting the procedures and practices provided for in its rules or otherwise available to the Tribunal which, in its opinion, offer the best opportunity for a fair, just and expeditious resolution of the merits of the applications.

2006, c. 30, s. 5 [To come into force June 30, 2008.]

41. (1) Orders of Tribunals — Where the Tribunal, after a hearing, finds that a right of the complainant under Part I has been infringed and that the infringement is a contravention of section 9 by a party to the proceeding, the Tribunal may, by order,

(a) direct the party to do anything that, in the opinion of the Tribunal, the party ought to do to achieve compliance with this Act, both in respect of the complaint and in respect of future practices; and

(b) direct the party to make restitution, including monetary compensation, for loss arising out of the infringement, and, where the infringement has been engaged in wilfully or recklessly, monetary compensation may include an award, not exceeding $10,000, for mental anguish.

(2) Order to prevent harassment — Where the Tribunal makes a finding under subsection (1) that a right is infringed on the ground of harassment under subsection 2(2) or subsection 5(2) or conduct under section 7, and the Tribunal finds that a person who is a party to the proceeding,

(a) knew or was in possession of knowledge from which the person ought to have known of the infringement; and

(b) had the authority by reasonably available means to penalize or prevent the conduct and failed to use it,

the Tribunal shall remain seized of the matter and upon complaint of a continuation or repetition of the infringement of the right the Commission may investigate the complaint and, subject to subsection 36(2), request the Tribunal to re-convene and if the Tribunal finds that a person who is a party to the proceeding,

(c) knew or was in possession of knowledge from which the person ought to have known of the repetition of infringement; and

(d) had the authority by reasonably available means to penalize or prevent the continuation or repetition of the conduct and failed to use it,

the Tribunal may make an order requiring the person to take whatever sanctions or steps are reasonably available to prevent any further continuation or repetition of the infringement of the right.

(3) [Repealed 1994, c. 27, s. 65(21).]

(4) Costs — Where, upon dismissing a complaint, the Tribunal finds that,

(a) the complaint was trivial, frivolous, vexatious or made in bad faith; or

(b) in the particular circumstances undue hardship was caused to the person complained against,

the Tribunal may order the Commission to pay to the person complained against such costs as are fixed by the Tribunal.

(5) Decision within 30 days — The Tribunal shall make its finding and decision within thirty days after the conclusion of its hearing.

Proposed Amendment — 41

41. Interpretation of Part and rules — This Part and the Tribunal rules shall be liberally construed to permit the Tribunal to adopt practices and procedures, including alternatives to traditional adjudicative or adversarial procedures that, in the opinion of the Tribunal, will facilitate fair, just and expeditious resolutions of the merits of the matters before it.

2006, c. 30, s. 5 [To come into force June 30, 2008.]

1994, c. 27, s. 65(20), (21); 2002, c. 18, Sched. C, s. 1, items 13–15

41.1 [Repealed 1995, c. 4, s. 3(3).]

42. (1) Appeal from decision of Tribunal — Any party to a proceeding before the Tribunal may appeal from a decision or order of the Tribunal to the Divisional Court in accordance with the rules of court.

(2) Record to be filed in court — Where notice of an appeal is served under this section, the Tribunal shall forthwith file in the Divisional Court the record of the proceedings before it in which the decision or order appealed from was made and the record, together with a transcript of the oral evidence taken before the Tribunal if it is not part of the record of the Tribunal, shall constitute the record in the appeal.

(3) Powers of court — An appeal under this section may be made on questions of law or fact or both and the court may affirm or reverse the decision or order of the Tribunal or direct the Tribunal to make any decision or order that the Tribunal is authorized to make under this Act and the court may substitute its opinion for that of the Tribunal.

Proposed Amendment — 42

42. (1) Statutory Powers Procedure Act — The provisions of the *Statutory Powers Procedure Act* apply to a proceeding before the Tribunal unless they conflict with a provision of this Act, the regulations or the Tribunal rules.

(2) Conflict — Despite section 32 of the *Statutory Powers Procedure Act*, this Act, the regulations and the Tribunal rules prevail over the provisions of that Act with which they conflict.

(3) [Repealed 2006, c. 30, s. 5. To come into force June 30, 2008.]

2006, c. 30, s. 5 [To come into force June 30, 2008.]

1994, c. 27, s. 65(23); 2002, c. 18, Sched. C, s. 1, items 16, 17

43. Settlements — Where a settlement of a complaint is agreed to in writing, signed by the parties and approved by the Commission, the settlement is binding upon the parties, and a breach of the settlement is grounds for a complaint under section 32, and this Part applies to the complaint in the same manner as if the breach of the settlement were an infringement of a right under this Act.

Proposed Amendment — 43

43. (1) Tribunal rules — The Tribunal may make rules governing the practice and procedure before it.

(2) Required practices and procedures — The rules shall ensure that the following requirements are met with respect to any proceeding before the Tribunal:

1. An application that is within the jurisdiction of the Tribunal shall not be finally disposed of without affording the parties an opportunity to make oral submissions in accordance with the rules.
2. An application may not be finally disposed of without written reasons.

(3) Same — Without limiting the generality of subsection (1), the Tribunal rules may,

(a) provide for and require the use of hearings or of practices and procedures that are provided for under the *Statutory Powers Procedure Act* or that are alternatives to traditional adjudicative or adversarial procedures;

(b) authorize the Tribunal to,

(i) define or narrow the issues required to dispose of an application and limit the evidence and submissions of the parties on such issues, and

(ii) determine the order in which the issues and evidence in a proceeding will be presented;

(c) authorize the Tribunal to conduct examinations in chief or cross-examinations of a witness;

(d) prescribe the stages of its processes at which preliminary, procedural or interlocutory matters will be determined;

(e) authorize the Tribunal to make or cause to be made such examinations of records and such other inquiries as it considers necessary in the circumstances;

(f) authorize the Tribunal to require a party to a proceeding or another person to,

(i) produce any document, information or thing and provide such assistance as is reasonably necessary, including using any data storage, processing or retrieval device or system, to produce the information in any form,

(ii) provide a statement or oral or affidavit evidence, or

(iii) in the case of a party to the proceeding, adduce evidence or produce witnesses who are reasonably within the party's control; and

(g) govern any matter prescribed by the regulations.

(4) General or particular — The rules may be of general or particular application.

(5) Consistency — The rules shall be consistent with this Part.

(6) Not a regulation — The rules made under this section are not regulations for the purposes of the *Regulations Act*.

Proposed Amendment — Conditional Amendment — 43(6)

On the later of the coming into force of S.O. 2006, c. 30, s. 5 [To come into force June 30, 2008.] and S.O. 2006, c. 21, Sched. F, s. 134 [In force July 25, 2007.], subsection 43(6) is replaced by the following:

(6) Not a regulation — The rules made under this section are not regulations for the purposes of Part III of the *Legislation Act, 2006*.

2006, c. 30, s. 11 [Conditions not yet satisfied.]

(7) **Public consultations** — The Tribunal shall hold public consultations before making a rule under this section.

(8) **Failure to comply with rules** — Failure on the part of the Tribunal to comply with the practices and procedures required by the rules or the exercise of a discretion under the rules by the Tribunal in a particular manner is not a ground for setting aside a decision of the Tribunal on an application for judicial review or any other form of relief, unless the failure or the exercise of a discretion caused a substantial wrong which affected the final disposition of the matter.

(9) **Adverse inference** — The Tribunal may draw an adverse inference from the failure of a party to comply, in whole or in part, with an order of the Tribunal for the party to do anything under a rule made under clause (3)(f).

2006, c. 30, s. 5 [To come into force June 30, 2008.]

44. (1) **Penalty** — Every person who contravenes section 9, subsection 33(11), or an order of the Tribunal, is guilty of an offence and on conviction is liable to a fine of not more than $25,000.

(2) **Consent to prosecution** — No prosecution for an offence under this Act shall be instituted except with the consent in writing of the Attorney General.

Proposed Amendment — 44

44. (1) **Tribunal inquiry** — At the request of a party to an application under this Part, the Tribunal may appoint a person to conduct an inquiry under this section if the Tribunal is satisfied that,

(a) an inquiry is required in order to obtain evidence;

(b) the evidence obtained may assist in achieving a fair, just and expeditious resolution of the merits of the application; and

(c) it is appropriate to do so in the circumstances.

(2) **Production of certificate** — A person conducting an inquiry under this section shall produce proof of their appointment upon request.

(3) **Entry** — A person conducting an inquiry under this section may, without warrant, enter any lands or any building, structure or premises where the person has reason to believe there may be evidence relevant to the application.

(4) Time of entry — The power to enter a place under subsection (3) may be exercised only during the place's regular business hours or, if it does not have regular business hours, during daylight hours.

(5) Dwellings — A person conducting an inquiry shall not enter into a place or part of a place that is a dwelling without the consent of the occupant.

(6) Powers on inquiry — A person conducting an inquiry may,

(a) request the production for inspection and examination of documents or things that are or may be relevant to the inquiry;

(b) upon giving a receipt for it, remove from a place documents produced in response to a request under clause (a) for the purpose of making copies or extracts;

(c) question a person on matters that are or may be relevant to the inquiry, subject to the person's right to have counsel or a personal representative present during such questioning and exclude from the questioning any person who may be adverse in interest to the inquiry;

(d) use any data storage, processing or retrieval device or system used in carrying on business in the place in order to produce a document in readable form;

(e) take measurements or record by any means the physical dimensions of a place;

(f) take photographs, video recordings or other visual or audio recordings of the interior or exterior of a place; and

(g) require that a place or part thereof not be disturbed for a reasonable period of time for the purposes of carrying out an examination, inquiry or test.

(7) Written demand — A demand that a document or thing be produced must be in writing and must include a statement of the nature of the document or thing required.

(8) Assistance — A person conducting an inquiry may be accompanied by any person who has special, expert or professional knowledge and who may be of assistance in carrying out the inquiry.

(9) Use of force prohibited — A person conducting an inquiry shall not use force to enter and search premises under this section.

(10) Obligation to produce and assist — A person who is requested to produce a document or thing under clause (6)(a) shall produce it and shall, on request by the person conducting the inquiry, provide any assistance that is reasonably necessary, including assistance in using any data storage, processing or retrieval device or system, to produce a document in readable form.

(11) **Return of removed things** — A person conducting an inquiry who removes any document or thing from a place under clause (6)(b) shall,

(a) make it available to the person from whom it was removed, on request, at a time and place convenient for both that person and the person conducting the inquiry; and

(b) return it to the person from whom it was removed within a reasonable time.

(12) **Admissibility of copies** — A copy of a document certified by a person conducting an inquiry to be a true copy of the original is admissible in evidence to the same extent as the original and has the same evidentiary value.

(13) **Obstruction** — No person shall obstruct or interfere with a person conducting an inquiry under this section.

(14) **Inquiry report** — A person conducting an inquiry shall prepare a report and submit it to the Tribunal and the parties to the application that gave rise to the inquiry in accordance with the Tribunal rules.

(15) **Transfer of inquiry to Commission** — The Commission may, at the request of the Tribunal, appoint a person to conduct an inquiry under this section and the person so appointed has all of the powers of a person appointed by the Tribunal under this section and shall report to the Tribunal in accordance with subsection (14).

2006, c. 30, s. 5 [To come into force June 30, 2008.]

1994, c. 27, s. 65(23); 2002, c. 18, Sched. C, s. 1, item 18

45. (1) **Acts of officers, etc.** — For the purposes of this Act, except subsection 2 (2), subsection 5(2), section 7 and subsection 44(1), any act or thing done or omitted to be done in the course of his or her employment by an officer, official, employee or agent of a corporation, trade union, trade or occupational association, unincorporated association or employers' organization shall be deemed to be an act or thing done or omitted to be done by the corporation, trade union, trade or occupational association, unincorporated association or employers' organization.

(2) **Opinion re authority or acquiescence** — At the request of a corporation, trade union, trade or occupational association, unincorporated association or employers' organization, the Tribunal in its decision shall make

known whether or not, in its opinion, an act or thing done or omitted to be done by an officer, official, employee or agent was done or omitted to be done with or without the authority or acquiescence of the corporation, trade union, trade or occupational association, unincorporated association or employers' organization, and the opinion does not affect the application of subsection (1).

Proposed Amendment — 45

45. Deferral of application — The Tribunal may defer an application in accordance with the Tribunal rules.

2006, c. 30, s. 5 [To come into force June 30, 2008.]

1994, c. 27, s. 65(23); 2002, c. 18, Sched. C, s. 1, item 19

Proposed Addition — 45.1–45.10

45.1 Dismissal in accordance with rules — The Tribunal may dismiss an application, in whole or in part, in accordance with its rules if the Tribunal is of the opinion that another proceeding has appropriately dealt with the substance of the application.

2006, c. 30, s. 5 [To come into force June 30, 2008.]

45.2 (1) Orders of Tribunal: applications under s. 34 — On an application under section 34, the Tribunal may make one or more of the following orders if the Tribunal determines that a party to the application has infringed a right under Part I of another party to the application:

1. An order directing the party who infringed the right to pay monetary compensation to the party whose right was infringed for loss arising out of the infringement, including compensation for injury to dignity, feelings and self-respect.
2. An order directing the party who infringed the right to make restitution to the party whose right was infringed, other than through monetary compensation, for loss arising out of the infringement, including restitution for injury to dignity, feelings and self-respect.
3. An order directing any party to the application to do anything that, in the opinion of the Tribunal, the party ought to do to promote compliance with this Act.

(2) Orders under par. 3 of subs. (1) — For greater certainty, an order under paragraph 3 of subsection (1),

(a) may direct a person to do anything with respect to future practices; and

(b) may be made even if no order under that paragraph was requested.

2006, c. 30, s. 5 [To come into force June 30, 2008.]

45.3 (1) Orders of Tribunal: applications under s. 35 — If, on an application under section 35, the Tribunal determines that any one or more of the parties to the application have infringed a right under Part I, the Tribunal may make an order directing any party to the application to do anything that, in the opinion of the Tribunal, the party ought to do to promote compliance with this Act.

(2) Same — For greater certainty, an order under subsection (1) may direct a person to do anything with respect to future practices.

2006, c. 30, s. 5 [To come into force June 30, 2008.]

45.4 (1) Matters referred to Commission — The Tribunal may refer any matters arising out of a proceeding before it to the Commission if, in the Tribunal's opinion, they are matters of public interest or are otherwise of interest to the Commission.

(2) Same — The Commission may, in its discretion, decide whether to deal with a matter referred to it by the Tribunal.

2006, c. 30, s. 5 [To come into force June 30, 2008.]

45.5 (1) Documents published by Commission — In a proceeding under this Part, the Tribunal may consider policies approved by the Commission under section 30.

(2) Same — Despite subsection (1), the Tribunal shall consider a policy approved by the Commission under section 30 in a proceeding under this Part if a party to the proceeding or an intervenor requests that it do so.

2006, c. 30, s. 5 [To come into force June 30, 2008.]

45.6 (1) Stated case to Divisional court — If the Tribunal makes a final decision or order in a proceeding in which the Commission was a party or an intervenor, and the Commission believes that the decision or order is not consistent with a policy that has been approved by the Commission under section 30, the Commission may apply to the Tribunal to have the Tribunal state a case to the Divisional Court.

(2) Same — If the Tribunal determines that the application of the Commission relates to a question of law and that it is appropriate to do so, it may state the case in writing for the opinion of the Divisional Court upon the question of law.

(3) Parties — The parties to a stated case under this section are the parties to the proceeding referred to in subsection (1) and, if the Commission was an intervenor in that proceeding, the Commission.

(4) Submissions by Tribunal — The Divisional Court may hear submissions from the Tribunal.

(5) Powers of Divisional Court — The Divisional Court shall hear and determine the stated case.

(6) No stay — Unless otherwise ordered by the Tribunal or the Divisional Court, an application by the Commission under subsection (1) or the stating of a case to the Divisional Court under subsection (2) does not operate as a stay of the final decision or order of the Tribunal.

(7) Reconsideration of Tribunal decision — Within 30 days of receipt of the decision of the Divisional Court, any party to the stated case proceeding may apply to the Tribunal for a reconsideration of its original decision or order in accordance with section 45.7.

2006, c. 30, s. 5 [To come into force June 30, 2008.]

45.7 (1) Reconsideration of Tribunal decision — Any party to a proceeding before the Tribunal may request that the Tribunal reconsider its decision in accordance with the Tribunal rules.

(2) Same — Upon request under subsection (1) or on its own motion, the Tribunal may reconsider its decision in accordance with its rules.

2006, c. 30, s. 5 [To come into force June 30, 2008.]

45.8 Decisions final — Subject to section 45.6 of this Act, section 21.1 of the *Statutory Powers Procedure Act* and the Tribunal rules, a decision of the Tribunal is final and not subject to appeal and shall not be altered or set aside in an application for judicial review or in any other proceeding unless the decision is patently unreasonable.

2006, c. 30, s. 5 [To come into force June 30, 2008.]

45.9 (1) Settlements — If a settlement of an application made under section 34 or 35 is agreed to in writing and signed by the parties, the settlement is binding on the parties.

(2) Consent order — If a settlement of an application made under section 34 or 35 is agreed to in writing and signed by the parties, the Tribunal may, on the joint motion of the parties, make an order requiring compliance with the settlement or any part of the settlement.

(3) **Application where contravention** — If a settlement of an application made under section 34 or 35 is agreed to in writing and signed by the parties, a party who believes that another party has contravened the settlement may make an application to the Tribunal for an order under subsection (8),

(a) within six months after the contravention to which the application relates; or

(b) if there was a series of contraventions, within six months after the last contravention in the series.

(4) **Late applications** — A person may apply under subsection (3) after the expiry of the time limit under that subsection if the Tribunal is satisfied that the delay was incurred in good faith and no substantial prejudice will result to any person affected by the delay.

(5) **Form of application** — An application under subsection (3) shall be in a form approved by the Tribunal.

(6) **Parties** — Subject to the Tribunal rules, the parties to an application under subsection (3) are the following:

1. The parties to the settlement.

2. Any other person or the Commission, if they are added as a party by the Tribunal.

(7) **Intervention by Commission** — Section 37 applies with necessary modifications to an application under subsection (3).

(8) **Order** — If, on an application under subsection (3), the Tribunal determines that a party has contravened the settlement, the Tribunal may make any order that it considers appropriate to remedy the contravention.

2006, c. 30, s. 5 [To come into force June 30, 2008.]

45.10 (1) Annual report — The Tribunal shall make a report to the Minister not later than June 30 in each year upon the affairs of the Tribunal during the year ending on March 31 of that year.

(2) **Report laid in Assembly** — The Minister shall submit the report to the Lieutenant Governor in Council who shall cause the report to be laid before the Assembly if it is in session or, if not, at the next session.

2006, c. 30, s. 5 [To come into force June 30, 2008.]

Part IV.1 — Human Rights Legal Support Centre

[Heading added 2006, c. 30, s. 6.]

45.11 (1) Centre established — A corporation without share capital is established under the name Human Rights Legal Support Centre in English and Centre d'assistance juridique en matière de droits de la personne in French.

(2) Membership — The members of the Centre shall consist of its board of directors.

(3) Not a Crown agency — The Centre is not an agent of Her Majesty nor a Crown agent for the purposes of the *Crown Agency Act.*

(4) Powers of natural person — The Centre has the capacity and the rights, powers and privileges of a natural person, subject to the limitations set out in this Act or the regulations.

(5) Independent from but accountable to Ontario — The Centre shall be independent from, but accountable to, the Government of Ontario as set out in this Act.

2006, c. 30, s. 6

45.12 Objects — The objects of the Centre are,

(a) to establish and administer a cost-effective and efficient system for providing support services, including legal services, respecting applications to the Tribunal under Part IV;

(b) to establish policies and priorities for the provision of support services based on its financial resources.

2006, c. 30, s. 6

45.13 (1) Provision of support services — The Centre shall provide the following support services:

1. Advice and assistance, legal and otherwise, respecting the infringement of rights under Part I.

2. Legal services in relation to,

   i. the making of applications to the Tribunal under Part IV,

   ii. proceedings before the Tribunal under Part IV,

   iii. applications for judicial review arising from Tribunal proceedings,

   iv. stated case proceedings,

v. the enforcement of Tribunal orders.

3. Such other services as may be prescribed by regulation.

(2) **Availability of services** — The Centre shall ensure that the support services are available throughout the Province, using such methods of delivering the services as the Centre believes are appropriate.

2006, c. 30, s. 6

45.14 (1) **Board of directors** — The affairs of the Centre shall be governed and managed by its board of directors.

(2) **Composition and appointment** — The board of directors of the Centre shall consist of no fewer than five and no more than nine members appointed by the Lieutenant Governor in Council in accordance with the regulations.

(3) **Appointment of Chair** — A Chair designated by the Lieutenant Governor in Council will preside at meetings.

(4) **Remuneration** — The board of directors may be remunerated as determined by the Lieutenant Governor in Council.

(5) **Duties** — The board of directors of the Centre shall be responsible for furthering the objects of the Centre.

(6) **Delegation** — The board of directors may delegate any power or duty to any committee, to any member of a committee or to any officer or employee of the Centre.

(7) **Same** — A delegation shall be in writing and shall be on the terms and subject to the limitations, conditions or requirements specified in it.

(8) **Board to act responsibly** — The board of directors shall act in a financially responsible and accountable manner in exercising its powers and performing its duties.

(9) **Standard of care** — Members of the board of directors shall act in good faith with a view to the objects of the Centre and shall exercise the care, diligence and skill of a reasonably prudent person.

2006, c. 30, s. 6

45.15 (1) **Government funding** — The Centre shall submit its annual budget to the Minister for approval every year in a manner and form, and at a time, specified in the regulations.

(2) Approved budget included in estimates — If approved by the Minister, the annual budget shall be submitted to Cabinet to be reviewed for inclusion in the estimates of the Ministry.

(3) Appropriation by Legislature — The money required for the purposes of this Act shall be paid out of such money as is appropriated therefor by the Legislature.

2006, c. 30, s. 6

45.16 Centre's money not part of Consolidated Revenue Fund — The Centre's money and investments do not form part of the Consolidated Revenue Fund and shall be used by the Centre in carrying out its objects.
2006, c. 30, s. 6

45.17 (1) Annual report — The Centre shall submit an annual report to the Minister within four months after the end of its fiscal year.

(2) Fiscal year — The fiscal year of the Centre shall be from April 1 to March 31 of the following year.

2006, c. 30, s. 6

45.18 (1) Audit — The Centre must ensure that its books of financial account are audited annually in accordance with generally accepted accounting principles and a copy of the audit is given to the Minister.

(2) Audit by Minister — The Minister has the right to audit the Centre at any time that the Minister chooses.

2006, c. 30, s. 6

PART V — GENERAL

46. Definitions — In this Act,

"board of inquiry" [Repealed 2002, c. 18, Sched. C, s. 7(1).]

"Commission" means the Ontario Human Rights Commission;

"Minister" means the member of the Executive Council to whom the powers and duties of the Minister under this Act are assigned by the Lieutenant Governor in Council;

"person" in addition to the extended meaning given it by Part VI (Interpretation) of the *Legislation Act, 2006*, includes an employment agency, an employers' organization, an unincorporated association, a trade or occupational association, a trade union, a partnership, a municipality, a board of police commissioners established under the *Police Act*, being chapter 381 of the Revised Statutes of Ontario, 1980, and a police services board established under the *Police Services Act*;

Proposed Addition — 46 "regulations"

"regulations" means the regulations made under this Act;

2006, c. 30, s. 7(1) [To come into force June 30, 2008.]

"Tribunal" means the Human Rights Tribunal of Ontario continued under section 35.

Proposed Amendment — 46 "Tribunal"

"Tribunal" means the Human Rights Tribunal of Ontario continued under section 32.

2006, c. 30, s. 7(2) [To come into force June 30, 2008.]

Proposed Addition — 46 "Tribunal rules"

"Tribunal rules" means the rules governing practice and procedure that are made by the Tribunal under section 43.

2006, c. 30, s. 7(3) [To come into force June 30, 2008.]

1994, c. 27, s. 65(24); 2002, c. 18, Sched. C, s. 7; 2006, c. 21, Sched. F, s. 136(2), Table 2

Proposed Addition — 46.1–46.3

46.1 (1) Civil remedy — If, in a civil proceeding in a court, the court finds that a party to the proceeding has infringed a right under Part I of another party to the proceeding, the court may make either of the following orders, or both:

1. An order directing the party who infringed the right to pay monetary compensation to the party whose right was infringed for loss arising out of the infringement, including compensation for injury to dignity, feelings and self-respect.
2. An order directing the party who infringed the right to make restitution to the party whose right was infringed, other than through monetary compensation, for loss arising out of the infringement, including restitution for injury to dignity, feelings and self-respect.

(2) Same — Subsection (1) does not permit a person to commence an action based solely on an infringement of a right under Part I.

2006, c. 30, s. 8 [To come into force June 30, 2008.]

46.2 (1) Penalty — Every person who contravenes section 9 or subsection 31(14), 31.1(8) or 44(13) or an order of the Tribunal is guilty of an offence and on conviction is liable to a fine of not more than $25,000.

(2) Consent to prosecution — No prosecution for an offence under this Act shall be instituted except with the consent in writing of the Attorney General.

2006, c. 30, s. 8 [To come into force June 30, 2008.]

46.3 (1) Acts of officers, etc. — For the purposes of this Act, except subsection 2(2), subsection 5(2), section 7 and subsection 46.2(1), any act or thing done or omitted to be done in the course of his or her employment by an officer, official, employee or agent of a corporation, trade union, trade or occupational association, unincorporated association or employers' organization shall be deemed to be an act or thing done or omitted to be done by the corporation, trade union, trade or occupational association, unincorporated association or employers' organization.

(2) Opinion re authority or acquiescence — At the request of a corporation, trade union, trade or occupational association, unincorporated association or employers' organization, the Tribunal in its decision shall make known whether or not, in its opinion, an act or thing done or omitted to be done by an officer, official, employee or agent was done or omitted to be done with or without the authority or acquiescence of the corporation, trade union, trade or occupational association, unincorporated association or employers' organization, and the opinion does not affect the application of subsection (1).

2006, c. 30, s. 8 [To come into force June 30, 2008.]

47. (1) Act binds Crown — This Act binds the Crown and every agency of the Crown.

(2) Act has primacy over other Acts — Where a provision in an Act or regulation purports to require or authorize conduct that is a contravention of Part I, this Act applies and prevails unless the Act or regulation specifically provides that it is to apply despite this Act.

48. Regulations — The Lieutenant Governor in Council may make regulations,

(a) prescribing standards for assessing what is undue hardship for the purposes of section 11, 17 or 24;

(a.1) prescribing the manner in which income information, credit checks, credit references, rental history, guarantees or other similar business practices may be used by a landlord in selecting prospective tenants without infringing section 2, and prescribing other similar business practices and the manner of their use, for the purposes of subsection 21(3).

(b) prescribing forms and notices and providing for their use.

(d) prescribing time limits for the production of documents and things requested in an investigation under clause 33 (3) (b);

(e) prescribing procedures for carrying out an investigation under section 33;

(f) prescribing matters that the Commission shall consider in deciding whether or not to endeavour to effect a settlement under subsection 33(1).

Proposed Amendment — 48

48. Regulations — **(1)** The Lieutenant Governor in Council may make regulations,

(a) prescribing standards for assessing what is undue hardship for the purposes of section 11, 17 or 24;

(a.1) prescribing the manner in which income information, credit checks, credit references, rental history, guarantees or other similar business practices may be used by a landlord in selecting prospective tenants without infringing section 2, and prescribing other similar business practices and the manner of their use, for the purposes of subsection 21(3).

(b) prescribing matters for the purposes of clause 43(3)(g);

(c) respecting the Human Rights Legal Support Centre;

(d) governing any matter that is necessary or advisable for the effective enforcement and administration of this Act.

(e) [Repealed 2006, c. 30, s. 9(1). To come into force June 30, 2008.]

(f) prescribing matters that the Commission shall consider in deciding whether or not to endeavour to effect a settlement under subsection 33(1).

(2) Human Rights Legal Support Centre — A regulation made under clause (1)(c) may,

(a) further define the Centre's constitution, management and structure as set out in Part IV.1;

(b) prescribe powers and duties of the Centre and its members;

(c) provide for limitations on the Centre's powers under subsection 45.11(4);

(d) prescribe services for the purposes of paragraph 3 of subsection 45.13(1);

(e) further define the nature and scope of support services referred to in subsection 45.13(1);

(f) provide for factors to be considered in appointing members and specify the circumstances and manner in which they are to be considered;

(g) provide for the term of appointment and reappointment of the Centre's members;

(h) provide for the nature and scope of the annual report required under section 45.17;

(i) provide for reporting requirements in addition to the annual report;

(j) provide for personal information to be collected by or on behalf of the Centre other than directly from the individual to whom the information relates, and for the manner in which the information is collected;

(k) provide for the transfer from specified persons or entities of information, including personal information, that is relevant to carrying out the functions of the Centre;

(l) provide for rules governing the confidentiality and security of information, including personal information, the collection, use and disclosure of such information, the retention and disposal of such information, and access to and correction of such information, including restrictions on any of these things, for the purposes of the carrying out of the functions of the Centre;

(m) specify requirements and conditions for the funding of the Centre and for the Centre's budget;

(n) provide for audits of the statements and records of the Centre;

(o) determine whether or not the *Business Corporations Act*, the *Corporations Information Act* or the *Corporations Act* or any provisions of those Acts apply to the Centre;

(p) provide for anything necessary or advisable for the purposes of Part IV.1.

2006, c. 30, s. 9 [To come into force June 30, 2008.]

1994, c. 27, s. 65(25); 1997, c. 24, s. 212

PART VI — TRANSITIONAL PROVISIONS

[Heading added 2006, c. 30, s. 10.]

49. Definitions — In this Part,

"effective date" means the day sections 4 and 5 of the *Human Rights Code Amendment Act, 2006* come into force;

"new Part IV" means Part IV as it reads on and after the effective date;

"old Part IV" means Part IV as it reads before the effective date.

2006, c. 30, s. 10

50. Orders respecting special programs — On the fifth anniversary of the effective date, all orders that were made by the Commission under subsection 14(2) before the effective date shall be null and void.

2006, c. 30, s. 10

51. Application of s. 32(3) — Subsection 32(3) applies to the selection and appointment of persons to the Tribunal on or after the day section 10 of the *Human Rights Code Amendment Act, 2006* comes into force.

2006, c. 30, s. 10

52. (1) Tribunal powers before effective date — Despite anything to the contrary in the old Part IV, the Tribunal may, before the effective date,

(a) make rules in accordance with the new Part IV, including rules with respect to the reconsideration of Tribunal decisions; and

(b) when dealing with complaints that are referred to it under section 36 of the old Part IV,

(i) deal with the complaint in accordance with the practices and procedures set out in the rules made under clause (a),

(ii) exercise the powers described in section 39 of the new Part IV, and

(iii) dispose of the complaint in accordance with section 40 of the new Part IV.

(2) Application — Sections 41 and 42 of the new Part IV apply to rules made under clause (1)(a).

(3) Tribunal decisions made before effective date — Despite anything in the old Part IV, the following applies before the effective date with respect to a complaint that is referred to the Tribunal by the Commission under section 36 of the old Part IV on or after the day section 10 of the *Human Rights Code Amendment Act, 2006* comes into force:

1. Section 42 of the old Part IV does not apply to a decision of the Tribunal made with respect to the complaint.

2. Sections 45.7 and 45.8 of the new Part IV apply to a decision of the Tribunal made with respect to the complaint.

2006, c. 30, s. 10

53. (1) Complaints before Commission on effective date — This section applies to a complaint filed with the Commission under subsection 32(1) of the old Part IV or initiated by the Commission under subsection 32(2) of the old Part IV before the effective date.

(2) Commission powers continued for six months — Subject to subsection (3) and despite the repeal of the old Part IV, during the six-month period that begins on the effective date, the Commission shall continue to deal with complaints referred to in subsection (1) in accordance with subsection 32(3) and sections 33, 34, 36, 37 and 43 of the old Part IV and, for that purpose,

(a) the Commission has all the powers described in subsection 32(3) and sections 33, 34, 36, 37 and 43 of the old Part IV; and

(b) the provisions referred to in clause (a) continue to apply with respect to the complaints, with necessary modifications.

(3) Applications to Tribunal during six-month period — Subject to subsection (4), at any time during the six-month period referred to in subsection (2), the person who made a complaint that is continued under that subsection may, in accordance with the Tribunal rules, elect to abandon the complaint and make an application to the Tribunal with respect to the subject-matter of the complaint.

(4) Expedited process — The Tribunal shall make rules with respect to the practices and procedures that apply to an application under subsection (3) in order to ensure that the applications are dealt with in an expeditious manner.

(5) Applications to Tribunal after six-month period — If, after the end of the six-month period referred to in subsection (2), the Commission has failed to deal with the merits of a complaint continued under that subsection and the complaint has not been withdrawn or settled, the complainant may make an application to the Tribunal with respect to the subject-matter of the complaint within a further six-month period after the end of the earlier six-month period.

(6) **New Part IV applies** — The new Part IV applies to an application made under subsections (3) and (5).

(7) **Disclosure of information** — Despite anything in the *Freedom of Information and Protection of Privacy Act*, at the request of a party to an application under subsection (3) or (5), the Commission may disclose to the party any information obtained by the Commission in the course of an investigation.

(8) **Application barred** — No application, other than an application under subsection (3) or (5), may be made to the Tribunal if the subject-matter of the application is the same or substantially the same as the subject-matter of a complaint that was filed with the Commission under the old Part IV.

2006, c. 30, s. 10

54. Settlements effected by Commission — Section 45.9 of the new Part IV applies to the enforcement of a settlement that,

(a) was effected by the Commission under the old Part IV before the effective date or during the six-month period referred to in subsection 53(2); and

(b) was agreed to in writing, signed by the parties and approved by the Commission.

2006, c. 30, s. 10

55. (1) **Where complaints referred to Tribunal** — This section applies to complaints that are referred to the Tribunal by the Commission under section 36 of the old Part IV before the effective date or during the six-month period referred to in subsection 53(2).

(2) **New Part IV applies** — On and after the effective date, the new Part IV applies to a complaint described in subsection (1) as though it were an application made to the Tribunal under that Part and the Tribunal shall deal with the complaint in accordance with the new Part IV.

(3) **Parties** — The Commission,

(a) shall continue to be a party to a complaint that was referred to the Tribunal before the effective date; and

(b) subject to subsection (4), shall not be a party to a complaint referred to the Tribunal during the six-month period referred to in subsection 53(2).

(4) Same, exceptions — The Commission shall continue as a party to a complaint that was referred to the Tribunal during the six-month period referred to in subsection 53(2) if,

(a) the complaint was initiated by the Commission under subsection 32(2) of the old Part IV; or

(b) the Tribunal sets a date for the parties to appear before the Tribunal before the end of the six-month period.

(5) Same — Nothing in subsection (3) shall prevent,

(a) the Tribunal from adding the Commission as a party to a proceeding under section 36 of the new Part IV; or

(b) the Commission from intervening in a proceeding with respect to a complaint described in subsection (1).

2006, c. 30, s. 10

56. (1) Regulations, transitional matters — The Lieutenant Governor in Council may make regulations providing for transitional matters which, in the opinion of the Lieutenant Governor in Council, are necessary or desirable to facilitate the implementation of the *Human Rights Code Amendment Act, 2006*.

(2) Same — Without limiting the generality of subsection (1), the Lieutenant Governor in Council may make regulations,

(a) providing for transitional matters relating to the changes to the administration and functions of the Commission;

(b) dealing with any problems or issues arising as a result of the repeal or enactment of a provision of this Act by the *Human Rights Code Amendment Act, 2006*.

(3) Same — A regulation under this section may be general or specific in its application.

(4) Conflicts — If there is a conflict between a provision in a regulation under this section and any provision of this Act or of any other regulation made under this Act, the regulation under this section prevails.

2006, c. 30, s. 10

57. (1) Review — Three years after the effective date, the Minister shall appoint a person who shall undertake a review of the implementation and effectiveness of the changes resulting from the enactment of that Act.

(2) Public consultations — In conducting a review under this section, the person appointed under subsection (1) shall hold public consultations.

(3) **Report to Minister** — The person appointed under subsection (1) shall prepare a report on his or her findings and submit the report to the Minister within one year of his or her appointment.

2006, c. 30, s. 10

ONT. REG. 290/98 — BUSINESS PRACTICES PERMISSIBLE TO LANDLORDS IN SELECTING PROSPECTIVE TENANTS FOR RESIDENTIAL ACCOMMODATION

made under the *Human Rights Code*

O. Reg. 290/98, as am. O. Reg. 31/00; 646/00; 284/05.

1. (1) A landlord may request credit references and rental history information, or either of them, from a prospective tenant and may request from a prospective tenant authorization to conduct credit checks on the prospective tenant.

(2) A landlord may consider credit references, rental history information and credit checks obtained pursuant to requests under subsection (1), alone or in any combination, in order to assess the prospective tenant and the landlord may select or refuse the prospective tenant accordingly.

(3) A landlord may request income information from a prospective tenant only if the landlord also requests information listed in subsection (1).

(4) A landlord may consider income information about a prospective tenant in order to assess the prospective tenant and the landlord may select or refuse the prospective tenant accordingly only if the landlord considers the income information together with all the other information that was obtained by the landlord pursuant to requests under subsection (1).

(5) If, after requesting the information listed in subsections (1) and (3), a landlord only obtains income information about a prospective tenant, the landlord may consider the income information alone in order to assess the prospective tenant and the landlord may select or refuse the prospective tenant accordingly.

2. (1) A landlord may require a prospective tenant to obtain a guarantee for the rent.

(2) A landlord may require a prospective tenant to pay a security deposit in accordance with sections 117 and 118 of the *Tenant Protection Act, 1997.*

3. In selecting a prospective tenant, a landlord of a rental unit described in paragraph 1, 1.1, 2 or 3 of subsection 5(1) or subsection 6(1) of the *Tenant*

Protection Act, 1997 may request and use income information about a prospective tenant in order to determine a prospective tenant's eligibility for rent in an amount geared-to-income and, when requesting and using the income information for that purpose only, the landlord is not bound by subsection 1(3) and (4).

O. Reg. 646/00, s. 1

4. Nothing in this Regulation authorizes a landlord to refuse accommodation to any person because of race, ancestry, place of origin, colour, ethnic origin, citizenship, creed, sex, sexual orientation, age, marital status, family status, handicap or the receipt of public assistance.

O. Reg. 31/00, s. 1; 284/05, s. 1

5. This Regulation comes into force on the day clause 48(a.1) of the Act comes into force.

ONT. REG. 642 — SEARCH AND ENTRY WARRANTS

made under the *Human Rights Code*

R.R.O. 1990, Reg. 642, as am. O. Reg. 22/92 (Fr.).

1. A search warrant under subsection 33(7) of the Act shall be in Form 1.

2. A warrant to enter under subsection 33(8) of the Act shall be in Form 2.

Form 1 — Warrant to Search under Subsection 33(7) of the *Human Rights Code*

Ontario
Human Rights
Commission

Commission ontarienne des droits de la personne

To
À ______________________________

WHEREAS, on the evidence upon oath or affirmation of
ATTENDU QUE, suivant le témoignage sous serment ou affirmation solennelle de ______________________________

I am satisfied that there are in
je suis convaincu(e) qu'il y a à/au ______________________________
(name and address of place)
(nom et adresse de l'endroit)

documents, namely
des documents, précisément ______________________________
(describe documents to be searched for)
(décrire les documents à perquisitionner)

and that there is reasonable ground to believe the documents will afford evidence relevant to a complaint by
et qu'il y a des motifs raisonnables de croire que ces documents constitueront une preuve pertinente à la plainte déposée par

____
(name(s) of complainant(s))
(nom du ou des plaignants)

against
contre ______________________________
(party against whom complaint is made)
(partie faisant l'objet de la plainte)

dated
le ______________________________

that
selon laquelle ______________________________
(describe nature of complaint)
(décrire la nature de la plainte)

____

____

____

This is therefore to authorize you to enter the place described above between the hours of ____________ and ____________
Pour ces raisons, la présente vous autorise à pénétrer dans l'endroit décrit ci-dessus entre ____________ *heures et* ____________ *heures*

and to search there for the documents described above and to remove them for the purpose of making copies of them or extracts from them.
et à perquisitionner les documents décrits ci-dessus et à les enlever pour en tirer des copies ou des extraits.

This warrant expires on
Le présent mandat expire le ______________________________, 19 ____

Issued at
Décerné à ______________________ on
le ______________________, 19 ____

____
Justice of the Peace
Juge de paix

103-074 (12/88)

Form 2 — Warrant to Enter under Subsection 33(8) of the *Human Rights Code*

Ontario
Human Rights
Commission

Commission ontarienne des droits de la personne

To
À ______________________________

WHEREAS, on the evidence upon oath or affirmation of
ATTENDU QUE, suivant le témoignage sous serment ou affirmation solennelle de ______________________________

I am satisfied that there is reasonable ground to believe it is necessary that
je suis convaincu(e) qu'il y a des motifs raisonnables de croire qu'il est nécessaire de pénétrer dans

____
(name and address of place)
(nom et adresse de l'endroit)

(check appropriate box)
(Cocher la case appropriée)

☐ which is being used as a dwelling, or
qui sert de logement, ou

☐ to which entry has been denied,
duquel l'accès a été refusé

be entered to investigate a complaint dated ______________________________
pour faire enquête sur la plainte du

by
déposée par ______________________________
(name(s) of complainant(s))
(nom du ou des plaignants)

against
contre ______________________________
(party against whom complaint is made)
(partie faisant l'objet de la plainte)

that
selon laquelle ______________________________
(describe nature of complaint)
(décrire la nature de la plainte)

____

____

____

This is therefore to authorize you to enter the place described above between the hours of ______________ and ______________
Pour ces raisons, la présente vous autorise à pénétrer dans l'endroit décrit ci-dessus entre ______________ *heures et* ______________ *heures*

and to investigate the complaint.
et à faire enquête sur la plainte.

This warrant expires on
Le présent mandat expire le ______________________________, 19 ______

Issued at
Décerné à ______________________________ on
le ______________________________, 19 ______

____
Justice of the Peace
Juge de paix

103-075 (10/88)

PART III — INDEX

D

Part IV — Other OHRC Publications

General

The following titles are only a portion of the publications developed by the Ontario Human Rights Commission. These documents and many more are available on the Commission's Web site (www.ohrc.on.ca) and many are also available from ServiceOntario Publications (www.publications.serviceontario.ca/ecom/) or from Government Information Centres and Service Ontario Kiosks across the province.

- Annual Reports (published each year by the Ontario Human Rights Commission)
- Human Rights at Work (2004)
- Hiring? A Human Rights Guide (1999)
- Complaint Service Guide (2007)

Position Papers

- An Intersectional Approach To Discrimination: Addressing Multiple Grounds In Human Rights Claims (2001)
- Human Rights Commissions And Economic And Social Rights (2001)
- Moving Towards Barrier-free Services: Final Report on the Restaurant Accessibility Initiative (2006)

Consultation Reports

- Human Rights And Public Transit Services In Ontario — Consultation Report (2001)
- Human Rights Issues In Insurance: Consultation Report (2001)
- Paying The Price: The Human Cost of Racial Profiling (2003)
- Strengthening Ontario's Human Rights System — What We Heard (Consultation Report) (2006)
- The Cost Of Caring: Report on the Consultation on Discrimination on the Basis of Family Status (2007)
- Time for Action: Advancing Human Rights for Older Ontarians (2001)
- The Opportunity To Succeed: Achieving Barrier-Free Education For Students With Disabilities (2001)

Brochures

- The Commission: What You Need to Know (Punjabi, Spanish, Tagalog and Urdu) (2001)
- Female Genital Mutilation: Questions and Answers (Arabic, Somalian, Swahili and Amharic) (1999)
- Aboriginal People and the Ontario Human Rights Code (2005)
- Age Discrimination: Your Rights and Responsibilities (2003)
- Disability and the Duty to Accommodate: Your Rights and Responsibilities (2006)
- Gender Identity: Your Rights and Responsibilities (2006)
- Hiring: Your Rights and Responsibilities (2001)
- Pregnancy and Breastfeeding: Your Rights and Responsibilities (2004)
- Racial Harassment: Your Rights and Responsibilities (Punjabi, Spanish, Tagalog and Urdu) (2001)
- Sexual Orientation: Your Rights and Responsibilities (2001)

Part V — For Further Information

For more information about the Ontario Human Rights Commission or these policy statements, please call 1-800-387-9080 (toll free) or in Toronto (416) 326-9511 (TTY: (416) 314-6526 (local) and 1-800-308-5561 (toll free), during regular office hours from Monday to Friday. You can also visit our Web site at www.ohrc.on.ca.

If A Human Rights Complaint is Made Against You

1. If the Commission receives a complaint against you, Commission staff will contact you to discuss the matter.

2. Commission staff will explain how the *Code* applies to the situation and how the complaint procedure works. Commission staff will work with you and the person making the complaint to try and resolve the concerns. The Commission also offers mediation services.

3. If the concerns cannot be resolved and mediation is not successful, the complaint may proceed to the investigation stage.

4. You can ask the Commission not to deal with the complaint under section 34 of the *Code* if:

   a) another Ontario law would be better suited to deal with the situation, such as the *Labour Relations Act*;

   b) you believe that the person making the complaint has no reasonable basis to support a claim of discrimination, or that the complaint is in bad faith, or that a remedy has already been obtained by the complainant somewhere else;

   c) the matter is outside the Commission's legal authority;

   d) the person making the complaint waited longer than 6 months from the last incident of discrimination to file a complaint.

5. The Commission is neutral and does not take sides in the complaint. Commission staff will assist you with questions about the complaint procedure. However, if you require legal representation or advice, please contact a lawyer.

If You Have a Human Rights Complaint

1. If you have a human rights complaint, you may contact the general inquiries line at 1-800-387-9080 or in Toronto at (416) 326-9511 from Mon-

day to Friday during office hours. A Commission staff person will tell you if your concerns are covered by the Ontario *Human Rights Code* (the "*Code*").

2. Commission staff will explain how the *Code* applies to your situation and how the complaint procedure works. Commission staff will work with you and the other party to resolve the concerns. The Commission also offers mediation services.

3. If you want the Commission to address your concerns, you should file a complaint within 6 months from the last incident of discrimination. This time limit is set out in section 34 of the *Code*.

4. "Filing a complaint" means that you have completed the Commission's complaint form and provided all requested details. You must have signed, dated and returned the form to the Commission.

5. When you file a complaint, Commission staff will work with you and the person/company you have filed against, to try and resolve the complaint through mediation.

6. The Commission may consider not to deal with a complaint under section 34 if:

a) another Ontario law would be better suited to deal with the situation, such as the *Labour Relations Act*;

b) you have no reasonable basis to support a claim of discrimination, or that you have made the complaint in bad faith, or that you have already obtained a remedy somewhere else;

c) the matter is outside the Commission's legal authority;

d) you have waited longer than 6 months from the last incident of discrimination to file a complaint.

7. The Commission is neutral and does not take sides in the complaint. Commission staff will assist you with questions about the complaint procedure. However, if you require legal advice, please contact a lawyer.

PLEASE NOTE: Until June 30, 2008, the Commission will continue to receive human rights complaints and refer appropriate cases to the Human Rights Tribunal of Ontario for a hearing. After that date, new human rights complaints will be filed directly with the Tribunal. Complaints already filed with the Commission will continue to be processed by the Commission until December 31, 2008, after which time a special procedure will be developed to deal with current complaints. For more information at that time, please refer to the Commission's Web site (www.ohrc.on.ca).

How to Reach Us at the Ontario Human Rights Commission

Tel: (416) 326-9511
Toll Free: 1-800-387-9080
TTY (Local): (416) 314-6526
TTY (Toll Free): 1-800-308-5561
Web Site: http://www.ohrc.on.ca
E-Mail: info@ohrc.on.ca

Head Office

Ontario Human Rights Commission
180 Dundas Street W., 7th Floor
Toronto ON M7A 2R9
Tel: (416) 314-4500
TTY: (416) 314-4493